PREPARE

TEACHER'S BOOK

Hilary Plass

Second Edition

Cambridge University Press
www.cambridge.org/elt

Cambridge Assessment English
www.cambridgeenglish.org

Information on this title: www.cambridge.org/9781108385961

First published 2015
Second Edition 2019

20 19 18 17 16 15 14 13 12 11 10 9 8 7 6 5 4

Printed in Malaysia by Vivar Printing

A catalogue record for this publication is available from the British Library

ISBN 978-1-108-38596-1 Teacher's Book with Downloadable Resource Pack (Class Audio, Video, Photocopiable Worksheets)
ISBN 978-1-108-43330-3 Student's Book
ISBN 978-1-108-38061-4 Student's Book and Online Workbook
ISBN 978-1-108-38095-9 Workbook with Audio Download

CONTENTS

	Introduction	4
	Student's Book overview	6
	Component line up	8
	The *Prepare* Exam Journey	10
	B1 Preliminary for Schools exam overview	11
	Student's Book contents	12
1	All about me	17
2	In fashion	25
CULTURE	Traditional clothes	33
3	My way of life	37
4	Champions	45
LIFE SKILLS	Physical well-being: Keeping fit	53
REVIEW 1		57
5	Call the police!	61
6	City life	69
CULTURE	New York City	77
7	Getting on	81
8	Going away	89
LIFE SKILLS	Interpersonal skills: Dealing with conflict	97
REVIEW 2		101
9	Shop till you drop	105
10	Taste this!	113
CULTURE	British food	121
11	A healthy future	125
12	Incredible wildlife	133
LIFE SKILLS	Social responsibility: Respecting the environment	141
REVIEW 3		145
13	Mixed feelings	149
14	On screen	157
CULTURE	The film industry	165
15	Digital life	169
16	Amazing science	177
LIFE SKILLS	ICT literacy: Staying safe online	185
REVIEW 4		189
17	Talented	193
18	The world of work	201
CULTURE	Special training	209
19	The written word	213
20	Seeing is believing	221
LIFE SKILLS	Critical thinking: Identifying reliable news	229
REVIEW 5		233

Extra activities (Student's Book) 236
Grammar reference and practice answer key 244
Workbook answer key and audioscripts 247
Student's Book audioscripts 261

DEAR TEACHERS

I'm delighted that you've chosen our official preparation materials to prepare for a Cambridge English Qualification.

We take great pride in the fact that our materials draw on the expertise of a whole team of writers, teachers, assessors and exam experts. These are materials that you can really trust.

Our preparation materials are unique in many ways:

- They combine the skills and knowledge of the teams at Cambridge Assessment English, who create the tests, and the teams at Cambridge University Press, who create the English Language Teaching materials.
- They draw upon the experience of millions of previous exam candidates – where they succeed and where they have difficulties. We target exercises and activities precisely at these areas so that you can actively 'learn' from previous test takers' mistakes.
- Every single task in our materials has been carefully checked to be an accurate reflection of what test takers find in the test.

In addition, we listen to what you tell us at every stage of the development process. This allows us to design the most user-friendly courses, practice tests and supplementary training. We create materials using in-depth knowledge, research and practical understanding. Prepare for Cambridge English Qualifications with confidence in the knowledge that you have the best materials available to support you on your way to success.

We wish you the very best on your journey with us.

With kind regards,

Pamela Baxter
Director
Cambridge Exams Publishing

PS. If you have any feedback at all on our support materials for exams, please write to us at cambridgeexams@cambridge.org

WELCOME TO PREPARE

STUDENT'S BOOK OVERVIEW

All reading texts are recorded, giving the option to listen and read or listen and check answers where appropriate.

Motivating, topic-based **texts** specifically chosen to engage and inform students.

Each unit begins with **About you**, where students can talk about themselves and their lives.

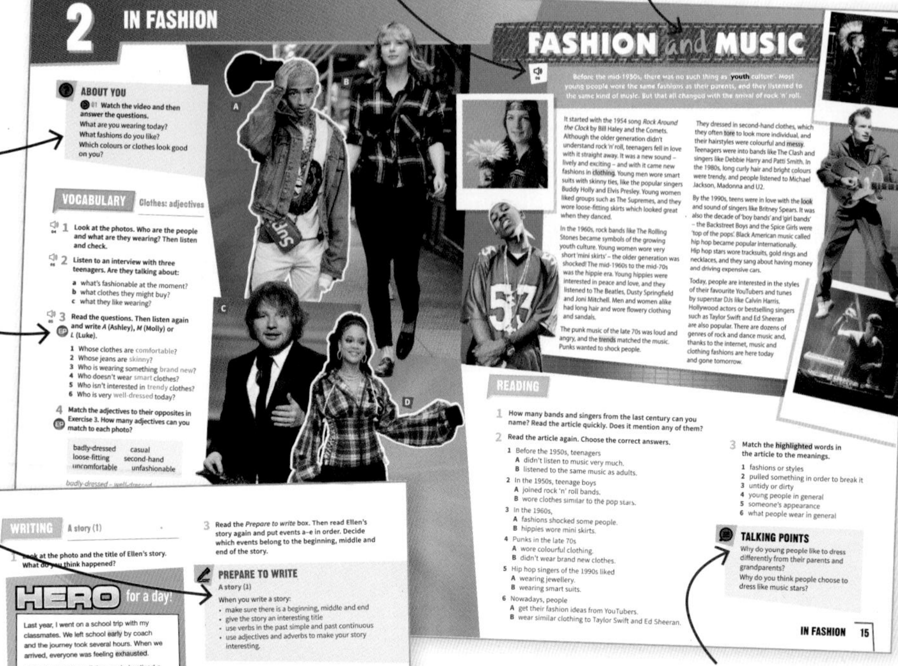

Vocabulary sets are informed by English Vocabulary Profile to ensure they are appropriate for the level.

Useful tips in **Prepare to write** help students learn to prepare, plan and check their writing.

Talking points provides opportunities to personalise language and encourage students to say what they think about the topic of the unit.

B1 Preliminary for Schools **exam tasks** are clearly marked by the exam icon.

In **Prepare to speak**, students learn useful words and phrases for effective communication.

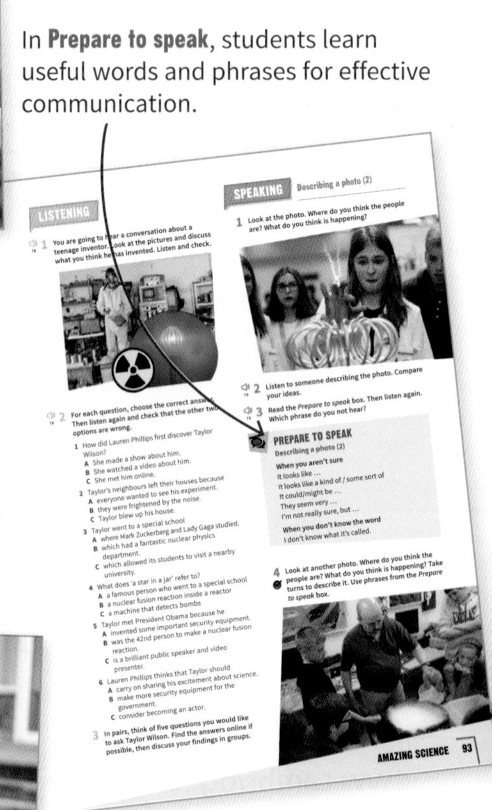

Clear **grammar presentation** and practice is extended in the Grammar reference and practice section at the back of the book.

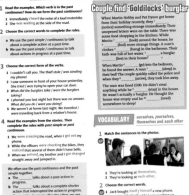

Common mistakes relevant to your students' level are identified in the grammar activities marked with the **Cambridge Learner Corpus icon.**

Video interviews show real teens giving their opinion on the topic of the unit. Each video comes with a worksheet containing comprehension and discussion questions.

There is a **Life Skills** or **Culture** lesson after every two units. The **Culture** lessons highlight interesting aspects of culture in English-speaking countries.

In the **videos** found in each Culture lesson, students can watch interesting documentaries about the Culture topics. Each video comes with a worksheet for students to complete as they watch.

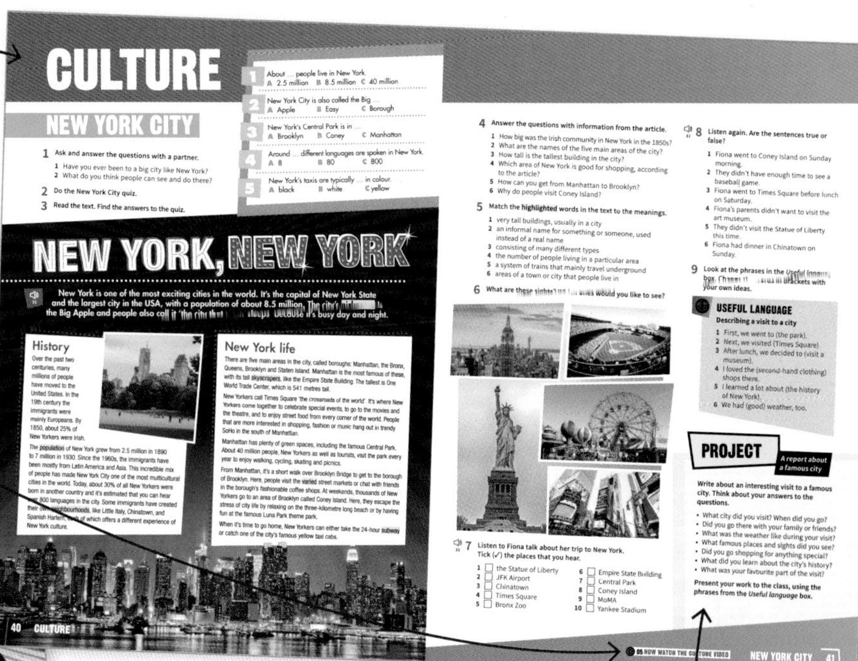

LIFE SKILLS CRITICAL THINKING

IDENTIFYING RELIABLE NEWS

FAKE NEWS

GET THE REAL FACTS!

PROJECT

IDENTIFYING RELIABLE NEWS 117

Life Skills lessons help students develop important skills for their everyday lives.

Projects in the Life Skills and Culture lessons encourage students to work together to create something fun and expand their learning.

REVIEW 2 UNITS 5–8

VOCABULARY

CRIME: THE FACTS AND THE FIGURES

GRAMMAR

How I met my best friend

Review pages after every four units give further practice of language, skills and exam tasks.

COMPONENT LINE UP

Student's Book

The Student's Book combines teen-appeal topics with preparation for the revised 2020 *B1 Preliminary for Schools* exam. With twenty lively core units, Reviews, Culture and Life Skills sections, a Vocabulary list, and a Grammar reference and practice section, the Student's Book has all the material you need to create interactive, personalised lessons. Full audio and extensive video to accompany the Student's Book is available for teachers online or to download.

CAMBRIDGE
PREPARE
WORKBOOK
WITH AUDIO DOWNLOAD
Gareth Jones
Second Edition
B1
LEVEL 4

Workbook with Audio Download

The Workbook gives additional practice of all the language from the Student's Book. It also provides students with comprehensive skills development work and further exposure to exam tasks. The Workbook is suitable for use both in the classroom and for homework. Learners can access and download the audio files from e-Source using the code provided.

4 CHAMPIONS
VOCABULARY Sports
READING
The amazing health benefits of snowboarding

Online Workbook

The Online Workbook, delivered via the Cambridge Learning Management System, is a digital version of the Workbook with interactive exercises and tasks which provide further practice of the language and skills in the Student's Book. The Online Workbook also allows you to track your students' progress, highlighting areas of strength and weakness for ongoing performance improvement.

CAMBRIDGE

PREPARE

TEACHER'S BOOK

WITH DOWNLOADABLE RESOURCE PACK

Hilary Plass

Second Edition

B1 LEVEL 4

Teacher's Book with Downloadable Resource Pack

The interleaved Teacher's Book contains complete teaching notes for all of the Student's Book tasks, in addition to answer keys and audioscripts. With a wealth of lesson ideas, warmers, coolers and extension tasks, the Teacher's Book helps you manage mixed ability classes and work with fast finishers. Information panels include background information about themes, topics and cultural events. Activities which practise the *B1 Preliminary for Schools* exam are clearly labelled and there is information about each exam task. Clear indications direct you to additional resources which support and extend learning.

The Downloadable Resource Pack, accessed via e-Source, includes Class Audio, Video and Photocopiable Worksheets. These provide an extensive suite of downloadable teacher's resources to use in class and include:

- Grammar worksheets (available at two levels of challenge: standard and plus)
- Vocabulary worksheets (available at two levels of challenge: standard and plus)
- Review Games
- Literature worksheets
- Speaking worksheets
- Writing worksheets
- Video worksheets
- Culture video worksheets

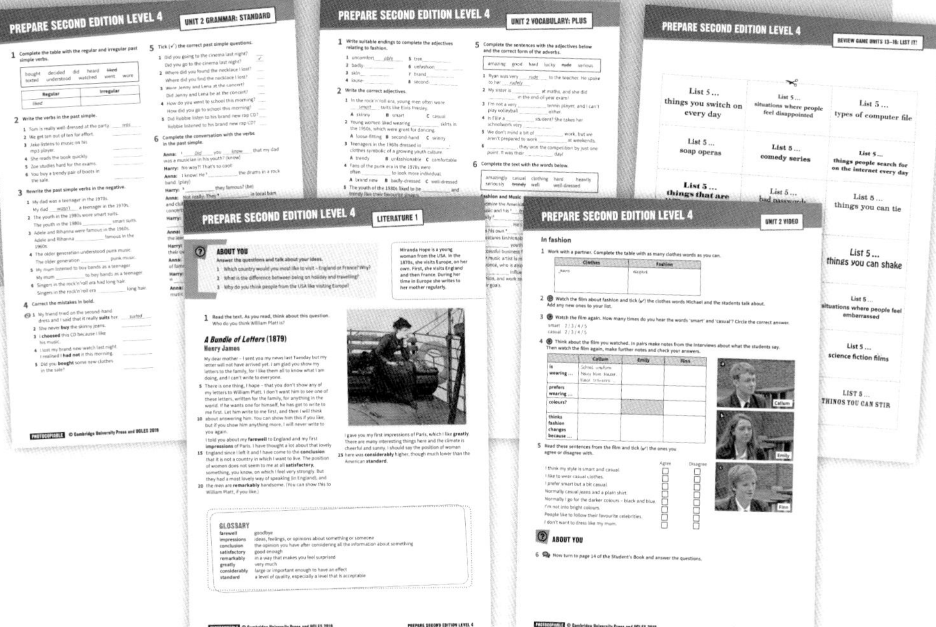

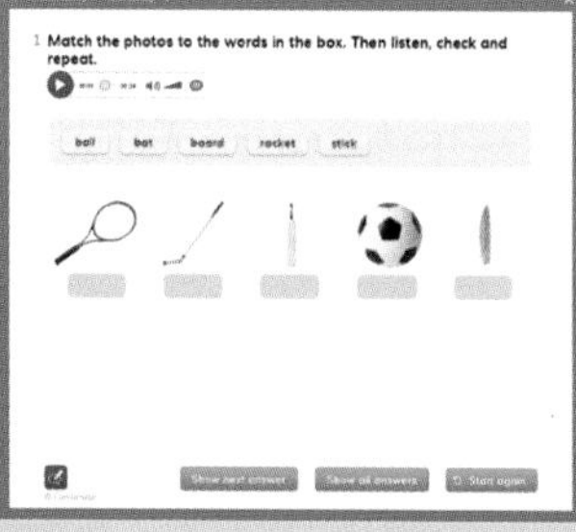

Presentation Plus

Presentation Plus is easy-to-use, interactive classroom presentation software that helps you deliver effective and engaging lessons. It includes all the Student's Book and Workbook content and allows you to present and annotate content, and link to the Photocopiable Worksheets.

Test Generator

The Test Generator allows you to download ready-made tests for each unit, term and end-of-year assessment or to build your own tests easily and quickly. All the tests are available at two levels of challenge: standard and plus, to help assess learners of mixed abilities.

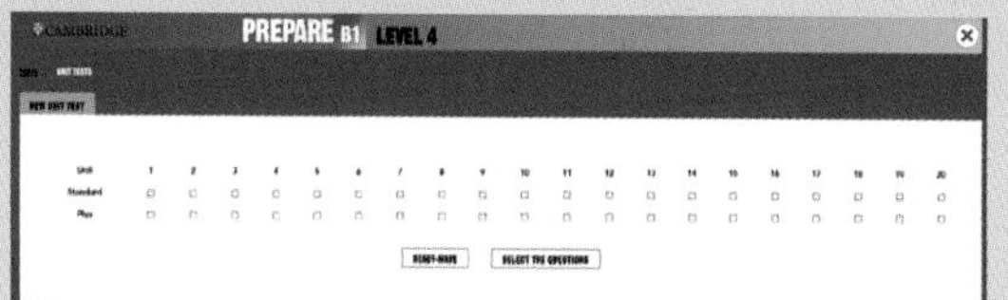

THE PREPARE EXAM JOURNEY

The *Prepare* Exam Journey combines teen-appeal topics with extensive preparation for Cambridge English Qualifications. Levels 4 and 5 of *Prepare* Second Edition take students on a two-year journey towards the revised 2020 *B1 Preliminary for Schools* exam. This approach builds confidence every step of the way from the first experiences of exam tasks to skills development; from language discovery to understanding how English works in the real world.

LEVEL 4

Prepare Level 4 gradually introduces authentic *B1 Preliminary for Schools* exam tasks, ensuring students become familiar with every part of the exam.

Exam tasks are discreetly labelled with the exam icon in **Level 4 Student's Book.**

3 Listen to the six conversations again. For each question, choose the correct answer.

1 You will hear two friends talking about a film. What do they say about it?
A The reviews of it are rather negative.
B They are too young to see it.
C Someone they know found it hard to follow.

Level 4 Workbook offers further exposure to each part of the exam.

10 **2 Listen to six conversations. For each question, choose the correct answer.**

1 You will hear a girl talking to a friend about a film they've seen.
How does she feel about it?
A confused by parts of the story
B impressed by the quality of the acting
C surprised by the way music was used in it

Information for each part of the exam is included in **Level 4 Teacher's Book.**

68 3 **B1 Preliminary for Schools Listening Part 2**
This exercise is based on Listening Part 2 which tests students' ability to listen for gist and to identify the speakers' attitudes, feelings and opinions. Students listen to six short unrelated extracts, each followed by three-option multiple-choice items. They hear the recording twice.

LEVEL 5

Prepare Level 5 provides complete coverage of the *B1 Preliminary for Schools* exam, driving students to exam success.

Each exam task is highlighted clearly in the *Prepare for the exam* features in **Level 5 Student's Book.**

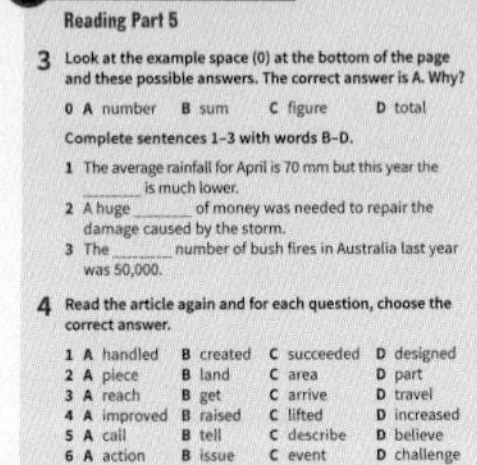

PREPARE FOR THE EXAM
Reading Part 5

3 Look at the example space (0) at the bottom of the page and these possible answers. The correct answer is A. Why?

0 **A** number **B** sum **C** figure **D** total

Complete sentences 1–3 with words B–D.

1 The average rainfall for April is 70 mm but this year the ______ is much lower.
2 A huge ______ of money was needed to repair the damage caused by the storm.
3 The ______ number of bush fires in Australia last year was 50,000.

4 Read the article again and for each question, choose the correct answer.

	A	B	C	D
1	handled	created	succeeded	designed
2	piece	land	area	part
3	reach	get	arrive	travel
4	improved	raised	lifted	increased
5	call	tell	describe	believe
6	action	issue	event	challenge

» PREPARE FOR THE EXAM PAGE 125

The *Prepare for the exam* section at the end of **Level 5 Student's Book** includes further guidance and support with practice tasks.

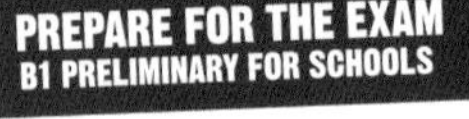

PREPARE FOR THE EXAM
B1 PRELIMINARY FOR SCHOOLS

Reading Part 4 Gapped text
(Unit 1, Unit 5)

1 **Read the text about Emily Hagins. What has she done since the age of 11?**
2 **Read the first paragraph and options A–H. Which sentence fits in gap 1? How do you know this is the correct answer?**
3 **Now read the exam instructions and complete the rest of the task.**

Five sentences have been removed from the article below. For each question, choose the correct answer. There are three extra sentences which you do not need to use.

EXAM INFORMATION
Reading Part 4
- You will read a text from which five sentences have been removed.
- The five sentences are placed after the text. They are not in the correct order. There are three extra sentences which are not needed.
- You need to read the text and then choose the sentence which best fits each gap.

EXAM TIPS
Read the whole text first. Then read the options and decide which one fits best. Read the sentences directly before and after each gap

Level 5 Workbook consolidates each exam task and includes Exam Tips.

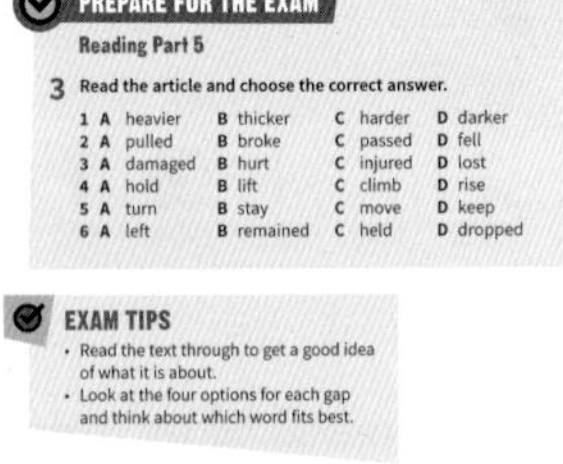

PREPARE FOR THE EXAM
Reading Part 5

3 Read the article and choose the correct answer.

	A	B	C	D
1	heavier	thicker	harder	darker
2	pulled	broke	passed	fell
3	damaged	hurt	injured	lost
4	hold	lift	climb	rise
5	turn	stay	move	keep
6	left	remained	held	dropped

EXAM TIPS
- Read the text through to get a good idea of what it is about.
- Look at the four options for each gap and think about which word fits best.

Level 5 Teacher's Book details each part of the exam and suggests teaching tips for the classroom.

PREPARE FOR THE EXAM

B1 PRELIMINARY FOR SCHOOLS
Reading Part 5
In this part, students are mainly tested on vocabulary, including precise meaning, collocations, fixed phrases and phrasal verbs. Some grammatical knowledge may be tested e.g. knowing which preposition comes after the correct word. The text contains six numbered spaces followed by a four-option multiple-choice cloze question for each space.

Tips Tell students that before they answer the questions, they should read the whole text to get an idea of the topic and general meaning. They should then look at each question, choosing the correct word for each space. Tell them to read the whole text again with their answers to check that it makes sense.

B1 PRELIMINARY FOR SCHOOLS EXAM OVERVIEW

PAPER / TIMING	PART	WHAT DO CANDIDATES HAVE TO DO?	PRACTICE IN LEVEL 4
Reading 45 minutes	**Part 1** Five 3-option multiple choice questions	Read five real-world notices, messages and other short texts for the main message.	Student's Book page 109 Workbook page 77
	Part 2 Five matching questions	Match five descriptions of people to eight short texts on a particular topic, showing detailed comprehension.	Student's Book page 87 Workbook page 61
	Part 3 Five 4-option multiple choice questions	Read a longer text for detailed comprehension, gist, inference and global meaning, as well as writer's attitude and opinion.	Student's Book page 55 Workbook page 37
	Part 4 Five gapped text questions	Read a longer text from which five sentences have been removed. Show understanding of how a coherent and well-structured text is formed.	Student's Book pages 25, 77 Workbook pages 17, 53
	Part 5 Six 4-option multiple choice cloze questions	Read a shorter text and choose the correct vocabulary items to complete gaps. An element of grammatical knowledge may be tested, e.g. complementation.	Student's Book pages 30–31, 37, 75, 119 Workbook page 25
	Part 6 Six open cloze questions	Read a shorter text and complete six gaps using one word for each gap. Show knowledge of grammatical structures, phrasal verbs and fixed phrases.	Student's Book pages 11, 53, 97, 99 Workbook pages 5, 68–69
Writing 45 minutes	**Part 1** An email	Write about 100 words, answering the email and notes provided. Candidates are assessed using four subscales: Content, Communicative Achievement, Organisation and Language.	Student's Book pages 23, 45, 89 Workbook pages 15, 31, 63
	Part 2 Choice between an article or a story	Write about 100 words, answering the question of their choosing. Candidates are assessed using four subscales: Content, Communicative Achievement, Organisation and Language.	Student's Book pages 35, 57, 67, 79 Workbook pages 23, 39, 47, 55
Listening 30 minutes	**Part 1** Seven 3-option multiple choice questions	Identify key information in seven short monologues or dialogues and choose the correct picture.	Student's Book page 61 Workbook page 43
	Part 2 Six 3-option multiple choice questions	Listen to six short dialogues and understand the gist of each.	Student's Book page 83 Workbook page 59
	Part 3 Six gap fill questions	Listen to a monologue and complete six gaps.	Student's Book page 49 Workbook page 35
	Part 4 Six 3-option multiple choice questions	Listen to an interview for a detailed understanding of meaning and to identify attitudes and opinions.	Student's Book page 115 Workbook pages 67, 83
Speaking 12–17 minutes Part 1: 2 minutes; Part 2: 3 minutes; Part 3: 3–4 minutes; Part 4: 3–4 minutes	**Part 1** Interlocutor asks questions to each candidate in turn	Respond to questions, giving factual or personal information.	Student's Book page 17
	Part 2 Extended turn	Describe one colour photograph, talking for about 1 minute.	Student's Book pages 71, 93
	Part 3 Discussion task with visual stimulus	Make and respond to suggestions, discuss alternatives and negotiate agreement.	Student's Book page 105
	Part 4 General conversation	Discuss likes, dislikes, experiences, opinions, habits, etc.	Student's Book page 105

UNIT	VOCABULARY	READING	GRAMMAR
1 ALL ABOUT ME page 10	Describing people Prefixes: *un-*, *in-*, *im-*	all.about.me ✔ Reading Part 6	Present simple and continuous
2 IN FASHION page 14	Clothes: adjectives Adverbs	Fashion and music	Past simple
Culture Traditional clothes page 18			
3 MY WAY OF LIFE page 20	Life events *too*, *enough*, *not enough*	Is teenage life better now than in the past?	Comparatives and superlatives *not as … as*
4 CHAMPIONS page 24	Sports Words with different meanings	Meet the new BMXers ✔ Reading Part 4	Past continuous
Life Skills Physical well-being: Keeping fit page 28			
Review 1 Units 1–4 page 30		✔ Reading Part 5	
5 CALL THE POLICE! page 32	Crimes and criminals *ourselves*, *yourselves*, *themselves* and *each other*	That isn't allowed here	Past simple and continuous
6 CITY LIFE page 36	City problems Compounds: noun + noun	City problems – teenagers' solutions ✔ Reading Part 5	*some*/*any*, *much*/*many*, *a lot of*, *a few* / *a little*
Culture New York City page 40			
7 GETTING ON page 42	*be*, *do*, *have* and *make* Phrasal verbs: relationships	Troublespot: don't get angry – get advice	*have to* and *must* *should*
8 GOING AWAY page 46	International travel Phrasal verbs: travel	We're off to Tokyo	Future: *be going to* and present continuous
Life Skills Interpersonal skills: Dealing with conflict page 50			
Review 2 Units 5–8 page 52		✔ Reading Part 6	
9 SHOP TILL YOU DROP page 54	Money and shopping Easily confused words: *pay*, *charge*, *cost*	Help! I just can't stop shopping! ✔ Reading Part 3	Present perfect The past participle of *go*: *been* and *gone*
10 TASTE THIS! page 58	Food and drink adjectives *look*, *taste*, *smell*	Ollie, don't eat that!	Present perfect and past simple *How long?* and *for*/*since*
Culture British food page 62			

LISTENING	SPEAKING	WRITING	VIDEO
		An online profile	
A conversation about fashion and music in the past	Talking about yourself Speaking Part 1		In fashion
			Trendsetters
		An informal email (1) Writing Part 1	Life events
A programme about sport	Describing a past event		
		A story (1) Writing Part 2	
An interview about living in the country	Agreeing and disagreeing		Modern life
			New York City
		An informal email (2) Writing Part 1	
A talk about a travel writing competition Listening Part 3	Making suggestions		
		A story (2) Writing Part 2	
Seven short conversations about food Listening Part 1	Ordering food		Taste this!
			International food in London

UNIT	VOCABULARY	READING	GRAMMAR
11 A HEALTHY FUTURE page 64	Body and health Illnesses and injuries: verbs	We will live for 1,000 years	*will* and *be going to*
12 INCREDIBLE WILDLIFE page 68	Animals Adverbs of probability	Weird animals	Modals of probability
Life Skills Social responsibility: Respecting the environment page 72			
Review 3 Units 9–12 page 74		Reading Part 5	
13 MIXED FEELINGS page 76	Adjectives: moods and feelings Adjectives: *-ed* or *-ing*	The worst day of the week Reading Part 4	*just*, *already* and *yet*
14 ON SCREEN page 80	TV and film Talking about films and shows	So you want to be in a film?	Relative clauses
Culture The film industry page 84			
15 DIGITAL LIFE page 86	Computer phrases Phrasal verbs: technology	Apps for learning English Reading Part 2	Present simple passive
16 AMAZING SCIENCE page 90	Doing experiments Phrasal verbs: science	The Ig Nobel Prize	Zero and first conditional
Life Skills ICT literacy: Staying safe online page 94			
Review 4 Units 13–16 page 96		Reading Part 6	
17 TALENTED page 98	Arts and entertainment Adjectives: *-al* and *-ful*	Who are the real artists? Reading Part 6	Reported commands
18 THE WORLD OF WORK page 102	Jobs Suffixes: *-er*, *-or*, *-ist*, *-ian*	I'm in charge	Second conditional
Culture Special training page 106			
19 THE WRITTEN WORD page 108	Things that you read *say*, *speak*, *talk* and *tell*	Signs, notices and messages Reading Part 1	Reported speech
20 SEEING IS BELIEVING page 112	Collocations: thinking *look (at)*, *see*, *watch*	Illusions everywhere	Past simple passive
Life Skills Critical thinking: Identifying reliable news page 116			
Review 5 Units 17–20 page 118		Reading Part 5	
Extra activities page 120			
Vocabulary list page 128			
Grammar reference and practice page 138			
List of irregular verbs page 158			

Key to symbols:
B1 Preliminary for Schools exam task   Video

LISTENING	SPEAKING	WRITING	VIDEO
		An article (1) Writing Part 2	Healthy future
A programme about animals at work	Describing a photo (1) Speaking Part 2		
		An article (2) Writing Part 2	Moods and feelings
Six conversations about TV and film Listening Part 2	Reaching agreement		
			History of Hollywood
		An informal email (3) Writing Part 1	
A conversation about a teenage inventor	Describing a photo (2) Speaking Part 2		
		A biography	Talented
Two conversations about problems	Discussing options Speaking Parts 3 and 4		I'm in charge
			Performing arts schools
		An online book review	
A university podcast Listening Part 4	Expressing surprise and disbelief		

1 ALL ABOUT ME

ABOUT YOU

What do you look like?
What type of person are you?

Alfie's family

Grace's family

Lucas's family

VOCABULARY Describing people

01 **1 Look at the photos and listen to three people talking about someone in their family. Who is each speaker describing?**

brother	dad	sister	mum

1 Lucas is describing his …
2 Alfie is describing his …
3 Grace is describing her …

2 Add the words to the table. EP

~~attractive~~ bald blonde curly dark elderly fair good-looking handsome middle-aged pretty straight teenage in his/her (early/late) twenties/thirties

Age	
Looks	*attractive*
Hair	

3 Describe someone in the photos. Can your partner guess who it is?

He's a teenage boy and he's good-looking.

Is it Alfie?

02 **4 Read the descriptions and choose the correct adjectives. Then listen and check.** EP

1 I think Lucas is really polite / careless. For instance, when he wants to borrow something, he always says please.
2 My brother's called Alfie. He takes my things without asking. He thinks he's funny / polite, but he doesn't make me laugh!
3 Grace is very miserable / friendly. I see her every morning on her way to school. She always says hello.
4 Alfie talks a lot – like his mum! He's sometimes a bit confident / careless with homework. I try to encourage him to check it, but he doesn't always do it.
5 Grace is a great friend. She's always smiling, and she's never miserable / polite. She really makes me laugh.
6 Lucas knows what he's good at, so he's quite a careless / confident boy. He can also be quite a lazy person though. His room is always really untidy!

5 Match the adjectives to their opposites in Exercise 4. EP

careful cheerful rude serious shy unfriendly

6 Which adjectives in Exercises 4 and 5 describe you?

7 Work in pairs. Describe someone you both know. Describe what they look like and what kind of person they are. Can your partner guess who it is?

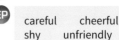

She's got straight hair and she's very confident.

Is it Ana?

1 ALL ABOUT ME

Unit Overview

TOPIC	Personal profiles
VOCABULARY	Describing people
READING	all.about.me
GRAMMAR	Present simple and continuous
VOCABULARY	Prefixes: *un-*, *in-*, *im-*
WRITING	An online profile
EXAM TASKS	Reading Part 6

Resources

GRAMMAR REFERENCE AND PRACTICE: SB page 138; TB page 244
WORKBOOK: pages 4–7
PHOTOCOPIABLE WORKSHEETS: Grammar worksheet Unit 1; Vocabulary worksheet Unit 1
TEST GENERATOR: Diagnostic test; Unit test 1

WARMER

In small groups, students have 30 seconds to brainstorm a list of adjectives to describe appearance and personality. Invite different groups to read out their lists. Write the adjectives on the board and award a point for each correctly spelled answer. Draw a stick person on the board and ask students to describe it. In pairs, students draw and describe their own stick people.

ABOUT YOU

Read the two questions and ask which question asks about your appearance (*the first one*) and what the other question asks about (*your personality*). Model the answers to the questions by answering them about yourself, for example 'I've got brown curly hair. I'm friendly and polite.'

VOCABULARY Describing people

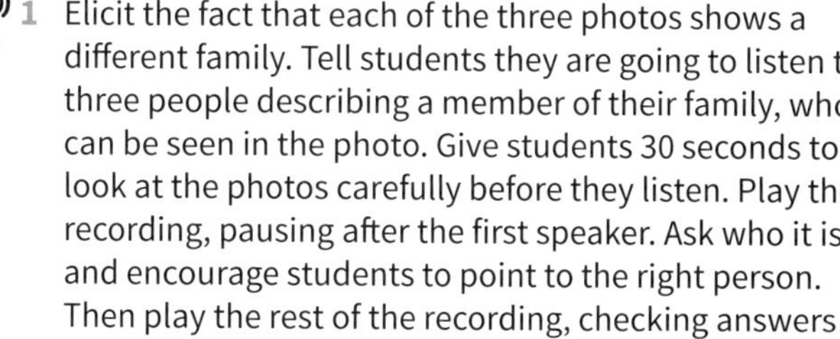

01 1 Elicit the fact that each of the three photos shows a different family. Tell students they are going to listen to three people describing a member of their family, who can be seen in the photo. Give students 30 seconds to look at the photos carefully before they listen. Play the recording, pausing after the first speaker. Ask who it is and encourage students to point to the right person. Then play the rest of the recording, checking answers after each speaker.

Answers

1 brother (the boy in the middle)
2 sister (the girl on the left)
3 dad (the man on the left)

» AUDIOSCRIPT TB PAGE 261

2 Tell students to look at the first adjective in the box, *attractive*, and ask what it describes (*looks*). Drill pronunciation. Students may have difficulty with *bald* /bɔːld/, *curly* /ˈkɜːli/, *straight* /streɪt/ and *thirties* /ˈθɜːtiz/. Check the meaning of each adjective using the people in the photos in Exercise 1. Ask, for example, 'Who's got curly hair?' and get students to point to the relevant person. Students complete the exercise in pairs. Check answers.

Answers

Age	elderly, middle-aged, teenage, in his/her (early/late) twenties/thirties
Looks	attractive, good-looking, handsome, pretty
Hair	bald, blonde, curly, dark, fair, straight

3 Ask two students to read out the example conversation. Using this as a model, describe another person from the photos using some of the new adjectives from Exercise 2. Students play the guessing game in pairs.

Possible answers

A: He's tall and middle-aged. He's got dark hair.
B: Is it Grace's dad?

02 4 Explain to students they are going to find out what type of people Lucas, Alfie and Grace are. Read out the first item and ask students to give you the correct answer. Ask them how they decided (by reading the following sentence, which gives an example of a person being polite: *he always says please*). Students complete the exercise in pairs. Play the recording, pausing after each item. Check the answers and the meaning of the adjectives. Ask students to find other adjectives in the sentences (*clever*, *great* and *lazy*) and check meaning.

Answers

1 polite 2 funny 3 friendly 4 careless 5 miserable 6 confident

» AUDIOSCRIPT TB PAGE 261

5 Go through the adjectives in the box and drill pronunciation. In pairs, students find the opposite adjectives in Exercise 4. Check answers.

Answers

careful – careless cheerful – miserable rude – polite serious – funny shy – confident unfriendly – friendly

6 Model the activity by describing yourself to the class. Choose a confident student and ask 'What about you?' Encourage them to use at least three adjectives. The student who answered then asks a classmate, and so on until several students have described themselves.

Answers

Students' own answers

7 Model the activity by describing someone in the class, adapting the example. Students work in pairs to describe and guess their classmates.

Answers

Students' own answers

READING

BACKGROUND INFORMATION

According to statistics from Statista.com and the UK Office for National Statistics, young people aged 8–15 spend 68 minutes a day on outdoor activities, sports and active travel (walking or cycling). Boys spend an average of 15 more minutes a day than girls. 75% of 12–15-year-olds use social media: 82% of young people have a Facebook account while 56% use Instagram. Internet users in the UK spend an average 114 minutes a day on social media.

1 Ask students to read the information and help them with any new vocabulary. They discuss the questions in pairs. Ask for feedback and then hold a short class discussion about question 2.

Answers

Students' own answers

2 Divide the students into three groups (A, B and C) and give them each a different profile to read. Tell group C not to worry about the missing words in their text about Alfie. Ask each group to match their profile to one of the activities in the box. Then put students into groups of three, with one student from each group A, B and C. Each student tells their group about the person whose profile they read. Students then read all three profiles and check that the people and activities are correctly matched. Check answers.

Answers

Lucas – technology
Grace – fitness
Alfie – going to the cinema

03 The Reading text is recorded for students to listen, read and check their answers.

3 **B1 Preliminary for Schools Reading Part 6**

In this part, candidates read a short text with six gaps and add the word that best fits each gap. This requires reading for detailed understanding at word and sentence level, and mostly tests knowledge of grammar. Most of the missing words are prepositions, pronouns, articles, auxiliary verbs, modal verbs, conjunctions, etc.

Explain to students that they have to complete each gap in Alfie's profile with one word. They should look at the words before and after the gap and think of one word which fits the gap. Look at the first gap together and ask students what sort of word goes after a subject and before a base form (*an auxiliary or a modal verb*). Ask them to complete the exercise and compare their answers with a partner before checking answers with the class. With the students, name the parts of speech used. Explain that these parts of speech are very typical of the words used in this kind of exercise.

MIXED ABILITY

For weaker students, monitor and help them to identify the correct part of speech for each gap. For example, we do not use the auxiliary *do* with the verb *to be* so they need a modal verb to fill the gap. Ask them to think about whether it will be positive or negative.

Answers

1 can (modal verb)
2 of (preposition)
3 them (pronoun)
4 in (preposition)
5 one (pronoun)
6 to (part of the infinitive)

4 Set a short time limit for students to read the profiles again and answer the questions. They compare their answers with a partner before checking answers as a class. Check understanding of any new words in the text. Encourage students to work out the meaning with a partner before confirming their ideas. New words may include *properly* (*correctly*) and *keen on* (*very interested in or enthusiastic about*).

Answers

1 Alfie 2 Grace 3 Lucas 4 Grace 5 Alfie 6 Lucas

5 Read the instructions. In pairs, students match the highlighted words and phrases with their meanings. Check answers and ask students to read out the sentences that contain the words and phrases.

Answers

1 take part (*taking part* in the text)
2 make progress (*making progress* in the text)
3 only child
4 code
5 be into (something) (*I'm into* in the text)
6 patient

FAST FINISHERS

Ask fast finishers to choose three of the words and phrases in Exercise 5 and write a sentence for each. Nominate students to read out their sentences. The class should decide whether they have used the word or phrase correctly.

TALKING POINTS

For the first question, take a class vote to find out who the class would most like to spend time with. Invite different students to explain why. Students discuss the second question in small groups. Monitor the discussions, giving positive feedback for interesting ideas.

COOLER

Ask students to find three sentences using *right* in the profiles:

- *Right* now, I'm taking part in a competition for young game designers.
- My friends and family say I'm a cheerful person. And they're *right*.
- I live … *right* opposite the school.

Ask students to work in pairs and discuss the meaning of *right* in each sentence. Listen to feedback as a class (*right now* means at the present moment; *they're right* means they are correct; *right opposite* means directly opposite). In small groups, students write another sentence for each of the meanings. Invite them to read their sentences out.

READING

1 **Read the information about part of a school website. Discuss the questions.**

1 Have you got something similar in your school?
2 What do you think of the idea?

BRYANS HIGH SCHOOL **all.about.me**

Would you like to meet other students at Bryans High School who share your hobbies and interests? It's easy with all.about.me.

1 Click here and create an account.
2 Post a photo and your profile – tell everyone about you, your interests and your plans.
3 Read about other students and click on 'Connect' to make new friends.

2 **Three students have posted information on *all.about.me*. Read the profiles below and ignore any gaps. Match each person to one interest.**

going to the cinema   fashion
technology   fitness

3 **Now read Alfie's profile again. Write ONE word for each gap.**

4 **Read the three profiles again. Write the correct name.**

1 ________ is interested in doing a job related to his/her hobby.
2 ________ is looking forward to learning a new activity.
3 ________ is learning a new skill with help from a relative.
4 ________ agrees with other people about his/her personality.
5 ________ would like to go to another country.
6 ________ might get a prize soon.

5 **Match the highlighted words and phrases in Lucas's and Grace's profiles with the meanings.**

1 be involved in an activity, with other people
2 become better
3 someone with no brothers or sisters
4 write computer programs
5 be very interested in something
6 able to stay calm and not get angry, especially when something takes a long time

TALKING POINTS

Who would you most like to spend time with – Alfie, Lucas or Grace? Why?
Is it important to have the same interests as your friends? Why? / Why not?

BRYANS HIGH SCHOOL
all.about.me

Hi everyone. I'm Lucas. I live with my parents, my sister and my two brothers. Some of my classmates think I'm quite serious, but I don't agree. I'm just a bit shy, and I'm quite independent. My main interest outside of school is computers and gaming. But I'm not just a gamer. Right now, I'm taking part in a competition for young game designers. So at weekends, I'm learning to code with my aunt. She's a professional coder. She's also a really patient teacher – I'm finding coding impossible at the moment!

CONNECT

Hello! I'm Grace. I live with my mum and dad. I'm an only child – so no brothers or sisters. My friends and family say I'm a cheerful person. And they're right. I think there's always something to smile about! In my free time, I'm into various typical teenage hobbies, but my favourite is sport. I'm in the school hockey and football teams. And this year I'm having tennis lessons. I'm really making progress, I think. In a few months, I'm going on a kayaking trip with my cousin. We've never done it before but we're really excited.

CONNECT

03

My name's Alfie. I live with my mum, dad and sister, Melissa, right opposite the school. I'm quite friendly and funny, but I [1] ________ be quite serious at times, too. One [2] ________ my biggest interests is film: thrillers, drama, science fiction – I don't mind. I like watching [3] ________ all. One day, I think I'd like to work [4] ________ film.

This year, I want to visit a film studio. There's [5] ________ near London where all eight Harry Potter films were made. My dream is [6] ________ fly to Hollywood and see a studio there.

CONNECT

ALL ABOUT ME 11

GRAMMAR Present simple and continuous

1 Match the examples to the rules.

1 Right now, I'm **taking part** in a competition for young game designers.
2 In a few months, I'm **going** on a kayaking trip with my cousin.
3 My friends and family **say** I'm a cheerful person.
4 This term, I'm **having** tennis lessons.
5 I **live** with my parents.

We use the present simple to talk about:
a facts.
b something that happens regularly.

We use the present continuous for:
c something that is happening right now or around now.
d temporary situations.
e future plans.

» **GRAMMAR REFERENCE AND PRACTICE PAGE 138**

2 Complete the sentences with the present simple or continuous form of the verbs in brackets.

1 I ________ (get) home at five o'clock every day.
2 Mum ________ (work) late this week.
3 Look at Dan. He ________ (not concentrate).
4 ____ you ________ (do) anything interesting next weekend?
5 She ________ (play) the guitar and the piano.
6 He always ________ (go) swimming on Saturdays.

3 Look at Exercises 1 and 2. Are these time words and phrases used with the present simple (PS) or present continuous (PC)?

at the moment / right now *PC*
never, sometimes, always
every day/week/year
this month/term/week
later, tomorrow, tonight
on Saturdays, at weekends
next week/weekend/month

4 Write six sentences about you. Use the time words and phrases in Exercise 3.

Right now, I'm having an English lesson.

5 Read the information about the verbs. Check the meaning of the verbs you don't know.

We don't use some verbs in continuous forms. These verbs are called **stative verbs** and include: *believe, hate, know, like, love, mean, need, own, prefer, understand, want.*
***I don't understand** this question.*
NOT *~~I'm not understanding~~ this question.*

6 Complete the sentences with the positive or negative form of the verbs in Exercise 5. Sometimes more than one answer is possible.

0 My uncle *owns* three cars.
1 Ruby's very friendly. We really ________ her.
2 I ________ how old he is. He looks about 14.
3 What ________ this word ________ ?
4 I'm feeling miserable today. I ________ cold weather.
5 You're speaking too quickly and I ________ you.

7 Choose the correct form of the verbs.

1 We *have / 're having* problems with the computers at the moment.
2 I *need / 'm needing* some new shoes.
3 I *write / 'm writing* to you about a trip we are planning in November.
4 Tonight she *goes / 's going* to the cinema with some friends.
5 This term I *have / 'm having* some extra maths lessons.
6 I *never forget / 'm never forgetting* my homework.

8 » **Work with a partner. Turn to page 120.**

VOCABULARY Prefixes: *un-*, *in-*, *im-*

1 Read the examples. Then write the opposites of the adjectives, 1–12.

EP

I'm finding coding **impossible** at the moment!
Lucas's room is always really **untidy**.
I'm quite **independent**.

1 kind	2 friendly	3 patient
4 expensive	5 known	6 polite
7 visible	8 healthy	9 well
10 fair	11 lucky	12 correct

2 Agree with these sentences. Use an adjective from Exercise 1 or its opposite.

0 **A:** I didn't recognise any of the actors in that film.
B: They were all *unknown*, I think.
1 **A:** Dad never waits for me!
B: You're right. He's very ________.
2 **A:** Mum's still in bed!
B: I know. She's feeling really ________.
3 **A:** It's important to wear bright clothing on a bike at night.
B: Yes, you need to be ________ to drivers.
4 **A:** We have to be home at 10.30. That's so early!
B: Yeah. It's really ________.
5 **A:** I can't believe you found your phone!
B: I know. I'm so ________.
6 **A:** The last question in the homework was hard!
B: Yes! I got the same answer as you, but Mrs Thomas said it was ________.

3 » **Work with a partner. Turn to page 120.**

GRAMMAR Present simple and continuous

WARMER

Dictate the following: 'My name is … I live in … I'm a teacher. I'm teaching right now. On Saturday morning I usually play tennis with my friend, but this Saturday we're playing in the afternoon because I'm going shopping in the morning.' Ask for volunteers to write each sentence on the board. Students name the tenses and say which refer to the present and which to the future.

1 Students look at the sentences and say which are in the present simple and which are in the present continuous. Read the rules and check understanding. In pairs, students match the examples to the rules. Check answers.

» **GRAMMAR REFERENCE AND PRACTICE ANSWER KEY TB PAGE 244**

Answers

1 c 2 e 3 b 4 d / c 5 a

2 Students read the first sentence and complete it with the correct verb form. They complete the exercise in pairs. Invite different pairs to read out the sentences. Ask stronger students to explain why the form they have chosen is correct. As a follow up, you can ask students to match the sentences to the rules in activity 1.

Answers

1 get (rule b) 2 is working (rule d) 3 isn't concentrating (rule c)
4 Are, doing (rule e) 5 plays (rule a) 6 goes (rule b)

3 In pairs, students underline the time expressions in Exercises 1 and 2. They read the first example and then complete the exercise in pairs.

Answers

Present simple
at the moment / right now
never, sometimes, always
on Saturdays / at weekends
every day/week/year
Present continuous
this month/term/week
later, tomorrow, tonight
next week/weekend/month

4 Students choose six words or expressions from Exercise 3. They read the example sentence and then write six sentences of their own on a piece of paper, using the time expressions they have chosen. Tell them not to write their name on the paper. Collect the papers and ask different students to read out one of the sentences for the class to guess who wrote it.

Answers

Students' own answers

5 Explain that some verbs, called *stative* verbs, are not used in continuous forms. Students read the list of verbs. Check understanding and read the example sentence. It might help students to group the verbs according to meaning, for example *hate, like, love, prefer*; *mean, understand*; *believe, know*; *need, want*. Other stative verbs similar to *own* that the students may know include *have, possess, belong*. Explain that this is not a complete set and they can add to the list when they learn new verbs.

6 Read the example. Students complete the exercise and compare their answers with a partner. Check answers.

Answers

1 like / love 2 don't know / don't believe 3 does, mean
4 hate / don't like 5 don't/can't understand

7 Point out the icon and explain that whenever students see this symbol it refers to the Cambridge English Corpus – in other words, the structures introduced here have been taken from a database of the language that is frequently used and most useful to students at this level. Students complete the exercise and compare answers with a partner. Check answers.

Answers

1 're having 2 need 3 'm writing 4 's going 5 'm having
6 never forget

8 Direct students to turn to page 120. In pairs, students write the questions. Check answers. Then the pairs ask and answer the questions. Invite students to tell the class what their partner answered. Check they use the third person forms correctly.

Answers

1 What subjects are you studying this year?
2 What are you doing after school today?
3 Do you own more than one mobile phone?
4 What TV programmes do you watch every week?
5 Do you prefer playing sport or watching TV?
6 What do you like doing on Sundays?
7 What music do you listen to regularly?
8 Are you having a party for your next birthday?

» **GRAMMAR WORKSHEET UNIT 1**

VOCABULARY Prefixes: *un-, in-, im-*

1 Remind students of the vocabulary exercises on page 10. Explain that we can make the opposite of some adjectives by using a prefix, for example *un-*, *in-* or *im-*. Read the examples, check understanding and ask students for the adjective forms without the prefix (*possible, tidy, dependent*). Then read the adjectives in the exercise and check understanding. Students complete the exercise individually before comparing answers with a partner. Check answers.

Answers

1 unkind 2 unfriendly 3 impatient 4 inexpensive
5 unknown 6 impolite 7 invisible 8 unhealthy 9 unwell
10 unfair 11 unlucky 12 incorrect

2 Read the example with the class. Students complete the exercise in pairs. Check answers.

Answers

1 impatient 2 unwell 3 visible 4 unfair 5 lucky 6 incorrect

3 Students turn to page 120. In pairs, they ask and answer the questions. Invite some students to share their answers with the class.

Answers

Students' own answers

» **VOCABULARY WORKSHEET UNIT 1**

WRITING An online profile

1 Elicit what an online profile is (*personal information about you and the things you like doing that appears on a website*). Find out when students last wrote an online profile. Check they understand the phrase 'most like you' = 'most similar to you'. Set a short time limit for students to read the profiles carefully and decide which person is most like them. Tell them not to worry about the underlined or highlighted words. Invite students to say who they are most like and why. Tell students to read the profiles again. Put them in small groups to make a list of the topics mentioned, for example their age and username, school, appearance, personality, hobbies, where they live, what they are learning to do, what their friends think about them. Find out which group identified the most topics.

Answers

Students' own answers

2 Direct students to the *Prepare to write* box and set a short time limit for them to find the phrases. Check answers.

Answers

Tom uses:
I'm (Tom)
I think I'm (quite intelligent and very friendly).
I'm really into (music)
Felicity uses:
My name's (Felicity)
I'm from (Australia)
My hobbies are (fashion, fashion and fashion)
I'm learning (to play the drums) at the moment
I'm (fairly confident)
I'm (a bit careless)
My friends say I'm (cheerful and friendly)

3 Put students in pairs to answer the questions. Tell them to look carefully at the underlined verbs in the two profiles.

MIXED ABILITY

Put students in mixed ability pairs to complete Exercise 3, encouraging stronger students to explain the rules from page 12, if necessary.

Answers

1 present simple
2 present continuous

4 Direct students to the highlighted words and ask 'What kind of words are these?' to elicit that they are adverbs. Direct students to the two headings in the table. Check what *stronger* and *weaker* mean (*more* and *less*). Monitor and help students to complete the table. Check answers.

Answers

Make adjectives weaker	Make adjectives stronger
quite	very
fairly	really
a bit	

5 Put students into small groups to write down as many of the adjectives for personality (from Exercises 4 and 5 on page 10) as they can in one minute. They exchange lists with another team and read out that list. Award points for each correct answer to find the winning team. Then read the instructions for Exercise 5 and model an example, such as 'I'm very cheerful'. Ask other students for an example of each sentence which is true for them. Then ask students to complete the sentences individually. Monitor and help as necessary. Give them time to share their answers with their group. Share some ideas as a class.

Answers

Students' own answers

6 Write the prompts on the board. Choose a confident student and say you are going to make some notes about them. Ask the class to say one or two positive things about the student and add notes to the appropriate point on the board. Students make their own notes about themselves. Put them in pairs to discuss their ideas.

Answers

Students' own answers

7 Students write their online profile, using the four bullet points to guide them, and the notes they made in Exercise 6. Ask them to use as much of the new language and vocabulary as they can, but not to make their profile too long (it doesn't matter if they don't use everything!). Monitor and help as they are working. Remind them to check their spelling and grammar. Ask confident students to read their profiles aloud.

Model answer

I'm Victor and I'm from Manchester in England. I love sport and I'm really into football. I play every day with my friends and I'm in the school team, too. There are two fantastic football teams in Manchester – it's a very good place for football! I'm quite confident and I like learning new things. At the moment I'm learning to play ice hockey. It's fairly difficult, but I know I can do it!

FAST FINISHERS

Ask fast finishers to write four more sentences using adjectives from Vocabulary Exercise 1 on page 12. They read out the sentences to the class omitting the adjective and the class has to guess the correct adjective.

COOLER

Play 'Guess the word' using *believe*, *hate*, *know*, *like*, *love*, *mean*, *need*, *own*, *prefer*, *understand* and *want*. Give students one minute to look at the verbs on page 12 and then tell them to close their books. Put them in small teams. Write short lines on the board to represent the letters of one of the verbs. Students work in teams and take turns to call out a letter. If the letter is in the word, write it where it occurs in the spaces. If the letter isn't in the word, write it on the board and cross it out. The first team to guess the word receives one point.

WRITING An online profile

1 Read the two online profiles. Which person is most like you? Why?

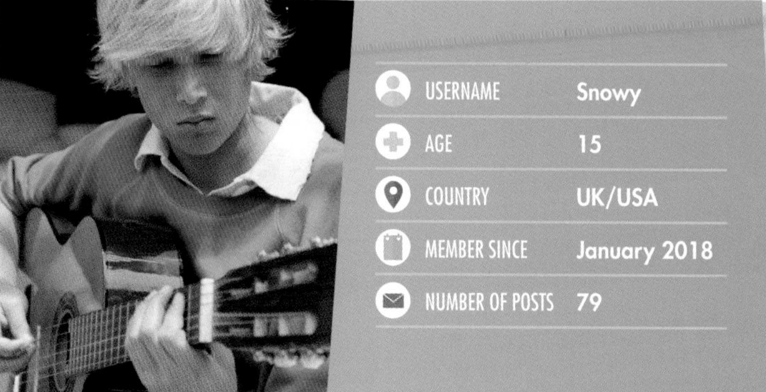

USERNAME	Snowy
AGE	15
COUNTRY	UK/USA
MEMBER SINCE	January 2018
NUMBER OF POSTS	79

I'm Tom, but my online name is Snowy – my hair is very blonde! I'm British, but I'm living in the USA right now because my parents are working here. I go to Carson High School in Boston.

I think I'm quite intelligent and very friendly. Some people disagree, of course! I'm really into music and I play the guitar. I practise every day and I'm starting to write my own songs. You can hear a few of them online.

USERNAME	Vogue
AGE	16
COUNTRY	Australia
MEMBER SINCE	March 2018
NUMBER OF POSTS	349

My name's Felicity, but everyone calls me Flic. I'm from Australia. My hobbies are fashion, fashion and fashion – especially from the 1970s and 80s. Oh, and I also love music. I'm learning to play the drums at the moment. They're really loud.

I'm fairly confident, but sometimes I'm a bit careless with my school work. My friends say I'm cheerful and friendly but I know that I can sometimes be impatient. I'm trying to change!

2 Read the *Prepare to write* box. Which phrases do Tom and Felicity use in their profiles?

PREPARE TO WRITE

An online profile

In an online profile:

- introduce yourself: *I'm …, My name's …, I'm from …*
- say what kind of person you are: *(I think) I'm very/quite …, My friends say I'm …, I can sometimes be …*
- talk about your hobbies and interests: *I'm interested in …, I'm (really) into …, My hobbies are …*
- say what you're learning at the moment: *At the moment I'm …, Right now I'm …*

3 Look at the underlined verbs in the profiles. What verb form do Tom and Flic use for:

1 their likes and dislikes, and things they do regularly?
2 things they're doing at the moment?

4 Look at the highlighted adverbs in the profiles. Add them to the table.

Make adjectives weaker	Make adjectives stronger
quite	

5 Complete the sentences for you.

1 I'm very …
2 I'm fairly …
3 Sometimes I'm quite …
4 My friends say I'm …
5 I think I can be a bit …

6 Make notes for your online profile. Use the ideas to help you.

- my name
- facts about me
- what I'm like
- hobbies and interests
- things I'm learning at the moment

7 Write your online profile.

- Use the plan and phrases in the *Prepare to write* box.
- Use adverbs to make adjectives stronger and weaker.
- Write about 80 words.
- Remember to check your spelling and grammar.

2 IN FASHION

ABOUT YOU

01 **Watch the video and then answer the questions.**

What are you wearing today?
What fashions do you like?
Which colours or clothes look good on you?

VOCABULARY Clothes: adjectives

04 **1** **Look at the photos. Who are the people and what are they wearing? Then listen and check.**

05 **2** **Listen to an interview with three teenagers. Are they talking about:**

a what's fashionable at the moment?
b what clothes they might buy?
c what they like wearing?

05 **3** **Read the questions. Then listen again and write** ***A*** **(Ashley),** ***M*** **(Molly) or** ***L*** **(Luke).** EP

1 Whose clothes are comfortable?
2 Whose jeans are skinny?
3 Who is wearing something brand new?
4 Who doesn't wear smart clothes?
5 Who isn't interested in trendy clothes?
6 Who is very well-dressed today?

4 **Match the adjectives to their opposites in Exercise 3. How many adjectives can you match to each photo?** EP

~~badly-dressed~~ casual
loose-fitting second-hand
uncomfortable unfashionable

badly-dressed – well-dressed

5 **Discuss the questions.**

1 What do you like wearing? What types of clothing do you never wear? Why?
2 Do you generally prefer smart or casual clothes? Why?
3 How important is it for you to wear trendy clothes?

A B C D

2 IN FASHION

Unit Overview

TOPIC	Fashion and clothes
VOCABULARY	Clothes: adjectives
READING	Fashion and music
GRAMMAR	Past simple
VOCABULARY	Adverbs
LISTENING	A conversation about fashion and music in the past
SPEAKING	Talking about yourself
EXAM TASKS	Speaking Part 1

Resources

GRAMMAR REFERENCE AND PRACTICE: SB page 139; TB page 244
WORKBOOK: pages 8–11
VIDEO AND VIDEO WORKSHEET: In fashion
PHOTOCOPIABLE WORKSHEETS: Grammar worksheet Unit 2; Vocabulary worksheet Unit 2
TEST GENERATOR: Unit test 2

WARMER

Put students into small groups to brainstorm articles of clothing. Give them a time limit. Compare answers. The group with the most items wins. Make sure students understand the vocabulary items that appear in the listening exercises: *bag*, *blouse*, *boots*, *cap*, *handbag*, *jacket*, *jeans*, *necklace*, *shirt*, *sleeve*, *suit*, *T-shirt*, *tie*, *top*, *tracksuit*, *trainers*, *trousers*.

ABOUT YOU

01 You can begin the class and introduce the topic of the unit by showing the video and asking students to complete the video worksheet. Then, read the questions in the *About you* box. Model answers to the questions to help understanding, for example 'Today I'm wearing trousers and a shirt. I like fashions from the 1960s. I look good in bright colours'. In pairs, students ask and answer the questions. If they find the second question difficult to answer, they could point to one of the pictures and say 'I like this fashion'. Ask for students to tell the class what their partner has answered. Make sure they use the third-person singular verbs correctly.

VOCABULARY Clothes: adjectives

04 1 Students look at the photos. They identify the people and describe what they are wearing. Play the recording, pausing after each description to check answers.

» AUDIOSCRIPT TB PAGE 261

Answers

A Jaden Smith, singer and actor – denim jacket, white T-shirt, white trousers, black cap (bag, necklaces)
B Taylor Swift, singer and actor – black shirt, black trousers (handbag)
C Ed Sheeran, singer – black suit, white shirt, black tie
D Rihanna, singer – trainers, trousers, black and white blouse

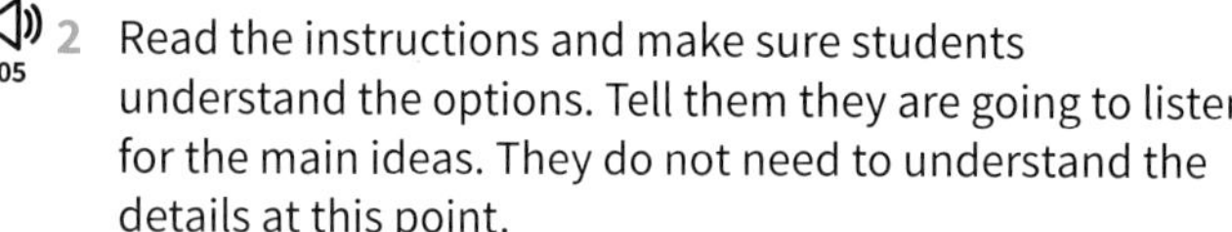

05 2 Read the instructions and make sure students understand the options. Tell them they are going to listen for the main ideas. They do not need to understand the details at this point.

Answers

c what they like wearing

05 3 Students read the questions. Check the meaning of the words in bold and ask what type of words they are (*adjectives*). Demonstrate meaning by pointing to items of clothing that you or a student are wearing or that are shown in the photos. Play the recording again. Students compare their answers with a partner. If necessary, play the recording once more. Check answers.

Answers

1 A 2 L 3 M 4 A 5 L 6 M

» AUDIOSCRIPT TB PAGE 261

4 Students match the adjectives to their opposites in Exercise 3. Check answers and pronunciation of the words in the box, paying attention to *dressed* /drest/, *casual* /ˈkæʒjuəl/ and *uncomfortable* /ʌnˈkʌmftəbl/. Students complete the second part of the exercise in pairs, matching the adjectives to the photos. Invite students to share their ideas with the class.

Answers

badly-dressed – well-dressed
casual – smart
loose-fitting – skinny
second-hand – brand new
uncomfortable – comfortable
unfashionable – trendy

FAST FINISHERS

Ask fast finishers to write a description of one of the photos, for example *He's wearing a smart suit and a narrow tie*. They read out their description for the class to guess which person is being described.

5 Ask students to read the questions and check understanding. Choose some stronger students to answer them briefly. Students ask and answer the questions in pairs. Monitor and join in with the discussions. Invite students to tell the class about their partner. Write any new vocabulary on the board.

Answers

Students' own answers

READING

BACKGROUND INFORMATION

In the 1960s, London was the centre of the fashion scene and was known as 'Swinging London'. Carnaby Street, in the centre of London's West End, was famous for its boutiques, and many pop stars and actors shopped there. The most famous designer at this time was Mary Quant, who is credited with inventing the mini skirt. She designed specifically for young people, encouraging them to wear whatever they felt like and to regard fashion as a game. The best-known designer associated with the punk era of the 1970s is Vivienne Westwood. In partnership with Malcolm McLaren, the manager of legendary punk band the Sex Pistols, she created clothes that were designed to shock.

1 Put students in groups to write down as many bands and singers as they know from the 20th century. Students read the article quickly to see if any of them are mentioned. Ask them to tell you names of bands or singers mentioned in the article and in which decade they were most famous (answers are in the article). Tell them not to worry about any unknown words at this point. Ask them to match the paragraphs with the photos (clockwise from top left: 1960s, 1970s, 1950s, today, 1990s).

Answers

Students' own answers

2 Elicit the key words in the questions and the answer options and ask students where they will find the answers in the text, for example question 1 – in the introduction or the first paragraph. Students read the text carefully and complete the exercise. Monitor and help, encouraging them to identify the part of the text where they can find each answer. Check answers, inviting different students to read out the relevant parts of the text.

Answers

1 B 2 B 3 A 4 B 5 A 6 A

06 The Reading text is recorded for students to listen, read and check their answers.

3 Set a short time limit for students to work individually to match the highlighted words to the meanings. They compare answers with a partner. Check answers as a class. Check understanding of any other new words in the text. Remind students that they should try to work out the meanings from the context. New words may include (paragraph 1) *straight away* – immediately, *lively* – full of energy and interest; (paragraph 2) *Men and women* ***alike*** – both men and women; (paragraph 3) *to be into* – to like or be interested in; (paragraph 5) *genre* /ˈʒɒnrə/ – type or category. Ask students what music they are into and encourage them to describe the fashions associated with it.

Answers

1 trends 2 tear (*tore* in the text) 3 messy 4 youth 5 look 6 clothing

TALKING POINTS

Check understanding of the questions with the class. Give students five minutes to work in pairs or small groups to note down some ideas about each question. Monitor and help with vocabulary. Ask the first question and encourage different students to offer their ideas, giving reasons for their opinions. Other students should react by adding ideas of their own, agreeing, disagreeing, etc. Repeat the process for the second question.

MIXED ABILITY

Allow weaker students to look at their vocabulary lists from page 14, Exercises 3 and 4, and page 15, Exercise 3, to help them. Remind them that questions asking *Why?* Should be answered with *Because …*

COOLER

Ask students to write a brief description on paper of what a classmate is wearing without giving their name or sex: *This person is wearing …* Collect the descriptions and share them out between other students. Ask for volunteers to read out the description. The class try to identify the person being described.

FASHION and MUSIC

06

Before the mid-1950s, there was no such thing as 'youth culture'. Most young people wore the same fashions as their parents, and they listened to the same kind of music. But that all changed with the arrival of rock 'n' roll.

It started with the 1954 song *Rock Around the Clock* by Bill Haley and the Comets. Although the older generation didn't understand rock 'n' roll, teenagers fell in love with it straight away. It was a new sound – lively and exciting – and with it came new fashions in clothing. Young men wore smart suits with skinny ties, like the popular singers Buddy Holly and Elvis Presley. Young women liked groups such as The Supremes, and they wore loose-fitting skirts which looked great when they danced.

In the 1960s, rock bands like The Rolling Stones became symbols of the growing youth culture. Young women wore very short 'mini skirts' – the older generation was shocked! The mid-1960s to the mid-70s was the hippie era. Young hippies were interested in peace and love, and they listened to The Beatles, Dusty Springfield and Joni Mitchell. Men and women alike had long hair and wore flowery clothing and sandals.

The punk music of the late 70s was loud and angry, and the trends matched the music. Punks wanted to shock people. They dressed in second-hand clothes, which they often tore to look more individual, and their hairstyles were colourful and messy. Teenagers were into bands like The Clash and singers like Debbie Harry and Patti Smith. In the 1980s, long curly hair and bright colours were trendy, and people listened to Michael Jackson, Madonna and U2.

By the 1990s, teens were in love with the look and sound of singers like Britney Spears. It was also the decade of 'boy bands' and 'girl bands' – the Backstreet Boys and the Spice Girls were 'top of the pops'. Black American music called hip hop became popular internationally. Hip hop stars wore tracksuits, gold rings and necklaces, and they sang about having money and driving expensive cars.

Today, people are interested in the styles of their favourite YouTubers and tunes by superstar DJs like Calvin Harris. Hollywood actors or bestselling singers such as Taylor Swift and Ed Sheeran are also popular. There are dozens of genres of rock and dance music and, thanks to the internet, music and clothing fashions are here today and gone tomorrow.

READING

1 **How many bands and singers from the last century can you name? Read the article quickly. Does it mention any of them?**

2 **Read the article again. Choose the correct answers.**

1. Before the 1950s, teenagers
   A didn't listen to music very much.
   B listened to the same music as adults.
2. In the 1950s, teenage boys
   A joined rock 'n' roll bands.
   B wore clothes similar to the pop stars.
3. In the 1960s,
   A fashions shocked some people.
   B hippies wore mini skirts.
4. Punks in the late 70s
   A wore colourful clothing.
   B didn't wear brand new clothes.
5. Hip hop singers of the 1990s liked
   A wearing jewellery.
   B wearing smart suits.
6. Nowadays, people
   A get their fashion ideas from YouTubers.
   B wear similar clothing to Taylor Swift and Ed Sheeran.

3 **Match the highlighted words in the article to the meanings.**

1. fashions or styles
2. pulled something in order to break it
3. untidy or dirty
4. young people in general
5. someone's appearance
6. what people wear in general

TALKING POINTS

Why do young people like to dress differently from their parents and grandparents?

Why do you think people choose to dress like music stars?

IN FASHION 15

GRAMMAR Past simple

1 **Read the examples and complete the rules with words from the box.**

1 They **listened** to the same kind of music.
2 They **didn't understand** rock 'n' roll.
3 What **did** they wear?

did	didn't	*-d* or *-ed*

We use the past simple to talk about finished past actions and states.
a Regular verbs end with ________ in the affirmative, but a lot of common verbs are irregular.
b We form negative sentences with ________ + infinitive.
c We form questions with ________ + infinitive.

» **GRAMMAR REFERENCE AND PRACTICE PAGE 139**

2 **Choose the correct words.**

1 I *choosed* / *chose* some new shoes for the party.
2 I *heard* / *heared* the new Harry Styles single.
3 My sister and I *enjoyed* / *enjoied* shopping last Saturday.
4 Did you *get* / *got* any new clothes?
5 He *read* / *red* the lyrics of the songs before he *sung* / *sang* them.
6 I didn't *met* / *meet* your friends at the concert.
7 When did you *go* / *went* shopping?
8 We *planned* / *planed* to go to a concert in Hyde Park but they cancelled it.

3 **Complete the sentences about you. Use the past simple positive or negative form of the verbs.**

1 I ________ (wear) jeans yesterday.
2 I ________ (get) clothes for my last birthday.
3 My parents ________ (buy) the clothes I'm wearing.
4 My family and I ________ (watch) TV last night.
5 My best friend ________ (text) me this morning.
6 We ________ (go) shopping last weekend.
7 I ________ (have) a music lesson last week.
8 I ________ (see) my friends last weekend.

4 **Complete the conversation with the past simple form of the verbs.**

A: Hey, where [1] ________ (you / get) that T-shirt? It's really cool!
B: My brother [2] ________ (give) it to me for my birthday.
A: I really like it. Where [3] ________ (he / find) it?
B: Well, he [4] ________ (not find) it exactly. He [5] ________ (design) it.
A: Really? How [6] ________ (he / do) that?
B: He [7] ________ (use) this app called UTme, on his phone. He [8] ________ (take) a photo and then added the colours and the writing. He [9] ________ (show) me the app. It's really cool.
A: Wow! I [10] ________ (not know) you could do that. Can you show me the app?

5 **Make questions about last weekend.**

0 what / you / do / last weekend?
What did you do last weekend?
0 you / go / shopping?
Did you go shopping?
1 which friends / you / meet?
2 you / play / any sports?
3 what / watch / on TV?
4 you / go / to bed late?

6 **In pairs, ask and answer the questions in Exercise 5.**

A: *What did you do last weekend?*
B: *We went to London.*
A: *Did you go shopping?*
B: *Yes, we did. / No, we didn't.*

VOCABULARY Adverbs

1 **We can form adverbs from adjectives. What are the adjective forms of the adverbs in the examples?**

1 Hip hop became popular **internationally**.
2 He shouted at us **angrily**.
3 You need to work **hard**.

2 **Complete the table with adverbs from the adjectives in the box.**

~~amazing~~	bad	careful	early
fast	good	healthy	heavy
honest	lazy	lucky	polite
quick	rude	serious	

+ *-ly*	*y* + *-ily*	Irregular adverbs
amazingly		

3 **Complete the sentences with adverbs formed from the adjectives.**

1 The sisters were chatting ________ (happy).
2 She was late, so she was walking ________ (fast).
3 You mustn't talk ________ (loud) in the cinema.
4 My grandma is old. She walks quite ________ (slow).
5 What did he say? He's talking very ________ (quiet).
6 I'm studying ________ (hard) for the exam.
7 He plays the piano really ________ (good).
8 Alana won the tennis match ________ (easy).

4 » **Work with a partner. Turn to page 120.**

GRAMMAR Past simple

WARMER

Introduce the past simple by saying what you did last weekend. Check how much students already know about the past simple by asking individuals what they did after school yesterday.

1 Books closed. Students call out verbs. Write them on the board in columns, according to whether they are regular (for example *walk*) or irregular (for example *go*). Elicit their past simple forms and ask students what they notice about the regular verbs (they end in *-ed*). It helps to group irregular verbs according to their patterns, for example *sing–sang*, *ring–rang*. With books open, students read the three sentences and complete the rules. Check answers. Elicit an example for each rule using the verbs on the board.

Answers

a *-d* or *-ed* b didn't c did

» **GRAMMAR REFERENCE AND PRACTICE ANSWER KEY TB PAGE 244**

2 Students read the first sentence and give the answer (*chose*). Remind them to think about irregular past tense forms and spelling rules. Students complete the exercise individually before comparing answers with a partner. Check answers and drill correct pronunciation.

Answers

1 chose 2 heard 3 enjoyed 4 get 5 read, sang 6 meet 7 go 8 planned

3 Ask students if any of them wore jeans yesterday. Elicit both a positive and a negative response. Students complete the exercise individually and share their answers with a partner. Check answers, eliciting both positive and negative responses for each verb.

Answers

1 wore / didn't wear 2 got / didn't get 3 bought / didn't buy 4 watched / didn't watch 5 texted / didn't text 6 went / didn't go 7 had / didn't have 8 saw / didn't see

4 Students say if the verbs in brackets are regular or irregular. Remind them of the rules for forming negatives and questions. Students complete the conversation. Invite different pairs to read out the conversation and check answers.

Answers

1 did you get 2 gave 3 did he find 4 didn't find 5 designed 6 did he do 7 used 8 took 9 showed 10 didn't know

5 Students look at the examples and explain why they are different (the first is an *open* or *information* question. The second is a *closed* or *Yes*/*No* question). Elicit other question words (*why*, *where*, *when*, *who*, and so on).

MIXED ABILITY

Put students in mixed ability pairs to complete Exercises 5 and 6.

Answers

1 Which friends did you meet? 2 Did you play any sports? 3 What did you watch on TV? 4 Did you go to bed late?

FAST FINISHERS

Ask fast finishers to write four more questions using prompts from Exercise 3, for example *Did you wear jeans yesterday?*

6 Nominate two students to read out the example questions and answers. Remind students of short answers: *Did you go to London?* ~~*Yes, I went.*~~ *Yes, I* ***did***; *No, I* ***didn't***. Students ask and answer the questions from Exercise 5. Invite different pairs to read out their conversations. Students give their own answers.

» **GRAMMAR WORKSHEET UNIT 2**

VOCABULARY Adverbs

1 Books closed. Write *slowly*, *quickly* and *beautifully* on the board. Explain that these words are adverbs and they tell us *how* we do something. Write *sing*, *speak*, *walk* on the board. Ask students to choose one verb and one adverb and write a sentence. Volunteers read their sentences, for example *Cristina speaks English beautifully. I walk very slowly*. Make sure the word order is correct. Students open their books and complete Exercise 1.

Answers

1 international 2 angry 3 hard

2 Ask students what they notice about how the adverbs are formed in Exercise 1 (*international* adds *-ly*, *angry* changes *y* to *i* and adds *-ly*, *hard* is irregular and does not change). Students complete the table in pairs. Write the three headings on the board and invite students to write the adverbs under the correct heading. Ask if they can think of any other adjectives ending in *-y* and add the adverb form to the second column (for example *easy*).

Answers

+ *-ly:* amazingly badly carefully honestly politely quickly rudely seriously

y + *-ily:* healthily heavily lazily luckily

Irregular adverbs: early fast well

3 Students complete the exercise individually and compare answers with a partner. Check answers.

Answers

1 happily 2 fast 3 loudly 4 slowly 5 quietly 6 hard 7 well 8 easily

4 Students turn to page 120. Check understanding of the adjectives. In pairs, students write as many sentences using the adverb forms as they can in five minutes and compare their answers with another pair. Students give their own answers.

» **VOCABULARY WORKSHEET UNIT 2**

LISTENING

1 Briefly revise clothes vocabulary from page 14. Ask students what they know about The Beatles and tell them to describe the clothes The Beatles are wearing in the picture. From left to right, they are John Lennon, Paul McCartney, Ringo Starr and George Harrison.

Possible answers

jackets, ties, scarves, shirts, trousers, shoes

07 2 Explain to students that they are going to listen to a conversation between Sara, a teenager, and her grandma. Students look at the photo and read the three options of what they are talking about. Play the recording and check answers.

Answer

b

» AUDIOSCRIPT TB PAGES 261–262

08 3 Before students do the exercise, ask them to predict the answers from what they remember from their first listen. Play the recording for students to choose the correct options. Allow them to compare answers with a partner before playing the recording again. Stop after each item to check answers.

Answers

1 didn't watch 2 listened to 3 on TV 4 dad

» AUDIOSCRIPT TB PAGE 262

09 4 Give students two minutes to read the sentences and predict the answers before they listen again. Play the second part of the conversation again for them to complete the sentences with the words in the box. Check answers.

Answers

1 blue, jeans
2 dresses, tights
3 hair, beards, loose-fitting
4 jacket

» AUDIOSCRIPT TB PAGE 262

SPEAKING Talking about yourself

1 Ask students to read the questions and discuss them with a partner. Monitor and help as necessary. Then nominate a student to answer the first question and name another student to answer the next question. Repeat the procedure for question 3.

Answers

Students' own answers

2 Ask students to read the questions about shopping and decide in pairs which option is correct. Check answers.

Answers

1 do you like 2 do you buy 3 do you usually 4 do

10 3 Read the instructions and play the recording for students to make notes. Invite different students to feed back to the class.

Answers

1 jeans
2 two or three times a month
3 the market
4 about £30 a month

10 4 Ask students to read the sentences with their partner and predict the kind of information that goes in each space (*verbs, time expressions*). Play the recording again for them to listen and complete the sentences. Check answers.

Answers

1 think 2 every week 3 don't like 4 always

10 5 Read the *Prepare to speak* box and ask students if they can add any more words or phrases to each point, for example *I sometimes*, *I love*, *In my opinion*, etc. Play the recording again for them to tick the phrases they hear. Check answers.

Answers

I like …
I think …
I usually …
I don't like …
because …
I always …

» AUDIOSCRIPT TB PAGE 262

6 **B1 Preliminary for Schools Speaking Part 1**

In this part, students' ability to give factual and personal information is tested. The interlocutor asks each candidate questions about their personal details, daily routines, likes and dislikes, past experiences and future plans. This part lasts for two to three minutes.

Put students into small groups and tell them to take turns to ask a question and invite each student to answer it. Monitor and join in the discussions. Invite different students to report back about their group's shopping habits.

Answers

Students' own answers

COOLER

Write the word *uncomfortable* on the board and put students into groups of three. They have three minutes to write down as many words of three or more letters as they can, using the letters in *uncomfortable*. Tell them they can only use the letters once in each of their words except for the letter *o*, which appears twice. Invite teams to read their lists. Award a point for each word and award a bonus point for any words which use more than four letters.

Possible answers

Three letters: are, cat, far, fat, for, not, one, ten; *four letters*: blue, boat, coat, comb, come, foot, form, four, from, late, moon, more, near, room, tune; *more than four letters*: comfort, comfortable, count, table, trouble

LISTENING

1 **Look at the photo. What do you know about The Beatles? What are they wearing in this photo?**

07 **2** **Listen to a conversation between Sara and her grandma. What does Sara's grandma talk about?**

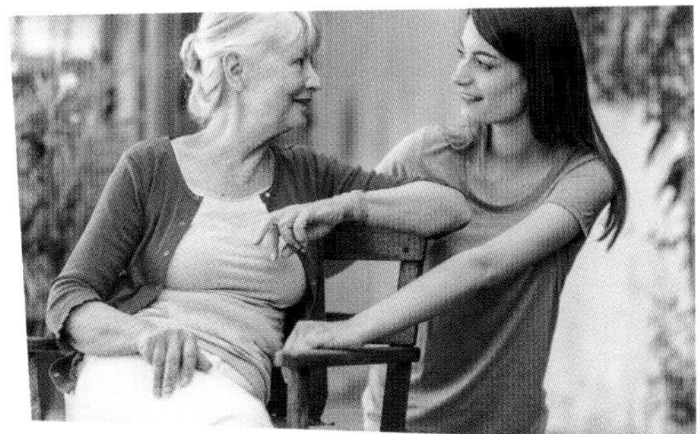

a her favourite band from the 1970s
b music and fashion in the 1960s
c women's clothes fashions in the 1960s

08 **3** **Listen to the first half of the conversation again. Choose the correct answers.**

1 People *watched / didn't watch* colour TV in the 1950s.
2 Sara's grandma *listened to / didn't listen to* pop music in the 1960s.
3 Sara's grandma watched The Beatles play *on TV / at a concert.*
4 Sara's *dad / grandma* still plays The Beatles' *Abbey Road* album.

09 **4** **Listen to the second half of the conversation again. Complete the sentences. Listen again and check.**

beards	blue	dresses	hair	jacket
jeans	loose-fitting	necklaces	tights	

1 Grandma's ________ jacket matches Sara's ________.
2 Girls wore short ________ and colourful ________ in the 1960s.
3 By the end of the 1960s, the fashion for men was for long ________, ________ and colourful, ________ clothes.
4 Grandma made her own ________.

SPEAKING Talking about yourself

1 **Discuss the questions.**

1 Do you enjoy shopping for clothes? Why? / Why not?
2 Who do you usually go shopping with?
3 What do you usually buy?

2 **Choose the correct words to make questions.**

1 What clothes *do you like / you like* wearing?
2 How often *you buy / do you buy* new clothes?
3 Where *do you usually / you do usually* buy your clothes?
4 How much *are / do* you spend on clothes?

10 **3** **Listen to Harry answering the questions in Exercise 2 and make notes on his answers.**

10 **4** **Listen again to Harry answering the questions and complete Harry's sentences. Listen again and check.**

1 I ________ jeans always look good.
2 I don't go shopping ________.
3 I ________ shopping in department stores because the clothes are too expensive.
4 I ________ spend more when I get money for my birthday.

10 **5** **Read the *Prepare to speak* box. Then listen again. Which phrases does Harry use?**

PREPARE TO SPEAK

Talking about yourself

When you answer questions:

- use the present simple and adverbs of frequency to talk about habits: *I usually …, I always …, I often …*
- add reasons for your answer: *because …*
- talk about your likes and dislikes: *I like …, I don't like …, I really like …*
- give your opinion: *I think …, I don't think …*

6 **Ask and answer the questions in Exercise 2. Use phrases from the *Prepare to speak* box.**

CULTURE

TRADITIONAL CLOTHES

A

1 **Discuss the questions.**

1. What four countries are part of the United Kingdom?
2. What are the nationalities of those four countries?
3. How do you think people dress in those countries? Do you know of any traditional clothes from the United Kingdom?

2 **Read the text. Match photos A–D to countries in the UK.**

UK CULTURE Traditional clothes

11

In many countries there are traditional clothes that people wear for special occasions, such as national holidays and popular folk festivals. The United Kingdom includes four different countries – England, Wales, Scotland and Northern Ireland – and each country has its own history and special customs.

One of the most traditional items of clothing in the UK is the kilt. There are many versions, but the most famous ones are the kilts that men wear in Scotland on special occasions. Traditional Scottish kilts are made with five metres of tartan, which is a fabric with vertical and horizontal lines in different colours. Many Scottish families have a tartan with their own special colours. At the front of their kilts, Scottish men usually wear a small bag called a sporran to carry money and personal items. Scottish women wear a tartan skirt with a blouse and a tartan cloth on their shoulders called a shawl. They may also wear tartan dresses.

B

England hasn't got a national folk costume, but some people wear special clothes for traditional events, such as Morris dancing shows. Morris dancers can wear many different things, but they typically have white or black trousers or breeches. Some people also wear hats and short jackets called waistcoats, with long, colourful ribbons that move when they dance. It's quite spectacular!

C

In Wales, some women wear a traditional costume on important occasions, such as St David's Day, on 1st March. On those special days, many women wear a long dress with a red shawl over their shoulders. However, the most unusual part of the costume is a tall, black hat. It looks like the very formal hats that men wore in the past. Welsh men haven't got a special costume for festivals, but they often wear old-fashioned trousers called breeches.

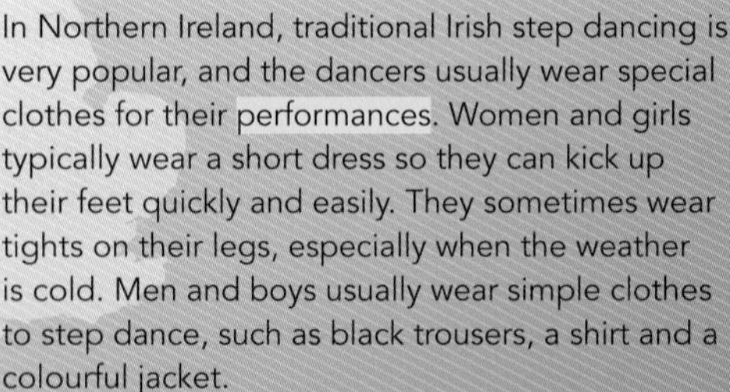

In Northern Ireland, traditional Irish step dancing is very popular, and the dancers usually wear special clothes for their performances. Women and girls typically wear a short dress so they can kick up their feet quickly and easily. They sometimes wear tights on their legs, especially when the weather is cold. Men and boys usually wear simple clothes to step dance, such as black trousers, a shirt and a colourful jacket.

D

18 CULTURE

CULTURE

Learning Objectives

- The students learn about traditional clothes in the United Kingdom.
- In the project stage, they create a poster about traditional clothes where they live.

Vocabulary

customs fabric items occasions performances spectacular

Resources

CULTURE VIDEO AND CULTURE VIDEO WORKSHEET: Trendsetters

BACKGROUND INFORMATION

The British royal family could be described as fashion trendsetters, although this is probably less true now than in the past. In the 17th century, women wore corsets to copy Queen Elizabeth I's slim figure and in the 21st century many women try to copy the styles worn by royals like Kate Middleton, wife of Prince William, and Meghan Markle, who is married to Prince Harry. In the 19th century, Queen Victoria wore black for mourning and the tradition of wearing black to funerals is a result of this. If you visit any stately homes or palaces in the United Kingdom, there are usually many articles of clothing on display, showing the importance of fashion to British history.

In the 20th century, styles and trends changed much more quickly than before. In the 1920s the *flapper girls* wore daring outfits, which reflected women's new freedoms such as equal voting rights with men. The Second World War was an event which influenced clothing. Women started wearing trousers because they were taking over jobs traditionally done by men. After the war ended, women in the 1950s began to wear more stylish clothing and, as the country became more prosperous, this was followed by the fashion explosion of 'Swinging Britain' in the 1960s.

WARMER

Anagrams: Write items of clothing on the board with the letters mixed up (for example *skirt*, *trousers*, *blouse*, *dress*, *tights*). This revises vocabulary from Unit 2 and prepares the students for the Culture lesson. Explain that the anagrams are all items of clothing. Give students three or four minutes to find the answers and check understanding.

1 Read the instructions and the first two questions. Students discuss the answers in small groups. Check answers with the class and check pronunciation. Tell students that they are going to learn about traditional clothes in the four countries of the United Kingdom. Read the third question and ask them to discuss it in their groups. Invite feedback from the groups.

Answers

1 England, Scotland, Wales, Northern Ireland
2 English, Scottish, Welsh, Irish
3 Students' own answers

2 Students look at the photos and read the text. They match the photos to the countries and check whether any of their ideas from Exercise 1 are mentioned. Set a time limit of three or four minutes. Tell students they do not need to understand every word but should read for general ideas. Check answers with the class.

Answers

A Northern Ireland
B Wales
C Scotland
D England

3 Read the instructions and the sentences. Ask students to identify the key words in each sentence. Students read the text again to find the answers, and correct the false sentences. Ask them to compare answers with a partner before checking answers with the class.

Answers

1 true
2 false (A shawl is a cloth that women wear on their shoulders. / A sporran is a bag worn by men.)
3 false (Only Welsh women wear tall black hats for special events.)
4 true
5 false (Morris dancers can wear many different things.)
6 false (Irish women sometimes wear tights when they do step dancing.)

11 The Reading text is recorded for students to listen, read and check their answers.

MIXED ABILITY

To help weaker students locate the information in the text, encourage stronger students to call out the key words in each question.

FAST FINISHERS

Ask fast finishers to write one more statement, which can be either true or false, for the rest of the class to answer.

4 Students find the highlighted words in the text. In order to match them to their meanings they should look at the context – the sentences immediately before or after the highlighted words. Check answers with the class and review any other new words or phrases in the text.

Answers

1 fabric 2 spectacular 3 occasions 4 customs 5 items 6 performances

5 Read the instructions and check understanding of *guards*. Ask students to describe the two photos and write key words on the board. Tell them that these are British guards who are called *Beefeaters*.

Answers

Students' own answers

12 6 Tell students they are going to listen to a presentation by a student about the Beefeaters. They are going to listen to it twice. The first time, they should match the names of the uniforms to the photos. Play the recording and check answers with the class. Ask whether any of the students have visited the Tower of London and seen the Beefeaters.

Answers

1 B 2 A

12 7 Students read the questions. Ask them to identify the key words and check understanding of the question words. Tell them to note down key words to help them answer the questions. Put students in pairs. Play the recording and give students time to compare their answers. If necessary, play it a second time. Check the answers with the class.

Answers

1 At the Tower of London
2 More than 500 years ago, in 1509
3 They always had beef to eat.
4 They wear the undress uniform on normal days and the state dress on special occasions.
5 a white b red c black

» AUDIOSCRIPT TB PAGE 262

8 Put students in pairs to complete the sentences in the *Useful language* box. Review answers with the class and remind students to write new vocabulary in their exercise books. Check pronunciation of *costumes* /ˈkɒstjuːms/ and *custom* /ˈkʌstəm/.

Answers

1 costumes 2 custom 3 dark 4 decorations 5 occasions 6 collar

PROJECT ***A poster about traditional clothes***

Tell students that they are going to work in groups to create a poster about traditional clothes where they live. Read the first three questions and check understanding. Put students into mixed ability groups to discuss them. Monitor and help as necessary. Encourage all members of each group to participate and remind them to speak in English. Ask for volunteers from each group to give feedback and write key vocabulary on the board. Repeat the procedure for the final two questions.

Students then plan their posters. They should share out the different tasks such as drawing or finding pictures, writing the text and designing the layout. Check their work is accurate.

Students create their posters and practise reading out the texts. Finally, they present their posters to the other students. Display the posters around the classroom for everyone to read. You could hold a class vote on the most interesting one.

PROJECT EXTENSION

In pairs or small groups, students choose another country and do some research into traditional clothes worn there. They could produce a short presentation, showing photos and giving brief explanations of the clothes, for example when they are worn, who wears them, what they are made of, and so on.

02 CULTURE VIDEO: Trendsetters

When students have completed the lesson, they can watch the video and complete the worksheet.

COOLER

Books closed. Read definitions in Exercise 4 and ask students to say the word. Say words in Exercise 8 and ask students to give a definition or a demonstration.

3 **Are the sentences true or false? Correct the false sentences.**

1 The kilt is traditionally a clothing item for Scottish men.
2 A sporran is a cloth that woman wear on their shoulders.
3 Welsh men and women wear tall black hats for special events.
4 Breeches are trousers that some men wear to festivals.
5 There's an official costume for all Morris dancers in England.
6 Irish women must wear tights when they do step dancing.

4 **Match the highlighted words in the text to the meanings.**

1 material for making clothes
2 very exciting to see and watch
3 special days or moments
4 normal habits in a culture
5 things or objects
6 shows for an audience

5 **Look at the guards in the photos. What are they wearing? Where do you think they work?**

A

B

6 **Listen to a presentation about the Beefeaters. Match the names of the uniforms to the photos.** 12

1 state dress uniform
2 undress uniform

7 **Listen again and answer the questions.** 12

1 Where can tourists usually see Beefeaters?
2 How long ago were the Beefeaters established?
3 Why are these special guards called Beefeaters?
4 When do the Beefeaters wear the two uniforms?
5 What colours are these parts of the state dress uniform?
   a collar
   b stockings
   c bonnet

8 **Read the *Useful language* phrases. Complete them with the words in the box.**

collar	costumes	custom
dark	decorations	occasions

USEFUL LANGUAGE

Talking about traditional clothes

1 People wear traditional ________.
2 This is a very important ________ in my country.
3 They wear ________ blue trousers.
4 The coat's got lots of gold ________.
5 For important ________ the (Beefeaters) wear (the state dress uniform).
6 There's a big ________ at the top of the coat.

PROJECT

A poster about traditional clothes

Create a poster about traditional clothes where you live. Use the questions below to help you.

- What festivals do people celebrate where you live?
- Do people wear special clothes on those occasions?
- What do those clothes look like? Are they popular?
- Are there any unusual uniforms where you live?
- Who wears those uniforms? What do they look like?

Present your poster to the class.

02 NOW WATCH THE CULTURE VIDEO

TRADITIONAL CLOTHES 19

3 MY WAY OF LIFE

ABOUT YOU

03 **Watch the video and then answer the questions.**

When did you learn to walk and talk?

How old were you when you learned to swim?

What are the most important events in a person's life?

VOCABULARY Life events

1 **Match six of the phrases to the photos.**

EP

be born get a degree get a driving licence get a job retire get married go to university
have children leave home leave school move home start school vote

2 **Put the life events in Exercise 1 in order. There is more than one possible answer. Then compare your answers.**

3 **Read the quiz. Which four events in Exercise 1 are not mentioned in the questions?**

Around the world: Age and events

1 In England, children usually start school when they are ________ .
A 4 B 5 C 6

2 In Belgium and Germany, students cannot leave school before they are ________ .
A 14 B 16 C 18

3 In some states in the USA, the youngest age you can get a driving licence is ________ .
A 14 B 16 C 17

4 In England, around ________ % of young people go to university. About 6% of these students leave university before the end of their course and don't get a degree.
A 33 B 43 C 53

5 In almost all European countries, ________ leave home before ________ .
A men, women B women, men

6 In the UK, children of ________ are allowed to get a part-time job.
A any age B 13 or over C 16 or over

7 In ________ , the average age at which women and men get married is 33.
A Spain B India C Japan

8 In Brazil you can vote in elections from the age of ________ .
A 16 B 18 C 21

13 **4** **Listen and choose Charlie's answers to the quiz.**

5 » **In pairs, choose *your* answers to the quiz. Then check your answers on page 120. Did you get more points than Charlie?**

6 **Look at the events in Exercise 1 again. Make six sentences with *I want to …* .**

I want to leave home before I'm 25. *I want to retire before I'm 40!*

7 **Discuss the questions.**

1 When can you leave school in your country?
2 At what age can you get a job?
3 How old do you have to be to get a driving licence?
4 What do you think is the best age to get married?
5 Is it important to go to university and get a degree? Why? / Why not?
6 Which of your relatives have retired?

3 MY WAY OF LIFE

Unit Overview

TOPIC	Comparing ways of life
VOCABULARY	Life events
READING	Is teenage life better now than in the past?
GRAMMAR	Comparatives and superlatives; *not as … as*
VOCABULARY	*too*, *enough*, *not enough*
WRITING	An informal email (1)
EXAM TASKS	Writing Part 1

Resources

GRAMMAR REFERENCE AND PRACTICE: SB page 140; TB page 244
WORKBOOK: pages 12–15
VIDEO AND VIDEO WORKSHEET: Life events
PHOTOCOPIABLE WORKSHEETS: Grammar worksheet Unit 3; Vocabulary worksheet Unit 3
TEST GENERATOR: Unit test 3

WARMER

Write *Life events* on the board and elicit its meaning (*important things that happen in our lives*). Brainstorm different life events as a class and write a list on the board, for example *start school*, *get married*.

ABOUT YOU

03 You can begin the class and introduce the topic of the unit by showing the video and asking students to complete the video worksheet. Then, read the questions in the *About you* box and check understanding. Students discuss the questions in pairs. For the third question, ask them to choose four or five of the events on the board and put these in order of importance. Invite students to tell the class about their partner.

VOCABULARY Life events

1 Students describe what is happening in each photo and read the life events in the box. Check any new words, for example *degree*, *driving licence*, *retire*, and pronunciation. Students match six of the phrases to the photos. Check answers with the class.

Answers

A start school
B get a degree
C get a driving licence
D get married
E move home
F vote

2 Students put the events in the box in order. They may have different ideas about this, so accept any reasonable answers. Refer students back to the list of life events on the board and compare it to the list in the box.

Possible answers

1 be born
2 start school
3 leave school
4 get a driving licence
5 vote
6 go to university
7 get a degree
8 leave home
9 get a job
10 get married
11 have children
12 retire
move home could happen at any stage

3 In pairs, students quickly read the quiz questions to find which events in Exercise 1 are not mentioned. Make sure students do not start answering the quiz questions yet.

Answers

be born retire have children move home

13

4 Students are going to listen to Charlie answering the quiz questions. First, read it as a class, checking any new words, for example *state* (*one of the parts that some countries, such as the US, are divided into*) and *average* (*most common*). Tell students to circle the answers Charlie chooses. Play the recording. Students compare answers with a partner. Play the recording again, pausing after each question to check answers. Discuss which facts the class found the most interesting / surprising.

Answers

1 A 2 C 3 B 4 A 5 B 6 A 7 C 8 B

» AUDIOSCRIPT TB PAGES 262–263

5 Ask students if they agree with Charlie's answers. In pairs, students look at the quiz again, choosing the answers they think are correct. They check the answers on page 120. Ask how many points Charlie got (*4*) and who got more points than him.

Answers

1 A 2 C 3 A 4 A 5 B 6 B 7 A 8 A

6 Refer students back to the life events in Exercise 1. Read the example sentences. Monitor and help as students write their sentences. Invite different students to read out their sentences. Ask them to listen out for the person whose answers are most similar to their own.

Answers

Students' own answers

7 Students discuss the questions in small groups. Invite one student from each group to report back to the class. Ask a different student from each group to discuss each question.

Answers

Students' own answers

READING

BACKGROUND INFORMATION

The first fully functional computer, the ENIAC, took three years to build. It was completed in 1946 and weighed nearly 50 tons. The first desktop computer went on sale in 1964 and cost about $3,500 – a huge amount of money at that time. The first laptop came onto the market in 1975 and weighed about 25kg! Smartphones were introduced in the early 2000s and the first smartphone with a touchpad in 2007.

1 Ask students to describe the photos and guess which image is from the past and which from the present. Refer them to the information at the top of the page and the title of the article. Ask them what information they think the texts will include. Read the instructions and set a short time limit for students to read the texts and answer the questions. Tell them not to worry about any unknown words at this point. Check answers. Find out whether their predictions about the texts were correct.

Answers

1 Simon 2 Emily

2 Students read the questions and answer options. They re-read the texts carefully and answer the questions. They compare answers with a partner. If they disagree, encourage them to find the section that answers the question. Check answers.

Answers

1 B 2 B 3 C 4 A 5 A 6 B

MIXED ABILITY

Support weaker students by telling them to underline key words in the questions and answer options and to look for synonyms in the text, for example *had* and *owned*.

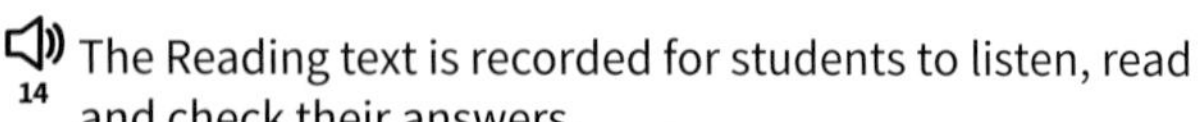

14 The Reading text is recorded for students to listen, read and check their answers.

3 Tell students to look at the highlighted words in the texts. Ask them if they are nouns, verbs, adjectives or adverbs (they are adjectives). Students work with a partner to match the words to their meanings. Check answers with the class. Check understanding of any other new words in the text. Encourage students to provide definitions if they know the words. New words may include *device* (*a machine such as a phone or computer that can be used to connect to the internet*), *essential* (*necessary*) and *bullying* (*intentionally trying to frighten someone who is smaller or weaker*).

Answers

1 unbelievable 2 relaxed 3 exhausted 4 awful 5 tiny 6 huge

FAST FINISHERS

Ask fast finishers to underline all the other adjectives in Simon's text (*different*, *greatest*, *simple*, *teenage*, *exciting*, *positive*, *healthy*, *active*, *free*, *safer*). In the Grammar section on page 22, they can identify those which are already in the comparative or superlative form (*safer* and *greatest*) and make the comparative and superlative forms of the other adjectives.

TALKING POINTS

Refer students to the two questions and tell them that you are going to hold a class discussion, but that first they should note down some ideas to talk about. Allow them five minutes to do this. Remind them to make notes only. They can do this individually or in pairs. Ask the first question, and encourage different students to offer their ideas, giving reasons for their opinions. Ask the second question and discuss ideas as a class.

COOLER

Write three ages on the board and tell students to guess which life event happened to you when you were each of those ages. Only answer the question if they form it correctly, for example *Did you get your driving licence when you were 21?* Students then write three ages of their own for their partner to guess what happened. In feedback, invite different students to tell the class about their partner.

Simon, 47, and his daughter Emily, 16, answer today's question …

Is teenage life better now than in the past?

home → life → teenagers

Simon Everything is so different from when I was a teenager. Technology is the greatest change. I had a computer – but only for games, really. And I remember my dad's first mobile phone in the car – it was huge! But the internet and smartphones changed teenage life forever. *We* wrote letters; *they* are texting each other all day. *We* bought a few CDs every month; *they've* got almost every song in the world – in a tiny device in their pocket! When we moved home, we often never saw old friends again. Now it's simple to stay in contact with anyone, anywhere. To me, teenage life looks more exciting than it was.

Not everything is positive, of course. I don't think teenagers now are as healthy as we were in the past. They don't do enough exercise. Without technology, we were more active and spent a lot of our free time outside. Roads were safer, of course, but it's unbelievable to think that often our parents didn't have any idea where we were!

Emily Yes, technology makes our lives easier and is now essential for entertainment and school. But it brings problems too – the worst are awful things like bullying on social media …

My problem is that teenage life is too busy now. On weekdays, as well as normal lessons, there are clubs at lunchtimes. Then after school on Mondays I have Spanish lessons, trumpet on Wednesdays and our band practises on Fridays. And weekends are just not long enough! On Saturday there's yoga club and on Sunday we often see relatives. Then there's homework, of course. Sometimes I'm exhausted on Sunday evenings!

The future will be harder for us, too. And I get worried about that. My friends and I feel the most important thing is to get a good degree – or we won't be able to leave home and get a job. And that means we have to get good marks in everything now. It's stressful.

I think my parents' teenage years were more relaxed than ours are today.

READING

1 Read the article quickly. Who thinks teenage life …

1 is better now? **2** was better in the past?

2 Read the article again. Choose the correct answers.

1 When Simon was a teenager,
A his dad owned a computer and a mobile phone.
B he owned a computer.
C he played games on his dad's phone.

2 Simon thinks that before the internet
A teenagers spent a lot of money on music.
B it was hard to stay friends with people you didn't see.
C teenagers enjoyed writing letters.

3 Why does Simon think that teenagers spent a lot of time outside?
A because their parents weren't worried about them
B because the roads weren't as dangerous
C because phones and computers didn't exist

4 Emily thinks that teenagers
A need technology for their school work.
B shouldn't use social media.
C aren't as happy as they were.

5 During the week, Emily
A has extra music and language lessons.
B never has time for lunch.
C doesn't do any sport.

6 Why does Emily think she has to go to university?
A because her friends want to go
B because jobs will be harder to find in the future
C because she always gets good marks at school

3 Match the highlighted words in the text to the meanings.

1 difficult to think is true
2 calm and not busy
3 very tired
4 very bad
5 very small
6 very big

TALKING POINTS

How was your parents' teenage life different from yours?
What problems can modern life bring for teenagers?

GRAMMAR Comparatives and superlatives

1 **Complete the table with the correct comparative and superlative adjectives. Check your answers in the article on page 21.**

Adjective	Comparative	Superlative
one-syllable adjectives		
big	bigger	the biggest
great	greater	1 ______
safe	2 ______	the safest
two-syllable adjectives with *-y*		
easy	3 ______	the easiest
other two-syllable and longer adjectives		
important	more important	4 ______
irregular adjectives		
good	5 ______	the best
bad	worse	6 ______
far	further	the furthest

2 **Read the examples. Then complete the rules with *comparative* and *superlative*.**

1 Teenage life looks more exciting than it was.
2 Technology is the greatest change.

We often use:
a *than* after ______ adjectives.
b *the* before ______ adjectives.

3 **Complete the facts with the comparative or superlative form of the adjectives. Remember to use *than* or *the*.**

IT'S A FACT!

1 ______ (old) woman in the world lived until she was 122.

2 The university with ______ (large) number of students, over four million, is in Delhi, India.

3 The average US teenage boy is 4 kg ______ (heavy) he was 25 years ago.

4 Research says that Norway is ______ (happy) country in the world and also one of ______ (good) countries for children to grow up in.

5 Homes in Hong Kong, China, are now ______ (expensive) in any other city in the world.

6 ______ (young) age at which people can vote in Scotland is 16.

7 The north of England is generally ______ (cheap) the south of England.

not as … as

4 **Read the example and choose the correct option.**

Teenagers aren't as healthy as they were in the past. (= *they were healthier in the past*)

We use ***not as … as*** to say that people or things are *the same* / *not the same*.

» GRAMMAR REFERENCE AND PRACTICE PAGE 140

5 **Compare the people and things with *not as … as*. Use the adjectives in the box or your own ideas.**

comfortable	hard	old	serious	untidy

0 English / maths *English isn't as hard as maths.*
1 children / adults
2 you / your best friend
3 your dad / your mum
4 you / one of your relatives

6 **Correct the mistake in each sentence.**

1 They live in a house bigger than us.
2 My mum is more relaxed that my dad.
3 Coffee is the more popular drink in the UK.
4 This area is more quiet than the city centre.
5 My most happiest time was when I lived abroad.
6 I'm not as taller as you.

VOCABULARY *too, enough, not enough*

1 **Read the examples and choose the correct options. Then match the rules to the sentences.**

EP

1 Weekends are just not long enough!
2 They don't do enough exercise.
3 Teenage life is too busy now.

a We use too *before* / *after* adjectives or adverbs to mean 'more than is necessary, possible, etc.'.
b We use enough *before* / *after* adjectives or adverbs to mean 'as much as is necessary'.
c We use enough *before* / *after* nouns.

2 **Write replies. Use *too* or *enough* and the words in brackets. Be careful with the position of *enough*.**

1 **A:** Did you buy the trainers?
B: No. They weren't ______ (big). They felt ______ (tight).
2 **A:** Why didn't you do the homework?
B: I didn't have ______ (time) and I was ______ (tired).
3 **A:** Are you getting a new laptop?
B: Yes. Mine is ______ (slow) and it hasn't got ______ (memory).

3 » Turn to page 120.

GRAMMAR Comparatives and superlatives

WARMER

Write *good–better–the best* on the board and ask students some questions about life events, saying, for example, 'Is it better to stay at home or leave home when you go to university?' 'What's the best age to get married?' Tell students we use comparatives and superlatives to compare two or more things or people.

1 Students complete the first two items and check their answers in the article on page 21. The forms for comparatives and superlatives are the same for most one-syllable adjectives but students need to be careful with the spelling. Elicit the differences.

- Most adjectives are like *great* and add *-er*, for example *long.*
- If the adjective ends with the pattern consonant–vowel–consonant, double the consonant in the comparative and superlative forms, for example *hot*. Note that the comparative of *new* is *newer*, because we never double the letter *w*.
- If the adjective ends with *e*, only the letter *r* is added, for example *brave.*

Repeat the procedure for item 3 and elicit the spelling rule. Repeat the procedure for item 4. Ask how many syllables *important* has (three) and elicit the rule: longer adjectives take *more* to make the comparative and *most* to make the superlative form. Elicit more examples, for example *useful*, *comfortable*. Finally tell students that some forms are irregular and have to be learned. Students complete items 5 and 6. Check answers.

Answers

1 the greatest 2 safer 3 easier 4 the most important
5 better 6 the worst

2 Students read the examples and complete the rules. Check answers.

Answers

a comparative b superlative

3 Check understanding of any new vocabulary. In mixed ability pairs, students complete the facts. Invite different students to read out each sentence. Ask the class which fact they think is the most interesting.

Answers

1 The oldest 2 the largest 3 heavier than
4 the happiest, the best 5 more expensive than
6 The youngest 7 cheaper than

not as … as

4 Read the example and ask students to find the sentence that this is paraphrased from in the text on page 21. Ask them if Simon thinks that children are healthier now (*no*). Ask them if he thinks children were healthier in the past (*yes*). Ask students if they agree with Simon and to give reasons. Students complete the rule. Give more examples using students and common facts, for example *Nadia isn't as tall as Belinda*; *[small town] isn't as big as [capital city].*

Answer

not the same

» GRAMMAR REFERENCE AND PRACTICE ANSWER KEY TB PAGE 244

5 Students look at the example. Give one of your own, for example *My mum isn't as old as my grandmother*. In pairs, students complete the exercise as a speaking activity. Invite different students to read out their sentences to the class.

Answers

Students' own answers

FAST FINISHERS

Ask fast finishers to write two more sentences using *not as … as*. They read them out and the class decides whether they are correct.

6 Read the instructions and do the first item together. Students complete the exercise in pairs. Check answers with the class.

Answers

1 They live in a **bigger house** than us.
2 My mum is more relaxed **than** my dad.
3 Coffee is the **most** popular drink in the UK.
4 This area is **quieter** than the city centre.
5 My **happiest** time was when I lived abroad.
6 I'm not as **tall** as you.

» GRAMMAR WORKSHEET UNIT 3

VOCABULARY *too, enough, not enough*

1 Students read the examples and find them in the article on page 21. Ask them to identify the parts of speech being described: *long* – adjective; *exercise* – noun; *busy* – adjective. Tell them to read the rules carefully, choose the correct option and match the rules with the sentences. Check answers.

Answers

a – before, sentence 3 b – after, sentence 1
c – before, sentence 2

2 Students read the conversations. Check understanding of any unknown words and whether the words in brackets are nouns or adjectives. Students complete the exercise in pairs. Invite pairs to read out the conversations.

Answers

1 big enough, too tight 2 enough time, too tired
3 too slow, enough memory

3 Point out to students that we can use *enough* in positive sentences as well as negative and give them some examples: *I have enough money to buy a new jacket*; *Is it warm enough to go swimming?* This construction is often followed by an infinitive. Students turn to page 120. Ask them which sentence is positive (*4*). Students complete the sentences with their own ideas and compare their answers with a partner. Invite students to read out their sentences to the class.

Answers

Students' own answers

» VOCABULARY WORKSHEET UNIT 3

WRITING An informal email (1)

1 Students are going to write an informal email. Check understanding of *informal* (*relaxed and friendly*). Students read Mark's email to Jamal. Ask them what questions Mark asks Jamal and tell them to identify the question words (*How? What's … like? What?*). Students read Jamal's notes and predict the content of his email to Mark. Ask them to tell you what Jamal recently did.

Answers

Jamal recently moved to a new area and started a new school.

2 Students read Jamal's reply and answer the question. Check the answer and then ask students to identify all the comparisons in the email (*brighter, bigger, not as big as, the largest, not as modern as, my best*).

Answers

No. Jamal doesn't tell Mark about his room.

3 Ask students which words Jamal uses to begin and end his email. See if students know any other ways to begin or end an email, before referring them to the *Prepare to write* box.

Answers

Hi Mark; It's great to hear from you.
Speak soon,

4 Ask students to read Jamal's letter again and underline six short forms. They compare answers with a partner. Check answers.

Answers

it's there's isn't they're aren't he's

5 Put students into pairs to complete the exercise. Invite different students to write the sentences on the board.

Answers

1 **He's** really nice and **we're** good friends.
2 **How's** school? I hope **you're** getting on well.
3 **I'm** getting to know everyone and **they're** all really friendly.
4 **We've** got tickets and **we're** going to a game together.

6 Remind students that some words and phrases are more informal than others. Ask them to look at the highlighted words in Jamal's letter and match them to the more formal equivalents. Check answers. Drill pronunciation of the new vocabulary.

Answers

1 I guess 2 really 3 's into 4 awesome 5 mate 6 loads

7 Students re-read Mark's email and Jamal's notes in Exercise 1. Put students into small groups to make notes before sharing ideas as a class.

8 **B1 Preliminary for Schools Writing Part 1**

In this part, students' control and range of language is tested. Students have to write an email of about 100 words in response to input which is similar to that provided in Exercise 1. The email provides the topic and there are notes to help students construct their response.

Refer students back to the *Prepare to write* box and tell them to use the notes in Exercise 1 in their email. Students write their email, using the notes they made in Exercise 7. Ask them to include some examples of comparative and superlative adjectives, and one example each of *too, not enough*, and *not as … as*. Remind students to write about 100 words and to check their spelling and grammar carefully. Monitor and help as they are working. Ask confident students to read their emails aloud.

MIXED ABILITY

Stronger students should be able to incorporate all of their notes in their reply. Weaker students can focus on giving just one piece of information per question.

Model answer

Hello Mark,
Congratulations on becoming captain! That's awesome.
Our new house is really nice and bigger than the old one. My bedroom's the smallest though – there's not enough space for all my things!
The town's not as big as my old town but there's lots to do. There's a cinema and a swimming pool, and you can play tennis and football. The pool can be too busy sometimes.
My new school is smaller than my old one, but the people are friendly and I've already got some new mates. I sit next to a guy called Oli in Science. He's funny and we get on really well.
Write soon,
Ben

COOLER

Tell students that time has passed and now Jamal is an old man. Play a memory game about events in Jamal's life. Start by saying 'Jamal learned to talk when he was two'. Ask a stronger student to repeat the sentence and then add a sentence of their own, for example *Jamal learned to talk when he was two. He started school when he was four.* Ask a third student to add another sentence, for example *Jamal learned to talk when he was two. He started school when he was four. He learned to swim when he was five*. Continue around the class with each student repeating the sentences in the correct order and adding one of their own. When someone makes a mistake, they're out of the game. Stop the game when there is a winner or after five minutes.

WRITING An informal email (1)

1 **Read the email Jamal received from his friend Mark and the notes he made. What did Jamal do recently?**

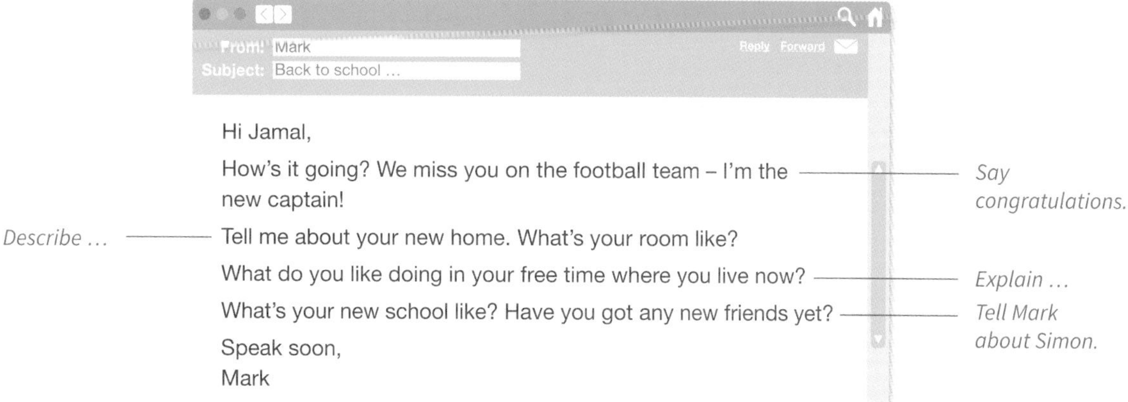
From: Mark
Subject: Back to school …

Hi Jamal,

How's it going? We miss you on the football team – I'm the new captain! — *Say congratulations.*

Describe … — Tell me about your new home. What's your room like?

What do you like doing in your free time where you live now? — *Explain …*

What's your new school like? Have you got any new friends yet? — *Tell Mark about Simon.*

Speak soon,
Mark

2 **Read Jamal's reply. Does Jamal answer all of Mark's questions?**

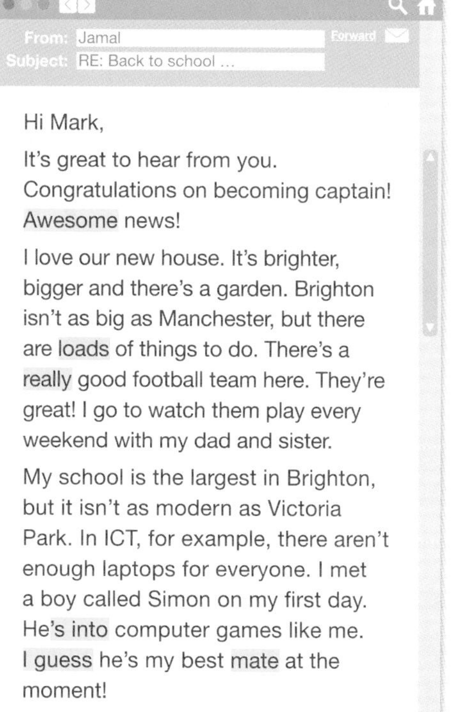
From: Jamal
Subject: RE: Back to school …

Hi Mark,

It's great to hear from you. Congratulations on becoming captain! Awesome news!

I love our new house. It's brighter, bigger and there's a garden. Brighton isn't as big as Manchester, but there are loads of things to do. There's a really good football team here. They're great! I go to watch them play every weekend with my dad and sister.

My school is the largest in Brighton, but it isn't as modern as Victoria Park. In ICT, for example, there aren't enough laptops for everyone. I met a boy called Simon on my first day. He's into computer games like me. I guess he's my best mate at the moment!

Speak soon,
Jamal

3 **Read the *Prepare to write* box. Which phrases does Jamal use to begin and end his email?**

PREPARE TO WRITE

An informal email (1)

In informal emails:

- use an informal phrase to begin your email: *Hi …, Hello …, It's great to hear from you*
- use short forms: *it's, he's, I'll*
- use informal words and expressions: *Great!, loads of things, He's into …, I guess …*
- use an informal phrase to end your email: *Love, Write soon, Speak soon, See you soon*

4 **Find six different short forms in Jamal's email.**

5 **Rewrite the sentences using short forms.**

1 He is really nice and we are good friends.
2 How is school? I hope you are getting on well.
3 I am getting to know everyone and they are all really friendly.
4 We have got tickets and we are going to a game together.

6 **Match the highlighted informal words and phrases in Jamal's email to the meanings.**

1 I think
2 very
3 likes
4 very good
5 friend
6 a lot

7 **Imagine you have moved to a new town and started a new school. Read Mark's email again and plan your reply. Use Jamal's notes in Exercise 1 to help you.**

8 **Write your email to Mark.**

- Use the phrases and tips in the *Prepare to write* box.
- Write about 100 words.
- Remember to check your spelling and grammar.

4 CHAMPIONS

ABOUT YOU

Which sports do you play regularly?
Which sports do you watch?

VOCABULARY Sports

1 (15) (EP) **Match the photos to some of the sports in the box. Then listen and check. Check the meaning of the other sports.**

athletics boxing climbing cycling gymnastics ice hockey ice skating jogging rugby squash surfing swimming table tennis tennis volleyball windsurfing

2 (16) **Listen to six interviews and match the sentence halves.**

1 We go
2 We do
3 I don't play
4 I go
5 My mates and I go
6 We never play

a athletics in the summer.
b cycling all the time.
c jogging quite often.
d ice hockey.
e tennis together.
f windsurfing on the lake.

3 **Add the sports from Exercise 1 to the table.**

do	go	play
athletics	*climbing*	*ice hockey*

4 **What other sports and activities can you think of? Add them to the table in Exercise 3.**

play basketball *go snowboarding*

5 **Do the quiz in pairs. The answers are all from Exercises 1 and 2.**

Answer the questions about the sports in Exercise 1.

Be quick! You've got a time limit of five minutes!

1 Which nine sports can you do on your own?
2 Which four sports are for two or four players?
3 Which three sports are for teams of more than four?
4 Which five sports do you do on or in water or ice?
5 In which two sports do you use a racket?
6 In which four sports is there a net?
7 Which sport is not in the Olympic Games?
   a cycling b table tennis
   c ice hockey d squash
8 What sports do people do in these competitions?
   a Wimbledon b Tour de France
   c IAAF World Championships

6 **Discuss the questions.**

1 What's your favourite sport? Why? When do you do it?
2 What are the most popular sports in your country?

4 CHAMPIONS

Unit Overview

TOPIC	Sports and sporting events
VOCABULARY	Sports
READING	Meet the new BMXers
GRAMMAR	Past continuous
VOCABULARY	Words with different meanings
LISTENING	A programme about sport
SPEAKING	Describing a past event
EXAM TASKS	Reading Part 4

Resources

GRAMMAR REFERENCE AND PRACTICE: SB page 141; TB page 244
WORKBOOK: pages 16–19
PHOTOCOPIABLE WORKSHEETS: Grammar worksheet Unit 4; Vocabulary worksheet Unit 4
TEST GENERATOR: Unit test 4

WARMER

Write *Sports* on the board. In pairs, students have one minute to make a list of sports. Students call out items from their lists. Write them on the board. Students decide which sports are team sports, which are played in groups of two or four people and which are individual.

ABOUT YOU

Students read the two questions. They ask and answer the questions in pairs. Invite students to tell the class about which sports their partner plays or watches.

VOCABULARY Sports

1 Refer students to the sports in the box and drill pronunciation of difficult words, for example *athletics* /æθˈletɪks/, *climbing* /ˈklaɪmɪŋ/ and *gymnastics* /dʒɪmˈnæstɪks/. Set a short time limit for students to match the sports to the photos and then play the recording for them to check their answers. Ask which sports from the box are not shown in the pictures (*athletics, climbing, ice skating, jogging, squash, swimming, tennis, windsurfing*).

15 *The answers are recorded for students to check and then repeat.*

Answers

A boxing B cycling C gymnastics D ice hockey E rugby
F surfing G table tennis H volleyball

16 2 Tell students to look at the first halves of the sentences and identify the three verbs (*go, do, play*). Students predict what the full sentences will be before they listen. Play the recording for students to complete the exercise. They compare answers with a partner before checking as a class.

Answers

1 f 2 a 3 d 4 c 5 b 6 e

» AUDIOSCRIPT TB PAGE 263

3 Refer students to the box in Exercise 1. See if they can work out the rules for *go* and *play*. For the sports that are left we use *do*. Students complete the table individually and compare their ideas with a partner. Check answers with the class.

Answers

do: boxing, gymnastics
go: cycling, ice skating, jogging, surfing, swimming, windsurfing
play: rugby, squash, table tennis, tennis, volleyball

4 Brainstorm other sports as a class and ask students to match them to the correct verb.

Possible answers

do: yoga, martial arts (karate, judo, etc.)
go: dancing, skiing, running
play: hockey, football

5 Put students into mixed ability pairs and tell them to choose a team name. Ask them what the title *Race against the clock* means. Tell them to read the questions. Check understanding of *on your own, racket* and *net*. One of each pair writes the team name and question numbers on a piece of paper. Students have five minutes to answer the questions. Monitor and help as necessary. After five minutes the pairs exchange papers and call out the answers. Confirm the answers and tell students to award one point for each correct answer.

Answers

1 athletics, climbing, cycling, gymnastics, ice skating, jogging, surfing, swimming, windsurfing
2 boxing, squash, table tennis, tennis
3 ice hockey, rugby, volleyball
4 ice hockey, ice skating, surfing, swimming, windsurfing
5 squash, tennis
6 ice hockey, table tennis, tennis, volleyball
7 d (squash)
8 a tennis b cycling c athletics

6 Invite different students to say which sports they do and when they do them. Encourage them to give reasons. Find out how many students like doing the same activities. Have a class vote on students' favourite sports. Discuss which sports people enjoy playing or watching most in your country. Ask how people celebrate when their team wins a big competition.

Answers

Students' own answers

READING

1 Ask students to describe the photo and read the title of the article. Ask them whether they have tried this sport or if they would like to. Find out if anyone in the class or a family member has a BMX bike. Then, ask students to predict what the text will be about. Read the questions and give students a few minutes to read the text quickly and answer the questions. Tell them to ignore the spaces for now.

Answers

1 teenage girls
2 racing

2 **B1 Preliminary for Schools Reading Part 4**

In this part, five sentences have been removed from the text. In addition there are three distractor sentences, which are not needed. This part tests students' ability to read for gist and understand text structure.

Do the first item together. Ask students to read the first two paragraphs and then read options A to H. In pairs, students decide on the correct option (*D*). Ask for volunteers to tell you which option they chose. Tell them the correct option and ask why (*the context – both the meaning and the use of* she *to refer to Olivia*). Explain that students should look at the sentences immediately before and after the space to understand the meaning. They should also look for related words in these sentences, for example *brother – boys*, and pronouns. Remind them that pronouns replace nouns, so they should look in the previous sentence to find out which nouns they are replacing. Students complete the exercise in pairs. Check answers with the class and, in each case, ask how students decided on the correct option and rejected other options. Check understanding of *pedal* (*to push the pedals of a bicycle with your feet*).

Answers

1 D 2 G 3 A 4 B 5 F
not needed: C, E, H

MIXED ABILITY

Help weaker students by pairing them with stronger students and monitoring as they do the exercise. Encourage them to identify meaning, related words and what the pronouns refer to.

17 The Reading text is recorded for students to listen, read and check their answers.

3 Tell students to read the definitions 1–5 and find the highlighted words in the article. They should try to work out their meaning from the context. Then they read the definitions and match them to the words. Ask them to compare their ideas with a partner. Check answers.

Answers

1 gears 2 stunts 3 track 4 helmet 5 guards

FAST FINISHERS

Tell fast finishers to find synonyms or write definitions for *smart*, *knowledge*, *seat*, *crazy* and *elbow*, which all appear in the article. Ask them to read out their definitions for the class, who try to guess the word and find it in the text. Check understanding of any other words or expressions in the text.

TALKING POINTS

Divide the class into two halves and subdivide each half into small groups. Ask one half to discuss the first set of questions, and the other half to discuss the second set of questions. Hold a short class discussion. Ask students who discussed each question to offer their opinions, and ask the other half of the class to say whether they agree, and why or why not.

COOLER

Jumbled words. Choose six or eight sports from Vocabulary Exercise 1 on page 24 and write them on the board as anagrams, i.e. the letters are in the wrong order. In pairs, students solve the anagrams and find the sports.

READING

1 Read the text quickly and answer the questions.

1 Who are the new BMXers?
2 Do they like racing or 'freestyle' BMX?

17

Did you think that BMX racing was just for men? Think again …

Meet the new BMXers

It was a dark, rainy, winter's day at the National Cycling Centre in Manchester (UK) and I was taking photographs of the girls' BMX team. They were riding around the track with apparently no fear. They all obviously had a real passion for the sport.

Olivia, aged 15, has long, brown hair. She's smart and confident, and the way she was smiling showed how much she loved it. How did she first become interested in BMX? [1] ________ . Although all the racers were boys, she knew instantly it was the sport for her. 'It's not harder for girls to get into the sport,' she said – anyone can do it. 'BMX gives you knowledge. When you come to the track, you learn something new every day.'

So what is a BMX? A BMX is a bike with small wheels and a low seat. Small wheels actually go faster than big wheels at speeds of up to 20 km/h. [2] ________ These mean that a bike can travel quickly without the rider using their legs too much. But there are no gears on a BMX, so the rider has to pedal a lot to go fast. [3] ________ .

Some BMXers love doing jumps and crazy stunts – this is called 'freestyle'. Other riders prefer racing. BMX races are fast but short. [4] ________ Both riding styles have something in common: riders fall off their bikes a lot. That's why they all wear a helmet, as well as knee and elbow guards under their racing clothes.

Many people think that BMX is scary or dangerous, but fear isn't a thought that goes through this BMX team's minds. [5] ________ They don't see the difference between male and female, not while they are out on the track doing what they enjoy the most.

2  **Read the article again. Five sentences have been removed from the text. For each space choose the correct sentence. There are three extra sentences which you do not need to use.**

A She laughed because some of the riders were moving their legs so quickly.
B They usually only last for about 40 seconds.
C BMX race bikes can be very expensive.
D She was watching her older brother race.
E They weren't worried by the rain either.
F They see BMX as a fun sport, a way of life, a good social activity.
G Normal bikes have at least 20 gears.
H This is the biggest problem with BMX races.

3 Match the **highlighted** words in the text to the meanings.

1 part of a bicycle that controls the speed of the wheels
2 tricks or difficult jumps on a bike
3 a path, often circular, used for races
4 a hard hat that protects your head
5 things you wear to protect parts of your body when playing a sport

TALKING POINTS

Should schools offer the same sports to girls and boys? Or are some sports for boys and others for girls?

Do you think there is too much sport on TV? Why? / Why not?

GRAMMAR Past continuous

1 **Read the examples. Then choose the correct words to complete the rules.**

1 I was taking photographs of the girls' BMX team.
2 They were riding around the track.

a We use the past continuous to talk about actions in progress at a particular time in *the present* / *the past*.
b We form the past continuous with the correct *present* / *past* form of *be* and the *infinitive* / *-ing* form of the verb.

» GRAMMAR REFERENCE AND PRACTICE PAGE 141

2 **Choose the correct form of the verbs to make past continuous sentences.**

1 They *were wearing* / *were wear* dark helmets.
2 He *isn't playing* / *wasn't playing* ice hockey last night.
3 My friends *wasn't talking* / *weren't talking* about sports.
4 What was he *doing* / *do* on the court?
5 *Were* / *Was* she watching the games?
Yes, she *was* / *were*.
6 Mark *is climbing* / *was climbing* yesterday.
7 My parents *was going* / *were going* to a bike race.
8 Were they *listening* / *listen* to the match?
No, they *weren't* / *wasn't*.

3 **Look at the picture of a park last Saturday morning. Write positive and negative past continuous sentences about what the people were and weren't doing.**

0 Kim / play tennis / swim
Kim was playing tennis. She wasn't swimming.
1 Adam and Pete / run / skate
2 Myla / throw a ball / hit a ball
3 Karl and Liam / play squash / kick a ball
4 Megan and Ana / cycle / climb
5 Lucy / catch a ball / do athletics

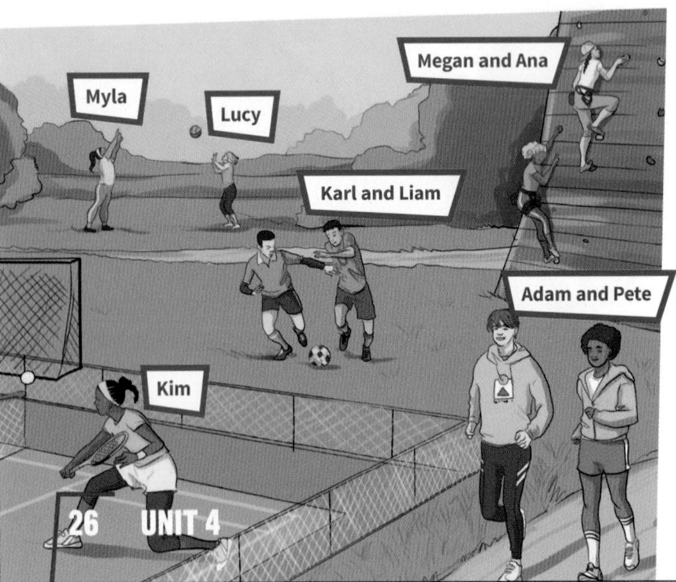

4 **Write questions in the past continuous.**

0 you / do / sports at 3.30 yesterday?
Were you doing sports at 3.30 yesterday?
1 what / you / do / at 8.30 yesterday evening?
2 you / read / at 10.30 / yesterday evening?
3 what / you / wear / last / Sunday?
4 you / sleep / at midnight last night?
5 you / have / breakfast at 8.00 this morning?
6 what / do / five minutes ago?

5 **Ask and answer the questions in Exercise 4.**

VOCABULARY Words with different meanings

1 **Read the sentences. Choose the correct meaning of the words.**

EP

1 I did the extra maths exercise. Did you?
a noun: physical activity to get stronger
b noun: written work to practise something
2 Does this tracksuit fit you?
a verb: be the right size
b adjective: healthy and strong
3 Who won the Chelsea–Arsenal match?
a verb: be the same
b noun: a sports competition
4 The Bulls won the basketball game by 20 points.
a noun: the score (e.g. the number of goals/ baskets) at the end of a match
b verb: indicate using your finger
5 The basketball team has got a new trainer.
a noun: a sports shoe
b noun: a person who prepares players for an event
6 I can't work out what to do next.
a verb: to exercise to make the body stronger
b verb: to find the answer to a problem
7 We got a coach to the volleyball match.
a noun: a type of bus
b noun: someone who teaches people a sport
8 We train at the football club twice a week.
a noun: a long, thin vehicle that travels on rails
b verb: to practise a sport

2 **Complete the sentences. Use the correct form of the words in Exercise 1.**

0 This green colour *matches* your top.
1 You aren't ________ enough. Do some ________ !
2 We go jogging with the rugby ________ every day, but we never ________ in the gym.
3 I can't see the captain. Can you ________ to her?
4 I bought some white ________ but they don't ________ me. They're a size 7 but I take an 8.
5 I need help with the last ________ on page 144.
6 How many ________ has your team got? Did they play any ________ last week?
7 Let's get a ________. The railway station is closed, so there aren't any ________ today.
8 I can't ________ how to play this game.

3 **» Work with a partner. Student A turn to page 121. Student B turn to page 126.**

GRAMMAR Past continuous

WARMER

Write *Yesterday* on the board and write times of the day down the left-hand side, for example 8.00, 10.30, etc. Tell students 'At 8.00 I was driving to school'. Ask a stronger student what they were doing at 8.30. They then pick another student and another time and ask the question. Write the answers on the board using the third person and repeat the sentences, for example *At 1.30 Hayley was having lunch*. Underline the verbs.

1 Students read the example sentences, taken from the reading text on page 25, and underline the verbs. Refer them to the box and tell them to complete the rules. Check answers.

Answers

a the past
b past, *-ing*

» GRAMMAR REFERENCE AND PRACTICE ANSWER KEY TB PAGE 244

2 Elicit the negative and question forms of *be* in the past simple. Remind students of the short answers to *Yes/No* questions. Students choose the correct options.

Answers

1 were wearing
2 wasn't playing
3 weren't talking
4 doing
5 Was, was
6 was climbing
7 were going
8 listening, weren't

3 Students look at the picture of people in the park. Read the example. Students read the prompts and find the people in the picture. Remind them that it is from last Saturday, so all their answers must be in the past tense. Put them into pairs to write the sentences. Monitor and help as necessary. Check answers.

Answers

1 Adam and Pete were running. They weren't skating.
2 Myla was throwing a ball. She wasn't hitting a ball.
3 Karl and Liam weren't playing squash. They were kicking a ball.
4 Megan and Ana weren't cycling. They were climbing.
5 Lucy was catching a ball. She wasn't doing athletics.

4 Read the example and tell students to re-read the questions in Exercise 2 (4, 5 and 8). Students complete the exercise in mixed ability pairs. Monitor and help as necessary. Check answers with the class. Ask students to underline the time expressions in the sentences. Explain that we say *yesterday morning / afternoon / evening* but *last night*.

Answers

1 What were you doing at 8.30 yesterday evening?
2 Were you reading at 10.30 yesterday evening?
3 What were you wearing last Sunday?
4 Were you sleeping at midnight last night?
5 Were you having breakfast at 8.00 this morning?
6 What were you doing five minutes ago?

FAST FINISHERS

Ask fast finishers to write two more sets of prompts and exchange them with another student to write the questions.

5 In pairs, students ask and answer the questions. Remind them of the short answers to *Yes/No* questions. Ask some students to tell the class about their partner.

Answers

Students' own answers

» GRAMMAR WORKSHEET UNIT 4

VOCABULARY Words with different meanings

1 Write *watch* on the board. Elicit both of its meanings and what parts of speech these are (*noun, verb*). Tell students that there are many words in English which have the same spelling but different meanings and parts of speech (for example verb, noun, adjective). Put students into pairs to read the sentences and definitions and discuss them. Explain that both meanings of the word are correct, but only one is correct for the context. Invite different students to give their answers.

Answers

1 b 2 a 3 b 4 a 5 b 6 b 7 a 8 b

2 Students complete the exercise in pairs. Explain that they may need to change the form of the word, as in the example. Invite different students to read out the sentences. Ask if they can think of any other words that have more than one meaning, for example *light* (*noun, verb, adjective*), *notice* (*verb, noun*), *like* (*verb / noun, preposition*). Ask if they know any words like this in their own language.

Answers

1 fit, exercise
2 coach, work out / train
3 point
4 trainers, fit
5 exercise
6 points, matches
7 coach, trains
8 work out

3 Put students into pairs and tell them one of them is A and one is B. Student A turns to page 121 and student B to page 126. Read the instructions and ask two students to read out the example. Give them a few minutes to look at the words in the second question before starting the activity. Explain that A and B have different lists of words. Monitor and help as necessary.

Answers

Students' own answers

» VOCABULARY WORKSHEET UNIT 4

LISTENING

BACKGROUND INFORMATION

Manchester and Liverpool are both in north-west England and both have famous football teams. Manchester has Manchester United and Manchester City; Liverpool has Liverpool and Everton. Sunderland is a smaller city in north-east England. The football team was formerly in the First Division, now known as the Premier League. Their last big title was the FA Cup in 1973.

18 **1** Tell students to look at the three photos. Ask what they can see and if they like the photos. Read the instructions and ask them what *photo of the week* means. Accept any reasonable suggestions, for example *the most popular / the best / the photo everyone talked about*. Play the recording and check the answer. Ask students what happened next.

Answers

Photo C. The football hit the beach ball and then went into the net.

18 **2** In pairs, students tell each other what they remember from the story. Refer them to the list of statements a–f and tell them to put the events in the order in which they heard them. Play the recording again for them to check their answers.

Answers

a 5 b 3 c 1 d 2 e 6 f 4

18 **3** Tell students to read the sentences and complete them with the correct city. Play the recording again for them to check their answers. Check answers with the class.

Answers

1 Manchester
2 Liverpool
3 Sunderland
4 Liverpool
5 Sunderland, Liverpool

» AUDIOSCRIPT TB PAGE 263

SPEAKING Describing a past event

1 Ask students to describe the pictures in Listening, Exercise 1. Then tell them to read the questions and discuss them with a partner. Listen to feedback as a class.

Answers

Students' own answers

19 **2** Play the recording for students to listen and answer the questions. Invite different students to answer the questions. Then ask 'Which sports did they talk about?' (*football and athletics*).

Answers

Max watched an event and Rachel took part in an event.

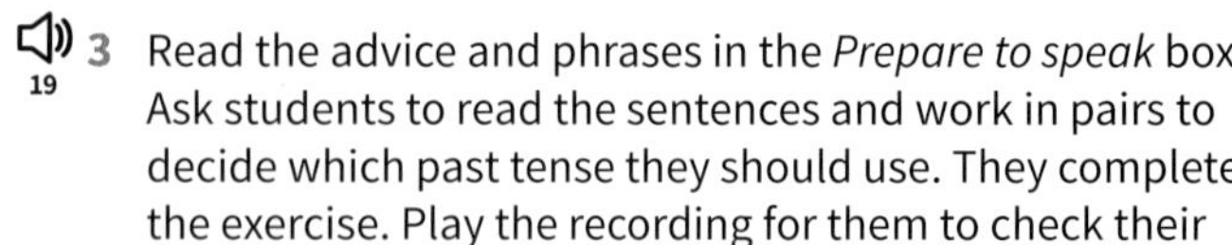

19 **3** Read the advice and phrases in the *Prepare to speak* box. Ask students to read the sentences and work in pairs to decide which past tense they should use. They complete the exercise. Play the recording for them to check their answers. Listen to feedback as a class.

Answers

1 were winning
2 scored
3 were watching
4 came

19 **4** Students listen again to the recording from Exercise 2 and tick ✓ the phrases they hear.

Answers

It was the best … ever

19 **5** Invite suggestions from the class as to how the sentences could be completed. Then play the recording for students to listen and complete the sentences. They check answers with a partner.

Answers

1 I was very happy because I support Real Madrid.
2 I really enjoyed taking part because it was my first time.

» AUDIOSCRIPT TB PAGES 263–264

6 Brainstorm some important national or international sporting events and write them on the board. Point to one of the events and ask students to say what happened. Set a short time limit for them to read the questions and choose a local, national or international event and make notes individually. Monitor and help as necessary and remind them to think of phrases from the *Prepare to speak* box which they can use.

Answers

Students' own answers

MIXED ABILITY

Support weaker students by suggesting answers and helping them with verb tenses and word order.

7 Monitor and join in as students discuss the questions in small groups. Give positive feedback when they use phrases from the *Prepare to speak* box and for the correct use of the past simple and past continuous. Invite different students to tell the class about the sports events their group discussed.

Answers

Students' own answers

COOLER

Play a mime game about what students were doing at different times in the past. Ask, for example, 'What was I doing last Sunday morning?' and mime an activity. Invite different students to ask similar questions and mime the answer for the class to guess.

LISTENING

🔊 18 **1** **Listen to the show and look at photos A–C. Which is the photo of the week? What happened next?**

🔊 18 **2** **Number the events in the order you hear them. Then listen again and check.**

a The football went into the goal.
b The Sunderland player kicked the football.
c A fan threw a beach ball onto the field.
d A Sunderland player was running towards the goal.
e The referee decided to allow the goal.
f The football hit the beach ball.

🔊 18 **3** **Listen again. Complete the sentences.**

Liverpool (x3)	Manchester	Sunderland (x2)

1 The *Sports Review* studio is in ________.
2 A ________ fan threw a beach ball onto the field.
3 ________ won the match 1–0.
4 The ________ players weren't playing well.
5 Chloe thought ________ played better than ________.

SPEAKING Describing a past event

1 **When was the last time you watched a sports event (in person or on TV) or took part in one? What was it?**

🔊 19 **2** **Listen to Max and Rachel talking about sports. Who took part in an event? Who watched one?**

🔊 19 **3** **Read the *Prepare to speak* box. Complete the sentences with the past simple or past continuous form of the verbs. Then listen again and check.**

1 Manchester City ________ (win) for most of the game.
2 Real Madrid ________ (score) two goals in the last five minutes.
3 Lots of people ________ (watch) the competition.
4 I ________ (come) third in one race.

PREPARE TO SPEAK

Describing a past event

When you describe a past event:

- use the past simple to talk about the main things that happened
- use the past continuous to talk about actions in progress
- add your opinion: *It was an amazing …, It was really exciting, It was the best … ever, It was so cool, I really enjoyed …*
- add reasons for your opinion: *because …*

🔊 19 **4** **Listen to the whole recording again. Which phrase from the *Prepare to speak* box do they *not* use?**

🔊 19 **5** **Complete the reasons that Max and Rachel give. Listen again to check.**

1 I was very happy because …
2 I really enjoyed taking part because …

6 **Think about a recent sports event. Read the questions and plan your answers.**

1 What was the event and when was it?
2 Did you watch it or take part in it?
3 What happened during the event?
4 What was the final result?
5 Did you enjoy it? Why? / Why not?

7 **Ask and answer the questions in Exercise 6. Use the past simple and past continuous, and use phrases from the *Prepare to speak* box.**

LIFE SKILLS PHYSICAL WELL-BEING

KEEPING FIT

LIFE SKILLS

Keeping fit

Fitness is an important part of a healthy lifestyle. If you want to keep fit, you need to care for your body and do physical activity every day.

1 **Ask and answer the questions with a partner.**

1 What activities do you enjoy doing in PE class?
2 What physical activities do you do in your free time?

2 **Read the text quickly. Match the sentences with the types of training.**

1 It's good for warming up before exercising.
2 It's exercise that gives you stronger muscles.
3 It's a typical activity for professional athletes.
4 It includes physical activities like cycling.

3 **Read the text again and answer the questions.**

1 How can lifting smaller weights help you keep fit?
2 What two ways can people lift weights at the gym?
3 How does aerobic exercise keep your heart healthy?
4 What type of training can help you cycle faster?
5 Why is balance important for some types of exercise?
6 Why is interval training a good idea for tennis players?

4 **Match the highlighted words in the text to the meanings.**

1 regular programme of activities
2 stop something from happening
3 in a good or correct way
4 move something to a higher place
5 pull something to make it longer
6 ability to exercise for a long time

20 **5** **Listen to Anna and Tom talking about their fitness habits. Who is usually more active?**

20 **6** **Listen again. Complete the sentences with one or two words.**

1 Tom usually plays ________ after school.
2 Tom sometimes goes to ________ with friends.
3 Anna's got ________ practice twice a week.
4 Anna also ________ on Tuesdays and Fridays.
5 Tom and Paul usually play ________ at the weekend.
6 Anna says Tom should ________ with his friend Danny.

7 **Complete the *Useful language* phrases with the words in the box.**

about	active	after school
could	go swimming	stairs

USEFUL LANGUAGE

Making a fitness plan

1 I usually play (basketball) ________.
2 I don't usually ________ on weekdays.
3 I do ________ an hour of exercise most days.
4 I'm not very ________ at weekends.
5 I ________ ride my bike to school more often.
6 We should always walk up the ________.

28 LIFE SKILLS

LIFE SKILLS

Learning Objectives

- The students learn about ways of keeping fit.
- In the project stage, they make an exercise plan.

Vocabulary

lift prevent properly routine stamina stretch

BACKGROUND INFORMATION

Tai Chi is a Chinese martial art that has been practised for two or three centuries (its origins are unclear) for both defence training and its health benefits. Although it was initially developed as a martial art, it is also practised for a variety of other personal reasons such as stress management and fitness. As a result, there are many different forms, both traditional and modern, depending on the objectives of those who practise it. Some training forms are especially known for having quite slow movements. The health benefits were widely promoted in the early 20th century and Tai Chi has developed a worldwide following, often of people with no interest in martial training. Medical studies of Tai Chi support its effectiveness as an alternative exercise and a form of martial arts therapy. It is claimed that focusing the mind on the movements of the form helps to develop a state of mental calm and clarity. Along with the health benefits attributed to Tai Chi training, aspects of traditional Chinese medicine are taught to advanced students in some schools.

WARMER

Anagrams: Write some sports activities on the board with the letters mixed up, for example *gymnastics*, *volleyball*, *windsurfing*. This revises the vocabulary from Unit 4 and prepares the students for the Life Skills lesson. Explain that the anagrams are all connected with sport. Give students three or four minutes to find the answers. If they find it difficult, underline the first letter of each word.

LIFE SKILLS

Keeping fit

Students read the text. Check understanding of *fit* and *fitness*. Ask students if they agree with the statement and whether they do a physical activity every day, seven days a week.

1 Read the questions. Students answer them in pairs and then report back to the class. Write key words on the board. Find out what the most popular activities in the PE class and after school are.

Answers

Students' own answers

2 Ask students what they think are the best ways of keeping fit. They look at the pictures on page 29 and read the title of the text. They read the questions and then read the text quickly to find the answers. Tell them not to worry about any new vocabulary at this stage. They compare answers with a partner. Check answers with the class and ask if any of their ideas were included.

Answers

1 flexibility training
2 weight training
3 sport-specific training
4 aerobic training

3 Students read the questions and underline the key words. They then read the text more carefully to find the answers. Encourage them to use their own words and not simply copy from the text. Monitor and help as necessary. Students compare answers with a partner. Check answers with the class. Ask if any of them do any of these activities, know someone who does them or can add any more information. Ask if they think there are any risks involved and discuss the importance of coaches and experts when doing keep-fit activities for the first time.

Answers

1 You can lift them more times, which helps you exercise for a longer time.
2 They can use weight machines or free weights.
3 It makes your heart work harder.
4 Interval training
5 So you don't fall down.
6 Because they start and stop a lot during matches.

21 The Reading text is recorded for students to listen, read and check their answers.

MIXED ABILITY

To support weaker students, tell them that they can copy the relevant information from the text and they do not need to put it into their own words.

FAST FINISHERS

Ask fast finishers to write two more questions about the text for the rest of the class to answer.

CONTINUED ON PAGE 54

4 Students find the highlighted words in the text. In order to match them to their meanings, they should look at the context of the words, including the sentences immediately before or after them. Then they match the words to their definitions and compare answers with a partner. Check answers with the class. Check any other new words or phrases, such as *balance*, *muscle*, *warm up* and pronunciation, for example *aerobic* /eəˈrəʊbɪk/, *martial* /ˈmɑːʃəl/, *muscle* /ˈmʌsl/, *stamina* /ˈstæmɪnə/ and *weight* /weɪt/.

Answers

1 routine 2 prevent 3 properly 4 lift 5 stretch 6 stamina

20 5 Explain to students that they are going to listen to two American friends talking about their fitness habits and how they keep fit. Students read the question. Play the recording. They discuss the answer in pairs. Check the answer as a class and ask students to explain how they know that Anna does more exercise. (*Tom only does about 20 minutes exercise at the gym and he doesn't do much exercise at the weekends.*)

Answer

Anna is usually more active.

20 6 Students read the incomplete sentences and, in pairs, add any missing information they can remember. Remind them that they can only use one or two words in each sentence. Play the recording again so they can check and add any extra words. Check answers with the class. Ask if they can remember what else Tom does at the weekends (*goes skateboarding*) and what he and Anna decide to do to get more physical exercise (*ride their bikes to school*, *walk up the stairs*). Play the recording again if necessary. Ask if students can think of more everyday activities Anna and Tom could do.

Answers

1 basketball
2 the gym
3 volleyball
4 goes swimming
5 computer games
6 go cycling

» **AUDIOSCRIPT TB PAGE 264**

7 Put students into pairs to read the words in the box and to complete the sentences in the *Useful language* box. Check the answers with the class and ask students to use the sentence structures to talk about themselves with a partner. If necessary, write a model on the board: *I usually (play) …, I don't usually … on weekdays, I do … of exercise …, I'm (not) very … at weekends, I should …, We should always ….* Ask for volunteers to share their partner's ideas with the class.

Answers

1 after school
2 go swimming
3 about
4 active
5 could
6 stairs

PROJECT ***An exercise plan***

Tell students that they are going make a realistic exercise plan. In groups, they discuss whether they do enough exercise, whether they should do more and how much time they have available for exercising. Then, in pairs, they read the questions and make notes. Monitor and help as necessary, reminding them to answer all the questions and to add any ideas of their own. Students write out their plan, check the grammar and vocabulary, and practise reading it. Finally, they present their plans to the other students. This could lead into a class discussion on the theme of keeping fit and physical well-being.

PROJECT EXTENSION

Students design a survey to find out people's keep-fit habits. Together, they draw up a chart with boxes for each type of activity, when it is done, and for how long. It could be a class survey or students could ask other students, family members and teachers. Then they pool all their information and make a final chart to display in the classroom. It should not display names but could be divided into age groups or categories, for example classmates, other students, teachers, family, friends.

COOLER

Write the four headings from the Reading text (*weight training*, *aerobic training*, *flexibility training*, *sport-specific training*) on the board and ask students to write a sentence about each, giving their opinion and saying whether they would like to do this activity, and why or why not.

4 ways to keep fit

21

Scientists say that people should do one hour of physical activity every day. It can be sports, exercise or everyday activities, such as walking. In the USA, only 25% of teenagers do enough physical activity, and that's a problem. In addition, teens need three types of training to keep fit: weight, aerobic and flexibility training. They also need to train well for specific sports. Good coaches understand athletes' needs and help them to train properly.

1

Weight training gives you stronger, healthier muscles. If you lift big weights, your muscles get larger. You can also use smaller weights and lift them more times. This trains your body to exercise for a longer time. At the gym, some people use weight machines, but other people prefer free weights. In both cases, they must lift the weights carefully to prevent accidents.

2

Aerobic training is good for you because it makes your heart work harder. You can do light exercise for a longer time, such as cycling slowly for an hour. This gives you stamina so you can exercise longer. You can also cycle hard for five minutes and then rest for a minute. Then you cycle for another five minutes and rest again. This is interval training and it helps you become faster.

3

Flexibility training is also important for fitness. For example, athletes need to warm up and stretch their muscles before they exercise. Martial arts, such as Tai Chi, are great for flexibility training. People also need balance for these activities so they don't fall down. In flexibility training, it's best to go slowly and be careful. You don't want to hurt yourself!

4

Sport-specific training is a special exercise routine that helps athletes play one sport better. For example, professional football players run a lot and do extra weight training for their legs. In contrast, tennis players do more exercises for their arms. They also stop and start a lot during matches, so interval training is helpful for them. This is when you quickly change between doing high-intensity exercise and low-intensity exercise.

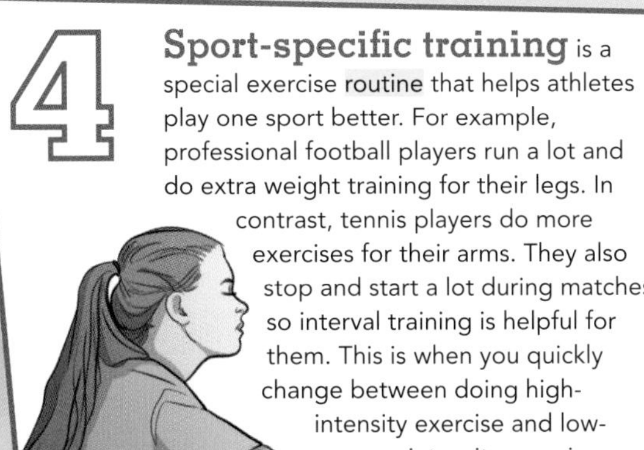

PROJECT

An exercise plan

Make a plan for doing exercise in your free time. Think about the questions and make notes.

- What sports can you do after school?
- What other exercise can you do on school days?
- What activities do you usually do at the weekend?
- What sports or exercise can you do with friends?
- What other activities can help you to keep fit?

Present your exercise plan to the class.

KEEPING FIT 29

REVIEW 1 UNITS 1–4

VOCABULARY

1 Write the opposite adjectives.

1 What's wrong? You look **miserable**. You're usually very c________ on Fridays.
2 Diana's very **polite.** She's never r________.
3 'Is Jacob **confident**?' 'No, he's quite s________.'
4 It was **careless** of you to lose your phone again. You need to be more c________ with your things.
5 Marcus is really **friendly** today. He can sometimes be quite u________!

2 Find the words (→ ↘ ↗ ↓).

u	p	r	e	t	y	i	n	e	u	d	w
g	o	o	d	l	o	o	k	i	n	g	t
f	w	t	r	e	n	d	y	a	f	b	e
a	e	u	o	b	n	o	h	d	a	r	e
i	c	o	b	a	r	d	l	r	s	a	n
s	m	a	r	t	n	a	n	r	h	n	a
t	i	i	s	o	b	e	n	i	i	n	s
r	p	n	c	u	d	g	r	d	o	p	m
a	t	e	e	n	a	g	e	p	n	r	a
i	s	e	o	k	a	l	d	e	a	e	r
g	e	l	d	e	r	l	y	e	b	t	w
h	b	c	a	s	a	l	g	i	l	t	t
t	s	k	i	n	y	c	u	r	e	y	e

Find words to describe someone's:

age
1 t *eenage*
2 e________

looks
3 p________
4 g________-l________

hair
5 b________
6 c________
7 s________
8 b________

clothes
9 c________
10 s________
11 u________
12 t________
13 s________-h________
14 b________n________

3 Choose two correct options for each verb.

1 **play** volleyball boxing rugby ice skating
2 **do** surfing gymnastics athletics cycling
3 **go** table tennis climbing squash jogging
4 **leave** home school to university married
5 **get** born married university a degree
6 **have** children home confident long hair
7 **get** school a child a job a driving licence

4 Read the text opposite and choose the correct word for each space. For each question, choose A, B, C or D.

	A	B	C	D
1	be	get	take	have
2	tiny	few	little	narrow
3	teams	coaches	members	teachers
4	finish	miss	stop	retire
5	method	road	kind	way
6	degree	university	grade	practice

GRAMMAR

1 Complete the conversations. Use the present simple or continuous, or the past simple or continuous form of the verbs.

1 **A:** I ________ (spend) a lot of time on homework at the moment.
B: Me too. It's unbelievable! Last term, we ________ (not have) as much work.
2 **A:** Why ____ you ________ (stop) having guitar lessons?
B: I ________ (not make) any progress and I didn't like the teacher.
3 **A:** Why ____ Tom ________ (be) so unfriendly at the moment?
B: I ________ (not know). He usually ________ (say) hello in the mornings.
4 **A:** ________ (you / go) cycling next Saturday?
B: No. I ________ (usually / go) cycling on Saturdays, but I ________ (lose) my helmet yesterday.
5 **A:** How old ________ (be) you when you ________ (get) your driving licence?
B: Eighteen. But I ________ (not own) a car until I was 25.
6 **A:** I ________ (send) you loads of messages last night but you ________ (not read) any of them.
B: No, sorry. I ________ (train) for a swimming competition. It's on Sunday. ____ you ________ (come) to watch?

Overview

VOCABULARY	Describing people; Prefixes: *un-*, *in-*, *im*; Clothes: adjectives; Adverbs; Life events; *too, enough, not enough*; Sports; Words with different meanings
GRAMMAR	Present simple and continuous; Past simple; Comparatives and superlatives; *not as … as*; Past continuous
EXAM TASKS	Reading Part 5

Resources

PHOTOCOPIABLE WORKSHEETS: Grammar worksheets Units 1–4; Vocabulary worksheets Units 1–4; Review Game Units 1–4; Literature worksheet; Speaking worksheet; Writing worksheet

WARMER

Bring some magazine photos of people to class. Put students in groups and give each group a photo. Ask each group to write adjectives describing the person's age, looks, hair, clothes and personality (they should use their imagination for this!). Join groups together and ask them to share their photos and say which adjectives they used. Monitor and help as necessary. Bring the class together and write some of the adjectives for each category on the board.

VOCABULARY

1 Read the instructions and set a time limit for students to complete the exercise. They compare answers with a partner. Check answers with the class.

Answers

1 cheerful 2 rude 3 shy 4 careful 5 unfriendly

2 Students look at the four categories. In pairs, they look at the first letters of the words and suggest answers. They do the word search and find the words. Check answers as a class. Then, students describe themselves to their partner using adjectives from Exercises 1 and 2.

Answers

2 elderly 3 pretty 4 good-looking 5 bald 6 curly 7 straight 8 blonde 9 casual 10 smart 11 unfashionable 12 trendy 13 second-hand 14 brand new

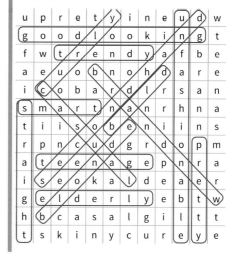

u	p	r	e	t	y	i	n	e	u	d	w
g	o	o	d	l	o	o	k	i	n	g	t
f	w	t	r	e	n	d	y	a	f	b	e
a	e	u	o	b	n	o	h	d	a	r	e
i	c	o	b	a	r	d	l	r	s	a	n
s	m	a	r	t	n	a	n	r	h	n	a
t	i	i	s	o	b	e	n	i	i	n	s
r	p	n	c	u	d	g	r	d	o	p	m
a	t	e	e	n	a	g	e	p	n	r	a
i	s	e	o	k	a	l	d	e	a	e	r
g	e	l	d	e	r	l	y	e	b	t	w
h	b	c	a	s	a	l	g	i	l	t	t
t	s	k	i	n	y	c	u	r	e	y	e

3 Give students five minutes to revise the collocations concerning life events on page 20 and the sports on page 24. Ask them to look at the list of verbs on the left and explain that two of the four options can be used with each verb. They complete the exercise and compare answers with a partner. Check answers with the class and ask students what verbs they could use with the incorrect options.

Answers

1 volleyball, rugby
2 gymnastics, athletics
3 climbing, jogging
4 home, school
5 married, a degree
6 children, long hair
7 a job, a driving licence

FAST FINISHERS

Ask fast finishers to add at least two more correct options connected with sport for the first three verbs, for example *play football*, *tennis*; *do yoga*, *exercise*; *go cycling*, *windsurfing*.

CONTINUED ON PAGE 58

4 **B1 Preliminary for Schools Reading Part 5**

In this part, reading for understanding of vocabulary and lexico-structural patterns in the text is tested. Students read a text of 120–150 words with six gaps. They choose the word that best fits the gap.

Tell students to read the text ignoring the gaps. Ask for a quick summary of what it is about. Ask the students to look at each gap, say which part of speech fits each space and suggest a possible answer. Accept all reasonable suggestions. While students complete the exercise, monitor and give help where necessary. They compare answers with a partner. Check answers with the class. Ask students if they can give any synonyms or brief definitions for each word or, for number 2, the expression (e.g. *take part* – join in an activity, participate).

Answers

1 C 2 A 3 B 4 D 5 D 6 A

GRAMMAR

1 Read the instructions and quickly revise the formation of each tense, including negatives and question forms, using a regular verb such as *to play*. In pairs, students test each other on the past simple forms of the irregular verbs in Vocabulary, Exercise 3 and in this exercise. Give students a few minutes to revise the use of the present simple, present continuous and past continuous tenses in the Grammar reference sections for Units 1 and 4 on pages 138 and 141. Tell them to read the conversations and decide if the verbs are referring to the present, the past or the future. They must also decide whether to use a simple or a continuous tense and take care to use the correct form of the verb. They complete the conversations and compare answers with a partner. Check answers with the class and ask stronger students to explain the tense use if there are any problems.

Answers

1 'm spending, didn't have
2 did, stop, wasn't making
3 is, being, don't know, says
4 Are you going, usually go, lost
5 were, got, didn't own
6 sent, didn't read, was training, Are, coming

2 Ask students how to form comparatives and superlatives. Give them some example adjectives, such as *new*, *big*, *nice*, *happy*, *useful*, *expensive*. Read the sentences and ask them which adjectives are irregular: *good*, *bad*. Check spelling rules and tell students to check how the comparative and superlative are used in the Grammar reference for Unit 3 on page 140, in particular the use of *than* and *(not) as … as*, and the use of *the* with superlatives. Make sure students understand the instructions. They complete the exercise and compare answers with a partner. Check answers as a class.

Answers

1 as messy as
2 better
3 the warmest
4 more comfortable than
5 curlier than
6 not as patient
7 the worst
8 as tall / the same height

MIXED ABILITY

Help weaker students with the *as … as* structure. Draw two stick figures, one taller than the other. Write their ages: 14 and 13 years old. Write two sentences: *A is taller than B. B isn't as old as A.* Then ask the students to write one negative sentence using *as … as* and one positive sentence using a comparative. The sentences must have the same meaning as the original sentences. Tell them they will need to change the subject of the sentence in each case: *B isn't as tall as A. A is older than B.*

3 Put students in pairs to complete this exercise. If they disagree on the correct form, each student should justify their choice by referring to the grammar rule that should be applied. Check answers with the class and ask stronger students to explain the grammar rules.

Answers

1 's meeting 2 sent 3 best 4 needed

4 Students complete this exercise in pairs. Tell them there is only one mistake in each sentence. They should agree about the mistake and how to correct it. Check answers with the class and, if necessary, ask stronger students to explain the mistakes.

Answers

1 We **have** fun when we are together.
2 I didn't **hear** my phone so I missed your call.
3 Our new home is **nearer** the school.
4 My dad **didn't go** to university.

COOLER

Ask students to think about Units 1–4. Write some questions on the board: *Which activities did you enjoy? What was difficult / easy for you? What are you good at? What errors do you need to work on?* Ask students to write their answers. Invite some students to share their answers and have a class discussion about each question.

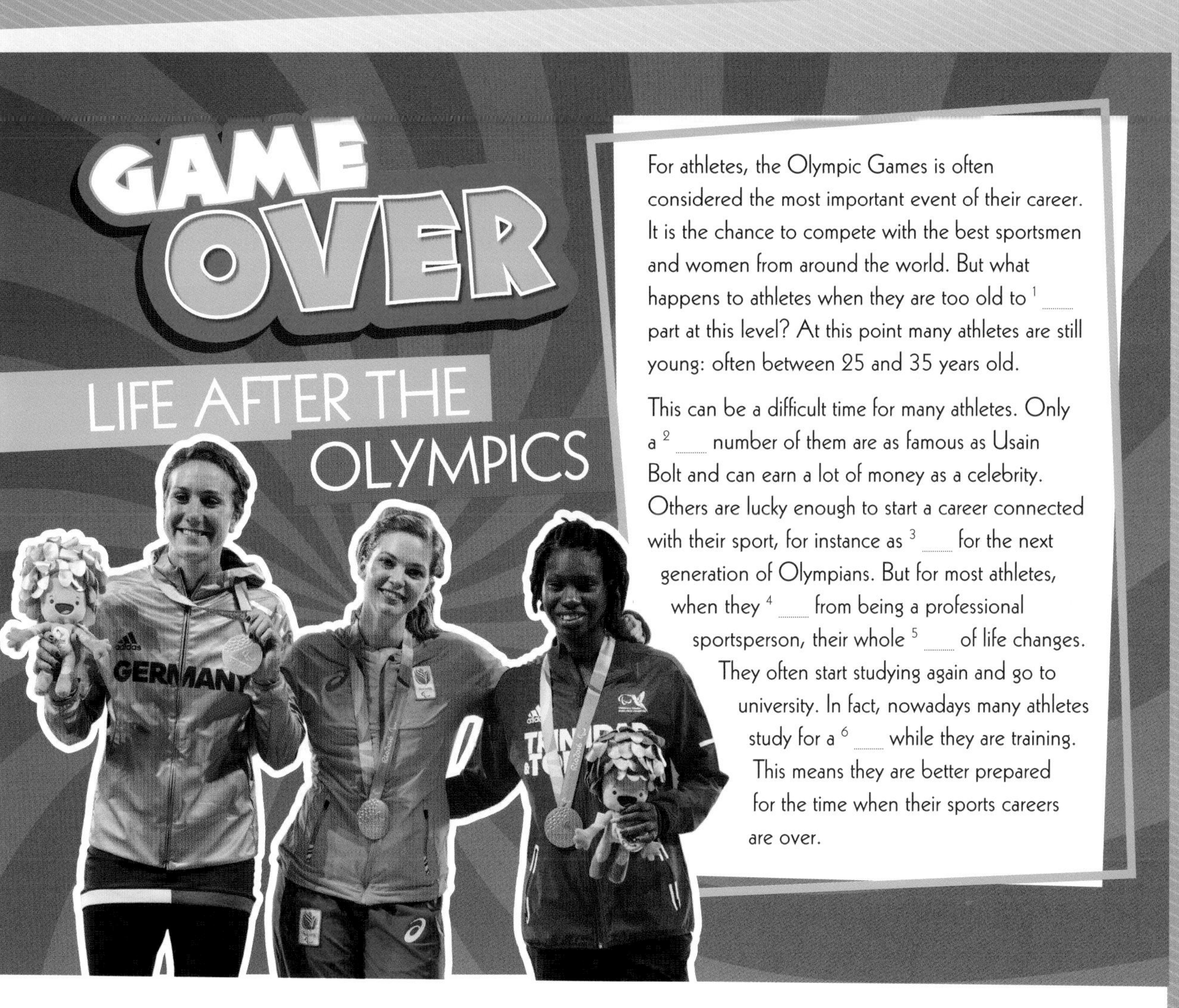

For athletes, the Olympic Games is often considered the most important event of their career. It is the chance to compete with the best sportsmen and women from around the world. But what happens to athletes when they are too old to [1] ____ part at this level? At this point many athletes are still young: often between 25 and 35 years old.

This can be a difficult time for many athletes. Only a [2] ____ number of them are as famous as Usain Bolt and can earn a lot of money as a celebrity. Others are lucky enough to start a career connected with their sport, for instance as [3] ____ for the next generation of Olympians. But for most athletes, when they [4] ____ from being a professional sportsperson, their whole [5] ____ of life changes. They often start studying again and go to university. In fact, nowadays many athletes study for a [6] ____ while they are training. This means they are better prepared for the time when their sports careers are over.

2 **Complete the second sentence so that it means the same as the first. Use no more than three words.**

1 Your room is messier than mine. — My room isn't ____ yours.
2 I'm not as good at climbing as my dad. — My dad is ____ at climbing than me.
3 I don't own a warmer jacket. — This is ____ jacket I own.
4 My old boots aren't as comfortable as these ones. — These boots are ____ my old ones.
5 My hair isn't as curly as my sister's. — My sister's hair is ____ mine.
6 You're more patient than me. — I'm ____ as you.
7 There isn't a player on the team as bad as me. — I'm ____ player on the team.
8 My brother and I are the same height. — I'm ____ as my brother.

3 **Choose the correct words.**

1 Tonight she *meet* / *'s meeting* some friends at the cinema.
2 Thank you for the gift you *sent* / *send* me recently.
3 She got the *better* / *best* mark in the class.
4 I was looking online because I *needed* / *was needing* some new clothes.

4 **Correct the mistake in each sentence.**

1 We are having fun when we are together.
2 I didn't heared my phone so I missed your call.
3 Our new home is more near the school.
4 My dad wasn't going to university.

UNITS 1–4 31

5 CALL THE POLICE!

ABOUT YOU

How much crime is there in your town or city?
Which crimes are the biggest problem where you live?

VOCABULARY Crimes and criminals

1 EP **Match the crimes to the photos.**

burglary hacking pickpocketing
shoplifting theft vandalism

22 **2** **Listen to six people talking about crime and decide which crime the speakers are talking about.**

23 **3** EP **Complete the sentences with the missing crimes from Exercise 1 and the correct type of criminals in the box. Use the plural form where necessary. Then listen and check.**

burglar hacker pickpocket shoplifter thief vandal

1 Three weeks ago a ______ stole over 100 million email addresses and passwords from a bank in the United States. Experts believe that ______ costs businesses over two trillion dollars every year.
2 We have a problem with ______ in our area. ______ have smashed the window of my parents' car three times in the last year.
3 We think that only 10% of ______ are professionals. For these people ______ is a job. They typically rob large stores and steal expensive items like designer clothes or bags.
4 I'd like to report the ______ of a car. I saw it happen. And I can describe the ______.
5 Please be careful of ______ in crowded areas. ______ is common at stations.
6 My neighbour doesn't know when the ______ happened. The ______ took TVs, computers, things like that.

4 EP **Read the example and complete the definitions with the verbs *steal* and *rob*.**

Professional shoplifters typically **rob** large stores and **steal** expensive items like designer clothes or bags.

1 Thieves ______ something from a place or person.
2 Thieves ______ a place or a person of something.

5 **Complete the sentences with the correct form of *steal* or *rob*.**

1 The thief ______ my phone from the table in the café.
2 Do any of these photos show the man who ______ you?
3 My parents once came home and a burglar was ______ their flat. He ran away immediately.
4 Is downloading films the same as ______ them?

5 CALL THE POLICE!

Unit Overview

TOPIC	Crime and the law
VOCABULARY	Crimes and criminals
READING	That isn't allowed here ...
GRAMMAR	Past simple and continuous
VOCABULARY	*ourselves, yourselves, themselves* and *each other*
WRITING	A story (1)
EXAM TASKS	Writing Part 2

Resources

GRAMMAR REFERENCE AND PRACTICE: SB page 143; TB page 244
WORKBOOK: pages 20–23
PHOTOCOPIABLE WORKSHEETS: Grammar worksheet Unit 5; Vocabulary worksheet Unit 5
TEST GENERATOR: Unit test 5

WARMER

Review the past simple by playing a story game. Start the story by saying 'Last night I woke up at 3 o'clock. There was a noise downstairs!' Invite a confident student to add a sentence to the story, using the past simple. This student then nominates another student to add the next sentence. Continue around the class. After a few minutes invite the class to think of suggestions for the ending.

ABOUT YOU

Write the word *crime* on the board. Check understanding. Ask students if they think crime is a problem in their town or city and what kind of crimes happen there. In pairs or small groups, ask students to decide which crimes are the biggest problems where they live. As they may not have the vocabulary to talk about this before doing Exercise 1, accept the crimes in L1 at this point. You could also write the translations on the board. Invite feedback from the groups and ask the other students if they agree.

VOCABULARY Crimes and criminals

1 Ask students to describe the photos and say what is happening in each one. Elicit that these actions are crimes. Read the words in the box and check pronunciation, particularly *burglary* /ˈbɜːgləri/ and *vandalism* /ˈvændəlɪzəm/. In pairs, students match the crimes to the photos. Tell students to guess if they are not sure about the meaning of the words. Check answers with the class.

Answers

A hacking B shoplifting C burglary D pickpocketing E vandalism F theft

22

2 Read the instructions and tell students they will hear the recording twice. Play the recording and put students in pairs to discuss their answers. Play it again, pausing between each item, for them to check their answers. Check answers with the class.

Answers

1 hacking 2 vandalism 3 shoplifting 4 theft 5 pickpocketing 6 burglary

» AUDIOSCRIPT TB PAGE 264

23

3 Explain that the words in Exercise 1 refer to crimes and the words in the box in this exercise refer to the people who commit these crimes. Check pronunciation, for example *thief* /θiːf/. Put students into pairs to complete the sentences, which have been taken from Exercise 2. Tell them to think carefully about the meaning of each sentence and whether the words they need are singular or plural. Check answers and ask students to guess the meaning of *smash* (sentence 2) and *crowded* (sentence 5).

Answers

1 hacker, hacking
2 vandalism, Vandals
3 shoplifters, shoplifting
4 theft, thief
5 pickpockets, Pickpocketing
6 burglary, burglar/burglars

» AUDIOSCRIPT TB PAGE 264

4 Write *rob* and *steal* on the board and ask students for the past tenses (*robbed* and *stole*). Read the example sentence, taken from Exercise 3, and then ask students to complete the rules.

Answers

1 steal 2 rob

5 Read the sentences and check understanding. Students complete the exercise and compare answers with a partner. Check answers with the class and remind them of the spelling rule for *rob* – they have to double the final *b* in the *-ing* and *-ed* forms.

Answers

1 stole 2 robbed 3 robbing 4 stealing

READING

BACKGROUND INFORMATION

Chewing gum has been banned on the streets of Singapore since 1992. Lee Kuan Yew, the first prime minister of Singapore, wanted the nation to have a clean environment. He apparently said, 'If you can't think because you can't chew, try a banana'. The ban remains one of the best-known aspects of life in Singapore, along with the country's laws against litter, graffiti, jaywalking (crossing the street at a place where it is not allowed), spitting, expelling 'mucus from the nose' and urinating anywhere but in a toilet. If it is a public toilet, you are legally required to flush it.

1 Read the title and the information about Singapore. Ask students to suggest reasons for why it is illegal to chew gum and if they agree with the ban. Ask for brief answers to the two questions in the introduction. Tell students they are going to read about some rules and laws in different countries. Ask them to describe the photos and say what the illegal activity might be. Tell them to read the three stories as quickly as possible and complete the sentences. Set a time limit of five minutes. Check answers with the class and check understanding of key vocabulary (*pedestrian crossing*, *swimming cap*, *bell*).

Answers

1 look at your phone on a pedestrian crossing.
2 wear a swimming cap in public swimming pools.
3 have a bell.

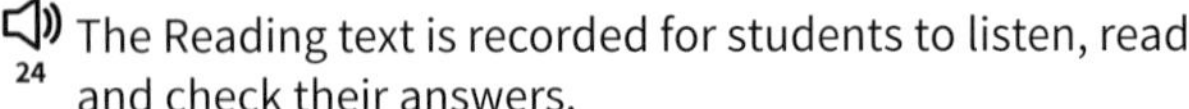

24 The Reading text is recorded for students to listen, read and check their answers.

2 Ask students to read the sentences. Then they re-read the article carefully, say if the sentences are correct or incorrect, and modify the incorrect ones. Students compare their answers with a partner, referring back to the article where necessary. Invite different students to give the answers.

Answers

1 false (Her mum suggested it.)
2 true
3 false (He didn't understand what the two lifeguards were shouting in Italian.)
4 true
5 false (He didn't have a bicycle back in the UK.)
6 true

3 Encourage students to use the context to work out the meanings of the highlighted words.

Put students into pairs to complete the sentences. Check answers. Nominate a student to read the first sentence and name another student to read out the next sentence. Continue until all the sentences have been read out. Point out that *fine* can be used as a verb or a noun. Check understanding of any other new words in the stories. Encourage stronger students to give their meanings. New words may include *unfair* (not morally right) and *look something up* (to find a particular piece of information by looking in a reference book or online).

Answers

1 fined 2 Illegal 3 The law 4 compulsory 5 fine 6 rule

MIXED ABILITY

Encourage weaker learners to name the parts of speech of the highlighted words and identify the parts of speech needed to complete the spaces. If they still need help, tell them that three are nouns, two are adjectives and one is a verb.

FAST FINISHERS

Ask fast finishers to choose two words from the text and to use them in sentences which demonstrate their meaning. Check their sentences and ask the students to come and write them on the board, leaving a space where the word from the text goes. Other students should work out the missing word.

TALKING POINTS

Refer students to the first question and put them in small groups to exchange ideas. Monitor and help as necessary. Ask for feedback and have a class vote on the most unusual law.

Students then discuss the second question in their groups. Discuss their ideas as a class and encourage students to give reasons for their opinions. Have a class vote on the most unpopular rule.

COOLER

Write *shoplifter* on the board with the letters in a circle. In teams, students write as many words of three or more letters as they can think of, using the letters from the word. Set a time limit of three minutes. They can only use each letter once in each word. The team with the longest list is the winner.

Possible answers

felt file fish fit help hole life lift lip self ship shoe shop sit the those top

That isn't ALLOWED HERE ...

In Singapore, few people chew gum on the streets. You can't bring it into the country and you can only buy it from the chemist's with an ID card! What unusual rules or laws have you come across around the world? And how did you find out about them?

I was away with my parents in Honolulu, Hawaii last year. One afternoon, we were leaving a restaurant when it started raining hard. My mom suggested visiting the Natural History Museum as we were directly opposite it. We were crossing the road, when I got out my phone. I wasn't really thinking. I wanted to check my messages. Anyway, almost immediately I heard the noise of a loud motorbike. My first thought was: phone thief! But when I looked up, I saw a police officer. We looked at each other for a few seconds and then I noticed she was pointing at my phone! I had no idea, but it's actually illegal to look at your mobile phone on a pedestrian crossing in Honolulu. I'm only 16 but I had to pay a $15 fine! It was really unfair!

Alexa, San Diego, US

We went camping in Italy last year and the campsite had a huge pool. When we arrived, my brother and I got changed straight away and jumped in. We were really enjoying ourselves when suddenly we heard a loud noise. Everyone was looking at us and two lifeguards were shouting in Italian. There was probably a rule about jumping in, we thought. It *was* quite crowded. But then the lifeguards started pointing to their heads. For a few seconds we were really confused. Then we realised: *everyone* was wearing swimming caps! We looked it up online later. It's actually the law there. Even my dad had to wear one, and he's completely bald!

Martin, Dublin, Ireland

When my dad got a job in Sydney, Australia, we moved there from the UK for two years. We were living close to the centre and Dad started going to work by bike. He didn't even have one back in the UK! We knew that bike helmets are compulsory in Australia. And Dad always wore one. So when the police stopped him and some other cyclists at a traffic light one morning, he was feeling relaxed. But can you believe this? While the officers were checking the bikes, they noticed that several of them didn't have bells – including Dad's. And all bikes must have them in the city. They were each fined $106 – about £60! That feels so unfair.

Louise, Brighton, UK

24

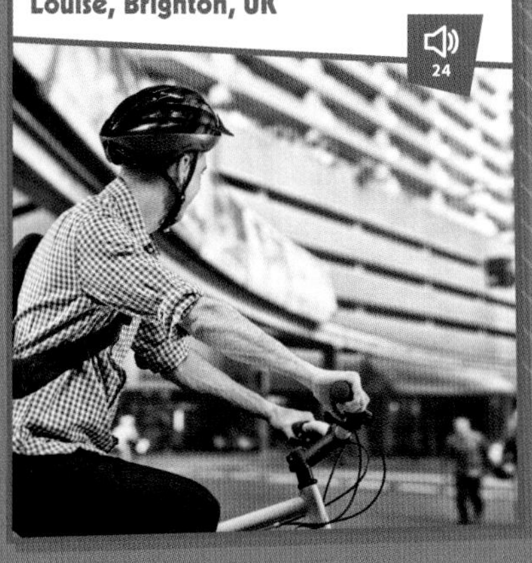

READING

1 **Read the stories quickly. Complete three sentences about each story.**

1 In Honolulu, Hawaii, you mustn't …
2 In Italy, you must …
3 In Sydney, Australia, all bikes must …

2 **Read the stories again. Are the sentences true or false?**

1 Alexa had the idea to go to the museum.
2 The police officer stopped Alexa near the museum.
3 Martin and his brother understand Italian.
4 Jumping into the pool was allowed at the campsite.
5 Louise's dad has always been into cycling.
6 Her dad had to pay $106.

3 **Complete the sentences with the highlighted words in the stories.**

1 We were once ______ for cycling at night without lights.
2 ______ downloading of music, TV and films is a common problem throughout the world.
3 ______ in Brazil says that everyone between 18 and 70 must vote in an election.
4 At my school, it's ______ to wear the uniform.
5 The minimum ______ for driving and texting in the UK is £200.
6 There's a ______ in our house about using phones at the dinner table.

TALKING POINTS

Do you know any unusual laws?
What rules do you disagree with at your school?

GRAMMAR Past simple and continuous

1 **Read the examples. Which verb is in the past continuous? How do we form the past continuous?**

1 Immediately I heard the noise of a loud motorbike.
2 She was waiting at the side of the road.

2 **Choose the correct words to complete the rules.**

a We use the past *simple / continuous* to talk about a completed action at a past time.
b We use the past *simple / continuous* to talk about actions in progress at a past time.

3 **Choose the correct form of the verbs.**

1 I couldn't call you. The thief *stole / was stealing* my phone!
2 I saw someone in front of your house yesterday. She *tried / was trying* to open your car door.
3 What *did the burglars take / were the burglars taking*?
4 I phoned you last night but there was no answer. What *did you do / were you doing*?
5 We weren't at home last night. We *travelled / were travelling* back from a relative's house.

4 **Read the examples from the stories. Then complete the rules with *past simple* or *past continuous.***

1 We were crossing the road, when I got out my phone.
2 While the officers were checking the bikes, they noticed that several of them didn't have bells.
3 When we arrived, my brother and I got changed straight away and jumped in.

We often use the past continuous and the past simple together.
a The _____ talks about a past action in progress.
b The _____ talks about a completed shorter action that interrupted the action in progress.
c If one action happens after the other, we use the _____ for both actions.

» GRAMMAR REFERENCE AND PRACTICE PAGE 142

5 **Correct the mistake in each sentence.**

1 I read a book when a woman screamed.
2 We are talking when a policeman asked me my name.
3 We went to my house and we were watching TV.
4 When I walked near the river, I saw a dog in the water.
5 While we're waiting for the bus, I heard a cry.
6 He was quite tall and wears a loose-fitting tracksuit.

6 **Complete the story with the past simple or past continuous form of the verbs.**

Couple find 'Goldilocks' burglar

When Martin Holtby and Pat Dyson got home from their holiday recently, they [1] _____ (notice) something strange immediately. Their unopened letters were on the table. There was some food shopping in the kitchen. While Martin [2] _____ (look) around the house, he [3] _____ (find) more strange things. A man's clothes [4] _____ (hang) in the bathroom. Their bath was full of hot water. [5] _____ a burglar _____ (live) in their house?

When Martin [6] _____ (go) into the bedroom, he found the answer. A man [7] _____ (sleep) in their bed! The couple quickly called the police and when they [8] _____ (arrive), they took him away.

The man was fined £200. He didn't steal anything while he [9] _____ (stay) in the house. He wasn't actually a burglar. He thought the house was empty and he [10] _____ (need) somewhere to sleep!

VOCABULARY *ourselves, yourselves, themselves* and *each other*

1 **Match the sentences to the photos.**

EP

1 They're looking at themselves.
2 They're looking at each other.

2 **Choose the correct words.**

EP

1 Jack bought itself / himself a new phone.
2 I cut myself / itself while I was washing up.
3 Did you teach myself / yourself the guitar?
4 Did you and Sara hurt herself / yourselves?
5 Sam and I made myself / ourselves a snack.
6 Thanks for the party! Everyone really enjoyed ourselves / themselves.

3 **Complete the sentences with the correct pronoun from Exercise 2 or *each other*.**

1 They walked past _____ without saying a word.
2 Josie introduced _____ to everyone.
3 Tom and I often argue with _____.
4 I need to buy a present for Tom. We always give _____ presents on our birthdays.
5 Did you all enjoy _____ last weekend?

4 » **Work with a partner. Turn to page 121.**

GRAMMAR Past simple and continuous

WARMER

Write several verbs on the board, for example *watch*, *play*, *buy*, *meet*. Ask students to guess what you were doing at 7 o'clock yesterday evening using the verbs on the board or any others they can think of.

1 Ask students to name the tenses in the two examples (*past simple and past continuous*). Revise positive, negative and question forms of the past continuous.

Answers

Example 2 is the past continuous. We form the past continuous with *was / were* and the *-ing* form of the verb.

2 In pairs, students read the sentences and complete the rules. Check answers.

Answers

a simple b continuous

3 Put students into mixed ability pairs to complete the exercise. Check answers and ask students to explain their choices.

Answers

1 stole
2 was trying
3 did the burglars take
4 were you doing
5 were travelling

4 Tell students to read sentences 1 and 2 and say which action happened first. Ask if the first action had finished before the second action started (*no*). Repeat for the third sentence and ask if the first action had finished before the second action started (*yes*). Students complete the rules in pairs. Check answers as a class. Explain that we often use *while* to introduce the past continuous. Ask students to find more example sentences from the Reading passages on page 33.

Answers

a past continuous
b past simple
c past simple

» GRAMMAR REFERENCE AND PRACTICE ANSWER KEY TB PAGE 244

5 Remind students to look at the rules in Exercise 4. Students complete the exercise and compare answers with a partner. Check answers.

Answers

1 I **was reading** a book when a woman screamed.
2 We **were** talking when a policeman asked me my name.
3 We went to my house and we **watched** TV.
4 When I **was walking** near the river, I saw a dog in the water.
5 While we **were** waiting for the bus, I heard a cry.
6 He was quite tall and **was wearing** a loose-fitting tracksuit.

6 Read the title and check understanding of *Goldilocks*. Students complete the exercise in pairs. Check answers by inviting different students to read the story one sentence at a time.

Answers

1 noticed 2 was looking 3 found 4 were hanging
5 Was, living 6 went 7 was sleeping 8 arrived 9 was staying
10 needed

MIXED ABILITY

Tell weaker students to identify the five main events or actions first and put them in the past simple. Then they should go back and put the other verbs in the past continuous. They re-read the story to make sure the past continuous verbs describe an action or event that was in progress.

» GRAMMAR WORKSHEET UNIT 5

VOCABULARY *ourselves, yourselves, themselves* and *each other*

1 Ask students to say what they can see in the pictures. Bring a mirror to class and use it to reinforce picture B. For example, hand it to a student and ask the class 'Who is Damien looking at?' Explain that when the subject and the object of the sentence is the same person, we use *-self*. Elicit the forms for each person and write them on the board. Ask students the difference between *yourself* and *yourselves*. Explain that *each other* is used to show that each person in a group of two or more people does something to the others.

Answers

1 B 2 A

2 Monitor and help as students choose the correct words before comparing answers with a partner. Check answers.

Answers

1 himself 2 myself 3 yourself 4 yourselves 5 ourselves
6 themselves

3 Do this exercise as an auction. Put students into teams. Each group has £100 to spend. Write three options on the board for each item, for example *1 each other, themselves, yourselves*; *2 ourselves, each other, themselves*, etc. Give the teams a few minutes to decide which option is correct. Open the bidding and sell each option to the highest bidder. Keep a record of price and buyers on the board. The winners are the team with the most correct answers and the most money left.

Answers

1 each other
2 herself
3 each other
4 each other
5 yourselves

4 Tell students to turn to page 121 and read the questions. In pairs, students ask and answer the questions. Monitor and help as necessary. Ask different students to tell the class their partner's answers.

Answers

Students' own answers

» VOCABULARY WORKSHEET UNIT 5

WRITING A story (1)

1 Tell students that they are going to write a story and that they will first read one as an example. Ask them what they think the story is about by looking at the title and the photo.

Possible answers

A story about someone who prevents a pickpocketing or helps to catch a pickpocket

2 Set a short time limit for students to read the story and see if their ideas were correct. Tell them to ignore the highlighted words. Ask if they can suggest a better title, for example *A brave girl!*

Answers

Students' own answers

3 Ask students to give their opinions of Ellen's story, giving reasons, in small groups. They discuss what makes a story good or bad. The groups share their ideas with the class. Read the *Prepare to write* box. In their groups, ask the students to decide whether Ellen's story follows these tips. Explain that it is important to think carefully about the logical order of events when writing a story. Tell them to look at the events from Ellen's story, put them in order and identify which sentences refer to the beginning, the middle and the end of the story. Check answers.

Answers

The order is e, c, (beginning); a, b, (middle); d (end).

4 Revise the uses of the past simple and past continuous. Ask students to underline examples of the tenses in Ellen's story. They compare answers with a partner before checking as a class. Ask if the main events of the story are in the past simple or past continuous (*past simple*).

Answers

Past simple: went, left, took, arrived, noticed, realised, shouted, heard, looked, started, were, ran, caught, was, was
Past continuous: was feeling, was getting, was standing, was happening, was trying, was talking

5 Students look at the highlighted words, say whether they are adverbs or adjectives and how they know (*adverbs describe verbs, adjectives describe nouns*). Point out that many adverbs end in *-ly*. They complete the exercise. Check answers and ask which word can be an adjective or an adverb (*early*).

Answers

adjectives: exhausted, early (second example)
adverbs: early (first example), suddenly, immediately, luckily, soon

6 Read the instructions and write the opening sentence on the board. Put students into small groups to discuss the questions. Invite groups to share their ideas with the class. Students plan their story individually.

7 Monitor and help as students compare their ideas in pairs. Encourage them to suggest ways to improve each other's story.

8 **B1 Preliminary for Schools Writing Part 2**

In this part, students are assessed on content, communicative achievement, organisation and language. Students can choose to write a story, as in this task, or an article, of about 100 words.

Students write their story, using the notes they made in Exercise 6. Remind them to include examples of the past simple and past continuous, and some adjectives and adverbs. Tell them to write about 100 words and to check their spelling and grammar carefully. Monitor and help as necessary. In groups, students take turns to read out their stories. Each group should choose one story to share with the class.

FAST FINISHERS

Ask fast finishers to exchange stories with each other. Tell them to write an alternative ending. Nominate one or two individuals to read the story aloud.

Model answer

False alarm!
While I was closing my curtains one night, I noticed something unusual. A man was standing in the street. He was looking at the building opposite. Suddenly he jumped onto a wall outside the house and then he climbed through an open window. Immediately, I called the police. 'Please come quickly,' I said, 'I think he's a burglar.' Two minutes later, the police arrived and arrested him. Next day a police officer came to my house. 'Thank you for calling us,' she said. 'Fortunately he wasn't a burglar. He was trying to get into his house. He left his keys and his phone inside.'

COOLER

Play 'Consequences'. In groups of four, each student takes a strip of paper. Write *title*, *beginning*, *middle* and *end* and the names *Beanie and Tog* on the board and tell students that they are going to write a story about Beanie and Tog (they can be people or animals). They must listen to the instructions carefully. They must not speak or show their paper to another student. At the top of the paper, each student writes a title. They fold the paper over so the title is hidden and pass it to the student on their left. Repeat the procedure for the beginning, middle and end of the story. Students unfold the strips of paper and read the stories. Ask each group to choose the best story to read to the class.

WRITING A story (1)

1 **Look at the photo and the title of Ellen's story. What do you think happened?**

HERO for a day!

Last year, I went on a school trip with my classmates. We left school early by coach and the journey took several hours. When we arrived, everyone was feeling exhausted.

While I was getting off the coach, I noticed a man in his early twenties. He was standing really close to one of my friends. Suddenly, I realised what was happening. The man was trying to steal my friend's purse from her bag!

I immediately shouted to my friend. The man heard me, and for a few seconds we looked at each other. Then he started running. Luckily, there were two police officers nearby. They ran after the pickpocket and soon they caught him.

The next day, there was a story about it online and everyone was talking about it. I was a hero!

2 **Read Ellen's story. What do you think of the title for her story? Can you think of a better title?**

3 **Read the *Prepare to write* box. Then read Ellen's story again and put events a–e in order. Decide which events belong to the beginning, middle and end of the story.**

PREPARE TO WRITE

A story (1)

When you write a story:

- make sure there is a beginning, middle and end
- give the story an interesting title
- use verbs in the past simple and past continuous
- use adjectives and adverbs to make your story interesting.

a Ellen saw the pickpocket.
b The police caught the pickpocket.
c Ellen got off the coach.
d The story appeared on the internet.
e The coach left school.

4 **Look at Ellen's story again. How many verbs can you find in the past simple and past continuous?**

5 **Look at the highlighted words in Ellen's story. Which are adjectives and which are adverbs?**

6 **You are going to write a story which must begin with the sentence 'While I was closing my curtains one night, I noticed something unusual'. Plan the events in your story. Use the questions to help you.**

- Where does the story take place?
- What happens at the beginning? What did you notice?
- What are the main events?
- What happens in the end?

7 **Compare your ideas with a partner. Can you improve your plan?**

8 **Write your story.**

- Begin the story with the sentence in Exercise 6.
- Use the tips in the *Prepare to write* box.
- Write about 100 words.
- Remember to check your spelling and grammar.

6 CITY LIFE

ABOUT YOU

04 **Watch the video and discuss the questions.**

Would you prefer to live in a big city or a village? Why?

What are the good and bad things about where you live?

VOCABULARY City problems

25 **1 Match the words to the photos A–F. More than one word can match some photos. Then listen and check.** EP

crowds graffiti green spaces
pollution power cut
public transport rubbish
rush hour traffic jam

2 Complete the sentences with some of the problems in Exercise 1.

0 If we leave for the shopping centre early, we can avoid the *crowds* . It gets really busy there by lunchtime.
1 There was a ________ in our building last night. We had to use torches to see.
2 Can you take out the ________? They'll collect it tomorrow morning.
3 There's a huge problem with ________ in our city from cars and lorries. Many of the buses are electric now.
4 There is always a ________ outside our school in the mornings. More children should walk to school. It's dangerous!
5 I go to school by ________. I often catch the bus but there's also a train.
6 We never go on the underground during the ________ in summer. The trains get too hot.

26 **3 Listen to four people describing where they live. Answer the questions about each person.**

- Do they live in a city or in a village?
- What problem from Exercise 1 is each person talking about? Choose from the words in the box.

graffiti green spaces public transport rush hour

27 **4 Listen and write one or two words in each space.**

1 There's a lot of graffiti on a ________ near the man's house.
2 When the girl lived in a village, she ________ to school.
3 The boy usually gets ________ into the city.
4 The woman says she avoids ________ during the rush hour.

5 Complete the sentences about where you live. Use the problems in Exercise 1. Discuss your sentences in pairs.

1 There's a serious problem with …
2 We don't have a problem with …
3 There are lots of …
4 There isn't/aren't enough …
5 One of my favourite places is …
6 One thing I don't like is …

6 CITY LIFE

Unit Overview

TOPIC	City life and country life
VOCABULARY	City problems
READING	City problems – teenagers' solutions
GRAMMAR	*some/any, much/many, a lot of, a few / a little*
VOCABULARY	Compounds: noun + noun
LISTENING	An interview about living in the country
SPEAKING	Agreeing and disagreeing
EXAM TASKS	Reading Part 5

Resources

GRAMMAR REFERENCE AND PRACTICE: SB page 143; TB page 244
WORKBOOK: pages 24–27
VIDEO AND VIDEO WORKSHEET: Modern life
PHOTOCOPIABLE WORKSHEETS: Grammar worksheet Unit 6; Vocabulary worksheet Unit 6
TEST GENERATOR: Unit test 6

WARMER

Write these questions on the board: *Do you like where you live? Why / Why not? Have you ever lived in a different place? Which place do you prefer? Why?* Put students into small groups to discuss the questions before discussing them as a whole class. Encourage them to give reasons for their answers.

ABOUT YOU

04 You can begin the class and introduce the topic of the unit by showing the video and asking students to complete the video worksheet. Read the first question. Invite opinions from the class and write key vocabulary on the board. In pairs, students answer the second question. They write the heading *Where I live* on a piece of paper and divide the page into two columns with the headings *Good things* and *Bad things*. Give them three minutes to create the list. Then put pairs into groups of four to compare their lists. Share some ideas as a class.

MIXED ABILITY

Give weaker students prompts, for example *traffic, fresh air, cinemas*.

VOCABULARY City problems

1 Students briefly describe the photos. Read the words in the box, discussing the meaning of any unfamiliar vocabulary and then tell students to match the words and phrases to the photos. Play the recording for them to check their answers. Check pronunciation, for example *graffiti* /grəˈfiːti/, *pollution* /pəˈluːʃən/ and *public* /ˈpʌblɪk/.

Answers

25

The answers are recorded for students to check and then repeat.
A graffiti, rubbish
B crowds, public transport, rush hour
C green spaces
D pollution
E power cut
F traffic jam

2 Read the example sentence. Tell students to look at the words in Exercise 1 again. They should read the sentences carefully before filling in the spaces, and try to work out the meaning of any new words from the context. Students complete the exercise and compare ideas with a partner. Ask individual students to read out the sentences and ask the class if they are correct. Check understanding of any new words, for example *torch* and *underground*.

Answers

1 power cut 2 rubbish 3 pollution 4 traffic jam 5 public transport 6 rush hour

26

3 Read the instructions, the questions and the words in the box. Ask students which problems they think are connected to city life and which to village life. Play the recording and tell students to discuss their answers with a partner. If necessary, play it a second time. Check answers and ask students if their predictions were correct. Ask them which words or expressions helped them to identify whether the speaker was talking about a city or a village. Check pronunciation of *village* /ˈvɪlɪdʒ/.

Answers

Question 1. Speaker 1: city; Speaker 2: village; Speaker 3: village; Speaker 4: city
Question 2. Speaker 1: rush hour; Speaker 2: public transport; Speaker 3: graffiti; Speaker 4: green spaces

» AUDIOSCRIPT TB PAGES 264–265

27

4 Tell students to read the sentences and fill the spaces with what they remember from the recording in Exercise 3. Play the recording again and ask students to compare answers with a partner before checking as a class. Check understanding of *get a lift* and *avoid*.

Answers

1 bus stop 2 walked 3 a lift 4 the underground

» AUDIOSCRIPT TB PAGE 265

5 Ask students to think about the problems where they live. Tell them to re-read the lists they made in *About you* and the words in Exercise 1. Set a short time limit for them to write sentences. They discuss their answers in pairs. Monitor and give positive feedback. Ask different students to tell the class about their partner's answers.

Answers

Students' own answers

READING

BACKGROUND INFORMATION

Ben Gulak was born in 1989 and, like Ann, he loved inventing things as a child. In partnership with Ryan Fairhead, he helped develop the DTV Shredder: a small, light vehicle which can be used in snow, mud or sand.

Ann Makosinski, born 1997, has won several awards. After finishing school she went on to study at the University of British Colombia. She has made some improvements to the torch, including the ability to store electricity and adaptability into a headlamp. She also invented the e-Drink which converts wasted heat from hot drinks into electricity. It can be used to charge portable electronic devices.

1 Briefly elicit some problems of living in a city. Tell students that they are going to read about two teenagers who have solved similar problems by inventing something. Ask them to look at the title of the article and the pictures and to guess what the teenagers invented. Set a short time limit for students to scan the article quickly to find out whether their ideas are correct.

Answers

The boy invented a scooter and the girl invented a torch.

2 **B1 Preliminary for Schools Reading Part 5**

In this part, students read a text of 120–150 words with six gaps. They choose the word that best fits the gap. The task tests reading for understanding of vocabulary meaning and use, as well as lexico-grammatical patterns. (See also Review 1.)

Ask students to look at each gap, say which part of speech fits and suggest a possible answer. Accept all reasonable suggestions and remind students that verbs should be in the past tense. While students complete the exercise, monitor and give help where necessary. They compare answers with a partner. Check answers with the class. Ask students if they can give synonyms or brief definitions for each word. You could also give example sentences containing some of the words, for example *Scientists have* ***developed*** *a new drug against cancer. Children* ***develop*** *into adults. Do you have Internet* ***access****? I don't have* ***access*** *to that kind of information. She has three children to* ***support***.

Answers

1 A 2 B 3 A 4 D 5 C 6 D

28 The Reading text is recorded for students to listen, read and check their answers.

3 Put students in pairs to predict the missing information before they read the article again. Read each sentence as a class and ask which parts of speech fit the space (*noun, adjective or verb*) and their forms (for example *comparative adjective, verb in the infinitive*). Students read the article again and complete the sentences. Remind them to read carefully to find the answers. Check answers by inviting different students to read out the completed sentences.

Answers

1 China, Canada
2 more petrol
3 air pollution
4 electricity
5 to invent
6 to study
7 body heat
8 invention

4 Tell students to look at the highlighted words in the text. Ask them to work in pairs to guess the meaning of the words from the context. Take feedback from the class. Then ask students to read the definitions and match them to the highlighted words. They can try replacing the highlighted word with the definition to check whether the answer is correct. Check answers.

Answers

1 main 2 fact 3 design 4 shocked 5 powerful 6 instead

FAST FINISHERS

Ask fast finishers to choose four of the words and write sentences using them. They read them out to the class replacing the word with *beep*. The class supplies the word.

TALKING POINTS

Divide the class into groups of four to discuss the questions and brainstorm ideas. Each group should appoint one member to make a note of the ideas. Monitor and help as necessary. As a class, students share what they discussed and talk about their ideas for the second question (for example reducing their carbon footprint, using alternative sources of energy, recycling). Write key vocabulary on the board. Have a class vote on the best ideas.

COOLER

Bring a paper clip or draw one on the board. In small groups, students think of ten ways to use it apart from keeping sheets of paper together, for example bookmark, screwdriver for glasses, wrap cotton wool around it to clean small spaces such as laptop keyboards, to unclog small holes such as salt and pepper pots, keep a plastic bag closed, etc. Share ideas and have a class vote on the most original idea.

READING

1 **Look at the photos. What do you think these teenagers invented? Read the article quickly and check your answers. Ignore any spaces.**

City problems – TEENAGERS' SOLUTIONS

28

These two teenagers noticed two everyday problems in cities. And they decided to do something about them.

While Ben Gulak was visiting Beijing, China, he was **shocked** at the air pollution in the city. He soon realised one of the **main** causes: transport. In Ben's home town in Canada, the traffic is quite light, but Beijing has a lot of traffic. Some people drive cars, but a lot of people ride scooters. They're cheaper and they don't need much petrol. They're also lighter and easier to drive through traffic jams. There is one problem: petrol scooters can produce ten times more air pollution than cars.

Back in Canada, Ben started thinking about the problem. He wanted to **design** a new type of transport – something as small as a scooter, but cleaner. He called his invention the Uno – a motorbike which looks like … half a motorbike! It doesn't use any petrol – just electricity.

Ben won a prize for his invention and now he's completed three different versions of the bike. Will we one day see it on our roads?

When Ann Makosinski was young, she only had a few toys to play with. **Instead**, she loved inventing new things from rubbish around the house. They didn't work, of course, but Ann soon [1] ______ an interest in science and electronics.

The idea for her first successful invention came from a friend in the Philippines. Ann, who is half Filipino, half Canadian, [2] ______ that her friend was doing badly at school. The [3] ______ was that she couldn't study at night because there wasn't any electricity. Ann was amazed to discover that many people, over a billion in fact, don't have [4] ______ to electricity. And then she remembered a **fact** from her science class: the heat in a person means each of us is like a walking 100W light bulb. So Ann designed a torch that uses just the heat from a human hand. It wasn't as **powerful** as a normal torch and only [5] ______ a little light. But Ann's invention won an international science competition with a prize of $25,000 to [6] ______ her education in the future.

2 **Now read the part about Ann Makosinski again and choose the correct word for each space. For each question, choose A, B, C or D.**

	A	B	C	D
1	A developed	B grew	C made	D increased
2	A informed	B heard	C told	D called
3	A trouble	B event	C complaint	D rule
4	A opportunity	B way	C chance	D access
5	A did	B brought	C produced	D achieved
6	A own	B carry	C keep	D support

3 **Read the article again and complete the sentences with one or two words in each space.**

1. Ben was on holiday in ______ but he is actually from ______.
2. Cars use ______ than scooters.
3. Scooters create more ______ than cars.
4. The Uno is cleaner than a normal scooter because it uses ______.
5. When she was a child, Ann used rubbish ______ new things.
6. Ann's friend wasn't doing well at school because it was impossible ______ at night.
7. Ann's torch works by changing ______ into electricity.
8. Ann won $25,000 for her ______ of the torch.

4 **Match the highlighted words in the article to the meanings.**

1. largest
2. something you know is true
3. plan something before making it
4. surprised and upset
5. very strong
6. in place of something else

TALKING POINTS

What problem or situation would you like to solve where you live?

How could you improve the problem or situation?

GRAMMAR *some/any, much/many, a lot of, a few / a little*

1 **Read the examples. Then complete the rules with *some* or *any*.**

1 Some people drive cars.
2 The Uno doesn't use any petrol.
3 Have you got any ideas?

We use:
a ________ before nouns in positive sentences.
b ________ before nouns in negative sentences and in questions.

2 **Complete the sentences with *some* or *any*.**

1 Do you need ________ help with the rubbish?
2 I like ________ graffiti but not all of it.
3 There's ________ heavy traffic on the motorway.
4 Is there ________ information about bus times?
5 There isn't ________ electricity at the moment. I think there's a power cut.
6 I've got ________ rubbish here. Where can I put it?

3 **Read the examples. Then complete the rules with the words.**

1 Beijing is like a lot of big cities around the world.
2 The city has a lot of traffic.
3 A lot of people ride scooters.
4 Scooters don't need much petrol.
5 When Ann was young, she only had a few toys.
6 Many people don't have access to electricity.
7 Ann's torch only produced a little light.

a We use *many*, ________ and ________ to talk about large amounts.
b We don't usually use *much* or *many* in positive sentences: *There is ~~much~~* ***a lot of*** *time.*
c We use ________ and ________ to talk about small amounts.
d We don't use *a few* or *a little* in negative sentences: *He hasn't got ~~a little~~* ***much*** *money.*

» **GRAMMAR REFERENCE AND PRACTICE PAGE 143**

4 **Look at the underlined nouns in the examples in Exercise 3. Are they countable or uncountable?**

5 **Complete the table with *a lot of*, *a little* and *much*.**

Countable nouns	Uncountable nouns
There aren't many cities.	There isn't [1] ________ water.
There are a lot of scooters.	There's [2] ________ traffic.
There are a few people.	There's [3] ________ petrol.

6 **Choose the correct words.**

1 **A:** Do you like living in the country?
B: Mostly. There are *a few / a little* bad things. There isn't *many / much* entertainment.
2 **A:** I got *much / a lot of* tips from my aunt about visiting the UK.
B: My brother gave me *a little / a few* information about *a / some* good things to see in the UK.
3 **A:** Have you got *a few / some* minutes? I'm doing a questionnaire on pollution.
B: I'm sorry. I haven't got *much / many* time. Are there *many / much* questions?
4 **A:** Do you have *some / any* problems with crime?
B: There's *a little / a few* graffiti, but not really.

7 **Think about your perfect place to live and complete the sentences. Compare your ideas.**

1 My perfect place to live has got *a lot of / a few …*
2 There are *some / a lot of …*
3 There aren't *any / a lot of …*
4 It hasn't got *much / many …*
5 There's only *a little …*

VOCABULARY Compounds: noun + noun

1 **Make a word from A and B for each photo 1–8 below.**

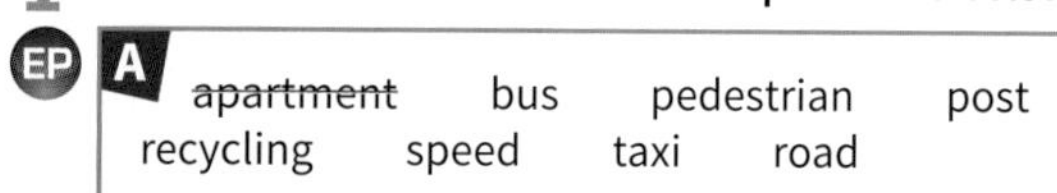

A ~~apartment~~ bus pedestrian post recycling speed taxi road

B bin box ~~building~~ crossing limit rank sign stop

1 *apartment building*

2 **Compete the sentences with the correct compound from Exercise 1.**

1 There's a lot of people at the ________. Maybe we should catch a bus instead.
2 What's the ________ on motorways?
3 Can you take this letter to the ________ for me?
4 I live on the fourth floor of that ________.
5 It's compulsory for cars to stop at a ________.
6 Is this your ________? Is it OK to put plastic in it?
7 Let's meet at the ________. There are lots that go into the centre from there.
8 The ________ says turn right.

3 » **Work with a partner. Turn to page 121.**

GRAMMAR *some/any, much/many, a lot of, a few / a little*

WARMER

On the board, write *some, any, much, many, a lot (of); a few, a little*. Use people, personal objects and objects in the classroom to practise the words, for example pictures, desks, chairs, students, teachers, water, money, coins, etc. Ask questions such as 'Is/Are there any…? How many/much…?' Write at least one example next to each quantifier.

1 Students read the examples, taken from the Reading on page 37, and say if they are positive, negative or questions. Complete the rules as a class.

Answers

a some b any

2 Students use the rules in Exercise 1 to complete the sentences with *some* or *any* and compare answers with a partner. Check answers.

Answers

1 any 2 some 3 some 4 any 5 any 6 some

3 Refer students to the examples on the board from the Warmer. In pairs, students read the sentences and complete the rules. Invite different students to read out each rule and match it to a sentence

Answers

a much, a lot of c a few, a little

» GRAMMAR REFERENCE AND PRACTICE ANSWER KEY TB PAGE 244

4 Refer students to the examples on the board again and ask them which items are countable. Remind them that most plurals end in *-s* but some are irregular, for example *people* is the plural form of *person*. It is countable and takes a plural verb. Ask them if they can remember any other irregular plurals, for example *child–children, man–men, woman–women*. Draw attention to the underlined words in Exercise 3. Tell students to decide in pairs whether the words are countable or uncountable. Check answers with the class.

Answers

countable: cities, people, toys
uncountable: traffic, petrol, light

5 Read the instructions and tell students to refer back to Exercises 3 and 4 to help them complete the table with the rules for uncountable nouns. Check answers. Point out that *a lot of* is used with both countable and uncountable nouns.

Answers

1 much 2 a lot of 3 a little

FAST FINISHERS

Fast finishers look back at the vocabulary in Exercise 1, page 36, and say whether the nouns are countable or uncountable.

Countable: crowd, green space, power cut, rush hour, traffic jam

Uncountable: graffiti, pollution, public transport, rubbish

6 Put students into mixed ability pairs. Read out each item and count down ten seconds for them to decide on the correct option. After ten seconds, invite students to call out the answers. Award one point for each correct answer to find the winning pair. Invite pairs to read out the conversations.

Answers

1 a few, much
2 a lot of, a little, some
3 a few, much, many
4 any, a little

7 Ask students to think about the perfect place to live and ask some of them for ideas. They can be as imaginative and creative as they want! Read the sentence beginnings. Students complete the sentences individually. Monitor and help as necessary. Put students into mixed ability pairs to compare their perfect places. Invite different students to tell the class about their partner's perfect place.

Answers

Students' own answers

» GRAMMAR WORKSHEET UNIT 6

VOCABULARY Compounds: noun + noun

1 Tell students to describe the photos. They may not know the compound nouns at this point, but should be able to describe the pictures. Check pronunciation of *building* /ˈbɪldɪŋ/. Put students into pairs to complete the exercise. Tell them that the word in A always comes before the word in B. Check answers and ask students to explain meanings, for example *speed limit* (*the fastest speed that a vehicle is allowed to travel on a particular road*).

Answers

1 apartment building 2 bus stop 3 pedestrian crossing
4 post box 5 recycling bin 6 speed limit 7 taxi rank
8 road sign

2 Tell students to read the whole sentence before they decide on the correct compound from Exercise 1. They complete the exercise and compare answers with a partner. Check answers as a class.

Answers

1 taxi rank 2 speed limit 3 post box 4 apartment building
5 pedestrian crossing 6 recycling bin 7 bus stop 8 road sign

3 Students turn to page 121. Ask individual students to read out each question and check understanding. In pairs, students ask and answer the questions. Monitor and help as necessary. As a class, invite students to share their partner's answers.

Answers

Students' own answers

» VOCABULARY WORKSHEET UNIT 6

LISTENING

1 Write *Living in the country* on the board as a heading. Under the heading, write *advantages* and *disadvantages*. In pairs, students brainstorm ideas for each column. Invite students to share their ideas and say whether they would prefer to live in the country or the city. Write key points on the board.

Answers
Students' own answers

29 2 Read the instructions. Students are going to hear part of an interview with Bess and her teacher, Mr Evans. Ask students what they think they will discuss. Play the recording for students to find out whether Bess and her teacher agree or disagree with each other. Listen to feedback as a class, eliciting any phrases that helped them decide, for example *Maybe you're right* and *I completely agree*. Ask students if their predictions were correct.

Answers
In general they agree.

29 3 In pairs, students read the sentences and choose the correct option. Play the recording again for them to listen and check. Check answers. Play the recording once more and ask students to make notes on what Bess and Mr Evans like about where they live (*Mr Evans: his village is green, he knows all his neighbours, and there are lots of things to do. Jess: she has more fun in the city and thinks there are more things to do, like going to the cinema*). Ask students to tell their partner who they agree with, and why. Share some ideas as a class.

Answers
1 country
2 lived
3 sometimes
4 public transport
5 worse
6 recycling

» AUDIOSCRIPT TB PAGE 265

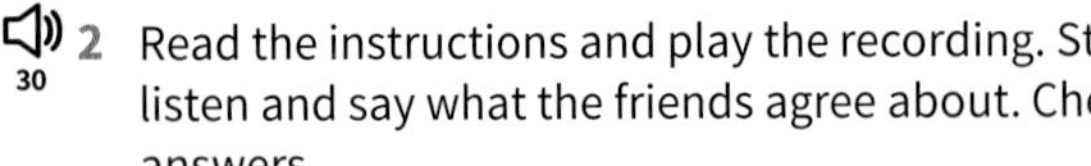

SPEAKING Agreeing and disagreeing

1 Students describe the two photos. Write key words on the board.

Answers
Students' own answers

30 2 Read the instructions and play the recording. Students listen and say what the friends agree about. Check answers.

Answers
In the city, there are too many cars and there's a lot of rubbish.

30 3 Write *agreeing* and *disagreeing* on the board. Ask students to make a list of any phrases they know for agreeing and disagreeing, for example *I think*. Take feedback from the class and write the phrases under the headings. Students look at the *Prepare to speak* box and compare the phrases to the ideas on the board. Ask them what Alice and Oliver agreed and disagreed about (*agreed: meet people, crowds, rush hour, pollution, traffic, rubbish; disagreed: where it's better to live, that the countryside is boring*). Play the recording again. Students make a note of who says the phrases. Check answers.

Answers

Giving your opinion
Personally, I think ... O
I (don't) think ... A
It seems to me ... O
If you ask me, ... A
Asking for an opinion
What do you think? O
Do you agree? O
Agreeing
That's true. A
Yes, maybe you're right. O
I completely agree with ... O
Disagreeing
I'm not sure I agree. A

» AUDIOSCRIPT TB PAGES 265–266

4 Read the instructions and give students a few minutes to make notes. In pairs, they discuss their ideas using the phrases from the *Prepare to speak* box. Monitor and help as necessary.

Answers
Students' own answers

5 Read the five options. Put students into new pairs and ask them to agree on two topics from the list. Explain that they should work individually to make a list of their opinions. Monitor and help as necessary.

MIXED ABILITY

Ask weaker students to write the four sentence beginnings for giving an opinion from the *Prepare to speak* box and complete them with their own ideas. Tell them to practise saying the sentences so they feel more confident when they have the discussion in Exercise 6.

6 Students share their opinions with their partner. They should prepare and practise a conversation about their topics. Remind them to use the questions and phrases from the *Prepare to speak* box. Monitor and join in, giving positive feedback for interesting ideas. Invite pairs to hold their conversation in front of the class. After each conversation, encourage the rest of the class to say which points they agree or disagree with and why.

Answers
Students' own answers

COOLER

Ask students how many of the compound nouns from Vocabulary, page 38, they remember. Write the first letter and dashes showing the number of letters of some new nouns which are all connected with city and country life. In small groups, they have to guess the words. If they cannot guess, add some more letters to help them or play 'Hangman'. Suggested compounds: health centre, post office, police station, post office, public library, shopping mall, swimming pool.

LISTENING

1 What are the advantages and disadvantages of living in the country?

29 2 Listen to an interview with Bess and Mr Evans. In general, do they agree or disagree?

29 3 Read the sentences carefully and check any new words. Then listen again and choose the correct words.

1 Mr Evans lives in the *country* / *city.*
2 Bess *lives* / *lived* in the same place as Mr Evans.
3 Mr Evans thinks Bess is *sometimes* / *never* late for school.
4 Mr Evans thinks villages need better *roads* / *public transport.*
5 Bess thinks the problem with rubbish is *worse* / *better* where she lives now.
6 Bess thinks we should do more *cleaning* / *recycling* in this country.

SPEAKING Agreeing and disagreeing

1 Look at the two photos below. What can you see?

30 2 Listen to Alice and Oliver talking about the places. What do they agree on?

30 3 Read the *Prepare to speak* box. Then listen again.

Which phrases do Alice and Oliver use? Write *A* or *O* next to each phrase.

PREPARE TO SPEAK

Agreeing and disagreeing

Giving your opinion
Personally, I think …
I (don't) think …
It seems to me …
If you ask me, …

Asking for an opinion
What do you think?
Do you agree?
Do you think …?

Agreeing
That's true.
Yes, maybe you're right.
I completely agree with …

Disagreeing
I'm not sure I agree.
I don't think so.
I don't agree.

4 Discuss which place in the photos below you would prefer to live in. Use phrases from the *Prepare to speak* box to agree and disagree.

5 Prepare your ideas on two of the topics below.

1 going to the cinema / watching films at home
2 going to a concert / listening to music on headphones
3 cycling / using public transport
4 living in an apartment building / living in a house
5 holidays at the beach / holidays in cities

6 Discuss the topics in Exercise 5. Use phrases from the *Prepare to speak* box to agree and disagree.

CULTURE

NEW YORK CITY

1 **Ask and answer the questions with a partner.**

1 Have you ever been to a big city like New York?
2 What do you think people can see and do there?

2 **Do the New York City quiz.**

3 **Read the text. Find the answers to the quiz.**

1 About … people live in New York.
A 2.5 million B 8.5 million C 40 million

2 New York City is also called the Big …
A Apple B Easy C Borough

3 New York's Central Park is in …
A Brooklyn B Coney C Manhattan

4 Around … different languages are spoken in New York.
A 8 B 80 C 800

5 New York's taxis are typically … in colour.
A black B white C yellow

NEW YORK, NEW YORK

31

New York is one of the most exciting cities in the world. It's the capital of New York State and the largest city in the USA, with a population of about 8.5 million. The city's nickname is the Big Apple and people also call it 'the city that never sleeps' because it's busy day and night.

History

Over the past two centuries, many millions of people have moved to the United States. In the 19th century the immigrants were mainly Europeans. By 1850, about 25% of New Yorkers were Irish.

The population of New York grew from 2.5 million in 1890 to 7 million in 1930. Since the 1960s, the immigrants have been mostly from Latin America and Asia. This incredible mix of people has made New York City one of the most multicultural cities in the world. Today, about 30% of all New Yorkers were born in another country and it's estimated that you can hear over 800 languages in the city. Some immigrants have created their own neighbourhoods, like Little Italy, Chinatown, and Spanish Harlem, each of which offers a different experience of New York culture.

New York life

There are five main areas in the city, called boroughs: Manhattan, the Bronx, Queens, Brooklyn and Staten Island. Manhattan is the most famous of these, with its tall skyscrapers, like the Empire State Building. The tallest is One World Trade Center, which is 541 metres tall.

New Yorkers call Times Square 'the crossroads of the world'. It's where New Yorkers come together to celebrate special events, to go to the movies and the theatre, and to enjoy street food from every corner of the world. People that are more interested in shopping, fashion or music hang out in trendy SoHo in the south of Manhattan.

Manhattan has plenty of green spaces, including the famous Central Park. About 40 million people, New Yorkers as well as tourists, visit the park every year to enjoy walking, cycling, skating and picnics.

From Manhattan, it's a short walk over Brooklyn Bridge to get to the borough of Brooklyn. Here, people visit the varied street markets or chat with friends in the borough's fashionable coffee shops. At weekends, thousands of New Yorkers go to an area of Brooklyn called Coney Island. Here, they escape the stress of city life by relaxing on the three-kilometre long beach or by having fun at the famous Luna Park theme park.

When it's time to go home, New Yorkers can either take the 24-hour subway or catch one of the city's famous yellow taxi cabs.

40 CULTURE

CULTURE

Learning Objectives

- The students learn about the history, people and famous sights of New York City.
- In the project stage, they write a report about a visit to a famous city and present it to the class.

Vocabulary

neighbourhoods nickname population skyscrapers subway varied

Resources

CULTURE VIDEO AND CULTURE VIDEO WORKSHEET: New York City

BACKGROUND INFORMATION

New York City was founded in 1624 by the Dutch, but the English seized it in 1664 and changed the city's name from New Amsterdam to New York. It is often considered to be the cultural, financial and media capital of the world. The Metropolitan Opera House and Broadway, which is made up of over 40 theatres, are both located in Manhattan. The New York Stock Exchange, the world's largest stock exchange, is on Wall Street in Lower Manhattan. Two of America's most influential newspapers and four major television channels are based in the city. It is also the home to the headquarters of the United Nations.

New York has many famous sports teams including the New York Yankees and New York Mets baseball teams, and the Brooklyn Nets and New York Knicks basketball teams.

The city attracts millions of tourists each year. Apart from the major tourist destinations mentioned in this unit, there are famous events such as Macy's Thanksgiving Day Parade and the St. Patrick's Day parade.

WARMER

In pairs or small groups, students write a list of cities in the USA. Set a time limit and then ask each group to name a city. The group with the highest number of cities is the winner. Ask the groups if they know any facts about each place, for example 'San Francisco' – *the Golden Gate Bridge*, 'Atlanta' – *1996 Olympics*, 'New York' – *the Statue of Liberty*, 'Los Angeles' – *the home of Hollywood*, etc.

1 Read the questions and find out which cities students have visited. In their groups, they share ideas about what people can see and do in New York City. Monitor and help with vocabulary as necessary. Invite students to share their ideas with the class and write key words on the board but do not give any feedback at this stage. Ask them to describe the photos of New York on page 40.

Answers

Students' own answers

2 Students read the questions. Set a time limit of two minutes for them to do the quiz and compare ideas with a partner. Do not confirm correct answers at this stage.

Answers

Students' own answers

3 Students read the text and check their answers to the quiz. Ask them to find the answers in the text and read them out.

Answers

1 B 2 A 3 C 4 C 5 C

4 Read the instructions and the questions. Students identify the key words in each question. They read the text again to find the answers. They compare answers with a partner before checking them with the class. Ask students what they have learned about New York and what they found most interesting or surprising.

Answers

1 It was about 25% of the population.
2 Manhattan, The Bronx, Queens, Brooklyn and Staten Island
3 541 metres
4 SoHo, in the south of Manhattan
5 Take a short walk over Brooklyn Bridge.
6 To escape the stress of city life by relaxing on the beach or having fun at Luna Park theme park

31 The Reading text is recorded for students to listen, read and check their answers.

MIXED ABILITY

To help weaker students locate the information in the texts, ask them to predict which section of the text will give them the answer to each question: *History* or *New York life*.

FAST FINISHERS

Challenge fast finishers to write two more questions for the rest of the class to answer.

5 Students find the highlighted words in the text. In order to match them to their meanings they should look at the context, focusing on the sentences immediately before or after the highlighted words. Check the answers with the class and check any other new words or phrases in the text. Ask students if they or anyone in their family has a nickname.

Answers

1 skyscrapers 2 nickname 3 varied 4 population 5 subway 6 neighbourhoods

6 Students describe the photos and, if they can, identify them (*the Empire State building, the Yankee baseball stadium, the Statue of Liberty, the amusement park on Coney Island, Times Square*). In pairs, they say which places they would like to visit and why. Students give their own answers.

32 7 Tell students that they are going to listen to a conversation between Fiona and her friend Dan and tick all the places Fiona and Dan mention. Ask different students to read out each of the places on the list. Tell students the answers are not in the same order as the list. Play the recording. Students compare answers with a partner. Check answers with the class. Ask students if anywhere that is not on the list was mentioned (*Fifth Avenue, Brooklyn, the Museum of Chinese in America, Liberty Island, Hard Rock Café*).

Answers

Places mentioned: 1, 3, 4, 6, 8, 9, 10 (not in that order)

32 8 Students read the sentences. Ask them to identify the key words, particularly time expressions, and check understanding. Put students into pairs. Play the recording and give them time to compare their answers. If necessary, play it a second time. Check the answers with the class and ask students to correct the false sentences. Ask them what *JFK* and *MoMA* stand for (John Fitzgerald Kennedy, Museum of Modern Art).

Answers

1 false (They went on Saturday morning.)
2 true
3 false (She visited Times Square on Saturday evening.)
4 true
5 true
6 false (She had lunch in Chinatown.)

» **AUDIOSCRIPT TB PAGE 266**

9 Write *in*, *on* and *at* on the board. Call out some time expressions and ask students to choose the correct preposition. Put students in pairs to read the phrases in the *Useful language* box. Tell them to change the words in brackets and use their own ideas instead, for example what they did in their home town last weekend. Monitor and help as necessary. Students give their own answers.

PROJECT ***A report about a famous city***

Read the instructions and the questions. Check understanding. Tell students that they are going to make a report about their visit to a famous city. First, they think of a city they have visited either in their own country or abroad. Then they should write answers to the questions. Tell them to add their own ideas, too. In pairs, they share their ideas with a partner and make suggestions about each other's ideas. Monitor and help as necessary. Ask the class to think about how they will introduce their presentation, for example *I'm going to talk about London, which I visited last summer. I'm going to talk about the history of London, the places I visited and the things I did.*

Students write their reports, including phrases from the *Useful language* box. Remind them to use some interesting adjectives, too, and to say what they liked best about the city. Put students in pairs and tell them to exchange reports and read their partner's report. Encourage them to give feedback on each other's work. Ask for volunteers to read their reports to the class. Ask students which city they would most like to visit and why.

PROJECT EXTENSION

Tell students they are going to write a tourist brochure for their hometown or, if they live in the country, the nearest town or city. Tell them to use the text about New York as a guide and to write about the geography and history of the town as well as interesting sights and places to visit. If they have internet access, they could do some research online. They could also include pictures in their brochure. Display the finished brochures in the classroom.

CULTURE VIDEO: New York City

05 When students have completed the lesson, they can watch the video and complete the worksheet.

COOLER

Ask students to write three questions about New York, taken from the text on page 40. Elicit some question words and write them on the board. With books closed, students ask and answer their questions in small groups.

4 Answer the questions with information from the article.

1 How big was the Irish community in New York in the 1850s?
2 What are the names of the five main areas of the city?
3 How tall is the tallest building in the city?
4 Which area of New York is good for shopping, according to the article?
5 How can you get from Manhattan to Brooklyn?
6 Why do people visit Coney Island?

5 Match the highlighted words in the text to the meanings.

1 very tall buildings, usually in a city
2 an informal name for something or someone, used instead of a real name
3 consisting of many different types
4 the number of people living in a particular area
5 a system of trains that mainly travel underground
6 areas of a town or city that people live in

6 What are these sights? Which ones would you like to see?

7 Listen to Fiona talk about her trip to New York. Tick (✓) the places that you hear.

32

1 ☐ the Statue of Liberty
2 ☐ JFK Airport
3 ☐ Chinatown
4 ☐ Times Square
5 ☐ Bronx Zoo
6 ☐ Empire State Building
7 ☐ Central Park
8 ☐ Coney Island
9 ☐ MoMA
10 ☐ Yankee Stadium

8 Listen again. Are the sentences true or false?

32

1 Fiona went to Coney Island on Sunday morning.
2 They didn't have enough time to see a baseball game.
3 Fiona went to Times Square before lunch on Saturday.
4 Fiona's parents didn't want to visit the art museum.
5 They didn't visit the Statue of Liberty this time.
6 Fiona had dinner in Chinatown on Sunday.

9 Look at the phrases in the *Useful language* box. Change the words in brackets with your own ideas.

USEFUL LANGUAGE

Describing a visit to a city

1 First, we went to (the park).
2 Next, we visited (Times Square)
3 After lunch, we decided to (visit a museum).
4 I loved the (second-hand clothing) shops there.
5 I learned a lot about (the history of New York).
6 We had (good) weather, too.

PROJECT

A report about a famous city

Write about an interesting visit to a famous city. Think about your answers to the questions.

- What city did you visit? When did you go?
- Did you go there with your family or friends?
- What was the weather like during your visit?
- What famous places and sights did you see?
- Did you go shopping for anything special?
- What did you learn about the city's history?
- What was your favourite part of the visit?

Present your work to the class, using the phrases from the *Useful language* box.

05 NOW WATCH THE CULTURE VIDEO

7 GETTING ON

ABOUT YOU

When you have a problem, who do you ask for help? Friends or family? Why?
Do you consider any members of your family to be a friend as well?

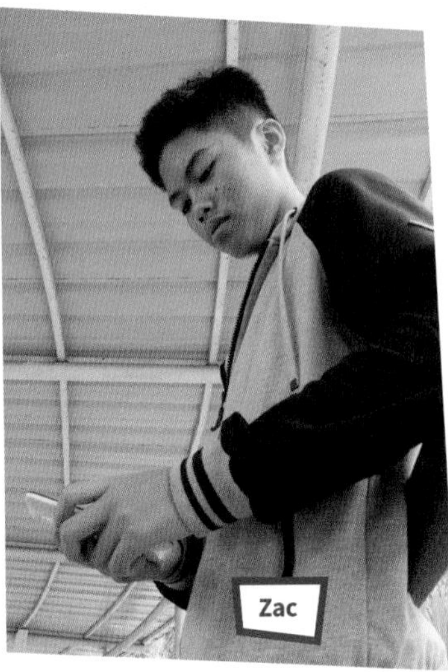

VOCABULARY *be, do, have* and *make*

33 **1 Look at the photos and listen to two conversations. Complete the sentences with the correct name.**

1 ________ has a problem with family.
2 ________ has a problem with non-family members.

33 **2 Choose the correct option to complete the sentences. Then listen again and check.**

EP

1 He *does / makes* me angry.
2 You're always *making / having* problems with him.
3 We *had / made* an argument this morning.
4 *I'm / I've* annoyed with him!
5 *Are you / Have you* on your own?
6 Why don't we *make / do* something later?
7 You need to *make / have* fun.
8 Can you *make / do* me a favour?
9 What *is / has* wrong?
10 It's hard to *do / make* friends.
11 It *doesn't / isn't* my fault.
12 You *have / are* lots in common.

3 Complete the table with the phrases in Exercise 2. Can you add any more?

be	*be annoyed*
do	
have	
make	

4 Complete the sentences with the correct positive or negative form of *be*, *do*, *make* or *have*.

1 Oh, no! Something ________ wrong with the TV. It isn't working!
2 Can you ________ me a favour, please?
3 Some people find it easy to ________ new friends.
4 I'm really sorry that the glass broke, but it ________ my fault!
5 You should talk to someone if you ________ problems.
6 Let's ________ something together on Saturday.
7 Our coach ________ really annoyed with the referee at our last match.
8 What were they saying? Were they ________ an argument?
9 Thanks for your party last night. We ________ a lot of fun.
10 I get on OK with Noel, but we ________ much in common.
11 My cousin is always rude. She ________ me really angry.
12 Is Piper feeling OK? She ________ on her own again.

5 Discuss the questions.

1 Who or what makes you angry?
2 When and why do you have arguments?
3 When do you like being on your own?
4 How do you have fun? Who with?
5 What do you have in common with your best friends?

7 GETTING ON

Unit Overview

TOPIC	Relationships
VOCABULARY	*be*, *do*, *have* and *make*
READING	Troublespot: don't get angry – get advice
GRAMMAR	*have to* and *must*; *should*
VOCABULARY	Phrasal verbs: relationships
WRITING	An informal email (2)
EXAM TASKS	Writing Part 1

Resources

GRAMMAR REFERENCE AND PRACTICE: SB page 144; TB page 245
WORKBOOK: pages 28–31
PHOTOCOPIABLE WORKSHEETS: Grammar worksheet Unit 7; Vocabulary worksheet Unit 7
TEST GENERATOR: Unit test 7; Term test 1

WARMER

Refer to the unit title and check understanding. Give some example sentences, for example *I get on really well with my best friend. I don't get on well with my little sister*. Write *Relationships* on the board and check understanding (*the way two people or groups feel and behave towards each other*). Discuss different kinds of relationships that people have, for example with friends, family and teachers. Ask students who they get on well with.

ABOUT YOU

Ask students what type of everyday problems they have with friends, family and teachers, for example being untidy, coming home late, doing homework, arguing with friends or family members, sharing possessions, etc. Students read the first set of questions and discuss them in pairs. Hold a brief class discussion about whether students prefer to talk to friends or family and why. Ask them if they talk to different people about different problems. In pairs, students discuss the question about whether family members can also be friends. Invite feedback and write key words on the board.

VOCABULARY *be, do, have* and *make*

 33

1 Students describe the four photos and read the two sentences. Explain that the first conversation is between Megan and Zac and the second one is between Rachel and Thomas. Play the recording for students to complete the sentences and ask them to compare answers with a partner. Check answers with the class.

Answers

1 Megan 2 Thomas

 33

2 Students read the sentences from the conversations in Exercise 1 and identify which four verbs are used (*be*, *do*, *have* and *make*). Ask them to decide on the correct option in each sentence and compare ideas with a partner. Play the recording again for them to check their answers.

Answers

1 makes 2 having 3 had 4 I'm 5 Are you 6 do 7 have 8 do 9 is 10 make 11 isn't 12 have

» AUDIOSCRIPT TB PAGE 266

3 Students look at the example in the table and complete the table with phrases from the sentences in Exercise 2. Write the verbs on the board as headings and invite different students to come and write the phrases in the correct column. Ask for more examples for each verb and add their suggestions to the list, for example *be hungry*, *do homework*, *have a good time*, *make the bed*. Note that we can also say *be angry*.

Answers

be: be annoyed, be on your own, be wrong, be someone's fault
do: do something, do someone a favour
have: have problems, have an argument, have fun, have something in common
make: make someone angry, make friends

4 Students read the sentences. Check understanding of any new vocabulary. They complete the sentences in pairs, using the examples in Exercise 2 to help them. Remind them to use the correct tense of the verbs (present simple, present continuous or past simple) and think about whether they are positive or negative. Check answers with the class.

Answers

1 is 2 do 3 make 4 wasn't 5 are having 6 do 7 was 8 having 9 had 10 don't have 11 makes 12 is

5 Read the questions and check understanding. Ask students for examples of what makes them angry. Put students into small groups to discuss the questions and encourage them to answer in full sentences using the expressions in Exercise 2, and to provide reasons for their answers. Monitor and join in with the discussions. Invite feedback from the class.

Answers

Students' own answers

READING

BACKGROUND INFORMATION

In a recent survey parents were asked to rate the biggest problems for adolescent children. Nearly 60% said excessive screen time was a major problem. They also identified stress and anxiety related to modern lifestyles and the unreal expectations parents may have about their children, particularly concerning performance at school. Other concerns included a lack of physical activity, internet safety, an unhealthy diet and bullying.

1 Books closed. Ask students to tell their partner what kinds of things annoy them or cause them problems. Ask them where people can get advice if they don't want to speak to someone they know, for example an internet forum. Books open. Tell students to look at the title of the internet forum and ask what they think it is about. Ask them for a synonym for *trouble* /ˈtrʌbl/ (*problems, difficulties or worries*). Set a short time limit for students to read the three problems and answer the question. Ask them which family members Dylan and Alex are having problems with (*little brother, parents*).

Answer

Kaitlin

2 Ask students to read the text again carefully and to fill in the missing names in the sentences. Remind them not to worry about any words they don't know at this point. Students complete the exercise individually and then compare answers with a partner. Check answers. Ask students to justify their answers with evidence from the text. Ask them to tell you, for example, what Alex's mistake was and whose decision he doesn't agree with, etc.

Answers

1 Alex 2 Kaitlin 3 Dylan 4 Kaitlin 5 Alex 6 Dylan

3 Tell students to read the advice in the *What you think …* box and match two pieces of advice to each problem. Invite different pairs to say what they think. Ask which verb is often used to give advice (*should*).

Answers

Kaitlin: A and F
Dylan: B and E
Alex: C and D

34 The Reading text is recorded for students to listen, read and check their answers.

4 In pairs, students read the three problems again and decide what advice they would give to each person and why. Ask for their opinion of the advice given in the box. Review their ideas as a class.

Answers

Students' own answers

MIXED ABILITY

Tell weaker students to give advice to just Alex about how to deal with his parents and his friends. Stronger students can give advice to all three teenagers.

5 Point to each of the highlighted words in the text and ask students to say what parts of speech they are (*behave*, *trust*, *apologise* and *lock* are verbs; *fair* is an adjective; *password* is a noun). Ask students to look at the meanings and work in pairs to match each word to its definition. Check answers by reading the definitions and encouraging students to call out the correct words. Check understanding of any other new words in the text. These may include *credit* (*money on your phone*), *hang out* (*spend a lot of time in a particular place or with a particular group of people*), *fall out with* (*argue with, stop being friends with*) and *sensible* (*behaving in a responsible way*).

Answers

1 password
2 lock
3 apologise
4 fair
5 behave (*behave themselves* in the text)
6 trust

FAST FINISHERS

Ask fast finishers to choose four words from Exercise 5 and write sentences using them. They replace the word with a space. Their partner reads the sentences and guesses the words. In whole-class feedback, they can test the other students.

TALKING POINTS

Read the first question and put students into groups to discuss them. Ask if they use any forums, which ones they use and if they get good advice. Tell them to think about the points in favour of and against internet forums. For example, *for*: there is a lot of advice from different people who have had similar experiences; *against*: the people who offer advice are not experts and may not know the best way to deal with the situation. Tell each group to nominate a spokesperson to share the group's opinion with the class. Take a class vote on whether internet forums are a good place to get advice or not. Discuss the second question as a whole class.

COOLER

On the board draw a small circle, a key, a small box and a dot. Tell students to draw some pictures very quickly, using one of the symbols as a basis for each drawing. Underneath each picture they should write one or two adjectives. The interpretations are how they see different aspects of themselves. The first picture represents themselves, the second is their friends, the third is their family and the fourth is their future. Students share their pictures with a partner and the class.

READING

TROUBLESPOT

don't get angry – get advice

1 **Read problems 1–3 quickly. Who isn't annoyed with a family member?**

34

LOGIN HOME ASK US VIDEOS LINKS

1 KAITLIN, 15, DERBY

I'm quite a shy person and I haven't got a lot of friends. I was walking home from school yesterday, when I saw some boys from my class. They were laughing at me. One of them said, 'She's always on her own!' and he pointed at me. It was unbelievable! Why do I have to be with someone all the time? What's wrong with being on your own?

2 DYLAN, 14, PENZANCE

My little brother is really annoying. Yesterday, I found him in my room. He knows he mustn't go in there. And he was reading my diary! It made me really angry. Then we had an argument because he took my phone. He sent about 50 texts and now I haven't got any credit. Help!

3 ALEX, 15, LONDON

My best mates, Sasha and Mandy, are just like me. They're often late and they forget things, but they behave themselves (most of the time!). I was hanging out with them last Saturday and I had to get home by 10 pm, but we were having fun and I didn't realise the time. I was a bit late because they didn't have to get home until 11 pm.

Now my parents say I can't spend time with my mates because they can't trust me, and I have to get home by 9.30 pm. It isn't fair! I don't want to fall out with my parents, but they think I'm still a child. What should I do?

What you think ...

A I agree. Sometimes you don't have anything in common with other people, and that's fine.

B He should apologise. Maybe you should lock your door.

C You shouldn't get angry. It's important to talk to your parents. Then you'll understand why they're worried.

D You must show them you can change, so try to be really sensible for a month – or forever!

E Maybe you should put a password on your phone.

F Friendship is important, but you don't have to be with someone all the time. It's good to be independent.

2 **Read the problems again and complete the sentences with the correct names, *Kaitlin*, *Dylan* or *Alex*.**

1 .... has a problem as a result of a mistake.
2 .... had a problem after class one day.
3 .... had an unwelcome visitor.
4 .... likes being alone sometimes.
5 .... doesn't agree with someone else's decision.
6 .... can't use something essential.

3 **Read the problems again and then read advice A–F in the 'What you think ...' section. Match two pieces of advice to each person.**

4 **What advice would *you* give to each person?**

5 **Match the highlighted words to the meanings.**

1 a secret word that protects you online
2 shut something with a key
3 say sorry to someone
4 treating people in a way that is right
5 be polite and not do things that are unhelpful
6 believe someone is good, reliable and honest

TALKING POINTS

Are internet forums good places to get advice? Why? / Why not?

In what ways can you help or support your friends when they have problems?

GRAMMAR *have to* and *must*

1 Read the examples. Then complete the rules.

1 You **must** show them you can change.
2 He knows he **mustn't** go in there.
3 I **have to** get home by 9.30 pm.
4 You **don't have to** be with someone all the time.
5 Last Saturday, I **had to** get home by 10 pm.
6 My mates **didn't have to** get home until 11 pm.

a We use *have to* and ________ to talk about rules and things that are necessary.
b We use ________ when something isn't allowed by a rule.
c We use *don't have to* when something isn't necessary. We use ________ when something wasn't necessary in the past.
d We use ________ for rules in the past.
e Remember: *You **mustn't** go.* = You aren't allowed to go. *You **don't have to** go.* = It isn't necessary for you to go.

2 Make two sentences for each idea. Compare your answers.

0 things you have to do at school
I have to wear a uniform. I have to study for my exams.
1 things you don't have to do at school
2 things you mustn't do at school
3 things you must do at home
4 things you mustn't do at home
5 things you had to do when you were younger
6 things you didn't have to do when you were younger

should

3 Read the examples. Then complete the rules.

1 What **should** I do?
2 He **should** apologise.
3 You **shouldn't** get angry.

We use:
a ________ to say something is a good idea.
b ________ to say something isn't a good idea.
c ________ in questions to ask for advice.

» GRAMMAR REFERENCE AND PRACTICE PAGE 144

4 Take turns to read out the problems and give advice. Use *You should* or *You shouldn't*.

1 I can never find my phone.
2 I find it hard to make friends.
3 I have a lot of arguments with my cousins.
4 My parents think everything is my fault.
5 My sister/brother uses my things without asking.

5 Correct the mistake in each sentence.

1 We wanted to chat, but we must go to school.
2 I'm sorry we had ask you.
3 In my opinion, all schools has to have a uniform.
4 Studying is great, but you don't have to sit down all day.
5 I don't must go to bed early at weekends.

VOCABULARY Phrasal verbs: relationships

1 Read the examples. Then match the phrasal verbs in 1–8 to the meanings a–h.

EP

1 We **hang out** in the park after school.
2 Do you **get on** well with your sister?
3 I **get together** with my mates on Saturdays.
4 I don't want to **fall out** with my parents.
5 Let's play on my computer. **Come round** at 4.30.
6 Friends should always **look after** each other.
7 Did your cousins **make up** after they had that argument?
8 The band were together for a year, but then they **split up**.

a have a good relationship and not argue
b spend a lot of time somewhere
c end a relationship
d visit someone in their home
e make sure someone is well or happy
f become friends again after a disagreement
g spend time with, or go to meet, a friend
h have an argument with someone

2 Complete the sentences with the phrasal verbs from Exercise 1.

1 I don't ________ very well with my brother. We had a big argument last week. I don't know if we'll ever ________.
2 Some of my friends ________ at the youth centre, but I don't go there.
3 Tom and Harriet weren't together for long. They ________ after six weeks.
4 I know you're nervous, but you mustn't worry. I'll ________ you.
5 I always ________ with my friends after school, but they never ________ to my place.
6 It isn't a serious problem, and I'm sure we won't ________ about it.

3 Discuss the questions.

1 When do you and your mates get together? Where do you usually hang out?
2 What kind of people do you get on with?
3 How should friends look after each other?

4 » Work with a partner. Student A, turn to page 121. Student B, turn to page 126.

GRAMMAR *have to* and *must*

WARMER

Tell students about the rules of your job, for example 'I don't have to wear a uniform but I must wear smart clothes. I have to speak English at work. I mustn't be late'. Include one example each of *have to*, *must*, *don't have to* and *mustn't*. Write the sentences on the board. Ask different students to come and underline the verbs.

1 Tell students to read the examples, adapted from the Reading on page 43. In pairs, they complete the rules. Invite different students to read out the completed rules. Ask them to match the sentences on the board to the rules. Point out that *must* does not have a past form.

Answers

a must
b mustn't
c didn't have to
d had to

2 Read the example sentences and ask for more examples, such as *I have to do homework*. Read the sentence beginnings and ask students to match them to the rules in Exercise 1 (*1 c, 2 b, 3 a, 4 b, 5 d, 6 c*). In pairs they write two sentences for each idea. Invite different students to read out their sentences. Ask the class to decide whether they have chosen the correct verbs.

Possible answers

1 At school, I don't have to stay for lunch.
2 I mustn't run in the corridors.
3 At home, I must help my parents.
4 I mustn't be rude to my brother.
5 When I was younger I had to keep my toys tidy.
6 I didn't have to make my bed.

FAST FINISHERS

Tell fast finishers to write an extra sentence for each idea.

should

3 Ask students what word was used in the box on page 43 to give advice (*should*). Students read the three examples. Complete the rules as a class. Ask for an example of giving advice using *shouldn't*, such as *You shouldn't eat too much sugar*.

Answers

a should b shouldn't c should

» **GRAMMAR REFERENCE AND PRACTICE ANSWER KEY TB PAGE 245**

4 Read out the first sentence and invite students to offer advice, using *should* and *shouldn't*. Students complete the exercise in pairs. Invite different pairs to read out the sentences and the advice they gave.

Possible answers

1 You should always keep it in the same place.
2 You should join a club and be friendly.
3 You shouldn't get angry. You should try to stay calm.
4 You should try to explain your point of view.
5 You should explain why you're annoyed.

5 Students read the sentences, paying careful attention to the meaning. They correct the mistakes and compare answers with a partner. Check answers with the class.

Answers

1 We wanted to chat, but we **had to** go to school.
2 I'm sorry we had **to** ask you.
3 In my opinion, all schools **have to** / **should** have a school uniform.
4 Studying is great, but you **shouldn't** sit down all day.
5 I don't **have to** go to bed early at weekends.

» **GRAMMAR WORKSHEET UNIT 7**

VOCABULARY Phrasal verbs: relationships

1 In pairs, students read the sentences and try to work out the meanings of the verbs in blue. Remind them that they saw *hang out* and *fall out* in the Reading on page 43. Do not feed back at this stage, but ask what they notice about the words (*they have two parts*). In their pairs, students read the definitions and match them to the phrasal verbs. Check answers and check irregular past tenses: *come–came*, *fall–fell*, *get–got*, *hang–hung*, *make–made*, *split–split*.

Answers

1 b 2 a 3 g 4 h 5 d 6 e 7 f 8 c

2 In pairs, students complete the sentences using the phrasal verbs from Exercise 1. They can only use each verb once. Invite different students to read out the sentences.

Answers

1 get on, make up 2 hang out 3 split up 4 look after
5 get together, come round 6 fall out

3 Check understanding. Each student writes down their answers to the questions. In pairs students ask each other *Yes/No* questions to find out the answers, for example *Do you get on with your sister? Do you hang out at the park?* Ask students to tell the class about their partner.

Answers

Students' own answers

4 Divide the class in half, A and B. Put A students in pairs and tell them to turn to page 121. Group B students work in pairs, too, and turn to page 126. Each pair is going to read five sentences which are not in order and which contain parts of the phrasal verbs from Exercise 1. Tell them to read their sentences and decide which word or words could go immediately before or after each sentence. Then put each A pair with a B pair to put the story in the correct order. The A pairs start the story with sentence b, which begins *Once upon a time*. Each pair can only see their own sentences. Volunteers read out their sentences and ask if the class agrees. Together, the groups decide on an ending for the story.

Answers

1 b, g, c, h, d, i, a, j, e, f
2 Students' own answers

» **VOCABULARY WORKSHEET UNIT 7**

WRITING An informal email (2)

1 Ask students how they communicate with friends or family in other countries, for example send postcards, letters or emails, phone or use Skype or Facetime, chat online, etc. Tell them that they are going to write an informal email to a friend. They read Ana's email and answer the questions. Check answers. Check understanding of *look forward to* and remind students that it is followed by a noun or a verb in the *-ing* form.

Answers
Ana lives in Spain.
Nicole lives in England.

2 Ask students to look at the notes Nicole wrote next to Ana's email and ask what kind of information they think Nicole will give in her reply, for example what the weather's like in England, what Ana needs to bring. Students complete the exercise and compare their ideas with a partner. Check answers with the class.

Answers
1 Me too! – I'm really looking forward to your visit too!
2 Explain – February is the coldest month here in the UK!
3 Suggest – Remember to pack a hat, gloves and your warmest coat. You should also bring some money for shopping and going out.
4 Tell Ana – You don't have to do homework, but during the trip it's a good idea to make a note of things to tell your classmates in Spain.

3 Read the points in the *Prepare to write* box and ask students to find the phrases in Nicole's email. They compare answers with a partner before checking as a class. Ask how Nicole starts and ends her email (*Hi Ana, Bye for now!*).

Answers
Remember to …
You should …
it's a good idea to …

4 Set a short time limit for students to complete the sentences and compare answers with a partner. Check answers.

Answers
1 a good idea
2 remember to
3 to hear from you
4 wait to see you again
5 should

5 Tell students that Sam is coming to visit them. Ask them to read Sam's email and find the questions. Divide the class into small groups and assign each one a question from the email: *What's the weather like at this time of year in your country? What should I bring with me? What (gift) would your family like?* Ask them to brainstorm ideas. Then form new groups of three, including a student who discussed each question. They tell the rest of their group what they discussed. Invite feedback from each group and write ideas on the board. Put students into pairs to plan the advice that they will give to Sam for each topic.

Answers
He asks four questions, including *How are you?*

6 **B1 Preliminary for Schools Writing Part 1**

In this part, students are awarded marks for content, communicative achievement, organisation and language. Students have to write an email of about 100 words in response to input which is similar to that provided in Exercise 1. The email provides the topic and there are notes to help students construct their response. (See Unit 3.)

Tell students to write their own reply to Sam. Remind them to answer all of Sam's questions and to use the tips from the *Prepare to write* box, including each of the three phrases for giving advice. They should write about 100 words.

Monitor and help as necessary. Then ask students to work in pairs to check each other's spelling and grammar. Invite different students to read out their replies.

MIXED ABILITY

Weaker students should concentrate on using the phrases in the *Prepare to write* box but give them a lower word count of 60–70 words.

Model answer
Hi Sam,
I'm fine, thanks. How are you? It's great that you're coming to visit Italy. It's warm here in July, so you should bring summer clothes. Remember to bring your swimming things, because our school's got a swimming pool. It's a good idea to bring a jacket, too, because sometimes it rains and it's cool in the evenings.
You should also bring some money. We can go shopping and go to the cinema.
Thanks for offering to bring a gift for my family! How about some English sweets or biscuits? We love things like that!
I can't wait to see you again.
Francesca

COOLER

Practise the phrasal verbs from page 44 (*hang out, get on, get together, fall out, come round, look after, make up, split up*). Say one of the verbs for students to call out the preposition to complete the phrasal verb. Then read out the definitions from Exercise 1 on page 44 in a random order for students to call out the correct phrasal verb.

WRITING An informal email (2)

1 Read the email. Where do Ana and Nicole live?

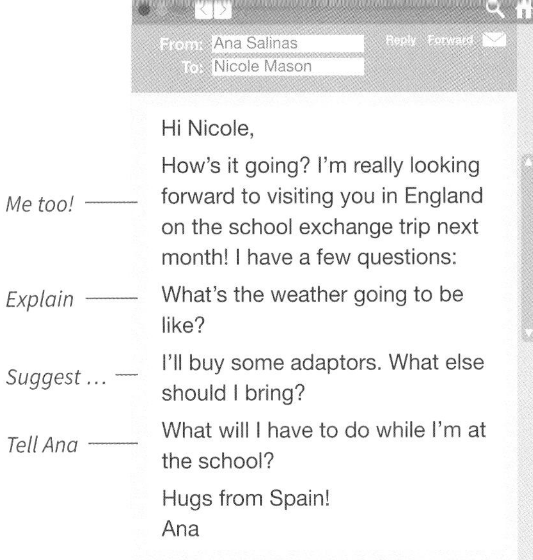
From: Ana Salinas
To: Nicole Mason
Reply Forward

Hi Nicole,

How's it going? I'm really looking forward to visiting you in England on the school exchange trip next month! I have a few questions: — *Me too!*

What's the weather going to be like? — *Explain*

I'll buy some adaptors. What else should I bring? — *Suggest …*

What will I have to do while I'm at the school? — *Tell Ana*

Hugs from Spain!
Ana

2 Read Nicole's reply to Ana. Underline the parts of Nicole's email that match the four notes in Exercise 1.

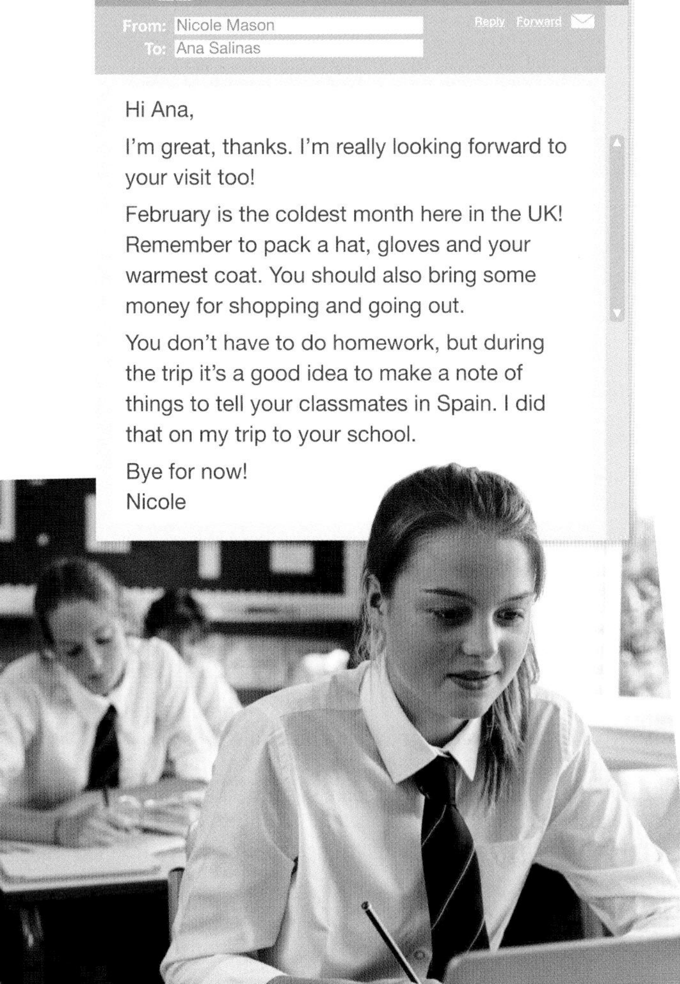
From: Nicole Mason
To: Ana Salinas
Reply Forward

Hi Ana,

I'm great, thanks. I'm really looking forward to your visit too!

February is the coldest month here in the UK! Remember to pack a hat, gloves and your warmest coat. You should also bring some money for shopping and going out.

You don't have to do homework, but during the trip it's a good idea to make a note of things to tell your classmates in Spain. I did that on my trip to your school.

Bye for now!
Nicole

3 Read the *Prepare to write* box and find the phrases that are in Nicole's email.

PREPARE TO WRITE

An informal email (2)

In replies to emails:

- start with a greeting: *How's it going?, How are you?, It's great to hear from you.*
- answer all of the questions you were asked
- to give advice, use: *You should / shouldn't …, Remember to …, It's a good idea to …*
- end with a closing phrase: *I'm really looking forward to your visit / to meeting you / to seeing you, I can't wait to meet you / see you again.*

4 Complete the sentences using phrases from the *Prepare to write* box.

1 It's very cold here in winter so it's ________ to visit in summer.
2 I know you love cycling, so ________ bring a helmet and gloves.
3 Thank you for your email. It's great ________ again.
4 We got together two years ago but I didn't see you last year, so I can't ________.
5 The weather changes all the time, so you ________ pack an umbrella and sunglasses!

5 Read the email from Sam. How many questions does he ask?

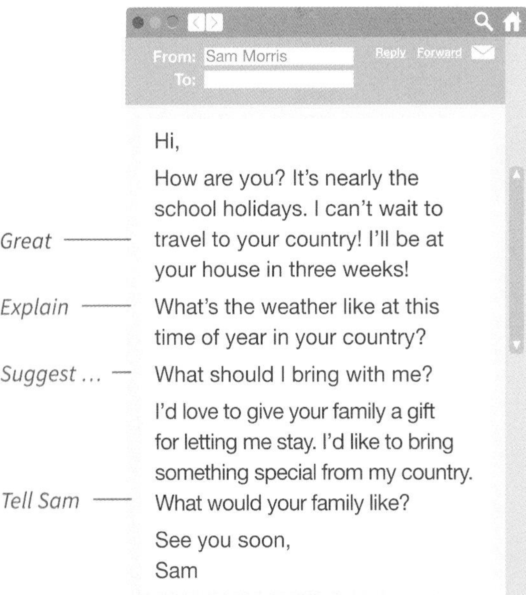
From: Sam Morris
To:
Reply Forward

Hi,

How are you? It's nearly the school holidays. I can't wait to travel to your country! I'll be at your house in three weeks! — *Great*

What's the weather like at this time of year in your country? — *Explain*

What should I bring with me? — *Suggest …*

I'd love to give your family a gift for letting me stay. I'd like to bring something special from my country. What would your family like? — *Tell Sam*

See you soon,
Sam

6 Write your email to Sam.

- Use the notes beside Sam's email.
- Use the tips in the *Prepare to write* box.
- Write about 100 words.
- Check your spelling and grammar.

8 GOING AWAY

ABOUT YOU

Has your family ever travelled abroad?
Where did you go?
Where in the world would you most like to visit? Why?

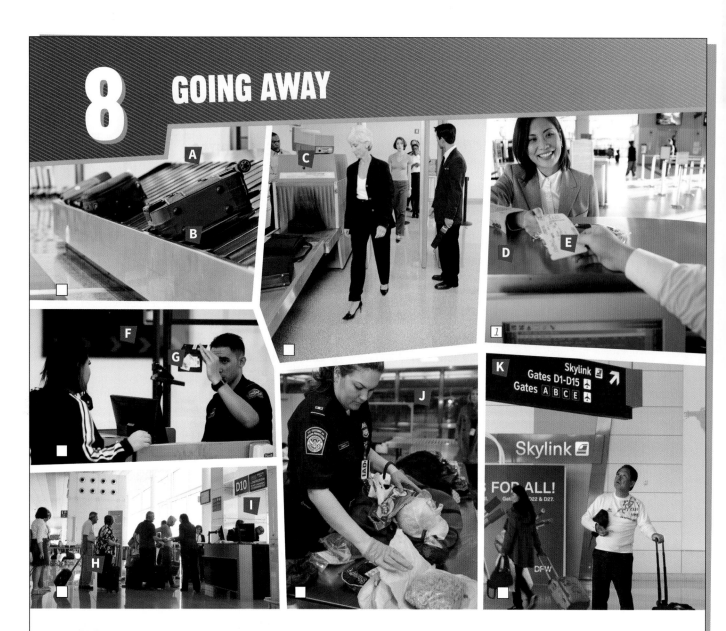

VOCABULARY International travel

1 **Match the words in the box with A–K in the photos.** EP

baggage	baggage hall	
boarding pass	check-in desk	
customs	departure gate	
passport	passport control	
queue	security check	sign

2 **Work in pairs. Number the photos in order and then use them to describe what you do at an international airport.**

1 You arrive at the airport and you go to the check-in desk. You show …

35 **3** **Listen and check your answers to Exercise 2.**

4 **Complete the sentences with words from Exercise 1.**

1 You have to show your ________ and your ticket at the check-in desk.
2 There's often a ________ for the security check.
3 You need to follow the ________ to your departure gate, where your ________ and your ________ are checked.
4 As you walk through customs, officers might ask to check inside your ________.

5 **Discuss the questions.**

1 What's the difference between a boarding pass and a ticket?
2 What's the difference between a security check and a customs check?
3 What are the best and worst things about air travel?

8 GOING AWAY

Unit Overview

TOPIC	Travel
VOCABULARY	International travel
READING	We're off to Tokyo
GRAMMAR	Future: *be going to* and present continuous
VOCABULARY	Phrasal verbs: travel
LISTENING	A talk about a travel writing competition
SPEAKING	Making suggestions
EXAM TASKS	Listening Part 3

Resources

GRAMMAR REFERENCE AND PRACTICE: SB page 145; TB page 245
WORKBOOK: pages 32–35
PHOTOCOPIABLE WORKSHEETS: Grammar worksheet Unit 8; Vocabulary worksheet Unit 8
TEST GENERATOR: Unit test 8

WARMER

Write *Going away* on the board and brainstorm reasons why people travel, for example to visit friends and family, go on business and go on holiday. Ask students to say which is their favourite holiday destination and why. Write key words on the board.

ABOUT YOU

Discuss the first question as a class to find out which families have travelled abroad and where they went. Put students into small groups to discuss the second question before discussing it as a class. Find out which country is the most popular, and nominate individuals to explain why. Ask students whether they enjoy travelling, either abroad or in their own country, and why / why not.

VOCABULARY International travel

1 In pairs, students look at the words in the box and discuss the meanings. After a few minutes, check understanding and drill pronunciation, paying attention to *baggage* /ˈbæɡɪdʒ/, *boarding* /ˈbɔːdɪŋ/, *customs* /ˈkʌstəmz/, *departure* /dɪˈpɑːtʃə/, *queue* /kjuː/, *security* /sɪˈkjʊərəti/ and *sign* /saɪn/. Tell students to look at the photos and find the airport words. Invite different students to use the words to describe each photo. In pairs, students match the words in the box with the photos. Check answers with the class.

Answers

A baggage hall B baggage C security check D check-in desk
E boarding pass F passport control G passport H queue
I departure gate J customs K sign

2 Read out the example sentence and ask students to say what the next step is. They continue in pairs, using the photos to help them. Remind them to use the words in Exercise 1. Monitor and help as necessary. Invite different students to say what happens next and nominate others to continue but do not give any feedback at this stage.

3 Explain to students that they are going to listen to instructions about what to do at an international airport. They should listen and find out if their answers to Exercise 2 are in the correct order. Play the recording and let students check their answers. Check answers with the class.

Answers

The order is:
1 top right – You go to the check-in desk and get your boarding pass.
2 top centre – You go through the security check.
3 bottom left – You go to the departure gate.
4 middle left – You arrive and go through passport control.
5 top left – You go to the baggage hall and collect your baggage.
6 bottom middle – You go through customs.
7 bottom right – You walk out into Arrivals.

» AUDIOSCRIPT TB PAGES 267–268

4 Put students into pairs to complete the exercise. Ask individual students to read out their sentences and ask the class if the answers are correct.

Answers

1 passport
2 queue
3 signs, boarding pass / passport, passport / boarding pass
4 baggage

5 Put students into pairs and read out the questions. Suggest that students write definitions for the words in question 1. In question 2, they should think about the purpose of the checks and when they take place. For question 3, they should think about the best and worst things for people travelling by plane and also for the environment.

Answers

1 You buy a ticket in a travel agent's or online. This covers a whole journey of one, two or more flights. The boarding pass is your seating ticket for an individual flight.
2 The security check is to stop people taking anything dangerous onto a plane before a flight. The customs check happens after a flight. Customs officers check that you have paid tax on things that you are bringing into the country. They are also looking for anything that's illegal.
3 Students' own answers

READING

BACKGROUND INFORMATION

Roppongi is a wealthy district in the centre of Tokyo. The nightlife is popular with both locals and foreigners. Internet cafés in Japan provide more than just internet service. They're also stocked with manga comics and magazines. However, internet café customers in Tokyo aren't only there for the online access or the comics, but because a night in an internet cafe is cheaper than getting a room at a regular hotel or taking a taxi home after the trains stop running. Harajuku is known internationally as a centre of Japanese youth culture and fashion. Shopping and dining options include many small, youth-oriented, independent boutiques and cafés, but the neighbourhood also has many larger international chain stores and luxury shops.

1 Ask students what they know about Tokyo and find out if anyone has been there. Read the question. Students read Olivia's blog entry and compare their answer with a partner. Check the answers. Check understanding of *sightseeing* (*visiting places that are interesting because they are historical, famous, etc.*). Ask them if Olivia wants to look around the shops. Ask students if they have any other suggestions of things to do in Tokyo.

Answers

sightseeing, visit a cat café, try gaming

2 Ask students to look at the headings, photos and labels in the online guide, and find out how much they know about Japanese food, *manga* comics and *anime*. Tell them they will find out more when they read the guide. Read out the question and set a short time limit for students to find the answers.

Answers

paragraphs 2 and 4

3 Explain to students that they are going to read the guide in more detail this time. Tell them to look at each question and predict the paragraph where they will find the answer. Explain that it is not essential to understand every word but they should try to work out the meaning of new words from the context. Monitor and help as necessary and tell students to compare answers with a partner. Check answers as a class and ask students to explain how they chose the correct option in each question. Check any new vocabulary (for example, hedgehog).

Answers

1 C 2 A 3 D 4 B 5 C

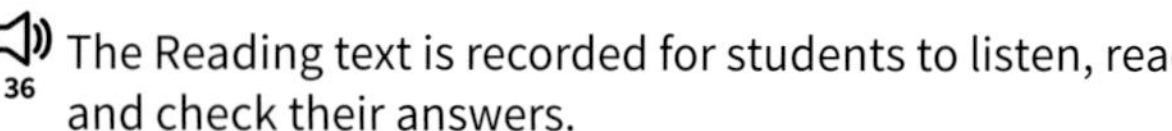
36 The Reading text is recorded for students to listen, read and check their answers.

MIXED ABILITY

Advise weaker students to read each paragraph and check all four options carefully to work out which ones are incorrect and why. Then they should check that the remaining option is the correct one.

FAST FINISHERS

Ask fast finishers to write definitions for *trendy*, *character* (both in paragraph 3), *block* and *kitten* (both in paragraph 4). They read out the definition and paragraph number and the rest of the class find the correct word.

TALKING POINTS

Put students into small groups to discuss the questions about Tokyo. Monitor and help as necessary before inviting feedback as a class. Write key words on the board. Discuss the question about sightseeing in your country as a class. Make a list of interesting places on the board and have a class vote on the best places to visit.

COOLER

Ask students to call out a list of things they need to take with them for a beach holiday. Accept all reasonable suggestions. Write the items on the board. Then divide the class into small groups of three to make a list of things of the ten most important items. They can add anything that is not on the list. Ask the groups to share their lists and see if they agree.

READING

36

1 Read Olivia's blog entry. What does she plan or intend to do in Tokyo?

2 Read the online guide to Tokyo. Which paragraphs mention things that are in the blog?

WE'RE OFF TO TOKYO
Posted 3.16 pm

I can't wait! We're leaving on Saturday – a taxi is picking us up at 8 am and we're going straight to the airport. We're going to have a great time! On the first day, we're going sightseeing in and around the Roppongi district. We're going to visit a cat café and have a go at gaming. Apart from that, I'm not sure. Mum says we're going to look around the shops but I'm not so sure about that. I've found this great guide to the city, but has anyone got other suggestions?

Olivia Burton

CITY MAP

- PLACES TO VISIT
- THINGS TO DO
- WHERE TO STAY

1 *FAST FOOD HEAVEN* › **THE STREETS ARE FULL OF RESTAURANTS** selling noodles and sushi. Noodles look like spaghetti and they're served with fried meat, seafood or vegetables. Sushi is rice served with uncooked fish or vegetables. The flavours are incredible. You can even take a class to learn how to prepare your own sushi.

2 *TECH CULTURE* › **IF YOU WANT TO DISCOVER** the Japanese love of technology, spend some time in a gaming café. Try the Internet Comic Café Manboo, where you can admire thousands of *manga* comics for sale as well as play all the latest computer games. They rent rooms with sofas where gamers can lie down after long sessions. They even have showers – you'd probably need one after an 8-hour overnight gaming session!

3 *FASHIONISTAS* › **BE SURE TO VISIT** the Harajuku district. It's where all the trendy Japanese teens hang out, so be prepared! You're going to see a lot of people wearing 'cosplay' clothing. Cosplay is short for 'costume play' and it's a Japanese pop tradition. Girls and boys dress in incredible costumes inspired by their favourite anime (manga cartoon) or computer game character.

4 *WEIRD AND WONDERFUL* › **TOKYO IS FULL OF UNUSUAL THINGS** to see and do. It's hard to walk a block in Tokyo without seeing loads of vending machines! Most sell cold drinks but others sell things like dog food, umbrellas and hamburgers! How about going to one of the famous cat cafés, where you can play with a cat or a kitten while you drink your coffee? There are around 60 cat cafés in Tokyo! There's even a hedgehog café in Roppongi.

3 **Read the online guide again and choose the correct answers.**

1 What is sushi?
   - **A** a meat and rice dish
   - **B** fresh fish and vegetables
   - **C** rice with fish or vegetables
   - **D** a type of noodle

2 At Manboo, you can't
   - **A** buy modern sofas.
   - **B** play computer games all night.
   - **C** get manga comics.
   - **D** have a shower.

3 What happens in the Harajuku district?
   - **A** Teens play computer games.
   - **B** People go to cosplay cafés.
   - **C** Japanese pop stars hang out.
   - **D** People wear unusual clothes.

4 A vending machine is something that
   - **A** makes drinks.
   - **B** sells drinks.
   - **C** cooks food.
   - **D** sells sushi.

5 Tokyo's cat cafés
   - **A** serve Japanese tea.
   - **B** have hedgehogs as well.
   - **C** are well-known.
   - **D** are in the Roppongi district.

TALKING POINTS

Would you like to visit Tokyo? What would you like to see and do there?
What sightseeing would you recommend to visitors to your town or country?

GRAMMAR Future: *be going to* and present continuous

1 **Read the examples. Then complete the rules with *be going to* or *present continuous*.**

1 We're going to look around the shops.
2 We're leaving on Saturday.
3 Be prepared! You're going to see a lot of people wearing 'cosplay' clothing.

We use:
a ________ to talk about future plans and arrangements, usually with a specific time reference (for example, *next week, in August*).
b ________ for things we intend to do some time in the future, sometimes with a non-specific time reference (for example, *one day, some time*).
c ________ when we predict things that we know are likely.

» GRAMMAR REFERENCE AND PRACTICE PAGE 145

2 **Complete the conversation with the correct form of *be going to* and the verbs in brackets.**

Olivia: We [1] ________ (fly) to Tokyo on holiday! I'm really looking forward it.
Zayne: I was in Japan a few years ago. Tokyo's amazing. You [2] ________ (have) a great time! What [3] ________ (you / do)?
Olivia: We [4] ________ (visit) a cat café.
Mum: And we [5] ________ (go) shopping!
Olivia: What? I [6] ________ (not walk) around the shops! I [7] ________ (find) a good gaming café.
Zayne: [8] ________ (you / try) sushi with fish?
Mum: No way! I [9] ________ (not eat) uncooked fish!

3 **Choose the correct form of the verbs.**

1 Next month, I *going to* / *'m going to* return your bicycle.
2 We *'re going to* / *going to* visit Argentina
3 They aren't going to *meet* / *met* at the bus stop.
4 I *'m going to working* / *'m going to work* in a sports shop. That's my plan.
5 You're going to *come* / *coming* to the UK one day.
6 They *aren't going* / *not going* to join us.

4 **Make sentences with the present continuous or *be going to.***

0 we / visit / Turkey one day
We're going to visit Turkey one day.
1 I / get / the bus at 6.45 pm
2 I / cycle / to your house next time
3 they / not buy / a new TV
4 we / walk / home after school today
5 The sky is dark and cloudy. I think / it / rain
6 we / not catch / the 5.30 train / tomorrow

5 **Make notes about your plans and arrangements for next weekend. Use the ideas in the box or your own ideas. Discuss your plans and arrangements in pairs.**

go shopping   go to a gig or to the cinema   hang out in town   meet some friends   study   visit my grandparents   watch a football match

A: *What are you doing next weekend?*
B: *I'm going shopping on Saturday. I'm going to buy some new jeans.*

VOCABULARY Phrasal verbs: travel

1 **Read the sentences. Choose the correct meanings of the phrasal verbs.**

1 We're going away at the weekend.
a staying at home **b** visiting another place
2 They set off at 9.30 this morning.
a left a hotel **b** started a journey
3 When are you getting back?
a arriving in another place
b returning
4 What time did the plane take off?
a leave the ground **b** arrive after a flight
5 We're going to check in early.
a arrive at a hotel or for a flight
b reserve a hotel or a flight
6 See you at 4.00. My flight is getting in at 3.45.
a arriving **b** leaving
7 I can't wait to look around Moscow.
a visit a place and look at the things in it
b feel happy that something is going to happen
8 My dad is going to pick up my mum at the station.
a call **b** collect

2 **Complete the questions. Use the correct form of the phrasal verbs in Exercise 1.**

1 What time do you ________ for school every morning?
2 Who normally ________ you and your friends from school?
3 Do you usually ________ or stay at home in the holidays?
4 Do you like ________ old places?
5 What time do you ________ from school in the afternoon?
6 When did you ________ from your most recent holiday? Where did you go to?
7 How do you feel when your flight ________ and lands?
8 Can you explain what you have to do when you ________ to a hotel?

3 **Ask and answer the questions in Exercise 2.**

4 » **Work with a partner. Turn to page 121.**

GRAMMAR Future: *be going to* and present continuous

WARMER

Draw an open double page of a diary on the board and write the days Monday to Sunday. Write some appointments and events in note form, for example *doctor*, *cinema*, *basketball*, *wedding*. Explain that this is your diary for next week and ask students what you're doing on a particular day to elicit the present continuous.

1 Tell students to read the sentences, taken from the Reading on page 47, and elicit the verb forms in each one. In pairs, students complete the rules, referring back to the example sentences for help. Ask which sentence matches each rule (*1–b, 2–a, 3–c*). Ask students if they have definite plans for the weekend to elicit the present continuous. Ask them what they're going to do when they get home today to elicit answers with *be going to*.

Answers

a present continuous
b be going to
c be going to

» **GRAMMAR REFERENCE AND PRACTICE ANSWER KEY TB PAGE 245**

2 Ask students what they remember about Olivia's blog post on page 47. Students read the conversation and fill the spaces using *be going to* and the verbs in brackets. Remind them to include the correct form of *be*, to use contractions where possible and to use *to* before the infinitive. They compare answers with a partner. Check answers with the class.

Answers

1 're going to fly
2 're going to have
3 are you going to do
4 're going to visit
5 're going to go
6 'm not going to walk
7 'm going to find
8 Are you going to try
9 'm not going to eat

3 Read the instructions and tell students to complete the exercise and then compare answers with a partner. Check answers with the class and ask individual students why they rejected the incorrect form.

Answers

1 'm going to
2 're going to
3 meet
4 'm going to work
5 come
6 aren't going

4 Students read the example sentence. Check understanding of *one day*. They underline the time references in the prompts. Refer them to the rules in Exercise 1 as they write the sentences and then compare answers with a partner. Invite different students to read out the sentences.

Answers

1 I'm getting the bus at 6.45 pm.
2 I'm going to cycle to your house next time.
3 They aren't going to buy a new TV.
4 We're walking home after school today.
5 The sky is dark and cloudy. It's going to rain.
6 We aren't catching the 5.30 train tomorrow.

FAST FINISHERS

Ask fast finishers to write two sets of prompts as in the exercise, one for the present continuous and one for *be going to*. They exchange them with another fast finisher to write the sentences using the correct tense.

5 Ask two students to read the example conversation aloud. Tell them to look carefully at Speaker B's response and elicit why the different forms are used. Students look at the activities and make notes which are true for them. They discuss their plans with a partner. Invite pairs to repeat their conversations for the class. Find out who has similar plans.

Answers

Students' own answers

» **GRAMMAR WORKSHEET UNIT 8**

VOCABULARY Phrasal verbs: travel

1 Remind students of the phrasal verbs about relationships from Unit 7. In this exercise they are going to learn some phrasal verbs about travel. In pairs, they read the sentences and choose the correct definitions. Check answers and the past tenses of irregular verbs: *go–went, set–set, get–got, take–took*. Ask students for the opposite of *take off* and *check in* (*land, check out*).

Answers

1 b 2 b 3 b 4 a 5 a 6 a 7 a 8 b

2 Students read the sentences. They complete the exercise, thinking carefully about the correct form of the phrasal verb. Invite different students to read out their sentences and check answers as a class.

Answers

1 set off 2 picks up 3 go away 4 looking around 5 get in
6 get back 7 takes off 8 check in

3 Model the activity by asking a confident student the first question. In small groups, students ask and answer the questions. Invite students to tell the class about members of their group.

Answers

Students' own answers

4 Students turn to page 121 and read the instructions. Tell them to be imaginative and to use as much travel vocabulary as they can. Ask individual students to read out their sentences.

Answers

Students' own answers

» **VOCABULARY WORKSHEET UNIT 8**

LISTENING

1 Tell students to look at the photo and read the questions. Accept any reasonable suggestions and ask them if they would enjoy this activity.

Answers

Students' own answers

2 Tell students they are going to hear some information about a travel competition. First, they are going to complete some notes to help them. Ask students to read the notes and think about what kind of information could go in each space. Invite different students to share their ideas.

MIXED ABILITY

Put weaker students with stronger students who can help them with their note-taking.

Answers

1 a place name
2 a period of time
3 something of interest when you travel
4 a number
5 a month
6 personal information, for example a phone number, a photo, an address

37 3 **B1 Preliminary for Schools Listening Part 3**

In this part, students' ability to listen for specific information is tested. It consists of a monologue and a set of notes with some missing information which may be one or two words, a number, or a date or a time from the recording. Students hear the recording twice.

Tell students they are going to complete a competition entry. They are going to hear a teacher telling his students about the competition. Tell them to listen carefully because they will hear more than one possible answer for each of the spaces. For example, more than one country is mentioned but only one is the destination of the trip. Play the recording. Students complete the notes and compare answers with a partner.

37 4 Play the recording again for students to check their answers. Invite different students to read out the notes. If necessary, play the recording a third time pausing after each answer and asking students to identify the distractors. For example, in the first space, the other countries which are mentioned (*Cambodia*, *Peru* and *South Africa*) have been destinations in the past. Ask the class whether they would like to enter the competition and to say why or why not.

Answers

1 Canada
2 weeks
3 (the) culture
4 1,500
5 February
6 email address

AUDIOSCRIPT TB PAGE 267

SPEAKING Making suggestions

1 Ask students to read the two questions and ask why the tenses are different (*present simple for regular activities, present continuous for definite plans*). In pairs, students discuss the two questions. Invite different students to tell the class about their partner.

Answers

Students' own answers

38 2 Tell students that they are going to listen to a conversation between two friends who are planning what to do at the weekend. Ask them to predict what activities they might talk about. Play the recording for students to listen and check their ideas.

Answers

They decide to visit the National Football Museum.

38 3 Books closed. Brainstorm a list of phrases which could be used to make suggestions and write them on the board. Then ask students to read the phrases in the *Prepare to speak* box and compare them to their own ideas. Play the recording for students to make a note of the phrases they hear. They compare their answers to the phrases in the box and say which one they didn't hear.

Answers

... might be a better idea.

» AUDIOSCRIPT TB PAGE 267

4 Put students in new pairs and set a short time limit for them to choose three activities to talk about. Check understanding of the activities in the box and explain that they can use these ideas or their own ideas. Monitor and help as necessary.

Answers

Students' own answers

5 Monitor as students discuss the ideas, giving positive feedback when they use phrases from the *Prepare to speak* box. Ask different pairs what they have decided to do, and encourage them to give further information using *be going to* or the present continuous, for example *We're visiting a cool museum on Saturday. We're going to eat lunch in a cafe, too.* Ask some of them to repeat their conversation in front of the class.

Answers

Students' own answers

COOLER

Describe an activity from Exercise 4, for example 'I'm feeling quite hot and I'm having a delicious ice cream. Where am I?' (*the beach*). Whoever answers correctly takes a turn to describe where they are using the present continuous for the rest of the class to guess. Try to ensure as many students as possible take a turn at describing where they are.

LISTENING

1 Look at the photo and make predictions.

1 Where do you think this is?
2 What is the person doing?
3 Where is the person going?

2 Read the notes and look at the spaces. What kind of information is needed for each space?

TRAVEL WRITING Competition

First prize: Trip to (1) ________.

Length of trip: two (2) ________.

Competition details

What you must mention: the people, (3) ________ and the local environment.

Maximum number of words to write: (4) ________.

Closing date of competition: 19th (5) ________.

What information to include when you apply: (6) ________.

37 3 Listen and complete the notes.
Compare answers with your partner.

37 4 Listen again to check, and correct any mistakes.

SPEAKING Making suggestions

1 Discuss the questions in pairs.

1 What do you usually do at the weekend?
2 What are you planning to do next weekend?

38 2 Listen to two friends planning their weekend. What do they decide to do?

38 3 Read the *Prepare to speak* box. Then listen again. Which phrase don't you hear?

PREPARE TO SPEAK

Making suggestions

Suggesting ideas
Why don't we ...?
What about ...?
How about ...?
We could ...

Agreeing with ideas
That's a good idea.
That sounds great!

Disagreeing with ideas
I'm not sure.
The problem with that is ...
... might be a better idea.

Making a decision
Yes, let's do that.

4 Work in pairs. Choose three possible activities for the weekend. Use the ideas in the box or your own ideas.

go walking in the mountains
go to the beach
hang out in a country park
go sightseeing
visit a cool museum

5 Discuss the three activities and agree what to do. Use phrases from the *Prepare to speak* box.

LIFE SKILLS INTERPERSONAL SKILLS

DEALING WITH CONFLICT

LIFE SKILLS

Dealing with conflict

We never have exactly the same ideas or opinions as our friends or family members. We often disagree with people and sometimes we get angry or have arguments. When that happens, we need to deal with conflict in a positive way and work together to solve the problem.

1 Ask and answer the questions with a partner.

1 Do you get along well with most people?
2 What things make you feel upset or angry?
3 What do and your friends argue about?

2 Read the text quickly. Match the titles (A–D) to four of the tips.

A Live and learn
B Be clear and kind
C Stay calm
D Think together

Friends *and* arguments

Tips for dealing with conflict

What happens when you and your friends argue? How should you react when they get angry or upset with you? Follow these helpful tips to deal with conflict in your friendships and find a solution that works for everyone.

1 ________. When we're angry, we might say or even scream things that aren't kind. It's always better to keep cool and think carefully before we speak. Count to ten in your head, and if you can't relax, then walk away. Sometimes you have to do that!

2 Listen first. Give the other person a chance to speak without interrupting them. You have to listen carefully and pay attention to your friend's face and body language. Try to imagine how your friend is probably feeling at that moment.

3 ________. You have to be honest about your thoughts and feelings. Explain the problem clearly and say what you need from your friend. You should choose your words carefully and try to be nice to the other person. You don't want to start a new argument!

4 Admit your mistakes. Remember that even the best people make mistakes and nobody is perfect. It's OK to make mistakes, but we have to admit them and then say we're sorry. We should also forgive other people when they apologise for their own mistakes.

5 ________. Two heads are always better than one. You should have a conversation with your friend about how you could solve the problem. And you don't have to keep it a secret. You can get help from another friend or an adult if that's helpful.

6 Cool down. After you've had a serious argument, it's good to relax and cool down. When you feel better, you should go for a walk with your friend or maybe you can do something fun. Why not play a sport or watch your favourite TV show together?

7 ________. Arguments are a normal part of life, and we don't have to worry about every disagreement. But we should try to learn from them. After all, we don't want to repeat the same mistakes again! Think about what happened, and remember that lesson for the future.

LIFE SKILLS

Learning Objectives

- The students learn about ways of dealing with conflicts.
- In the project stage, they write and act out a dialogue about resolving a conflict.

Vocabulary

admit body language disagreement interrupting scream solve

BACKGROUND INFORMATION

It can help to know the origin of a conflict when deciding how best to deal with it. According to experts, conflict arises from three main sources: limited resources such as time, money and property; unlimited basic needs such as belonging, power, freedom and fun; different values such as beliefs, priorities and principles. Equally, there are three basic responses. One response involves either denying the existence of a conflict or simply giving in. The opposite response is to resort to verbal or physical aggression. While these may be natural reactions, they are unlikely to lead to a satisfactory outcome. A potentially more successful approach involves listening, understanding, respecting and resolving, as discussed in the Reading text in this unit. Many of these ideas, known as choice theory, were developed by the American psychiatrist William Glasser (1925–2013).

WARMER

Revise vocabulary, including phrasal verbs, from Unit 7. Suggested words: *annoyed*, *apologise*, *fault*, *trust* (verb); suggested phrasal verbs: *fall out*, *get on*, *make up*, *split up*. Divide the words and phrasal verbs into two groups, A and B, and write them on the board. Divide the class in half and assign them one list each. In pairs, students write four sentences, each one using a word in their list. Bring the class together and ask for volunteers to read out their sentences.

LIFE SKILLS

Dealing with conflict

Students read the text. Check understanding of *deal with (take action in order to achieve something or find the answer to a problem) and solve (find the answer to a problem)*. Ask students if they agree and what might happen if two people or groups don't solve the problems they have with each other.

1 Read the questions, check understanding of *upset* (*the state of being unhappy, annoyed or worried*), and explain that *get along well* means the same as *get on well*. Students discuss them in pairs and then report back to the class. Write key words on the board.

Answers

Students' own answers

2 Students read the title of the text and read the introduction. They look at the four headings before reading the text quickly and matching them to the four tips with missing headings. Tell them not to worry about any new vocabulary at this point. They compare answers with a partner. Check answers with the class and ask students to give reasons for their answers. Ask them to describe what is happening in the photos (*two girls appear to be in the middle of a disagreement; two boys, one is speaking and the other is listening, so maybe they are trying to deal with a conflict*).

Answers

A 7 B 3 C 1 D 5

39 The Reading text is recorded for students to listen, read and check their answers.

TEACHING NOTES FOR STUDENT'S BOOK PAGE 51

3 Students read the sentences and underline the key words. They read the text more carefully to identify the similar ideas. Monitor and help as necessary. Check answers as a class.

Answers

1 Remember that even the best people make mistakes and nobody is perfect. (Tip 4)
2 After you've had a serious argument, it's good to relax and cool down. (Tip 6)
3 When we're angry, we might say or even scream things that aren't kind. (Tip 1)
4 (After all,) we don't want to repeat the same mistakes again! (Tip 7)
5 Try to imagine how your friend is probably feeling at that moment. (Tip 2)
6 You can get help from another friend or an adult if that's helpful. (Tip 5)

MIXED ABILITY

Put students into mixed ability pairs to look at the heading of each tip, 1–7, and predict where they might find similar ideas to the sentences in the exercise.

4 Students read the six options and match them to the highlighted words in the text. They should look at the context, including the sentences immediately before or after the highlighted words. Ask for volunteers to read out the definitions and give the correct answer.

Answers

1 admit 2 interrupting 3 solve 4 disagreement 5 scream 6 body language

FAST FINISHERS

Ask fast finishers to choose three words from the following list and write a definition for each one: *forgive* (*stop feeling angry with someone for something they have done*), *chance* (*opportunity*), *cool down* (*become calm*), *ignore* (give no attention to someone or something), *keep cool* (*stay calm*), *walk away* (*stop taking part in a difficult situation*).

5 In small groups, students discuss the questions. Monitor and help as necessary. As a class, discuss which conflicts are the most frequent, for example arguing about borrowing and lending possessions or about not being reliable. Compare different ways to deal with a particular conflict, such as reacting aggressively as opposed to listening and being sensitive to each other's needs. Students give their opinions about the tips in the text. Ask them which they think are most useful and if they can think of any other ways of dealing with conflict.

Answers

Students' own answers

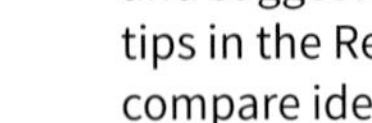

6 Students read the questions, look at the photo of Michael and suggest why he could be upset. Remind them of the tips in the Reading text. Play the recording. Students compare ideas with a partner.

Answers

Michael is upset with Amy because she is late, and she is often late.
Yes, they use some of the suggestions. They both make an effort to calm down. Michael is honest about his feelings. They try to laugh about it and they make suggestions for how to improve the situation in the future, and they go for a walk.

7 Students read the questions and, in pairs, write down any information they can remember. Play the recording again so they can check what they have written and add any extra information. Check answers with the class. Play the recording again, if necessary. Point out how important tone of voice is. Apart from the words Michael and Amy use, we can learn a lot about how they feel from the way they sound. Play the first two lines of the conversation and elicit how Michael is feeling (*annoyed, impatient*) and how Amy sounds (*in a hurry, out of breath*). Continue in the same way. Divide the class into two groups, one group is Michael and the other is Amy. Students repeat the conversation line by line, copying the intonation. Then the groups exchange roles.

Answers

1 half past five
2 her sister
3 thirty minutes ago / five o'clock
4 She listens to music or chats on her phone and forgets about the time.
5 Michael suggests sending Amy a text to remind her, and she offers to set an alarm on her phone and to call Michael if she is going to be late.
6 He wants to go for a walk and go to a comic shop.

» AUDIOSCRIPT TB PAGE 267

8 Put students into pairs to read the words in the box and to complete the sentences in the *Useful language* box. Check the answers with the class and put students into pairs to practise saying the sentences with appropriate intonation.

Answers

1 always 2 tired 3 Why 4 about 5 fault 6 idea

PROJECT ***Resolving a conflict***

Tell students that they are going write a dialogue about resolving a conflict. Ask them to choose a situation and imagine that two of their friends are having an argument about it. They are going to discuss the situation and think about how they can help their friends to deal with the problem in the best way. Then they are going to write a conversation and act it out in pairs. First, they read the questions and discuss their ideas. Tell them it's a good idea to make notes of their ideas. They write their conversation and act it out. Remind them to use the vocabulary from the Reading text and the *Useful language* box. Monitor and help as necessary. Ask different pairs to act out their conversation for the class. While they listen, the class should decide on which suggestions are the most helpful. Depending on the time available, they could repeat this with another situation.

PROJECT EXTENSION

In small groups, students make a poster with their top tips for resolving conflicts. Encourage them to use pictures and graphics to make their posters attractive. Display them in the classroom and have a vote on the best poster.

COOLER

Have a brief discussion about the importance of non-verbal language, such as body language and facial expressions, to show our feelings. Explain that students are going to use body language to express how they are feeling, and give them an example yourself. The class guesses how you are feeling. Ask for volunteers to continue the activity. If they need help, write different feelings on pieces of paper, for example *angry, bored, cheerful, friendly, impatient, miserable, patient, serious, shy, stressed, unfriendly*.

3 Match the sentences to similar ideas in the text.

1 Nice people sometimes do things that aren't right.
2 You should do something to make you feel calm after an argument.
3 We sometimes say bad things to people when we're angry.
4 We don't want to have the same problem twice.
5 Try to put yourself in the other person's place.
6 A third person could help you find an answer.

4 Match the highlighted words in the text to the meanings.

1 say that something is true or real
2 stopping someone who is speaking
3 find the answer to something or stop a problem
4 when people have a different opinion about something
5 shout something very loudly, in a high voice
6 movements and positions of your body and face that show other people how you are feeling, without using words

5 Discuss the questions.

1 When was the last argument you had with a friend? What did you argue about?
2 How did you deal with the conflict? Did you use any tips from the article?

40 **6 Listen to a conversation. Why is Michael upset with Amy? Do they use any of the suggestions in the article to find a solution?**

40 **7 Listen again and answer the questions.**

1 What time did Amy arrive?
2 Who has got Amy's bicycle right now?
3 When did Michael and Amy plan to meet?
4 Why does Amy usually arrive late?
5 What solutions do Michael and Amy discuss?
6 What does Michael want to do right now?

8 Complete the *Useful language* phrases with the words in the box.

about always fault idea tired why

USEFUL LANGUAGE

Dealing with conflict with a friend

You've ________ got an excuse.
I'm getting ________ of this.
________ are you so angry?
I'm sorry ________ that.
It wasn't my ________.
I've got an ________.

PROJECT

Resolving a conflict

Work with a partner. Write a dialogue about two friends who are having an argument. Use the situations and questions below to help you.

- forgetting someone's birthday
- not inviting someone to a party
- borrowing and losing something
- always arriving ten minutes late

1 Who are the people in your dialogue?
2 What are the people arguing about?
3 Which person started the argument?
4 How could they solve the problem?
5 What can they do after the argument?

Act out your dialogue for the class.

DEALING WITH CONFLICT 51

REVIEW 2 UNITS 5–8

VOCABULARY

1 Complete the information with the pairs of words.

burglary / burglars hacking / hacker
pickpocketing / pickpockets
shoplifting / shoplifters vandalism / vandals

The average [1] ________ takes less than ten minutes. About 30% of [2] ________ enter a home through an open door or window of an apartment.

[3] ________ is very common near signs that warn about the problem. The reason is that when people see these signs, they check their important possessions. [4] ________ can then see where these possessions are and follow the people until they get their chance to steal them.

[5] ________ in many areas has decreased since the introduction of mobile phones. Some researchers believe that mobile phones are so entertaining that [6] ________ aren't as likely to go out, get bored and break or damage something.

According to American research, 75% of [7] ________ are adults, and 25% of them are under 18. And [8] ________ is actually more common among shop workers than customers!

The youngest [9] ________ in the world was five-year-old Kristoffer von Hassel. He discovered a way to use his father's video game account without knowing the password. His [10] ________ earned him $50 and four free games from the video games company.

2 Match the beginnings of the sentences 1–4 to two correct endings a–h.

1 I am …
2 I am doing …
3 We have …
4 He makes …

a on my own.
b me really happy.
c something tonight.
d a lot of things in common.
e friends easily.
f fun together.
g you a favour.
h never wrong.

3 Use a word from each box to make a compound noun to match the definitions 1–8.

baggage boarding check-in departure
green power public traffic

cut desk gate hall jam
pass spaces transport

1 the place at an airport where passengers get on a plane
2 a card that a passenger must have to get on a flight
3 buses, trains, etc. that anyone can use
4 a queue of cars, lorries, etc. that are moving slowly or not moving at all
5 the place at an airport where you show your ticket and leave large suitcases
6 a temporary problem when there isn't any electricity
7 areas of grass, trees, etc. usually in a city, where people can walk, play sport and enjoy themselves.
8 the place at an airport where you collect your suitcases after a flight

GRAMMAR

1 Choose the correct word.

1 There isn't ________ crime in my neighbourhood.
A many **B** much **C** some
2 My sister and I are having ________ arguments at the moment.
A a lot of **B** many **C** a little
3 We did ________ sightseeing on holiday, but we mainly relaxed on the beach.
A a few **B** much **C** a little
4 I'm taking out the rubbish. Have you got ________?
A any **B** a lot of **C** many
5 I made ________ new friends at the party.
A any **B** a little **C** a few
6 How ________ boarding passes have you got in your hand?
A a lot of **B** many **C** much
7 There's ________ amazing graffiti under the bridge.
A some **B** any **C** a few
8 There's ________ traffic on the roads this evening.
A a lot of **B** many **C** much
9 There isn't much serious crime where I live, but there's ________ vandalism.
A a little **B** any **C** much

REVIEW 2 UNITS 5–8

Overview

VOCABULARY	Crimes and criminals; *ourselves, yourselves, themselves* and *each other;* City problems; Compounds: noun + noun; *be, do, have* and *make*; Phrasal verbs: relationships, International travel; Phrasal verbs: travel
GRAMMAR	Past simple and continuous; *some/any, much/many, a lot of, a few / a little*; *have to* and *must*; *should*; Future: *be going to* and present continuous
EXAM TASKS	Reading Part 6

Resources

PHOTOCOPIABLE WORKSHEETS: Grammar worksheets Units 5–8; Vocabulary worksheets Units 5–8; Review Game Units 5–8; Literature worksheet; Speaking worksheet; Writing worksheet

WARMER

Anagrams. Choose some vocabulary items from Units 5–8 and write them on the board with the letters mixed up. In pairs, students solve the anagrams. If they find it difficult, underline the first letter of each word. The first pair to solve them all is the winner.

VOCABULARY

1 Read the words in the box and check pronunciation, particularly *burglar* /ˈbɜːglə/ and *vandalism* /ˈvændəlɪzəm/. Make sure students understand that the first word of each pair is the crime and the second word is the person who commits the crime. In pairs, they take turns to describe the crimes in the box. Listen to feedback as a class and then ask them to read and complete the information. The students compare answers with a partner. Review answers with the class and ask whether any of these facts and figures surprised them.

Answers

1 burglary 2 burglars 3 Pickpocketing 4 Pickpockets 5 Vandalism 6 vandals 7 shoplifters 8 shoplifting 9 hacker 10 hacking

2 Write *be annoyed*, *do your homework*, *have problems* and *make someone angry* on the board. Give students a time limit of two minutes to add more words to the list. Read the instructions. Students complete the exercise and compare answers with a partner. Check answers with the class. In pairs, they discuss what things or people make them happy.

Answers

1 a, h
2 c, g
3 d, f
4 b, e

3 Read the instructions together. In pairs, students match the words to make compound nouns. Check answers. Then they read and complete the definitions. Ask which refer to international travel (*1, 2, 5 and 8*) and which to city life (*3, 4, 6 and 7*). Check answers with the class and check understanding and pronunciation of vocabulary, for example *baggage* /ˈbægɪdʒ/, *boarding* /ˈbɔːdɪŋ/ and *queue* /kjuː/. Ask students if they can remember any other vocabulary connected with city life and international travel.

Answers

1 departure gate
2 boarding pass
3 public transport
4 traffic jam
5 check-in desk
6 power cut
7 green spaces
8 baggage hall

FAST FINISHERS

Ask fast finishers to write definitions for two of the following: *rush hour*, *bus stop*, *passport control*, *customs check*. They read out their definitions and the rest of the class guess the words.

GRAMMAR

1 Write *some/any*, *much/many*, *a lot of*, *a few / a little* on the board. Draw a table and ask students to copy and complete it with the correct quantity words.

	countable: cars	uncountable: traffic
positive ✓		
negative –		
question ?		

Students read the sentences and decide which of the nouns after each space are countable and which are uncountable. They complete the exercise and compare answers with a partner. Check answers with the class.

Answers

1 B 2 A 3 C 4 A 5 C 6 B 7 A 8 A 9 A

2 Ask students to describe the photo. Elicit the forms of the past simple and past continuous, including negative and question forms. Give students two minutes to check the use of these tenses in the Grammar reference for Unit 5 on page 142. Ask them to look at the verbs in brackets and give the past forms of the irregular verbs (*hit–hit, fall–fell, find–found, take–took, see–saw, stand–stood*). They complete the exercise and compare answers with a partner. Review answers and elicit the appropriate rules for use from stronger students.

Answers

1 hit 2 stopped 3 was falling 4 was working 5 found
6 was taking 7 was moving 8 saw 9 were standing
10 appeared

3 On the board, write *have / has to, don't have to / doesn't have to, had to, didn't have to, must, mustn't, should, shouldn't*. In pairs, students use the modals to write five sentences about school, for example *Yesterday we didn't have to do any homework. You should always be friendly to new students*. Monitor and help with ideas and vocabulary as necessary. Invite some students to read out their sentences. The rest of the class say if they are grammatically correct. Students read the instructions and complete the exercise. They compare answers with a partner. Check answers with the class and refer them to the Grammar reference for Unit 7 on page 144, if necessary.

Answers

1 don't have to
2 I should split up
3 didn't have to
4 must (only) pick up
5 Should we come round

4 Write *definite plan* and *intention* on the board. Tell students to think about what they plan to do after school today. Ask volunteers to tell you and ask the class if these are definite plans or intentions. Ask which tense we use for each and write them on the board using the correct tense, for example *I'm meeting my friends at 6 o'clock. I'm going to do my homework and watch TV*. Read the instructions and explain that the sentences all refer to the future. Tell them to use contractions where possible. Students complete the exercise and check answers with a partner. Review answers with the class and refer them to the Grammar reference for Unit 8 on page 145, if necessary.

Answers

1 's going to steal
2 're getting
3 'm going away
4 're going to get
5 aren't coming round
6 are going to find out, 's going to be / you're going to be in

5 Students complete the exercise individually and then compare answers with a partner. If they disagree, each student should justify their choice by referring to the grammar rule that should be applied. Check answers with the class and invite stronger students to explain the grammar rules.

Answers

1 going to ask
2 should
3 a little
4 saw

6 Elicit the structures students have studied in Units 5–8: the past simple and continuous; the future with *be going to* or the present continuous; words describing quantity with countable and uncountable nouns; describing obligation using *have to*, *had to*, *must* and *should*. Students complete the exercise in pairs. They should agree about the mistake and how to correct it. Check answers with the class.

Answers

1 Last week we **had to** do three tests.
2 When we **were travelling** to Cambridge, the car broke down.
3 I think **I'm** going to visit your house.
4 When I was younger, I spent **a lot of** money on sweets.

7 **B1 Preliminary for Schools Reading Part 6**

In this part, candidates read a short text with six gaps. They have to think of which word best fits each gap. This requires reading for detailed understanding at word and sentence level, and mostly tests knowledge of grammar. Most of the missing words are prepositions, pronouns, articles, auxiliary verbs, modal verbs, conjunctions, etc. (See also Unit 1.)

Explain to students that they should first read the text ignoring the gaps to find out what it is about. For each gap they have to write the missing word. Look at the first gap with the students. They should look at the words before and after the gap and think of one word which fits the gap. Ask them if they can think of any other words that could fit (*No*). Tell them that this applies to gaps 1, 3, 4 and 5 – only one word will fit. For gaps 2 and 6 there is a choice of two words which have similar meanings, and both are correct. Students complete the exercise and compare answers with a partner before checking answers as a class. With the students, name the parts of speech used. Explain that these parts of speech are very typical of the words used in this kind of exercise.

Answers

1 it (pronoun)
2 When/Once (adverb)
3 herself (reflexive pronoun)
4 lot (noun)
5 few (determiner)
6 like/as (preposition)

MIXED ABILITY

Help weaker students by pairing them with stronger students to complete the exercise.

COOLER

Ask students to think about Units 5–8. Ask, 'Which activities did you enjoy? What are you good at? What was difficult / easy for you? What are you going to do to improve your English?' Ask the students to think of three things they could do and to write down their answers. Invite some students to share their answers and have a class discussion about each question. Share ideas on how they can improve their weaker areas.

2 Complete the story. Use the past simple or past continuous form of the verbs.

On a cold January morning, Flight 1549 [0] *was taking off* (take off) from a New York airport when it [1] ________ (hit) some birds. The engines [2] ________ (stop) almost immediately. Captain Sullenberger quickly realised that the plane [3] ________ (fall) very fast. There was only one place he could land the plane: on the Hudson River in the middle of New York!

Steven Day is a photographer. That morning he [4] ________ (work) on his computer when someone passed his desk. 'What's that?' they asked, pointing to something on the river. Steven [5] ________ (find) his camera. At first, he didn't know what he [6] ________ (take) pictures of. 'It [7] ________ (move) down the river, like a boat,' he said. When he looked closely, he [8] ________ (see) it was a plane. People [9] ________ (stand) on its wings in the middle of the river!

The next day Stephen's photograph [10] ________ (appear) in newspapers and on websites all over the world.

3 Complete the second sentence so that it means the same as the first. Use three or four words including the word in brackets.

1 It isn't necessary to take your passport. (have)
You ________ take your passport.
2 What's your advice about splitting up with Francesca?
Do you think ________ with Francesca? (should)
3 It wasn't necessary for them to print their boarding passes.
They ________ print their boarding passes. (have)
4 Taxi drivers are only allowed to pick up passengers at the rank.
Taxi drivers ________ passengers at the rank. (must)
5 Is it a good idea for us to come round after dinner? (should)
________ after dinner?

4 Complete the sentences with the correct form of *be going to* or the present continuous.

1 That woman near the bags is behaving oddly. I think she ________ (steal) something.
2 We ________ (get) together on Saturday. Are you free?
3 I ________ (go away) on holiday in the last two weeks of August.
4 You drive too fast. One day you ________ (get) a fine.
5 I've changed my plans. My friends ________ (not come round) this evening any more.
6 Mum and Dad ________ (find out) about this and there ________ (be) trouble.

5 Choose the correct words.

1 One day I'm *asking* / *going to ask* you for a favour.
2 In my opinion, young people *have to* / *should* stay at school until they are 18.
3 We've got *a little* / *a few* time before we need to set off.
4 We *saw* / *were seeing* the crowds of people when we were leaving my apartment building.

6 Correct the mistake in each sentence.

1 Last week we must do three tests.
2 When we travelled to Cambridge, the car broke down.
3 I think I going to visit your house.
4 When I was younger, I spent much money on sweets.

7 For each question, write the correct answer. Write one word for each gap.

How I met my best friend

A few years ago we moved to a new city, so I had to change schools. On the first day at my new school, I was really nervous. I find [1] ________ hard to make new friends and hardly said a word to anyone for hours. [2] ________ the morning break started, I went outside and stood on my own. I was feeling really lonely.

Towards the end of break, a girl walked up to me. She introduced [3] ________ as Monica and started chatting right away. She was also quite new at the school and we soon discovered we had a [4] ________ in common. We watched the same TV shows, listened to similar types of music, and we were both learning to play the guitar. Also, we lived just a [5] ________ minutes' walk from each other!

Monica and I have been really good friends since that day. Naturally we sometimes argue [6] ________ everyone does, but we're very close.

UNITS 5–8 53

9 SHOP TILL YOU DROP

ABOUT YOU

Do you get pocket money for helping at home?
How often do you go shopping? What do you like buying?

VOCABULARY Money and shopping

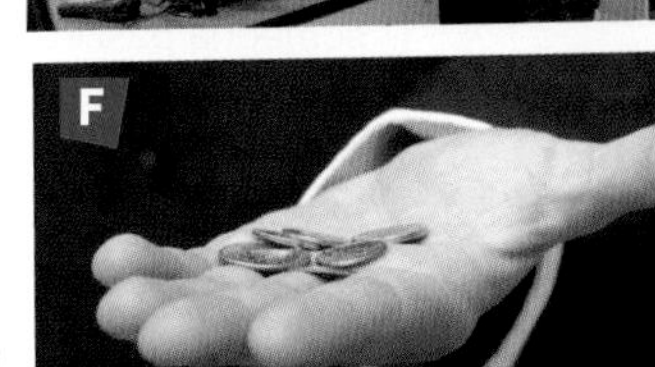

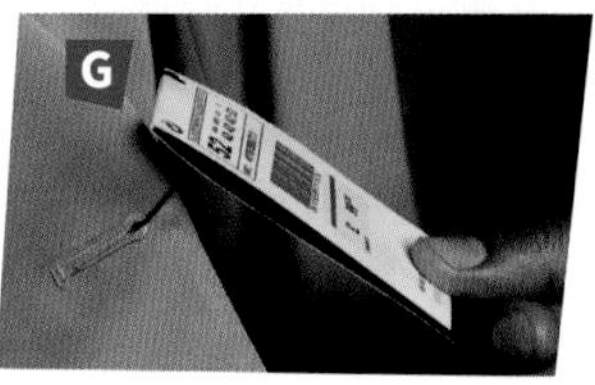

1 EP **Read the quiz questions. Match the words to photos A–H. Two words or phrases match one of the photos.**

MONEY WIZARD OR MONEY WASTER?

1. Do you **save up** for things?
   a Yes, I'm always saving up for something.
   b Sometimes, but not often.
   c No, I never save up for anything.
2. Have you got a **bank account**?
   a Yes. I save my money in mine.
   b Yes, but I never use it.
   c No way. I'm not old enough!
3. Do you always look at the **price** of things before buying them?
   a Of course.
   b I don't always check with small things like a drink.
   c Not really. If I want something, I buy it.
4. Do you look for **special offers**?
   a All the time.
   b Sometimes. But if I really want something, I don't care.
   c Not really. Life is too short!
5. Do you ever decide not to buy something while you're waiting at the **checkout**?
   a Often. I realise I don't need something and put it back.
   b Sometimes.
   c Not really.
6. Do you always check your **change**?
   a Always. Shop assistants often make mistakes.
   b Sometimes.
   c Hardly ever.
7. Do you keep **receipts** in case you need to **take something back**?
   a I keep everything.
   b Only for expensive things.
   c Never.
8. What do you do with old clothes, DVDs and other stuff?
   a I throw them in the bin.
   b I usually **give** everything **away**.
   c I sell them to friends or online.

2 41 **Listen to Gemma and Leo, and read the quiz again. Write *G* next to Gemma's answers for the quiz. Do you think Gemma is a Money Wizard or a Money Waster?**

3 **Complete the sentences with words from the quiz.**

1 The assistant at the ________ gave me too much ________.
2 I want to open a ________ so that I can put money in there and ________ to buy a new phone.
3 Look! Those jumpers are on ________ this week – there's 25% off the normal ________!
4 I tried to ________ the shoes ________ to the shop, but I didn't have the ________, so they wouldn't accept them!
5 Why don't you ________ your old clothes ________ to a charity shop?

4 » **Do the quiz and discuss your answers in pairs. Then read the key on page 122. Do you agree?**

9 SHOP TILL YOU DROP

Unit Overview

TOPIC	Shopping and money
VOCABULARY	Money and shopping
READING	Help! I just can't stop shopping!
GRAMMAR	Present perfect; The past participle of *go*: *been* and *gone*
VOCABULARY	Easily confused words: *pay, charge, cost*
WRITING	A story (2)
EXAM TASKS	Reading Part 3; Writing Part 2

Resources

GRAMMAR REFERENCE AND PRACTICE: SB page 146; TB page 245
WORKBOOK: pages 36–49
PHOTOCOPIABLE WORKSHEETS: Grammar worksheet Unit 9; Vocabulary worksheet Unit 9
TEST GENERATOR: Unit test 9

WARMER

Put students into small groups to discuss these questions:

- Do you like going shopping?
- Who do you go shopping with?
- Where do you go?

Ask each group to nominate a spokesperson to tell the class about their group's shopping habits. Ask them what they think the unit title means (*shop until you are too tired to shop any longer*).

ABOUT YOU

Check understanding of *pocket money*. Do the first question as a class survey. Ask students to stand up and talk to as many of their classmates as possible, asking them the questions and making a note of their name and answers. Put the students into groups to look at their notes and find the most popular jobs that are done at home for pocket money. They stay in the groups to discuss the other questions. Monitor and help as necessary. Ask groups to share their answers with the class. Write key vocabulary on the board.

VOCABULARY Money and shopping

1 Put students into pairs to read the quiz questions and match the photos to the words in blue. Check answers and understanding. Elicit parts of speech (noun or verb).

MIXED ABILITY

Put students into mixed ability pairs for this exercise and ask stronger students to explain the meanings of each phrase to the weaker students.

Answers

1 save up – F
2 bank account – A
3 price – G
4 special offers – B
5 checkout – D
6 change – F
7 receipts, take something back – H
8 give something away – C

41

2 Tell students that they are going to listen to Gemma and Leo doing a quiz called *Money Wizard or Money Waster?* Ask what they think the terms mean (*good with money*; *bad with money*) and to which category students think they belong. Read the instructions and tell students to read the quiz. Check understanding of any difficult vocabulary, for example *not care, put back, receipt*. Check pronunciation of *receipts* /rɪˈsiːts/. Play the recording and tell students to compare answers with a partner. Check answers with the class and elicit that Gemma is good with money, so she's a Money Wizard. If necessary, play the recording again.

Answers

1 a 2 b 3 a 4 a 5 c 6 b 7 b 8 c

» AUDIOSCRIPT TB PAGES 267–268

3 Play a game. Divide students into groups of five. Each student in the group copies one sentence from Exercise 3 onto a piece of paper, including the spaces. They then write the correct answer on the back of the paper (you will need to check that their answers are correct).

Students take turns to hold up their sentence for their group to read and say the missing words. They tell their group whether their answers are correct.

Answers

1 checkout, change
2 bank account, save up
3 special offer, price
4 take, back, receipt
5 give, away

4 Put students into pairs to do the quiz and find out whether they are Money Wizards or Money Wasters. They ask and answer the questions. Encourage them to provide additional information, for example what kind of special offers they look for (clothes, games, etc.). Then they read the key on page 122 and say whether they agree with their result and why.

Answers

Students' own answers

READING

BACKGROUND INFORMATION

The phenomenon of shopping for pleasure came with the emergence of a middle class in 17th- and 18th-century Europe. Shops became important places for people to meet and socialise. In the late 18th century, shopping arcades opened in Britain and Europe. Stores had glass exterior windows so people could window shop. Department stores opened across Britain, the USA and Europe from the mid-19th century including Harrods of London in 1834, Macy's of New York in 1858 and Galeries Lafayette of Paris in 1905.

1 Tell students to read the title and the introduction in italics. Check understanding of *shopaholic* (*someone who is addicted to shopping*). Ask them why Alison was asking for help (*because she shopped too much and wanted to stop*). Students read the three statements and scan the article quickly to find the answer. Check the answer and ask students to indicate where the statements come in the passage.

Answers

Statement 2 is not true.

2 **B1 Preliminary for Schools Reading Part 3**

In this part, students' ability to understand both the detailed and global meaning of a text is tested. Students also need to demonstrate understanding of the writer's purpose, attitude and opinion. This part consists of a text of up to 360 words followed by five four-option multiple-choice questions.

Ask students to read the questions and options carefully and to predict the answers before they read the article again. Check understanding of *persuade* (*make someone agree to do something*), *encourage* (*make someone more likely to do something*), *inform* (*tell someone about something*) and *warn* (*advise someone not to do something*). You could write the words and definitions in a random order on the board for students to match. Students read the article and decide on the correct options. Tell them to ignore the highlighted words at this point. Students compare answers with a partner and explain why they chose them. Check answers.

Answers

1 C – the article isn't trying to encourage, persuade or warn readers. It tells the story of one person, and how she overcame her addiction.
2 D – the article tells us she bought hundreds of things online.
3 B – this paraphrases *Soon after* [shopaholics] *buy something, they think they've made a mistake and start to feel miserable.*
4 D – A is wrong because she still goes shopping, B is wrong because it is not mentioned and C is wrong because she asks 'Do I need it?' and walks away if not.
5 A – The text mentions her mum helped her to realise she had a problem and then that her parents helped her with her problem. She doesn't say anything about borrowing from friends or family. She mentions price tags but only to explain why she bought some trainers. She talks about being able to control herself in shops – not avoiding going to them.

42 The Reading text is recorded for students to listen, read and check their answers.

3 Students read the definitions 1–5 and find the highlighted verbs in the article. They should look carefully at the context of the verbs as this will help them understand the meaning. They complete the exercise and compare answers with a partner. Check answers as a class. Elicit the grammar of these verbs, for example word order with the object: *pay* ***someone / something*** *back, run out (of* ***something)***; whether followed by *-ing* or infinitive: *regret* + ***-ing***; dependent prepositions: *suffer (from)*.

Answers

1 pay back (*pay them back* in the text)
2 afford
3 regret
4 run out of (*ran out of* in the text)
5 suffer from

FAST FINISHERS

Ask fast finishers to write definitions of *jewellery* (paragraph 1), *research* (paragraph 3) and *anxious* (paragraph 4). They read them out and the class tries to find the word.

TALKING POINTS

Put students into groups of four to discuss the questions. Then ask one pair from each group to move to another group and compare their ideas. Encourage them to use the verbs in Exercise 3. Monitor and help as necessary. Hold a short class discussion, inviting students to share their ideas. Write new vocabulary on the board.

COOLER

Divide students into teams of three and write *shopaholic* on the board. They have five minutes to write down things families buy on a shopping trip, starting with each of the letters in the word. Provide examples, such as *sugar, oranges*. After five minutes, ask one student from each group to write their shopping lists on the board. Award points for each answer which is correctly spelled, and a bonus point for each answer that no other team has thought of.

HELP! I just can't stop ... SHOPPING!

42

Have you ever bought something and then changed your mind? For Alison Jenson, 23, this used to happen several times a week. Alison was a shopaholic. She just couldn't stop shopping and she loved special offers.

Alison's bedroom is full of stuff. 'I've been to every shop in Birmingham, I think,' says Alison. She picks up some trainers. The price tag is still on them. 'I paid £20 for these. They cost £40 originally, so they were half price,' she says. 'But I've never worn them.' Alison's problem wasn't just clothes. She bought jewellery, make-up and hundreds of other small things online. She hasn't used any of them!

According to experts, we all feel excited when we buy something new. For shopaholics, it's a little different. Soon after they buy something, they regret buying it and start to feel miserable. So they buy themselves something else to feel happier.

Psychologists first described the problems of shopaholics in 1915. However, there was very little research on the subject until recently. Now, doctors think thousands of people suffer from the problem, both men and women, and the situation is getting worse. There are also more teenage shopaholics now, although most young people don't have enough money to go shopping very regularly.

Alison knew she had a problem. 'I often bought something every day. It was usually something small, but I just needed to buy it,' she says. 'When I ran out of money, I started using credit cards. Unfortunately, I couldn't pay them back and the charges quickly became a problem. When I couldn't go shopping, I felt anxious. Then one day, my mum just looked at all the stuff in my room and said, "Alison, this is crazy!" She was right. I needed some big changes in my life.'

Alison's parents helped with her problem and she now feels she has changed. She no longer thinks she's a shopaholic. 'When I want to buy something in a shop, I ask myself two questions,' she says. 'Do I need it? Can I afford it? The answer to both questions is usually "no", so I walk away. It's great!'

READING

1 Read the article quickly. Which statement is not true?

1 Alison's parents know about her problem.
2 Alison's problem is a very modern one.
3 More people are shopaholics now than fifty years ago.

2 Read the article again. Choose the correct answers.

1 What is the purpose of the article?
  A to persuade people to go shopping less
  B to encourage people to get help if they have a problem
  C to inform people about a problem
  D to warn people about the dangers of shopping
2 What did Alison especially like buying?
  A sneakers and other items of clothing
  B discounted items
  C anything she could take back to a local shop
  D things she could order on the internet
3 What do experts say about shopaholics?
  A They feel more excited than other people when they shop.
  B They soon feel unhappy after they have bought something.
  C Shopping is the only way they can feel happy.
  D They feel unhappy when they are paying for things.
4 What is Alison's attitude to shopping now?
  A She doesn't often want to buy things now.
  B She doesn't enjoy shopping now.
  C She still buys things she doesn't need.
  D She is in control of her shopping now.
5 What advice might Alison give to someone who has a problem with shopping?
  A Ask someone you are close to for help.
  B Never borrow money from friends or family.
  C Always look at the price carefully.
  D Avoid going to shops.

3 Match the highlighted verbs to their meanings.

1 give someone the money that you borrowed from them
2 be able to buy or do something because you have enough money or time
3 feel sorry about a situation, especially something that you wish you had not done
4 finish, use or sell all of something so that there is none left
5 have an illness or other health problem

TALKING POINTS

How do you feel when you buy something new?
What was the last thing you bought that you didn't need?
What advice can you give for saving money?

GRAMMAR Present perfect

1 **Read the examples and complete the rules with the words in the box.**

1 I've **been** to every shop in Birmingham.
2 She **hasn't used** any of them.
3 I've **never worn** them.
4 **Have** you **ever bought** something and then been unhappy with it?
Yes, I **have**. / No, I **haven't**.

ever	-ed	past participle	never

a We use the present perfect to talk about experiences in our life.
b The positive form is: *have / has* + ________.
c The negative form is: *have / has* + *not* or ________ + ________.
d We often use ________ in questions.
e Regular past participles end in ________ and are the same as the past simple form.

2 **Write the infinitive of these regular and irregular past participles. Use the list of irregular verbs on page 158 to help you.**

chosen	heard	lent	made
paid	read	travelled	tried
worn	written		

3 **Complete the sentences with the present perfect form of the verbs.**

1 My sister ________ (win) lots of competitions.
2 My grandparents ________ (never / buy) anything online.
3 I ________ (never / use) a credit card. I'm not old enough!
4 My brother ________ (never / borrow) any money from me.
5 We ________ (visit) Ireland. My aunt lives there.
6 Tim and I ________ (never / have) an argument.
7 You ________ (not / meet) my brother.
8 I ________ (never / steal) anything in my life!

4 » Turn to page 122.

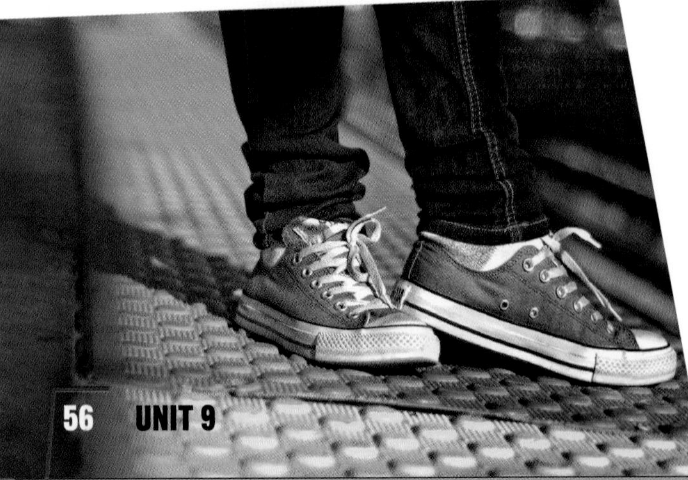

The past participle of *go*: *been* and *gone*

5 **Match the examples to the meanings.**

1 My brother's **gone** to the shops.
2 My brother's **been** to the shops.

a My brother went to the shops earlier but he isn't there now.
b My brother is travelling to the shops or he's at the shops now.

» GRAMMAR REFERENCE AND PRACTICE PAGE 146

6 **Complete the sentences with the correct present perfect form of *go*.**

1 ________ you ever ________ to London?
2 Sally isn't here. She ________ swimming.
3 Rob ________ home. He wasn't feeling well.
4 You're late! Where ________ you ________?
5 I ________ never ________ to Spain but I'd like to go.
6 Where ________ Dad ________? I can't find him anywhere.

VOCABULARY Easily confused words: *pay*, *charge*, *cost*

1 **Read the examples. Complete the definitions with *pay*, *charge* or *cost (of)*.**

1 I **paid** £10 for these.
2 These trainers **cost** £40 originally.
3 They **charge** £1.50 for a small bottle of water!
4 My brother enjoys his job but the **pay** is terrible.
5 The **cost of** repairing my phone was over £100.
6 The **charges** quickly became a problem.

a *Charge* is the amount of money that a business asks for something, especially a service.
b ________ is the amount of money someone receives for doing a job.
c The ________ something is the amount of money you pay for it.
d Products ________ an amount of money to buy.
e Sellers ________ an amount of money for a product or service.
f Customers ________ sellers an amount of money for a product or service.

2 **Choose the correct word.**

1 How much do they *charge / cost* for delivery on that website?
2 I only *paid / charged* £20 for these trainers.
3 How much does it *pay / cost* to go by train?
4 The job is hard but the *cost / pay* isn't bad.
5 My parents couldn't believe the *charge / cost* of food on holiday. It was really expensive.
6 Students can visit the exhibition free of *charge / pay*.

3 » Work with a partner. Turn to page 122.

GRAMMAR Present perfect

WARMER

Play Bingo! Write a list of irregular verbs in random order on the board. In pairs, students choose six of them and write them down. Call out the infinitives. If it is on a pair's list, they write the past participle. The first pair to complete all six past participles calls 'Bingo!'. Check their answers. If they are all correct, they are the winners.

1 Students look at examples 1–4 and complete rules a–e with the words in the box. Check answers and apply the rules to the sentences. Explain that we can't use the past simple in these situations either because none of them has finished or because we don't know when they happened. Ask for the infinitive forms of *been / worn / bought* (*be*, *wear*, *buy*). Do not explain the difference between *have gone* and *have been* at this stage.

Answers

b past participle c never, past participle d ever e *-ed*

2 Students read the list of past participles and say which are regular (*try* and *travel* – although students do have to apply spelling rules). In pairs, students write the infinitive forms. Check answers and ask them the past simple of *choose* and *write*.

Answers

chosen – choose
heard – hear
lent – lend
made – make
paid – pay
read – read
travelled – travel
tried – try
worn – wear
written – write

3 Students complete the sentences in pairs, paying attention to the use of *has / hasn't* with third-person singular subjects. Check answers with the class.

Answers

1 has won 2 have never bought 3 've never used
4 has never borrowed 5 've visited 6 've never had
7 haven't met 8 've never stolen

4 Students turn to page 122. In pairs, they write the past participles of the verbs in brackets. Check answers. Students read and answer the questions individually, putting a tick ✓ or a cross × in the *You* column. Next read the example conversation. In their pairs, students ask and answer the questions and complete the *Your partner* column. Remind them to use short answers. Invite students to tell the class about their partner.

Answer

2 lent 3 taken 4 lost 5 received 6 regretted 7 bought
8 saved
Students' own answers

The past participle of *go*: *been* and *gone*

5 Write *be* and *go* on the board and ask students what the past participles are. They read sentences 1 and 2 and match them to the meanings. Check answers. Explain that in this context *been* is used as a past participle for *go*. Ask students which preposition follows *been* when it is used with this meaning (*to*).

Answers

1 b 2 a

» GRAMMAR REFERENCE AND PRACTICE ANSWER KEY TB PAGE 245

6 Students complete the sentences individually and compare answers with a partner. Check answers with the class.

Answers

1 Have, been 2 has gone 3 has gone 4 have, been
5 have, been 6 has, gone

MIXED ABILITY

Weaker students work in pairs. Tell them to ask themselves 'Is the person there now (use *gone*) or have they come back?' (use *been*). 'Does the question mean *ever in your life*?' (use *been*).

» GRAMMAR WORKSHEET UNIT 9

VOCABULARY Easily confused words: *pay, charge, cost*

1 Write *pay*, *charge* and *cost* on the board. Ask students if they are verbs or nouns. Elicit that they can be both. Check past tenses and past participles of the verbs and explain that *pay* as a noun is uncountable. Check pronunciation of *charged* /tʃɑːdʒd/ and *charges* /ˈtʃɑːdʒɪz/. Ask students to read the example sentences and say if the words are used as verbs or nouns. They do the same with the definitions before completing the exercise in pairs. Check answers with the class.

Answers

a Charge (noun) b Pay (noun) c cost of (noun) d cost (verb)
e charge (verb) f pay (verb)

2 Students complete the exercise and compare answers with a partner. Check answers with the class.

Answers

1 charge 2 paid 3 cost 4 pay 5 cost 6 charge

3 Students turn to page 122. Read the questions and ask whether the words *pay*, *charge* and *cost* are used as verbs 1–3 or nouns 4–6. Check understanding and put students into pairs to complete the exercise. Invite students to tell the class about their partner.

Answers

Students' own answers

» VOCABULARY WORKSHEET UNIT 9

WRITING A story (2)

1 Put students into pairs to think of something interesting that might happen on a shopping trip. Invite suggestions from the class, but do not confirm their ideas at this point. In pairs, students look at the photos and read the first sentence of the story. Give them a few minutes to discuss what they think happens in the story. Invite some pairs to share their ideas. Do not give feedback at this stage.

Answers

Students' own answers

2 Set a short time limit for students to read the first two paragraphs of Jamie's story. Invite a stronger student to provide a summary of the story, and then ask the class whether any of their predictions were correct.

Answers

Students' own answers

3 Put students into small groups to discuss what they already know about how to write a story – for example the first sentence should be interesting so that people want to read the rest of the story. Invite some suggestions from the class and then ask them to compare their ideas to the tips in the *Prepare to write* box. Students read the whole story and answer the question. Ask them to identify the three parts of the story.

Answers

Yes, it does.

4 Ask students to work in pairs to decide what the highlighted words in the text mean, using the context to help them. Invite different students to give their answers but do not confirm them at this point. Tell them to complete the exercise and check their ideas. You could get students to write their own sentences using the highlighted words.

Answers

1 enter
2 looked up
3 sent back
4 noticed

5 Ask students to cover the *Prepare to write* box and call out the time adverbs and phrases in Jamie's story. They uncover the box and check. Ask students to group the words and phrases into sequencers (*first*, *then*, *soon*, … *later*, … *after that*), words followed by subject + verb (*when*, *while*) and adverbs (*suddenly*). Tell them that *as soon as* is also followed by subject + verb and check meaning. Students find the time adverbs and phrases in the story and complete the exercise. They compare answers with a partner. Check answers, inviting students to explain their choices.

FAST FINISHERS

Ask fast finishers to write another sentence with two options for another fast finisher to complete. They can write the sentences on the board for the rest of the class to do.

Answers

In the story: *then, soon, while, a few days later, A few weeks after that*
1 as soon as
2 later
3 while
4 suddenly
5 First
6 When

6 Give students time to think of ideas and plan their story. Remind them to think of a good beginning, middle and end to their story. Monitor and help as necessary. Ask students to compare ideas with a partner and make suggestions about each other's story about how it might be improved.

7 **B1 Preliminary for Schools Writing Part 2**

In this part, content, communicative achievement, organisation and language is tested. Students can choose between writing a story, as in this task, or an article, of about 100 words. (See also Unit 5.)

Students write their story. Remind them to include interesting verbs and time expressions.

Tell them to write about 100 words and to check their spelling and grammar carefully. Monitor and help as necessary. In groups, students take turns to read out their stories. Each group should choose one story to share with the class. Take a class vote on the best story.

Model answer

While I was leaving the shop, the security guard stopped me. Everyone was looking at me and I felt very embarrassed. The guard asked me to follow her into her office. Then she asked 'Have you bought anything here today?' I felt so frightened that I couldn't remember. She asked me to open my bag and show her what was inside. As soon as I put my hand in my bag I remembered. 'Yes,' I replied, 'I bought a scarf for my mum. It's her birthday tomorrow. I'm sure I paid for it.' Finally I found the receipt in my purse. I was so happy I almost hugged the guard!

COOLER

Tell students that they are going to tell a story as a class. Divide the class into groups and ask them to think of an opening sentence. Invite them to share ideas and write the sentences on the board. Take a class vote for the story they would like to tell. Read out the opening sentence and follow it with another. Invite students to think of the next sentence. Students who wish to provide a sentence raise their hands. Accept any sentences that follow on from the previous sentence, and continue the story in this way. Remind them to use interesting verbs, time adverbs and phrases. Tell students when it is time to finish the story, and invite different endings. Ask which ending they like best.

WRITING A story (2)

1 **Look at the pictures and read the first sentence of the story. What do you think happens in the story?**

I've never enjoyed shopping for clothes.

2 **Read the first few sentences of Jamie's story and check your ideas.**

> I've never enjoyed shopping for clothes. It takes ages, and when I get home I always regret buying something, and then I have to take it back. So one day I decided to try doing it online.
>
> I looked up the website of my favourite clothes shop and soon I had everything I needed. And there were lots of special offers too! While I was paying for everything, I noticed a competition. I could win the money I paid for my clothes. I've never been lucky, but I decided to enter.
>
> A few days later the clothes arrived. Unfortunately, *nothing* fitted me apart from some socks. So I sent back everything ... except for the socks.
>
> A few weeks after that, I got an email. I was one of the winners in their competition. I got back everything I paid for the clothes online. And how much was that? £4.99!

3 **Read the *Prepare to write* box. Then read the story again. Does it have a clear beginning, middle and end?**

PREPARE TO WRITE
A story (2)

When you write a story:

- make sure there is a beginning, middle and end
- use interesting verbs to describe the actions of the story
- use time adverbs and phrases to describe when things happened: *first, then, when, while, soon, a few days later, a few weeks after that, suddenly.*

4 **Match the highlighted verbs in the story to the meanings.**

1 take part in a competition
2 found by looking on a computer
3 returned something to a shop by post
4 saw

5 **Find five time adverbs and phrases in the story. Then choose the correct time adverbs in the sentences.**

1 I called my friend *as soon as / while* the accident happened.
2 About ten minutes *then / later*, I finally arrived home.
3 He discovered the truth *while / then* he was reading some old letters.
4 She *when / suddenly* had a brilliant idea!
5 I needed a new jacket. *Soon / First*, I tried looking online.
6 *When / While* I got to school, it was already nine o'clock.

6 **Read the task and plan your story.**

Your English teacher has asked you to write a story.
Your story must begin with one of these sentences:

- *My dad handed me a big bag from a department store.*
- *While Chloe was looking at the website, she saw the special offer.*
- *While I was leaving the shop, the security guard stopped me.*

7 **Write your story.**

- Use the tips in the *Prepare to write* box.
- Write about 100 words.
- Remember to check your spelling and grammar.

10 TASTE THIS!

ABOUT YOU

06 **Watch the video and then answer the questions.**

What are your favourite types of food?
Is your diet healthy? Why?
What's the most unusual food you've ever tried?
Do you think it's good to try lots of different food and drink?

A 

B 

D 

E 

C 

F G 

H 

VOCABULARY Food and drink adjectives

1 **Look at the photos. Which of the foods have you tried? Did you like them?**

43 2 **Listen to the first part of a conversation. What is Isla asking Ali to do?**

44 3 **Listen to the second part of the conversation. Number the photos in the order of the taste test.**

45 4 **Match the adjectives to the foods in Isla's project. Then listen and check.**
EP

1 juicy	**a** curry
2 sour	**b** pineapple
3 raw	**c** lemon juice
4 spicy	**d** salmon
5 bitter	**e** bread
6 sweet	**f** vegetables
7 frozen	**g** cake
8 fresh	**h** coffee

46 5 **Match the foods that Ali tasted to the adjectives he used to describe them. Then listen again and check.**
EP

delicious disgusting horrible tasty

1 pineapple
2 sushi
3 lemon juice
4 curry

6 **Discuss the questions.**

1 What's the most delicious food you've ever eaten?
2 What's the most disgusting food you've ever tried?
3 What food do you eat raw?
4 What spicy food do you eat?
5 Do you often eat vegetarian meals?
6 Do you eat a lot of sweet things?

10 TASTE THIS!

Unit Overview

TOPIC	Food and drink
VOCABULARY	Food and drink adjectives
READING	Ollie, don't eat that!
GRAMMAR	Present perfect and past simple; *How long?* and *for/since*
VOCABULARY	*look, taste, smell*
LISTENING	Food and cooking
SPEAKING	Seven short conversations about food
EXAM TASKS	Listening Part 1

Resources

GRAMMAR REFERENCE AND PRACTICE: SB page 147; TB page 245
WORKBOOK: pages 40–43
VIDEO AND VIDEO WORKSHEET: Taste this!
PHOTOCOPIABLE WORKSHEETS: Grammar worksheet Unit 10; Vocabulary worksheet Unit 10
TEST GENERATOR: Unit test 10

WARMER

Write *Food and drink* on the board and divide it into three columns – *healthy*, *not sure*, *unhealthy*. Ask students to call out different items of food and drink and say which column they belong to. Have a class discussion, particularly about the items in the *not sure* column.

ABOUT YOU

06 You can begin the class and introduce the topic of the unit by showing the video and asking students to complete the video worksheet. Read the questions and check understanding. Put students into small mixed ability groups and ask them to appoint a spokesperson. Monitor and help as necessary as they answer the four questions. Listen to feedback as a class and write key vocabulary on the board. Have a class vote on favourite foods and most unusual foods.

VOCABULARY Food and drink adjectives

1 Put students into pairs to identify the food in the photos. Check understanding and if necessary explain that curry is a spicy dish from the Indian sub-continent which is very popular in Britain. Check pronunciation of *curry* /ˈkʌri/, *juice* /dʒuːs/, *salmon* /ˈsæmən/ and *vegetables* /ˈvedʒtəbəlz/. Ask students which items they have tried and if they liked them. Find out who has tried the most food from the photos.

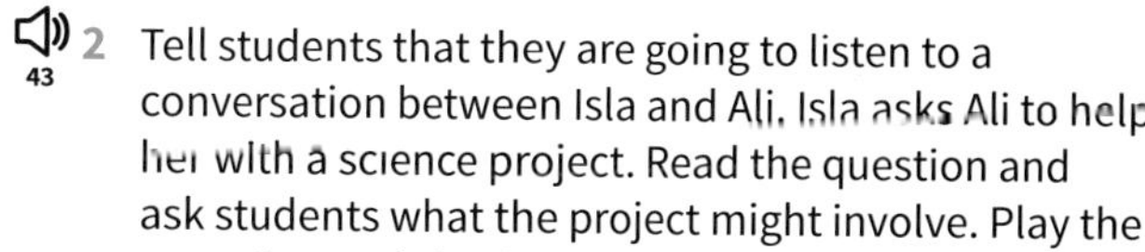

43 2 Tell students that they are going to listen to a conversation between Isla and Ali. Isla asks Ali to help her with a science project. Read the question and ask students what the project might involve. Play the recording and check the answer. Ask students if their predictions were correct.

Answers

She is asking him to taste different types of food with his eyes covered (a blind taste test).

» AUDIOSCRIPT TB PAGE 268

44 3 Read the instructions and play the recording. In pairs, students number the photos in the order in which they hear them. Check answers.

Answers

1 D 2 F 3 B 4 E 5 A 6 H 7 C 8 G

» AUDIOSCRIPT TB PAGE 268

45 4 Read the list of adjectives. Check understanding and check pronunciation of *sour* /saʊə/, *raw* /rɔː/ and *spicy* /ˈspaɪsi/. Students complete the exercise in pairs. They can only use each adjective once. Check answers as a class.

Answers

1 b 2 c 3 d 4 a 5 h 6 g 7 f 8 e

» AUDIOSCRIPT TB PAGE 268

46 5 Tell students to look at the four adjectives and decide whether they are positive or negative. Check pronunciation of *delicious* /dɪˈlɪʃəs/. Students complete the exercise in pairs. Play the recording again for them to check their answers.

Answers

1 delicious 2 disgusting 3 horrible 4 tasty

» AUDIOSCRIPT TB PAGE 268

6 Read the questions and check understanding. Check pronunciation of *vegetarian* /vedʒɪˈteəriən/. In groups of six, each student chooses a different question. They take turns to ask their question to the group and make a note of the answers. Monitor and help as necessary. Review feedback as a class and write key words on the board. Encourage students to give reasons for their answers.

Answers

Students' own answers

READING

BACKGROUND INFORMATION

Insect-eating is common in cultures in most parts of the world, including Central and South America, Africa, Asia, Australia and New Zealand, but uncommon in North America and Europe. There are 1,900 registered edible insect species and about 2 billion insect consumers living in 80% of the world's nations. Some companies are trying to introduce insects into Western diets as a solution to the environmental damage caused by livestock production. Insects such as crickets are a complete protein and contain about the same amount of protein as soybeans. They also have dietary fibre, mostly unsaturated fat and some vitamins and essential minerals

1 Ask students for examples of unusual food they talked about in Vocabulary, on page 58. They read the title and the first paragraph and say how old Ollie was, what he tried to eat and when he started writing his blog (one year old, his brother's pet turtle (/ˈtɜːtl/), two years ago). Direct them to the picture of the turtle. Students look at spaces 1–5 and identify what is missing from the text (*the interview questions*). They read questions a–e and predict which one comes first. Set a short time limit for students to scan the text, complete the exercise and compare answers with a partner. Check answers with the class and ask students to justify their answers. Ask them to name the items in each photo – the answers are in the interview.

Answers

1 b 2 a 3 d 4 e 5 c

MIXED ABILITY

Tell weaker students to underline the key words in each question and scan the paragraphs for a key word or synonym. If they cannot find the answer quickly, they should move on to the next question and then come back to the more difficult ones.

2 Write some key words from each paragraph on the board. Students cover the text and say what they remember about the interview. They read the sentences and decide what information goes in each space, for example whether the missing word is a number, an adjective or something else. Students read the text and complete the sentences in pairs. Invite different students to read out the sentences and check understanding.

Answers

1 two 2 dad 3 carry 4 disgusting 5 meat 6 can 7 sweet 8 ill

FAST FINISHERS

Ask fast finishers to write three sentences, a mix of correct and incorrect, using information from the interview. They read out their sentences and the class decides if they are correct or incorrect. They rewrite the incorrect sentences.

47 The Reading text is recorded for students to listen, read and check their answers.

3 Ask students to find the words in the text and to decide in pairs what they mean. They choose the correct definition for each word. Check answers with the class and ask them to justify their answers. Check pronunciation of *recipe* /ˈresɪpi/.

Answers

1 a 2 a 3 b 4 a 5 b

TALKING POINTS

Read the questions and ask the class for suggestions. In small groups students discuss the second question. One person from the group makes notes of the group's ideas on a piece of paper under the headings *Yes, because* and *No, because*. Monitor and help as necessary. The groups share their ideas with the class, giving their reasons. Have a class discussion and take a vote.

COOLER

Pronunciation. Write headings on the board: *bread*, *curry*, *juice*, *raw*, *sour*, *spice*. Check pronunciation. Underneath, in random order, write the following words: *bed*, *door*, *flower*, *goose*, *hour*, *hurry*, *loose*, *more*, *mousse*, *nice*, *price*, *red*, *rice*, *said*, *shower*, *worry*, *your*. Students match the words with the headings according to their sound. Listen to feedback as a class and ask students if they can add any more words under each heading.

OLLIE, DON'T EAT THAT!

When Ollie James was one, his brother had a tiny pet turtle. One day, it disappeared. Then Ollie's mum noticed a turtle's leg, hanging out of Ollie's mouth! This was the beginning of Ollie's interest in very unusual types of food. And, don't worry, the turtle was fine! Now, aged 16, Ollie's eaten everything from ants to zebra. And for the last two years, he's written about them on his blog: 'Ollie, Don't Eat That!'

47

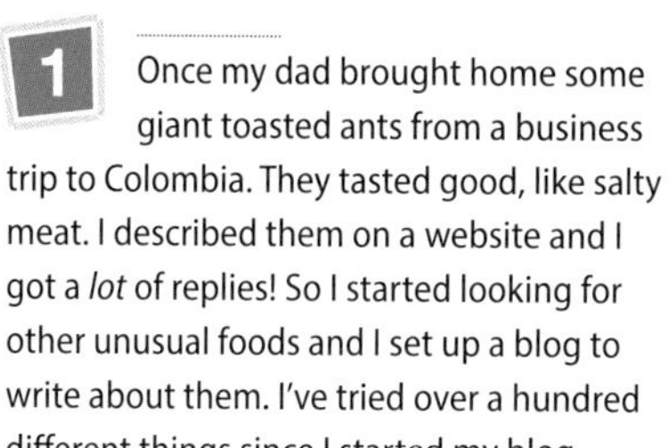

1 .... Once my dad brought home some giant toasted ants from a business trip to Colombia. They tasted good, like salty meat. I described them on a website and I got a *lot* of replies! So I started looking for other unusual foods and I set up a blog to write about them. I've tried over a hundred different things since I started my blog.

2 .... The strangest is durian fruit, from South East Asia. It's actually illegal to carry them on public transport in some countries because they smell disgusting – like old fruit and rubbish. However, they taste incredible – sweet and creamy. I've also cooked with unusual ingredients. I found a recipe for an ostrich curry online, and last week I made that. An ostrich is a bird, but its meat is dark red. I expected a strong flavour, but it isn't as meaty as lamb. I got it from an ostrich farm in England.

3 .... That's definitely the cheeseburger in a can. A reader sent it to me from Germany. It tasted like a really low-quality vegetarian burger. It looked horrible and it tasted worse. I really couldn't finish it.

CHEESEBURGER

4 .... Oh, my favourite is miracle berries, from Africa. They taste bitter, and after you eat them anything that's sour tastes sweet! Lemon juice, for example, tastes like sweet lemonade!

5 .... Not once. I'm always careful that the food is safe. My parents check everything. They've tried lots of things too. They loved my ostrich curry!

READING

1 Read the interview quickly. Match questions a–e to spaces 1–5.

a What's the most interesting thing you've ever eaten?
b Why did you start your website?
c Have you ever been ill because of something you've tried?
d And what about the most disgusting?
e What's the best food you've tried?

2 Complete the sentences with one word in each space.

1 Ollie started his blog .... years ago.
2 Ollie's .... gave him the toasted ants.
3 In some countries, it's against the law to .... durian fruit on public transport
4 The smell of durian fruit is ....
5 Ollie recently made a curry with some ostrich ....
6 Ollie didn't eat all of the cheeseburger in a ....
7 Miracle berries make sour things taste ....
8 Ollie has never been .... from eating foods for his blog.

3 Find these words in the article. Then match them to their meanings.

1 giant
  a very large
  b very small
2 recipe
  a instructions for cooking something
  b a book about food
3 flavour
  a how food or drink smells
  b how food or drink tastes
4 lamb
  a meat of a young sheep
  b a type of fruit
5 low-quality
  a something that's very good
  b something that isn't very good

TALKING POINTS

What food or drink from your country would you like Ollie to try?
Do you think more people will eat insects in the future? Why? / Why not?

TASTE THIS! 59

GRAMMAR Present perfect and past simple

1 **Read the examples. Then complete the rules with *present perfect* or *past simple*.**

1 Ollie's eaten everything from ants to zebra.
2 I made an ostrich curry last week.

a We use the ________ to ask or talk about experiences in our life.
b We use the ________ (often with a past time phrase) to ask or say exactly when something happened.
c We do not use past time phrases with the ________.

2 **Choose the correct form of the verbs.**

1 We enjoyed the party, but there *hasn't been* / *wasn't* anything to eat.
2 Macy *had* / *'s had* an argument with her best friend yesterday.
3 We eat meat, but we *went* / *'ve been* to vegetarian restaurants lots of times.
4 *Did you ever cook* / *Have you ever cooked* a meal for your friends?
5 It was Mum's birthday on Sunday and we *went* / *'ve been* out to a restaurant.
6 I *never ordered* / *'ve never ordered* pizza online.

3 **Ask and answer questions using the present perfect with *ever* and the past simple.**

0 go to a concert? – Who / see?
1 make anyone angry? – Who / be / it?
2 eat out with your friends? – Where / go?
3 win anything? – What / win?

A: *Have you ever been to a concert?*
B: *Yes, I have.*
A: *Who did you see?*
B: *I saw Calvin Harris last year.*

How long? and *for/since*

4 **Read the examples. Then complete the rules with the words in the examples.**

1 How long has Ollie had a blog? He's had a blog for two years.
2 He's tried over a hundred different things since he started his blog.

We use:
a ________ to ask a question in the present perfect about a period of time.
b ________ to say when something started.
c ________ to give the period of time something has continued.

» GRAMMAR REFERENCE AND PRACTICE PAGE 147

5 **Write *for* or *since* for these time phrases.**

three weeks	this morning	a long time
2018	Monday	a few years
four o'clock	midday	

6 **Complete the sentences about you.**

0 I *'ve been* (be) at this school for three years
1 I ________ (not miss) a lesson since ________.
2 We ________ (be) in this classroom for ________.
3 I ________ (not eat) anything since ________.
4 Our teacher ________ (work) here for ________.
5 I ________ (not do) an exam since ________.
6 I ________ (live) in this town for ________.

7 **Correct the mistake in each sentence.**

1 Yesterday I have left my phone at your house.
2 Hi! I didn't see you for a long time.
3 I know her since 2010.
4 On my last birthday I've got a lot of presents from my friends.
5 Have you ever visit London?
6 Two weeks ago I've watched a tennis match.

8 **In pairs, ask questions with *How long …?* Answer them with *for* or *since*.**

0 you / know / your best friend?
1 you / have / your phone?
2 you / be / in this class?
3 you / live / in your home?

A: *How long have you known your best friend?*
B: *I've known my best friend for …*

VOCABULARY *look, taste, smell*

1 EP **Read the examples. What type of word can we use after the verbs *look*, *taste* and *smell*?**

1 It looked horrible.
2 They taste bitter.
3 It smells disgusting.

2 **Complete the sentences with the correct form of *look*, *taste* or *smell* and an adjective from the box.**

disgusting	clean	exhausted	bitter
delicious	upset	~~new~~	

0 Those trainers *look new*. When did you buy them?
1 What are you cooking? It ________!
2 My coffee ________. Did you put sugar in it?
3 These socks don't ________. Put them in the washing machine.
4 You all ________. Did you go to bed late last night?
5 Mum ________. You should apologise.
6 This burger ________. I'm not going to finish it.

3 » Work with a partner. Turn to page 122.

GRAMMAR Present perfect and past simple

WARMER

Divide the board into two columns: *last week* and *this week*. Give a personal example for each column, for example *Last week I went to the cinema*; *This week I've marked your homework*. Ask students to add examples of their own and write them in the correct column, correcting the verb tense if necessary. Ask students what the difference is (*last week is finished, this week is not*).

1 Ask students what they remember about the difference between the present perfect and the past simple. Read out the examples. Students read and complete the rules in pairs. Check answers.

Answers

a present perfect b past simple c present perfect

2 In mixed ability pairs, students read the sentences and choose the correct option. Invite different students to read out the sentences and explain the reason for their choice (see possible answers in brackets).

Answers

1 wasn't (the party is finished)
2 had (this happened yesterday)
3 've been (an experience in life)
4 Have you ever cooked (an experience in life)
5 went (this happened on Sunday)
6 've never ordered (an experience in life)

3 Remind students of the rules in Exercise 1 and of short answers. In pairs, students write the questions. Check they are correct. Students ask and answer them with their partner.

Answers

1 Have you ever made anyone angry? Who was it?
2 Have you ever eaten out with your friends? Where did you go?
3 Have you ever won anything? What did you win?

MIXED ABILITY

Write the present perfect and past simple question forms on the board for weaker students to refer to (*present perfect:* Have you ever + *past participle*; *past simple: question word* + did + *person/pronoun* + *infinitive*).

FAST FINISHERS

Ask fast finishers to write two more sets of questions. They share them with another fast finisher or with the class.

How long? and *for/since*

4 Read the example sentences with the students and ask them to match the sentences to the rule. Check answers.

Answers

a How long b since c for

» GRAMMAR REFERENCE AND PRACTICE ANSWER KEY TB PAGE 245

5 Students read the time expressions. In pairs, one student finds the time phrases that use *for* and their partner does the same for *since*. They compare answers and discuss any differences of opinion. Check answers.

Answers

for: three weeks, a long time, a few years
since: this morning, 2018, Monday, four o'clock, midday

6 Read the example. Students complete sentences 1–6 so that they are true for them. Check the verb tenses.

Answers

1 haven't missed, students' own answers
2 've been, students' own answers
3 haven't eaten, students' own answers
4 has worked, students' own answers
5 haven't done, students' own answers
6 have lived, students' own answers

7 Students find the mistakes and correct them. Check answers with the class and ask students to give reasons.

Answers

1 Yesterday I **left** my phone at your house.
2 Hi! I **haven't seen** you for a long time.
3 I've **known** her since 2010.
4 On my last birthday **I got** a lot of presents from my friends.
5 Have you ever **visited** London?
6 Two weeks ago **I watched** a tennis match.

8 Remind students of the question form *How long?* and read the example conversation. In pairs, students write questions using the prompts, then ask and answer the questions.

Answers

1 How long have you had your phone? I've had my phone for / since …
2 How long have you been in this class? I've been in this class for / since …
3 How long have you lived in your home? I've lived in my home for / since …

» GRAMMAR WORKSHEET UNIT 10

VOCABULARY *look, taste, smell*

1 Read the heading and explain that these are the senses we most often use when we cook and eat. Students read the examples and identify which part of speech is used after the verbs (*adjectives*).

2 Read the adjectives in the box and the example. Check understanding. In pairs, students read and complete the sentences using each adjective only once.

Answers

1 smells/looks delicious 2 tastes bitter 3 look/smell clean
4 look exhausted 5 looks upset 6 tastes disgusting

3 Students turn to page 122. Check understanding. Students take turns to choose an item and describe it without naming it, using the adjectives in the box or their own ideas, for example *They taste delicious and juicy* (*strawberries*). Point out that some items are plural. Students give their own answers.

» VOCABULARY WORKSHEET UNIT 10

LISTENING

1 Read the questions. Put students into small groups to discuss them. Invite students to share their group's experiences.

Answers
Students' own answers

2 **B1 Preliminary for Schools Listening Part 1**

In this part, students' ability to listen for specific information is tested. It consists of seven short 'daily life' extracts, each with a question and three pictures. Students listen and choose the picture that answers the question. They hear the recording twice.

Tell students that they are going to listen to seven people talking about food. Ask them to read the questions, look at the pictures and work in pairs to make a list of words they might hear. Monitor and help as necessary. Ask students to call out the words and write them on the board. Do not give feedback at this point.

Answers
Students' own answers

48 3 Read the instructions. Students read the questions. Check understanding of *available* and *ingredients*. Play the first extract and ask students to choose A, B or C. Check the answer with the class and ask students if they heard any of the words they listed in Exercise 2. Play the recording again and ask students to listen for key words. Play the whole recording, pausing after each extract. Ask students to compare answers with a partner. Then play it again without pausing. Check answers using the same procedure as for question 1. Play the recording again if necessary and discuss why the other two pictures in each question are incorrect.

Answers
1 C 2 A 3 A 4 B 5 C 6 C 7 A

» AUDIOSCRIPT TB PAGE 269

SPEAKING Ordering food

1 Students read the menu. Check understanding and revise saying prices, for example *The cheese sandwich is/costs three pounds fifty. Extras are/cost fifty p*. In pairs, students ask and answer the questions with their partner. Invite different students to give their answers. Check pronunciation of *onion* /ˈʌnjən/, *mixed* /mɪkst/ and *sparkling* /ˈspɑːklɪŋ/.

Answers
1 vegetarian
2 £9
3 There are two different sizes.

2 Tell students to read the questions and then play the recording. Allow them to compare their answers with a partner before checking as a class.

Answers
a veggie pizza, a green salad and a small cola
£12.50

3 Read out the questions and phrases from the *Prepare to speak* box for the students to repeat. Encourage them to copy your intonation. Play the recording again for them to listen for the phrases and to make a note of who says them. Check answers. Point out the use of *I'll have* and *I'd like* when ordering food.

Answers
What can I get you? (Server)
And to drink? (Server)
Eat in or take out? (Server)
Here's your change. (Server)
Could I have … , please? (Emma)
I'll have … , please. (Emma)
I'd like … , please. (Emma)
Here you are. (Emma)

» AUDIOSCRIPT TB PAGE 269

4 Students read the menu and make a note of their order. In pairs, they take turns to be the server and the customer. Monitor and help as necessary. Give positive feedback when they use phrases from the *Prepare to speak* box.

Answers
Students' own answers

5 Invite pairs to act out their conversation in front of the class. Ask others to repeat the orders that were placed. Give positive feedback for good intonation.

Answers
Students' own answers

COOLER

Start a chain sentence of unusual foods from A to Z. Say *I've never eaten ants*. The next student repeats the first sentence and adds an unusual food beginning with B, the next student with C, and so on. If they cannot think of an unusual food, they can add any food item. Suggestions: *ants*, *berries*, *curry*, *durian*, etc.

LISTENING

1 Have you ever made a meal for anyone? Who was it for? What did you make?

2 You are going to listen to some short extracts. Read the questions and look at the pictures. What words might you hear in each extract?

1 What did the girl cook when she was young?

2 Where does the boy get his recipes from?

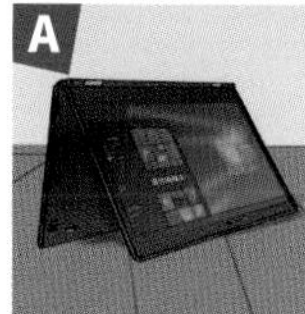

3 Who is a vegetarian?

4 Which dish is only available today?

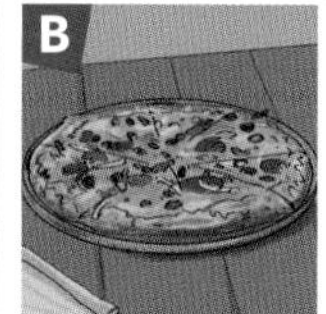

5 Which food does Lizzie dislike?

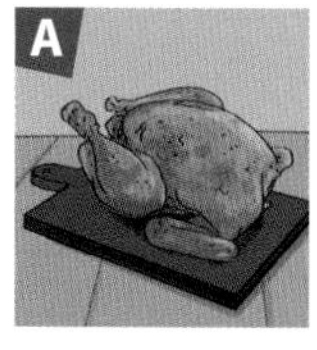

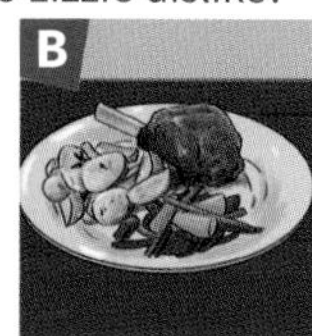

6 Which ingredient do they need to buy?

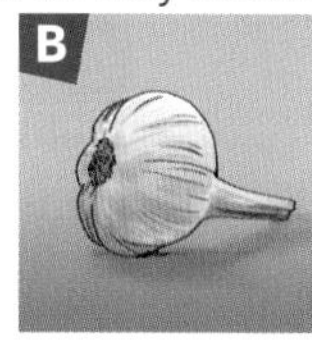

7 What do the couple decide to have for dinner?

48 3 Listen and choose the correct picture A, B or C. Listen again and check.

SPEAKING Ordering food

1 Look at the menu below and answer the questions.

1 What do you think 'veggie' means?
2 How much is a spicy beef pizza with olives?
3 Why are there two prices for cola?

49 2 Listen to the conversation. What does Emma order? How much is her meal?

49 3 Read the *Prepare to speak* box. Then listen again. Which phrases do Emma and the server use?

PREPARE TO SPEAK

Ordering food

Phrases the server uses	Phrases the customer uses
What can I get you?	Could I have … , please?
What would you like?	I'll have … , please.
And to drink?	I'd like … , please.
Anything else?	Have you got any … ?
Eat in or take out?	Here you are.
Here's your change.	

4 Look at the menu again and decide what you would like to order. In pairs, practise ordering food. Use phrases from the *Prepare to speak* box.

5 Act out your conversation for the class.

Sandwiches / Panini	
Cheese	£3.50
Tuna	£4.00
Chicken	£4.00
Roast beef	£4.75

Pizza	
Margherita	£6.50
Veggie – peppers, onions, olives	£8.00
Spicy beef – beef, red peppers, onion, chilli	£8.50

Extras (50p each): mushrooms, chilli, olives, etc.

All pizzas include cheese and tomato

Salads	
Green salad	£3.00
Mixed salad	£4.00
Tuna salad	£5.50
Grilled chicken	£6.00

Drinks	
Tea	£2.00
Coffee	£2.50
Fresh orange juice	£2.50
Still/sparkling water	£1.50
Cola	£1.50/£2.00

TASTE THIS! 61

CULTURE

BRITISH FOOD

1 **Answer the questions.**

1. What do you think British people eat in a typical day?
2. What do you know about traditional British dishes?
3. Do you think British food is very different from food in your country?

2 **Read the text quickly. Match the underlined food to photos A–G.**

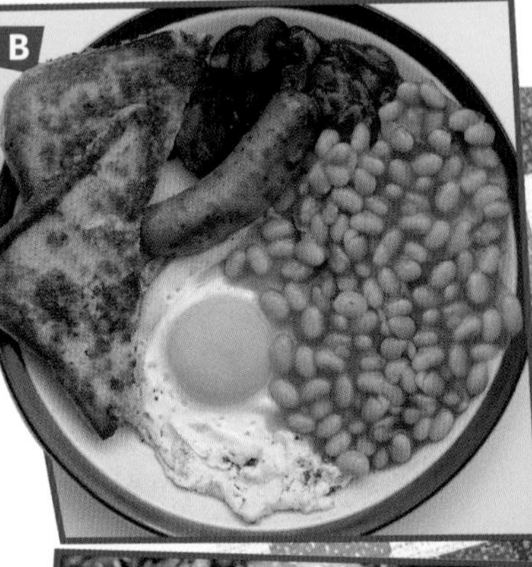

50

Many tourists are quite surprised by all the delicious food they can find in the UK. In the past, many visitors had a bad opinion of British cooking, but that was often because they ate in cheap restaurants that only served food for tourists. Fortunately, things have changed in recent years and now tourists can find many types of good quality food all over the country.

Typical favourites

You can find excellent traditional British food in the thousands of cafés, restaurants and takeaways around the UK. A typical café dish, and perhaps the best-known abroad, is the 'full English breakfast'. That's eggs, sausage, tomatoes, beans and fried bread. If you want something hot for lunch in a café, try the meat or vegetarian pies on offer.

A classic summer dish is ploughman's lunch, which is a cold dish of bread, butter, cheese, pickled onion and salad. On Sundays, it's typical to have a roast dinner with friends and family. Roast beef, lamb or chicken is served with potatoes and boiled vegetables such as carrots and broccoli, and gravy is poured on top. Gravy is a thick, brown sauce and it's delicious!

Takeaways are really popular in the UK. These are small shops that sell hot food that customers take home or eat on the street. Fish and chips has been a British takeaway favourite for a long time. They fry the fish in batter (a mixture of flour and water) and it's often served with peas, and, of course, lots of chips!

Many places in the UK have local specialities. In Scotland, Cullen skink is a creamy soup with fish, potatoes, onions, and milk. In Wales, one of the most popular dishes is called Welsh rarebit. It's hot cheese on toast. And for dessert you can try some bara brith. It's a sweet bread with fruit and spices.

Since the 1950s, many immigrants have come to Britain from all over the world and they have brought lots of international dishes with them: curry from India and Pakistan, pizza and pasta from Italy, along with dishes from China, Japan, Egypt, Mexico and many other places. Curry, in particular, has become so popular that it is often called a 'national dish' of the UK.

With all of these choices, tourists nowadays won't have any problems eating in the UK. Their biggest challenge will be deciding what to eat!

CULTURE

Learning Objectives

- The students learn about British food.
- In the project stage, they write a food guide for tourists visiting their town or city.

Vocabulary

challenge perhaps pickled specialities takeaways

Resources

CULTURE VIDEO AND CULTURE VIDEO WORKSHEET: International food in London

BACKGROUND INFORMATION

In Roman times, Britain was known for its fertile soils and advanced methods of animal breeding. After the Romans, Anglo-Saxon England developed meat and herb stewing techniques. The Norman invasion brought with it continental influences and exotic spices but following the Protestant Reformation in the 16th and 17th centuries British food became plainer and simpler. That all changed in the 18th and 19th centuries when the British Empire was influenced by Indian cuisine. Later, during the World Wars of the 20th century, the government introduced rationing, which was not fully abolished until almost ten years after the war ended, so a whole generation grew up without tasting ingredients which had previously been very common. However, in the later 20th century, there was an increase in the availability of good quality fresh products from all over the world, and many sections of the British population varied their diets and selected dishes from other cultures.

Some British food and drink products now have Protected Geographical Status under European Union Law. This means they are recognised as genuine local or regional products and they are protected from imitations. The United Kingdom has a total of 65 products with protected status, including 15 cheeses.

WARMER

Play an alphabet game with food products. Each student repeats the list and adds a new product, for example *apples*, *bread*, *carrots*, *doughnuts*, *eggs*, etc. Any student who makes a mistake or cannot think of a product is out.

1 Read the first question. On the board, write *breakfast*, *lunch*, *dinner*, *snacks*. Elicit the meaning of *snack*: a small amount of food you eat between meals or sometimes a light meal. In groups, students make a list under each category. Tell them to decide which are *sweet* and which are *savoury* (the opposite of *sweet*). Ask the groups to read out their lists and write the items on the board. Ask the second question. Students may know about fish and chips and roast dinners. Read the third question and ask for suggestions about similarities and differences between British food and food from their country.

Answers

Students' own answers

2 In pairs, students describe the seven photos, say what they think they are, whether they are sweet or savoury and when British people would eat them. Ask them to read the text quickly and match the underlined food to the photos. Check answers as a class.

Answers

A Welsh rarebit
B full English breakfast
C fish and chips
D bara brith
E roast dinner (roast beef)
F Cullen skink
G ploughman's lunch

3 Read the six sentences. Check understanding and pronunciation of *variety* /vəˈraɪəti/ (*things that are different from each other*) and *recipe* /ˈresɪpi/ (*a list of ingredients and instructions about how to cook something*). Students read the text carefully, decide if the sentences are true or false and correct the false ones. They compare answers with a partner. Check answers as a class.

Answers

1 false (There are many types of food.)
2 false (On Sundays, it's typical to have a roast dinner with friends and family.)
3 false (Fish and chips is a takeaway favourite.)
4 false (It's a Scottish dish.)
5 true
6 true

50 The Reading text is recorded for students to listen, read and check their answers.

MIXED ABILITY

To help weaker students locate the information in the texts, ask them to predict which section will give them the answer to each question: *the introduction*, *Typical favourites*, *Local dishes* or *International options*.

FAST FINISHERS

Ask fast finishers to write two more *True/False* sentences for the rest of the class to answer.

4 Ask students to look at the highlighted words in the text and to try to work out their meanings from the context. They then complete the exercise by matching the words to their meanings. Check answers with the class and check any other new words and phrases.

Answers

1 pickled 2 specialities 3 takeaway (*takeaways* in the text)
4 perhaps 5 challenge

51 5 Ask students to describe the four photos and guess what each dish contains. Ask if they can name any of the dishes and say whether they are sweet or savoury. Students read the questions. Play the recording. They compare answers with a partner. Check answers with the class.

Answers

1 In London
2 They are trying to decide what to have for lunch.
3 The first curry restaurant opened in London more than 200 years ago.

51 6 Students read the sentences and fill any of the spaces they remember from the recording. Play the recording again for them to complete the sentences. They compare answers with a partner. Check answers with the class. Ask students to say what other food words they heard in the recording: *fish and chips*; *roast beef*; *beef, vegetables and mashed potato* (the ingredients of cottage pie); and play it again if necessary. They name the dishes in the four photos (*mashed potato, chicken tikka masala, cottage pie and trifle*) and say which they would most like to try.

Answers

1 beefburgers
2 chicken
3 spicy
4 sausages, potatoes
5 sweet dish
6 fruit, cake

» **AUDIOSCRIPT TB PAGES 269–270**

7 Students read the sentence beginnings in the *Useful language* box. Check understanding of the modal verbs *would*, *could*, *might (not)*. In pairs, they answer the questions. Monitor and help as necessary. Listen to feedback as a class, allowing students to express their opinions and to agree and disagree with each other. Write key words on the board.

Answers

Students' own answers

PROJECT ***A food guide***

Read the instructions and the six questions. Check understanding. In pairs, students discuss the questions and agree on what to include in their food guide. Encourage them to give reasons for the advice they give in the answers to questions 3, 5 and 6. They write their food guides, remembering to include phrases from the *Useful language* box. Monitor and help as necessary. Invite volunteers to read their guides to the class.

PROJECT EXTENSION

Tell students to imagine they run a restaurant serving local food to tourists who are visiting their town or city. Ask them to write a menu of starters, main dishes and desserts, with their prices. They should add short explanations of the dishes if necessary and make their menus look attractive. Display the finished menus in the classroom.

07 **CULTURE VIDEO: International food in London**

When students have completed the lesson, they can watch the video and complete the worksheet.

COOLER

Students write three sentences about their favourite food without saying its name, for example *It's made of …*, *I usually eat it (for Sunday lunch / in the morning)*, etc. In pairs or small groups, they read out their sentences and the other students try to guess the food.

3 **Are the sentences true or false? Correct the false sentences.**

1 At the moment, British food hasn't got much variety.
2 Nowadays, British people don't eat roast dinners.
3 People usually cook fish and chips at home.
4 Cullen skink is an English dish that has fish and potatoes.
5 Welsh rarebit is a recipe that hasn't got any meat or fish.
6 British food has become more varied because of immigration.

4 **Match the highlighted words in the text to the meanings.**

1 kept in vinegar or salty water
2 famous dishes
3 a place that cooks and sells food for people to eat somewhere else
4 maybe, possibly
5 something difficult

51 **5** **Listen to Emily and her cousin Andrew, who is from the USA. Answer the questions.**

1 Where are Emily and Andrew now?
2 What decision are they trying to make?
3 What historical event does Emily talk about?

51 **6** **Listen again. Complete the sentences with one or two words.**

1 At first, Andrew suggests they have ________ for lunch.
2 Emily thinks some ________ tikka masala would be good.
3 Andrew says he isn't a big fan of ________ dishes.
4 Bangers and mash are ________ with mashed ________.
5 Emily says that cottage pie isn't a ________.
6 Trifle is made with ________, ________ jelly and cream.

7 **Read the *Useful language* phrases. Complete them with ideas about food in your country.**

USEFUL LANGUAGE

Discussing possibilities

1 A famous dish in our country would be …
2 A popular local speciality might be …
3 Visitors could perhaps try …
4 A popular fast food here would be …
5 Some tourists might not like …
6 People who like desserts might want to try …

PROJECT

A food guide

Write a food guide for tourists who visit your town or city. Use the questions below to help you.

- What food is popular in your country?
- What are the local specialities where you live?
- Which restaurants should tourists try in your area?
- What fast food is popular where you live?
- What desserts or sweets should visitors have?
- What other food might people want to try?

Present your guide to the class. Then post your work at school where other people can see it.

07 NOW WATCH THE CULTURE VIDEO

11 A HEALTHY FUTURE

ABOUT YOU

08 **Watch the video and then answer the questions.**

Are you generally quite healthy?

Have you ever broken an arm or a leg? What happened?

Do you think most people would like to live to be 1,000 years old? Why? / Why not?

VOCABULARY Body and health

52 **1 Match the words to the parts of the body A–N. Then listen and check.**

EP

ankle back cheek chest chin
elbow finger forehead knee
neck shoulder throat thumb toe

2 Complete the table with the words from Exercise 1. Add more parts of the body you can see in the photo.

head	*chin, …*
body	*back, …*
leg	*ankle, …*
arm	*elbow, …*

53 **3 Listen to three conversations. Match the speakers to the sentences.**

Sam Kelly Josh

a ________ might be ill.
b ________ had an accident and is injured.
c ________ has sore legs and arms after doing sport.

4 Discuss the illnesses and injuries. What parts of the body do they affect?

EP

aches broken (a) cold (a) cough
(a) cut earache (a) fever flu
sore stomach ache toothache

53 **5 Complete the sentences with words from Exercise 4. There is one word you don't need. Listen again and check.**

1 Sam played tennis yesterday and now she's got **(a)** ________ in her arms, legs and back.
2 Kelly's got a headache, and she has a **(b)** ________ inside her mouth. She says her cheek's **(c)** ________. She needs to go to the dentist because she has **(d)** ________. The other girl hurt her thumb, but it wasn't **(e)** ________.
3 Josh feels very hot, so he thinks he's got a **(f)** ________. Dora thinks that Josh might be getting a **(g)** ________. Josh has a sore throat and a **(h)** ________. Last night he had **(i)** ________, too. He hopes he hasn't got **(j)** ________.

6 In pairs, compare the illnesses and injuries you've had.

A: *I've had a fever.*
B: *Me too. I had a high temperature last year.*

11 A HEALTHY FUTURE

Unit Overview

TOPIC	Health, illnesses and injuries
VOCABULARY	Body and health
READING	We will live for 1,000 years
GRAMMAR	*will* and *be going to*
VOCABULARY	Illnesses and injuries: verbs
WRITING	An article (1)
EXAM TASKS	Writing Part 2

Resources

GRAMMAR REFERENCE AND PRACTICE: SB page 148; TB page 245
WORKBOOK: pages 44–47
VIDEO AND VIDEO WORKSHEET: Healthy future
PHOTOCOPIABLE WORKSHEETS: Grammar worksheet Unit 11; Vocabulary worksheet Unit 11
TEST GENERATOR: Unit test 11

WARMER

In pairs, give students three minutes to make a list of as many parts of the body as they can. Take feedback from the class and write the body parts on the board.

ABOUT YOU

08 You can begin the class and introduce the topic of the unit by showing the video and asking students to complete the video worksheet. This unit focuses on common, non-serious illnesses and injuries. In pairs, students discuss the first two questions. Remind them to think carefully about tense use. Ask for feedback from the class and write key words on the board. Discuss the third question briefly as it will be examined in more depth later in the unit.

VOCABULARY Body and health

1 Read out the words in the box and drill pronunciation, paying attention to *ankle* /ˈæŋkl/, *elbow* /ˈelbəʊ/, *knee* /niː/, *throat* /θrəʊt/ and *thumb* /θʌm/. Students point to the corresponding part of their body. In pairs, students match the body parts to the letters on the picture. Play the recording for them to check answers.

52

Answers

The answers are recorded for students to listen and check.
A forehead B shoulder C elbow D finger E thumb F back
G toe H ankle I knee J chest K neck L throat M chin
N cheek

2 Students look at the examples in the table and complete the lists in pairs. Check answers and ask students to add any other parts of the body to the table.

Answers

head: cheek, chin, forehead
body: back, chest, neck, throat
leg: ankle, knee, toe
arm: elbow, finger, shoulder, thumb

53 3 Ask students what symptoms they have when they feel ill, to describe the last time they fell over, and if they have ever had a sports injury. Explain that they are going to listen to three different conversations about people who are not feeling well. Read the names and the sentences. Check understanding. Play the first conversation and pause for students to decide on the correct sentence. Repeat the process for the remaining conversations. Check answers.

Answers

a Josh b Kelly c Sam

» AUDIOSCRIPT TB PAGE 270

4 Books closed. In small groups, give students two minutes to write a list of illnesses and injuries. Make a list on the board. Students compare the words on the board to the words in the box. Drill pronunciation, paying attention to *cough* /kɒf/ and *stomach ache* /ˈstʌmək ˌeɪk/, and check understanding. Ask which two words are adjectives (*broken* and *sore*).

Answers

Students' own answers

53 5 In pairs, students complete the sentences. Play the recording for them to check their answers and work out which word they did not need. Review answers with the class.

Answers

1 a aches
2 b cut c sore d toothache e broken
3 f fever g cold h cough i earache j flu
(Stomach ache is not needed.)

» AUDIOSCRIPT TB PAGE 270

6 Nominate two students to read out the example conversation. Ask which tenses are used (*past perfect and past simple*) and why. Remind students to use the list of illnesses and injuries on the board and in Exercise 4 to talk about their own experiences. Students ask and answer the questions in pairs. Invite students to talk about their partner's experiences.

Answers

Students' own answers

READING

BACKGROUND INFORMATION

Dr Aubrey de Grey (born 1963) is an English scientist who studies old age and the process of ageing. His research focuses on whether medicine can prevent the aging process by reversing seven types of molecular and cellular damage caused by essential metabolic processes. Stuart Jay Olshansky (born 1954) is a professor at the University of Illinois in Chicago. The focus of his research is concerned with estimating the upper limits of human life. He is a supporter of scientific attempts to prolong human's *healthy* life-span as compared to increasing the overall length of life.

1 Tell students to look at the layout and the title to decide what kind of text it is and what it is about (*an online news report about living for 1,000 years*). Ask students how long people generally live now and who is the oldest person they know. They scan the first paragraph to find the name of the man in the photo. Set a short time limit for students to read the text and comments and answer the question. Ask them to summarise Dr de Grey's ideas and Professor Olshansky's opinion. (Dr De Grey believes that humans will live for 1,000 years but Olshansky disagrees.)

Answers

Damian from London

2 In pairs, students first decide what the highlighted words mean from the context before matching them to meanings 1–5. Check answers. Check understanding of any other new words in the text. Encourage other students to provide definitions if they can.

Answers

1 drugs 2 disease 3 damaged 4 alive 5 predict

FAST FINISHERS

Ask fast finishers to write definitions for *rather* in paragraph 2 (*more exactly*), *research* in paragraph 2 (*detailed study of a subject in order to discover new information*) and *evidence* in paragraph 3 (*proof that something is true or exists*). They read them out and the class finds the correct words.

3 Go through the questions and check understanding. Discuss the type of answers required. A question with *how* is asking about a process. A question with *what* is asking for a fact, a prediction or an opinion. A question with *why* is asking for a reason, usually starting with *because*. Ask students where they can find each answer, whether in paragraph 1, 2, or 3 or in the comments box. Encourage students to use their own words when they write their answers rather than simply copying the text. Give them plenty of time to complete the exercise. Monitor and help as necessary. Ask students to compare answers with a partner before checking answers as a class. Bear in mind that it is more important to have the correct and relevant information than to be grammatically perfect.

Answers

1 People used to die at the age of 50 and now many people live until 90 or longer.
2 Dr de Grey believes that soon people will be able to live to 1,000 years.
3 Old age, or the diseases of old age
4 He claims that we will be able to look after and repair damaged bodies in the same way as we do cars.
5 The population would grow quickly.
6 They will die in accidents.
7 They were both scientists who thought they knew how to live for ever.
8 She thinks it would be boring.
9 He'd like a cure for cancer first.

MIXED ABILITY

Weaker students do not need to write complete sentences for the answers. It is more important that they can find the relevant information and write the key words. Monitor and help as necessary.

54 The Reading text is recorded for students to listen, read and check their answers.

TALKING POINTS

Discuss the article as a class. Ask students what they think of Dr de Grey's ideas, Professor Olshansky's opinion and the comments from Simone, Hannah and Damian. Encourage students to give reasons for their answers. Write key words and ideas on the board. Tell students to write down two reasons in favour of living to be 1,000 and two against. Students share their ideas. Have a class vote on how many students would like to live to be 1,000.

COOLER

Write these prompts on the board: *cars*, *houses*, *students*, *mobile phones*, *food*. Then write these time expressions: *in 2020*, *in 100 years*, *in 1,000 years*. Students work in small groups to make predictions about the prompts using each of the time expressions. Provide an example first. Say 'In 2020, cars will be the same as they are now. In 100 years, they will be much faster and cleaner. In 1,000 years, cars will be able to fly!' Monitor and join in with the discussions, helping with ideas and language where necessary.

HOME | UK NEWS | WORLD NEWS | OPINION | VIDEO | PICTURES

We will live for **1,000 years**

How long do you expect to live? One hundred years ago, people died at the age of about 50. These days, people often live for 90 years or more, and doctors predict that most teenagers alive today will live to be over 100. But one scientist, Dr Aubrey de Grey, thinks that medicine will soon allow people to live to the age of 1,000.

Dr de Grey says that most people die from old age, or rather from a disease that old people's bodies are unable to fight. But, he says: 'I think we're close to keeping people so healthy that at the age of 90, they'll wake up every day in the same physical state as they were at the age of 30.' Dr de Grey believes that doctors can look after the human body in the same way that we look after things like old cars. Scientists have invented drugs that can completely repair old or damaged parts of our bodies. Their research suggests that people who take these drugs aren't going to get old or die from common diseases. Their bodies are going to stay healthy – and young. De Grey's plans mean there might be a lot more people on the planet, but de Grey says that doesn't matter, because our priority should be health not population. 'We still need to give people the best healthcare that we can,' and de Grey is going to continue to do exactly that through his research. However, Dr de Grey warns that people won't live for ever. Although people won't die from the diseases of old age, they'll still have accidents, such as car crashes.

Many scientists disagree. All through history, scientists have predicted that we will live for ever, says Professor S. Jay Olshansky. A Chinese scientist, Ko Hung, said 1,700 years ago that eating very little would help people to live for ever, but he died at the age of 60. The English scientist Roger Bacon thought we could live for ever by eating gold, but he died aged 78. There's a long list of promises, says Professor Olshansky, but there's no evidence that people will ever live for 1,000 years.

Comments (43)

I don't believe this. Anyway, who wants to live that long? Life will become very boring after a few hundred years!
Simone, Peterborough, UK

People love the idea of living for ever, but I think it's impossible. I'm going to look after my own health, and forget about Dr de Grey.
Hannah, Sydney, Australia

Dr de Grey is probably right. I think I'll find out more about these drugs! But millions of people die every year from cancer, for instance, and we can't even cure that yet. Let's cure cancer first!
Damian, London, UK

READING

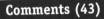

1 Read the news report and the comments quickly. Who agrees with Dr de Grey?

2 Match the highlighted words in the article to the meanings.

1 medicines
2 an illness
3 broken, hurt
4 the opposite of *dead*
5 say something will happen

3 Read the news report again and answer the questions.

1 How has the length of human lives changed in the past 100 years?
2 How does Dr de Grey think the length of human lives will change in the future?
3 What do most people die from today?
4 Why does Dr de Grey compare human bodies with cars?
5 How might Dr de Grey's ideas affect the human population?
6 What will people die from if they don't die from disease?
7 What do Ko Hung and Roger Bacon have in common?
8 What is Simone's opinion about living for ever?
9 What would Damian prefer scientists to work on?

TALKING POINTS

What do you think of Dr de Grey's ideas? Do you agree or disagree with Professor Olshansky? Why? / Why not?
Would you like to live to be 1,000? Why? / Why not?

GRAMMAR *will* and *be going to*

1 Match the examples to the rules.

1 Medicine **will allow** people to live to the age of 1,000.
2 Their research suggests that people **aren't going to die** from common diseases.
3 De Grey **is going to continue** to do exactly that.
4 I think **I'll find out** more about these drugs.

We use *will* …
a to predict the future generally.
b when we decide to do something while we are speaking.

We use *be going to* …
c to talk about something we have already decided to do.
d to predict the future based on something we can see or know now.

» **GRAMMAR REFERENCE AND PRACTICE PAGE 148**

2 Choose the correct verb form.

1 I'm glad you *'ll visit* / *'re going to visit* in June.
2 Let's have a snack. I *'m going to get* / *'ll get* us some popcorn.
3 No, I don't want to come out, thanks. I *'ll have* / *'m going to have* an early night.
4 There isn't a cloud in the sky. It *won't rain* / *isn't going to rain*!
5 I *'ll go* / *'m going to go* and visit my cousins in the summer. We've already bought the tickets.
6 In my opinion, scientists *are going to find* / *will find* a cure for all cancers soon.
7 You should watch this film. I think you *'ll like* / *'re going to like* it.
8 Speak clearly or the children *won't understand* / *aren't going to understand* you.

3 Complete the sentences. Use the *will* or *be going to* future form of the verb in brackets.

1 Hey, I ________ (help) you pick up these books.
2 Do you think we ________ (find) life on other planets?
3 I've decided about the party. I ________ (not come). I have to study this evening.
4 Oh, no, look at those cyclists. They ________ (crash)!
5 Don't worry about me. I ________ (see) the doctor tomorrow.
6 It's late, I think I ________ (go) home now.

4 Read the questions and prepare your answers. Then ask and answer the questions.

1 Is it going to rain later?
2 What are you going to do at the weekend?
3 Do you think you'll go to university?
4 What kind of job do you think you'll do?
5 Where will you live when you're older?

VOCABULARY Illnesses and injuries: verbs

1 How many verbs can you match with 1–3?

EP

break catch cut feel get
have hurt injure be

1 a cold 2 sick 3 your leg

2 Choose the two correct answers.

0 I was quite ill yesterday, but I'm __ better now.
A catching (B) feeling (C) getting
1 Ouch! My throat __ .
A injures B feels sore C hurts
2 My sister __ ill last night.
A was B caught C felt
3 He's never __ flu.
A caught B had C felt
4 I've __ my ankle.
A broken B caught C injured
5 Be careful. Don't __ your thumb.
A cut B get C hurt
6 My uncle __ his shoulder last week.
A got B broke C hurt

55 **3 Complete the conversations with the correct form of the verbs. Then listen and check.**

break hurt injure

Doctor: What seems to be the problem?
Zac: My finger really [1] ________ . I [2] ________ it last night when I was playing football.
Doctor: Let me see. Can you move it at all?
Zac: Yes, a bit.
Doctor: OK, so you haven't [3] ________ it. But we need to …

catch feel have (got) have (got)

Niall: What are you going to do this weekend?
Anna: Not much! I [4] ________ flu. I started to [5] ________ ill on Thursday, and now I'm exhausted. I [6] ________ a fever at the moment, and aches in my arms and legs.
Niall: Is anyone else in your family ill?
Anna: No, but my sister was ill last week, so maybe I [7] ________ it from her.

4 » **Work with a partner. Student A turn to page 123. Student B turn to page 126.**

66 UNIT 11

GRAMMAR *will* and *be going to*

WARMER

Books closed. Ask students to say what they remember about the article from Reading, page 65. Confirm their answers by repeating them back using *will* or *be going to* where appropriate, for example *People will live to be 1,000 years old*; *Drugs are going to help us to stay young and healthy*.

1 Books open. Tell students to read the four sentences and look at the future forms in bold carefully. Ask them what they think the difference is between *will* and *be going to*. Put students into pairs to match the rules to the sentences. Check answers.

Answers

1 a 2 d 3 c 4 b

» GRAMMAR REFERENCE AND PRACTICE ANSWER KEY TB PAGE 245

2 Books closed. Check that students remember the rules for *will* and *be going to*. Books open. Ask students to choose *will* or *be going to* in each of the sentences. Monitor and help as necessary. Invite different students to read out a completed sentence and match it to the correct rule in Exercise 1.

Answers

1 're going to visit 2 'll get 3 'm going to have
4 isn't going to rain 5 'm going to go 6 will find 7 'll like
8 won't understand

3 In mixed ability pairs, students read the sentences and complete them using the correct forms. Ask individual students to read out their answers and invite the class to say whether they are correct or not and match them to the rules in Exercise 1.

Answers

1 'll help 2 'll find 3 'm not going to come
4 're going to crash 5 'm going to see 6 'll go

4 Ask students to read the questions. Elicit which future form is used in each question and why. Students work individually to make notes to answer the questions. Encourage them to think of reasons where appropriate. Ask students to number the questions 1–5 in terms of how interesting they are. In pairs, they ask and answer the questions, starting with the most interesting one. Monitor and help as necessary. Give positive feedback for interesting answers and the correct use of *will* and *be going to*. Invite pairs to ask and answer each question in front of the class.

Answers

Students' own answers

FAST FINISHERS

Ask fast finishers to match the questions to the rules in Exercise 1. They can explain them to the class after feedback for Exercise 4.

» GRAMMAR WORKSHEET UNIT 11

VOCABULARY Illnesses and injuries: verbs

1 Revise the illnesses and injuries vocabulary from page 64. Ask students to look at the verbs in the box and at the words 1–3. Ask which one is an adjective (*sick*). Decide as a class which verbs go with each of the words 1–3.

Answers

1 catch a cold, get a cold, have a cold
2 feel sick, get sick, be sick
3 break your leg, cut your leg, hurt your leg, injure your leg

2 Ask students to look at the example sentence and explain why *catch* is not used with *better* (it means to get an illness or a disease). Put students in pairs to decide which two answers fill each space. Ask them to compare their answers with another pair's. Check answers with the class. Explain that *hurt* has two meanings. It can mean the same as *injure*: to cause pain, as in *hurt your leg*; it also means to be or feel painful, as in *my throat hurts*.

Answers

1 B, C
2 A, C
3 A, B
4 A, C
5 A, C
6 B, C

55 3 Read the instructions. Tell students to read the conversations and complete them in pairs. Check understanding of *exhausted* (very tired). Play the recording for students to check their answers. Ask different students to read out the text sentence by sentence.

Answers

1 hurts
2 injured
3 broken
4 've got / have
5 feel
6 've got / have
7 caught

» AUDIOSCRIPT TB PAGE 270

4 Put students into pairs, A and B. Student A turns to page 123 and Student B turns to page 126. They read the instructions and the example. Students cannot say what is wrong with them. They can only mime and give one verbal hint. Their partner can only ask *Yes/ No* questions to find out the problem. Ask two strong students to act out Student A's situation. The class can help by suggesting questions to ask. Give students a few minutes to think of some health problems. Remind them that we use *my* / *your* when referring to parts of the body. Monitor and help as necessary.

Answers

Students' own answers

» VOCABULARY WORKSHEET UNIT 11

WRITING An article (1)

1 Ask students to look at the pictures and check understanding of *keep fit*. Put them into small groups to discuss the question. Invite different students to talk about a member of their group and ask the class to guess who it is. Write key words on the board.

Answers
Students' own answers

2 Students read the notice and discuss their ideas in pairs before feeding back to the class. Monitor and help as necessary. Ask them why they think sport is important and make a list of sports on the board, for example swimming, cycling, running, going to a gym, etc.

Answers
Students' own answers

3 Read the instructions. Set a short time limit for students to read the article and find out whether their own ideas are mentioned. Ask them if they have taken part in a triathlon or anything similar. Check understanding of any new words and expressions.

Answers
Students' own answers

4 Read the advice in the *Prepare to write* box. Students do the matching exercise. Ask them if the main article answers all the questions in the notice (*yes*).

Answers
1 B 2 C 3 A

5 Read the three possible titles for the article. Check understanding of *encourage* (*suggest someone does something you believe will be good for them*). Students re-read the article and choose the best title. Check the answer and ask students to explain why they rejected the other titles.

Answer
2 How to stay fit and healthy

6 Read the instructions and the notice. Check understanding of *avoid* (*to choose not to do something*). In pairs, students discuss their ideas and make notes before feeding back as a class. Monitor and help as necessary. Ask students for examples of unhealthy foods, for example hamburgers, crisps, drinks that contain a lot of sugar, and so on. Ask them what a healthy diet should include and if they think their diet is healthy. Finally, ask for suggestions of how to avoid unhealthy food.

Answers
Students' own answers

7 **B1 Preliminary for Schools Writing Part 2**
In this part, students are assessed on content, communicative achievement, organisation and language. Students can choose between writing an article, as in this task, or a story, of about 100 words. (See also Units 3 and 9.)

Read the advice and remind students that their article should have an introduction, a main part and a conclusion. They should answer the three questions and think of a good title. Tell students to avoid simply writing a list of healthy foods. For example, they could give reasons why these foods are healthy, and they could also include some foods which are unhealthy. Students write their article and check spelling and grammar. Invite some students to read their article to the class.

MIXED ABILITY

Help weaker students by asking them to think of a good title and an opening sentence. Give them sentence openers for each of the three points, for example *A healthy diet should include…*, *I think my diet is…*, *I'm going to / I'll try to…* Then they should think of a sentence to write as a conclusion.

Model answer
Eat well and stay well!
We all know that eating a lot of sweets and fast foods like crisps and burgers is bad for our health but it can be difficult to avoid them.
A healthy diet should include plenty of fruit and vegetables. We shouldn't eat processed food or drinks that contain a lot of sugar. I think my diet is quite healthy but I sometimes eat things that are not good for me. I'm going to eat an apple every day and I'll try not to eat snacks between meals.
If you want to stay healthy you can eat fast foods sometimes, but remember not every day!

COOLER

Ask students to mime different activities that help them keep fit, for example swimming, yoga, running, etc. Have a pile of cards ready with suggestions for students who cannot think of a healthy activity. Students take turns and the class guesses the activity.

WRITING An article (1)

1 What do you do to keep fit during the summer holidays?

2 Read the notice. What should your article include? What suggestions would you make?

You see the following notice in a magazine.

ARTICLES WANTED!

Doing sport is healthy, but routines can be hard to follow. Why is sport important? What sports are you going to do this holiday? How will you make sure you do them regularly?

Write an article answering these questions. We will publish the most interesting articles in our magazine.

3 Read the article that a student has written. (It is not in the correct order.) Does it include any of your suggestions?

A I find it's a good idea to have a goal, like a race, because a goal gives you a reason to do sports regularly.

B People know that doing sport is healthy, but they often say they don't have time to do it.

C Doing sports is a great way to keep fit. It's good for your heart and it makes your body strong and healthy. There's a triathlon in my town at the end of the holiday, and I'm going to compete in it! A triathlon is a race where you have to swim, then cycle, and then run. So this holiday I'm going to train for the triathlon. I'm going to train with a group of friends. That way we will be able to encourage each other to carry on.

4 Read the *Prepare to write* box. Match the parts of the article 1–3 below with paragraphs A–C in Exercise 3.

PREPARE TO WRITE

An article (1)

Organise your article into paragraphs:

1 Introduction
2 Main article: answer each question from the exam task
3 Conclusion

Then write a title that will help readers to understand the *whole* article.

5 Read the article in the correct order. Then choose the best title.

1 Encourage your friends
2 How to stay fit and healthy
3 You should do a triathlon

6 Read the notice. What should your article include? Make notes of your suggestions.

You see this notice in a health and fitness magazine.

ARTICLES WANTED!

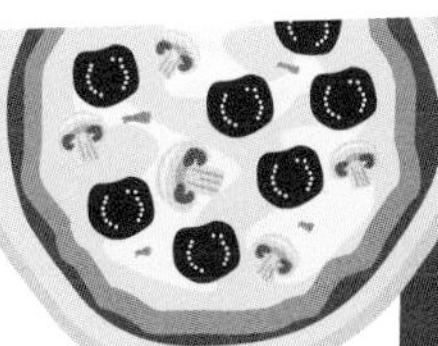

We know we should avoid fast food and sweets, but it can be hard to do. What should a healthy diet include? How healthy is your diet? How can you avoid unhealthy food?

Write an article answering these three questions. We will publish the most interesting articles in our magazine.

7 Write your article.

- Use your notes from Exercise 6.
- Follow the structure and instructions in the *Prepare to write* box.
- Use *be going to* and *will* to explain your decisions and predictions.
- Use language for giving advice: *It's a good idea to, Remember to, You should*
- Write about 100 words.
- Remember to check your spelling and grammar.

12 INCREDIBLE WILDLIFE

ABOUT YOU

What is your favourite animal? Why?
Which of these animals have you seen? Where?
Which of them can you see in your country?

VOCABULARY Animals

56 **1** Look at the quiz. Match the animals to the photos. Then listen and check.

EP

ant bat bee butterfly deer donkey eagle
fly fox frog mosquito shark wolf worm

57 **2** Do the quiz. Then listen and check.

3 Describe an animal without saying its name. Can your partner guess what it is?

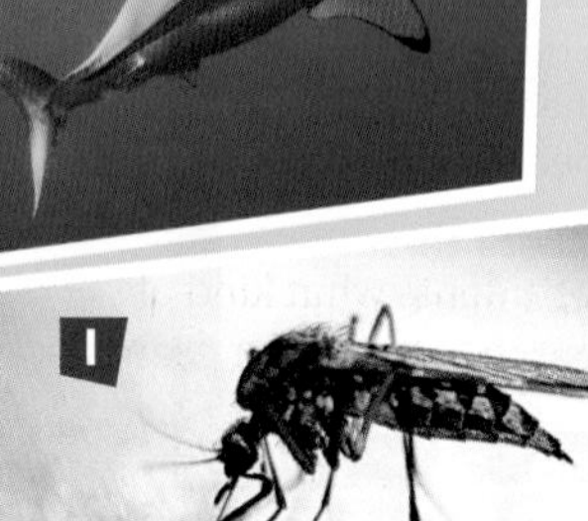

The CREATURES Quiz

Guess which animal ...

1 can grow mushrooms.
A ant B bee C parrot D worm

2 kills the most humans every year.
A mosquito B shark C snake D tiger

3 uses sound to find food.
A ant B bat C donkey D frog

4 loves the smell of toothpaste.
A bear B deer C fox D parrot

5 communicates by dancing.
A butterfly B bee C eagle D kangaroo

6 can't recognise itself in a mirror.
A dog B dolphin C elephant D monkey

7 doesn't drink much water.
A camel B donkey C giraffe D wolf

8 usually lives alone.
A bat B bee C fly D whale

9 is not frightened of lions.
A cat B dog C donkey D rat

10 can't fly.
A ant B bat C parrot D penguin

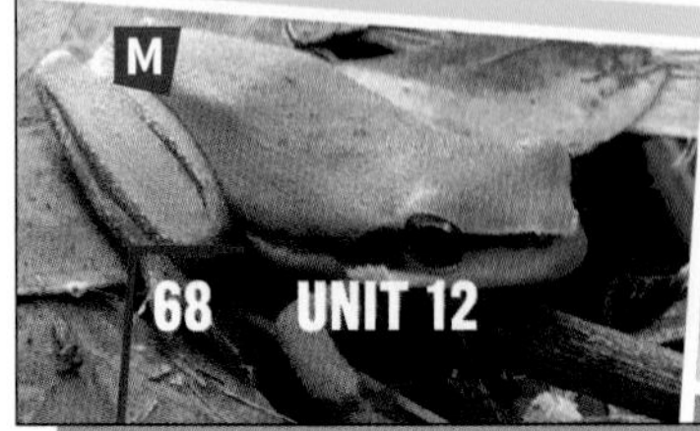

68 UNIT 12

12 INCREDIBLE WILDLIFE

Unit Overview

TOPIC	Animals, their characteristics and qualities
VOCABULARY	Animals
READING	Weird animals
GRAMMAR	Modals of probability
VOCABULARY	Adverbs of probability
LISTENING	A programme about animals at work
SPEAKING	Describing a photo (1)
EXAM TASKS	Speaking Part 2

Resources

GRAMMAR REFERENCE AND PRACTICE: SB page 149; TB page 245
WORKBOOK: pages 48–51
PHOTOCOPIABLE WORKSHEETS: Grammar worksheet Unit 12; Vocabulary worksheet Unit 12
TEST GENERATOR: Unit test 12

WARMER

Put students into small teams and tell them to write three headings: *mammal*, *bird* and *reptile* on a sheet of paper. Check understanding. Explain that you are going to read out a list of mammals, birds and reptiles and that they have to write them in the correct column. Tell them not to worry about spelling. Read out the animals, birds and reptiles from Exercise 3 which are not included in Exercise 1.

Answers

Mammals – tiger, bear, kangaroo, dog, dolphin, elephant, monkey, camel, giraffe, whale, cat, rat
Birds – parrot, penguin
Reptile – snake

ABOUT YOU

Students ask and answer the first question in pairs. Listen to feedback as a class. For the other questions, students point to the animals in the pictures and say where they saw them, for example *In a zoo*. It does not matter at this stage if they cannot name them. As a class, decide which animals can be seen in your country.

VOCABULARY Animals

1 Ask students to look at the words and drill pronunciation, paying attention to *mosquito* /mɒˈskiːtəʊ/, wolf /wʊlf/ and worm /wɜːm/. Ask them which four are insects (*ant, bee, fly, mosquito*). Put them in pairs to match each word to a photo. Play the recording for students to listen and confirm their answers. Check answers with the class.

56

Answers

The answers are recorded for students to listen and check.
A donkey B fox C eagle D wolf E ant F fly G shark
H worm I mosquito J bat K bee L deer M frog N butterfly

57

2 Divide students into teams and ask them to choose a name. Write the team names on the board. One member of each team writes the numbers 1–10 on a sheet of paper. Ask them to read the questions but not the options. Check understanding. Books closed. Read out each question and the four options twice. Give students 15 seconds to decide on their answer and write it down. Books open. Ask students to check they have written down the right letter, but tell them not to change their answers. Get students to swap their sheets with another team. Play the recording for them to check and mark the answers. The team with the most points is the winner.

Ask some follow-up questions and play the recording again – for example: 'What disease do mosquitoes carry? How many people does the disease kill each year? What should you do with your toothpaste if there are bears around? What do bees communicate when they dance? What's the difference between dogs and the other three animals? Why don't giraffes need to drink much water? Why don't donkeys run away from lions?' Ask students which facts surprised them and if they know any other surprising facts about any of these animals (e.g. penguins only live in the southern hemisphere). You could also open out the discussion and ask, for example, if there are any other birds that can't fly (*kiwi, ostrich*).

Answers

1 A 2 A 3 B 4 A 5 B 6 A 7 C 8 C 9 C 10 D

» AUDIOSCRIPT TB PAGES 270–271

3 Read the instructions and ask students what kind of information they can give about the animal, for example appearance, where it lives, what it eats, particular habits (such as it sleeps in winter, it hunts at night, and so on). Demonstrate the activity by describing one of the animals in the pictures for the class to guess. Say, 'This animal is a mammal but it can fly like a bird.' (*A bat.*) Students work in pairs, describing animals for their partner to guess. Stop them after a few minutes and invite different students to describe an animal for the class to guess.

Answers

Students' own answers

READING

BACKGROUND INFORMATION

There are around 8.7 million species on our planet. 86% of land species and 91% of marine species remain undiscovered. Bob May, a zoologist at the University of Oxford, says 'Knowing how many plants and animals there are on the planet is absolutely fundamental … Without this knowledge, we cannot even begin to answer questions such as how much diversity we can lose while still maintaining the ecosystem services that humanity depends upon.'

1 Read the title of the article and check understanding of *wild* (*not looked after by people, unlike a cow or a pet cat*) and *weird* /wɪəd/ (*very strange*). In pairs, students describe the animals in the photos. Listen to feedback as a class and write key vocabulary on the board. Encourage students to make guesses about what kinds of animals they are, for example *It's a kind of monkey, maybe it's a kind of fish*, etc. Answer questions 2 and 3 the same way, encouraging the students to make guesses. Accept all reasonable suggestions. Check understanding and pronunciation of *species* /ˈspiːʃiz/ and explain that the singular and plural forms are the same.

Answers

Students' own answers

2 Ask students to read the article quickly and see if their guesses in Exercise 1 were correct. Tell them not to worry about the three spaces or about any words they don't know, but to focus on the general meaning of each paragraph. In pairs, they match the animal names to the pictures. Check answers with the class.

Answers

1 pufferfish
2 golden poison dart frog
3 star-nosed mole
4 slow loris
5 lamprey
6 blobfish

3 Read the sentences and check understanding. Point out that in this context *funny* means *strange*, not something that makes you laugh. Set a short time limit for students to match the sentences to the spaces. They compare answers with a partner before checking as a class.

Answers

1 C 2 B 3 A

58 The Reading text is recorded for students to listen, read and check their answers.

4 Ask students to look at the highlighted words and try to work out their meanings from the context. Then tell them to match each word to its meaning. Check answers as a class and check understanding of any other new words in the text. Encourage other students to provide definitions if they can. New words may include *mole* (a small animal that lives underground), *tentacle* (long sensitive parts of an animal used for feeling, holding things, getting food and moving), *risk* (a possible danger) and *chef* (a professional cook).

Answers

1 harmless 2 poison 3 blind 4 pretty 5 the ground 6 shape

5 In pairs, students read and discuss the questions from what they can remember, without looking at the article. Then they read the article again, looking carefully for the specific information. Check answers as a class. Ask if any of the students would like to eat pufferfish.

Answers

1 Because the water pressure 1,000m underwater pushes its body into more of a fish shape.
2 Because it's a fish that drinks the blood of another fish.
3 To feel for and eat worms.
4 By biting them: it has poison in its mouth.
5 It has poison on its back.
6 Because it tastes delicious.

MIXED ABILITY

Help weaker students by reminding them to answer *Why?* questions with *because* and the two other questions by looking for which parts of these two animals are poisonous. They do not have to write complete sentences but just need to write the key words to demonstrate they have understood the text.

FAST FINISHERS

Ask fast finishers to write three sentences, a mix of correct and incorrect, taken from the text. They read them to the class who decide if they are correct or incorrect.

TALKING POINTS

Ask students to estimate how many different animals and plants there are in the world. Accept all and any guesses, however small or large! Ask students if they knew that we have only discovered about 20% of them and ask for suggestions as to why this is the case. In pairs or small groups, students discuss the second question. Monitor and help as necessary. Invite students to describe their animal or draw it on the board for the class to guess. Have a class vote on the most dangerous animal and the weirdest-looking one. Write key words on the board.

COOLER

Ask students to write anagrams of four animals found in this unit. They should write the letters in a jumbled order in a circle on a piece of paper. Demonstrate with an example on the board. In pairs or small groups they exchange papers with another student and solve the anagrams.

Weird animals

58

Animals > wild **weird** wonderful

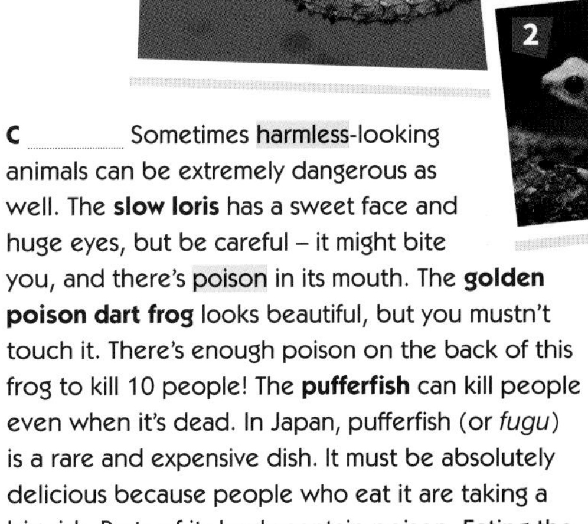

A ________ They think that at least 80% of animal and plant life on Earth could still be unknown. And of the known animals, there are some pretty unbelievable species.

B ________ The **blobfish** could be the world's ugliest animal. Out of the water, it has a face like an old man because its body is soft and full of fat. It looks more like a 'normal' fish 1,000m underwater because the water pressure pushes its body into shape. The **lamprey** looks like it might be something out of a horror film! Actually, it's a fish, and in this picture its mouth is open. To eat, the lamprey bites another fish and drinks the blood – like a vampire. As its name suggests, the **star-nosed mole** looks like it has a star on its face! In fact, those are tentacles around its nose. It lives under the ground and is almost blind. It moves slowly and uses its tentacles to feel for worms in the dark. Once its tentacles find a worm, it can eat it in 0.25 seconds!

C ________ Sometimes harmless-looking animals can be extremely dangerous as well. The **slow loris** has a sweet face and huge eyes, but be careful – it might bite you, and there's poison in its mouth. The **golden poison dart frog** looks beautiful, but you mustn't touch it. There's enough poison on the back of this frog to kill 10 people! The **pufferfish** can kill people even when it's dead. In Japan, pufferfish (or *fugu*) is a rare and expensive dish. It must be absolutely delicious because people who eat it are taking a big risk. Parts of its body contain poison. Eating the wrong part can cause death, and only special chefs are allowed to prepare it. Still, around 100 people die every year from eating *fugu*.

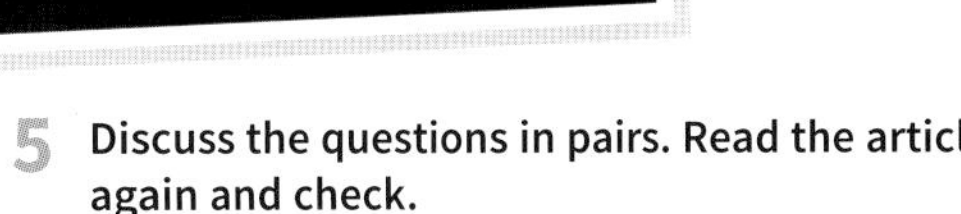

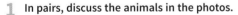

READING

1 In pairs, discuss the animals in the photos.

1 What kinds of animal are they?
2 Where do they live?
3 What is interesting about them?

2 Read the paragraphs quickly and check your answers to Exercise 1. Then match the bold animal names with the photos.

3 Match the sentences to spaces A–C.

1 What animals do you think are the most dangerous – a snake, a spider, perhaps a shark?
2 There are some very funny-looking animals out there.
3 Scientists discover hundreds of new and unusual animals every year.

4 Match the highlighted words in the article to the meanings.

1 not dangerous
2 a substance that can kill you if you eat it
3 unable to see
4 quite, but not completely or extremely
5 the surface of the earth
6 the physical form of something

5 Discuss the questions in pairs. Read the article again and check.

1 Why does the blobfish look less ugly 1,000 m underwater?
2 Why is the lamprey similar to a vampire?
3 Why does the star-nosed mole need tentacles?
4 How can the slow loris hurt people?
5 How can the golden poison dart frog kill people?
6 Why do people eat pufferfish?

TALKING POINTS

Why have we discovered only 20% of the world's animals and plants?
What other weird-looking or dangerous animals can you think of?

GRAMMAR Modals of probability

1 **Look at the photo and read the conversation. Then complete the rules with the bold verbs.**

A: This looks like it **might** be a plant.
B: Or it **could** be a stick.
A: No, wait. It **can't** be a stick. It's got eyes.
B: Yes, and antennas.
A: And it's got six legs, so it **must** be some sort of insect.

a We use ________ / ________ + infinitive to talk about things that are possible.
b We use ________ + infinitive to talk about things that we think are certain.
c We use ________ + infinitive to talk about things that are impossible.

» **GRAMMAR REFERENCE AND PRACTICE PAGE 149**

2 **Choose the correct option.**

1 That bird *could* / *can't* be a penguin. It flew onto the roof.
2 Our dog hasn't moved all day. He *could* / *can't* be ill.
3 Be careful. I can hear a mosquito. It *might* / *must* bite you.
4 Something is eating food from the bins. There aren't any wolves around here, but it *can't* / *could* be a fox.
5 It's big and it's got brown fur. It *can't* / *might* be a bear.
6 The cat's asleep. She *can't* / *must* be sleepy today.
7 It's got four legs, so it *could* / *can't* be a snake.
8 I can hear a voice speaking, but there's nobody here. It *must* / *can't* be that parrot!

59 **3** **Listen to sounds 1–8. In groups, discuss what the sounds *can't*, *might* or *must* be.**

4 **Look at the photos and discuss what animals they *can't*, *might* or *must* be.**

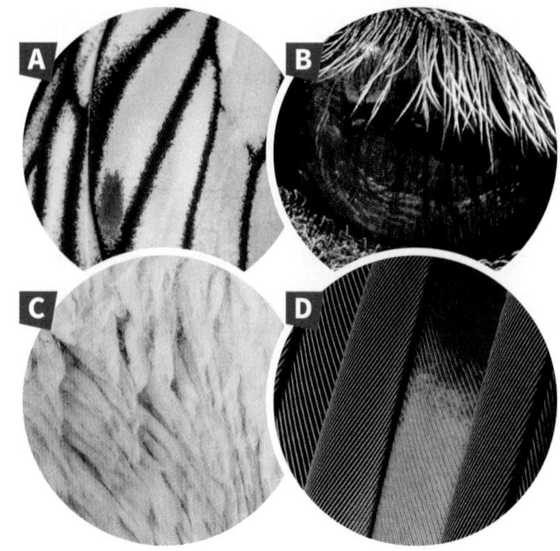

A: *It has some red on it, so it can't be a tiger.*
B: *It could be a bird …*
A: *Oh, I know. It must be a … !*

VOCABULARY Adverbs of probability

1 **Read the examples. Complete the diagram with the bold adverbs.**

EP

1 It has fur. It's **definitely** an animal of some kind.
2 It isn't in water, so it's **definitely not** a fish.
3 It's very small, so it's **probably** an insect.
4 I'm not sure what it is. **Perhaps** it's a bird of some kind.

NO ←→ YES

1 ________ *probably not* 2 ________ / *maybe* 3 ________ 4 ________

2 **Look at the photos and discuss what they might be. They both have a connection to this unit. Use adverbs of probability. Check your ideas on page 123.**

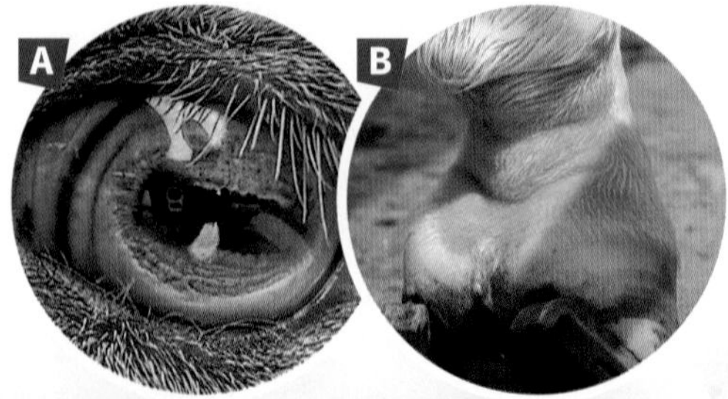

3 » **Work with a partner. Student A turn to page 123. Student B turn to page 127.**

GRAMMAR Modals of probability

WARMER

Wrap up a box in paper, write a name on it (for example your name or another teacher's) and put it on your desk. On the board, write *It can't be* ×, *it could / might be ??*, *it must be* ✓. Ask students to guess what's inside the package and who it is for. If they don't have many ideas, ask questions, for example 'Could it be a football? Who is it for?' Do not correct their use of modals of probability at this point.

1 Ask students to look at the photo and say what they think it might be (*a stick insect*). Ask two students to read out the conversation. Students complete the rules in pairs. Check answers with the class. Refer them back to the Warmer and the questions on the board.

Answers

a might / could
b must
c can't

» GRAMMAR REFERENCE AND PRACTICE ANSWER KEY TB PAGE 245

2 Put students in pairs and tell them to read the sentences carefully. They should refer to the rules in Exercise 1 to help them choose the correct option. Monitor and help as necessary. Ask each pair to compare answers with another pair before checking answers with the class.

Answers

1 can't 2 could 3 might 4 could 5 might 6 must 7 can't 8 must

FAST FINISHERS

Fast finishers choose two animals from pages 68 and 69 and write two sentences about each of them using *It must be a … because …* and *It can't be a … because …*

59 3 Write on the board: *It can't be… It could be… It might be… It must be*. Play the first sound. Ask students to make a suggestion for each of the options on the board and give a reason, if they can, for example *It can't be a bee, because a bee is too small. It could be a bear because it is loud! It might be an elephant. It must be a tiger because it sounds like a big cat*. Play the second sound. Students work in small groups to discuss the noise and make sentences using all four modals of probability. Encourage stronger students to give a reason if they can. Repeat the process with the other sounds.

Answers

1 a tiger
2 birds
3 a basketball game
4 an egg frying
5 heavy rain
6 a motorboat
7 a plane taking off
8 an audience clapping and cheering

4 Tell students to look at the photos and ask two students to read out the example conversation. Put students in new pairs to discuss the photos. Monitor and help as necessary. Give positive feedback for the correct use of modals of probability. Invite pairs to hold their conversations in front of the class. Take a vote on the most convincing suggestions.

Answers

Students' own answers
(A is part of a butterfly's wing. B is the eye of a donkey. C is a sheep. D is parrot feathers.)

» GRAMMAR WORKSHEET UNIT 12

VOCABULARY Adverbs of probability

1 Ask students to read the sentences and discuss the meaning of the words in bold with a partner. Copy the probability line on the board while they are working. Feed back as a class.

Tell students to look at the line on the board and ask them what the *yes* and *no* mean (*yes* – I'm certain it is; *no* – I'm certain it isn't). Invite different students to come to the board and write the adverbs in the correct place along the line. Point out word order: *perhaps* and *maybe* go at the beginning of a sentence; *probably* and *definitely* go in the same place as frequency adverbs.

Answers

1 definitely not 2 perhaps 3 probably 4 definitely

2 Ask students to describe the photos. Tell them that they are both related to the topic of the unit. Put students into pairs to make suggestions about the photos using the adverbs of probability. Monitor and help as necessary. Invite suggestions from the class, reminding students to use the adverbs of probability. They can check their ideas on page 123 to see if they were correct.

Answers

A the eye of a goat
B a horse's leg

3 Put students in pairs and label them A and B. Student A turns to page 123 and Student B to page 127. They read the instructions and the example. Give a couple of examples about yourself, for example 'I studied at … My father is from …', and ask students to react, using an adverb of probability. Tell them to write five true and five false sentences. Their partner has to guess which are true and which are false, using an adverb of probability. Ask some students to share their partner's sentences with the class.

Answers

Students' own answers

» VOCABULARY WORKSHEET UNIT 12

LISTENING

1 Write *Animals at work* on the board and elicit examples of animals which work with humans, for example dogs help the police. Set a short time limit for students to read the introduction. Check understanding of vocabulary, for example *wheelchair* and *army*. Students look at the photos and work in pairs to make suggestions about how rats and bees might help humans.

Answers
Students' own answers

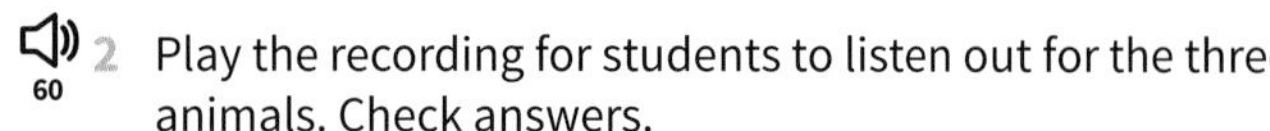

60 2 Play the recording for students to listen out for the three animals. Check answers.

Answers
They talk about dogs, rats and bees.

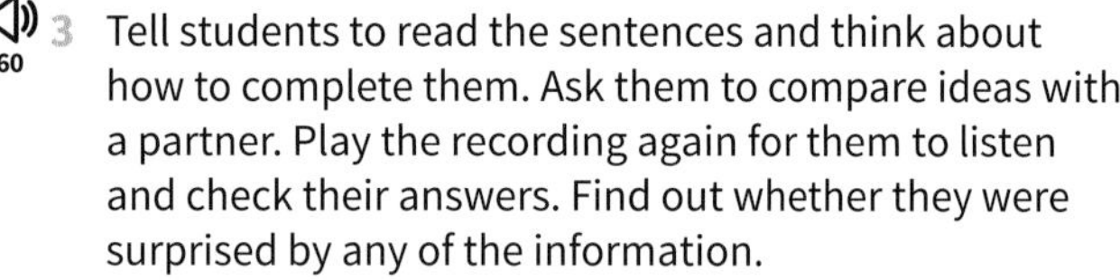

60 3 Tell students to read the sentences and think about how to complete them. Ask them to compare ideas with a partner. Play the recording again for them to listen and check their answers. Find out whether they were surprised by any of the information.

MIXED ABILITY
Pair weaker students with stronger students for this listening exercise. Encourage the weaker student to name the animal and the stronger student to explain how they know and which key words helped them.

Answers
1 Rats 2 Dogs 3 Bees 4 Rats 5 Dogs 6 Bees

» **AUDIOSCRIPT TB PAGE 271**

4 Put students into small groups. Read the questions and ensure they know who Donna and Riley are. Monitor and join in as they discuss the questions. Give positive feedback for interesting ideas. Then give each student in the group a number and ask all students with the same numbers to form a new group. Set a short time limit for them to share their ideas before holding a whole-class discussion.

Answers
Students' own answers

SPEAKING Describing a photo (1)

1 Remind students that we use the present continuous to say what is happening in a photo. Put them into pairs to describe what they can see and suggest how dogs might help people. Remind them to use modals and adverbs of probability. Invite them to share their ideas but do not confirm them at this point.

Answers
Students' own answers

61 2 Play the recording for students to listen and check, and ask if any of their ideas were mentioned.

Answers
Students' own answers

61 3 Tell students to read the phrases in the *Prepare to speak* box. Go through each one, and then ask students to complete the sentences. Sometimes more than one answer may be correct. Play the recording again for students to check their answers. Check answers as a class.

Answers
1 probably
2 left
3 Maybe / Perhaps
4 right
5 might
6 Perhaps / Maybe

» **AUDIOSCRIPT TB PAGE 271**

4 Monitor as students describe the photo in pairs, giving positive feedback when they use phrases from the *Prepare to speak* box. Invite different students to say a sentence about the photo using one of the phrases.

Answers
Students' own answers

5 **B1 Preliminary for Schools Speaking Part 2**

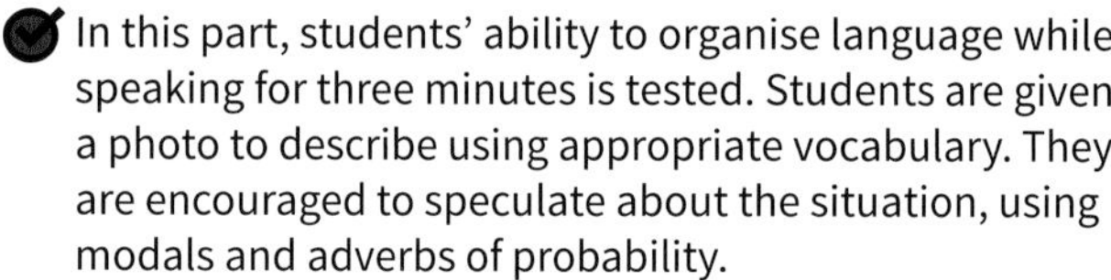

In this part, students' ability to organise language while speaking for three minutes is tested. Students are given a photo to describe using appropriate vocabulary. They are encouraged to speculate about the situation, using modals and adverbs of probability.

Students turn to page 124. Give them a few minutes to think about what they are going to say, but tell them not to write anything down. They take turns to describe the photo using phrases from the *Prepare to speak* box on page 71. Bring the class together and invite students to say one sentence each about the photo. Give positive feedback for use of phrases from the *Prepare to speak* box.

Answers
Students' own answers

COOLER
On the board, write *It can't be / It might be / It could be / It must be a … because …* Draw part of an animal on the board and ask students to guess what it is using the modals. Students then work in small groups taking turns to draw part of an animal and guess what it is. Monitor and help as necessary. You may need to supply extra words as the game is in progress, for example *claw*, *sharp teeth*, *tail*, *paw*, *whisker*, *trunk*, *wing*, *beak*, *hoof / hooves*, *fins*, *stripes*, *spots*, etc.

LISTENING

1 Read the TV guide and look at the photos. In pairs, discuss how the animals might help people.

ANIMALS at work

We're always hearing stories in the news about how we need to save the planet's wildlife. But sometimes humans need help too. In today's show we look at how clever creatures can help people to live normal lives – for example, people who are blind, or wheelchair users – as well as how animals help the emergency services and army to keep us safe.

60 **2 Listen to the show. Which three animals do they talk about?**

60 **3 Listen again. Complete the sentences with *Dogs*, *Rats* or *Bees*.**

1 ________ avoid a problem because they aren't as heavy as humans.
2 ________ can bring things to people.
3 ________ can help find dangerous chemicals.
4 ________ can help find bombs that are under the ground.
5 ________ can help with buying things.
6 ________ are cheaper to train than other animals.

4 Discuss the questions.

1 In what ways do you think Riley has improved Donna's life?
2 In what other ways can animals improve people's lives?
3 Is it fair to use animals to help us in dangerous situations? Why? / Why not?

SPEAKING Describing a photo (1)

1 Look at the photo. What do you think is happening?

61 **2 Listen to someone describing the photo and check your ideas.**

PREPARE TO SPEAK

Describing a photo (1)

Saying what you can see	Guessing what's happening
I can see …	Perhaps …
There's …	Maybe …
On the left/right, …	It's probably …
In the middle …	They might be …

61 **3 Read the *Prepare to speak* box. Then complete the sentences about the photo using words from the box. Listen again and check.**

1 The dog is ________ a rescue dog.
2 On the ________, one person is digging down into the snow.
3 ________ they're looking for someone.
4 The other person's on the ________.
5 He ________ be the dog's trainer.
6 ________ the dog has found the person.

4 Work with a partner. Take turns to describe the photo in Exercise 1. Use phrases from the *Prepare to speak* box.

5 » Work with a partner. Turn to page 124.

LIFE SKILLS SOCIAL RESPONSIBILITY

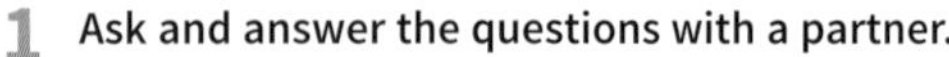

RESPECTING THE ENVIRONMENT

LIFE SKILLS

Respecting the environment

The environment is the natural world around us. It includes the land, water and air where plants and animals live. People also need the environment to live, so we must work together to protect and care for our natural home.

1 **Ask and answer the questions with a partner.**

1 How often do you use public transport?
2 Does your family recycle at home?
3 Do you like spending time in natural areas?

2 **Read the text quickly. What are the three Rs?**

Caring for our world

62

Many countries have programmes to care for the environment, but ordinary people can also help in everyday ways. For example, we can follow the three Rs: reduce, reuse and recycle. We can also care for natural areas and teach others about environmental protection to keep our world clean, beautiful and healthy.

Reduce, reuse, recycle

The first way to help the environment is to ***reduce*** any resources that you use. For example, you can turn off the water while brushing your teeth, and have a short shower instead of a long one.

Turning off lights and other electrical items when they aren't needed also saves energy. And eating less meat eat can help the environment too - it takes ten times more energy to produce beef compared with vegetables.

Perhaps the biggest change we can make is reducing how much plastic we use. Try to buy food that is not wrapped in plastic and buy a reusable bottle for water instead of buying water in plastic bottles.

We must also ***reuse*** things more often. For example, when we're going to go to the supermarket, we can take reusable bags. If we do that, we won't need plastic bags, which usually end up in the rubbish. Other things can also be reusable, such as batteries. If we use rechargeable batteries, we won't need new ones all the time. We can also sell or give away things that we don't want, like old clothes or books, so other people can reuse them.

The third rule is to ***recycle*** as much as possible. If we recycle paper and cardboard, we won't need to cut down so many trees. Many sorts of plastic, metal and glass are also recyclable. If we recycle those old materials, it will save resources and use less energy than creating new materials. Look out for recycling bins in your neighbourhood and separate materials correctly when you recycle.

Protect and teach

In addition to the three Rs, we need to care for natural spaces, such as parks. We should always throw paper, plastic and other litter into the correct rubbish bins. When we go camping, we mustn't feed any wild animals, such as ducks. We don't want them to follow people around for food. And if we make a fire to cook our food, we must be careful so we don't start any forest fires.

We can also inform other people about the need for environmental protection. We can make presentations at school and collect money for environmental organisations. Finally, we can celebrate special occasions about nature, such as Earth Day on 22nd April.

LIFE SKILLS

Learning Objectives

- The students learn about protecting the natural world around us.
- In the project stage, they plan an environmental campaign and make a presentation or video about it.

Vocabulary

inform litter ordinary resources sorts

BACKGROUND INFORMATION

The first Earth Day, also known as Mother Earth Day, was celebrated in the USA in 1970 as a protest against a big oil spill near the Californian coast in 1969. It is often considered to be the birth of the modern environmental movement. Across America, 20 million people participated in the first day of action and it led to the creation of the United States Environmental Protection Agency. The next Earth Day took place in 1990 and was a global event. Thanks to the internet, by the year 2000 the organisers were able to reach out to people in 184 countries around the world, with the actor Leonardo DiCaprio acting as host. In 2010, Earth Day became the largest non-religious observance in the world and now many countries celebrate it every year with the participation of more than a billion people. It is a day of action that can change human behaviour and influence policy makers.

WARMER

Write *The environment* on the board and then write the headings *1 My environment – school and home*, *2 Cities* (remind students they studied this in Unit 6), *3 The world*. In pairs, students think of at least two environmental problems for each heading, for example *1 – litter, too much food packaging, wasting food*, *2 – lack of green spaces, pollution from cars and factories*, *3 – over-fishing, cutting down forests*. Take feedback from the class and write key words on the board. Ask students if they can suggest solutions for any of the problems.

 **LIFE SKILLS**

Respecting the environment

Students read the text. Check understanding. Ask students if they agree and what might happen if we don't work together to protect and care for the environment.

1 Read the questions and check understanding of *recycle* (*convert waste products into things we can use again*). Students discuss them in pairs and then report back to the class. Have a class discussion on the benefits of using public transport and separating products for recycling. Find out what activities students like to do when they spend time in natural areas.

Answers

Students' own answers

2 Students look at the photos and say how they show ways of respecting the environment.

They read the title and the subheadings of the text and answer the question. Ask them to read the text quickly and explain what is meant by *reduce*, *reuse* and *recycle*. Tell them to ignore any new vocabulary at this stage.

Answers

The 3 Rs are reduce, reuse, recycle.

3 Students read the sentences and, in pairs, suggest one or two words to fill each space. They read the text more carefully to find the answers. Monitor and help as necessary. Check answers with the class.

Answers

1 (everyday) ways 2 reduce 3 reusable 4 energy 5 (rubbish) bins 6 forest fires

62 The Reading text is recorded for students to listen, read and check their answers.

MIXED ABILITY

Ask weaker students to read the incomplete sentences and predict where in the text they will find the information – in the introduction or in which of the paragraphs in the body of the text. Tell them to scan each paragraph and look for key words.

4 Students read the highlighted words in the text. They should look at the context to try to work out the meaning, including the sentences immediately before or after the highlighted words. Then they match the words to their definitions and compare answers with a partner. Check answers with the class.

Answers

1 sorts 2 inform 3 litter 4 ordinary 5 resources

FAST FINISHERS

Ask fast finishers to choose two of the words and write a sentence including each. They read out their sentences to the rest of the class, omitting the word. The class guesses the missing word.

63 5 Tell the students they are going to listen to a podcast called *Green Teens*. They will hear an interview with a person involved in environmental campaigns. Check pronunciation and understanding of *campaign* /kæmˈpeɪn/ (*a series of organised activities or events intended to achieve a result*). Ask them to predict what problems there might be in the park. Play the recording. Students compare answers with a partner. Check answers with the class and find out whether their predictions were correct. Ask students if there are similar problems in any parks or green spaces where they live.

Answers

The main problems are people leaving litter and people breaking trees.

63 6 Students read the sentences and, in pairs, say if they are true or false from what they remember of the recording. Play the recording again so they can check their answers and correct the false statements. Check answers with the class. Ask for extra information, saying, 'What does Hannah teach?' (*science*), 'How often does she do campaigns?' (*every year*), 'What else do people do in the park?' (*go camping*), 'Why, does Hannah think, are people breaking trees?' (*maybe for fun*), 'What kind of video are the students making?' (*a comedy*), 'What are the main characters called?' (*Treeboy and Greengirl*) and 'What else are the students doing?' (*collecting donations for the park to plant some new trees and put up signs saying* Don't drop litter *and* Please use the bins). Play the recording again if necessary.

Answers

1 false (She's a teacher.)
2 false (They haven't finished it yet.)
3 true
4 false (People are breaking the trees.)
5 true
6 false (They want to put it on the internet.)

>> **AUDIOSCRIPT TB PAGES 271–272**

7 Put students into pairs to read the words and to complete the sentences in the *Useful language* box. Check answers as a class. Ask for suggestions of any other questions and sentences students can use for brainstorming ideas.

Answers

1 could 2 think 3 possible 4 sure 5 else 6 idea

PROJECT ***An environmental campaign***

Ask students what they think about the campaign that Hannah is organising. Explain that they are going to work in groups to produce a similar campaign to solve a local environmental problem. They answer the first question individually. In groups, they share their ideas, brainstorm the second question and agree on an issue before deciding what sort of campaign would be fun to do. Monitor and help as necessary. Students should think about their skills as a group and how they could use them to create a campaign, for example taking photos, making videos, making a computer presentation, writing a persuasive text or slogan, and so on.

Advise them to think about the content and suggest a structure: introduction, explain the problem, suggest a solution and say how it would benefit the environment. They write the text for their presentation or video and review it for any mistakes with grammar and vocabulary. If they are making a presentation, they decide what to put on each slide. Remind the students that visual images have more impact than words, so there should not be too much text on each slide. They decide who is going to talk about each slide or each part of the video and have a practice run-through before sharing it with the class. Have a class discussion about the campaigns and vote on the best one.

PROJECT EXTENSION

Ask students to find out about Earth Day in their country: how it is celebrated, how many people and organisations take part, what kind of activities they do and what is planned for the next Earth Day. If it has never been celebrated or it is hard to find out information, they could explore how to get people interested and who they could contact to help organise an event.

COOLER

Ask students to write down four things they are going to do to help protect or respect the environment. They can use ideas from the unit or their own ideas but they must be realistic and practical. Invite volunteers to read out their ideas to the class.

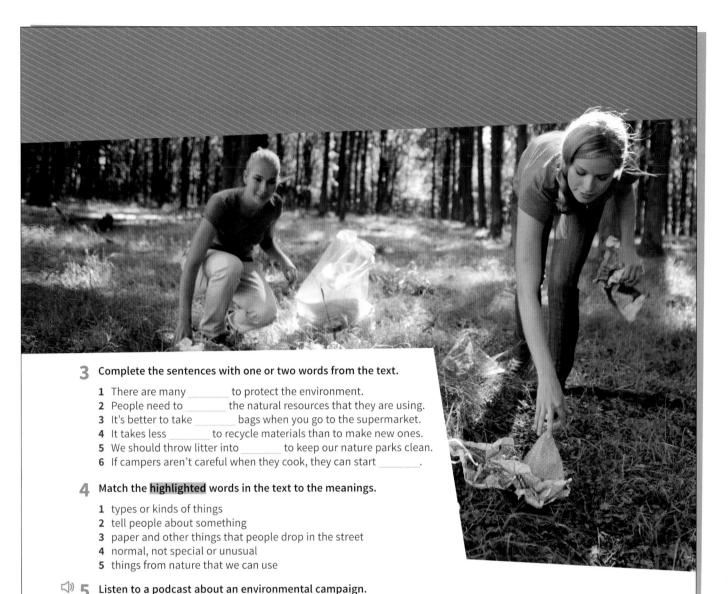

3 Complete the sentences with one or two words from the text.

1 There are many ________ to protect the environment.
2 People need to ________ the natural resources that they are using.
3 It's better to take ________ bags when you go to the supermarket.
4 It takes less ________ to recycle materials than to make new ones.
5 We should throw litter into ________ to keep our nature parks clean.
6 If campers aren't careful when they cook, they can start ________.

4 Match the highlighted words in the text to the meanings.

1 types or kinds of things
2 tell people about something
3 paper and other things that people drop in the street
4 normal, not special or unusual
5 things from nature that we can use

5 Listen to a podcast about an environmental campaign. What are the two main problems in the park?

63

6 Listen again. Are the sentences true or false?

63

1 Hannah works for an organisation that protects the environment.
2 The students have finished making their video.
3 Lots of young people go hiking in the nature park.
4 Some people are burning the trees in the park.
5 The main characters of the film are superheroes.
6 They're only going to show the film at school.

7 Complete the *Useful language* phrases with the words in the box.

could else idea possible
sure think

USEFUL LANGUAGE

Brainstorming ideas

1 I think we ________ make a poster.
2 What do you ________ we should do?
3 Do you think that's ________?
4 I'm not ________ about that.
5 What ________ can we do?
6 That's a great ________.

PROJECT *An environmental campaign*

Work in groups. Brainstorm ideas for an environmental campaign and then make a presentation or video. Use the questions below to help you think.

- What environmental topics interest you?
- Are there any environmental issues in your area?
- Do the people in your area recycle enough?
- What sorts of campaign would be fun to do?
- Are you good at taking photos or making videos?
- Could you create a computer presentation?

Share your presentation or video with the class. Then vote on the best idea.

REVIEW 3 UNITS 9–12

VOCABULARY

1 Complete the crossword.

Across

1 keep money until you have enough to buy something (4, 2)
4 You might do this to something when you don't want it any more. (4, 2, 4)
5 the place where you pay in a supermarket (8)
8 something that is cheaper for a period of time (7, 5)
9 You might do this when you buy something and then decide you don't like it. (4, 2, 4)

Down

2 the amount of money something costs (5)
3 a place where you put your money to keep it safe (4, 7)
6 a piece of paper that a shop assistant gives you when you buy something (7)
7 the money you get back at the 5 (6)

2 Match four words in the box to each topic.

bitter	chin	cough	cut	deer
flu	forehead	fresh	mosquitoes	
raw	shoulder	sour	stomach ache	
toe	eagles	wolves		

1 Describing food and taste: _____, _____, _____, _____
2 The body: _____, _____, _____, _____
3 Health: _____, _____, _____, _____
4 Animals: _____, _____, _____, _____

3 Complete the sentences with the words in Exercise 2. Use two words from each topic.

1 I've had a _____ for over a week. It's really making my throat sore.
2 This chocolate isn't very nice. It's too _____.
3 Unlike most other birds, female _____ are larger than the males.
4 Can you feel my _____? I think I've got a temperature.
5 _____ are the most dangerous insects in the world.
6 I don't buy fruit here. It isn't _____ enough.
7 You haven't got a cold. You've caught _____.
8 I was carrying a heavy bag today and now my _____ really hurts.

GRAMMAR

1 Complete the conversations. Use the past simple or present perfect form of the verbs.

1 **A:** _____ you ever _____ (see) a shark?
B: No, I haven't. But last year I _____ (swim) with dolphins on holiday.
2 **A:** How long _____ Ruth _____ (have) stomach ache?
B: It started yesterday. She _____ (not eat) anything since then.
3 **A:** We _____ (go) to a Japanese restaurant last weekend.
B: I _____ never _____ (try) Japanese food.
4 **A:** James and Tom _____ (be) over 20 minutes late this morning.
B: _____ they ever _____ (arrive) at school on time? They're always late!

2 Choose the correct verbs.

1 **A:** Don't buy those trainers now. I think they *'ll / 're going to* have lots of special offers soon.
B: I know, but mine are really uncomfortable. I *'ll / 'm going to* buy these ones now.
2 **A:** Is Paul interested in coming? Tell him we *'ll / 're going to* leave in ten minutes.
B: I don't think he *'ll / 's going to* want to watch that film. But I'll ask.
3 **A:** Our teacher *will / is going to* have a baby in June. She told us today.
B: Really? That's nice news. I *'ll / 'm going to* send her a card.
4 **A:** I *'ll / 'm going to* take my new jacket back to the shop today. It's too small.
B: I *'ll / 'm going to* come with you! I've got nothing else to do today.

REVIEW 3 UNITS 9–12

Overview

VOCABULARY	Money and shopping; Easily confused words: *pay, charge, cost*; Food and drink adjectives; *look, taste, smell*; Body and health; Illnesses and injuries: verbs; Animals; Adverbs of probability
GRAMMAR	Present perfect; The past participle of *go*: *been* and *gone*; Present perfect and past simple; *How long?* and *for/since*; *will* and *be going to*; Modals of probability
EXAM TASKS	Reading Part 5

Resources

PHOTOCOPIABLE WORKSHEETS: Grammar worksheets Units 9–12; Vocabulary worksheets Units 9–12; Review Game Units 9–12; Literature worksheet; Speaking worksheet; Writing worksheet

WARMER

Write the topics *money and shopping*, *illnesses*, *body* and *animals* on the board. Divide the class into four groups and assign each group a topic. Give them two minutes to write as many words connected with their topic as they can. Then ask each group in turn, except the group who wrote the list, to call out a word for the first topic. If the group responsible for that topic has the word on their list, they score a point. If not, the other group scores a point. Repeat until there are no more suggestions for that topic. Repeat with the other three topics. The group with the most points is the winner.

VOCABULARY

1 Read the instructions and tell the students that all the words are connected with money and shopping. Set a time limit for them to complete the crossword. They compare answers with a partner. Review answers with the class. Check pronunciation of *receipt* /rɪˈsiːt/.

Answers

Across
1 save up 4 give it away 5 checkout 8 special offer 9 take it back
Down
2 price 3 bank account 6 receipt 7 change

2 Students read the words in the box and look at the topics. They add the words to the correct topic and compare answers with a partner. Check answers with the class. Ask for the singular of *wolves* (*wolf*) and whether *deer* is singular or plural (*both – it's an irregular plural, like* sheep). Check pronunciation, including *sour* /saʊə/, *raw* /rɔː/, *cough* /kɒf/, *stomach ache* /ˈstʌmək ˌeɪk/, *mosquito* /mɒˈskiːtəʊ/ and *wolves* /wʊlvz/.

Answers

1 bitter, fresh, raw, sour
2 chin, forehead, shoulder, toe
3 cough, cut, flu, stomach ache
4 deer, mosquitoes, eagles, wolves

3 Tell students to read the sentences ignoring the spaces. Then they complete the sentences using words in Exercise 2 and compare answers with a partner. Check answers with the class. Check understanding of the words in Exercise 2 not used in this exercise by asking fast finishers to read out their sentences.

Answers

1 cough 2 bitter 3 eagles 4 forehead 5 Mosquitoes 6 fresh 7 flu 8 shoulder

FAST FINISHERS

Ask fast finishers to write two sentences using the words in Exercise 2 that they have not used in this exercise.

GRAMMAR

1 Elicit the forms of the past simple and present perfect, including negative and question forms. In pairs, students test each other on the past simple and past participle of the irregular verbs in the exercise: *see – saw, seen*; *swim – swam, swum*; *have – had, had*; *eat – ate, eaten*; *go – went, gone / been*; *be – was / were, been*. Check pronunciation of *arrived* /əˈraɪvd/ and *tried* /traɪd/. Give students a few minutes to revise the use of the past simple and the present perfect tenses in the Grammar reference for Unit 10 on page 147. Then students complete the conversations and compare answers with a partner. Review answers as a class and ask stronger students to explain the tense use if there are any problems.

Answers

1 Have, seen, swam
2 has, had, hasn't eaten
3 went, 've, tried
4 were, Have, arrived

MIXED ABILITY

Support weaker students by allowing them to check the Grammar reference for Unit 10 on page 147 while they are doing the exercise.

CONTINUED ON PAGE 146

2 Elicit the forms of the future with *will* and the future with *be going to*, including negative and question forms. Elicit the uses of each form and refer students to the Grammar reference section for Unit 11 on page 148. Write the uses on the board: *will* – general predictions about the future, decisions made while we are speaking; *going to* – intentions, predictions based on something we can see or know. Ask for an example sentence for each use. Students complete the exercise and compare answers with a partner. Check answers with the class.

Answers
1 'll, 'm going to
2 're going to, 'll
3 is going to, 'll
4 'm going to, 'll

3 On the board write *I'm sure it's true* ✓ *Perhaps it's true ? I'm sure it isn't true* ×. Ask students to rewrite the sentences using the modal verbs *must*, *could / might* and *can't*. (*It must be true. It could / might be true. It can't be true.*) Explain that they are going to do the same thing in the exercise, using the verb in brackets. They complete the exercise and compare answers with a partner. Check answers with the class.

Answers
1 It might be broken.
2 It can't be fresh.
3 He could have a cold.
4 He must know your sister.
5 It might be a rat.

4 Put students into pairs to complete this exercise. Tell them to read the sentences carefully and think about which grammar rule they need to apply. If they disagree with their partner about the correct option, encourage them to justify their choices. Review answers as a class and ask stronger students to explain the grammar rules.

Answers
1 'm going
2 have I
3 might
4 for

5 Tell students that the mistakes can all be found in the verb forms and ask them to underline all the verbs. They compare with a partner and check that they have identified all of them. They complete the exercise in pairs. They should agree about the mistake and how to correct it and then rewrite the sentences correctly. Check answers with the class and, if necessary, ask stronger students to explain the mistakes.

Answers
1 This change **can't** be correct.
2 We**'ve been** friends since I was six.
3 I think **you'll** like it when you see it.
4 **Have you** heard about the concert?

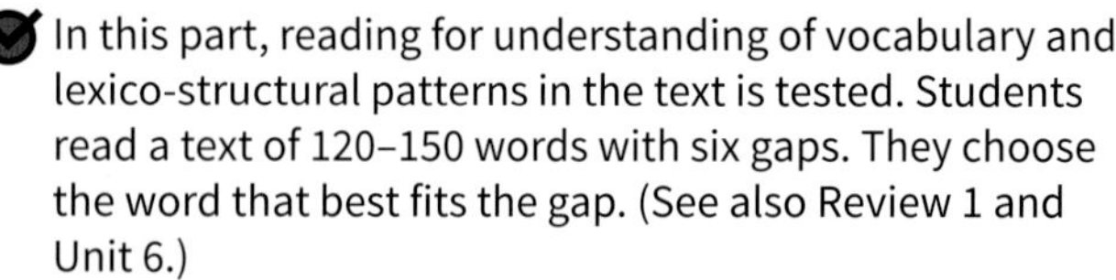

6 **B1 Preliminary for Schools Reading Part 5**

In this part, reading for understanding of vocabulary and lexico-structural patterns in the text is tested. Students read a text of 120–150 words with six gaps. They choose the word that best fits the gap. (See also Review 1 and Unit 6.)

Tell students to read the text, ignoring the missing words. Ask for a quick summary of what it is about (*foods you should eat when you're ill*). Ask students to look at each gap, say which part of speech would fit and suggest a possible answer. Accept all reasonable suggestions. While students complete the exercise, support and give help where necessary. They compare answers with a partner. Check answers with the class. Use this as an opportunity to do some vocabulary work on collocations and dependent prepositions, for example *to fall*, *feel* or *get* ***ill*** but *to catch* or *get* ***an illness***; *to complain* ***about/of*** but to *suffer* ***from***.

Answers
1 A 2 B 3 D 4 C 5 A 6 B

COOLER

Ask students to think about Units 9–12. Write some questions on the board: *Which activities did you enjoy? What was difficult / easy for you?* Ask students to write their answers. Discuss ways of learning collocations, such as using mind maps, writing example sentences, making vocabulary cards, using a highlighter pen to remind yourself of mistakes you make regularly, testing yourself once a week or, in pairs, testing each other, etc. Ask students which ideas they think are the most useful.

3 **Write a sentence that means the same as the second sentence. Use the verb in brackets.**

1 He can't move his arm. *Perhaps it's broken.* (might)
2 It tastes disgusting. *I'm sure it isn't fresh.* (can't)
3 He's got a cough and a sore throat. *Perhaps he has a cold.* (could)
4 My brother often goes to that café. *I'm sure he knows your sister.* (must)
5 It looks bigger than a mouse. *Perhaps it's a rat.* (might)

4 **Choose the correct words.**

1 This summer I *'ll go* / *'m going* to England with my friends.
2 Sorry, *I* / *have I* met you before?
3 I'm not sure at the moment, but I *can* / *might* be a bit late tomorrow.
4 I've known him *for* / *since* a long time.

5 **Correct the mistake in each sentence.**

1 This change mustn't be correct. You've given me more money than I gave you!
2 We are friends since I was six.
3 I think you like it when you see it.
4 You have heard about the concert?

6 **Read the text and choose the correct word for each space. For each question, choose A, B, C or D.**

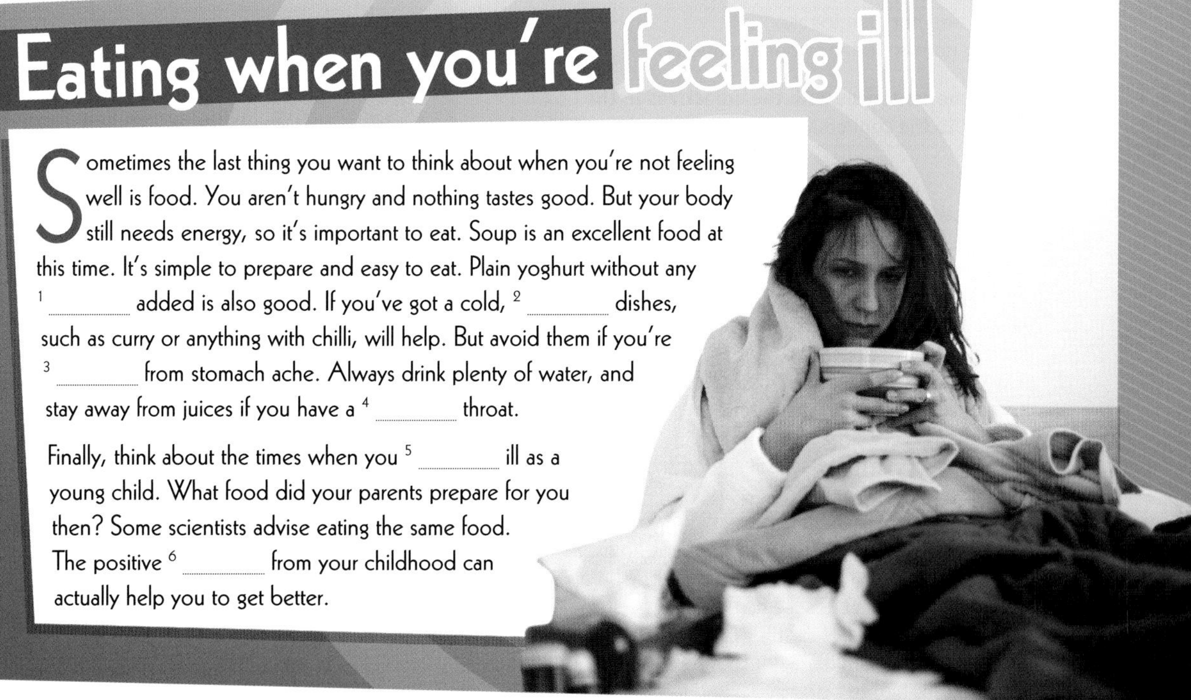

Eating when you're feeling ill

Sometimes the last thing you want to think about when you're not feeling well is food. You aren't hungry and nothing tastes good. But your body still needs energy, so it's important to eat. Soup is an excellent food at this time. It's simple to prepare and easy to eat. Plain yoghurt without any [1] ________ added is also good. If you've got a cold, [2] ________ dishes, such as curry or anything with chilli, will help. But avoid them if you're [3] ________ from stomach ache. Always drink plenty of water, and stay away from juices if you have a [4] ________ throat.

Finally, think about the times when you [5] ________ ill as a young child. What food did your parents prepare for you then? Some scientists advise eating the same food. The positive [6] ________ from your childhood can actually help you to get better.

	A	B	C	D
1	flavour	recipe	change	sour
2	juicy	spicy	raw	frozen
3	supporting	experiencing	complaining	suffering
4	cut	broken	sore	hurt
5	fell	went	had	caught
6	records	memories	rules	minds

13 MIXED FEELINGS

ABOUT YOU

09 **Watch the video and then answer the questions.**

Are you usually in a good mood?

What kind of things put you in a bad mood?

VOCABULARY Adjectives: moods and feelings

1 **Read the social media posts and choose the correct adjectives.**

2 **Match the adjectives you didn't choose in Exercise 1 with the definitions.**

a feeling or showing thanks
b unhappy because something was not as good as you hoped
c very surprised
d very tired
e worried and not able to relax
f showing no fear of dangerous situations

64 **3** **Complete the sentences with the adjectives in the box. Then listen to the conversations and check.**

amazed	brave	confused	disappointed
embarrassed	exhausted	grateful	hopeful
proud	relaxed	scared	stressed

1. Ben's mum feels really ________ because he got to the final of the tennis competition. Tom is ________ because he didn't win.
2. Vicky is feeling ________ because she had football training all afternoon. However, she agrees to go to the shop for her dad and he is very ________.
3. Freddy is ________ that Sadie designed the rugby poster. It looks so professional. But he's also ________. He doesn't understand why Sadie is interested in rugby.
4. Anna is feeling ________ because she's got an exam tomorrow. Harry thinks she'll work better if she's ________.
5. Lucas feels ________ because he made some stupid mistakes in his exam. He's still ________ that he has passed.
6. Dan is ________ to tell his sister that he broke her phone. His mum tells him to be ________ and tell her now.

4 **Complete the sentences. Then compare them with your partner's.**

1. I get embarrassed when …
2. On Friday afternoons, I usually feel …
3. At the weekend, I sometimes feel …
4. I get stressed when …
5. I feel a bit disappointed when …
6. I'm scared of …

Ellen Gardner

165 friends

Your friends' recent activity

7 minutes ago
Alfie Dale
is feeling [1] *scared / grateful.*
I'm at home by myself. Maybe this wasn't the night to watch a horror film!

22 minutes ago
Evie Turner
is feeling [2] *proud / brave.*
Incredible game, Brighton ♥ ! Next week Chelsea!

1 hour ago
Lily Gates
is feeling [3] *stressed / relaxed.*
Sunday night is film night in our house. I'm on the sofa with some snacks!

1 hour ago
Ollie Parks
is feeling [4] *confused / amazed.*
OK. Does anyone want to explain the ending of Sherlock to me? I didn't understand it at all!

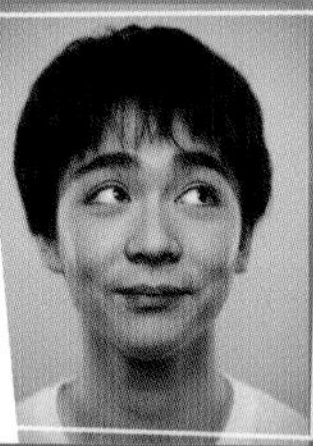

2 hours ago
Jack Forrest
is feeling [5] *exhausted / embarrassed.*
I thought that Sydney was the capital of Australia! Oops!

2 hours ago
Grace Buxton
is feeling [6] *disappointed / hopeful.*
I scored 92% in the practice maths test! I'm feeling pretty good about the real exam now.

13 MIXED FEELINGS

Unit Overview

TOPIC	Moods and feelings
VOCABULARY	Adjectives: moods and feelings
READING	The worst day of the week
GRAMMAR	*just*, *already* and *yet*
VOCABULARY	Adjectives: *-ed* or *-ing*
WRITING	An article (2)
EXAM TASKS	Reading Part 4; Writing Part 2

Resources

GRAMMAR REFERENCE AND PRACTICE: SB page 150; TB page 245
WORKBOOK: pages 52–55
VIDEO AND VIDEO WORKSHEET: Moods and feelings
PHOTOCOPIABLE WORKSHEETS: Grammar worksheet Unit 13; Vocabulary worksheet Unit 13
TEST GENERATOR: Unit test 13

WARMER

Write *Feelings* on the board and elicit its meaning (*emotions*). Brainstorm a list of feelings as a class and write them on the board. Write *I feel … when …* and ask one or two students to complete the sentence using the feelings on the board. Next, students write two sentences on a piece of paper. Collect the pieces of paper and distribute them randomly among the students. Students take turns to read out the information and the class guess who wrote it. Ask them what they think the unit title means (*to be unsure of your feelings or opinions about something*).

ABOUT YOU

09 You can begin the class and introduce the topic of the unit by showing the video and asking students to complete the video worksheet. Then, read the questions in the *About you* box and students answer the questions. Write *Good mood* and *Bad mood* as headings on the board with faces to indicate *happy* and *sad*. Tell students to discuss the first question in pairs. Then ask for a show of hands to find out who is usually in a good mood and who is often in a bad mood. Ask students to work in small groups to discuss the things that put them in a bad mood or a good mood. Invite them to share their answers with the class. Write key words on the board.

VOCABULARY Adjectives: moods and feelings

1 Tell students to look at the text and say what kind of website it is (*social media*). Ask them if they use social media websites, what kind of information they share online and if they use emojis or adjectives to show their feelings. Ask students to look at the first comment and elicit how Alfie is feeling. They complete the exercise in pairs. Check answers.

Answers

1 scared 2 proud 3 relaxed 4 confused 5 embarrassed 6 hopeful

2 Read the instructions and the definitions. Students complete the exercise in pairs. Invite different students to read out each definition and say which adjective it matches.

Answers

a grateful b disappointed c amazed d exhausted e stressed f brave

64 3 Tell students to compare the list on the board from the Warmer to the adjectives in the box. Read the adjectives and check pronunciation, paying particular attention to *-ed* endings, for example *exhausted* /ɪɡˈzɔːstɪd/ and *stressed* /strest/. Ask students to read the sentences and check understanding. In pairs, they complete the exercise. They can only use each adjective once. Play the recording, pausing after each speaker for students to check their answers. Invite different students to read out the completed sentences. Point out that *scared* is followed by *of*.

Answers

1 proud, disappointed
2 exhausted, grateful
3 amazed, confused
4 stressed, relaxed
5 embarrassed, hopeful
6 scared, brave

» AUDIOSCRIPT TB PAGE 272

4 Read the sentence beginnings and ask students about the people in the recordings. Elicit why Lucas was embarrassed, Anna stressed, Tom disappointed and Dan scared. Invite suggestions from the class about when and why someone might feel embarrassed. Students complete the sentences, writing about themselves, and compare ideas with a partner. Monitor and join in with the discussions. In whole-class feedback, invite different students to tell the class something about their partner.

Answers

Students' own answers

FAST FINISHERS

Tell fast finishers to choose two more adjectives and write prompts as in Exercise 4 for their partner to complete. They can share their partner's answers with the class after feedback to Exercise 4.

READING

BACKGROUND INFORMATION

The first written use of the term *weekend* appeared in a British magazine in 1879. Sunday was the day of worship but, in 1908, the first five-day working week was introduced to allow Jewish workers to worship on Saturday, known as the Sabbath, in New England in the USA. In 1926, Henry Ford shut down his car factories on Saturday and Sunday but it was not until 1940 that the two-day weekend was adopted throughout the USA. Many Muslim countries used to consider Thursday and Friday as their weekend but some countries replaced this with Friday and Saturday, to allow for Friday prayers and to coincide more with international financial markets. Some countries with Muslim-majority or large Muslim populations, such as Indonesia, Lebanon, Turkey, Tunisia and Morocco, have a Saturday and Sunday weekend with a long midday break on Friday for prayers. In Israel, the weekend is Friday and Saturday. Brunei Darussalam is the only country that has two separate days off, Friday and Sunday.

1 Students read the title of the article and say which are the worst and best days of the week for them. Invite students to share their opinions and give reasons for their answers. Set a short time limit for students to read the article and see if their answers agree with the research.

Answers

The research says that Wednesday is the worst day of the week for most people, and Sunday is the happiest day of the week.

2 **B1 Preliminary for Schools Reading Part 4**

In this part, five sentences have been removed from the text and the students have to put them back in the correct place. In addition there are three distractor sentences, which are not needed. This part tests students' ability to read for gist and understand text structure. (See also Unit 4.)

Check understanding of the sentences A–H. Do the first item together. Ask students to read the first paragraph and decide on the correct option. Ask volunteers to tell you which option they chose. Tell them the correct option (*G*) and ask why it is correct (*The first paragraph talks about Monday, so the missing sentence probably continues with the same subject*). Ask students which paragraph talks about how the professors did their research (*2*) and which paragraph talks about the results of the research (*3*). Tell them to read the sentences and predict which are about doing research (*C, D, E*) and which are about the results (*A, B, F, H*). Explain that students should look at the sentences immediately before and after the gaps in order to make their choice. Students complete the exercise in pairs. Check answers with the class and, in each case, ask how students decided on the correct option.

Answers

1 G 2 D 3 C 4 A 5 F
Extra sentences: B, E, H

MIXED ABILITY

Pair weaker students with stronger students and monitor as they do the exercise. Ask them to identify meaning, related words and what the pronouns refer to.

65 The Reading text is recorded for students to listen, read and check their answers.

3 Ask students to look at the highlighted words in the text, including the *Comments* section, and guess their meanings from the context. They match the words to the definitions.

Answers

1 came up with
2 analysed
3 surprising
4 put off
5 dreadful
6 according to

TALKING POINTS

Put students into pairs to discuss one of the questions. Monitor and join in with the discussions, helping where necessary. Put pairs together to make groups of four (i.e. a pair who discussed each question). Ask them to share their ideas and opinions. Then ask the whole class to comment on both questions. Write key vocabulary on the board. Have a class vote on each of the questions.

COOLER

Give each student a day of the week and arrange them in groups of different days (if your class divides into seven, organise them this way; if not, smaller groups are fine). Ask students to talk about what they do on the day they were given, for example *On Saturdays I go to dance classes in the morning and visit my grandparents in the afternoon. I go out with my friends in the evening*. Monitor and help as they are working. Invite different students to tell the class about someone in their group.

The WORST day of the week

65

Ask someone who goes to school from Monday to Friday for the worst day of their week and many people will say Monday. On Mondays the fun of the weekend has just finished and the week has just begun. [1] ________

However, two maths professors in the USA have just completed research that tells us more about the worst day of our week. Peter Dodds and Christopher Danforth analysed 10 million sentences on social networking websites like Facebook and Twitter. [2] ________ Then, the professors came up with a system of scores for words, between 1 and 9. They gave positive words like 'hopeful' and 'relaxed' high scores. Negative words, like 'stressed' and 'exhausted', got low scores. [3] ________

Their results could change your life – or at least your week! According to the professors, Sunday is the happiest day of the week. [4] ________ Monday is actually the second happiest day of the week. People haven't forgotten about their weekends yet. And the worst day of the week for most people is ... Wednesday! [5] ________ As a result, their memory of the previous weekend has gone, and there are two more days before the next one.

The research found another surprising fact: people between 45 and 60 are the happiest people online, but the most miserable group is ... teenagers!

Comments

Ryan, *Cambridge*	Sunday evening is definitely the worst evening of my week. I always put off starting my homework until then and I have to work until midnight.
Omar, *Riyadh*	It's different here. Our schools are closed on Friday and Saturday. So I think my worst day is probably Tuesday.
Anna, *Kraków*	I agree with this research. I always feel dreadful on Wednesday mornings.

READING

1 **What's your worst day of the week? And the best? Read the article quickly and see if your answers agree with the research.**

2 **Read the article again. Five sentences have been removed from the text. For each space choose the correct sentence. There are three extra sentences which you do not need to use.**

- **A** On that day, people think and write about the fun things they did the day before – on Saturday.
- **B** That's why it's most people's favourite day.
- **C** Finally, they used these numbers to decide how happy people were on each day.
- **D** All of these included the phrase 'I feel' or 'I'm feeling'.
- **E** It was the result of four years' work.
- **F** Most people have already been at school or work for two days.
- **G** Everyone is back at school, or work, and the next weekend is in five days' time.
- **H** There is just one more day before the weekend.

3 **Match the highlighted words in the article to the meanings.**

1. thought of (an idea or plan)
2. examined the details of something carefully
3. not expected
4. decide to do something at a later time
5. terrible
6. as said by someone

TALKING POINTS

Would it be a good idea to have two separate days off every week, instead of a weekend? Why? / Why not?

What's your worst day of the week? Why?

GRAMMAR *just, already* and *yet*

1 Read the examples. Then complete the rules with *just, already* and *yet*.

1 On Mondays the week has just begun.
2 People haven't forgotten about their weekends yet.
3 Most people have already been at school or work for two days.
4 Have you finished your homework yet?

We often use *just, already* and *yet* with the present perfect to talk about recent actions.
a ______ means that something happened before now or sooner than expected.
b ______ means a short time ago.
c ______ means that the speaker expected something to happen before now.

2 Choose the correct words.

1 **A:** Have you told your parents *just* / *yet*?
B: No. I wasn't feeling brave enough last night.
2 **A:** I'm so proud of you. I've *already* / *yet* told everyone at my work.
B: Dad! I'm getting embarrassed!
3 **A:** You look relaxed.
B: Yes. I've *yet* / *just* been for a swim.
4 **A:** I'm confused about question 6.
B: Hold on! I haven't finished question 5 *yet* / *already.*

3 Look at the examples in Exercise 1 again and complete the rules.

We use [1] ______ and [2] ______ in positive sentences. They come after *have* and before the past participle.
We use [3] ______ in negative sentences and questions. It comes at the end of the sentence.

» **GRAMMAR REFERENCE AND PRACTICE PAGE 150**

4 Make sentences using the present perfect and *just, already* and *yet*.

1 We / hear / some amazing news. (just)
2 I / put off / my dentist's appointment once. I can't do it again. (already)
3 Ella isn't stressed! It's eleven o'clock and she / not / get up (yet)
4 Do I have to come? I / sit down and I'm absolutely exhausted. (just)
5 you / try / Jack's cake? (yet)
6 My phone was fully charged this morning and it / run out / of battery. (already)

5 Correct the mistake in each sentence.

1 We just see your advertisement.
2 I haven't already bought a new book.
3 Did I tell you about my holiday yet?
4 I already asked a friend of mine.
5 He just has moved to a new house.
6 I haven't been yet there.

6 Kate is getting ready for a party. Look at the picture. Say what Kate *has already done* and what she *hasn't done yet*. Use the words in the box.

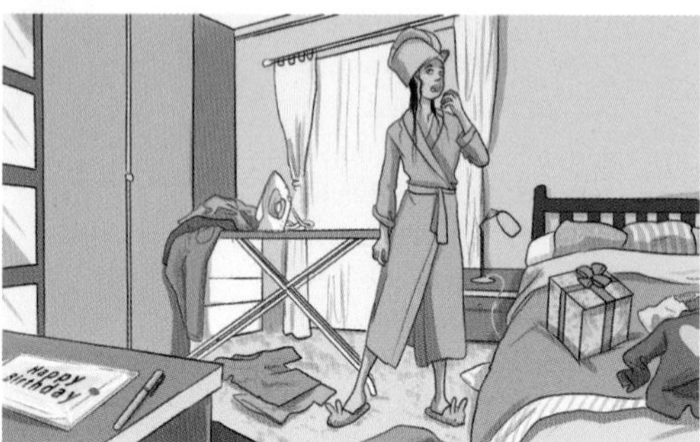
Happy Birthday

have a shower	write the birthday card
wrap the present	iron her clothes
tidy her room	wash her hair

VOCABULARY Adjectives: *-ed* or *-ing*

1 Look at the picture and the examples. Complete the rules with *-ed* or *-ing*.

EP

This story is really confusing.
Yes, I'm completely confused!

a Adjectives with ___ describe how a person feels about something.
b Adjectives with ___ describe the things, person, or situation that causes the person's feeling.

2 Complete the adjectives with *-ed* or *-ing*.

1 I'm tidying my room and I'm bor___.
2 Are you feeling relax___ after your holiday?
3 I want to go to bed. I've had a really tir___ day.
4 I think my brother's failed his driving test. He looks really disappoint___.
5 That's really annoy___. I've just bought that game and now it's 50% off.
6 When my mum sings, it's really embarrass___.

3 » Turn to page 123.

GRAMMAR *just, already* and *yet*

WARMER

Revise *-ed* adjectives by asking students to choose one and mime it for the others to guess. Demonstrate first with a volunteer and then put students into small groups to continue. One student writes down each adjective the group have guessed. The group with the longest list is the winner.

1 Ask students what they have done in the last half hour and what they have and haven't done today. Write their answers on the board, adding and underlining *just*, *already* and *yet*, for example *We've just had lunch. We've already had maths. We haven't had social sciences yet.*

Books open. Students read the sentences, taken from the Reading on page 77, and complete the rules. Check answers.

Answers

a already b just c yet

2 Put students into mixed ability pairs to read the conversations and decide which option is correct. Tell them to look back at Exercise 1 for help. Invite students to read the completed sentences, explaining their answers.

Answers

1 yet 2 already 3 just 4 yet

3 Students re-read the sentences in Exercise 1 and say if they are positive, negative or a question. Complete the rules as a class. Point out that *just* and *already* go in the same position as frequency adverbs like *usually* and *often*.

Answers

1 just / already
2 just / already
3 yet

» GRAMMAR REFERENCE AND PRACTICE ANSWER KEY TB PAGE 245

4 Elicit which tense is used with *just*, *already* and *yet* in Exercises 1 and 2 (*present perfect*) and how it is formed. Review past participles of the verbs in Exercise 4. Write the first prompt on the board and construct the sentence as a class. Students complete the exercise in pairs, paying attention to the rules. Monitor and help as necessary. Check answers with the class.

Answers

1 We've just heard some amazing news.
2 I've already put off my dentist's appointment once.
3 It's eleven o'clock and she hasn't got up yet.
4 I've just sat down and I'm absolutely exhausted.
5 Have you tried Jack's cake yet?
6 My phone was fully charged this morning and it's already run out of battery.

5 Explain that there is one mistake in each sentence. Do the first item together. In pairs, students complete the exercise. Check answers and make sure students understand the mistakes, which are mainly tense use or word order. Accept both corrections for sentence 2.

Answers

1 We**'ve just seen** your advertisement.
2 I **haven't** bought a new book **yet**. / **I've already** bought a new book.
3 **Have I told** you about my holiday yet?
4 I**'ve already** asked a friend of mine.
5 He**'s just** moved to a new house.
6 I haven't been **there yet**.

6 Ask students to imagine they're going to a birthday party and ask them what they might need to do before they go, for example choose their clothes, buy a present, etc. Students read the words in the box and compare them with their ideas. Read the instructions. Students put a ✓ next to the things Kate has already done and a × next to the things she hasn't done yet. They have 30 seconds to memorise the picture and the actions. Students then work in pairs to write six sentences about Kate using *already* and *yet*. Monitor and help as necessary. Check answers.

Answers

She's already had a shower.
She hasn't written the birthday card yet.
She's already wrapped the present.
She hasn't ironed her clothes yet.
She hasn't tidied her room yet.
She's already washed her hair.

» GRAMMAR WORKSHEET UNIT 13

VOCABULARY Adjectives: *-ed* or *-ing*

1 Students look at the image and read the speech bubbles. They read the rules and complete them. Check answers. Revise the *-ed* adjectives from the Vocabulary on page 76 and explain that most of them can have both endings. However, two are different: *stressed* – ~~*stressing*~~ *stressful*, *scared* – ~~*scearing*~~ *scary*.

Answers

a *-ed* b *-ing*

2 Students read the sentences and decide which form of the adjectives is needed to complete them. They compare answers with a partner. Check answers with the class. Elicit other adjectives which can have both endings, for example *interested / interesting, excited / exciting*.

Answers

1 bored 2 relaxed 3 tiring 4 disappointed 5 annoying 6 embarrassing

3 Direct students to turn to page 123. They read the sentences and decide which form of the adjectives is needed to complete them. They complete the exercise individually and add two more questions. They compare answers with a partner. Check answers and understanding. Finally, they ask and answer the questions.

Answers

1 tiring 2 disgusting 3 confusing 4 amazing 5 annoyed 6 relaxed 7 embarrassed 8 worrying

» VOCABULARY WORKSHEET UNIT 13

WRITING An article (2)

1 Students read the notice and say which is their favourite day of the week. Ask volunteers to read out the three questions.

Answers
Students' own answers

2 Students read the article quickly. Check understanding of vocabulary, for example *be into*, *challenging*. They re-read the article more carefully, write notes on the answers to the three questions and compare answers with a partner. Check answers.

Answers
Best day: Sunday
Activities: gets up late, looks online for project ideas, goes climbing, has dinner with relatives, watches a film
Feelings: excited, full of energy, relaxed

3 Ask students how the writer gets the reader's attention and makes the article interesting. Go through the *Prepare to write* box and ask students to find phrases used in the article. Check answers and ask if they can add any more phrases, for example *In my view*. Ask what adverbs the writer uses instead of *very / very much*: *absolutely*, *really*, *perfectly*.

Answers
Are you one of those people who looks forward to weekends?
I absolutely love Sundays.
When I wake up, I feel excited and full of energy.
I think it's a challenging sport, but it's also really exciting.
In my view, it's a perfectly relaxing end to my favourite day.

4 Students read the three notices and beginnings of articles. Check understanding. In pairs, students match the notices to the beginnings. Take feedback from the class and ask students to justify their answers.

Answers
1 A 2 C 3 B

5 Students read sentences a–f. Check understanding. In pairs, they match the sentences to notices 1–3 in Exercise 4 and compare answers with another pair. Check answers with the class and ask students to justify their choices. Next, ask students to identify the adverbs and adjectives in sentences a–f: *incredibly grateful*, *absolutely exhausted*, *toughest*. Ask them to identify time expressions: *by the weekend*, *as soon as*, *Thursdays*. Finally ask them to find phrases giving opinions: *I would say that*, *I don't think*, *For me*.

Answers
a 2 b 3 c 1 d 3 e 1 f 2

6 **B1 Preliminary for Schools Writing Part 2**

In this part, students are assessed on content, communicative achievement, organisation and language. Students can choose between writing an article, as in this task, or a story of about 100 words.

Ask students to choose which article they are going to write and group students who choose the same article together. They plan their article individually and then share their ideas with the group. Remind students to follow the advice in the *Prepare to write* box. They should also think of a good title. They write their article and check spelling and grammar. Monitor and help as necessary.

MIXED ABILITY

Help weaker students by asking them to think of a good title and an opening sentence. Suggest sentence openers for each of the three points. Then they should think of a sentence to write as a conclusion. Encourage them to use expressions and phrases from the examples given on this page.

FAST FINISHERS

Fast finishers should exchange articles and give positive feedback on ways to make the article more interesting for the reader.

Model answer
A busy week!
Do you have trouble getting to the end of the week? This might be because teenagers nowadays are busier than ever, according to the experts.
After a great weekend with my friends and family, I usually wake up feeling happy and full of energy on Monday mornings. But the feeling doesn't last long. By Wednesday I'm always tired and stressed because I haven't finished my homework yet. Sometimes I haven't even started it!
On Thursday I feel better because it's nearly the weekend, when I can play football and hang out with my friends. I think these things are important because all work and no play make life very boring!

COOLER

On the board write the word *embarrassed* but mix up the letters. In pairs, students make words of three or more letters. They cannot repeat any letters (except *e*, *r* and *s*, which appear twice). Tell them there is one word that they have learned in this unit which uses all the letters. The pair with the longest list is the winner. Give bonus points to any pair who has found the word with all the letters.

Possible answers
bad, bar, bead, bed, bee, bread, dare, dear, dream, mad, made, read, sad, same, sea, seed

WRITING An article (2)

1 **You see this notice on an English-language website. What's *your* favourite day of the week?**

ARTICLES WANTED!

Everyone has a favourite day of the week. What day of the week do you like the best? What do you do on this day that makes it your favourite day of the week? How do you feel?

Tell us what you think!

Write an article answering these questions and we will publish the most interesting on our site.

2 **Read the article. Write notes of the answers to the questions in the notice in Exercise 1.**

Friday? Saturday? No, it's …

Are you one of those people who looks forward to weekends? I am. And I absolutely love Sundays.

A typical Sunday starts around nine-thirty in my house. When I wake up, I feel excited and full of energy. I'm really into making stuff at the moment. I look online for ideas for projects.

My dad and I have just joined a climbing centre, so we go there on Sunday afternoons. I think it's a challenging sport, but it's also really exciting. Then, in the early evening, my aunt, uncle and cousins come round for a meal. After they leave, we watch a film together as a family. In my view, it's a perfectly relaxing end to my favourite day.

3 **Read the *Prepare to write* box. Find the phrases used in the article.**

PREPARE TO WRITE
An article (2)

Ask questions to get the reader's attention:

Do you … ?
Have you ever …?
Are you one of those people who …?
Can you imagine …?

Make your article interesting:

I **absolutely love** Sundays.
When I wake up, I feel excited and **full of energy.**
It's a **perfectly relaxing** end to my favourite day.

Give your own opinion:

I think … For me, … I would say that …

4 **Read these notices (1–3) and match them to the beginnings of students' articles (A–C).**

ARTICLES WANTED!

1 Bored!
We all get bored sometimes. It's part of life. What kinds of things do you find boring? Do you ever get bored in your spare time? Do you think being bored can ever be good for you?

2 An amazing person
We all know someone amazing. Perhaps it's an incredible musician, a talented sportsperson, or even a member of your family. Who do you think is amazing? Why do you think this? Have you ever told this person what you think about him or her?

3 Your week
According to experts, teenagers nowadays are busier than ever. Do you find your school week tiring? Which day is the worst? What do you do to relax out of school?

A Are you one of those people who jump out of bed in the morning, full of energy? I am definitely not.

B Can you imagine spending six hours in a car without anyone to talk to? I did this every day for a week last summer.

C Do you ever think about all the things your parents do for you? It's easy to forget sometimes.

5 **Which article 1–3 in Exercise 4 could each of these sentences be from? Match two possible sentences to each article.**

a I'm incredibly grateful to her for all her help and she knows that.
b By the weekend, I am absolutely exhausted.
c As soon as that show starts, I switch off the TV.
d I would say that Thursdays are my toughest days.
e I don't think people should have to go to museums until they're an adult.
f For me, this person is my mum.

6 **Write an article. Use one of the notices in Exercise 1 or 4.**

- Organise your article into paragraphs (see *Prepare to write* page 67).
- Use phrases from the *Prepare to write* box.
- Write about 100 words.
- Remember to check your spelling and grammar.

14 ON SCREEN

ABOUT YOU

What films have you seen recently?
What are your favourite TV shows?

A

B

C

THE HOUSE
Watch the housemates 24/7
on Channel45.tv

D

E

F

G

H

I

J

K

L

VOCABULARY TV and film

1 **Match the photos to the TV and film genres in the box.**

action thriller	animation	chat show	comedy
crime drama	documentary	horror film	period drama
reality show	science fiction	soap opera	the news

A – action thriller

66 **2** **Listen and check your answers to Exercise 1.**

3 **Are the genres in Exercise 1 a TV show, a film, or both?**

4 **Complete the definitions with genres from Exercise 1. Then, in pairs, write one-line definitions of the other seven genres.**

1 A ________ is a film or TV show that gives information about a subject.
2 A ________ is a TV drama series about people's daily lives.
3 A show or film about the future is called ________.
4 A ________ is a show or film with a story that takes place in the past.
5 A ________ is a TV show where someone interviews guests on various topics.

5 **In pairs, think of one example for each of the genres from Exercise 1.**

The *Toy Story* films are animations.

Yes, and so are the *Despicable Me* films.

6 **Complete the sentences with the genres that you like and dislike. Compare your opinions in groups.**

1 I'm a big fan of …
2 I can't stand …
3 I love …
4 I'm not a big fan of …
5 I'm really into …
6 I'm not into …

14 ON SCREEN

Unit Overview

TOPIC	Films and television
VOCABULARY	TV and film
READING	So you want to be in a film?
GRAMMAR	Relative clauses
VOCABULARY	Talking about films and shows
LISTENING	Six conversations about TV and film
SPEAKING	Reaching agreement
EXAM TASKS	Listening Part 2

Resources

GRAMMAR REFERENCE AND PRACTICE: SB page 151; TB pages 245–246
WORKBOOK: pages 56–59
PHOTOCOPIABLE WORKSHEETS: Grammar worksheet Unit 14; Vocabulary worksheet Unit 14
TEST GENERATOR: Unit test 14; Term test 2

WARMER

Check understanding of *on screen*. Ask students for some types of films and TV shows, for example *comedy*, *quiz shows*, and then put students into small groups to write a list. They share their lists. Write the categories on the board.

ABOUT YOU

Find out what films students have seen recently and whether they watched them online, on TV or at the cinema. They say whether they enjoyed them and give reasons. For the second question, students decide on their favourite TV show and then walk around the class to find out if anyone else has chosen the same one. Share feedback as a class and have a class vote on the most popular show.

VOCABULARY TV and film

1 Students look at the TV and film genres in the box and compare them with the list on the board. Check meaning and pronunciation of *genre* /ˈʒɒnrə/ (*category or type*). In pairs, students match the words to the photos. Check answers but do not confirm them at this point.

2 Play the recording for students to check their answers, pausing after each one. Check answers and play the recording again to practise pronunciation.

66

Answers

The answers are recorded for students to listen and check.
A action thriller B comedy C reality show D crime drama
E period drama F the news G documentary
H science fiction I animation J soap opera K chat show
L horror

3 In pairs, students decide whether the genres are TV shows, films or both. Check answers.

Answers

action thriller: film
animation: film and TV show
chat show: TV show
comedy: film and TV show
crime drama: film and TV show
documentary: TV show
horror: film
period drama: film and TV show
reality show: TV show
science fiction: film and TV show
soap opera: TV show
the news: TV show

4 Students read the definitions. Check understanding. They complete the exercise. In pairs, they compare answers and write a one-sentence definition of the remaining genres. Check answers and invite students to read out their definitions.

Answers

1 documentary 2 soap opera 3 science fiction
4 period drama 5 chat show

Possible answers

An action thriller is an adventure film with heroes and bad guys.
An animation is a computer-generated cartoon show or film, often for younger children.
A comedy is a funny film or show that makes you laugh.
A crime drama is a film or show with police chasing bad guys.
A horror is a very scary film.
A reality show is a show with real people in (sometimes crazy) situations.
The news is a show in which someone reads information about important recent events and shows video clips.

5 Ask two students to read the conversation. In pairs, students think of at least one example for all the genres in Exercise 1. Ask students to give their examples and ask the rest of the class if they agree with the classification.

Answers

Students' own answers

6 Check understanding of the sentence beginnings. Ask volunteers to complete each one. In groups of three, students write numbers 1–6 on separate pieces of paper which are shuffled and placed face down. Students pick up a number and complete the corresponding sentence, giving reasons. A spokesperson from each group tells the class about their group's likes and dislikes.

Answers

Students' own answers

READING

BACKGROUND INFORMATION

Sylvester Stallone was an extra in Woody Allen's 1971 film, *Bananas,* before he got his big break with *Rocky.* Action star Arnold Schwarzenegger was an extra in the films *Hercules in New York* and *The Long Goodbye. Twilight* star Kristen Stewart's first role was a non-speaking part in the Disney Channel film *The Thirteenth Year*. She was eight years old.

Heath Ledger's first role was as an extra in the Australian film *Clowning Around* at the age of 13. He went on to star in one of the biggest franchises ever, *The Dark Knight* series. A 17-year-old George Clooney started his film career as an extra in the 1978 TV miniseries *Centennial,* which was about a group of early US settlers.

1 Ask students if any of them have been on TV or in a film. Ask for suggestions about how they might get a role in a film, and widen the discussion to talk about people in general. Write key words on the board. Tell students to look at the photograph, the title and the subtitle of Kameron's blog.

Answers

Students' own answers

2 Set a time limit for students to read the text quickly and find out if any of their ideas were correct. Ask stronger students to summarise Kameron's three suggestions (*become an extra by joining a casting website, contacting your local film board, taking acting classes*).

3 In pairs, students find the words in the text and complete the exercise. They can check their answers with another pair. You can also ask students to try to work out the meanings of the words from the context. Check answers and ask students for definitions or synonyms (see possible answers in brackets).

Answers

1 warning (something that tells or shows you something bad may happen)
2 appear (to perform in a play, film, etc.)
3 hire (to begin to employ)
4 in charge (having control or responsibility)
5 part (role in a play, film etc.)
6 support (to help)

4 Students read the questions. Check understanding of *volunteer* (*a person who works for free*) and *film board* (*a local organisation that supports a city or region's film industry*). Students answer them according to what they remember. Then they read the text carefully to check their answers and complete the exercise. Encourage them to use their own words and not just copy the text word for word. They compare answers with a partner. Check answers with the class and check any new vocabulary, for example *main, hang out, cool, join*.

Answers

1 He was an extra.
2 They act in films but they don't have a main part.
3 Because they can meet interesting people and help a local film director.
4 A director is in charge of the filming and a producer is responsible for the team, including hiring actors.
5 They can tell you if any directors need extras near where you live.
6 Because producers look for students in drama schools.
7 Because you often have to wait around for long periods.

67 The Reading text is recorded for students to listen, read and check their answers.

MIXED ABILITY

Support weaker students by telling them that the most important thing is to find the answer in the text. They do not need to use their own words but can copy the text word for word if necessary.

FAST FINISHERS

Ask fast finishers to make a list of the skills and qualities they would list about themselves for a casting website if they wanted to be an extra. They read them out to the class, who can add more ideas.

TALKING POINTS

Read the questions, check understanding and put students into small groups to discuss them. Monitor and help as necessary. Bring the class together to discuss the answers and find out which films or shows students would most like to appear in.

COOLER

In pairs, students write a definition of a genre of film or TV show. They read it to the class, who have to guess the genre.

READING

1 Discuss how you think people can get their first role in a film.

2 Read the text quickly. Did you think of the three ways that Kameron suggests?

SO YOU WANT TO BE **IN A FILM?** 67

HERE'S HOW ANYONE CAN DO IT …

My best friend and I have just appeared in a film! It sounds unbelievable, but the truth is: it was easy. We were extras, and anyone can be an extra. Extras act in films or TV shows, but they aren't the main actors. They might be people who are chatting in a restaurant, walking down a street or playing sports. Sometimes, with smaller films, people are happy to work for free as extras. Although you don't get paid, you get to hang out with cool people, learn about film making and support a local director. Also, film companies provide great lunches!

BY KAMERON BADGERS

There are three ways to get hired as an extra:

1 JOIN A CASTING WEBSITE I found a national website which producers and directors look through to find extras. It was free to join. I just had to send a photo and fill in a questionnaire about my skills and abilities, for example sports I'm good at, musical instruments I can play, and whether I have a motorcycle licence. A director is the person who is in charge of filming. A producer is responsible for the team that makes the film. Producers are interested in anyone, from babies to grandparents. Hopefully, you'll get something cool like a part in a reality show or a period drama!

2 CONTACT YOUR LOCAL FILM BOARD Film boards help local companies with things like money and the contacts they need to make a film. They'll also send you information about directors who are filming in your area.

3 TAKE ACTING CLASSES Drama schools are often the first place where producers look.

FINALLY, A FEW WORDS OF WARNING!

- Be prepared for long waits: you'll spend more time doing nothing than appearing in a scene.
- Forget advertisements that say they'll make you famous. They probably won't!
- Remember: this isn't your 'big chance' to become a star. Extras are there to do a job, not because they hope to 'show what they can do'.

3 Complete the sentences with the correct form of the highlighted words from the text.

1 The teacher gave her a ________ about being late.
2 Do you want to ________ in a video that I'm making?
3 The football team is going to ________ a new coach.
4 I'd like to talk to the person who's ________ here.
5 My brother played the ________ of a rock singer in a short film.
6 It's hard preparing for exams, but my teachers  ________ me in various ways.

4 Read the text again and answer the questions.

1 How did Kameron appear in a film?
2 What do extras do?
3 Why do volunteers like helping smaller film productions?
4 What's the difference between a producer and a director?
5 How can film boards help people who want to start acting?
6 Why should you take acting classes?
7 Why might it be boring to be an extra?

TALKING POINTS

Would you like to be an extra or even an actor? Why? / Why not?

What films or shows would you like to appear in?

GRAMMAR Relative clauses

1 **Read the examples. Then complete the rules with the words in the box.**

1 They'll send you information about directors **who** are filming in your area.
2 I found a national website **which** producers and directors look through.
3 A producer is responsible for the team **that** makes a film.
4 Local drama schools are often the first place **where** producers look.
5 Forget advertisements **that** say they'll make you famous.

~~that~~	that	where	which	who

We use relative clauses to explain who, what or where we are talking about. We use:
a *that* and ______ to talk about things.
b ______ and ______ to talk about people.
c ______ talk about places.

» **GRAMMAR REFERENCE AND PRACTICE PAGE 151**

2 **Read the text and choose the correct words.**

Frankenstein is a classic science fiction story. There are a lot of film versions, but *Frankenstein* was originally a novel [1] *that / who* was published in 1818. Many people think Frankenstein is a monster, but in fact the main character is a crazy scientist [2] *which / who* is called Dr Frankenstein. He's got a laboratory [3] *where / who* he is trying to create a beautiful, new kind of creature. Eventually, he makes a monster [4] *that / where* is huge – and ugly. Frankenstein's monster has got yellow and green skin, and a face [5] *where / which* is very frightening.

Boris Karloff played the part of the monster in a 1931 film version of the book. Karloff's monster had a big, square head with a white face and a metal bolt [6] *where / that* went through its neck. This 1931 film created the image of Frankenstein's monster [7] *that / who* most modern audiences are familiar with.

3 **Complete the sentences with *who*, *which* or *where*. Then tick (✓) the ones where *that* is also correct.**

0 This is a film about a weak boy *who* turns into a strong man. ✓
1 The Font Café is a quiet place ______ you can study.
2 Have you ever met anyone ______ can speak five languages?
3 My mum has a new car ______ I love.
4 I met a girl at the youth club ______ knows you.
5 Are there any places around here ______ I can charge my phone?

4 **Connect the sentences with relative pronouns.**

0 Mary Shelley was a British author. She wrote *Frankenstein* in 1818.
Mary Shelley was a British author who wrote Frankenstein in 1818.
1 *Stranger Things* is a brilliant series. I started watching it last week.
2 The *Fantastic Beasts* series was filmed in New York. It stars Eddie Redmayne and Katherine Waterston.
3 There's a new bookshop in the mall. You can buy English-language DVDs there.
4 Jennifer Lawrence is a Hollywood star. She has appeared in lots of great films.
5 Steven Spielberg is an incredible director. He has won three Oscars.
6 Cortlandt Alley is a tiny street in New York. They have filmed dozens of film scenes there.

VOCABULARY Talking about films and shows

1 **Match the sentence halves.**

EP
1 A **character** is
2 A **clip** is
3 A **plot** is
4 A **review** is
5 A **series** is
6 A **soundtrack** is
7 A **trailer** is

a a small part taken from a longer film or show.
b a report with an opinion of a film or show.
c the story in a film or show.
d a short video advertising a new film or show.
e a part which an actor plays.
f the music used in a film or show.
g individual programmes that use the same characters in different situations.

2 **Complete the sentences with words from Exercise 1.**

1 Homer is my favourite ______ in *The Simpsons*.
2 There's a new comedy ______ on tonight that I haven't watched, but there are ______ of the funniest scenes online.
3 Nothing happens in this film. The ______ is really boring.
4 Have you read any ______ of the new Marvel film? – No, but I've watched a ______ for it. It looks amazing.
5 The ______ has some great songs on it.

3 **Discuss the questions.**

1 Who's your favourite film or TV show character?
2 Do you read reviews before you choose a film to watch? Where?

4 » **Work with a partner.** **Turn to page 123.**

GRAMMAR Relative clauses

WARMER

Write some questions on the board and underline the relative pronouns, for example *This is a man who was president of the USA from 2009 to 2017. It's a game that two teams of eleven people play using a ball. It's a place where you go to watch films*. Students guess the answers. In small groups, they write three more questions using relative pronouns for the class to guess.

1 Read the sentences adapted from the Reading on page 81. Explain that they contain examples of *relative clauses*, which give us more information about nouns – the person, place or thing which we are talking about. We use words called *relative pronouns* to introduce these clauses. Students complete the rules and then identify who, what or where the relative pronouns in the examples are referring to. Check answers.

Answers

a which b that, who c where

» **GRAMMAR REFERENCE AND PRACTICE ANSWER KEY TB PAGES 245–246**

2 Ask students what they know about Frankenstein and whether they have seen any of the films. Encourage students who have read the story or seen a film to tell the class about it. Students read the text quickly to see if their ideas are correct. In pairs, they select the correct options referring to the rules in Exercise 1. Ask students to take turns reading out a sentence. The class decides whether the options chosen are correct and why or why not.

Answers

1 that 2 who 3 where 4 that 5 which 6 that 7 that

3 Read the example and refer back to the rules in Exercise 1. Students complete the exercise and check answers with a partner. Check answers with the class.

Answers

1 where 2 who (✓) 3 which (✓) 4 who (✓) 5 where

4 Explain that relative clauses can be used to join sentences together to make writing flow better. Students read the example. Ask them who *She* refers to and which word replaces *She* when the sentences are connected. Ask them to read sentence 1, say what *it* refers to in the second sentence and which relative pronoun or pronouns they can use to replace *it* when they connect the sentences. They complete the exercise in mixed-ability pairs. Check answers and refer back to the Grammar reference and practice page if necessary.

Answers

1 *Stranger Things* is a brilliant series **that/which** I started watching last week.
2 The *Fantastic Beasts* series, **which** stars Eddie Redmayne and Katherine Waterston, was filmed in New York.
3 There's a new bookshop in the mall **where** you can buy English-language DVDs.
4 Jennifer Lawrence is a Hollywood star **that/who** has appeared in lots of great films.
5 Steven Spielberg is an incredible director **who/that** has won three Oscars.
6 Cortlandt Alley is a tiny street in New York **where** they have filmed dozens of film scenes.

MIXED ABILITY

To provide extra practice for weaker students, and consolidation for stronger students, write some incorrect sentences on the board, for example *This is the jacket what I bought last week (which / that). That's the place that I grew up (where). Messi is a footballer when plays for Barcelona (who / that). Paris is the city what I'm going in summer (where)*. Put students in mixed ability pairs to correct the sentences.

» **GRAMMAR WORKSHEET UNIT 14**

VOCABULARY Talking about films and shows

1 Students read the words and give a definition of any that they already know. Check pronunciation: *character* /ˈkærəktə/, *review* /rɪˈvjuː/, *series* /ˈsɪəriːz/. Students complete the exercise and compare answers with a partner. Check answers. Ask students if they can add any more words, including vocabulary from the Reading on page 81. Point out that *series* can be singular or plural, the form is the same.

Answers

1 e 2 a 3 c 4 b 5 g 6 f 7 d

2 Read the sentences and check understanding. Students complete the exercise and compare answers with a partner. Check answers.

Answers

1 character
2 series, clips
3 plot
4 reviews, trailer
5 soundtrack

FAST FINISHERS

Ask fast finishers to write two more sentences with spaces. They work in pairs, asking and answering each other's questions.

3 Use the sentences in Exercise 2 to lead into the discussion. Put students into small groups and tell them to appoint one person to take notes and present them to the class. Encourage students to give reasons for their answers. Monitor and help as necessary before sharing feedback. Write key words on the board.

Answers

Students' own answers

4 Read the instructions and the example on page 123. Ask students to identify any relative clauses. Ask two students to read out the example conversation. Give students a few minutes to write their sentences and then carry out the activity. Invite some students to read out their sentences to the class.

Answers

Students' own answers

» **VOCABULARY WORKSHEET UNIT 14**

LISTENING

68

1 Read the instructions and the list of genres. Play the recording. Students match the conversations to the genre and compare answers with a partner. Check answers with the class.

Answers

a comedy – 6
b documentary – 3
c horror – 1
d period drama (not needed)
e reality show – 2
f the news – 5
g science fiction – 4

» AUDIOSCRIPT TB PAGES 272–273

2 Before listening to the recording for a second time, ask students to read the questions and possible answers in Exercise 3. In pairs, they underline key words to help them when they listen again. Remind them to read the questions carefully as they contain relevant and helpful information. Check answers and understanding of vocabulary, for example *rather*, *behave*, *unlikely*, *creature*, *set off*, *showing*.

68

3 **B1 Preliminary for Schools Listening Part 2**

In this part, students' ability to listen for gist and to identify the speakers' attitudes, feelings and opinions is tested. Students listen to six short unrelated extracts, each followed by three-option multiple-choice items. They hear the recording twice.

Tell students that they are going to listen to the extracts again. They should listen for the key words and then choose the correct answer for each conversation. Play the recording again, pausing after each conversation for students to choose the answer. Check answers and then play the recording again to help students who have had difficulties understanding why the answer they chose was incorrect.

Answers

1 B 2 C 3 B 4 C 5 C 6 A

» AUDIOSCRIPT TB PAGES 272–273

SPEAKING Reaching agreement

1 Check understanding of *Reaching agreement*. Students read the outlines of the four films in the online film menu. Check understanding. Ask students to say which of the films they would most like to see and why.

Answers

Students' own answers

69

2 Read the instructions. Play the recording for students to find out which film the friends choose. They compare their answer with a partner before checking as a class.

Answer

Jerry's Vacation

69

3 Write *Reaching agreement* on the board. Elicit phrases which are used to agree with other people and write them on the board. Tell students to read the phrases in the *Prepare to speak* box and compare their ideas. Play the recording again for them to make a note of the phrases they hear. Check answers.

Answers

It looks …
It sounds …
because …
Let's decide.
I think we're both happy with that.
Yes, that's a good choice.

» AUDIOSCRIPT TB PAGE 273

4 Students look back at the films and shows in Exercise 1 on page 80. They decide on three that they would like to watch. They discuss their choices with a partner and reach agreement on which one to watch. Remind them to use the words and phrases from the *Prepare to speak* box and to listen carefully to their partner's choices and reasons. Monitor and help as necessary. Invite different pairs to repeat their conversation in front of the class. The class listens for the phrases from the *Prepare to speak* box.

Answers

Students' own answers

COOLER

In pairs, students think of a popular film, TV show or series. They write four sentences about it without mentioning its name. The first sentence should be the most difficult, the second a little easier, and so on. They find another pair and read out the first sentence. If the other students guess it, they get four points; if they guess it after the second sentence they get three points, and so on. The pairs then move on and find another pair. Each pair can change pairs several times.

LISTENING

68 **1** **Look at the list of film and TV genres. Listen to six conversations and write the conversation number next to the genre. (There is one genre that you don't need.)**

a ___ comedy
b ___ documentary
c _1_ horror film
d ___ period drama
e ___ reality show
f ___ the news
g ___ science fiction

2 **Read the questions and possible answers in the exam task in Exercise 3. Underline the key words.**

68 **3** **Listen to the six conversations again. For each question, choose the correct answer.**

1 You will hear two friends talking about a film. What do they say about it?
A The reviews of it are rather negative.
B They are too young to see it.
C Someone they know found it hard to follow.

2 You will hear two friends talking about reality shows.
What annoys the girl about reality TV stars?
A They get paid too much.
B They behave badly in public.
C They are boring to listen to.

3 You will hear two friends talking about taking part in a short film.
The boy is unlikely to appear in the film because
A he didn't see the information about it.
B he doesn't want to go to the meeting about it.
C the producer won't pay people who appear in it.

4 You will hear two friends talking about a sci-fi film they've seen.
They agree that
A the creature was scary.
B the film was too long.
C the soundtrack was excellent.

5 You will hear two friends talking about the news.
They agree that
A there's too much politics in the news.
B they should stop watching the news.
C their attitudes to the news have changed.

6 You will hear two friends talking about going to the cinema.
What does the boy suggest?
A asking someone to get their tickets
B reading about the film before they set off
C seeing the last showing of the day

SPEAKING Reaching agreement

1 **You are going to watch a film with friends. Look at the menu. Which one would you like to watch? Why?**

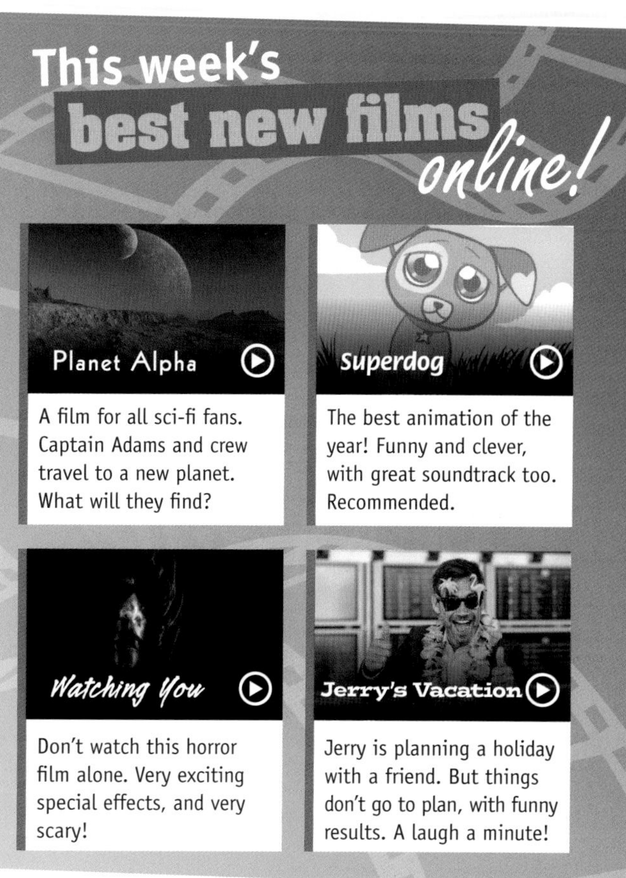

This week's
best new films
online!
Planet Alpha
A film for all sci-fi fans. Captain Adams and crew travel to a new planet. What will they find?
Superdog
The best animation of the year! Funny and clever, with great soundtrack too. Recommended.
Watching You
Don't watch this horror film alone. Very exciting special effects, and very scary!
Jerry's Vacation
Jerry is planning a holiday with a friend. But things don't go to plan, with funny results. A laugh a minute!

69 **2** **You will hear two friends talking about which film to watch. Which one do they choose?**

69 **3** **Read the *Prepare to speak* box. Then listen again. Which phrases do you hear?**

PREPARE TO SPEAK

Reaching agreement

Giving reasons	**Reaching agreement**
because …	Let's decide.
It's too …	Yes, that's a good choice.
It looks/sounds …	I think we're both happy with that.

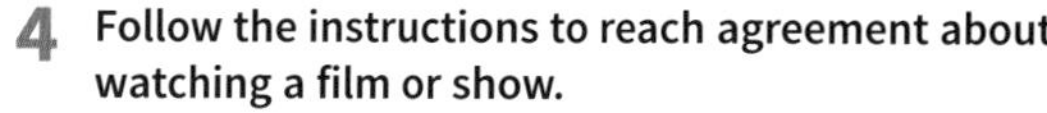

4 **Follow the instructions to reach agreement about watching a film or show.**

1 Look at the films and shows on page 80. In pairs, make a list of three that you would like to watch.
2 Discuss the films/shows, and reach agreement on which one to watch. Use phrases from the *Prepare to speak* box.

CULTURE

THE FILM INDUSTRY

1 **Ask and answer the questions with a partner.**

1 What's your favourite film?
2 What are some famous films from your country?
3 Who is the most famous film director from your country?

2 **Do the film quiz.**

FILM quiz
1 The Lumière brothers made the first ever film. What was the year?
A 1895 B 1905 C 1959
2 The first full-length film was The Story of the Kelly Gang. Where did they make it?
A the UK B the USA C Australia
3 The earliest films were silent. When was the first film with dialogue and music?
A 1927 B 1957 C 1987
4 Which famous fictional character has appeared in the most films?
A Mickey Mouse
B Sherlock Holmes
C James Bond
5 In which country do people go to the cinema most frequently?
A Iceland B the USA C Poland
MAJESTIC
84 CULTURE

70 **3** **Listen and check your answers.**

4 **Read the *World film facts* on page 85. Complete the sentences with the names of the countries.**

1 ________ makes the most films every year.
2 ________ has got the most cinema screens.
3 ________ celebrates the BAFTA awards.
4 ________ makes the most money in tickets.
5 ________ made Godzilla films popular.

5 **Answer the questions about the text.**

1 Which of the countries has the fewest screens?
2 Why do Hollywood studios make films in Canada?
3 What were Chinese films usually about in the past?
4 When did Japanese samurai films become popular?
5 Why are Bollywood films called *masala films*?
6 What type of film is *Sense and Sensibility*?

6 **Match the highlighted words in the text to the meanings.**

1 great, amazing
2 something that becomes popular
3 famous
4 formal celebrations
5 extremely large
6 plant products used to give food a special taste

71 **7** **Listen to Jack's presentation of the Japanese film *The Hidden Fortress*. Which characters in the box does Jack talk about?**

doctors farmers general king
monsters princess queen samurai

71 **8** **Listen again. Are the sentences true or false? Correct the false sentences.**

1 *The Hidden Fortress* was filmed in 1954.
2 All of the locations in the film are in Japan.
3 The story takes place about 200 years ago.
4 General Rokurota protects Princess Yuki.
5 The two farmers are quite serious characters.
6 At first, the film wasn't very popular in Japan.

CULTURE

Learning Objectives

- The students learn about the film industry in different countries.
- In the project stage, they give a presentation about a famous film to the class.

Vocabulary

ceremonies giant renowned spices terrific trend

Resources

CULTURE VIDEO AND CULTURE VIDEO WORKSHEET: History of Hollywood

BACKGROUND INFORMATION

Mickey Mouse is a cartoon character and the mascot of the Walt Disney Company, who has featured in over 130 short and full-length films. Other characters who often appear in the cartoons include Mickey's girlfriend, Minnie Mouse, his friends Goofy and Donald Duck and his pet dog, Pluto. Mickey first appeared in 1928 in one of the first cartoons with sound. The cartoons were originally in black and white but after the introduction of colour in 1935 Mickey usually wore red shorts, yellow shoes and white gloves. In 1978, Mickey became the first cartoon character to have a star on the Hollywood Walk of Fame.

Sherlock Holmes is a fictional detective who made his first appearance in 1887 in the novel *A Study in Scarlet*, written by Sir Arthur Conan Doyle. The first known film featuring Holmes is *Sherlock Holmes Baffled*, made in 1900 and lasting less than a minute. The English actor Basil Rathbone played Holmes in 14 films, starting with *The Hound of the Baskervilles*. Holmes and Dr Watson's adventures have also been the subject of comedies such as *The Private Life of Sherlock Holmes* and the highest-grossing Sherlock Holmes film to date is a comedy, *Sherlock Holmes: A Game of Shadows* (2011). It has made over $500 million worldwide.

James Bond is a British secret agent whose code number is 007. He was created by Ian Fleming in 1953. Between 1962 and 2015 a total of 24 James Bond films were made, starting with *Dr No*. The 24th was *Spectre*. Major actors in the series include the first James Bond, Sean Connery, who made seven James Bond films, Roger Moore, who also starred in seven, Pierce Brosnan and Daniel Craig, who have both played Bond four times. To date, the films have made over $13 billion at the box office.

WARMER

Review the genres of TV shows and films from page 80 by playing a guessing game. Put students in groups of six or eight and tell them to work in two teams of three or four. Each team chooses three or four genres, according to the number of students in the team. Students from each team take it in turns to explain one of the genres without using the word, for example without using the word *action* if they are describing an action film. The other team has to guess the genre. They have a 15-second time limit.

1 Read the questions and put students in small groups to discuss their ideas. As a class, invite them to share their answers. Ask how many students have seen the famous films from their country and if they know the names of films made by famous directors from their country.

Answers

Students' own answers

2 Ask students to read the quiz and work in pairs to answer the questions. Clarify any unknown vocabulary at this point. This may include *full-length film* (a film that is usually one and a half to two hours long) and *frequently* (often). Invite students to share their ideas, but do not confirm their answers at this point.

Answers

Students' own answers

70 3 Play the recording for students to check their answers to the quiz. Then check answers as a class. Find out which pairs got the most answers correct. Ask if they have seen any Mickey Mouse, Sherlock Holmes or James Bond films and what they know about these characters.

Answers

1 A 2 C 3 A 4 B 5 A

>> AUDIOSCRIPT TB PAGE 273

4 Ask students if every country in the world produces films, and why or why not (*no, some countries do not have the money or technology to do so*). Students read the names of the countries on page 85 and discuss in small groups whether they have seen any films from these countries. Review their findings as a class. Students read the sentence endings and scan the text to find the answers as quickly as they can. Tell them the information could be anywhere on the page, including in the information boxes on the left-hand side. They compare answers with a partner. Check answers with the class.

Answers

1 India 2 China 3 the UK 4 the USA 5 Japan

CONTINUED ON PAGE 166

5 Students look at the questions and read the *World film facts* more carefully to find the answers. They compare answers with a partner. Check answers with the class.

Answers

1 Japan
2 It's cheaper there.
3 serious, historical topics
4 in the 1950s
5 They have many ingredients, like masala spices.
6 a historical film about a famous novel

72 The Reading text is recorded for students to listen, read and check their answers.

6 Ask students to look at the highlighted words in the text and to try to work out their meanings from the context. Students then complete the exercise by matching the words to their meanings. Check answers with the class and check any other new words and phrases, for example *hit* (*a very successful film*), *ghost* (*the spirit of a dead person that appears to people who are alive*), *take place* (*happen, especially at a particular time*). Check pronunciation of *martial* /ˈmɑːʃəl/.

Answers

1 terrific 2 trend 3 renowned 4 ceremonies 5 giant
6 spices

FAST FINISHERS

Ask fast finishers to write two or three sentences, using words from the exercise. They read their sentences out, omitting the word. The class guesses the missing word.

71 7 Students look at photo from the film *The Hidden Fortress* on page 85. Tell them to scan the text about Japan and find out what it's about. Ask if any of them have seen any martial arts films and if they know anything about Japanese cinema in the 1950s. Explain that Jack is making a presentation to his class about the film. Read the list of characters in the box and check understanding, for example *samurai* (*a warrior, a member of a powerful military class in mediaeval Japan*). Play the recording and check answers.

Answers

princess, general, farmers, samurai
(NOT: doctors, king, monsters, queen)

71 8 In pairs, students read the sentences and mark them as true or false from what they remember of the recording. Play the recording again for them to listen and check their answers.

Answers

1 false (1958)
2 true
3 false (500 years ago)
4 true
5 false (They are funny characters.)
6 false (It was the fourth most popular.)

MIXED ABILITY

To support weaker students, play the recording again pausing after each of the answers. Ask students to try to repeat the exact words used.

» AUDIOSCRIPT TB PAGES 273–274

9 Students read the sentence beginnings in the *Useful language* box and complete them in pairs. You may need to write the director's name on the board.

Answers

1 Japan
2 Akira Kurosawa
3 Japan
4 in Japan / in the 16th century / 500 years ago
3 a princess and a general
5 the best foreign film at the Berlin Film Festival

PROJECT *A presentation about a film*

Read the instructions and ask the students to choose a film. This may be one they have seen and know about or one from the *World fact file* text. They can do this activity in pairs or individually. Students read the questions and then carry out their research online, making brief notes for each point. Students then create their presentations, using Microsoft PowerPoint or a similar program. Remind them to answer one question per slide. Tell them to include photos and a clip of the soundtrack.

Allow the students time to practise their presentations. If they are working in pairs, remind them to divide the information equally between them. Students then give their presentations. Ask the rest of the class to listen to each one carefully and to say at the end which film they would most like to see, and why.

PROJECT EXTENSION

Ask students to do some research about the film industry in their country. They should find out about its history, some facts about ticket sales and number of screens, famous films, actors and directors, any current trends, which films have been successful abroad, and so on.

10 CULTURE VIDEO: History of Hollywood

When students have completed the lesson, they can watch the video and complete the worksheet.

COOLER

Play 'Film charades'. Write some film titles on pieces of paper. Hold up the number of fingers that represent the number of words in the film title. Then act out each word. Hold up fingers to say which word you are describing, for example hold up two fingers for the second word. Students can call out the answer at any time. The first student to guess the film title correctly in English acts out another title. Continue until several students have had a turn.

1 The USA	40,000 Cinema screens; approximately $10 billion Ticket sales / year
2 China	41,000 Cinema screens; approximately $6.6 billion Ticket sales / year
3 Japan	3,500 Cinema screens; approximately $2.0 billion Ticket sales / year
4 India	10,000 Cinema screens; approximately $1.9 billion Ticket sales / year
5 The UK	4,200 Cinema screens; approximately $1.7 billion Ticket sales / year

World film facts: THE BIG FIVE

72

The USA

The biggest films studios in the USA are in Hollywood, California. However, many studios make their films in other states, like New York and Louisiana. Canadian locations, like Vancouver and Toronto, are also popular because it's cheaper to work there. The most renowned film awards in the USA are the Golden Globes and the Oscars. Both ceremonies take place in Los Angeles, California.

Big hits: *Black Panther, Jurassic World*

China

Chinese audiences watch many films from the USA, but they have a dynamic national industry too. In the past, Chinese films were often about serious, historical topics, but now studios also make horror films, thrillers, comedies and romances, with Chinese stars, of course! One of the most famous actresses is Yang Mi. She's also a pop singer and fashion model.

Big hits: *Monster Hunt, The Great Wall*

Japan

In the 1950s, Japan became famous for action-adventure films about martial arts, like *Seven Samurai* or *The Hidden Fortress*. In 1954, there was also a very popular film about a giant monster, called *Godzilla*. Audiences loved the film and it started a new trend. In more recent years, animated films, called anime, have become popular, as well as scary horror films about ghosts and other monsters.

Big hits: *Princess Mononoke, The Ring*

India

India makes more films than any other country per year. Many are Bollywood films, which combine love, drama, comedy and action with Indian music and dancing. Indians call them *masala films* because they have so many ingredients, like the masala spices that Indians use for cooking. Bollywood actors usually speak and sing in Hindi, but they often use English phrases too.

Big hits: *Sultan, Chennai Express*

The UK

Britain has made some of the world's most popular films, like the James Bond and Harry Potter series. They also make lots of historical films about famous novels, like *Sense and Sensibility* or *Jane Eyre*. If you like detective and crime stories, the Sherlock Holmes films are also terrific. The biggest prizes for British cinema are the BAFTA awards, which take place every year in London.

Big hits: *Casino Royale, Fantastic Beasts and Where to Find Them*

9 Read the *Useful language* phrases. Complete them with information about *The Hidden Fortress*.

USEFUL LANGUAGE

Talking films

1 It's a film from …
2 The director's name is …
3 It was filmed in …
4 The story takes place …
5 The main characters are …
6 The film won (the award for) …

PROJECT

A presentation about a film

Plan a presentation about a famous film that you like. Go online and find information about it. If possible, find photos and music from the film.

1 Where is it from? What type of film is it?
2 Who directed the film? Where was it filmed?
3 Where and when does the story take place?
4 Who are the main characters in the film?
5 Has the film won any important awards?
6 What do you like the most about the film?

Present your film to the class.

10 NOW WATCH THE CULTURE VIDEO

15 DIGITAL LIFE

ABOUT YOU

What do you use your phone or computer for? Make a list of things.

VOCABULARY Computer phrases

73 **1 Match the beginnings and ends of the quiz questions. Then listen and check.**

EP

74 **2 Listen to Jack's answers to the quiz. Alex asks follow-up questions to get more details. Complete the questions.**

1 What did *you do* ?
2 How did you ______ ?
3 How do you ______ ?
4 What kind of things ______ ?
5 What did ______ ?
6 Which apps do you use ______ ?
7 How many do you ______ ?
8 Which ones do you ______ the most?

74 **3 Complete the sentences about Jack with words from Exercise 1. Then listen again and check.**

1 Jack *deleted* a school project, but his dad helped him to get it back.
2 He got a ______ when he installed a game.
3 He uses a different ______ for each website.
4 He often ______ to funny videos or photos.
5 He has ______ for his name and found it in some football reports.
6 He ______ a lot of ______ and mainly uses Instagram.
7 He has ______ about ten ______ this week and has over 200 altogether.
8 He sometimes ______ and his favourites are the ones about science.

4 In pairs, take turns to answer the quiz questions in Exercise 1. If you can, use the follow-up questions in Exercise 2 to find out more information.

5 Tell the class something interesting you found out about your partner.

Sara got a virus on her dad's computer and they had to buy a new one.

YOUR digital WORLD

1 Have you ever deleted an
2 Have you ever had
3 Do you have a
4 Do you often share
5 Have you ever done
6 Do you upload
7 How many new apps have you
8 Do you ever download

a photos or videos to the internet to share with friends?
b different password for each website you use?
c important file by mistake?
d podcasts?
e a search for your own name online?
f a virus on your computer?
g installed on your phone this week?
h links to interesting websites with friends?

15 DIGITAL LIFE

Unit Overview

TOPIC	Technology and the digital world
VOCABULARY	Computer phrases
READING	Apps for learning English
GRAMMAR	Present simple passive
VOCABULARY	Phrasal verbs: technology
WRITING	An informal email (3)
EXAM TASKS	Reading Part 2; Writing Part 1

Resources

GRAMMAR REFERENCE AND PRACTICE: SB page 152; TB page 246
WORKBOOK: pages 60–63
PHOTOCOPIABLE WORKSHEETS: Grammar worksheet Unit 15; Vocabulary worksheet Unit 15
TEST GENERATOR: Unit test 15

WARMER

Write *Technology* on the board and elicit one or two examples to demonstrate meaning, for example *laptop* and *mobile phone*. Start a word association game with a confident student: say 'laptop' and then ask what associated word students think of. Accept *computer* or any laptop-related vocabulary as an answer, for example *mouse* or *tablet*. Students continue playing the game in small groups. In whole-class feedback, invite a student to start the game, nominating another to answer. Continue until several students have had a turn. Write key words on the board.

ABOUT YOU

In pairs, give students two minutes to make a list of all the things they use their phone, computer or tablet for. Share ideas and write them on the board. Have a class vote to find the most popular. Find out which social media students use.

VOCABULARY Computer phrases

73 1 Tell students that they are going to do a quiz but first they must match the beginnings and ends of the questions. Tell them to think carefully about sentence structure and use of prepositions as well as meaning. They complete the exercise in pairs. Play the recording for students to check their answers. Check understanding of the words in blue by asking for definitions or example sentences. Check pronunciation of *upload* /ʌpˈləʊd/ and *virus* /ˈvaɪərəs/.

Answers

1c 2f 3b 4h 5e 6a 7g 8d

» AUDIOSCRIPT TB PAGE 274

74 2 Read the instructions. Tell students that Alex asks one follow-up question for each of the questions in Exercise 1. Students refer back to Exercise 1, read the follow-up question beginnings in Exercise 2 and suggest endings for them. Accept all reasonable suggestions. Tell them they will hear the recording twice and will need two or three words to complete each question. Play the recording, pausing between each of the eight exchanges for students to complete the questions. Students compare answers in pairs. Play the recording again for them to check their answers and then check answers with the class.

Answers

2 get it 3 remember them 4 do you share 5 you find 6 to share them 7 have altogether 8 listen to

74 3 Ask students what they remember about Jack's answers to the questions in Exercises 1 and 2. Tell them to complete the sentences in Exercise 3 using the words in blue from the quiz. Read the example sentence. Tell them they may need to change the form of some of the words and that some of the answers consist of more than one word. They complete the exercise in pairs. Play the recording for them to check answers. Check answers with the class and check understanding.

Answers

2 virus
3 password
4 shares links
5 done a search
6 uploads, photos
7 installed, apps
8 downloads podcasts

» AUDIOSCRIPT TB PAGES 274–275

4 Students ask and answer the questions with their partner. Monitor and help as necessary. Encourage them to use the follow-up questions in Exercise 2 to get further information.

Remind them to listen carefully to what their partner tells them as they are going to report back to the class.

Answers

Students' own answers

MIXED ABILITY

Advise weaker students to take notes of their partner's answers to help them tell the class about their partner in Exercise 5.

5 Each student tells the class something interesting they found out about their partner, as in the example. Ask students how they can get better at using technology.

Answers

Students' own answers

BACKGROUND INFORMATION

An app is a computer program designed to run on a mobile device such as a phone or tablet. Teenagers juggle many different apps to find friends, post pictures and send messages and they change apps constantly, unlike adult users, who stay with the same apps. This is a headache for app developers because apps make money only when users are plugged in and absorbing adverts!

1 Find out whether students use language apps and whether they know any good ones for practising different skills, such as grammar or listening. They read about Emre and look at the underlined information carefully. Ask them what kind of app Emre needs.

Answers

Students' own answers

2 Students read points 1–3, which describe Emre's needs, and scan the first three app descriptions to find which apps match these requirements. Check answers and ask for evidence from each description. Check understanding of *challenging*. Hold a brief discussion about which app would be best for Emre and why. Find out which app students would like to use and why.

Answers

1 B (challenging activities), C (surprisingly hard)
2 B (video stories), C (listen to … stories)
3 A (Games last just a few minutes, so it's perfect for a bus ride), C (activity takes between five and ten minutes)
C is the best app for Emre.

3 Read the instructions and remind students of the key information underlined in Exercise 1. They read the text about Anna and ask what three things she wants. Check answers. Students continue in the same way for Luis, Evie and Filipe.

Answers

1 Anna: <u>needs more help with English vocabulary and grammar</u>, <u>bored of doing traditional exercises</u>, <u>activities that are quick to complete</u>
2 Luis: <u>would like to get better at understanding movies and TV shows in English</u>, <u>expects apps to look good</u>, <u>prepared to spend money on the right one</u>
3 Evie: <u>developing and revising her vocabulary</u>, <u>likes fun activities</u>, <u>enjoys competing against friends</u>
4 Filipe: <u>advanced level student</u>, <u>help him revise grammar</u>, <u>doesn't want to pay for an app</u>

4 **B1 Preliminary for Schools Reading Part 2**

In this part, reading for specific information and detailed comprehension is tested. Students match five descriptions of people to eight short, factual texts.

Students will read each text looking for the key features they identified in Exercise 3. As a class, students read description A and identify the key features: it practises vocabulary, so it could be of interest to Anna and Evie. However, there's no mention of grammar activities, so it isn't what Anna wants. The activities are enjoyable and you can also play against other users, so it would be suitable for Evie. Students continue the exercise in mixed ability pairs. Monitor and help as necessary. Check answers. Find out which app students would most enjoy using.

Answers

2 H 3 B 4 A 5 E
2 H: Themez
Fresh and unusual and uses games (Anna: bored of traditional exercises), teaches English through topics like science and history (Anna: enjoys all subjects but needs help with English), short games (Anna: wants activities that are quick to complete).
3 B: EnglishScene
Expensive but gets awesome reviews (Luis: prepared to spend money), high-quality and interesting video stories (Luis: get better at understanding movies and TV shows in English), simple but attractive design (Luis: expects apps to look good).
4 A: WordPowr
About learning words (Evie: interested in developing and revising her vocabulary), eight games which are very enjoyable (Evie: likes fun activities), can play online against other users (Evie: enjoys competing against friends).
5 E: Language lab
Costs nothing (Felipe: doesn't want to pay), of limited interest to anyone except high-level language learners (Felipe: advanced level student), grammar reference for each topic (Felipe: to help him revise grammar).

75 The Reading text is recorded for students to listen, read and check their answers.

FAST FINISHERS

Ask fast finishers to think of synonyms for *awesome*, *attractive*, *fairly*, *allow* and *huge*.

TALKING POINTS

Read the questions and put students in small groups to discuss them. Bring the class together to find out who uses apps for studying, how useful they are and what features they have. Discuss if students are prepared to pay for apps or not. This is a good opportunity to get students thinking about what they can do outside the classroom to improve their English skills. Encourage them to share information about apps and websites they use or other ways they practise English outside class.

COOLER

Write some vocabulary from pages 86 and 87 on the board but leave out the vowels, for example *vrs* (virus), *dlt* (delete). In small groups, students complete the words. The first group to complete the words and spell them correctly is the winner.

READING

1 **Emre wants an app to help him with learning English. Read about Emre and notice the key underlined information a–c.**

1 Emre often [a] finds language apps easy and wants some difficult practice. He [b] would like to improve his listening skills and he [c] intends to use the app on his short bus journey to and from school.

2 **Read the descriptions of the first three apps (A–C). Find two apps that do these things:**

1 mention difficult practice *B, C*
2 practise listening skills
3 are suitable for use on short journeys

Which app is best for Emre?

3 **Read about four more teenagers who want apps to help them with learning English. Underline three key pieces of information about each person.**

2 Anna enjoys all subjects but she needs more help with English vocabulary and grammar. She is bored of doing traditional exercises and is looking for an app with activities that are quick to complete.
3 Luis would like to get better at understanding movies and TV shows in English. He expects apps to look good and is prepared to spend money on the right one.
4 Evie's interested in developing and revising her vocabulary. She likes fun activities and she really enjoys competing against friends.
5 Filipe is an advanced level student and he would like an app to help him revise grammar. He doesn't want to pay for an app.

4 **Read the descriptions of the apps (A–H). Decide which app would be the most suitable for each teenager in Exercise 3. There are three apps you don't need.**

APPS FOR LEARNING ENGLISH

75

A **WordPowr** is all about learning words – nouns, verbs, everything. There are eight games, which are very enjoyable, but the best part is that you can also play online against other users. At less than the price of a coffee, the app is great value for money. Games last just a few minutes, so it's perfect for a bus ride. Turn down the annoying music, though!

B Although **EnglishScene** is expensive, the app is often given awesome reviews by its users. As soon as you use it, you can understand why. Everything about this app is professional, from the high-quality and interesting video stories, with challenging activities to support students in understanding them, to the simple, but attractive design.

C **Newscast** is a professional-looking app that helps you understand the news in English. You listen to and read stories, do some typical exercises about new words, even a little grammar, and then answer the questions. Each activity takes between five and ten minutes and is surprisingly hard.

D Practise the 3000 most frequent words in English with **PassWords3000**. This app is for low-level students working by themselves and includes a very common range of activity types. It's free, so sometimes you have to watch video advertisements to continue using it. New questions are added every month.

E **LanguageLab** costs nothing, but will be of limited interest to anyone except high-level language learners. The grammar reference for each topic is full of important details but the practice that follows is fairly typical. The app also allows you to compare your progress with friends on social networks.

F The design of **VidEnglish** isn't always clear and it seems to be mainly links to very high-level video clips from documentaries. The clips aren't downloaded with the app, so it's best to use when you have free wi-fi. There is a basic dictionary and the app is completely free, with no advertisements.

G The first thing you notice with **GrammarWise** is its professional-looking design. Everything about this app is easy to use. There are fun, animated grammar presentations and a huge choice of practice activities, with over 50 different grammar topics per level. You can try one topic for free but it costs to get access to the whole app.

H **Themez** is a fresh and unusual app. It uses games to teach grammar and vocabulary through topics like science and history. The app is perfect for when you only have a few minutes to practise, but at the moment you can only play by yourself.

TALKING POINTS

What apps do you use to help you with studying?
Do you mind paying for apps?

DIGITAL LIFE 87

GRAMMAR Present simple passive

1 **Read the examples. Then complete the rules with the words in the box.**

1 The app **is** often **given** awesome reviews **by** its users.
2 New questions **are added** every month.
3 The clips **aren't downloaded** with the app.
4 What **is** the app **called**?

be	by	past participle

a We use the passive when the person or thing that causes the action is unknown or unimportant.
b We form the present simple passive with the correct form of ________ and the ________ of the verb.
c When we include who or what did the action, we use ________.

» **GRAMMAR REFERENCE AND PRACTICE PAGE 152**

2 **Complete the text about Instagram. Use the present simple passive form of the verbs.**

Instagram is an online photo and video sharing app and [1] ________ (own) by Facebook.

The app is extremely popular and [2] ________ (use) by over 500 million people daily.

Over 95 million photos and videos [3] ________ (share) every day and a word or phrase [4] ________ (add) to the photo, called a 'tag'. Thousands of products [5] ________ (advertise) by companies on the app too. Users click a heart icon next to the photos they like the most. Around 50,000 'likes' [6] ________ (give) to photos and videos every *second* on Instagram!

3 » **Complete the questions with the present simple passive form of the verb. Then answer the questions with your own ideas. Turn to page 124 to check.**

1 Which type of program ________ (download) from the internet the most often?
2 Which password ________ (use) by people most often online?
3 Which celebrities ________ (search) for online the most often?
4 How much ________ (spend) on buying apps every year?
5 Which countries ________ most smartphones ________ (make) in?

4 **Correct the mistake in each sentence.**

1 My best friend called Luis.
2 This computer it's used by everyone in my family.
3 More computers need in our school.
4 My favourite game calls FIFA and costs about £50.
5 This phone is recommend for older people.
6 The virus was deleted some important files.

VOCABULARY Phrasal verbs: technology

1 **Complete the phrasal verbs.**

EP

1

5

2

6

3

7

4

8

look	plug	shut	switch
switch	take	turn	turn

1 ________ down
2 ________ in
3 turn on / ________ on
4 ________ up
5 turn off / ________ off
6 ________ out
7 ________ down
8 ________ up

2 **Complete the sentences with the correct form of the phrasal verbs in Exercise 1.**

0 Please *turn off / switch off* your mobile phones. The film is starting soon.
1 This TV isn't working. Can you check it is ________?
2 This app makes it easy to ________ the train times.
3 ________ that music! It's too loud!
4 Is there a problem? Try ________ the computer. Wait ten seconds, then ________ the computer again.
5 Don't forget to ________ your SIM card before you sell your phone.
6 Can you ________ the sound on the TV? I can't hear what they're saying.

3 » **Work with a partner. Turn to page 124.**

GRAMMAR Present simple passive

WARMER

Revise past participles playing noughts and crosses. Make a grid 3 × 3 and write an infinitive in each square. Divide the class in two. Each team chooses an infinitive and gives the past participle (including spelling!). The first team to get three in a row is the winner.

1 Students read the example sentences, taken from descriptions B, D and F on page 87, and the question. Ask students to identify the verb forms and the tense. Put them into pairs to complete the rules. Check answers and ask students to make the sentences active. Point out that we only know the subject for the first sentence so they will have to invent a subject for the other sentences and the question: *The app's users often give it awesome reviews. Someone adds new questions every month. People don't download the clips with the app. What do we call the app?*

Answers

b be, past participle
c by

» GRAMMAR REFERENCE AND PRACTICE ANSWER KEY TB PAGE 246

2 Ask students what they know about Instagram and if they use it. Ask them to complete the text using the present simple passive forms of the verbs. Remind them to think about whether the subjects are singular or plural and the correct past participle of each verb. Check answers and ask them if they found out anything new about Instagram. Encourage them to use the present simple passive form in their answers.

Answers

1 is owned
2 is used
3 are shared
4 is added
5 are advertised
6 are given

3 Do this exercise as a class. Invite students to call out the answers and ask the class if they agree. Ask them which question follows the word order used in Exercise 1 number 4 (5). Explain that in all the other questions, the question word or words are the subject of the question but in number 5 the subject is *most smartphones* and *Which countries* is the object. In pairs, students guess the answers and then turn to page 124 to check. Ask how many they got right and if any of the answers surprised them.

Answers

1 is downloaded (anti-virus)
2 is used (some people use *password* or *123456*)
3 are searched (in 2017, Meghan Markle and Gal Gadot)
4 is spent (in 2017, more than $200 billion)
5 are, made (China, South Korea, India, Taiwan)

4 Explain to students that there is one mistake in each sentence. They complete the exercise in pairs and then compare answers with another pair. Check answers with the class and make sure they understand why two of the verbs (*cost*, *deleted*) are active (Note: *cost* is never passive).

Answers

1 My best friend **is** called Luis.
2 This computer **is** used by everyone in my family.
3 More computers **are needed** in our school.
4 My favourite game **is called** FIFA and costs about £50.
5 This phone is **recommended** for older people.
6 The virus **deleted** some important files.

» GRAMMAR WORKSHEET UNIT 15

VOCABULARY Phrasal verbs: technology

1 Students look at the pictures. Write *turn* on the board. Ask them in which four pictures we can use *turn* (1, 3, 5 and 7). Ask if they know which other verb we can use in pictures 3 and 5 (*switch*) and for examples of other things we can *switch on / off*, for example phone, TV, speakers, lights, etc. Ask what *turn up* and *turn down* mean. Students complete the other four items in pairs. Check answers and understanding. Explain that, with all these verbs, if the object is a pronoun *it* must come between the verb and the particle: *turn it off*, *look it up*, etc. Ask students when they might do each of these actions.

Answers

1 turn 2 plug 3 switch 4 turn 5 switch 6 take 7 shut
8 look

2 Read the example. Monitor as students complete the exercise in pairs. Invite different students to read out the completed sentences.

Answers

1 plugged in
2 look up
3 Turn down
4 shutting down, turn/switch on
5 take out
6 turn up

FAST FINISHERS

Ask fast finishers to think of more things they can *turn up*, *turn down*, *shut down*, *plug in*, *take out* and *look up*. Ask them to make gapped sentences for *switch on* and *turn up*. In feedback, ask them to write their sentences on the board for the class to complete.

3 Students turn to page 124. Read the instructions and check understanding of the words in the two boxes. Ask a stronger student to mime an example. Monitor and help as necessary. Invite different students to mime some of their activities.

Answers

Students' own answers

» VOCABULARY WORKSHEET UNIT 15

WRITING An informal email (3)

1 Ask students what they remember about writing an informal email (see Units 3 and 7) and what kind of language is used. Tell them that they are going to write another informal email. Set a short time limit for them to read Abbie's email and find out why she is looking for new apps and podcasts. Check the answer.

Answers
Because she is visiting relatives in Scotland next week and she's going to be in the car for a long time.

2 Students identify Abbie's questions and look at Paul's notes next to her email. Then they read Paul's reply quickly to find out whether he answers Abbie's questions. Check the answer and explain any difficult vocabulary, for example *rollercoaster*. Ask if they think it is a good reply and encourage them to give reasons.

Answers
Yes, he does.

3 Set a short time limit for students to read Paul's email again and answer the first question. Check answers. Then ask students to identify the phrases which Paul uses to recommend the game and the podcast. Invite different students to read out the phrases from the email. Ask if they like Paul's recommendations.

Answers
the game 'Rollercoaster Tycoon': *You should try it.*
the podcast 'Reply All': *I'd recommend (Reply All).*

4 Read the *Prepare to write* box. Give students time to read Paul's email again and find the phrases from the box which he uses to give his opinion.

Answers
I think
I would say
in my opinion

5 Students read the instructions and the sentence beginnings. Ask them for ideas about what makes a game app or podcast good and write key words and phrases on the board, for example *they're exciting / challenging*, *they discuss unusual topics*, *they have good designs*, *they're easy to use*. Students complete the sentences individually before comparing their answers in mixed ability pairs. Encourage them to say whether they agree or disagree with their partner using the phrases from the Speaking exercises in Unit 14 (page 83). Share some ideas as a class, encouraging students to say whether they agree with each other or not and why.

Answers
Students' own answers

6 Ask students what they remember about how to start and end an informal letter or email. They look at how Paul begins and ends his email. Check answers. Ask students to suggest other ways to begin or end an informal letter or email, for example *Hello*, *Write soon*, *Bye for now*.

Answers
Hey Abbie
Have a great time!

7 Students read Abbie's email again and work individually to plan their reply, using Paul's notes to help them. Monitor and help as necessary.

MIXED ABILITY
Tell weaker students to look back at the *Prepare to write* boxes in Units 3 and 7 (pages 23 and 45) to help them.

8 **B1 Preliminary for Schools Writing Part 1**

In this part, students are awarded marks for content, communicative achievement, organisation and language. Students have to write an email of about 100 words in response to input which is similar to that provided in Exercise 1. The email provides the topic and there are notes to help students construct their response. (See also Units 3 and 7.)

Students write their email to Abbie. Remind them to use the tips in the *Prepare to write* box. Encourage them to include examples of the present simple passive and some of the new vocabulary from this unit. Tell them to write about 100 words. Monitor and help as necessary, reminding them to check spelling and grammar. Display the emails around the classroom for other students to read. Ask them which game they would like to play and which podcast they would like to listen to.

Model answer
Hi Abbie,
Lucky you, going to Scotland! I recommend a great app called *Road Trip Travel Games*. It has a variety of fun games that you can play on your own or with other members of your family.
I think another good game is *Build a Business*. You have to create a business, like a shop or a café. It's fun but it takes a long time.
Right now my favourite podcast is *411Teen* because lots of the ideas are supplied by teenagers so in my opinion the content is relevant and interesting.
Have a lovely time in Scotland!
Bye,
Luke

COOLER
Revise the phrasal verbs from page 88. Write the names of some items on the board and ask students which phrasal verbs can be used with them, for example *football results*, *radio*, *music*, *speakers*, etc. In pairs, they make a list. Check answers with the class and ask if they can add any more items.

WRITING An informal email (3)

1 **Read this email that Paul receives from his friend Abbie. Why is Abbie looking for new apps and podcasts?**

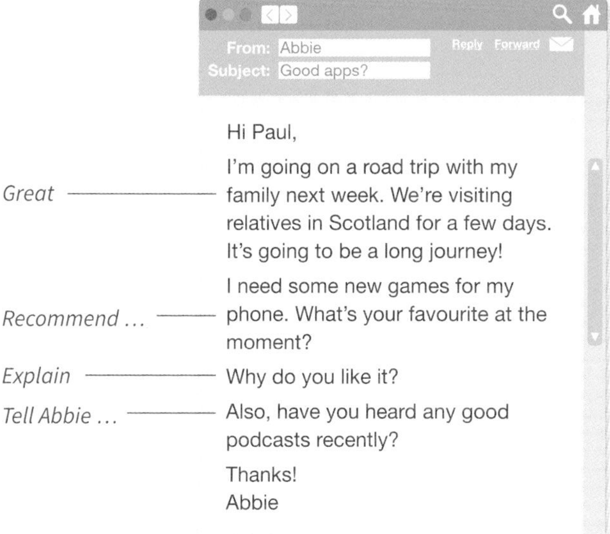
From: Abbie
Subject: Good apps?
Reply Forward

Hi Paul,

Great — I'm going on a road trip with my family next week. We're visiting relatives in Scotland for a few days. It's going to be a long journey!

Recommend … — I need some new games for my phone. What's your favourite at the moment?

Explain — Why do you like it?

Tell Abbie … — Also, have you heard any good podcasts recently?

Thanks!
Abbie

2 **Read Paul's reply. Does he answer all of Abbie's questions?**

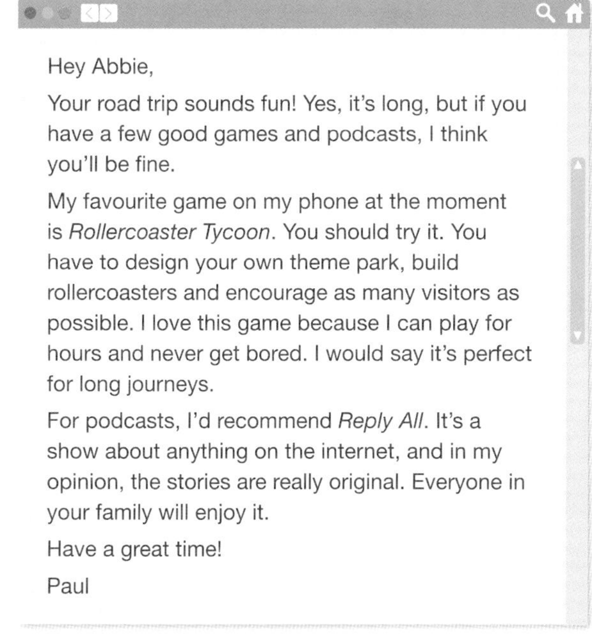
Hey Abbie,

Your road trip sounds fun! Yes, it's long, but if you have a few good games and podcasts, I think you'll be fine.

My favourite game on my phone at the moment is *Rollercoaster Tycoon*. You should try it. You have to design your own theme park, build rollercoasters and encourage as many visitors as possible. I love this game because I can play for hours and never get bored. I would say it's perfect for long journeys.

For podcasts, I'd recommend *Reply All*. It's a show about anything on the internet, and in my opinion, the stories are really original. Everyone in your family will enjoy it.

Have a great time!

Paul

3 **Which game and which podcast does Paul mention? What phrases does he use to recommend them to Abbie?**

4 **Read the *Prepare to write* box. Find three phrases that Paul uses to give his opinion.**

PREPARE TO WRITE

An informal email (3)

In an informal email:

- use phrases to give your opinion:
  I (really) think …
  I don't think …
  For me, …
  In my opinion, …
  I would say …
- use phrases to make suggestions and recommendations:
  You should … I recommend …
- remember to answer any questions
- remember to use an informal phrase to begin and end the email.

5 **Complete the sentences with your opinions about game apps and podcasts. Compare your opinions with a partner. Do you agree with your partner's opinions?**

1 In my opinion, …
2 I really think …
3 I would say …

6 **What informal phrases does Paul use to begin and end his email?**

7 **Read Abbie's email again and plan your reply. Use all Paul's notes in Exercise 1.**

8 **Write your email to Abbie.**

- Use the phrases and tips in the *Prepare to write box.*
- Write about 100 words.
- Remember to check your spelling and grammar.

16 AMAZING SCIENCE

EXPERIMENTS YOU CAN TRY AT HOME

MOVING A CAN WITHOUT TOUCHING IT

YOU WILL NEED:

- ✔ a balloon
- ✔ a tissue
- ✔ an empty drinks can

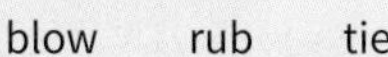

blow rub tie

- ★ **a** ______ air into the balloon and **b** ______ the end.
- ★ **c** ______ the filled balloon on your hair or on a tissue.
- ★ Put the can on the floor and hold the balloon near it.
- ★ **Pull the balloon away from the can slowly, and the can will move towards the balloon!**

HOW IT WORKS

The can moves towards the balloon because when you rub the balloon, it gets a negative [1] *electricity / electrical* charge. When you put the balloon near the can, the [2] *electricity / metal* in the can gets a small positive charge. The result is that the static [3] *electricity / air* in the balloon attracts the can.

KEEPING LIQUIDS APART

YOU WILL NEED:

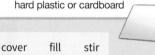

- ✔ two glasses
- ✔ salt
- ✔ food colouring
- ✔ a small piece of thin, hard plastic or cardboard

cover fill stir

- ★ **d** ______ the glasses with water.
- ★ Put two large spoons of salt into the first glass and **e** ______ it.
- ★ Add a few drops of food colouring into the other glass.
- ★ **f** ______ the glass of coloured water with the cardboard/plastic. Turn it upside down and put it on top of the glass of salt water. Pull the cardboard/ plastic out from between the glasses.
- ★ **The coloured water and the salty water won't mix!**

HOW IT WORKS

The coloured water and the salty water stay apart because salt water is heavier than [4] *normal / warm* water. The [5] *heavier / lighter* salt water stays at the bottom of the glass and the [6] *heavier / lighter* coloured water floats at the top.

GETTING AN EGG INTO A BOTTLE

YOU WILL NEED:

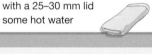

- ✔ an egg
- ✔ a towel
- ✔ a glass bottle with a 25–30 mm lid
- ✔ some hot water

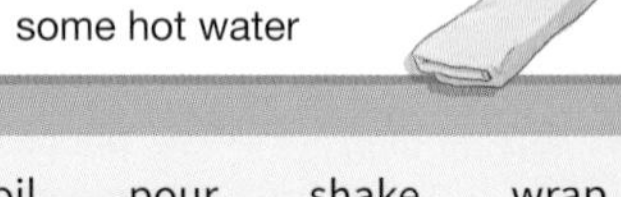

boil pour shake wrap

- ★ **g** ______ the egg for 4 minutes, until the white of the egg is hard but the yolk is soft. Let it cool. Then peel it.
- ★ **h** ______ the hot water into the bottle. Put on the lid, **i** ______ it in a towel and **j** ______ it well.
- ★ Take off the lid and pour out the water.
- ★ Put the egg in the opening of the warm bottle.
- ★ **After a few minutes the egg is pulled into the bottle.**

HOW IT WORKS

The egg is pulled into the bottle because the hot water in the bottle makes the bottle [7] *smaller / warm*, and the air in the bottle gets warm too. Hot air expands: it gets bigger and takes up more space than [8] *cold / hot* air. Cold air contracts, in other words it gets smaller and takes up less space than warm air. So as the air in the bottle goes back to room temperature, it gets [9] *smaller / warmer*, and so it pulls the egg into the bottle.

ABOUT YOU

Are you more into science or arts? Why?
What scientific experiments have you done at school?

VOCABULARY Doing experiments

1 **Look at the instructions for three experiments and complete a–j in the sentences with the words in each box.**

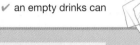

2 **Choose the correct words to complete the *How it works* explanation for each experiment. Then listen and check.** (76)

3 **In pairs, discuss the questions. Use one or more verbs from Exercise 1 in your answers.**

0 How do you make a candle go out? *You blow it.*
1 How do you make coffee?
2 What do you do when you add sugar to coffee?
3 How can you keep flies off your food?
4 How can you say no without speaking?
5 How can you keep your hands warm in cold weather?
6 What do people with long hair often need to do?
7 What can you do if your glass is empty?
8 What do you do with a present before giving it to someone?

90 UNIT 16

16 AMAZING SCIENCE

Unit Overview

TOPIC	Science
VOCABULARY	Doing experiments
READING	The Ig Nobel Prize
GRAMMAR	Zero and first conditional
VOCABULARY	Phrasal verbs: science
LISTENING	A conversation about a teenage inventor
SPEAKING	Describing a photo (2)
EXAM TASKS	Speaking Part 2

Resources

GRAMMAR REFERENCE AND PRACTICE: SB page 153; TB page 246
WORKBOOK: pages 64–67
PHOTOCOPIABLE WORKSHEETS: Grammar worksheet Unit 16; Vocabulary worksheet Unit 16
TEST GENERATOR: Unit test 16

WARMER

Write anagrams of school subjects on the board and ask students to find the words. Then decide if they belong to arts, sciences, social sciences or another category.

ABOUT YOU

Read the questions. In pairs, students discuss the first question, giving reasons. Bring the class together and find out which group is the majority – science or arts. For the second question, be ready to supply some science vocabulary! Find out if students remember a particular experiment and why, for example *the results were surprising*, *it was a bit dangerous*, *it was fun*, and so on. Put students into small groups to briefly discuss the three questions. Invite students to tell the class about a member of their group.

VOCABULARY Doing experiments

1 Students read the three headings. Ask if any of them know how to do these experiments. They look at the items they will need. Check understanding. Put students into groups of three. Give each group one of the experiments. They read the instructions and fill the spaces with the correct verb. Make new groups of three with one student from each of the original groups. They share their answers. With the class, check answers and pronunciation, for example *blow* /bləʊ/, *cover* /ˈkʌvə/, *rub* /rʌb/, *stir* /stɜː/ and *tie* /taɪ/. Check understanding of the verbs by asking different students to mime them. The class guesses which verb they are miming. Check understanding of any other vocabulary, for example *drop*, *upside down*, *peel*, *yolk* /jəʊk/. Ask students to work out their meaning from the context.

Answers

a blow b tie c rub
d fill e stir f cover
g boil h pour i wrap j shake

76

2 With books closed, ask students if they know how each experiment works. Write *might*, *could*, *must* and *can't* on the board and encourage students to use them in their explanations. Students stay in their new groups of three to complete the explanations. Play the recording for them to check and then check answers with the class. Check understanding of any other vocabulary, for example *attract*, *float*, *take up*. Tell students to try to work out their meaning from the context. Ask them if they can describe any other simple experiments. Remind them to use the present simple passive if appropriate.

Answers

1 electrical 2 metal 3 electricity
4 normal 5 heavier 6 lighter
7 warm 8 cold 9 smaller

» AUDIOSCRIPT TB PAGE 275

3 Read the instructions and the example. Ask students to read the questions and check understanding. In pairs, students ask and answer, making sure they use a verb from Exercise 1. They should use each verb at least once. Monitor and help as necessary. Invite individual students to read their answers and ask the rest of the class if they agree.

Possible answers

1 You **boil** water and **pour** the water onto the coffee granules.
2 You **stir** it.
3 You can **cover** the food with a plate.
4 You can **shake** your head.
5 You can **blow** on them or **rub** them together.
6 They need to **tie** it back.
7 You can **fill** it.
8 You **wrap** it.

FAST FINISHERS

Ask fast finishers to think of objects or things you can *drop*, *peel*, *add (to)* and *cool*. They name the objects and the class decides which of the four verbs can be used with each object.

READING

BACKGROUND INFORMATION

The Ig Nobel Prizes, which started in 1991, are presented by Nobel prize winners in a ceremony at Harvard University. Ten prizes are awarded each year in categories including the usual Nobel Prize categories of physics, chemistry, medicine, literature and peace, but also in other categories such as public health, engineering and biology. Some interesting prizes include:

2016 Medicine: if you have an itch on the left side of your body, you can relieve it by looking into a mirror and scratching the right side of your body (and vice versa).

2014 Arctic Science: how reindeer react to seeing humans who are disguised as polar bears.

2010 Medicine: symptoms of asthma can be treated with a rollercoaster ride.

1 Find out how much students know about the Nobel Prize, for example the categories, when it was first awarded (1901), where it is awarded (in Stockholm, Sweden, except for the Peace prize which is awarded in Oslo, Norway), etc. and if they know the names of any prize winners.

Answers

1 Prizes awarded each year for the most important work in physics, chemistry, medicine, literature, economics and work for peace.
2 Some famous prize winners are Marie Curie, Nelson Mandela, Albert Einstein, Mother Teresa, Alexander Fleming, Pablo Neruda, Martin Luther King, James Watson, Barack Obama.

2 Explain that there is an alternative Nobel Prize and ask students to tell you what it is called. Ask them to describe the pictures and suggest what people might have done to win it. Encourage students to think creatively! Write suggestions on the board. Give students three minutes to scan the text and check. Ask if any of their suggestions were correct.

Answers

1 Proved that if a cow has a name, it produces more milk.
2 Proved that when you drop a slice of toast, 80% of the time it falls buttered-side down.
3 Discovered that mosquitoes bite people less if there's some Limberger cheese nearby.
4 An experiment that made a frog float in the air.

3 Students read the questions and then read the article more carefully to find the answers. Encourage them to write the answers in their own words. Monitor and help as necessary. They compare answers with a partner. Check answers with the class.

77 The Reading text is recorded for students to listen, read and check their answers.

Answers

1 A Nobel Prize is an award for a great scientific achievement. An Ig Nobel Prize is an award for making people smile and making them think about science.
2 Probably because they feel less loved if they don't have a name.
3 Because it only has time to turn once before it reaches the floor.
4 Some mosquitoes carry malaria (which kills humans).
5 The discovery of graphene won a Nobel Prize because it is a great scientific achievement.

MIXED ABILITY

Help weaker students with questions 1–4 by providing some key words and partially completed sentences. For example:

1 … is an award for … and … is an award for …

2 Cows with … names feel … loved.

3 It only has time to …

4 Because they carry a … called …

4 In pairs, students look at the highlighted words in the text and try to work out their meanings from the context. Then they read the definitions and match them to the words. Check answers and check understanding of any other vocabulary, for example *headlines*.

Answers

1 float 2 aim 3 trap (*traps* in the text) 4 proof 5 drop
6 achievement (*achievements* in the text)

TALKING POINTS

Put students into small groups to brainstorm ideas. Encourage them to be as creative as they can. Monitor and join in the discussions. Then ask each group to choose their best idea and present it to the class, giving reasons for their choice. Write the ideas on the board and have a class vote on the best idea. Refer students back to the opening sentence of the article and ask them for their ideas about the biggest questions of our time. If they don't come up with many ideas, write some words to stimulate ideas on the board, for example *space*, *black holes*, *war and peace*, *climate change*, etc. Remind students to listen to each other, to agree and disagree and offer their own opinions. Write key words and ideas on the board.

COOLER

Write *physics* on the board and ask students what other words they can make from the same root, for example *physical*, *physician*. In pairs or small groups, ask students to do the same with *electric*, *history*, *invent*, *produce* and *science*. Set a time limit. The pair with the most correct words is the winner.

Possible answers

electricity, electrician, electrical
historic, historical, historian
invention, inventor, inventive
producer, product, productive
scientific, scientist

READING

1 **Discuss the questions.**

1 What is the Nobel Prize?
2 Do you know the names of anyone who has won a Nobel Prize?

2 **Look at the title of the article and the photos. What do you think people have done to win the Ig Nobel Prize? Read the text quickly and check.**

The *Ig* Nobel Prize

77

Science tries to answer the biggest questions of our time: 'If we explore nearby galaxies, will we find other forms of life?' or 'What will happen to the planet if we don't stop climate change?' The greatest scientific achievements are awarded a Nobel Prize: Alexander Fleming (penicillin), Marie Curie (radioactivity) and Albert Einstein ($E=mc^2$) are all Nobel Prize-winners. Science is serious, but scientists are only human and sometimes they want answers to questions like: 'Why do shower curtains blow towards you when you have a shower?' And so the Ig Nobel Prize was born, with the aim of making people smile first, and then think about science.

Here's a selection of scientific ideas that have won an Ig Nobel Prize

If a cow has a name, it produces more milk! Farmers have always known this, but now there's proof. Cows *without* names produce about 13,000 litres a year, but cows *with* names produce 13,500 litres. This is probably because the cows with names feel more loved by farmers.

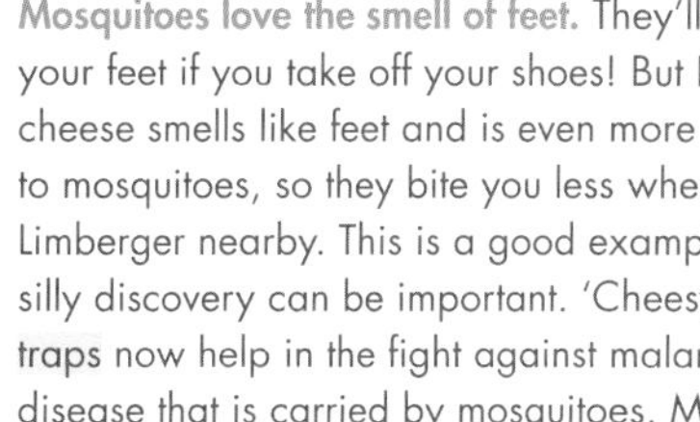

When you drop a slice of toast, it falls to the ground with the buttered side down 80% of the time, according to experiments. This is because it usually falls from table height and only has time to turn over once before it reaches the floor.

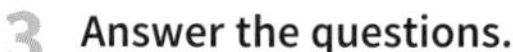

Mosquitoes love the smell of feet. They'll bite your feet if you take off your shoes! But Limberger cheese smells like feet and is even more attractive to mosquitoes, so they bite you less when there's Limberger nearby. This is a good example of how a silly discovery can be important. 'Cheesy' mosquito traps now help in the fight against malaria, a disease that is carried by mosquitoes. Malaria kills 500,000 people per year.

Only one person has won both an Ig Nobel and a Nobel Prize: Andre Geim made the headlines in 1997 for his 'flying frog' experiment, in which he made a frog float in the air! Then in 2010 he discovered graphene, a form of carbon that is one *atom* thick. Graphene is the thinnest and strongest substance known to man. There are no prizes for guessing which experiment won an Ig Nobel!

3 **Answer the questions.**

1 What's the difference between a Nobel Prize and an Ig Nobel Prize?
2 Why do cows without names produce less milk?
3 Why does toast fall with the buttered side down?
4 Why are some mosquitoes dangerous?
5 Which of Andre Geim's experiments do you think won a Nobel Prize? Why?

4 **Match the highlighted words in the article to the meanings.**

1 stay in the air without support
2 the reason for doing something
3 something for catching animals
4 information to show that something is true
5 allow something to fall
6 something difficult that you succeed in doing

TALKING POINTS

What 'problem' would you like the Ig Nobel Prize to solve?

What do you think are the biggest questions of our time? Why?

GRAMMAR Zero and first conditional

1 Read the examples and complete the rules.

1 If a cow **has** a name, it **produces** more milk.
2 Mosquitoes **bite** you less **when** there's cheese nearby.

Zero conditional
a We use the zero conditional for things that are *true* / *probable* or always happen.
b We use the present simple in *the first* / *both* clauses.
c The *If* or *When* clause can come first or second. The meaning is *different* / *the same*.

2 Complete the zero conditional sentences.

1 Water ________ (boil) when you ________ (heat) it to 100°C.
2 If you ________ (not add) sugar to this coffee, it ________ (taste) very bitter.
3 If you ________ (press) 'play', the music ________ (start).
4 When a player ________ (score) a goal, the fans ________ (go) crazy.
5 My journey to school ________ (be) quicker if I ________ (take) the bus.

3 Read the examples. Then choose the correct words to complete the rules.

1 What **will happen** to the planet **if** we **don't stop** climate change?
2 Mosquitoes **will bite** your feet **if** you **take off** your shoes.

First conditional
a We use the first conditional to talk about possible or probable *future* / *past* events.
b We use *if* + *present simple* / *past simple*, and *will* + infinitive.

4 Choose the correct words to make first conditional sentences.

1 If I light the candles, everyone *sing* / *will sing* 'Happy Birthday'.
2 What *will* / *do* you do if you get lost?
3 You *make up* / *will make up* if you shake hands.
4 Where will you go if it *will rain* / *rains* later?
5 The gift will look lovely if we *wrap* / *will wrap* it in some pretty paper.

5 Read the rule and choose the sentence that means the same.

Life will end **unless we stop** climate change. =
a Life will end **if we don't stop** climate change.
b Life will end **if we stop** climate change.

First conditional: ***if*** **and** ***unless***
We can use *unless* instead of *if*. *Unless* means *if not*.

» GRAMMAR REFERENCE AND PRACTICE PAGE 153

6 Complete the sentences with ***if*** **or** ***unless***.

1 ________ you fill the bottle, the experiment will work.
The experiment won't work ________ you fill the bottle.
2 The computer won't turn on ________ you enter the password.
________ you enter the password, the computer will turn on.
3 I won't cover the picnic ________ the rain gets worse.
I'll cover the picnic ________ the rain gets worse.
4 I hate soap operas. I'll watch TV with you ________ you turn to another channel.
________ you turn to another channel, I won't watch TV with you.

7 Correct the mistake in each sentence.

1 You want to start a fire, blow the flame gently at first.
2 Dad won't cook a pizza for you unless you'll text him later.
3 When it's OK with you, I'll come to your place after school.
4 Unless we'll meet before 8 pm, we won't have time to buy tickets.
5 Wrap yourself in a blanket you have a fever.

VOCABULARY Phrasal verbs: science

1 Match the sentence halves.

EP
1 We're trying to add
2 To do this experiment, cut
3 First, you need to carry
4 I can't work
5 If you have 1 trillion and you take
6 Be careful. Don't blow

a away 1 million, you get …
b up a sheet of paper into 1 cm strips.
c up the whole school!
d out the answer to this problem.
e out some experiments in a lab.
f up the number of atoms in this molecule.

2 Complete the sentences with the verbs above.

1 I can't ________ how to design this experiment.
2 If you ________ the units and divide by two, you get the answer.
3 We'll ________ the pizza into six slices.
4 We ________ lots of experiments last year.
5 This potassium won't ________ unless you get water on it.
6 If you have seventy-five and ________ ten, it leaves sixty-five.

3 » **Work with a partner. Turn to page 125.**

GRAMMAR Zero and first conditional

WARMER

Write on the board *What will happen if …?* and ask for suggestions to complete the question, for example *if you get home late, if you get 100% in your exams, if our team wins the league*, etc. Write the suggestions on the board and then put students into pairs to ask and answer the questions. Monitor and help as necessary.

1 Read the example sentences, adapted from the Reading on page 91. Explain that this sentence form is called a 'zero conditional'. Students read and complete the rules. They compare answers with a partner. Check answers.

Answers

1 true
2 both
3 the same

2 Students work in pairs to complete the exercise, using the present simple of the verbs in brackets. Invite different students to read out their sentences. Check understanding. Students look at the position of the comma in Exercises 2, 3 and 4. Elicit that it is used between clauses when the sentence starts with *If* or *When*.

Answers

1 boils, heat
2 don't add, tastes
3 press, starts
4 scores, go
5 is, take

3 Students are now going to talk about possible or probable future events using the first conditional. Students read the example sentences, complete the rules and compare answers with a partner. Check answers.

Answers

1 future
2 present simple

4 Do the first sentence as an example. Students complete the activity in pairs, referring to the rules in Exercise 3. Check answers and understanding.

Answers

1 will sing
2 will
3 will make up
4 rains
5 wrap

5 Write on the board: *What will happen if we don't stop climate change?* Ask students if it is zero conditional or first conditional and whether the *if* clause is positive or negative (*first conditional, negative*). Invite suggestions and encourage students to start their answers with the *if* clause. Students read the sentences and rule and decide which sentence, a or b, means the same. Check the answer. Ask a stronger student to change the question on the board using *unless*: *What will happen unless we stop climate change?*

Answers

sentence a

» **GRAMMAR REFERENCE AND PRACTICE ANSWER KEY TB PAGE 246**

6 Students make large cards with *if* and *unless* on them. Give pairs a few minutes to read the sentences and decide which word goes in each space. Remind them to refer to the rule in Exercise 5. Read out each sentence, pausing at the space for students to hold up the word they think is correct.

Answers

1 If, unless
2 unless, If
3 unless, if
4 if, Unless

7 In pairs, students read the sentences, find the mistakes and correct them, referring to the rules in Exercises 1, 3 and 5. Check answers and understanding.

Answers

1 **If** you want to start a fire, blow the flame gently at first.
2 Dad won't cook a pizza for you unless **you** text him later.
3 **If** it's OK with you, I'll come to your place after school.
4 Unless **we** meet before 8 pm, we won't have time to buy tickets.
5 Wrap yourself in a blanket **if** / **when** you have a fever.

» **GRAMMAR WORKSHEET UNIT 16**

VOCABULARY Phrasal verbs: science

1 Since a lot of these verbs are new, some of this will be guesswork but tell students to look for words that are connected. Do the first item together: *add* is connected to numbers, so the sentence ending will probably be a, which contains *1 million*, or f, which contains *the number*. In pairs, students complete the exercise. Go through the answers and then read out the definitions and ask students to match them to the phrasal verbs. Definitions: *add up* – put numbers together to make a total; *cut out* – remove a form or shape by cutting; *carry out* – do or complete something, for example an experiment; *work out* – find an answer or a solution; *take away* – subtract one number from another; *blow up* – cause to explode. Point out that all these verbs are separable, i.e. pronouns go between the verb and the particle: *add them up*, not ~~*add up them*~~. Nouns can go in this position or after the particle: *add the numbers up* / *add up the numbers*.

Answers

1 f 2 b 3 e 4 d 5 a 6 c

2 In pairs, students complete the sentences. Check answers as a class.

Answers

1 work out
2 add up
3 cut up
4 carried out
5 blow up
6 take away

3 In pairs, students write sentences using the phrasal verbs on page 125. Invite pairs to act out their sentences. The class guesses the sentence.

Answers

Students' own answers

» **VOCABULARY WORKSHEET UNIT 16**

LISTENING

1 Find out if any students have heard of Taylor Wilson. They describe the pictures and discuss what they think he invented. Explain that they are going to listen to an interview with an American woman, Lauren Phillips, who has made a documentary about him. Play the recording and check answers. Ask students for their reactions to his achievements.

Answers

He invented a nuclear fusion reactor.

2 Ask students to read the questions and choose the correct option, based on what they remember from the interview. If they are not sure of an answer, they should underline the key words. Tell them they will hear the recording twice. Play the recording and give students time to choose each option before comparing answers with a partner. Play it again for them to check their answers and make any changes. Check answers with the class. If necessary, play the recording again, pausing in the places relevant to both the correct and the incorrect options.

Answers

1 B 2 B 3 C 4 B 5 A 6 A

» **AUDIOSCRIPT TB PAGES 275–276**

3 In pairs, students think of questions for Taylor and, if possible, search for the answers online. Monitor and help as necessary. Put them into groups to discuss their findings and ask each group to share their results with the class. Write key words on the board.

Answers

Students' own answers

FAST FINISHERS

Ask fast finishers to write two or three more questions they would like to ask Taylor Wilson.

SPEAKING Describing a photo (2)

1 In pairs, students describe the photo and answer the questions. Invite different pairs to give their suggestions and write key words on the board but do not confirm answers at this point.

Answers

Students' own answers

2 Play the recording for students to listen and check and ask if any of their ideas were mentioned.

Answers

Students' own answers

3 Ask students to read the phrases in the *Prepare to speak* box. Elicit that they can use these phrases when they aren't sure about what's happening in a picture or when they don't know a word. Students listen to the recording again and make a note of which phrases from the *Prepare to speak* box are used. They work out which phrase isn't used.

Answers

It could/might be

» **AUDIOSCRIPT TB PAGE 276**

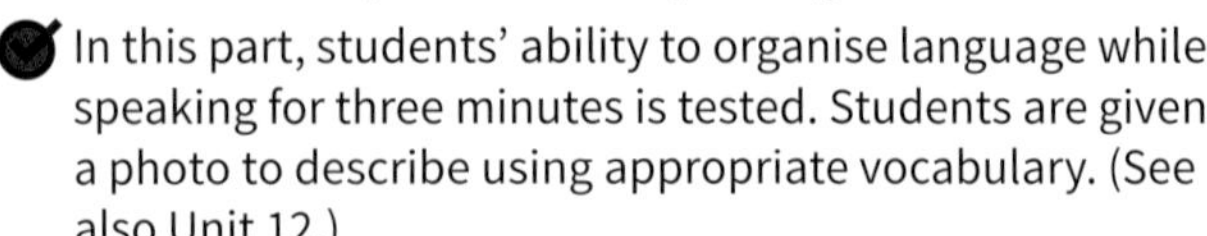

4 **B1 Preliminary for Schools Speaking Part 2**

In this part, students' ability to organise language while speaking for three minutes is tested. Students are given a photo to describe using appropriate vocabulary. (See also Unit 12.)

Students look at the picture and the questions. Ask students to work with a new partner. Give them a few minutes to think about what they are going to say, but tell them not to write anything down. Then they take turns describing the photo using the phrases from the *Prepare to speak* box. Bring the class together and invite students to say one sentence each about the photo. Give positive feedback for use of phrases from the *Prepare to speak* box.

Answers

Students' own answers

MIXED ABILITY

Tell weaker students to refer back to the *Prepare to speak* box in Unit 12 on page 71 and use some of the phrases as well as the phrases on this page. Tell them to write some key words and phrases down to help them when they are speaking.

COOLER

Write the phrasal verbs from the unit on one side of the board in random order, and the particles on the other side. In pairs, students match the verbs with the particles and make at least one sentence for each verb. Set a time limit. Students read out their sentences and the rest of the class says if the verbs are correct and used correctly.

LISTENING

78 **1** **You are going to hear a conversation about a teenage inventor. Look at the pictures and discuss what you think he has invented. Listen and check.**

78 **2** **For each question, choose the correct answer. Then listen again and check that the other two options are wrong.**

1 How did Lauren Phillips first discover Taylor Wilson?
 A She made a show about him.
 B She watched a video about him.
 C She met him online.

2 Taylor's neighbours left their houses because
 A everyone wanted to see his experiment.
 B they were frightened by the noise.
 C Taylor blew up his house.

3 Taylor went to a special school
 A where Mark Zuckerberg and Lady Gaga studied.
 B which had a fantastic nuclear physics department.
 C which allowed its students to visit a nearby university.

4 What does 'a star in a jar' refer to?
 A a famous person who went to a special school
 B a nuclear fusion reaction inside a reactor
 C a machine that detects bombs

5 Taylor met President Obama because he
 A invented some important security equipment.
 B was the 42nd person to make a nuclear fusion reaction.
 C is a brilliant public speaker and video presenter.

6 Lauren Phillips thinks that Taylor should
 A carry on sharing his excitement about science.
 B make more security equipment for the government.
 C consider becoming an actor.

3 **In pairs, think of five questions you would like to ask Taylor Wilson. Find the answers online if possible, then discuss your findings in groups.**

SPEAKING Describing a photo (2)

1 **Look at the photo. Where do you think the people are? What do you think is happening?**

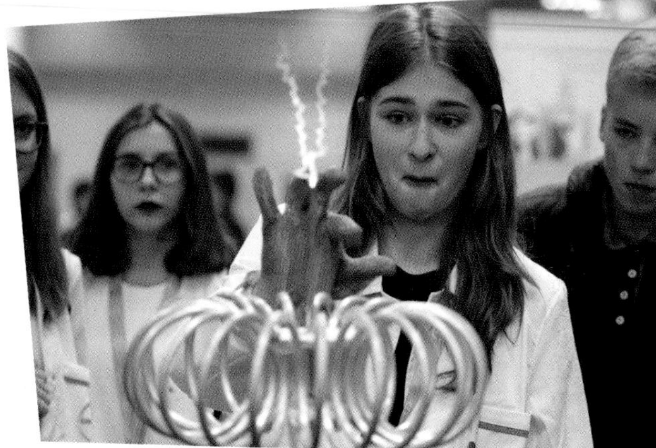

79 **2** **Listen to someone describing the photo. Compare your ideas.**

79 **3** **Read the *Prepare to speak* box. Then listen again. Which phrase do you not hear?**

PREPARE TO SPEAK

Describing a photo (2)

When you aren't sure
It looks like …
It looks like a kind of / some sort of
It could/might be …
They seem very …
I'm not really sure, but …

When you don't know the word
I don't know what it's called.

4 **Look at another photo. Where do you think the people are? What do you think is happening? Take turns to describe it. Use phrases from the *Prepare to speak* box.**

AMAZING SCIENCE 93

LIFE SKILLS ICT LITERACY

LIFE SKILLS

Staying safe online

We use the internet for many things, such as studying, communicating with friends and having fun online. The internet is a normal part of modern life, but we must use it carefully in order to stay safe and prevent problems.

STAYING SAFE ONLINE

1 Ask and answer the questions with a partner.

1. How many hours do you spend on the internet on a typical day?
   A less than 1 **B** 1 to 2 **C** 3 to 4 **D** more than 4
2. What electronic device do you use most often for going online?
   A smartphone **B** a tablet **C** a laptop **D** other
3. How much do you think you know about internet safety?
   A nothing **B** a little **C** quite a lot **D** a lot

80

2 Read the text quickly. Match photos A–D to four of the rules. How well do you follow these rules?

INTERNET SAFETY

The internet is useful and it can also be a lot of fun, as long as people use it responsibly.

Here are some basic rules that you should always follow to stay safe on the internet:

1 When you're online, you should protect information like your real name, address, phone number and date of birth. This information is too personal to share with everyone.

2 Don't accept any friend or chat requests from strangers on social media apps or websites. All your online contacts should be people that you already know and trust.

3 Be cautious about websites and apps that tell people your location. You don't want strangers to know where you are going or when you aren't home!

4 If you really want to meet a new online friend, you should always tell your parents first. They should know where you're going, and they may want to accompany you the first time.

5 Think very carefully before you share any personal photos or videos online. Just pause for a moment and ask yourself, 'Do I really want everyone in the world to see this?'

6 Don't share any photos or videos of your friends and other people unless you have their permission. Be polite and respect other people's privacy online.

7 Keep your passwords secret, so strangers can't access your email or other accounts. And don't choose an obvious password, like 123456. Choose something that people can't guess.

8 If you use social media, you shouldn't write nasty comments about people or the things they post online. Respect their feelings and don't be mean. You wouldn't want someone to say those things about you!

9 If you have any problems with other people online, ask an adult for help. It's better to talk with someone as soon as possible. Don't keep the problem a secret!

A

16 likes

B

Like Comment

I hate you

C

User ID:

Password:

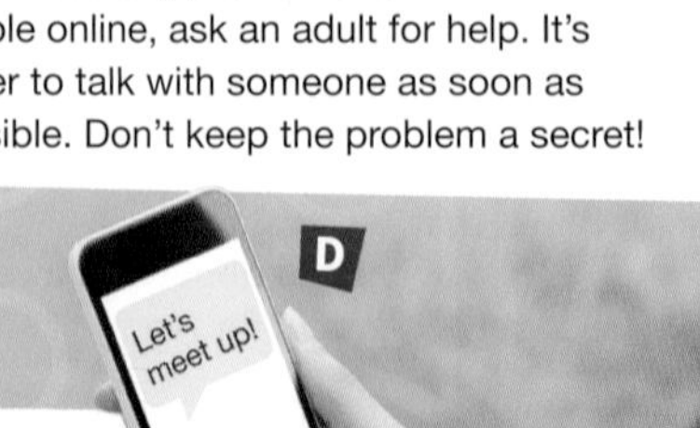

3 Match the highlighted words in the text to the meanings.

1. easy to guess
2. stop or wait
3. unkind or nasty
4. keep someone or something safe
5. where someone or something is

LIFE SKILLS

Learning Objectives

- The students learn about staying safe online.
- In the project stage, they make a poster about cyberbullying and the dangers of internet use.

Vocabulary

location mean obvious pause protect

BACKGROUND INFORMATION

Apart from staying safe online, many parents are worried that their children spend too much time online. A recent study by Oxford University concluded that using smartphones, computers and tablets as well as playing video games is actually beneficial as it may improve creativity, communication skills and development. Researchers found that up to four and a quarter hours a day was a healthy amount of time for 15-year-olds. However, some psychiatrists think children can become hyper-aroused by gadgets, a condition known as 'electronic screen syndrome'. Other studies suggest that teenagers should take a substantial break after 90 minutes of screen time. It has also been shown that using electronic devices before bedtime can have negative effects on sleep patterns. The researchers of the new study did agree that electronic devices should not be used as a substitute for sleep, exercise, environments and above all relationships with real (as opposed to virtual) people. Many people would argue that these are what young people need to develop into healthy adults.

WARMER

In pairs, students brainstorm the good and bad aspects of the internet. Ask for a couple of suggestions first, for example bad – *cybercrime such as hacking*, good – *being able to speak to family and friends who are far away*. Give students a few minutes to write down their ideas and then listen to feedback as a class. Write key vocabulary on the board and check understanding of *ICT* (*information and communication technology*).

LIFE SKILLS
Staying safe online

Students read the text. Check understanding. Ask students if they agree and whether they think online safety is an important issue.

1 In pairs, students ask and answer the questions and then report back to the class. Have a class discussion about how much time they spend online. Ask whether they think they spend too long online and what they consider to be a healthy amount of time. Find out how much they know about internet safety and where or from whom they learned this information, for example at school, from parents or friends, from online sites, etc.

Answers
Students' own answers

2 Students describe the photos and read the title of the article. Ask them to read the text quickly and match each photo to a rule. Check answers and have a discussion about how well students follow the rules themselves.

Answers
A 5 B 8 C 7 D 4

80 The Reading text is recorded for students to listen, read and check their answers.

3 Students find the highlighted words in the text. In order to match them to their meanings they should look at the context, including the sentences immediately before or after the highlighted words. Then they match the words to their definitions and compare answers with a partner. Check answers and new vocabulary with the class.

Answers
1 obvious 2 pause 3 mean 4 protect 5 location

FAST FINISHERS

Ask fast finishers to write definitions of *share* – have or use something at the same time as someone else; *cautious* – avoiding risks, being careful; *stranger* – a person you don't know; *accompany* – go with; *privacy* – someone's right to keep their personal matters secret.

4 In pairs, students read and answer the questions, using ideas from the text and their own ideas. Tell them they should read the text more carefully this time to find the answers. Monitor and help as necessary. Check answers with the class and discuss any ideas not in the text. Ask students their opinion of the rules and if they would add any more rules to protect themselves and others when they are online.

Answers

1 Your real name, address, telephone number, date of birth
2 Tell your parents first.
3 They will be able to use your accounts.
4 Everyone in the world can see them. / Students' own answers
5 When you already know the person.
6 You wouldn't like it if other people did that to you.

MIXED ABILITY

Ask weaker students to underline the key words in each question and then quickly scan each rule to find them. Then they should read the sentence containing the word or words and decide whether it answers the question.

5 In pairs, students read the comments and decide whether the young people are using the internet in an appropriate way. Ask them to give reasons for their answers. Review answers with the class and ask them if they would be upset if friends posted photos of them online without asking their permission first. Discuss why some people think it's OK to say things to a person online that they would never say to them directly.

Answers

Angela – no. She isn't following rule 6.
Daniel – yes.
Kelly – yes.
Samuel – no. He isn't following rule 8.

81 6 Tell the students they are going to listen to four young people talking about their online problems. First they read the sentences about the problems. Play the recording and give them time to decide on the correct option. They compare answers with a partner. Check answers with the class. Check that they understand *cyberbullying* – using the internet to frighten or harm another person. The person who does the action is a *cyberbully*.

Answers

1 Justin 2 Melissa 3 Laura 4 David

81 7 Explain that students are going to hear the recording again and that they should listen to find out how each person dealt with the problem. They read the sentences and, if they remember from the recording, write the correct name in each space. Play the recording for students to complete the spaces with the correct names. They compare answers with a partner. Check answers with the class and discuss the four problems and how each person dealt with them. Ask if they can suggest anything to help David, for example changing his settings about spam.

Answers

1 Laura 2 Justin 3 David 4 Melissa

>> AUDIOSCRIPT TB PAGE 276

8 In pairs, students read the words in the box and complete the sentences in the *Useful language* box. Check the answers with the class. Ask if students can think of any other expressions for giving advice, for example *It might be a good idea to …*

Answers

1 should 2 need 3 tell 4 opinion 5 best 6 important

PROJECT ***A poster about internet safety***

Explain that students are going to work in groups to produce a poster about cyberbullying. As a class, brainstorm the first question. In their groups, students discuss the other questions and make notes. Monitor and help as necessary. As a class, discuss where people could find more information about this problem and, if students are not sure, ask them to do some research online. Next, in their groups, students decide what information they are going to put on their poster and discuss the design, the layout and whether they are going to use any graphics. They make their posters, check grammar, vocabulary and spelling and present them to the class. Have a discussion about whether all the ideas are practical or not. Display the posters in the classroom or around the school.

PROJECT EXTENSION

In pairs, students write a dialogue. One of them is a victim of cyberbullying. The friend gives some advice. Encourage them to use expressions from the *Useful language* box. If possible, students record the conversation and then play it back to the class. In that way, they can practise several times and re-record parts of it until they are satisfied with the result.

COOLER

Ask students to choose four words from the unit and write them as anagrams, with the letters mixed up. Tell them to make sure they have spelled the words correctly before making them into anagrams and that they have included all the letters in their anagram. Put them in small groups to solve each other's anagrams.

4 **Answer the questions. Use ideas from the text.**

1 What type of information should you keep personal?
2 What must you do if you want to meet a new online friend?
3 Why shouldn't you tell other people your password?
4 What can happen if you share silly photos of yourself online?
5 When can you safely accept friendship requests online?
6 Why shouldn't you write bad things about other people?

5 **Read the comments. Are these people using the internet safely? Why? / Why not?**

Angela says
I love posting photos of my friends online. Sometimes they get angry with me, but I think it's funny.
posted 2h ago

Daniel says
I don't like it when strangers send me friend requests. I never answer, and I block them when I can.
posted 2h ago

Kelly says
I use a phone app that shows people where I am, but only my parents can see that information.
posted 2h ago

Samuel says
When people insult me online, I always insult them back. Sometimes it gets really nasty.
posted 2h ago

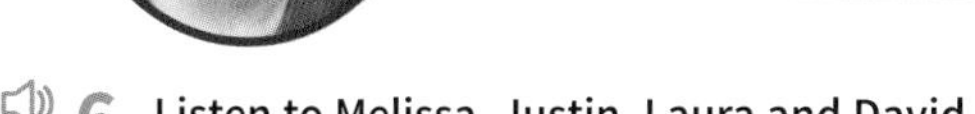

81 **6** **Listen to Melissa, Justin, Laura and David. Choose the correct answers.**

1 A boy posted comments about *Justin* / *David* on a social network.
2 Girls were making fun of *Laura* / *Melissa* because she looks different.
3 A boy was writing nasty emails about *Melissa* / *Laura* last year.
4 *David* / *Justin* always receives lots of emails from strangers.

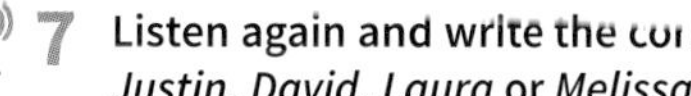

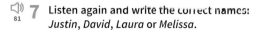

81 **7** **Listen again and write the correct names: *Justin*, *David*, *Laura* or *Melissa*.**

1 ________ didn't tell her parents about the cyberbullying.
2 ________ changed the privacy settings on his profile.
3 ________ has closed his email account five times already.
4 ________ got a new phone. Now she blocks messages from strangers.

8 **Complete the *Useful language* phrases with the words in the box.**

best	important	need
opinion	tell	should

USEFUL LANGUAGE

Giving advice

1 You ________ tell your parents right away.
2 I think people ________ to be more careful.
3 I'd ________ my friends not to be mean.
4 In my ________, people should be nicer.
5 The ________ thing to do is ask for permission.
6 It's ________ to keep your password secret.

PROJECT

A poster about internet safety

Make a poster about cyberbullying and the dangers of internet use. Give practical advice.

- What type of things do cyberbullies do?
- Why shouldn't people do these things?
- What can people do if they're being cyberbullied?
- Why is it important to talk about cyberbullying?
- Where could people find more information about this problem?

Present your poster to the class. Then display it at school.

REVIEW 4 UNITS 13–16

VOCABULARY

1 **Find the words (→ ↓ ↘) and complete the lists. You have got the first letter of each word.**

d	o	c	u	m	e	n	t	a	r	y	s
m	i	d	g	w	r	a	p	n	e	p	e
b	d	s	p	r	a	b	l	i	s	r	m
o	o	r	a	i	a	s	r	m	l	o	b
c	w	e	s	p	y	t	h	a	i	u	a
o	n	s	s	y	p	n	e	a	n	d	r
m	l	o	w	u	r	o	s	f	k	t	r
e	o	c	o	v	e	r	i	o	u	e	a
d	a	r	r	w	e	e	h	n	r	l	s
y	d	a	d	v	i	r	u	s	t	e	s
b	l	o	w	t	o	r	n	c	h	e	e
e	a	c	h	a	t	s	h	o	w	r	d
p	t	p	a	n	i	m	a	t	i	o	n

Adjectives: feelings
d______ e______
g______ p______

Computer words
p______ l______
v______ d______

TV and film
a______ c______
c______ d______

Doing experiments
b______ c______
s______ w______

2 **Complete the sentences with the words in the box.**

blow up characters confused deleted exhausted plot plug in search soap opera soundtrack stressed turn off work out

1 I did a ______ for a cheap ticket online, but there weren't any.
2 This ______ is on TV five times a week.
3 I've just run 15 km. I'm ______!
4 She's upset because she ______ her homework by mistake.
5 I'm ______. I can't ______ how to answer this question.
6 I'm feeling very ______ this evening. I need to sit down and relax.
7 Can you ______ this HDMI cable ______ to the back of the screen?
8 Have you heard the ______ from the new *Star Wars* film?
9 ______ the machine, quickly. This experiment's going to ______!
10 The ______ of *Stranger Things* is great; it always keeps you guessing what will happen next. I love the main ______ too.

GRAMMAR

1 **Complete the sentences. Use the correct form of the verbs.**

1 ____ you ______ this book yet? (read)
2 When I switch off the lights, it ______ always very dark in here. (be)
3 This table ______ of wood. (not make)
4 He never ______ much homework when he's in his room. (do)
5 Look! The teacher ____ just ______. (arrive)
6 Breakfast ______ every day between 7 and 10 am. (serve)
7 Don't worry. I'll remind her if she ______. (forget)
8 I'm not hungry. I ____ already ______ lunch. (have)
9 If you click 'yes', the film usually ______ quite quickly. (download)
10 Unless he arrives soon, we ______ leave without him. (have to)

2 **Make sentences.**

1 you / upload / your film / yet?
______
2 this film / not translate / into Spanish
______
3 Jon / just / shut down / his computer
______
4 if / I / fill / the kettle, / you / make / the coffee?
______
5 the app / open / when you / enter / your password
______
6 the British actors / not mention / in the reviews
______
7 the rubber ring / not float / unless / you / fill / it with air
______
8 Sonia / already / wrap / your present
______

REVIEW 4 UNITS 13–16

Overview

VOCABULARY Adjectives: moods and feelings; Adjectives: *-ed* or *-ing*; TV and film; Talking about films and shows; Computer phrases; Phrasal verbs: technology; Doing experiments; Phrasal verbs: science

GRAMMAR *just, already* and *yet*; Relative clauses; Present simple passive; Zero and first conditional

EXAM TASKS Reading Part 6

Resources

PHOTOCOPIABLE WORKSHEETS: Grammar worksheets Units 13–16; Vocabulary worksheets Units 13–16; Review Game Units 13–16; Literature worksheet; Speaking worksheet; Writing worksheet

WARMER

Divide the board into three columns, as in the example below, but mix up the order in each column. In pairs, students make sentences in the present passive. Challenge them to add one or two of their own.

Cars	make	by Ferrari
Films	produce	in Hollywood
Stamps	sell	at the post office
Tea	grow	in India
Big Macs	serve	at McDonalds
Presents	give	for birthdays
iPhones	make	by Apple

VOCABULARY

1 Students read the four headings and, in pairs, suggest words for each category starting with the given letters. They do the word search. Check answers. Ask students to choose a word from each category and make a sentence. In groups, they read out their sentences omitting the word. The other students guess the word.

Answers

Adjectives: feelings
disappointed embarrassed grateful proud
TV and film
animation chat show comedy documentary
Computer words
password link virus download
Doing experiments
blow cover shake wrap

d	o	c	u	m	e	n	t	a	r	y	s
m	i	d	g	w	r	a	p	n	e	p	e
b	d	s	p	r	a	b	l	i	s	r	m
o	o	r	a	i	a	s	r	m	l	o	b
c	w	e	s	p	y	t	h	a	i	u	a
o	n	s	s	y	p	n	e	a	n	d	r
m	l	o	w	u	r	o	s	f	k	t	r
e	o	c	o	v	e	r	i	o	u	e	a
d	a	r	r	w	e	e	h	n	r	l	s
y	d	a	d	v	i	r	u	s	t	e	s
b	l	o	w	t	o	r	n	c	h	e	e
e	a	c	h	a	t	s	h	o	w	r	d
p	t	p	a	n	i	m	a	t	i	o	n

2 Write *1 adjectives: feelings, 2 films and TV, 3 computer words* and *4 doing experiments* on the board. Read the words in the box and ask students to match them to a category. Answers: *1 confused, exhausted, stressed*; *2 characters, plot, soap opera, soundtrack*; *3 deleted, plug in, search, turn off*; *4 blow up, tie, work out*. Tell students they might need words from more than one category to complete the sentences. They complete the exercise and compare answers with a partner. Review answers and check understanding with the class.

Answers

1 search 2 soap opera 3 exhausted 4 deleted
5 confused, work out 6 stressed 7 plug in 8 soundtrack
9 Turn off, blow up 10 plot, characters

FAST FINISHERS

Ask fast finishers to choose two verbs from the list *look up, turn down, add up* and *work out*, and write a sentence for each. They read their sentences out, omitting the phrasal verb, and the rest of the class guesses the verb.

GRAMMAR

1 Do some general grammar revision of *just, already* and *yet*, considering meaning, position in the sentence and use with the present perfect. Revise the formation and use of zero and first conditionals and the use of *unless* to replace *if … not*. Remind students that they revised the present passive in the Warmer. Refer them to the Grammar reference sections for Units 13, 15 and 16 on pages 150, 152 and 153. Students read the sentences and complete them with the correct forms of the verbs in brackets. They compare answers with a partner. Check answers with the class and ask stronger students which grammar rule they are applying: present perfect with *just, already* and *yet*, present simple passive, zero conditional or first conditional.

Answers

1 Have, read 2 is 3 isn't made 4 does 5 has, arrived
6 is served 7 forgets 8 've, had 9 downloads 10 'll have to

CONTINUED ON PAGE 190

2 Tell students they are going to use the same grammar rules but this time they have to write sentences and questions from the prompt. Ask them to read the prompts and check understanding of the vocabulary, for example *rubber ring* (*an air-filled tube used as an aid to swimming*). Monitor and help as necessary while students complete the exercise. Check answers and, as in Exercise 1, ask stronger students which grammar rule they are applying.

Answers

1 Have you uploaded your film yet?
2 This film isn't / hasn't been translated into Spanish.
3 Jon has just shut down his computer.
4 If I fill the kettle, will you make the coffee?
5 The app opens when you enter your password.
6 The British actors aren't mentioned in the reviews.
7 The rubber ring won't float unless you fill it with air.
8 Sonia has already wrapped your present.

3 Revise the formation and use of relative clauses. Refer students to the Grammar reference section for Unit 14 on page 151. Read the instructions and tell students to read the first sentence carefully, looking out for positive and negative verbs and verb tenses. Remind them they can use a maximum of three words. Monitor and help as necessary while students complete the exercise. They check their answers with a partner. Review answers as a class and ask volunteers to offer any explanations necessary.

Answers

1 are produced
2 You won't
3 aren't installed
4 just finished
5 actor who plays
6 DVDs sold
7 comedy which/that you
8 can (only) use

MIXED ABILITY

Support weaker students by telling them which grammatical structures are needed in the second sentences: passive – 1, 3, 6; conditional – 2, 8; *just / already / yet* – 4; relative clause – 5, 7.

4 Remind the students of what they have reviewed in the Grammar section and elicit the different structures: relative clauses; present simple passive; zero and first conditional; *just*, *already* and *yet*. Students read the sentences carefully and complete the exercise. They compare answers with a partner. If they disagree on the correct form, each student should justify their choice by referring to the grammar rule that should be applied. Check answers with the class and ask stronger students to explain the grammar rules.

Answers

1 yet 2 'll have 3 that 4 's called

5 Explain that there is one mistake in each sentence and, as in Exercise 4, the mistakes concern the structures they have been reviewing. Put students in pairs to complete the exercise. If they disagree or are not sure what the mistake is, tell them to re-read the sentences carefully and think about which grammar rule is being tested. Check answers with the class and ask stronger students to explain the grammar rules.

Answers

1 I've just **spent** some money on lunch.
2 You'll like the pizza restaurant **which/that** is near my house.
3 My closest friend **is called** Simone.
4 If **you** have a problem, I'll help you.

6 **B1 Preliminary for Schools Reading Part 6**

In this part, candidates read a short text with six gaps and think of the word which best fits each gap. This requires reading for detailed understanding at word and sentence level, and mostly tests knowledge of grammar. Most of the missing words are prepositions, pronouns, articles, auxiliary verbs, modal verbs, conjunctions, etc. (See also Unit 1 and Review 2.)

Explain to students that they will read a short text with six gaps, but first they should read the text ignoring the gaps to find out what it is about. For each gap they have to write the missing word. Tell students that if they have no ideas about the missing word, they should underline the words directly before or after the gap and think about what kind of word is missing. For four of the gaps, only one word will fit. However, for gaps 4 and 6 there is a choice of two words which have the same or similar meanings, and both are correct. Ask students to complete the exercise and compare their answers with a partner before checking answers with the class. With the students, name the parts of speech used. Explain that these parts of speech are very typical of the words used in this kind of exercise.

Answers

1 are (auxiliary verb)
2 a (article)
3 few (quantifier)
4 made/produced (verb)
5 has (auxiliary verb)
6 that/which (relative pronoun)

COOLER

Ask students to think about Units 13–16. Ask questions such as, 'Which activities did you enjoy? What did you find difficult / easy? What could you do to improve your English?' Ask students to write down their answers, including at least three suggestions for how they could improve their language skills. Invite some students to share their answers and have a class discussion about each question. Share ideas on how they can improve their weaker areas, for example if they are having trouble with word order, they can copy some sentences and cut them up into individual words. They can also search for online exercises. If they need more practice with speaking, they can record themselves on their phone and send it to you or set up a conversation with a friend.

3 **Complete the second sentence so that it means the same as the first sentence. Use no more than three words.**

1. They produce most Indian films in Bollywood.
   Most Indian films ________ in Bollywood.
2. If you don't come to the cinema, you'll be really bored tonight.
   ________ be bored tonight if you come to the cinema.
3. This laptop doesn't install updates automatically.
   Updates ________ automatically on this laptop.
4. I finished watching the documentary a few minutes ago.
   I've ________ watching the documentary.
5. She's the new actress. She plays Juliet.
   She's the new ________ Juliet.
6. Do you sell DVDs here?
   Are ________ here?
7. This is a really funny comedy. You should watch it.
   This is a really funny ________ should watch.
8. Unless someone can remember the password, we can't use the computer.
   We ________ the computer if someone can remember the password.

4 **Choose the correct words.**

1. My friend hasn't arrived *already* / *yet*.
2. You *have* / *'ll have* fun if you come with us.
3. This is the computer game *that* / *who* I bought a few weeks ago.
4. I've been watching a series that *called* / *'s called Stranger Things*.

5 **Correct the mistake in each sentence.**

1. I've just spend some money on lunch.
2. You'll like the pizza restaurant where is near my house.
3. My closest friend calls Simone.
4. If you'll have a problem, I'll help you.

6 **For each question, write the correct answer. Write one word for each gap.**

PRIZES FOR YOUNG ENGINEERS

Any student between the ages of 12 and 19 can enter the *Young Engineers for Britain* competition. This is an annual event in which students [1] ________ challenged to be creative in developing their own idea. The aim of the competition is to design [2] ________ useful item that can eventually be produced and sold.

Ruth Amos won the prize a [3] ________ years ago for her invention, the 'StairSteady', which helps old people to go up and down stairs. It is [4] ________ from a strong metal and is very safe, as well as being simple to use. Ruth [5] ________ sold over 1,000 StairSteadys all around the country.

More recently, Matthew Hunter developed a product to charge a mobile phone [6] ________ will fit on a bicycle. He won the *Young Engineers' Duke of York Award* and received prize money of £1,000 for his invention.

17 TALENTED

ABOUT YOU

11 **Watch the video and then answer the questions.**

Have you ever tried creating art, playing music or performing on stage?

Do you know anyone who is young and talented?

VOCABULARY Arts and entertainment

1 **Look at the photos. What can you see? What are these places?**

2 **Listen to three conversations. Do they mention any of your ideas?** (82)

3 **Which words are related to which profession? Add the words to the table. Some words match more than one profession. Can you add any other words to the lists?** EP

audience biography director gallery novel painter painting poet poetry sculpture studio writer

Actor	*audience,*
Artist	
Author	

4 **Complete the articles with words in Exercise 3.**

YOUNG TALENT

There's an exhibition of new [0] *artists* called Young Talent at the university [1] ______ this month. It's mainly [2] ______ and drawings, but there are a few huge outdoor [3] ______ in the park next to it.

Secrets told

The best-selling [4] ______ Jenny Lee has written dozens of books over the years. Now it's time for us to read all about the secrets of Dr Lee's life in a new 600-page [5] ______ of the writer. It tells her life story, from her childhood in Singapore right up to the present day, and discusses in detail how she thought of ideas for her series of crime [6] ______, *What We See*.

Hollywood hopes

There's trouble in Hollywood this week for the *Project Z* movie. The main [7] ______ in the film won't work because they're unhappy with their pay and with the conditions in the [8] ______. However, time is money in show business, so the [9] ______, Frankie Jones, needs to show that he's in charge and end this argument quickly.

5 **Discuss the quiz questions.**

What's the difference between ...

1 a studio and a gallery?
2 an artist and a painter?
3 a novel and a biography?
4 an author and a poet?
5 a sculpture and a painting?

17 TALENTED

Unit Overview

TOPIC	Skills and talents
VOCABULARY	Arts and entertainment
READING	Who are the real artists?
GRAMMAR	Reported commands
VOCABULARY	Adjectives: *-al* and *-ful*
WRITING	A biography
EXAM TASKS	Reading Part 6

Resources

GRAMMAR REFERENCE AND PRACTICE: SB page 154; TB page 246
WORKBOOK: pages 68–71
VIDEO AND VIDEO WORKSHEET: Talented
PHOTOCOPIABLE WORKSHEETS: Grammar worksheet Unit 17; Vocabulary worksheet Unit 17
TEST GENERATOR: Unit test 17

WARMER

Write *talented* on the board and elicit its meaning (*having a natural ability to do something, especially without being taught*). Brainstorm a list of creative skills, for example drawing, writing, designing clothes, composing music, etc.

ABOUT YOU

11 You can begin the class and introduce the topic of the unit by showing the video and asking students to complete the video worksheet. Then, read the questions in the *About you* box. For the first question, ask for a show of hands for each activity and put students into groups containing a mix of experiences. They tell each other about one of the things they have tried. Encourage the other students to ask follow-up questions about their experiences. Invite students to tell the class about a member of their group. As a class, find out if any of the students know someone who is young and talented. Write key words on the board.

VOCABULARY Arts and entertainment

1 In pairs, students describe the pictures. Share ideas as a class and write key words on the board. Encourage students to give reasons for their answers.

Answers

Students' own answers

82 2 Play the recording for students to check if any of their ideas are mentioned. Ask them to listen for key words. They compare answers with a partner before checking as a class. Ask them which key words they heard.

Answers

Students' own answers

» AUDIOSCRIPT TB PAGE 276

3 Books closed. Draw three circles and write a profession inside each one: *actor*, *artist* and *author*. In pairs, students write down words connected to each heading. Add the words to create mind maps. Books open. Students read the words in the box. Check pronunciation, for example *audience* /ˈɔːdiəns/ and *sculpture* /ˈskʌlptʃə/. Students complete the table in pairs. Invite students to call out the words for each row, explaining their meaning or giving an example. Compare the answers with the mind maps on the board. Explain why 'studio' fits in two categories.

Answers

Actor: audience, director, <u>studio</u>
Artist: gallery, painter, painting, sculpture, <u>studio</u>
Author: biography, novel, poet, poetry, writer

4 Put students into groups of three to complete the texts, using the correct form of the words in Exercise 3. Each student in the group takes responsibility for one of the texts and then shares their answers with the rest of the group. Check answers as a class. Discuss what students enjoy doing best: going to art exhibitions, reading books or watching films.

Answers

1 gallery 2 paintings 3 sculptures 4 author 5 biography 6 novels 7 actors 8 studio 9 director

5 Give students a couple of minutes to review the vocabulary in Exercise 3. In groups, they write their answers and compare them with another group's. Make sure there is a range of abilities within each group. Check answers with the class.

Answers

1 A studio is where an artist works. A gallery is where an artist's work is displayed.
2 An artist can paint, draw, make sculptures and generally produce creative work. A painter paints pictures.
3 A novel is a book about imaginary people and events. A biography is the true story of someone's life, written by someone else.
4 An author is someone who writes a book, article, play, etc. A poet is someone who writes poetry.
5 A sculpture is made from solid materials, for example stone, metal, wood, clay. A painting is a picture done on paper or canvas using paints.

READING

BACKGROUND INFORMATION

Sia (born 1975 in Australia) has co-written songs for singers including Christina Aguilera, Beyoncé, Kylie Minogue, Flo Rida and Rihanna. In July 2014, her own sixth album went straight to No. 1 in the US *Billboard* 200 and, by 2016, it had sold 1 million copies worldwide.

Kendall Jenner and Kylie Jenner (born 1995 and 1997) are American models and television personalities. In 2014 and 2015, the Jenner sisters were on the *Time* magazine list of the most influential teens in the world.

Ben Cooke (born 1974) is an English stunt performer and fight coordinator. He acted as a stunt double for Daniel Craig in *Casino Royale*, *Quantum of Solace* and *Skyfall*.

Damien Hirst (born 1965) is an English artist. He became famous for a series of artworks in which dead animals (including a shark, a sheep and a cow) are preserved in formaldehyde, as well as the 'spot' paintings.

1 Ask students what they think the title of the article means: it suggests that a piece of work has been done by someone else and not the person named as its creator. Students look at the photos and subheadings, identify the people in the photos and suggest what art form they represent. Check understanding of *ghostwriter* (*someone who writes a book for another person, so that that person can pretend it is their own*) and *stunt double* (*someone skilled who does the dangerous actions in a film, taking the place of the lead actor*).

Answers

Sia (music), Kylie Jenner (books), Daniel Craig (acting), a colourful painting (art)

2 Students read the list of names. Find out whether they recognise any of them and what the people do. Give them a time limit to scan the article and answer the question. Check the answer.

Answer

They do secret work for celebrities who people might think have done the work themselves.

3 Students read the questions and choose the correct options. They read the article more carefully to check their answers. Tell them to ignore new vocabulary and the spaces in *The secret painter* at this point. Check answers. Ask if they are surprised by anything they found out.

Answers

1 A, C 2 A, C 3 B, C 4 B, C

4 **B1 Preliminary for Schools Reading Part 6**

In this part, candidates read a short text with six gaps. They decide which word best fits each gap. This requires reading for detailed understanding at word and sentence level, and mostly tests knowledge of grammar. Most of the missing words are function words. (See also Unit 1 and Reviews 2 and 4.)

Refer students to *The secret painter*. Explain that for each gap they have to write the missing word. Look at the example with the students. Look at the words before and after the gap and think of one word which fits it. Do the first item together. Ask students which word can go before *many* (*so* or *too*) and which one fits better with the meaning. They complete the exercise and compare answers with a partner. Check answers as a class and identify the parts of speech used. Explain that these parts of speech are very typical of the words used in this kind of exercise.

Answers

1 so (part of a quantifier)
2 to (part of infinitive)
3 too (adverb)
4 for (preposition)
5 by (preposition)
6 whose (relative pronoun)

83 The Reading text is recorded for students to listen, read and check their answers.

MIXED ABILITY

Help weaker students to identify the correct part of speech for each space. For example, for number 6, we need a subject before a verb. It must be a pronoun and so they need to look at the beginning of the passage to find who or what the pronoun refers to.

5 Ask students to look at the highlighted words and define them from the context. In pairs, students match the words to the definitions and compare them to the ones they created. Check answers.

Answers

1 toured 2 performers 3 perform 4 stunt double
5 publisher(s)

FAST FINISHERS

Ask fast finishers to write definitions for *successful*, *grow up*, *not mind*, *reputation*, *tournament*. Write the words on the board. The students read out their definitions and the class match them to the correct word.

TALKING POINTS

Put students into mixed ability pairs to discuss the questions. After a few minutes, invite pairs to share their ideas and hold a short class discussion. Write key words on the board.

COOLER

Students choose three words from the vocabulary on page 98 and make anagrams. In pairs, they solve each other's anagrams.

READING

WHO ARE THE REAL ARTISTS?

83

THE SONGWRITERS

When you hear a new song, you probably don't think about who wrote it. And although certain **performers** like Lady Gaga always write their own songs, hundreds of others **perform** songs written for them by songwriters. Sia is a famous singer who has **toured** the world several times and sold millions of her own albums. She's also a successful songwriter, who has written hits for Rihanna and other big stars. Next time you hear a song you love, why not look it up online and see who actually wrote it?

THE GHOSTWRITERS

Kylie Jenner and her sister Kendall were teenagers when they wrote their first science fiction novel, *Rebels: City of Indra*. But the Jenner sisters grew up as reality show stars, so how did they manage to write a book? The truth is, they didn't write it on their own. They had lots of ideas for the story, but they asked an author called Maya Sloan to write it with them. Sloan is also a ghostwriter who writes celebrities' books for them. Celebrities often use ghostwriters, either because they don't have time, or because they aren't natural writers. **Publishers** usually order ghostwriters not to talk about the books they've written for celebrities, but the Jenner sisters didn't mind anyone knowing about Maya Sloan.

THE STUNT DOUBLES

Daniel Craig has an action-hero reputation thanks to his performances as James Bond. But does the actor appear in all the dangerous scenes himself? Not always. Instead, a **stunt double** does lots of them. Ben Cooke was competing in a martial arts tournament when a producer saw him and advised him to become a stunt double. Ben Cooke looks a bit like Daniel Craig, so he became Craig's double. He's won a lot of prizes, including one for an incredible jump in *Casino Royale*.

THE SECRET PAINTERS

Damien Hirst produces hundreds of paintings every year. How does one man produce [1] ________ many? Like da Vinci and Michelangelo before him, he employs assistants in a studio. He usually tells them [2] ________ do the easy jobs, but they often do whole paintings [3] ________. Rachel Howard was 22 when she started working [4] ________ Hirst. According to Hirst, he only ever made five 'spot' paintings himself and the best spot painting is one painted [5] ________ Rachel! Nowadays, Rachel Howard doesn't work for Hirst. She is a well-known artist [6] ________ work fills galleries all around the world.

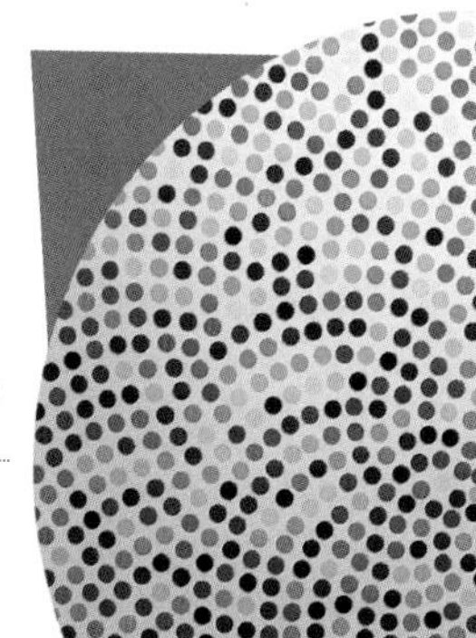

1 Look at the photos. Who or what can you see?

2 Read the article quickly. What do these people have in common?

Ben Cooke   Maya Sloan   Rachel Howard   Sia

3 Choose the correct answers. Read the article again and check.

1 Sia has written songs for ________ and ________.
   A herself **B** Lady Gaga **C** Rihanna
2 Maya Sloan is ________ and ________.
   A a ghostwriter **B** a reality show star **C** an author
3 ________ and ________ acted in *Casino Royale*.
   A James Bond **B** Daniel Craig **C** Ben Cooke
4 Painters like ________ and ________ had assistants.
   A Rachel Howard **B** Michelangelo **C** Damien Hirst

4 Now read 'The secret painters' again and think of the word which best fits each gap. Use only one word in each gap.

5 Match the **highlighted** words in the article to the meanings.

1 travelled around, playing in concerts or appearing at events
2 people who entertain others by acting, singing, dancing or playing music
3 act in a film or a play
4 somebody who does the difficult or dangerous scenes for an actor
5 a company, or the people, that produce books

TALKING POINTS

Do you think it's fair that famous people get others to do things for them? Why? / Why not?

Whose book would you most like to ghostwrite? Why?

GRAMMAR Reported commands

1 **Read the examples and choose the correct commands, a or b.**

1 The Jenner sisters **asked** a ghostwriter **to write** a novel with them.
  a 'Please write a book with us!'
  b 'Don't write our book, thanks.'
2 Publishers usually **order** ghostwriters **not to talk** about the books they've written.
  a 'You mustn't discuss these books with anyone!'
  b 'Feel free to talk about the books you've written.'
3 A film-maker **advised him to be** a stunt double.
  a 'You shouldn't be a stunt double!'
  b 'You should be a stunt double!'
4 He usually **tells them to do** the easy jobs.
  a 'Don't do the easy jobs.'
  b 'Do the easy jobs, please.'

2 **Complete the rules with *to* or *not*.**

We report:
a positive commands using a reporting verb + object pronoun + ____ infinitive.
The teacher ***ordered us to be*** *quiet.*
b negative commands using a reporting verb + object pronoun + ____ + *to* infinitive.
The teacher ***reminded us not to talk.***

>> GRAMMAR REFERENCE AND PRACTICE PAGE 154

3 **Choose the correct option.**

1 Why don't you *ask* / *tell* Tina to go to cinema with you?
2 I persuaded Lou *to not read* / *not to read* her poems!
3 I was crying, so my friend *said to me* / *told me* to calm down.
4 Go to the teacher and *tell to* / *ask* her for help.
5 The gallery attendant *told* / *said* us to be quiet.
6 Don't tell us what *do* / *to do*!
7 Dad *reminded* / *remembered* us to study for the test.
8 Who advised you *not print* / *not to print* your tickets?

4 **Complete the reported commands. Use the reporting verbs in brackets.**

0 **Mum:** '**Help** in the kitchen, please.'
  Mum *asked* them *to help* in the kitchen.' (ask)
1 **Karen:** 'You mustn't **touch** my things!'
  Karen ____ me ____ her things. (warn)
2 **Police officer:** '**Stop**!'
  A police officer ____ us ____. (order)
3 **Anna:** 'You must **be** more careful.'
  Anna ____ him ____ more careful. (tell)
4 **Sara:** 'You should**n't worry** so much.'
  Sara ____ her ____ so much. (advise)
5 **Diane:** 'Come on! It's time to **go**!'
  Diane ____ us ____. (persuade)
6 **Mrs Holt:** '**Don't hand in** the work late.'
  Mrs Holt ____ us ____ the work late. (remind)

5 **Read the example and notice how *your* changes to *their*. Then report the commands. Use the reporting verbs in brackets and change the pronouns if necessary.**

0 A teacher to her students: 'Remember to finish your homework before Friday.' (remind)
  The teacher reminded her students to finish their homework before Friday.
1 A father to his child: 'Don't run!' (tell)
2 A boy to his sister: 'Pass the salt, please.' (ask)
3 A girl to her brother: 'Get out of my room!' (order)
4 A woman to her daughter: 'Don't be late.' (warn)
5 A taxi driver to his passenger: 'Don't get out at the traffic lights.' (advise)
6 A boy to his friend: 'Watch the match with me! Go on, it'll be fun!' (persuade)

VOCABULARY Adjectives: *-al* and *-ful*

1 **Read the examples and answer questions a and b.**

EP
1 She's also a **successful** songwriter.
2 They aren't **natural** writers.
3 We were watching a **historical** drama.

a Which part of speech (verbs or nouns) do we use to make adjectives with *-al* and *-ful*?
b What spelling changes do you notice in examples 2 and 3?

2 **Complete the sentences with adjectives formed from the nouns in brackets.**

1 This exhibition is very ____. (colour)
2 I love the countryside. It's so ____. (peace)
3 That's a really ____ idea. (origin)
4 Ouch! My leg is still ____. (pain)
5 My brother's always smiling. He's very ____. (cheer)
6 The articles aren't at all ____. (politics)
7 I have three exams next week. It's very ____. (stress)
8 Is your apartment ____? (centre)

3 **>> Work with a partner. Student A turn to page 125. Student B turn to page 127.**

GRAMMAR Reported commands

WARMER

Give students some instructions to follow. Say, for example, 'Find a piece of paper and a pen. Write a short note. Make an aeroplane. Fly the plane to a friend. Open and read the message.' Elicit what you asked students to do in order and write the instructions on the board. Write a prompt on the board: *Our teacher told us to …* and ask a student to finish the sentence. Continue with the other orders.

1 Students read the example sentences and decide what the person giving the command actually said. In pairs, they choose the correct commands. Invite students to give their answers. Explain that the reporting verb can be used in any tense according to the context, for example *I'm going to tell him not to park his car there*.

Answers

1 a 2 a 3 b 4 b

2 Point out the negative form in example 2 in Exercise 1. Students read the sentences again and complete the rules in pairs. Check answers. Tell them we can use a noun in the same position as the pronoun, as in examples 1 and 2. There is a list of verbs that can be used in this way in the Grammar reference on page 154. Note that we cannot use *say* in this way.

Answers

a to b not

» GRAMMAR REFERENCE AND PRACTICE ANSWER KEY TB PAGE 246

3 Students choose the correct alternative, referring to the rules in Exercise 2. They should think carefully about word order in negative sentences. Students compare answers with a partner. Check answers with the class. We can also use question words between the object and the infinitive, as in question 6, especially with *tell*. Give some examples, such as: *Your teacher will tell you how to do the exercise.*

Answers

1 ask 2 not to read 3 told me 4 ask 5 told 6 to do
7 reminded 8 not to print

4 Explain that the sentence pairs show the command and the reported command. Check understanding of the reporting verbs. Students complete the exercise and compare answers with a partner. Check answers. Ask what they notice about the possessive adjective in question 1 and ask why it changes from *my* to *her*.

Answers

1 warned, not to touch
2 ordered, to stop
3 told, to be
4 advised, not to worry
5 persuaded, to go
6 reminded, not to hand in

5 Read the example. Students complete the exercise and compare answers with a partner. Check answers with the class and make sure students understand the pronoun changes in questions 3 and 6.

Answers

1 The father told his child not to run.
2 The boy asked his sister to pass (him) the salt.
3 The girl ordered her brother to get out of her room.
4 The woman warned her daughter not to be late.
5 The taxi driver advised his passenger not to get out at the traffic lights.
6 The boy persuaded his friend to watch the match (with him).

» GRAMMAR WORKSHEET UNIT 17

VOCABULARY Adjectives: *-al* and *-ful*

1 Write *-al* and *-ful* on the board. In small groups, give students one minute to make a list of adjectives for each ending. Read the example sentences and discuss the questions as a class. Students answer the questions. Check answers and add more spelling rules: nouns keep the final *e* with *-ful*, for example *care–careful*; nouns ending in *s*, delete the final *s* before adding *-al*, for example *mathematics–mathematical*.

Answers

a nouns
b 2) we delete the *e* at the end of *nature*
3) we change *y* to *ic* at the end of *history*

2 Students add *-al* or *-ful* to make adjectives. They complete the sentences and compare answers with a partner. Invite students to read out the completed sentences. Write the adjectives on the board for students to check spellings.

Answers

1 colourful 2 peaceful 3 original 4 painful 5 cheerful
6 political 7 stressful 8 central

FAST FINISHERS

Give fast finishers other nouns to make into *-al* and *-ful* adjectives, for example *beauty*, *culture* and *hope* (beautiful, cultural, hopeful).

3 Put students in pairs and assign A or B to each pair. A pairs turn to page 125 and B pairs to page 127. They read the sentences and complete them using adjectives formed from the nouns in the box. In new pairs consisting of one A and one B student, they ask and answer the questions, beginning with the most interesting one. Check the adjectives with the class and ask students to tell the class about their partner.

Answers

Student A
1 digital 2 musical 3 personal 4 professional 5 useful
6 hopeful
Student B
1 traditional 2 musical 3 environmental 4 cultural
5 helpful 6 stressful

» VOCABULARY WORKSHEET UNIT 17

WRITING A biography

1 Ask students what they know about Taylor Swift and if they like her music. Elicit what kind of books describe someone's life (*biographies and autobiographies*). Tell them they are going to read a short biography about Taylor Swift and elicit what kind of information it might include, for example where she was born and what she has done in her life so far. Tell them to read the text and compare it to their ideas.

Answers
Students' own answers

2 Find out whether students thought the biography was interesting and whether they learned anything new or interesting about Taylor Swift. In small groups, students discuss what makes a biography interesting. They report their ideas back to the class. Write key points on the board. Tell them to read the *Prepare to write* box and compare their ideas.

Possible answers
She lived on her family's Christmas tree farm.
She made her first album when she was 16.
She paid for an education centre in Nashville.

3 Give students one minute to read the biography again. Tell them to memorise as much information as they can. Books closed. Call out each of the dates in the text and ask the class to tell you what happened at that time in Taylor Swift's life. They can check their answers by looking back at the text.

Answers
1989 – She was born.
2004 – She moved to Nashville.
2006 – First album *Taylor Swift*.
2008 – Second album *Fearless*.
2017 – *Reputation* album.
2017 – One of her videos had 40 million views in 24 hours.

4 Students read the sentences and fill each space with one word. They are all time expressions. They compare answers with a partner before checking as a class. Point out that the expression *by the time* is often used with *already*.

Answers
1 at
2 as, as
3 as
4 Nowadays
5 By, time

5 Students are going to write their own biography. They can choose a famous person or someone they know. In pairs or small groups, students discuss the person they have chosen, answer the questions and decide on any other important information they want to include. If they have internet access, students could do some further research about their chosen person. If not, they should choose someone they already know a lot about. If several students have chosen the same celebrity, allow them to compare ideas.

MIXED ABILITY

Encourage weaker students to use each of the time expressions at least once and to think carefully about verb tenses. Tell them to read their finished biography twice: the first time to check content and the second time to check grammar and vocabulary.

6 Students write their biographies. Remind them to check their spelling and grammar and to use the tips and language in the *Prepare to write* box. Ask them to include an *-al* and *-ful* adjective, too. Encourage stronger students to include one or two reported commands, for example *Her mum told her not to become an actress*. Put students into groups to read each other's biographies. They should say what they found interesting or surprising. Display the biographies around the classroom for other students to read.

Model answer
Daniel Radcliffe is a successful British actor who was born in England in 1989. He decided that he wanted to act as a young child and appeared in his first TV programme at the age of ten. He auditioned for the role of Harry Potter in the year 2000, and the first film in the series was released in 2001. Daniel played Harry Potter for ten years.
Daniel didn't go to university because he wanted to act instead. Since the last Harry Potter film in 2011, he has been in several other films and starred in plays on Broadway in New York as well as in London. In 2007, he published several poems in *Rubbish*, an underground fashion magazine, but he used the name Jacob Gershon instead of his own name. He supports many charities and has won an award for his charity work. His favourite charity is a children's hospice in the south of England.

COOLER

Guessing game. Choose a famous person or someone you know well and write their name and three important dates from their life on the board. Students have to guess why these dates are significant. Only accept answers which are grammatically correct. Students then write down three significant dates from their own lives. Put them into small groups to guess what happened on each date. Invite students to choose an important date in their life and tell the class about it.

WRITING A biography

1 Look at the photo. What do you know about Taylor Swift? Read the biography and check your ideas.

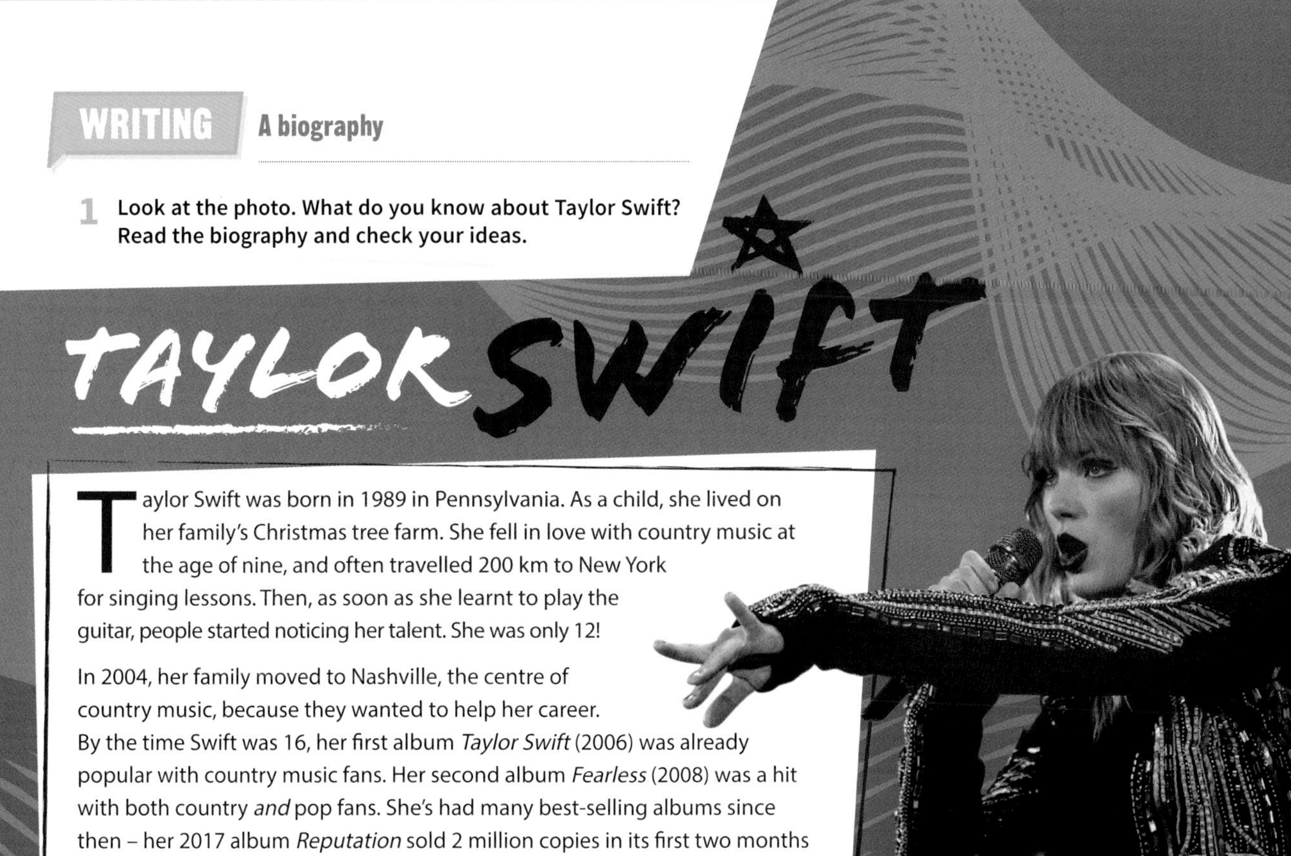

Taylor Swift was born in 1989 in Pennsylvania. As a child, she lived on her family's Christmas tree farm. She fell in love with country music at the age of nine, and often travelled 200 km to New York for singing lessons. Then, as soon as she learnt to play the guitar, people started noticing her talent. She was only 12!

In 2004, her family moved to Nashville, the centre of country music, because they wanted to help her career. By the time Swift was 16, her first album *Taylor Swift* (2006) was already popular with country music fans. Her second album *Fearless* (2008) was a hit with both country *and* pop fans. She's had many best-selling albums since then – her 2017 album *Reputation* sold 2 million copies in its first two months on sale. A video for a single from the album, *Look What You Made Me Do*, had over 40 million views in 24 hours, and the *Reputation* world tour earned over $400 million! Nowadays, Swift uses her success to help other people. She gives lots of money to charity, and she once paid $4 million for an education centre in Nashville.

2 Read the *Prepare to write* box, then read the biography again. What interesting facts do you learn about Taylor Swift?

PREPARE TO WRITE

A biography

When you write a biography, include:

- interesting or unusual facts about the person
- important dates from the person's life
- information about what the person did at different ages:
  As a child, …
  At the age of …
  As soon as he/she …
  By the time he/she was …
  Nowadays, …

3 How many important dates are mentioned in the biography? What happened in each year?

4 Write one word in each space. Use language from the biography in Exercise 1.

1 He left home ________ the age of 14.
2 She got married ________ soon ________ she was 21.
3 He started playing football ________ a young child.
4 ________, she's a well-known guitarist.
5 ________ the ________ he started at college, he was already in two bands.

5 You are going to write a biography. Choose a famous person or someone you know. Plan your biography and make some notes. Here are some ideas to help you.

- When was he/she born?
- What are the important dates in his/her life?
- What are his/her main achievements?
- What interesting facts do you know about him/her?

6 Write your biography.

- Use the tips in the *Prepare to write* box.
- Write about 150 words.
- Remember to check your spelling and grammar.

TALENTED 101

18 THE WORLD OF WORK

ABOUT YOU

12 Watch the video and then answer the questions.
What jobs do people you know do?
What job might you want to do? Why?

VOCABULARY Jobs

84 **1 Label the photos with the jobs in the box. Then listen and check.**

architect	babysitter	builder	coach	firefighter
hairdresser	journalist	lawyer	pharmacist	
politician	presenter	vet		

85 **2 Listen to six people describing their jobs. What are their jobs?**

3 Answer the questions, using the jobs you didn't use in Exercise 2.

Who …
1 explains the law to people and gives them advice?
2 designs buildings?
3 works in government?
4 introduces a TV or radio show?
5 gives people medicine?
6 writes news stories or articles for publications, radio or TV?

4 Discuss the questions.

Which jobs …
1 do you usually need to get a degree for?
2 are paid the highest?
3 do people mainly do in an office?
4 often mean working weekends?
5 would be the most interesting/boring?

18 THE WORLD OF WORK

Unit Overview

TOPIC	Work and jobs
VOCABULARY	Jobs
READING	I'm in charge
GRAMMAR	Second conditional
VOCABULARY	Suffixes: *-er*, *-or*, *-ist*, *-ian*
LISTENING	Two conversations about problems
SPEAKING	Discussing options
EXAM TASKS	Speaking Part 3; Speaking Part 4

Resources

GRAMMAR REFERENCE AND PRACTICE: SB page 155; TB page 246
WORKBOOK: pages 72–75
VIDEO AND VIDEO WORKSHEET: I'm in charge
PHOTOCOPIABLE WORKSHEETS: Grammar worksheet Unit 18; Vocabulary worksheet Unit 18
TEST GENERATOR: Unit test 18

WARMER

Put students into teams to brainstorm a list of jobs. They write one job for each letter of the alphabet, for example actor, builder, cleaner (they probably won't be able to think of a job for every letter, but they can have fun trying!). Set a strict time limit for this. Students exchange lists with another team. Ask one of the teams to read out the list they have in front of them, and ask the other teams to add any additional words. Write the jobs on the board, awarding a point for any job that no other team has thought of.

ABOUT YOU

12 You can begin the class and introduce the topic of the unit by showing the video and asking students to complete the video worksheet. Ask students to discuss the questions in small groups. Ask if they know anyone who does an exciting, difficult or dangerous job, and to discuss their dream job. Invite each group to tell the class about the people they discussed. Find out how many students in the class are interested in doing the same job, and if there are any jobs students would not like to do.

VOCABULARY Jobs

1 Students read the words in the box and compare them to the list they made in the Warmer. In pairs, they match the jobs to the photos. Play the recording for them to check their answers. Check answers with the class and then play the recording again to practise pronunciation.

84

Answers

The answers are recorded for students to listen and check.
A architect B builder C vet D politician E hairdresser F presenter G journalist H babysitter I lawyer J firefighter K pharmacist L coach

85

2 Read the instructions and explain that the people will not say the name of the job, so students must listen carefully to the descriptions and for key words. Play the recording, pausing between each description. Students compare answers with a partner. Play the recording again and ask students to make a note of the key words that helped them to decide.

Answers

1 vet 2 firefighter 3 babysitter 4 hairdresser 5 coach 6 builder

» AUDIOSCRIPT TB PAGES 276–277

3 Ask students to call out the remaining jobs from the box in Exercise 2. Invite stronger students to provide definitions for them. Put students into mixed ability pairs to read the definitions and match them to the jobs. Check answers.

Answers

1 a lawyer
2 an architect
3 a politician
4 a presenter
5 a pharmacist
6 a journalist

FAST FINISHERS

Tell fast finishers to write a question starting with *Who …?* about two of the following jobs: author, designer, film director, detective, DJ, model.

4 Read the questions and check understanding. Explain that students should list all the jobs in Exercise 1 for each question. Ask for suggestions for question 1. Put students into small groups to discuss the questions. Monitor and help as necessary. Check answers with the class and allow for class discussion to see if the groups agree.

Possible answers

1 lawyer, journalist, architect, politician, pharmacist, vet
2 lawyer, vet, presenter
3 lawyer, journalist, architect
4 firefighter, babysitter, coach, pharmacist, presenter
5 Student's own answers

READING

BACKGROUND INFORMATION

Originally called Takeover Day, Takeover Challenge, which started in 2004, is a national event organised by the Office of the Children's Commissioner for England, a public body in England responsible for promoting and protecting the rights of children. The aim of Takeover Challenge is to give children and young people the opportunity to work with adults and take part in making decisions. Each year about 50,000 children and young people work with a range of organisations from businesses, schools, police and fire services, newspapers, banks, TV and radio stations to charities, local councils, hospitals and government departments.

1 Students read the title of the article. Check understanding and ask students to read the introduction in the blue box. Ask them to suggest what a *Takeover Challenge* is. Students read the first two paragraphs of the article to see if their predictions were correct. Ask them to summarise the two aims of the event. Students look at the photos and suggest what jobs they represent. Set a short time limit for them to read about the three jobs to check their predictions. Check answers.

Answers

Sophie – headteacher
Simon – football coach
Alexandra – politician

2 Students read the questions. Check understanding and ask them to discuss what they remember about the text with a partner. Tell them to read the text more carefully and find the answers. Students compare answers with a partner, pointing to the section of the text where they found the information. Invite different students to give their answers.

Answers

1 It happens every year.
2 It gives young people experience in a wide range of jobs; adults can learn from young people's opinions and ideas.
3 She didn't like the meetings. There were so many meetings and some of them went on for ages.
4 He found it exhausting to train with fit professional players.
5 It is a 24/7 job and there's no time for lunch.
6 The text mentions: actor, sports star, musician, TV presenter, sports coach, journalist, (head) teacher, politician, school chef, professional football player, prime minister.

86 The Reading text is recorded for students to listen, read and check their answers.

MIXED ABILITY

Pair weaker students with stronger students to complete the exercise.

3 Ask students to cover Exercise 3 and look at the highlighted words in the text. In pairs, they look carefully at the context and write their own definitions. Invite different pairs to read out a definition for the rest of the class to say which word they are describing. Students then uncover Exercise 3 and complete the exercise. Check answers. Check understanding of any other new words in the text and discuss their meanings as a class.

Answers

1 a wide range
2 chance
3 ages
4 fresh
5 unforgettable
6 prime minister

TALKING POINTS

Set a short time limit for students to work in pairs to think of some ideas in response to each question. Then hold a class discussion. Tell them to listen carefully to each other and to agree and disagree politely. Encourage them to ask each other what they think, and to help each other with vocabulary, if necessary.

COOLER

Ask students to think of a job. In teams, students have to guess each other's jobs by asking *Yes/No* questions. Ask for suggestions for questions before they begin and write them on the board, for example *Do you work inside or outside? Do you wear a uniform? Do you need a degree?* etc.

READING

1 Read the introduction and look at the photos. What jobs do you think the three young people did? Read the article quickly and check.

86

If you could do any job for a day, what would it be? A famous actor? An amazing sports star? A well-known musician? *Takeover Challenge* offers thousands of young people this opportunity. Read more to find out how it works and hear about the experiences of Sophie, Simon and Alexandra.

I'M IN CHARGE

Takeover Challenge **is an annual event in English schools and about 50,000 young people 'take over' from adults and have a go at their jobs. They're in charge for just one day! Of course, it's difficult to make someone into a film or music celebrity. However,** ***Takeover Challenge*** **has offered young people the chance to be TV presenters, sports coaches, journalists, teachers and even politicians.**

The event has two aims. Firstly, it gives young people experience in a wide range of jobs. Secondly, adults can learn from young people's opinions and fresh ideas.

Sophie Cameron, 15, became the headteacher of her school. 'I'd go mad if I were a headteacher permanently,' she said. 'There were so many meetings and some of them went on for ages!' Sophie thinks she learned a lot. 'My favourite part of the day was meeting the school chef and approving the school menus for the week. It was a great opportunity to tell her what we really like eating!'

Simon Evans spent the day at Coventry Football Club. He became coach of the football team. 'Training with professional players was exhausting. They're really fit,' said Simon. 'I would do this job every day if I could. It was an unforgettable experience.'

Alexandra Shaw spent the day with a politician. She even went to a meeting with the prime minister! Alexandra thought that if everyone did a politician's job for a day, they'd be amazed. 'It isn't a nine-to-five job,' she said. 'It's 24/7. There isn't even any time for lunch!'

2 Read the article again. Answer the questions.

1 How often does *Takeover Challenge* happen?
2 Who does the day help? How?
3 What did Sophie dislike about her day?
4 What part of being a coach was difficult for Simon?
5 What surprised Alexandra about a politician's work?
6 What jobs does the article mention?

TALKING POINTS

Is *Takeover Challenge* a good idea? Why? / Why not?

What job would you like to 'take over' for a day?

3 Match the highlighted words in the article to the meanings.

1 a lot of different types
2 opportunity
3 a long time
4 new and different
5 exciting and impossible to forget
6 the leader of a government

GRAMMAR Second conditional

1 **Read the examples. Then complete the rules with the correct words.**

1 If everyone **did** a politician's job for a day, they'**d** be amazed.
2 If you **could** do any job for a day, what **would** it be?
3 I **would** do this job every day **if** I **could**.
4 I'**d** go mad **if** I **were** a head teacher permanently.

We use the second conditional to talk about an unlikely or impossible situation in the present or future, and its results.
a We form the second conditional with: *If* + ________, and ________ + infinitive
b The short form of *would* is ________.
c We can use *I* ________ instead of *I was* in the *if* clause of the second conditional.
d The *if* clause can come first or second in the sentence.

» **GRAMMAR REFERENCE AND PRACTICE PAGE 155**

2 **Match the sentence halves and choose the correct verbs.**

1 You probably *didn't* / *wouldn't* earn much money
2 I *get* / *'d get* paid a lot of money
3 *Did* / *Would* you be worried
4 If I *were* / *would be* the headteacher of my school,
5 If I *wanted* / *would want* to be a vet,
6 If Dad *worked* / *would work* nine-to-five in an office,

a if your dad *was* / *would be* a firefighter?
b he *got* / *'d get* very bored.
c if you *became* / *would become* a musician.
d what subjects *did* / *would* I have to study?
e if I *became* / *'d become* a lawyer.
f lessons *started* / *would start* at 10 am.

3 **Complete the second conditional sentences.**

1 You ________ (sleep) better if you ________ (do) more exercise.
2 If you ________ (fail) the end-of-year exam, what ________ your parents ________ (say)?
3 If my brother ________ (not take) my things, we ________ (not have) so many arguments.
4 You ________ (finish) your homework before dinner if you ________ (not waste) so much time on the internet.
5 If I ________ (can) live anywhere in the world, I ________ (choose) somewhere hot.
6 ________ you ________ (be) upset if your best friend ________ (not give) you a birthday present?

4 **Correct the mistake in each sentence.**

1 If I were you, I'll get a job as a babysitter.
2 Would you be a football coach if you would have the chance?
3 If you met her, you will really like her.
4 It will be fun if you came with me.
5 I would leave if I would find my job stressful.
6 If I would see them again, I could identify them.

5 **Complete the sentences with your own ideas. In pairs, compare your answers.**

1 If I were a journalist, *I'd write about fashion.*
2 If I could do any job for a day, …
3 If I had €100,000 to spend on equipment for my school, …
4 I wouldn't ever be bored again if …
5 If I were in charge of my school, …
6 My parents wouldn't be pleased if …
7 If I could be the coach of any team, …
8 If I were prime minister of my country, …

6 **Tell the class about your partner's answers in Exercise 5.**

If Luca could do any job for a day, he'd be a photographer.

VOCABULARY Suffixes: *-er*, *-or*, *-ist*, *-ian*

1 **Read the examples. Then make nouns for people from the words in the box.**

EP

1 He spent the day with a **politician**.
2 It isn't easy being a **teacher**.
3 Would you like to be a **journalist**?
4 I'd love to be a **film director** for a day!

~~act~~	art	clean	music
reception	run	visit	

actor

2 **Complete the words with the correct suffix and match them to the definitions.**

1 A blogg*er*
2 A competit…
3 A scient…
4 A football support…
5 A vegetar…
6 A guitar…
7 A novel…
8 A comed…
9 A goalkeep…

a competes in a competition.
b is an expert who studies or works in one of the sciences.
c is the player who stands in the goal.
d writes a blog.
e writes novels.
f plays the guitar.
g doesn't eat meat or fish.
h tells jokes.
i likes a particular football team and wants them to win.

3 » **Work with a partner. Turn to page 125.**

 Second conditional

WARMER

Remind students of their dream jobs from *About you* from page 102. On the board, write *If you could do any job, what would you choose?* Invite answers from students and write them on the board using the conditional. Find out if any students share the same dream.

1 Ask students what they remember about zero and first conditionals. Read out the example sentences. Ask concept questions to check understanding that the *if* clause refers to a situation that is unlikely or impossible, for example *Can everyone do a politician's job for a day? Can most people do any job they want for a day? Can Simon be a football coach every day? Is Sophie a headteacher?* Students read the examples and complete the rules. Check answers.

Answers

a past simple, would
b 'd
c were

» **GRAMMAR REFERENCE AND PRACTICE ANSWER KEY TB PAGE 246**

2 Students match the sentence halves and then, referring to the rules in Exercise 1, they choose the correct verb forms for each clause. They compare answers with a partner. Check answers with the class.

Answers

1 c You probably **wouldn't** earn much money if you **became** a musician.
2 e **I'd get** paid a lot of money if I **became** a lawyer.
3 a **Would** you be worried if your dad **was** a firefighter?
4 f If I **were** the headteacher of my school, lessons **would start** at 10 am.
5 d If I **wanted** to be a vet, what subjects **would** I have to study?
6 b If Dad **worked** nine-to-five in an office, he**'d get** very bored.

3 Remind students to apply the rules in Exercise 1 and encourage them to use contractions where possible. They complete the exercise individually. In mixed ability pairs, they compare answers. Check answers with the class.

Answers

1 'd sleep, did
2 failed, would, say
3 didn't take, wouldn't have
4 'd finish, didn't waste
5 could, 'd choose
6 Would, be, didn't give

4 Tell students to read the sentences carefully and refer to the rules if necessary. They compare answers with a partner. Check answers with the class.

Answers

1 If I were you, **I'd** get a job as a babysitter.
2 Would you be a football coach if you **had** the chance?
3 If you met her, you **would** really like her.
4 It **would** be fun if you came with me.
5 I would leave if I **found** my job stressful.
6 If I **saw** them again, I could identify them.

5 Students read out the sentence beginnings. Check understanding. Read the example and invite other students to suggest their own ideas. Students complete the exercise individually and then compare answers with a partner. Monitor and help as necessary. Give positive feedback for interesting answers and the correct use of the second conditional.

Answers

Students' own answers

MIXED ABILITY

Work with weaker students to decide which sentence endings will be in the conditional (2, 3, 5, 7, 8) and which will be in the past simple (4, 6).

6 Invite different students to tell the class about their partner, as in the example. Students give their own answers.

» **GRAMMAR WORKSHEET UNIT 18**

VOCABULARY Suffixes: *-er, -or, -ist, -ian*

1 Quickly review the list of jobs on page 102. Students read the examples and look at the words in bold. Point out that *-er* and *-or* are both pronounced /ə/. In pairs, students decide on the correct endings for the words in the box. Check answers. Remind students of the spelling rules for the consonant–vowel–consonant pattern, for example *runner*. Ask whether they can think of any other jobs with the different endings, for example *waiter, doctor, dentist, technician*. Record vocabulary.

Answers

artist cleaner musician receptionist runner visitor

FAST FINISHERS

Ask fast finishers to think of other jobs ending in the different suffixes, for example *banker, editor, psychiatrist, magician*.

2 Students complete the words and then match them to the definitions. They compare answers with a partner. Check answers and understanding with the class.

Answers

1 d A blogg**er**
2 a A competit**or**
3 b A scient**ist**
4 i A football support**er**
5 g A vegetar**ian**
6 f A guitar**ist**
7 e A novel**ist**
8 h A comed**ian**
9 c A goalkeep**er**

3 Students turn to page 125. Check understanding of the words in the box. Ask one student to mime one of the jobs. In pairs, students take turns to mime the remaining jobs for their partner to guess. They have a time limit of two minutes.

» **VOCABULARY WORKSHEET UNIT 18**

LISTENING

87 **1** Tell students that they are going to hear two conversations in which two young people, Allie and Evan, talk about a problem and ask for advice. Students read the questions in the table. Play the recording. Students compare answers with a partner before checking as a class. Ask if they can remember any key words or phrases that helped them answer the questions.

Answers

Allie never has any money. She is asking her friend Ben for advice.
Evan doesn't know which subjects to choose for next year. He is asking his teacher, Mrs Shaw, for advice.

87 **2** Ask students to read the sentences and check understanding. They underline key words and phrases and decide whether the sentences are correct or incorrect according to what they remember from the recording. Play the recording again for them to check their answers. Check answers with the class.

Answers

1 false (He might get a job in a year or so.)
2 false (They might say 'no'.)
3 true
4 false (She will speak to them tonight about it.)
5 true
6 false (Mrs Shaw suggests it and Evan agrees.)
7 true
8 true

» AUDIOSCRIPT TB PAGE 277

SPEAKING Discussing options

1 Ask students if any of them have weekend jobs and what they do. In pairs, they describe the pictures and say what is happening in each one. Listen to feedback as a class and write key vocabulary on the board. In pairs, students discuss which job they would prefer to do and why. Have a show of hands to find out which job is the most popular.

Answers

gardening babysitting doing housework
working in an office waitressing/working in a café
walking dogs

88 **2** Tell students that they are going to hear two friends discussing the jobs Nicole could do and deciding which one would be best. Tell them to number the pictures in the order they are mentioned (*1 walking dogs, 2 gardening, 3 doing housework, 4 working in an office, 5 babysitting, 6 working in a café*). Play the recording and then check the answer. Students listen again and say why the café job is suitable and why the others are not. Play the recording again and check answers. Check understanding of *tip* (*extra money for someone who has provided you with a service to thank them*).

Answers

working in a café

88 **3** Books closed. Write the four headings from the *Prepare to speak* box on the board. In small groups, students brainstorm any phrases they know for each one. Invite students to share their ideas and write the phrases on the board. Books open. Ask students to compare the phrases on the board to those in the *Prepare to speak* box. Play the recording again for them to make a note of the phrases they hear. Students compare answers with a partner before checking as a class.

Answers

Making suggestions
What about …?
What do you think about …?
If I were you/him/her, …
Agreeing
Yes, you're right.
That's true.
Maybe you're right.
Disagreeing
I'm not so sure.
The problem with … is…
… might be better.
Reaching agreement
Yes, that's a good choice.

» AUDIOSCRIPT TB PAGE 277

4 B1 Preliminary for Schools Speaking Part 3

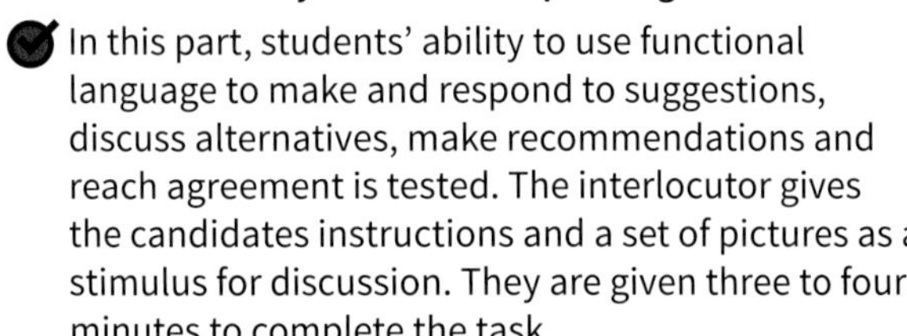
In this part, students' ability to use functional language to make and respond to suggestions, discuss alternatives, make recommendations and reach agreement is tested. The interlocutor gives the candidates instructions and a set of pictures as a stimulus for discussion. They are given three to four minutes to complete the task.

Read the instructions. Give students a few minutes to prepare their ideas and then complete the task in pairs. Monitor and give positive feedback for using phrases from the *Prepare to speak* box and for interesting ideas. Invite students to share their conclusions with the class.

Answers

Students' own answers

5 B1 Preliminary for Schools Speaking Part 4

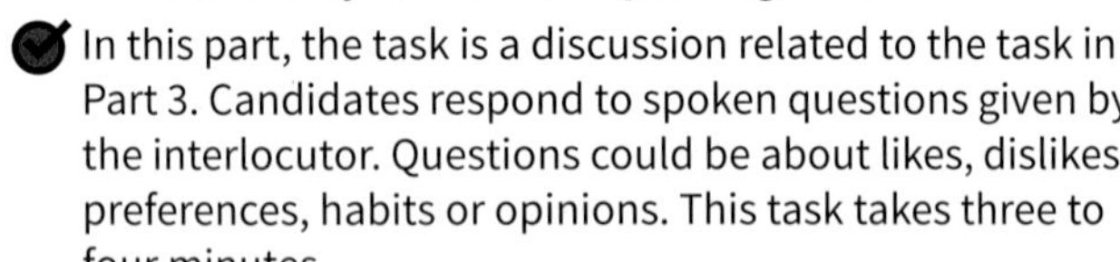
In this part, the task is a discussion related to the task in Part 3. Candidates respond to spoken questions given by the interlocutor. Questions could be about likes, dislikes, preferences, habits or opinions. This task takes three to four minutes.

Read out the questions and ask each pair to choose one group: 1, 2 or 3. Encourage them to give reasons for their opinions and to listen and respond to each other. Monitor and help as necessary. Invite students to tell the class about their groups' opinions.

Answers

Students' own answers

COOLER

Write some problems on pieces of paper, for example a friend borrowed money and didn't pay it back; you didn't do your homework, etc. In small groups, students choose a piece of paper, read the problem and give advice.

LISTENING

87 **1 Listen to two conversations about problems and complete the table.**

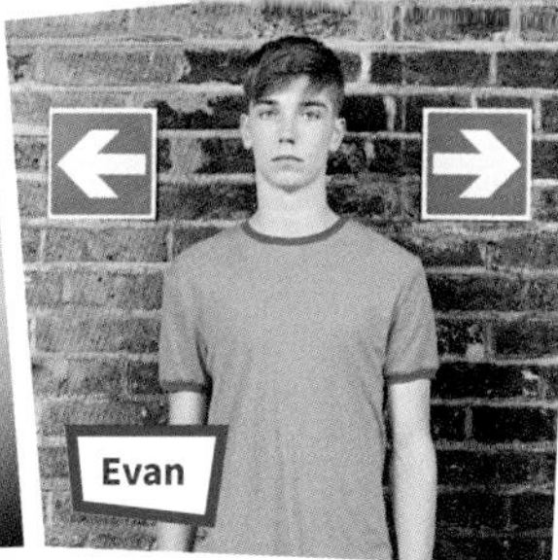

	Conversation 1: Allie	Conversation 2: Evan
What is his/her problem?		
Who is he/she asking for advice?		

87 **2 Listen again. Are the sentences true or false?**

Conversation 1

1 Ben has already got a weekend job.
2 Allie's parents said she is allowed to get a weekend job.
3 Ben thinks Allie might be able to earn some money at home.
4 Allie wants to avoid asking her parents about a weekend job.

Conversation 2

5 Evan knows what he wants to study at university.
6 Evan has already done some research online.
7 Mrs Shaw thinks Evan should choose a wide range of subjects.
8 Mrs Shaw thinks that ten subjects might be too many for Evan.

SPEAKING Discussing options

1 Look at the picture. Nicole is thinking about getting a weekend job. Which jobs is she thinking about?

88 **2 Listen to two friends discussing the jobs that Nicole could do. Which one do they agree would be best for Nicole?**

88 **3 Read the *Prepare to speak* box. Then listen again. Which phrases do you hear?**

4 Work with a partner. Talk together for three minutes about the different jobs Nicole could do and decide which would be best. Use the phrases in the *Prepare to speak* box.

5 In pairs, discuss the questions.

1 Would you like to have a weekend job?
2 Which job would you choose? Why?
3 Do you think students should have weekend jobs? Why? / Why not?

PREPARE TO SPEAK

Discussing options

Making suggestions
What about ...?
I think ... might be a good idea
What do you think about ...?
If I were you/him/her, ...

Agreeing
Yes, you're right.
That's true.
Maybe you're right.
I see what you mean.

Disagreeing
No, I don't agree.
I'm not so sure.
The problem with ... is ...
... might be better.
But don't you think ...?

Reaching agreement
Yes, that's a good choice.

CULTURE

SPECIAL TRAINING

1 Ask and answer the questions with a partner.

1 What activities do you enjoy in art class?

2 What after-school activities do you enjoy?

2 Read the article. Complete it with the words in the box.

acrobatics companies dancers fashion regular training

SCHOOLS *FOR THE ARTS*

Most schools offer a variety of subjects and activities for students, but some schools offer additional training in certain areas, such as the performing and visual arts. In this way, schools can help students develop their artistic talents from an early age and have greater success in their future profession.

89

THE ROYAL BALLET SCHOOL

For ballet dancers, one of the best training centres in the world is The Royal Ballet School, in London, England. The school only accepts the most talented [1] __________ , who must complete eight years of full-time training. There are 225 students, aged 11–19, and most of them live together in boarding houses. On school days, they start at 8.30 am and finish at 4.00 pm. They have two hours of ballet classes and four hours of [2] __________ subjects. Students also have ballet practice after school and on Saturdays. It's a lot of work, but the results are incredible.

IDYLLWILD ARTS ACADEMY

Located in the mountains about 100 miles from Los Angeles, the Idyllwild Arts Academy is a boarding school for young artists. It offers [3] __________ in visual arts, like drawing, painting, sculpture, photography and cinema, along with programmes for the performing arts, like music, dance and theatre. There is even a special department for young [4] __________ designers. Every year, more than 300 students from about 25 countries attend Idyllwild, and it has become one of the most famous arts schools in North America. The school's quiet, rural location also makes it a very peaceful and beautiful place to learn.

THE NATIONAL CIRCUS SCHOOL

If you'd like to join the circus, you should apply to the National Circus School in Montreal, Canada. Since it was founded in 1981, the school has offered training in [5] __________ , theatre, dance, juggling and other circus arts. About 150 people study there every year and 30 of them are teen students in the high school programme. In a typical week, they have twenty hours of circus classes and twenty hours of regular classes. After finishing the programme, many students find work in circus [6] __________ , such as the Cirque du Soleil. That's the dream of every circus artist!

CULTURE

Learning Objectives

- The students learn about special arts training.
- In the project stage, they give a presentation about an unusual training school to the class.

Vocabulary

accept apply attend boarding school incredible profession

Resources

CULTURE VIDEO AND CULTURE VIDEO WORKSHEET: Performing Arts Schools

BACKGROUND INFORMATION

For most young people with ambitions to become professional performing artists, a good academic education in a mainstream school is probably the best, but for those few with exceptional talents, specialist schools can offer the best of both worlds. Although acting does not depend on early specialism, for those wanting to be classical dancers or musicians, professional early training is fundamental. The entry levels to specialist schools are very high. For example, at Tring Park School for the Performing Arts in the UK, candidates, who are aged 13 or under, take part in a dance class, recite a poem, sing a song and play an instrument. In addition, they must display a piece of artwork. They also take academic tests in maths and English.

The UK government-funded Music and Dance Scheme provides scholarships for over 700 boys and girls with outstanding talent in music or ballet. Children aged eight and over (or 11 in the case of dance schools) can be considered for fund aid and, if successful, will receive specialist training as well as a good academic education. The scheme covers eight specialist independent schools in England – four music schools and four dance schools.

WARMER

Write *performing and visual arts* on the board. Ask for one or two examples and then put students in pairs or small groups to write a list. Set a time limit. Take feedback from the whole class and write key words on the board. Possible answers could include dance, ballet, music, acting, singing, circus arts, drawing, painting, sculpture, photography, cinema, etc.

1 Read the questions and put students in pairs to answer them. As a class, invite them to share their answers. Ask students if they think arts classes are important and useful and encourage them to explain why or why not. Find out which are the most popular after-school activities.

Answers

Students' own answers

2 Students look at the photos and read the title of the article and the words in the box. They then read the article and fill in the spaces. Check answers with the class. Check understanding of *acrobatics* (*performing difficult physical acts, such as walking on a wire high above the ground*) and pronunciation of *ballet* /ˈbæleɪ/.

Answers

1 dancers 2 regular 3 training 4 fashion 5 acrobatics 6 companies

89 The Reading text is recorded for students to listen, read and check their answers.

3 Students read the questions and then read the article in detail. They mark the sentences true or false, correct the false ones and compare answers with a partner. Check answers with the class.

Answers

1 false (Only the most talented dancers can attend.)
2 true
3 true
4 false (It also offers programmes for performing arts and fashion design.)
5 false (It has 30 high school students.)
6 false (That company is only one example.)

4 Ask students to look at the highlighted words in the text and guess their meaning from the context. Then they complete the exercise by matching the words to their meanings. Check answers with the class and check any other new words and phrases. Ask students if they would like to attend any of these places and what they would like to study.

Answers

1 apply 2 attend 3 accepts 4 profession 5 boarding school 6 incredible

FAST FINISHERS

Ask fast finishers to write definitions of three of the following words: *boarding house* (a place where you sleep and have your meals), *boarding school* (a school where students live as well as study), *located* (in a particular place), *rural* (in the countryside, not the town), *found* (start an organisation or institution), *juggling* (throwing several items in the air to entertain people). They read out their definitions and the class guesses the word.

90 5 Students look at the picture of Carolina, read the questions and suggest what her special talent is. Play the recording. Students answer the questions and compare answers with a partner. Check answers with the class.

Answers

1 She's a ballet dancer.
2 at the Royal Ballet School in London
3 at a ballet school in Russia

90 6 Students read the sentence beginnings and in pairs complete them with anything they remember from the recording. Point out that *advantages* and *disadvantages* are plural so they should listen for more than one example of each. Play the recording again and give students time to complete the sentences. Check answers with the class. Ask them about the other numbers they heard in the interview (*17, three, seven*) and why they were mentioned (*Carolina is 17 now, she's loved ballet since she was three, she had her first real lesson when she was seven*). If necessary, play the recording again.

Answers

1 promised to buy her a pink ballet dress.
2 it was her first time away from home.
3 it's one of the best ballet schools in the world; she trains with some of the best dancers in the world every day; she's doing what she loves.
4 she couldn't speak Russian at first and she didn't know anybody there; her whole body hurts at the end of the day; she misses her friends and family.

» AUDIOSCRIPT TB PAGES 277–278

MIXED ABILITY

To support weaker students, play the recording again, pausing after each of the answers. Ask students to try to repeat the exact words used.

7 Students read the phrases in the *Useful language* box. Check understanding. Students complete the sentences and compare answers with a partner. Invite feedback from the class and write key words on the board.

Answers

Students' own answers

PROJECT ***Research a training school***

Read the instructions and ask students if they know of any unusual training schools in their country or anywhere in the world. If not, ask them to use the internet to find out some information and then choose a training school. Tell them their presentation should include answers to the five questions and any other interesting information they can find. They read the questions and then carry out their research online, making brief notes for each point. Students then write their presentations. Remind them to include an introduction saying what they are going to talk about. Allow them time to practise their presentations in pairs. Students then give their presentations in small groups. Invite some students to give their presentations to the class. Ask the rest of the class to listen to each one carefully and say which school they would most like to attend, and why.

PROJECT EXTENSION

In pairs, students are going to record an interview. One of them is a radio journalist and the other one is a student at the training school they made their presentation about. Encourage them to either write the full interview first or write the questions and make notes of the answers. If necessary, play the recording from Exercise 5 again to remind students of the questions. If possible, record the interviews and then play them back to the class.

13 **CULTURE VIDEO: Performing Arts Schools**

When students have completed the lesson, they can watch the video and complete the worksheet.

COOLER

Books closed. Divide the class into three groups, one for each of the training schools described in the article on page 106. The groups write at least three sentences about each school. Then put students in groups of three so that there is one student from each of the original groups in each group of three. Each student reads out what they have written and the others have to say if it is correct and add any other information the student has not included. Then they open their books and check.

3 Are the sentences true or false? Correct the false sentences.

1 Any students who like dance can attend The Royal Ballet School.
2 Royal Ballet School students must also practise at the weekend.
3 The Idyllwild Arts Academy isn't in the centre of Los Angeles.
4 Idyllwild only offers programmes for visual arts students.
5 The National Circus School has about 150 high school students.
6 Everyone who does the circus programme joins the Cirque du Soleil.

4 Match the highlighted words in the text to the meanings.

1 ask for permission, usually in writing
2 be present or go to a place or event
3 agrees to take someone or something
4 work or job that someone chooses
5 a school where students live and study
6 very good, surprising

5 Listen to an interview with Carolina Woods. Answer the questions. (90)

1 What is Carolina's special talent?
2 Where did she start studying when she was 11?
3 Where did she decide to study when she was 15?

6 Listen again and complete the sentences. (90)

1 Carolina didn't like her first ballet class, but then her parents …
2 Her first week at The Royal Ballet School was hard because …
3 The advantages of studying in Russia are …
4 The disadvantages of studying in Russia are …

7 Read the *Useful language* phrases. Complete them with information about your own school.

USEFUL LANGUAGE

Describing schools

1 The school is located in …
2 There are about … students.
3 The school offers classes in …
4 Students can also … after school.
5 On a typical day, students …
6 The advantages/disadvantages are …

PROJECT Research a training school

Find information about an unusual training school in your country or anywhere in the world. Make a presentation about the school and its programmes.

1 Where is the school located?
2 How many students attend the school?
3 What can young people study there?
4 What do students do on a typical day?
5 What are the advantages and disadvantages?

Make your presentation to the class.

13 NOW WATCH THE CULTURE VIDEO

19 THE WRITTEN WORD

ABOUT YOU

Do you like reading? What do you read?
Do you prefer printed magazines or digital ones? Why?

VOCABULARY Things that you read

91 **1 Match the words with the photos. Then listen and check.**

EP

advert article brochure e-book graphic novel note notice paper poster sticker

92 **2 Listen to four short conversations. What things that you read are they talking about?**

3 Complete the sentences.

1. I don't want to carry the novel I'm reading around the whole time, so I read ________.
2. I read an interesting ________ in this magazine all about how to relax before exams.
3. My dad buys a ________ six days a week, even though the news is at least a day old.
4. There's a big ________ in the corridor all about World Book Day.
5. Your parcel was posted in the States. Look, there's a customs ________ stuck on it.
6. I like looking at the ________ in magazines, but they don't persuade me to buy anything.

4 Where can you see the following? Include things that you can read from Exercises 1 and 2 as well as other words you know.

1. an advert
2. an article
3. instructions
4. poetry
5. a review

5 Discuss the questions.

1. How often do you read each of the things from Exercise 1?
2. Is most of what you read printed or digital?
3. What are the advantages and disadvantages of reading printed material as opposed to digital?

108 UNIT 19

19 THE WRITTEN WORD

Unit Overview

TOPIC	Genres of written texts
VOCABULARY	Things that you read
READING	Signs, notices and messages
GRAMMAR	Reported speech
VOCABULARY	*say*, *speak*, *talk* and *tell*
WRITING	An online book review
EXAM TASKS	Reading Part 1

Resources

GRAMMAR REFERENCE AND PRACTICE: SB page 156; TB page 246
WORKBOOK: pages 76–79
PHOTOCOPIABLE WORKSHEETS: Grammar worksheet Unit 19; Vocabulary worksheet Unit 19
TEST GENERATOR: Unit test 19

WARMER

Brainstorm things you can read, for example novels, newspapers, magazines, labels, shopping lists, notes, text messages, poetry, textbooks, etc. Write the list on the board.

ABOUT YOU

Read out the first question. Students share their ideas and preferences in small groups. Share feedback as a class and write key words on the board. As a class, discuss the question about printed and digital magazines and ask students to give reasons for their choices.

VOCABULARY Things that you read

1 Ask volunteers to describe one of the photos. The rest of the class call out the letter. Read the words in the box. In pairs, students match the words to the photos. Play the recording for them to check their answers. Play it again to practise pronunciation, especially *advert* /ˈædvɜːt/, *article* /ˈɑːtɪkl/ and *brochure* /ˈbrəʊʃə/. Check that students are familiar with all of the items and ask them what kind of information they might give, for example a *poster* might give information about an event such as a concert. You could also bring some examples into the classroom.

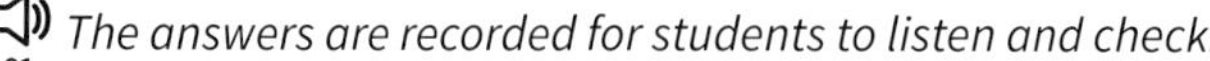

91 *The answers are recorded for students to listen and check.*

Answers

A note
B e-book
C sticker
D paper
E advert
F poster
G graphic novel
H brochure
I article
J notice

92 2 Explain that the speakers do not mention the reading matter by name, but all the items are in Exercise 1. Play the recording. Ask volunteers to suggest answers. Do not give feedback at this point but play the recording again, asking students to make a note of key vocabulary. Check answers and ask students what key vocabulary they wrote down, for example for conversation 1 *novel*, *pictures*, *comic*.

Answers

1 graphic novel 2 note 3 brochure 4 notice

» AUDIOSCRIPT TB PAGE 278

3 Students read the sentences. Check understanding of any new vocabulary. In pairs, students complete the sentences using words in Exercise 1. Check answers and ask students about their experiences with these items, for example if they use e-books.

Answers

1 e-books 2 article 3 paper 4 poster 5 sticker 6 adverts

FAST FINISHERS

Tell fast finishers to choose an item from the list on the board from the Warmer activity and write a definition for the class to guess.

4 Check understanding. Elicit some places where adverts can be seen using vocabulary from Exercises 1 and 2 as well as students' own ideas. In small groups, students write a list for each item. Set a time limit. Listen to feedback from the class and write suggestions on the board.

Answers

1 poster, brochure, notice, paper, sticker
+ students' own answers: e.g. magazine, tablet / online, TV
2 paper
+ students' own answers, e.g. tablet / online, magazine
3 article, note, notice, poster, paper
+ students' own answers: e.g. whiteboard, coursebook, label, leaflet
4 e-book, poster
+ students' own answers: e.g. book, notebook
5 article, paper
+ students' own answers: e.g. magazine, tablet / online

5 Check understanding of the questions. Remind students of frequency expressions, such as *often*, *hardly ever*, *once a week*, etc. In pairs, they discuss the first two questions and make a list of advantages and disadvantages for question 3. Invite students to share their answers to the first two questions and then have a class discussion about question 3. Divide the board into sections and note the advantages and disadvantages of the two media, print and digital.

Answers

Students' own answers

READING

1 Explain to students that they are going to identify various short texts and discuss where each one might be seen. Look at the example together. Set a time limit of four or five minutes for students to discuss the other texts in pairs. Check answers with the class and ask them to give reasons for their answers.

Answers

1 notice – in a school
2 text message – on a phone
3 note – on a desk, on a book or in a bag
4 sticker – at a beach, by the entrance to a swimming pool
5 competition – in a magazine or online

2 Check understanding of *CV* (*short for 'curriculum vitae'; a document describing your qualifications and experience, which you send to an employer you want to work for*). Students read the questions and the email. They answer the questions and compare their answers with a partner. Check answers with the class and refer them to the three-option multiple-choice question on the right.

Answers

1 We should discuss what qualifications and experience you can include …
2 Jon is going to write his own CV.
3 She discussed what people need to do to apply for the job.

3 **B1 Preliminary for Schools Reading Part 1**

In this part, students' ability to read for gist is tested. They read five very short unrelated texts including signs, messages, postcards, notes, emails and labels, and then choose from three options.

Students read the five texts and the three options for each one. Tell them to read the options carefully in order to eliminate the two incorrect options and choose the correct one. Set a time limit of five minutes. Students compare answers with a partner. Check answers with the class and ask students to justify their choices and explain why the other two options are incorrect. Ask them the meaning of *knock* in text 1 (*to repeatedly hit something, producing a noise*) and check understanding of any other vocabulary and phrases in the texts.

Answers

1 B 2 A 3 C 4 A 5 B

93 The Reading text is recorded for students to listen, read and check their answers.

MIXED ABILITY

Put weaker students with stronger students to check answers and ask stronger students to explain why they rejected the incorrect options.

TALKING POINTS

Ask students if they have ever written a CV and if so what its purpose was and who they sent it to. In pairs or small groups, they discuss what qualifications and experience they could include. To give it a clearer purpose, you could ask them what they would put in a CV to apply for the job in the bike shop. Discuss answers with the class and write their answers on the board. Then discuss which of the points mentioned would be suitable and which would be unnecessary or unsuitable.

In pairs or small groups, students discuss the second set of questions. In addition, ask them to talk about how they found out about the competition and why they decided to enter it. Monitor and help as necessary before inviting students to tell the class about their partner. Find out if some types of competition are more popular than others and why.

COOLER

Divide the class into small teams. Write words describing things that can be read on the board, omitting the vowels, for example *brchr* (brochure), *ntc* (notice). Students work together to write the complete word. Award a point to teams which spell the words correctly. The winner is the team with the most points.

READING

1 **Look at the texts 0–5 below. What kind is each one? In pairs, discuss where you think you might see them.**

0 *email – on your tablet or laptop*

2 **Look at the example (0) again and answer these questions.**

1 Underline the part of the email where Paula offers to help Jon.
2 Who is going to write Jon's CV?
3 What did Paula discuss with the bike shop manager?

93 **3** **Look at texts 1–5 again. What does each one say? Choose the correct answer, A, B or C.**

0

I called the bike shop about the job advert. The manager said he wanted people to send a CV. We should discuss what qualifications and experience you can include when you write yours.

Paula

1

STAFF ONLY

Students are not permitted in the staff room. Please knock on the door if you need to speak to a teacher.

2

Don't worry, Deb, everyone makes mistakes. Mum and Dad told me they wouldn't get angry, but you have to come home to talk about everything. Love you, sister!

3

Soph,
Mum said she could take us to the cinema later. Why don't we get together after school and walk to mine? Mum said she was working till 6.30. She can drive us to the cinema after that.
Georgia

4

Children under the age of 16 must be accompanied by an adult.

5

Win a trip to Barcelona!

We've hidden the football in this photo. Put a 'X' where you think the ball was and win a holiday!

Includes tickets to see an FC Barcelona match. To enter, complete your details and send us the picture.

Name ....
Address ....
....
Email ....

0 Paula is offering to
(A) help Jon with his CV.
B write Jon's CV.
C introduce Jon to the manager.

1 **A** Students can only go into the staff room with a teacher.
B Students can speak to teachers outside the staff room.
C Students can't speak to members of staff.

2 **A** Deb has done something wrong.
B Deb's parents miss her.
C Deb's sister is in trouble.

3 **A** Georgia and Soph are going to walk to the cinema.
B Georgia is going to meet Soph and her mum at the cinema.
C Georgia and Soph are going to watch a film after school.

4 At this pool
A you must be at least 16 to swim alone.
B you have to be 16 or younger.
C children can't swim at the same time as adults.

5 You can win a competition
A to go on tour with FC Barcelona.
B by finding the location of a ball.
C by emailing a picture.

TALKING POINTS

What qualifications and experience could you put on your CV?

Have you ever entered a competition? What for? Did you win?

GRAMMAR Reported speech

1 Match the speech bubbles to the examples.

a I can take you later.

b We won't get angry.

c I want people to send a CV.

d I'm working till 6.30.

1 The manager said he wanted people to send a CV.
2 They told me they wouldn't get angry.
3 Mum said she was working till 6.30.
4 Mum said she could take us to the cinema later.

2 Match the examples 1–4 in Exercise 1 to the tense changes a–d in the box.

We use reported speech to repeat what someone said earlier. We change the tense in reported speech.

Direct speech →	**Reported speech**
a present simple	past simple
b present continuous	past continuous
c *can*	*could*
d *will*	*would*

We also often change pronouns:
'*I make films.*' → *He said* **he** *made films.*
Remember: *say* + ~~object~~; *tell* + object.
He said ~~me~~ *he made films.* → *He told* **me** *he made films.*

» **GRAMMAR REFERENCE AND PRACTICE PAGE 156**

3 Choose the correct options.

1 Katy *says* / *said* she liked reading graphic novels.
2 Dexter *told* / *told us* he would leave us a note.
3 Adam told me he *is reading* / *was reading* an e-book.
4 Tatum *said me* / *said* she couldn't read my handwriting.
5 Sally *told* / *said* me there were some adverts online.
6 Cosmo said the noticeboard *will* / *would* be full soon.
7 Jude *said* / *told* he was coming to the party.
8 Caz said *I* / *she* was getting some stickers.

4 Complete the second sentence so that it has the same meaning as the first. Use one, two or three words.

0 **Clare:** 'I love writing about fashion.'
Clare said that *she loved writing* about fashion.
1 **Ewan:** 'I don't want to write about sport!'
Ewan told me he ________ to write about sport.
2 **Anita:** 'My article will be really funny.'
Anita said her article ________ really funny.
3 **Paul:** 'I'm writing about the cafeteria.'
Paul told us that he ________ about the cafeteria.
4 **James:** 'The story can't be true.'
James said the story ________ true.
5 **Sophie:** 'The photos look amazing.'
Sophie told me the photos ________ amazing.
6 **Dan:** 'You'll enjoy the movie.'
Dan told me that I ________ the movie.
7 **Sarah:** 'There won't be any more shows in that series.'
Sarah said there ________ any more shows in that series.
8 **Chris:** 'I'm not listening to a word you say!'
Chris said that he ________ to a word she said.

5 Report what the people said.

I don't read print magazines very often. I prefer reading online. It's free and I can choose from thousands of websites. I'll start my own website one day.

Louisa said she didn't read print magazines very often. …

Sandra can help us put up some posters. She does it every day, and she knows all the best places. She'll be a graphic designer one day!

Pavel said that Sandra could …

VOCABULARY *say, speak, talk* and *tell*

1 Read the examples. Then match the verbs to the uses.

Can you speak Turkish?
I said, 'Hello.'
I've told you the answer.
I'm talking about blogs.

1 speak	a someone something
2 say	b about something or to someone
3 tell	c something
4 talk	d a language

2 Choose the correct verbs.

1 What did you *tell* / *say*?
2 I can *say* / *speak* English.
3 I *spoke* / *told* him my phone number.
4 She was *talking* / *telling* about you.
5 Nobody *told* / *said* anything.
6 Did you *talk* / *tell* to Mr Marsh?
7 Can anyone here *speak* / *say* German?
8 Please *tell* / *say* us the truth.

3 » **Work with a partner. Student A turn to page 125. Student B turn to page 127.**

GRAMMAR Reported speech

WARMER

Dictate the following sentences: 'I'm an author. I'm writing my fourth novel. My next novel will be about a superhero. He can read people's minds.' Ask for volunteers to write them on the board. Then ask students to report what you said, using the third person: *Our teacher said he / she was an author*, and so on, helping them with tenses and pronouns if necessary.

1 Remind students about the reported commands they learned in Unit 17. Now they are going to learn about reported speech using the verbs *say* and *tell*. Students read the example sentences and match them to the speech bubbles.

Answers

1 c 2 b 3 d 4 a

2 Students match the examples in Exercise 1 to the rules. Check answers. Read the rules about pronoun changes and the use of *say* and *tell*. Students will have more practice with these verbs in the Vocabulary section.

Answers

1 a 2 d 3 b 4 c

» GRAMMAR REFERENCE AND PRACTICE ANSWER KEY TB PAGE 246

3 In pairs, students choose the correct option, referring to the rules and examples in Exercises 1 and 2. Check answers with the class and ask students to explain their choices.

Answers

1 said
2 told us
3 was reading
4 said
5 told
6 would
7 said
8 she

4 Students look at the example. Elicit what has changed (*the pronoun* I *to* she *and the tense from present simple* love *to past simple* loved; *no speech marks are necessary*). Do the first sentence as a class. Students complete the sentences in pairs. Invite different students to read out the completed sentences. Explain that the use of *that* to introduce reported speech is optional.

Answers

1 didn't want
2 would be
3 was writing
4 couldn't be
5 looked
6 would enjoy
7 wouldn't be
8 wasn't listening

MIXED ABILITY

Help weaker students by asking them to name the tenses, say which tense they change to in reported speech and whether they are positive or negative.

5 Students look at the first picture and read the speech bubble. Ask questions about Louisa, for example 'Does she read magazines often? What does she read instead? What does she want to do one day?' Students read the example sentence about Louisa. Ask what is different about the second speech bubble (*one person is talking about another*). Students read the example sentence and complete the exercise in pairs. Check answers.

Answers

Louisa said she didn't read print magazines very often. She said she preferred reading online. She said that it was free and that she could choose from thousands of websites. She said she would start her own website one day.
Pavel said that Sandra could help them put up some posters. He said that Sandra did it every day, and that she knew all the best places. Pavel said that Sandra would be a graphic designer one day.

FAST FINISHERS

Ask fast finishers to work together to write another speech bubble. They then write it on the board (encourage them to draw a little picture, too) for the class to report.

» GRAMMAR WORKSHEET UNIT 19

VOCABULARY *say, speak, talk* and *tell*

1 Write *say*, *speak*, *talk* and *tell* on the board. Explain that the meanings of the words are similar, but they aren't used in the same way. Students read the example sentences and look at the verbs in blue. They match the uses to the verbs. Check answers.

Answers

1 d 2 c 3 a 4 b

2 In pairs, students choose the correct option in each sentence, using the examples in Exercise 1 to help them. Invite different students to read out the completed sentences.

Answers

1 say 2 speak 3 told 4 talking 5 said 6 talk 7 speak 8 tell

3 Put students into pairs and assign A or B to each pair. A pairs turn to page 125 and B pairs to page 127. Check understanding of *backwards* (*in reverse order*), *equivalent* (*with the same meaning*) and *gap* (*a short silence, when nobody is speaking*). Students complete the questions. In new pairs consisting of one A and one B student, they ask and answer the questions. Finally, check the reporting verbs with the class and ask some students to tell the class about their partner.

Answers

Student A
1 speak 2 tell 3 say 4 speak / talk 5 speak / talk 6 say
Student B
1 speaking / talking 2 told 3 say 4 speak 5 speak / talk 6 say

» VOCABULARY WORKSHEET UNIT 19

WRITING An online book review

BACKGROUND INFORMATION

Anthony Horowitz (born 1955) is an English novelist and screenwriter specialising in mystery and suspense. His work for young adult readers includes The Diamond Brothers series, the Alex Rider series and The Power of Five series. He has also written a James Bond novel called *Trigger Mortis* (2015). Eoin Colfer (born 1965) is an Irish author of children's books. The first novel in the Artemis Fowl series was published in 2001 and became a *New York Times* Best Seller.

1 Tell students that they are going to write an online book review and check understanding of *review* (*a report on a website that gives an opinion about a new book, film, etc.*). Discuss the questions briefly as a class.

Answers

Students' own answers

2 Find out if students have ever read or heard of *Crocodile Tears* by Anthony Horowitz, and if so, what it is about. Ask them what kind of information is usually included in a book review to elicit ideas, for example *title*, *a description of the story*, and write them on the board. Students compare their own ideas with those on the list. They read the review quickly and tick the information which is included. Tell them that it is not important to understand all the vocabulary. Listen to feedback as a class. Check understanding and pronunciation of *author* /ˈɔːθə/ (*the writer of a book, article, play, etc.*) and *character* /ˈkærəktər/ (*a person represented in a film, play or story*).

Answers

1 the title of the book
2 the author's name
4 the name of the main character
6 a description of part of the story
8 his own opinion of the book

3 Ask if students think the review is good or bad and why the reviewer does not describe the ending. Set a short time limit for students to read the tips in the *Prepare to write* box and find them in the review.

Answers

a *Crocodile Tears* by Anthony Horowitz
b Alex Rider
c *It's a great book!, I think it's a very exciting story*
d Sentences 4 to 8 … *I won't write more in case you read the book!*

4 Students look at the picture and read the review of *Artemis Fowl*. They say whether the reviewer liked the book and how they know this (*a really good fantasy novel*; *it's a really exciting story*; *I'll definitely read the rest of the series*). They read the words in the box and complete the review in pairs. Check answers with the class. Find out if anyone has read the book and if they would like to. Ask if they like book series which have the same character in them and which ones they have read, for example Harry Potter.

Answers

1 written 2 author 3 character 4 incredible 5 thought

5 Students are going to write an online book review. They choose a book and discuss it with a partner. Monitor and help as necessary, particularly with vocabulary, and encourage them to help each other with ideas. Ask them if they think it is OK to write a bad review and explain that this is fine, but it is important to explain why and try to find positive points, too, if possible.

6 Students write their book review. They should write about 100 words. Remind them to use the tips in the *Prepare to write* box and to check their spelling and grammar carefully after they have finished writing. Students exchange reviews with their partner and decide if they would like to read the book.

Model answer

I've just read a book called *I am still alive* by Kate Alice Marshall. It's a thriller set in an isolated part of a Canadian forest.
The main character is a 16-year-old girl, Jess Cooper, who is living in a cabin with her father after her mother's death in a car crash. After three men murder her father and destroy the cabin, she has to learn to survive on her own. At the same time, she wants revenge for her father's death and she is sure that the killers will return.
I really liked the book because I admire Jess and the story is very exciting!

COOLER

Do a quick revision quiz of the unit. In groups, students write one question for each page in the unit. Ask for some suggestions, for example *What's a graphic novel? Where are Georgia and Soph going? Complete this sentence with the correct verb: I ______ four languages. True or false: you should include the ending of a book in a book review.* They exchange their questions with another group. Award points for each correct answer to find the winning team.

WRITING An online book review

1 Do you read reviews of books or films online? Do you ever write reviews?

2 Read the review quickly. Tick (✓) the information that Sachin includes.

1 the title of the book
2 the author's name
3 information about the author
4 the name of the main character
5 the story of the whole book
6 a description of part of the story
7 details about how the story ends
8 his own opinion of the book

REVIEW
Crocodile Tears
by Anthony Horowitz

I've just read *Crocodile Tears* by Anthony Horowitz. It's a great book! The main character is a teenager called Alex Rider. He's a spy for the British government. Alex visits a farm in England that belongs to a criminal. The criminal is called Desmond McCain and he's creating a new type of crop that can kill people. He's planning to cause lots of problems around the world using the crops. Suddenly, McCain catches Alex! I think it's a very exciting story, but I won't write more in case you read the book!

Sachin Patel

3 Read the *Prepare to write* box and find features a–d in Sachin's review.

PREPARE TO WRITE
An online book review

In an online book review:

a include the title of the book and the author
b include the name of the main character(s)
c give your opinion of the book
d include some details of the story, but avoid 'spoilers' – and don't say how the book ends!

4 Read an online review of *Artemis Fowl*. What is the writer's opinion of the book? Complete the review with the words in the box.

author	character	incredible
thought	written	

Artemis Fowl
by Eoin Colfer

I've just read a really good fantasy novel called *Artemis Fowl*. It was [1] ________ by Eoin Colfer, an Irish [2] ________. The main [3] ________ is a teenage boy called Artemis Fowl II. He comes from a family of criminals and he does all sorts of awful things to make his family richer. He isn't a very nice person, but that doesn't matter because the story is [4] ________. It was the first in a series of eight books. I [5] ________ it was a really exciting story, and I'll definitely read the rest of the series.

RATING: ★★★★☆

5 You are going to write an online book review. Think about a book that you like and plan your review. Use the notes to help you.

- What is the title of the book?
- Who is the author?
- Who is the main character?
- What happens in the story?
- What is your opinion of it?

6 Write your online book review.

- Use the tips in the *Prepare to write* box.
- Write about 100 words.
- Remember to check your spelling and grammar.

20 SEEING IS BELIEVING

ABOUT YOU

Look at the pictures on this page. Have you ever seen any of these pictures before?
Do you know the name for these types of pictures?
What other examples have you seen?

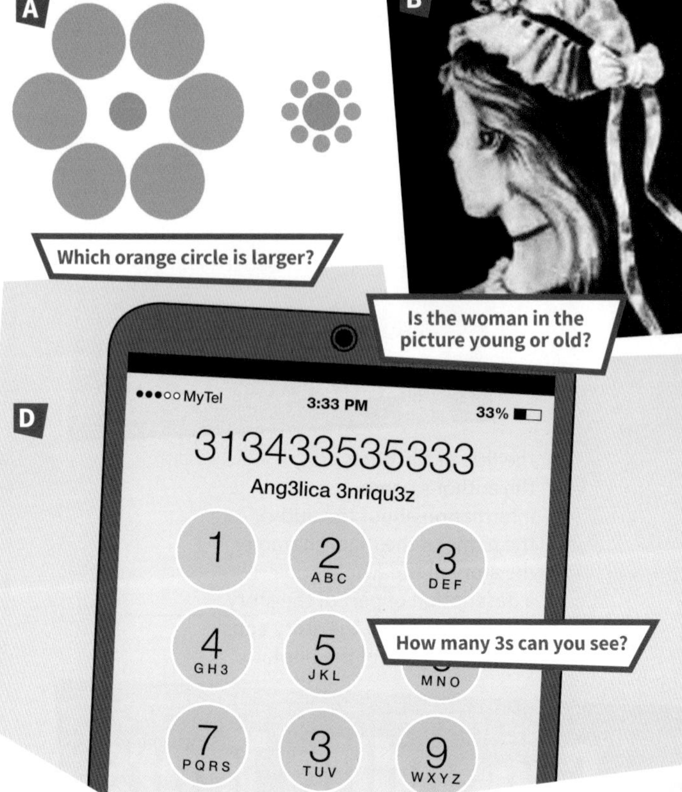

VOCABULARY Collocations: thinking

1 Work in pairs. Look at the pictures and answer the questions.

94 **2** Listen to five short conversations. Match them to the pictures.

94 **3** Match the sentence halves. Then listen again and check.

EP
1 I lost
2 Can you give me
3 It didn't cross
4 I've just had a
5 I'm having
6 Make up
7 You have to use

a second thoughts now.
b your imagination to see the second person.
c your mind!
d concentration!
e a hint?
f thought.
g my mind to look there.

4 Complete the sentences with the correct form of the collocations in Exercise 3.

0 I've just *had a thought*. Why don't you get some work as a babysitter?
1 It's time to ________. Are you coming or not?
2 I wanted to watch that new comedy show. But now I've read the reviews I'm ________.
3 As soon as I fell in the water, the thought of sharks ________.
4 Question ten is impossible and Mrs Thomas wouldn't even ________.
5 I can't do my homework while I watch TV. I ________.
6 I find it hard to write stories because I'm not good at ________.

E

blue	green	yellow
pink	red	orange
purple	black	grey
white	brown	

Can you say the colours of each word without saying the word itself?

5 In pairs, ask and answer the questions.

1 Do you find it difficult to make up your mind about things? Or are you good at making decisions?
2 What causes you to lose concentration while you are studying at home or at school?
3 When was the last time you had second thoughts about something?
4 What school subjects allow you to use your imagination? Do you use your imagination out of school?

20 SEEING IS BELIEVING

Unit Overview

TOPIC	Optical illusions
VOCABULARY	Collocations: thinking
READING	Illusions everywhere
GRAMMAR	Past simple passive
VOCABULARY	*look (at), see, watch*
LISTENING	A university podcast
SPEAKING	Expressing surprise and disbelief
EXAM TASKS	Listening Part 4

Resources

GRAMMAR REFERENCE AND PRACTICE: SB page 157; TB page 246
WORKBOOK: pages 80–83
PHOTOCOPIABLE WORKSHEETS: Grammar worksheet Unit 20; Vocabulary worksheet Unit 20
TEST GENERATOR: Unit test 20; Term test 3; End of Year test

WARMER

Ask students what they think the unit title means. Do they agree? Can you trust everything you see? Encourage them to think about images on the internet, the use of Photoshop, and so on.

ABOUT YOU

Students look at the pictures and say if they have seen any of them before. Ask if they know what they are called (*optical or visual illusions*) and if they have seen any other examples. Check pronunciation of *illusion* /ɪˈluːʒən/.

VOCABULARY Collocations: thinking

1 In pairs or small groups, students discuss what they can see and answer the questions. They do not have to agree! As a class, discuss these optical illusions. Tell students that not everyone agrees about how they work. If you have internet access, there are plenty of good websites showing more optical illusions, not all of them static.

Answers

Students' own answers

94

2 Tell students that they are going to listen to five short conversations between two people who are discussing the pictures. They should match each conversation to the correct picture. Play the recording, pausing between each conversation for students to make their choice. They compare their answers with a partner. Check answers with the class.

Answers

1 E 2 C 3 D 4 A 5 B

94

3 In pairs, students match the sentence halves, which are all taken from the recording. Tell students not to worry if they are unsure of the answers and the meanings because they will hear the recording again to check. Play the recording again and pause after each conversation for students to check their answers. Check answers with the class. Ask stronger students to explain the meaning of each expression and write key words on the board; *lose concentration* and *use your imagination* are fairly clear but students may need help with the remaining expressions: *give a hint* – give a small indication or suggestion to help someone find an answer or a solution; *cross your mind* – suddenly think of something (more frequent in the negative form); *have a thought* – think of something, often suddenly or unexpectedly; *have second thoughts* – change your opinion; *make up your mind* – make a decision.

Answers

1 d 2 e 3 g 4 f 5 a 6 c 7 b

» AUDIOSCRIPT TB PAGE 278

4 Read the example. Put students in mixed ability pairs to complete the sentences with the correct form of each collocation. Remind them to think about verb forms and personal pronouns. Students compare answers with another pair before checking answers as a class.

Answers

1 make up your mind
2 having second thoughts
3 crossed my mind
4 give me / us a hint
5 lose concentration
6 using my imagination

5 Read the questions and check understanding. Students discuss them in pairs. Encourage them to give reasons for their answers when appropriate. Monitor and join in with the discussions, helping where necessary. Students share their ideas and find out about the rest of the class.

Answers

Students' own answers

READING

BACKGROUND INFORMATION

Human beings see with both our brain and our eyes, and the human brain puts images together because it has learned to expect certain things. When we look at an object, the information passes through various circuits of neurons until it reaches and is processed by the visual cortex in our brain. Films are a good example, because a film consists of a series of still photographs which are then shown at high speed, creating an illusion of movement. Computer screens consist of tiny red, green and blue dots which we actually see as a wide range of colours. Some illusions can be dangerous. Our sense of balance is closely related to our visual world, so when pilots fly at night or in a cloud they cannot tell whether the plane is increasing or decreasing its altitude or if it is turning left or right. As a result, pilots have to depend on the plane's instruments to give them accurate information.

1 Students read the title of the article and the three options for the main topic. Set a short time limit for them to read the article quickly. Take a class vote on the main topic. Ask students to explain why A is correct and B and C are incorrect.

Answers

A

MIXED ABILITY

To support weaker students, tell them to read the first paragraph to find the answer and then the opening sentences of the remaining paragraphs to confirm that their answer is correct.

2 Read the instructions and the questions and check understanding. Students underline the key words in each sentence and then read the article carefully and complete the exercise. Students compare their answers with a partner. Nominate a student to give their answer, reading out the part of the text that provides the answer, and correcting any incorrect statements at the same time. This student then nominates another student to answer the next question. Continue until all the statements have been read out. Ask students to suggest why the New Year's card was used in a car advert, and if they can find the animal in the photo .

Answers

1 true
2 false (He designed it for a New Year's card.)
3 false (Several celebrities bought the dress.)
4 true (In the photo, the animal hiding is a snake (a viper) which is wrapped round the branch.)
5 true (They cause drivers to go more slowly.)
6 false (It is probably healthier to use smaller plates instead of larger ones as we think we are eating more food on smaller plates.)

95 The Reading text is recorded for students to listen, read and check their answers.

3 Ask students to find the words in the article and identify which part of speech they are. In pairs, ask them to work out their meanings from the context. Then tell them to read the definitions and match them to the words. Check answers with the class. Ask them which word can also be used as a noun; if they are not sure, tell them to read the last line of the article (*trick*). Discuss the article as a class. Ask students if they were surprised by anything they read.

Answers

1e 2b 3a 4c 5d

FAST FINISHERS

Ask fast finishers to provide definitions of *pattern* (*a repeated design*), *puzzle* (*a problem or question that you have to answer by using your skill or knowledge*) and *waste* (*use something badly when there is a limited amount of it*).

TALKING POINTS

Read the questions and put students in small groups to discuss them. Monitor and help as necessary. Ask groups to share their ideas with the class and write key words on the board. Have a vote on their favourite optical illusion.

COOLER

Write the following sentences and definitions of expressions with *mind* on the board and ask students to match them:

1 What's the first word that comes into your mind?
2 Don't make up your mind yet.
3 Do you mind if I open the window?
4 Mind the iron – it's very hot!
5 Can you mind my bag while I go to the toilet?

A be careful
B look after
C make a decision
D bother or upset someone
E think of

Answers

1E 2C 3D 4A 5B

READING

1 **Read the article quickly. Choose the main topic of the article.**

A The ways optical illusions are used
B How optical illusions work
C Optical illusions in nature

2 **Read the article again. Are the sentences true or false?**

1. Scientists can't fully explain optical illusions.
2. Akiyoshi Kitaoka designed his optical illusion for a car advertisement.
3. Alexander McQueen only made one of his striped 'optical illusion' dresses.
4. Animals use optical illusion to hunt for food.
5. The road safety illusions have been successful.
6. The plate illusion means it is probably healthier to use larger plates instead of smaller ones.

95

Illusions everywhere

Optical illusions often use light, colour and patterns to trick our brains into seeing something that isn't there. The Ancient Greeks studied them over 2,000 years ago, yet scientists still don't completely understand how they work. One explanation is that our brains are trying to understand so much information that they have to make guesses about some of it. Optical illusions happen when these guesses are wrong.

They might seem like only fun puzzles, but optical illusions have practical uses too. Here are some everyday examples – from advertising and nature to restaurants and on the roads.

In advertising, optical illusions are useful to get people to pay attention. Look at this picture by Akiyoshi Kitaoka, a Japanese professor of Psychology. Kitaoka created it while he was making a New Year's card for his family and friends. The picture was later used in a car advertisement. Can you guess why?

On roads, several countries have used optical illusions to encourage people to drive more safely. For instance, these pedestrian crossings were painted on roads in China. From a distance, they look 3D and the research shows that this causes drivers to go more slowly near the crossings.

In fashion, optical illusions are used to change our appearance. This dress was designed by the famous fashion designer, Alexander McQueen. But it wasn't designed just to look good. The narrow black and white lines create an illusion, and the person appears slimmer than they are. Several celebrities bought one.

In the natural world, some animals need optical illusions to stay alive. Many butterflies, snakes and spiders are a similar colour to the place where they live. They don't want their enemies to see them – and eat them. They can also use their colour to catch other animals themselves. Can you see the animal hiding in this picture? What is it?

Researchers have found that one simple illusion could help us to eat, and also waste, less food. In experiments, the same amount of food was served on two plates: one small and one large. When people were asked to estimate the amount of food on each plate, they usually said the same thing: there was more food on the smaller plate. Restaurants sometimes use this trick too – if we think we are getting more food, then a meal looks better value for money.

3 **Match the highlighted words in the text to the meanings.**

1 trick	**a** stop something or someone from escaping
2 appears	**b** seems
3 catch	**c** make someone more likely to do something
4 encourage	**d** watch, listen to or think about something carefully
5 pay attention (to something)	**e** make someone believe something that is not true

TALKING POINTS

What practical uses of optical illusions have you seen?

What are your favourite optical illusions from the unit so far?

GRAMMAR Past simple passive

1 **Match the examples to the passive forms.**

1 The picture **was used** in a car advertisement.
2 In fashion, optical illusions **are used** to change our appearance.
3 This dress **wasn't** just **designed** to look good.

a present simple positive
b past simple positive
c past simple negative

2 **Look at the examples and complete the rules.**

ACTIVE:
A Japanese professor **created** the picture.
PASSIVE:
The picture **was created by** a Japanese professor.

In the past simple passive:
a we use *was* / ________ + (not) + ________ participle.
b if we want to say the person/thing that did the action, we use ________.

» GRAMMAR REFERENCE AND PRACTICE PAGE 157

3 **Read the first part of an article and choose the correct forms of the verb.**

Street painting first [1] *appeared / was appeared* in the 16th century in Italy. The painters [2] *called / were called* 'madonnari' and they [3] *painted / were painted* pictures of well-known characters on the pavement.

In 1984, 3D pavement art [4] *invented / was invented* by the American, Kurt Venner. When you look at 3D pavement art from a certain place, it looks like it is 3D! A few years later, a TV documentary [5] *made / was made* Kurt and his work famous. He [6] *asked / was asked* to make 3D art for adverts, festivals and museums. This 3D pavement art [7] *didn't do / wasn't done* by Kurt, but by Julian Beever, a British pavement artist.

4 **Complete the second part of the article. Use the past simple active or passive form of the verbs.**

Between 1790 and 1820, over 150 kilometres of canals [1] ________ (build) in London to help transport materials. Nowadays, cyclists and pedestrians share the path next to these canals, but some cyclists ride too fast. Recently, 3D pavement art [2] ________ (use) to make the path safer. A large 3D hole [3] ________ (paint) on it by two local artists. As cyclists approached the painting, it [4] ________ (look) like there was a huge hole in the path. Many cyclists stopped or [5] ________ (start) to ride more slowly. Then they [6] ________ (give) information about safer cycling!

5 **Correct the mistake in each sentence.**

1 He born in Paris and he died in London.
2 This house it's built in the 16th century.
3 Yesterday we were met to have lunch together.
4 The medicine was tasted terrible.
5 The film we saw yesterday called *Now You See It*.
6 We were allow to eat in the classroom.

VOCABULARY *look (at), see, watch*

1 **Read the examples. Match the verbs *look (at)*, *see* and *watch* to their meanings.**

EP

1 **Look at** this picture by Akiyoshi Kitaoka.
2 They don't want their enemies to **see** them.
3 I wanted to **watch** that new comedy show.

a ________: notice people or things with your eyes
b ________: pay attention to something, usually for a short time and especially something that isn't moving.
c ________: pay attention to something, usually for a longer time and especially something that is moving.

2 **Complete the sentences with the correct form of *look (at)*, *see* and *watch*.**

1 Did you ________ that white van? It was going really fast.
2 ________ the whiteboard and copy the words.
3 It crossed my mind today that I haven't ________ your brother for ages.
4 ________ my hands carefully and I'll show you how the trick was done.
5 ________! That guy is shoplifting!
6 I'm exhausted. I was ________ films all night.
7 The World Cup final was ________ by over a billion people around the world.

3 » **Work with a partner. Turn to page 125.**

GRAMMAR Past simple passive

WARMER

Write three or four sentences with facts from previous units on the board, using the past simple passive but leaving out the past participle, for example Crocodile Tears *was (written) by Anthony Horowitz. Taylor Swift's video from* Reputation *was (seen) by 40 million people. Some of Damien Hirst's artworks were (painted) by his assistants*. Students supply the missing words. Ask them what part of speech they are.

1 Students read the sentences adapted from the article on page 113 and underline the verb forms. They match them to the passive forms. Check answers and ask what they remember from Unit 15 about using the passive and when it is used (*when the person or thing that causes the action is unknown or unimportant*). Ask questions about the sentences in Exercise 1, for example if we know who used the picture in the advertisement.

Answers

1 b 2 a 3 c

2 Students look at the active and passive examples in Exercise 2. Complete the rules as a class. Ask them to find four more examples of the past simple passive in the article on page 113 (*This dress was designed*; *pedestrian crossings were painted*; *food was served*; *people were asked*).

Answers

1 were, past
2 by

» GRAMMAR REFERENCE AND PRACTICE ANSWER KEY TB PAGE 246

3 Students describe the photo. In pairs, they read the first part of the article and choose the correct options, referring to the rules in Exercise 2. Explain that the verbs are all in the past simple but some are active and some are passive. Invite students to read out the sentences and the class to say if they are correct.

Answers

1 appeared
2 were called
3 painted
4 was invented
5 made
6 was asked
7 wasn't done

4 Students describe the photo and read the second part of the article. This time they have to write the correct past simple form of the verbs in brackets. Invite students to read out the sentences and explain their answers. Find out what students think of the idea and elicit other ways in which pavement art could be used to educate people, for example to encourage them not to drop litter.

Answers

1 were built 2 was used 3 was painted 4 looked 5 started 6 were given

MIXED ABILITY

Support weaker students by reading the text as a class. Students decide whether the active or passive form is needed for each space. Ask stronger students to explain why. All students can then complete the exercise individually.

FAST FINISHERS

Ask fast finishers to write two sentences in the past simple, one active and one passive. Suggest some verbs they could use: *design*, *invent*, *make*, *produce*. They exchange their sentences with another fast finisher, who rewrites the active sentences in the passive and the passive sentences in the active.

5 In pairs, students read the sentences carefully to find and correct the mistakes. They compare answers with another pair. Ask volunteers to write the corrected sentences on the board.

Answers

1 He **was born** in Paris and he died in London.
2 This house **was built** in the 16th century.
3 Yesterday we **met** to have lunch together.
4 The medicine **tasted** terrible.
5 The film we saw yesterday **was called** *Now You See It*.
6 We were **allowed** to eat in the classroom.

» GRAMMAR WORKSHEET UNIT 20

VOCABULARY *look (at), see, watch*

1 Write the verbs *look (at)*, *see* and *watch* on the board and ask students if they know the difference between their meanings and how they are used. Students read the examples and match them to their meanings. They compare answers with a partner. Check answers. Ask for examples of things you can *look at*, for example a picture, a view, a clock; and things you can *watch*, for example television, a race, a film.

Answers

a see b look at c watch

2 Monitor as students work in pairs to complete the sentences. Then invite different students to read out the completed sentences.

Answers

1 see 2 Look at 3 seen 4 Watch 5 Look 6 watching 7 watched

3 Students turn to page 125. Read the first question and check understanding of the words in the box. Give students a few minutes to write their sentences using the ideas from the box or their own ideas. Then put them in pairs and read the second question. Set a time limit for them to mime their sentences and ask for volunteers to mime some of their sentences for the class to guess.

Answers

Students' own answers

» VOCABULARY WORKSHEET UNIT 20

LISTENING

1 Bring a pack of cards to class. Ask students if they are interested in magic and if they like seeing magic tricks. Read the questions and put students into small groups to discuss them. As a class, ask them to share their answers, and write key words on the board. If any of the students know any card tricks, ask them to demonstrate them to the class.

Answers

Students' own answers

2 Students read the description of the podcast. Elicit some question words and write them on the board. Elicit a question the presenter might ask and write it on the board. In pairs, students write four or five more questions. Ask for volunteers to read them out.

Possible answers

1 Why are you interested in magic?
2 When did you start practising magic?
3 What kind of places do you perform in?
4 How many people come to your shows?
5 Do you have to practise a lot?

96

3 Ask students to listen for the questions the presenter asks. Play the recording and give them time to make notes. Check answers and ask students if their predictions were correct.

Answers

How did you get started as a magician?
Where have you performed?
Have you created any of your own tricks?
Do you practise tricks a lot?
Do you ever tell anyone how you do your tricks?
Would you like to be a professional magician one day?

96

4 **B1 Preliminary for Schools Listening Part 4**

In this part, students' ability to identify specific information, detailed meaning and attitude or opinion is tested. It consists of a longer monologue or interview and six multiple-choice questions with three options. Students hear the recording twice.

Ask students to read the questions and choose the correct option, based on what they remember from the interview. If they are not sure, they can underline the key words. Tell them they will hear the recording twice. Play the recording and give students time to choose each option before comparing answers with a partner. Play it again for them to check their answers and make any changes. Check answers with the class. If necessary play the recording again, pausing in the places relevant to both the correct and the incorrect options.

Answers

1 B 2 B 3 A 4 A 5 C 6 B

» **AUDIOSCRIPT TB PAGES 278–279**

SPEAKING Expressing surprise and disbelief

1 Ask students to describe the photo. If necessary, help them with vocabulary. They should remember the verb *float* and some may know the verb *levitate*. Ask how they would feel if they saw someone float. Elicit adjectives, for example *surprised*, *amazed*, etc. Ask them for adjectives to describe the trick, for example *incredible*, *amazing*, *unbelievable*, etc. Elicit any phrases they know for expressing disbelief and write them on the board.

Answers

Students' own answers

97

2 Tell students they are going to listen to Mark and Lucy talking about Thomas, who performs magic tricks. They read the two sentences. Play the recording and check the answer.

Answer

b

97

3 Read the phrases in the *Prepare to speak* box and compare them to the expressions on the board. Play the recording again. Ask students to listen for the phrases Mark and Lucy use and to notice the intonation. Play the recording again for students to make a note of the phrases they hear. Check answers. Play it again, pausing after each of the phrases for the students to repeat with the correct intonation.

Answers

You won't believe this but …
Are you serious?
That just isn't possible.
I couldn't believe my eyes.
No way!

» **AUDIOSCRIPT TB PAGE 279**

4 Ask students to read the quiz questions and answers and check understanding. Tell them to do the quiz individually and then work in pairs to persuade their partner that their answer is correct. Tell them to use phrases from the *Prepare to speak* box. Monitor and help as necessary. As a class, ask a few pairs for their answers to each question but do not confirm them at this point. Students give their own answers.

5 Students turn to page 127 to check their answers. As a class, check understanding, find out how many they got right and ask them which answers surprised them most.

Answers

1 A and C
2 A
3 A and C
4 C
5 A and B

COOLER

Students write three sentences about the unit: which activity they liked most, which they liked least, and what they found most surprising. Discuss their ideas as a class, asking them to give reasons for their choices.

LISTENING

1 In pairs, discuss the questions.

1 Do you know the names of any famous magicians?
2 What are the best magic tricks you've seen?
3 Can you do any magic tricks?

2 Read the description of the podcast. In pairs, write five questions that you think the presenter might ask.

The University Podcast

LATEST EPISODE:

33 Mysteries of the mind

Play   More episodes …

This week's show is all about mysteries of the mind. And we start with an interview with Amelia Rogers, a first-year French and Spanish student at the university. Amelia is also a member of the University Magic Club, whose recent show was reviewed very well by this podcast in episode 31.

96 **3 Listen to the podcast. Did the presenter ask any of the questions you wrote in Exercise 2?**

96 **4 Listen to the interview again. For each question, choose the correct answer.**

1 Amelia became interested in magic because
  A her older brother used to enjoy it.
  B she was told she was naturally good at it.
  C she was given a magic set on her birthday.

2 Amelia's favourite performances have been
  A at children's parties.
  B in competitions she won.
  C during her time at university.

3 Amelia thinks creating your own tricks is
  A less important than how you perform them.
  B impossible for people with her level of experience.
  C necessary if you want to become famous.

4 What does Amelia say about practising tricks?
  A She does it in lots of different places.
  B Her friends aren't interested in helping.
  C It's something she prefers doing alone.

5 What does Amelia say about explaining to other people how she does tricks?
  A She thinks it's a bad idea because people can't keep secrets.
  B She sometimes does it with her closest friends.
  C She only ever does it with other magicians.

6 What are Amelia's plans for the future?
  A She wants to be a professional magician.
  B She wants to concentrate on her studies.
  C She wants to work abroad.

SPEAKING

Expressing surprise and disbelief

1 Look at the photo. How would you feel if you saw someone do this?

97 **2 Listen and decide which sentence is true.**

a Mark doesn't believe Lucy.
b Lucy doesn't believe Mark.

97 **3 Read the *Prepare to speak* box. Then listen again. Which phrases do Mark and Lucy use?**

PREPARE TO SPEAK

Expressing surprise and disbelief

You won't believe this, but …
I find that hard to believe.
You're joking!
Are you serious?
No way!
I can't/couldn't believe my eyes.
That just isn't possible.

4 Work in pairs. Discuss the quiz questions together. Use the language in the *Prepare to speak* box.

The No Way! quiz

1 Which two events happened in the same year?
A The Eiffel Tower in Paris was finished.
B Contact lenses were invented.
C The Japanese company Nintendo was started.

2 Which law is true in parts of Australia?
A You are only allowed to own a pet rabbit if you are a magician.
B Cats aren't allowed to make a noise after 9 pm.
C You must attend classes before you can own a dog.

3 When the *Mona Lisa* was stolen in 1911, who did the police think the thief was?
A a French poet
B a museum guard
C Picasso

4 How thick would a piece of paper be if you folded it in half 42 times?
A It would be about 2 metres thick.
B It would be as tall as a house.
C It would be thick enough to reach the moon.

5 Which two people were born in the same year?
A Marilyn Monroe, the film actress
B Queen Elizabeth II
C Pelé, the Brazilian footballer

5 » **Turn to page 127 and check your answers to the quiz. Which answers surprised you the most?**

LIFE SKILLS CRITICAL THINKING

IDENTIFYING RELIABLE NEWS

LIFE SKILLS

Identifying reliable news

We can get news from many sources. We can ask people we know and we can turn on the radio or TV. We can also use the internet to find out what's happening. However, we can't trust everything we see or hear. We need to identify reliable sources that we can believe and trust.

1 **Ask and answer the questions with a partner.**

What sources of information help you stay up to date?

- my parents
- teachers and other adults
- my friends at school
- newspapers and magazines
- news on the radio or TV
- internet websites and apps
- other sources

Which sources of information above do you believe the most? Why do you think they are better than other sources?

2 **Read the text quickly. Match the questions (a–e) to the expert's answers.**

a Why do people create fake news?
b How can we avoid or identify fake news?
c Is fake news only a recent problem?
d What other negative effects can fake news have?
e What does the phrase 'fake news' mean?

3 **Match the sentences to similar ideas in the introduction and paragraphs 1–5.**

1. New technology, like the internet, makes it easier to share fake news.
2. You should always check the facts if a news story sounds false.
3. We can get information about the news from lots of places.
4. Fake news stories can change opinions about people and companies.
5. A fake story can become famous if lots of people share it online.
6. Some websites use fake news to get more visitors and make money.

4 **Match the highlighted words in the text to the meanings.**

1. funny stories that people tell
2. give or supply something
3. notice or understand something
4. topic or subject
5. very new and up-to-date
6. have a bad effect on something

98 **5** **Match the photos (A–D) to the topics (1–4). Then listen to four people talking about fake news. Which topics do they discuss?**

A

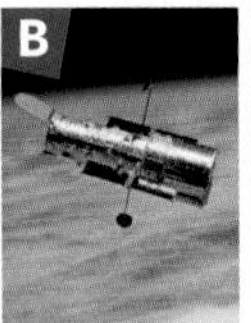
B

C

D

1. a food that sounds disgusting
2. stories about health and medicine
3. celebrities and their private lives
4. something surprising in space

98 **6** **Listen again and answer the questions.**

1 A In the astronomy article, what did scientists see on Mars?
B Why might NASA want to keep the story secret?
2 A Who did the article say the actor had married?
B Why was it impossible for them to be married?
3 A Why didn't the company like the phrase 'strange pink liquid'?
B What happened after the report was shown on TV?
4 A What health products are fake stories often about?
B What are the fake news writers really trying to do?

7 **Complete the *Useful language* phrases with the words in the box.**

cases	discuss	issue	serious
share	solution		

USEFUL LANGUAGE

Discussing a problem

1. It can be a ________ problem.
2. There have been many ________ of this.
3. It's quite an important ________.
4. We need a ________ to this problem.
5. People shouldn't ________ fake news.
6. It'd be good to ________ it at school.

LIFE SKILLS

Learning Objectives

- The students learn about how to tell the difference between reliable and fake news.
- In the project stage, they organise an information campaign about fake news.

Vocabulary

damage issue jokes modern provide realise

BACKGROUND INFORMATION

Fake news is certainly not new! For example, in the 13th century BC the Egyptian pharaoh, Rameses the Great, spread false news by saying the Egyptians had won a huge victory over their enemies, the Hittites, which was later shown to be untrue.

According to 2018 statistics, 80% of Americans aged 18–29 thought that fake news is a major problem. Another survey concluded that young people tended to trust their families more than teachers, news media and friends as a source of accurate news. However, over 30% of children and teenagers in the USA had shared a news story in the previous six months and later found out it was fake.

Buzzfeed, an American Internet media and news company, found that fake news stories on Facebook about the 2016 US presidential election were more popular than the top election stories from major media outlets. However, another study found that, although a large number of people were exposed to fake news, they actually read or watched far more sources of reliable news. The impact that fake news had on them was actually relatively small.

WARMER

Ask students if they have read any news stories in the past week and what they were about. Ask why they chose to read them, for example the topic was one they were already interested in, the article had a catchy headline or an interesting photograph. Ask them if there are topics they never read about and why or why not. Write key vocabulary on the board.

LIFE SKILLS

Identifying reliable news

Students read the text. Check understanding and pronunciation of *reliable* /rɪˈlaɪəbl/ (*able to be trusted or believed*) and *source* /sɔːs/ (*someone or something that supplies information*). Ask students if they agree and if they think this is an important issue.

1 Check understanding of *up to date* (*having the most recent information*). In pairs, students discuss the questions and then report back to the class. Have a class discussion about what sort of news they get from each source and then, as a class, discuss which sources they believe most and why. Write key words on the board.

Answers

Students' own answers

2 Read the title of the article and ask students what they think it is about. Students read the five questions, read the text quickly and match the questions to the expert's answers. Tell them not to worry about any new vocabulary at this stage. Students compare answers with a partner. Check answers and ask students to give reasons for their choices.

Answers

a 3 b 5 c 2 d 4 e 1

3 Students read the sentences. Then, they read the text more carefully to find which paragraph, including the introduction, has a similar idea. Monitor and help as necessary. Students compare answers with a partner. Check answers with the class and ask students to read out the sentences that express the same idea.

Answers

1 paragraph 2 (sentence 3)
2 paragraph 5 (sentence 1)
3 introduction (sentence 2)
4 paragraph 4 (sentence 2)
5 paragraph 1 (sentence 3)
6 paragraph 3 (sentence 2)

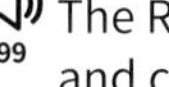

The Reading text is recorded for students to listen, read and check their answers.

MIXED ABILITY

Ask weaker students to underline the key words in each sentence and then quickly scan the introduction and each paragraph to find them. Then they should read the paragraph containing the word or words and decide whether it has a similar idea.

FAST FINISHERS

Ask fast finishers to write three *True/False* sentences taken from the text. They read them out and the rest of the class has to identify the false ones and correct them.

CONTINUED ON PAGE 230

4 Students read the highlighted words in the text. They should think about the context, including the sentences immediately before or after the highlighted words, in order to work out their meaning. Then they match the words to their definitions and compare answers with a partner. Check answers with the class and clarify the pronunciation of *damage* /ˈdæmɪdʒ/. Check understanding of any other new vocabulary, for example *rumour* (*something a lot of people are talking about although they do not know if it is true*), *headline* (*the title of a news story, printed in large letters above it*) and *protect* (*keep someone or something safe from something that is dangerous or bad*).

Answers

1 jokes 2 provide 3 realise 4 issue 5 modern 6 damage

5 Students look at the four photos and match them to the topics. Tell students they are going to listen to four young people talking about fake news stories on each topic. In pairs, students predict what the stories might be about. Play the recording and check answers. Ask students if their predictions were correct.

Answers

1 D – Ben (speaker 3)
2 C – Katy (speaker 4)
3 A – Marc (speaker 2)
4 B – Jade (speaker 1)

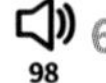

6 In pairs, students read the questions and answer any that they can remember from the recording. Play the recording again, pausing between each speaker so students can write their answers. Ask students if they have read or heard any fake news about each topic. Ask them if they believed it at first and if they asked themselves the four questions in paragraph 5 of the Reading text. Talk about the possible consequences of people believing fake news about these topics and ask whether some of the topics are more serious or dangerous than others.

Answers

1 A a secret city
1 B Because people would be scared.
2 A a supermodel
2 B They had never met.
3 A It sounded horrible.
3 B The TV programme had to pay the company because its image was damaged.
4 A medicines, superfoods or exercise machines
4 B They want to sell their products.

» **AUDIOSCRIPT TB PAGE 279**

7 Put students into pairs to read the words in the box and complete the sentences in the *Useful language* box. Check the answers with the class. Ask students to suggest other vocabulary and expressions that could be used to discuss problems.

Answers

1 serious 2 cases 3 issue 4 solution 5 share 6 discuss

PROJECT ***A campaign about fake news***

Explain that students are going to work in groups to organise an information campaign about fake news. The objectives of the campaign are to persuade young people that fake news can be damaging or even dangerous, and to help people identify and avoid fake news. Read the questions and put students into groups to discuss them and make notes. They should agree on a definition of fake news. Tell them to think of at least two answers to each of the other questions. Monitor and help as necessary. As a class, discuss where they could find more information about this problem and, if students are not sure, ask them to do some research online. Next, in their groups, students decide what information they are going to use for their campaign and how they are going to present it, for example a presentation, a poster or a brochure. They discuss the design, the layout and if they are going to use any graphics. They write the text and check grammar, vocabulary and spelling. Finally, they present their campaign to the class. Have a discussion about whether all the ideas are realistic and practical or not. Depending on the format chosen for the campaign, display the results in the classroom or around the school

PROJECT EXTENSION

In pairs or small groups, students do some research to find the most widely shared false news stories in the past year either in their country or around the world. They write a summary saying when and where the news appeared, how often it was shared, what the story was about and what effect it had. They present their work to the class.

COOLER

Write four topics from the lesson on the board, for example *celebrities*, *science*, *food*, *medicine* and ask students to write a convincing false news story about one of the topics. It should have a fake headline and be about four or five sentences long. Ask volunteers to read out their stories.

99

FAKE NEWS

GET THE **REAL FACTS!**

We need to know what's happening around us in the world, and there are many ways to get news. We can read print media, such as newspapers and magazines, or we can use digital media, like TV and the internet. However, we have to think carefully about the information those sources provide and watch out for a problem called 'fake news'.

01 ________?

When people talk about fake news, they mean false stories that we sometimes find in the media. For example, a website might post an article with false information about a famous celebrity. Then the story might be shared on social media and go viral before people realise that it's false.

THE PRESIDENT IS AN ALIEN

02 ________?

The phrase 'fake news' isn't new. In fact, it's more than 100 years old. And of course, rumours and false stories have existed since people started using language! However, fake news is becoming more common today because modern technology makes communication faster and easier than before.

03 ________?

In some cases, people invent fake stories to have fun and make jokes, but fake news can also be used to get attention. For example, websites might use fake headlines to attract more readers so they can earn more money. In some cases, fake news gets more attention than real news, and that's not funny!

04 ________?

Another negative effect of fake news is that people can stop trusting the media because they don't know who is really telling the truth. Fake news stories can also damage the image of a person or company. For instance, a fake story about a restaurant could suggest that its food is unhealthy or dangerous. Similarly, fake news about other cultures makes people feel negatively about them and changes public opinion.

05 ________?

To protect yourself against fake news stories, ask yourself four questions: who, what, where and why.

Who wrote the story? Are they experts on the issue? Do you trust them to tell the truth?

What do other people say? Check the facts with other sources and people that you trust.

Where has this story appeared? Did you find it on a website that usually tells the truth?

Why has this story appeared? Is it a joke or is it serious? What is the writer trying to do?

Think carefully about these questions before you share any news on social media. But don't be too negative. Some people tell the truth!

Actress Pippa Cox says she hates her fans

PROJECT

A campaign about fake news

Organise an information campaign about fake news for your school. Use the questions to help you plan your campaign.

- Can you define fake news in a simple, clear way?
- Have there been any fake news stories in your area?
- Why do some people believe fake news so easily?
- How can young people avoid or identify fake news?
- How can schools help students notice fake news?
- How can websites be useful for stopping fake news?

Present your work to the class. Then display it in your school.

REVIEW 5 UNITS 17–20

VOCABULARY

1 Choose the odd one out in each group of words. Explain your answer.

1	novel	biography	author	e-book
2	actor	audience	painter	writer
3	sticker	painting	poetry	sculpture
4	artist	director	studio	poet
5	article	gallery	notice	brochure

2 Complete the jobs with the missing vowels. Then answer the questions.

b _ bys _ tt _ r	pr _ s _ nt _ r
f _ r _ f _ ght _ r	j _ _ rn _ l _ st
_ rch _ t _ ct	ph _ rm _ c _ st

Who …

1 has the most dangerous job? ________
2 works with children? ________
3 writes about the news? ________
4 designs buildings? ________
5 introduces radio or TV shows? ________
6 sells medicines? ________

3 Complete the words in the mini-conversations.

1 A: We have to finish this essay by tomorrow but I'm *so* tired. I keep losing my **c**________ and I can't think of anything to write!
B: Your problem isn't being tired, you just need to pay more **a**________ in class.

2 C: So what do you want for your birthday? Give us a **h**________!
D: No way, I want a surprise. You know me well enough, just use your **i**________.

3 E: I have £12 to spend but I can't make up my **m**________ what to buy. I was going to get a poster for my room but now I'm having second **t**________.
F: Hey, I've just had a **t**________. What about one of these graphic **n**________? The plots are supposed to be amazing.

4 Complete the sentences. Use the noun or adjective form of the words in brackets.

-al -er -ful -ian -ist -or

1 Katy doesn't eat meat. She's ________. (vegetable)
2 There's a new ________ on this site who is really funny. (blog)
3 I love the soundtrack to that film, but the acting isn't very ________. (nature)
4 My sister is a brilliant ________. (piano)
5 How many ________ are there in this year's marathon? (compete)
6 I've hurt my leg. It's really ________. (pain)

GRAMMAR

1 Read the first sentence. Then complete the second sentence using the verbs in the box.

~~advised~~	asked	persuaded
ordered	warned	

0 'You should publish that story.'
His friends *advised* him *to publish* the story.

1 'Sit down!'
The teacher ________ the students ________.

2 'Be careful when you do question five.'
The teacher ________ the students ________ with question five.

3 'Can you help me?'
Harry ________ Charlotte ________ him.

4 'You really should enter the art competition.'
My mum ________ me ________ the art competition.

2 Complete the sentences. Use the second conditional form of the verbs.

0 My cousins don't live near me, so I don't see them.
If my cousins lived near me, …
I would see them.

1 Marcia doesn't invite me to her parties, so I don't invite her to mine.
If Marcia invited me to her parties, …

2 They talk all the time, so they're always in trouble.
They wouldn't always be in trouble if …

3 I never do exercise, so I'm not fit.
If I did exercise, …

4 He doesn't work hard, so he never gets good marks.
He'd get good marks if …

5 She doesn't like TV, so she plays computer games all the time.
If she liked TV, …

REVIEW 5 UNITS 17–20

Overview

VOCABULARY	Arts and entertainment; Adjectives: *-al* and *-ful*; jobs; Suffixes: *-er*, *-or*, *ist*, *ian*; Things that you read; *say*, *speak*, *talk* and *tell*; Collocations: thinking; *look (at)*, *see*, *watch*
GRAMMAR	Reported commands; Second conditional; Reported speech; Past simple passive
EXAM TASKS	Reading Part 5

Resources

PHOTOCOPIABLE WORKSHEETS: Grammar worksheets Units 17–20; Vocabulary worksheets Units 17–20; Review Game Units 17–20; Literature worksheet; Speaking worksheet; Writing worksheet

WARMER

On a sheet of paper, each student writes their name and four sentences about themselves, one in the present simple, one in the present continuous, one with *can* and one with *will*. First, elicit some example sentences and write them on the board. For example *Emma: I like studying English, I'm going cycling on Sunday, I can ride a bike, I'll do my homework this evening*. Ask stronger students to report what Emma said, and write the verbs on the board: She said she *liked*, *was going*, *could*, *would*. Students write their sentences. Collect the sheets of paper and redistribute them. Ask students to report what is on their paper without saying the student's name. The rest of the class guesses who wrote the sentences.

VOCABULARY

1 Write *Arts and entertainment* and *Things that you read* on the board and elicit some words for each category. In pairs, students read the groups of words and find the odd one out. They compare with another pair and explain their answers. Check answers with the class. Check understanding and pronunciation, particularly *audience* /ˈɔːdiəns/, *sculpture* /ˈskʌlptʃə/, *article* /ˈɑːtɪkl/ and *brochure* /ˈbrəʊʃə/.

Answers

1 An **author** is a person who writes things; the others are things that an author might write.
2 An **audience** is a group of people who are entertained by the other three.
3 A **sticker** is not a creative art form; the other three are.
4 A **studio** is a place; the other words are people who might work in a studio.
5 A **gallery** is a place for exhibitions; the other three are things that you read or write.

2 Students complete the jobs with the missing vowels and answer the questions. Check answers as a class. Check pronunciation, for example *architect* /ˈɑːkɪtekt/ and *journalist* /ˈdʒɜːnəlɪst/.

Answers

1 firefighter 2 babysitter 3 journalist 4 architect 5 presenter 6 pharmacist

3 Tell students they are going to complete the conversations with phrases about thinking from Unit 20, apart from the final space. They complete the exercise. Review answers and ask for definitions of the verb phrases.

Answers

1 concentration, attention
2 hint, imagination
3 mind, thoughts, thought, novels

4 Students read the suffixes in the box and say which ones are endings for adjectives and which for nouns. They complete the sentences using the correct form of the words in brackets. Check answers and check the words are spelled correctly.

Answers

1 vegetarian 2 blogger 3 natural 4 pianist 5 competitors 6 painful

FAST FINISHERS

Ask fast finishers to write adjectives from *peace* and *origin*, and nouns from *comedy*, *act*, *science* and *teach*. They write a definition for each word and the rest of the class tries to guess the word.

GRAMMAR

1 Read the example and remind students of the structure of reported commands. Write on the board: subject + verb + object + infinitive. They read the sentences, decide which verb to use in each item and complete the sentences. Check answers as a class.

Answers

1 ordered, to sit down
2 warned, to be careful
3 asked, to help
4 persuaded, to enter

2 Elicit the structure and use of the second conditional (*if* + past tense, *would* + infinitive) and remind students that the *if* clause can go either first or second in the sentence. Read the example and elicit that the negative verb becomes positive in the conditional sentence. Similarly, positive verbs become negative, so students need to look carefully at the verbs and think about meaning. Students complete the exercise using contractions where possible. Check answers as a class.

Answers

1 I'd invite her to mine.
2 they didn't talk all the time.
3 I'd be fit.
4 he worked hard.
5 she wouldn't play computer games all the time.

3 On the board write *Eoin Colfer wrote* Artemis Fowl, and ask students if the sentence is active or passive. Tell them to make it passive (Artemis Fowl *was written by Eoin Colfer*). Write Fearless *record Taylor Swift 2008* and ask students to write a passive sentence (Fearless *was recorded by Taylor Swift in 2008*). Explain that they are going to complete the second sentences using grammatical structures from Units 17–20. They complete the exercise and compare answers with a partner. Monitor and help as necessary. Review answers as a class.

Answers

1 painted by
2 was sold
3 she couldn't imagine
4 wouldn't paint
5 'm going to

MIXED ABILITY

Support weaker students by telling them which grammatical structures are needed in the second sentences: past simple passive – 1, 2; reported speech – 3, 5; second conditional – 4.

4 Ask students what part of speech the options are (*verbs*). Elicit typical mistakes often made with verb forms, for example incorrect tense, incorrect ending for present simple or present perfect third person, incorrect past tense or past participle, confusion between active and passive forms, whether a verb is followed by a pronoun, incorrect verb, etc. Put students into pairs to complete the exercise. If they disagree, they should explain their choice by referring to the grammar rule that should be applied. Check answers with the class and ask volunteers to explain the grammar rules.

Answers

1 asked 2 wanted 3 tell 4 was

5 Ask students what part of speech the mistakes are (*verbs*). Remind them of the typical mistakes they discussed in Exercise 4. Students complete the exercise in pairs and justify their correction by referring to the appropriate grammar rule. Check answers with the class and, if necessary, ask stronger students to explain the mistakes.

Answers

1 The driver stopped the bus and **warned** Lisa to sit down.
2 If you came with me to the concert, it **would** be more fun for me.
3 Someone **told** us it was too late to get a bus.
4 The medicine **tasted** horrible but it made me feel better.

6 B1 Preliminary for Schools Reading Part 5

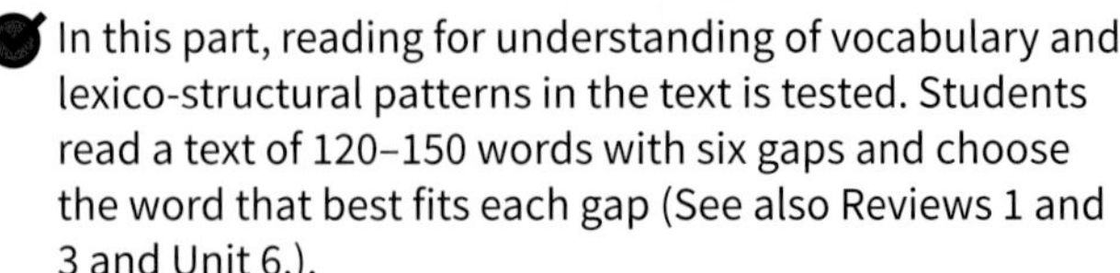

In this part, reading for understanding of vocabulary and lexico-structural patterns in the text is tested. Students read a text of 120–150 words with six gaps and choose the word that best fits each gap (See also Reviews 1 and 3 and Unit 6.).

Students read the text ignoring the gaps. Ask for a quick summary of what it is about (*it's an advert for a short course for students to develop skills in performing arts*). Then students look at each gap, say which part of speech would fit and suggest a possible answer. Accept all reasonable suggestions. Tell students that if they are unsure which is the correct answer, they should start by deleting the ones that they are certain are incorrect. They can then guess between the ones that are left. While students complete the exercise, monitor and give help where necessary. They compare answers with a partner. Check answers with the class. Use this as an opportunity to do some vocabulary work on collocations with *make* and *take*, for example make *an effort*, *an excuse*, *a note*; take *care of*, *charge*, *a photo*.

Answers

1 C 2 D 3 D 4 A 5 A 6 A

COOLER

Ask students to think about Units 17–20. Write some questions on the board: *Which activities did you enjoy? What was difficult / easy for you?* Ask students to write their answers. Discuss ways of having contact with English during the school holidays, such as watching series with English subtitles, listening to podcasts, doing online exercises, using opportunities to practise with native speakers who are visiting their country or if students go abroad. Ask students which they think are the most useful for them and if they can recommend websites, series, etc.

3 **Complete the second sentence so that it means the same as the first. Use no more than three words.**

1 Leonardo da Vinci painted the *Mona Lisa*.
The *Mona Lisa* was ________ Leonardo da Vinci.
2 In 2017, a collector sold *Salvator Mundi* by da Vinci for US$400 million!
In 2017, *Salvator Mundi* by da Vinci ________ for US$400 million!
3 'I can't imagine life without my phone,' said Nina.
Nina said ________ life without her phone.
4 I don't think you should paint your bedroom black.
If I were you, I ________ your bedroom black.
5 Joe said he was going to the exhibition later.
'I ________ the exhibition later,' said Joe.

4 **Choose the correct words.**

1 The teacher *asked* / *asked to* us to work together.
2 If they *would want* / *wanted* to watch a film, they'd need to use my spare screen.
3 I wanted to *say* / *tell* you that I have a new game.
4 This series *was* / *is* filmed in 2017.

5 **Correct the mistake in each sentence.**

1 The driver stopped the bus and warns Lisa to sit down.
2 If you came with me to the concert, it will be more fun for me.
3 Someone tells us it was too late to get a bus.
4 The medicine was tasted horrible but it made me feel better.

6 **Choose the correct word for each space. For each question, choose A, B, C or D.**

DEVELOP YOUR *talents!*

Many teenagers dream of becoming celebrities – do you?

If you have a [1] ________ talent for acting, dancing or singing, why not attend our two-week course and develop all three! Students are taught in small groups to allow you to [2] ________ progress quickly. For the first three days, you will concentrate on the three areas – acting, dancing and singing – with a full day for each skill. The rest of the course is all about the challenges of performing live. On the final afternoon, you will take [3] ________ in a show in front of a real [4] ________, which is always exciting. Past students [5] ________ it's the most fun they've ever had.

The course starts on 15th July and there are ten six-hour classes altogether. To book, simply complete your details on the other side of this [6] ________ and send it in!

	A	B	C	D
1	central	cultural	natural	traditional
2	do	get	have	make
3	away	back	off	part
4	audience	character	presenter	performer
5	say	speak	talk	tell
6	advert	paper	novel	sticker

EXTRA ACTIVITIES

UNIT 1 GRAMMAR, PAGE 12

8 **Make questions with the present simple or present continuous. Then ask and answer them.**

1 What subjects / you / study / this year?
2 What / you / do / after school / today?
3 you / own / more than one mobile phone?
4 What TV programmes / you / watch / every week?
5 you / prefer / playing sport or watching TV?
6 What / you / like / doing on Sundays?
7 What / music / you / listen to / regularly?
8 you / have / a party for your next birthday?

UNIT 1 VOCABULARY, PAGE 12

3 **Discuss these questions.**

1 Do you ever get **impatient** with anyone?
2 Are you ever **unkind** to people? Who?
3 Do you think you're generally **lucky** or **unlucky**?
4 Do you think your parents are sometimes **unfair**?
5 Do you think you're an **independent** person?
6 How often are you **unwell**?

UNIT 2 VOCABULARY, PAGE 16

5' **4** **In pairs, write as many sentences as possible using the adverb forms of the adjectives in the box. You have a time limit of five minutes!**

accurate amazing beautiful brave dangerous early easy excited happy hard last perfect safe secret urgent

We met secretly.

Compare your sentences with other pairs. Who has the most sentences?

UNIT 3 VOCABULARY, PAGE 20

5 **Quiz answers**

1 In England, the majority of children start school the September before their fifth birthday. However, education is not obligatory until the age of five.
2 In Belgium and Germany, students cannot leave school until they are 18.
3 In some states in the USA, the youngest age you can get a driving licence is 14. However, there are often a lot of rules for drivers of this age. For example, in South Dakota young drivers cannot drive between 10 pm and 6 am.
4 In England, 33% of young people go to university after leaving school. Around 6% of these students leave university before they get a degree. The most common reason for leaving is that students don't have enough money.
5 In almost all European countries, women leave home before men. In Italy, over 50% of men leave home in their thirties.
6 In the UK, you can get a job at the age of 13. You can work a maximum of 12 hours a week and 25 hours a week in the holidays.
7 In Spain, the average age at which women and men marry is 33. In India it is 22. In Japan it is 28.
8 In Brazil, the minimum voting age is 16. Between the ages of 18 and 70 in Brazil, it is obligatory to vote.

UNIT 3 VOCABULARY, PAGE 22

3 **Complete the sentences with your own ideas. Then compare your answers with a partner.**

1 I never have enough ________.
2 I don't ________ because I'm too ________.
3 My parents sometimes aren't ________ enough.
4 I'm ________ enough to ________.
5 Our school isn't ________ enough and it's too ________.

UNIT 4 VOCABULARY, PAGE 26

3 Student A

Read the instructions and play the game.

- **a** You are going to explain some words in English without saying the word itself. Student B has to guess each word. Student B can ask questions.
- **b** Read the example.
- **c** You have a time limit of five minutes! How many can you explain?

0 ~~trainer~~	**4** rugby
1 coach	**5** athletics
2 exercise	**6** match (noun)
3 fit (adjective)	**7** squash

Example:
A: *This is a noun for a person. They help sports players.*
B: *Is it a manager?*
A: *No. They help the players to get better at their sport.*
B: *A coach?*
A: *No, but it's very similar to a coach!*
B: *A trainer?*
A: *Yes!*

Listen to Student B and guess the words. You can ask questions. You have a time limit of five minutes! How many words can Student B explain?

UNIT 5 VOCABULARY, PAGE 34

4 Ask and answer the questions with a partner.

1. Do you and your friends buy each other birthday presents?
2. Do you usually enjoy yourself at parties?
3. How do you and your friends greet each other in the mornings?
4. Are you good at introducing yourself to new people?
5. Have you ever taught yourself a new skill?
6. Do you and your teachers email each other?

UNIT 6 VOCABULARY, PAGE 38

3 Ask and answer the questions with a partner.

1. Where's the nearest post box to your home?
2. What's the speed limit near your school? Is it too high?
3. How often do cars stop at pedestrian crossings?
4. What do you do while you are waiting at bus stops?
5. How many recycling bins are there in your school?
6. How many different types of road sign can you think of?

UNIT 7 VOCABULARY, PAGE 44

4 Student A

In pairs, put your sentences and Student B's sentences in the correct order to form a story. Don't look at each other's sentences. Read the story together and check.

- **a** **on** very well – in fact, they fell in love. They knew that their relationship would be difficult, because Juliet was a Capulet and Romeo was a Montague, and their families would never **make**
- **b** *Once upon a time*, in a town called Verona in Italy, there were two families, the Montagues and the Capulets. The families **had**
- **c** **out** many years ago. One day, a young man from the Montague family called Romeo was **hanging**
- **d** **round** to their house for a party, so Romeo and his friends decided to go in masks. Then Romeo could **get**
- **e** **up** because their love was perfect. They wanted to be together and **look**

Read the story together and discuss how you think the story ends.

UNIT 8 VOCABULARY, PAGE 48

4 In pairs, write as many sentences as possible using the phrasal verbs in the box. You have a time limit of three minutes!

check in	get back	get in	go away
look around	pick up	set off	take off

My mum picks up my dad if he works late.

Compare your sentences with other pairs. Who has the most correct sentences?

EXTRA ACTIVITIES

UNIT 9 VOCABULARY, PAGE 54

4 **Key for quiz**

Mostly **a**) answers: You think very carefully about what you spend your money on and you probably find all the best offers. But are you too careful? Money isn't the most important thing in life!

Mostly **b**) answers: The way you think about money is probably just right. You don't waste it, but you don't let it control your life.

Mostly **c**) answers: You need to start thinking about money or you're going to be short of cash your whole life! You don't *have to* spend everything you have. What about saving a bit?

UNIT 9 GRAMMAR, PAGE 56

4 **Complete the questions with the correct past participles. Then complete the table for you with ✓ (Yes) or ✗ (No).**

Have you ever …	You	Your partner
1 *sold* (sell) anything online?		
2 ______ (lend) anyone any money?		
3 ______ (take) anything back to a shop?		
4 ______ (lose) your phone?		
5 ______ (receive) too much change in a shop?		
6 ______ (regret) buying anything?		
7 ______ (buy) anything you can't afford?		
8 ______ (save) up to buy anything?		

Ask and answer the questions in Exercise 4. Complete the table for your partner.

A: *Have you ever sold anything online?*
B: *Yes, I have. Lots of times.*

UNIT 9 VOCABULARY, PAGE 56

3 **Ask and answer the questions with a partner.**

1. Do you think museums should charge for admission or be free? Why?
2. What's the most you've paid for a small bottle of water?
3. How much does it cost to go to the cinema in your town or city?
4. Will pay be important to you in your future choice of job?
5. Do you know the cost of a typical flat or house in your area?
6. Have you ever eaten at a restaurant free of charge?

UNIT 10 VOCABULARY, PAGE 60

3 **Work in pairs. Check you understand the meaning of the items.**

Student A
Choose an item to describe using *look, taste* or *smell.* Use the adjectives or your own ideas.

Student B
Can you guess what your partner is describing?

Items

a chilli a flower an ice lolly fireworks honey mustard strawberries

Adjectives

amazing delicious disgusting freezing fresh juicy soft spicy sweet

UNIT 11 VOCABULARY, PAGE 66

4 Student A

- **Say the sentence and act the injury. Student B has to guess what's wrong. (Student B can only ask questions that have *Yes/No* answers.)**

Say: "Ow, my head!"
Act: Put one hand over your right eye and moan with pain.
Answer: You walked into a door and cut your forehead.

B: *Have you got a fever?*
A: *No, I haven't.*

- **Guess what's wrong with Student B. You can only ask questions that have *Yes/No* answers.**
- **Take turns to invent and act out more illnesses and injuries.**

UNIT 12 VOCABULARY, PAGE 70

2 **Photo A is the eye of a goat. Photo B is a horse's foot.**

UNIT 12 VOCABULARY, PAGE 70

3 Student A

- **Write ten sentences about yourself, your family, friends or where you live. Five sentences should be true and five sentences should be false.**

My family originally comes from ... .
My brother can speak ... .

- **Read your sentences one at a time. Student B has to guess which are true and which are false using adverbs of probability.**

A: *My family originally comes from Ireland.*
B: *That's* ***definitely not*** *true! You have a Spanish surname, so you must come from a Spanish-speaking country.* ***Perhaps*** *your family originally comes from Spain.*
A: *You're right! / No, my family originally comes from Colombia.*

- **Listen to Student B's sentences. Guess which are true and which are false using adverbs of probability: *definitely* (*not*), *perhaps*, *probably*.**

UNIT 13 VOCABULARY, PAGE 78

3 **Complete the sentences with the *-ed* or *-ing* adjective form of the words. Then write two more questions using *-ed* or *-ing* adjectives. In pairs, ask and answer the questions.**

1. Which day of your week is the most ________ (tire)?
2. What's the most ________ (disgust) thing you've ever eaten?
3. Which school subject do you find the most ________ (confuse)?
4. What's the most ________ (amaze) fact you know?
5. Who was the last person you got ________ (annoy) with?
6. When was the last time you felt completely ________ (relax)?
7. How often do you feel ________ (embarrass) by your parents?
8. What's the most ________ (worry) thing happening in the world at the moment?

UNIT 14 VOCABULARY, PAGE 82

4 **In pairs, write a few sentences about the words in the box, without actually using the words.**

~~clip~~ character plot review
series soundtrack trailer

Example: clip
This is a short video that comes from a longer show or film.
You can watch it on your phone or on your computer.
Usually they show the best parts of a show or film.

Take turns to read your sentences to other pairs of students. How quickly can they guess the word?

A: *This is a short video that comes from a longer show or film.*
B: *Is it a trailer?*
A: *No. You can watch it on your phone or ...*
B: *Is it a clip?*
A: *Yes!*

EXTRA ACTIVITIES

UNIT 12 SPEAKING, PAGE 71

Take turns to describe the photo. Use phrases from the *Prepare to speak* box.

UNIT 15 GRAMMAR, PAGE 88

3
1. The most common type of program that people download is anti-virus software. This is software to check for computer viruses.
2. The most common passwords are often quite simple. Many people just use the word 'password' or the numbers '123456'.
3. This will change every year, but in 2017, the top ten included the Hollywood actors Meghan Markle and Gal Gadot.
4. This figure is increasing every year, but in 2017, we spent more than $200 billion on apps.
5. Most smartphones are made in China, South Korea, India and Taiwan.

UNIT 15 VOCABULARY, PAGE 88

3 **Take turns to mime an activity using the verbs in Box A and the words in Box B. Can your partner guess what you are doing?**

A

look up	plug in	shut down
switch/turn off	switch/turn on	turn down
turn up	take out	

B

your fitness tracker	your games console
a hairdryer	your laptop
a light	the TV
your phone	a printer
a memory card from a phone	
the weather on your phone	

UNIT 16 VOCABULARY, PAGE 92

3 **In pairs, write sentences using the phrasal verbs in the box.**

add up blow up carry out
cut up take away work out

Act them out. Can the class guess your sentences?

UNIT 17 VOCABULARY, PAGE 100

3 **Student A**

Complete the questions using adjectives formed from the nouns in the box. Then ask Student B the questions.

digit hope music person
profession use

1 What ________ device could you not live without?
2 Can you play any ________ instruments?
3 Do you tell your friends about your problems, or keep ________ issues to yourself?
4 Would you like to be a ________ artist or musician? Why? / Why not?
5 What's the most ________ advice you've ever received?
6 What things do you feel most ________ about in the future?

Answer Student B's questions.

UNIT 18 VOCABULARY, PAGE 104

3 **Work in pairs. Check you understand the meaning of the words in the box.**

an actor an artist an author
a banker a composer a baker
a dentist a driver an electrician
a film director a headteacher a musician
a pianist a politician

Take turns to mime a person in the box. Can you / your partner guess all the words in two minutes?

UNIT 19 VOCABULARY, PAGE 110

3 **Student A**

Complete the questions using *say, speak, talk* and *tell*. Then ask Student B the questions.

1 How many languages can you ________?
2 Can you ________ me what your favourite film is?
3 Can you ________ the alphabet backwards in English?
4 Which celebrity would you most like to ________ to? Why?
5 Who do you ________ to when you're in trouble?
6 Can you ________ the English equivalent of your name, or any of your friends' names?

Answer Student B's questions.

UNIT 20 VOCABULARY, PAGE 114

3 **Write two sentences for each of 1–3 below. Use the ideas in the box or your own.**

1 You're looking at …
2 You've just seen …
3 You're watching …

a famous actor in the street.
someone steal a car.
a fly in your meal at a restaurant.
a poster about a concert.
the pictures in a recipe book.
a soap opera.
an incredibly exciting football match.
an eagle in the sky.
a clip from your favorite TV show.
a school notice about exam results.

Work in pairs. Take turns to mime one of your sentences. Can your partner guess your sentence exactly?

EXTRA ACTIVITIES 125

EXTRA ACTIVITIES

UNIT 4 VOCABULARY, PAGE 26

3 Student B

Read the instructions and play the game.

a You are going to listen to Student A explain some words in English without saying the word itself. You have to guess each word. You can ask questions.
b Read the example.
c You have a time limit of five minutes! How many can Student A explain?

Example:
A: *This is a noun for a person. They help sports players.*
B: *Is it a manager?*
A: *No. They help the players to get better at their sport.*
B: *A coach?*
A: *No, but it's very similar to a coach!*
B: *A trainer?*
A: *Yes!*

Explain these words without saying the word itself. Student A has to guess each word. You have a time limit of five minutes! How many can you explain?

0 ~~trainer~~
1 BMX
2 champion
3 jogging
4 point (noun)
5 train (verb)
6 windsurfing
7 work out (noun)

UNIT 7 VOCABULARY, PAGE 44

4 Student B

In pairs, put your sentences and Student A's sentences in the correct order to form a story. Don't look at each other's sentences. Read the story together and check.

f **after** each other forever. So, the day after the party, they got married in secret.
g **arguments** and fought all the time. No one can remember exactly why, but the two families **fell**
h **out** with his friends in Verona when they heard about a party at the Capulets' house. Romeo loved a Capulet girl called Rosaline, so he wanted to go to the party to see her. But the Capulets would never let a Montague **come**
i **together** with Rosaline and the Capulets would never know. At the party, Romeo didn't speak to Rosaline. Instead, he met a girl called Juliet. Romeo and Juliet **got**
j **up** and accept their relationship. After the party, Romeo went into the garden and talked to Juliet through her bedroom window. 'But, soft!' he said. 'What light through yonder window breaks? It is the east, and Juliet is the sun.' They knew they'd never **split**

Read the story together and discuss how you think the story ends.

UNIT 11 VOCABULARY, PAGE 66

4 Student B

- **Guess what's wrong with Student A. You can only ask questions that have *Yes/No* answers.**
- **Say the sentence and act the illness. Student A has to guess what's wrong. (Student A can only ask questions that have *Yes/No* answers.)**

Say: 'Oh, I feel terrible!'
Act: Fold your arms, lean forward with your eyes closed and moan.
Answer: You feel very sick.

B: *Have you injured your arm?*
A: *No, I haven't.*

- **Take turns to invent and act out more illnesses and injuries.**

UNIT 12 VOCABULARY, PAGE 70

3 **Student B**

Write ten sentences about yourself, your family, friends or where you live. Five sentences should be true and five sentences should be false.

My family originally comes from … .
My brother can speak … .

Listen to Student A's sentences. Guess which are true and which are false using adverbs of probability: *definitely* (*not*), *perhaps*, *probably*.

A: *My family originally comes from Ireland.*
B: *That's* ***definitely not*** *true! You have a Spanish surname, so you must come from a Spanish-speaking country.* ***Perhaps*** *your family originally comes from Spain.*
A: *You're right! / No, my family originally comes from Mexico.*

Read your sentences one at a time. Student A has to guess which are true and which are false using adverbs of probability.

UNIT 17 VOCABULARY, PAGE 100

3 **Student B**

Complete the questions using adjectives formed from the nouns in the box. Then ask Student A the questions.

culture environment help music stress tradition

1 Can you cook any ________ dishes from your country or region?
2 Can you play any instruments, or aren't you very ________?
3 Are you worried about ________ issues like global warming?
4 Do you like ________ TV shows about art and literature?
5 What's the most ________ advice you've ever received?
6 Have you been in any ________ situations recently? What happened?

Answer Student A's questions.

UNIT 19 VOCABULARY, PAGE 110

3 **Student B**

Complete the questions using the correct form of *say, speak, talk* and *tell*.

1 What would you do if someone was ________ during a film at the cinema?
2 Have you ever ________ your best friend your most secret of secrets?
3 What would you ________ if you saw someone stealing in a shop?
4 Can you ________ any other languages apart from English?
5 What do you ________ about when there's a gap in a conversation?
6 Can you ________ the names of any American states / British cities? How many?

Answer Student A's questions.

Now ask Student A your questions in Exercise 1.

UNIT 20 SPEAKING, PAGE 115

5 **Answers to quiz**

1 A and C. In 1889, the Eiffel tower was finished and the company Nintendo was started. At that time, Nintendo made card games.
Contact lenses were invented by Leonardo Da Vinci in around 1508. But they weren't actually produced until 1888 in Germany.

2 A is true in Queensland. In this area of Australia, rabbits cause a lot of damage in the wild. There is also a 2,000-mile fence around this area to stop animals like rabbits getting into Queensland.
B is true in parts of the USA.
C was true until 2017 in Switzerland.

3 A and C. The police first thought the painting was stolen by Guillaume Apollinaire, a French poet and a friend of the Spanish painter, Picasso. They also believed that Picasso was involved.

4 C In theory, if you could fold a piece of paper 42 times, it would be thick enough to reach the moon. However, it is almost impossible to fold a piece of paper more than seven times.

5 A and B. They were both born in 1926. Pele was born in 1940.

GRAMMAR REFERENCE AND PRACTICE ANSWER KEY

UNIT 1 PRESENT SIMPLE AND CONTINUOUS

PRESENT SIMPLE

1 **1** Do you prefer **2** chooses, doesn't like **3** don't see, live **4** does he go **5** don't want **6** doesn't play, watches **7** Does he know **8** studies

PRESENT CONTINUOUS

2 **1** 'm/am cycling **2** isn't watching **3** are you doing, 're/are watching, 're/are studying

3 **1** I'm sitting **2** We're going **3** is playing **4** doesn't play **5** they're playing **6** I believe **7** we're having **8** I want **9** they get **10** we're eating

UNIT 2 PAST SIMPLE

1 **1** saw **2** was **3** Did you go **4** went **5** drove **6** did you wear **7** were **8** did you sit **9** did your ticket cost **10** didn't pay **11** won **12** were

2 **1** Was she late again?
2 I didn't like Andrea's new dress.
3 We slept really well last night.
4 Did you find my bag?
5 He wore his new trainers.
6 They didn't know about Bill Haley and the Comets.

3 **1** walked **2** wanted **3** weren't **4** knew **5** decided **6** had **7** was **8** didn't eat **9** caught **10** started **11** came

UNIT 3 COMPARATIVES AND SUPERLATIVES

1 **1** slower than, noisier **2** harder than, better **3** more fashionable, cheaper than **4** faster than, warmer **5** more attractive than, funnier than **6** wetter, windier than **7** more confused, more complicated than **8** brighter, more colourful

2 **1** isn't as tiring as football. **2** aren't as clean as electric cars. **3** aren't as fit as most ballet dancers. **4** aren't as healthy as salads. **5** as much work this week as last week.

3 **1** the coolest, the cheapest **2** the best, the worst **3** the safest, the most interesting **4** the lightest, the biggest, the heaviest **5** the most brilliant, the most creative **6** the closest, the cosiest **7** the most untidy / the untidiest, the most charming **8** the most sociable, the liveliest

UNIT 4 PAST CONTINUOUS

1 **1** was dreaming **2** were you playing **3** weren't watching **4** Were you talking **5** wasn't doing **6** was sitting **7** Were we using **8** were chatting **9** wasn't looking, was shouting **10** wasn't asking, was explaining

2 **1** were lying **2** were arguing **3** was telling **4** were listening **5** was making **6** wasn't listening **7** was looking **8** were waiting **9** wasn't selling

3 **1** were Derek and Armando arguing about **2** was Henri telling a story about **3** were Penelope and Doris doing **4** was Doris making **5** was Margherita listening to **6** were waiting to buy an ice cream (from the ice cream van)

4 **1** Derek and Armando weren't arguing about music, they were arguing about football.
2 Henri wasn't describing the scenery in Florida, he was telling a story about his holiday (in Florida).
3 Penelope and Doris weren't waving at Henri, they were listening to him.
4 Margherita wasn't taking a photo of the other students, she was looking at the ice cream van.

UNIT 5 PAST SIMPLE AND CONTINUOUS

1 **1** was watching **2** waited **3** watched **4** were waiting **5** talked **6** were talking **7** emailed **8** were emailing

2 **1** didn't hear, was wearing **2** all celebrated, got **3** found, was working **4** broke, was learning **5** was driving, got **6** opened, discovered **7** was chatting, went, heard **8** emailed, was mending, didn't check

3 **1** was snowing **2** slipped **3** fell off **4** was picking up **5** saw **6** was moving **7** jumped **8** hit **9** wasn't standing **10** told

4 **1** I visited my friends. Afterwards, I took the bus home.
2 Luke walked into the door because he wasn't looking ahead.
3 It was snowing at lunchtime, so I didn't go for a walk.
4 I wasn't hungry, so I didn't have anything to eat.
5 My sister crashed into a traffic light when she was riding her scooter.
6 I was thinking about the holidays. Then suddenly, I realised the time.

UNIT 6 *SOME/ANY, MUCH/MANY, A LOT OF, A FEW / A LITTLE*

1 **1** d **2** a **3** f **4** b **5** e **6** c

2 **1** any **2** some **3** any **4** any **5** some **6** any

3 **1** many **2** much **3** any **4** a few **5** a lot of **6** many **7** some **8** any **9** a lot of **10** a little

4 **1** much, a few **2** a little, much **3** much **4** a few, much **5** a few, many **6** many **7** a little, a few **8** many, a few **9** many, much **10** much, a few

UNIT 7 *HAVE TO* AND *MUST*; *SHOULD*

1 **1** should **2** should **3** must **4** don't have to **5** should **6** mustn't **7** should

2 **1** mustn't text our friends in lessons. **2** should read through your work before you show it to anyone. **3** doesn't have to wear **4** should I buy **5** didn't have to book seats for the concert. **6** shouldn't wear your best shirt when you mend your bike. **7** have to / must wear seat belts.

UNIT 8 FUTURE: *BE GOING TO* AND PRESENT CONTINUOUS

1 **1** it's going to take **2** we're organising **3** I'm going to get **4** I'm going to ask **5** I'm taking, I'm going to do **6** We're catching, We're going to play **7** It's going to rain **8** We're meeting

2 **1** Are you going to go **2** are you going to wear **3** 's/is going to be **4** 'm/am going to buy **5** Are you going to take **6** 'm/am going to give **7** 's/is going to be **8** 'm/am not going to find **9** 'm/am going to tell

3 **1** 's/is going to arrest him. **2** 's/is going to fall over it / the bin. **3** 're/are going to burn. **4** isn't going to sleep well. **5** 's/is going to win. **6** aren't going / 're/are not going to win.

UNIT 9 PRESENT PERFECT

1 **1** hasn't eaten **2** 's/has never written **3** have known **4** 's/has never beaten **5** 've/have flown **6** hasn't given, haven't texted **7** 's/has fallen, hasn't hurt, 's/has torn **8** 's/has gone, 's/has forgotten

2 **1** Have you finished **2** 've/have found **3** haven't read **4** 've/have been **5** 've/have borrowed **6** Have you tidied **7** haven't **8** 've/have made **9** 've/have had **10** have you been **11** 've/have been **12** 've/have bought **13** Have you ever seen **14** haven't

UNIT 10 PRESENT PERFECT AND PAST SIMPLE; *HOW LONG?* AND *FOR/SINCE*

1 **1** a **2** b **3** b **4** a **5** b **6** a

2 **1** I've made **2** has gone **3** cooked, haven't met **4** hasn't come, I asked **5** didn't enjoy, was

3 **1** since, for **2** for, since **3** for, since **4** since, for **5** since, for

4 **1** 've/have been **2** 've/have enjoyed **3** was **4** started **5** saw **6** arrived **7** thought **8** haven't missed **9** had **10** gave **11** didn't leave / haven't left **12** 've/have entered **13** 've/have had **14** haven't won

UNIT 11 *WILL* AND *BE GOING TO*

1 **1** will help **2** I'm going to help **3** is going to save / will save **4** I'll feel **5** is going to leave **6** is going to run **7** will be / are going to be **8** I'll go

2 **1** is going to be **2** 'll help **3** are you going to do **4** 'm going to have **5** 'm going to lie **6** 'll walk **7** 'll use **8** 'll lend **9** won't weigh **10** will take **11** 'll put **12** won't care

3 **Possible answers**

1 Lucy's going to win.

2 He's going to be sick.

3 His sister will help him.

4 They're going to look great.

5 They're / The burgers are going to burn. / She's going to burn the burgers / them.

6 He's going to go to university.

UNIT 12 MODALS OF PROBABILITY

1 **1** He/Jon must be cold.

2 They / The potatoes must be ready to eat by now.

3 This (parcel) must be my new phone.

4 It must be broken.

2 **1** He/The cat might be hungry.

2 It might be in the car.

3 He/She / My teacher might speak three languages.

3 Yes, you can use *could* instead of *might*.

4 **1** It/This fish can't be fresh.

2 That coat can't belong to you.

3 You can't feel tired.

5 **1** can't be **2** can't be **3** could be **4** might be **5** must be **6** could be **7** can't be **8** could be

UNIT 13 *JUST*, *ALREADY* AND *YET*

1 **1** just **2** yet **3** just **4** just **5** yet

2 **1** The lesson has already begun.

2 Have you been to the new shopping centre yet?

3 This parcel has just arrived for you.

4 I haven't saved much money for my holiday yet.

5 It's only eleven o'clock but everyone's already gone home.

6 My parents have just bought a new car.

7 Have you done this exercise yet?

8 We've just finished the last sentence.

3 **1** S **2** D **3** S **4** D **5** S

4 **1** He's already bought some new pens.

2 He hasn't set his alarm for 7 a.m. yet.

3 He hasn't decided what to wear yet.

4 He's already texted his mates about meeting after the exam.

5 He's already asked his mum/mother to give him a lift to school.

UNIT 14 RELATIVE CLAUSES

1 **1** who **2** which **3** which **4** which **5** who **6** which **7** who **8** who

2 **1** which was really funny **2** who lived in an old bus **3** who was called Millie Moop **4** who was always unkind to him **5** where Mr Scratch lived **6** where Millie put shampoo into a toothpaste tube **7** which you need to see to understand **8** who hasn't seen it

3 1 This is a photo of my friend who/that wants to be a TV presenter.
2 We have a goldfish who/that is called Bubbles.
3 That man wrote a song which/that everyone knows.
4 I visited the house where John Lennon lived as a boy.
5 Do you remember the woman who/that had 20 cats?
6 Our teacher gave us some exercises for homework which/that no one could understand.
7 I have a neighbour who/that is a famous designer.
8 Kington is a small town near where I grew up.

UNIT 15 PRESENT SIMPLE PASSIVE

1 **1** P **2** A **3** P **4** P **5** A

2 **1** always gives me money **2** grow all our **3** visit **4** use **5** uses

3 **1** is needed to enter **2** is cleaned (by my brother) **3** aren't sent to prison **4** are stolen every day **5** is played **6** 'm/am not allowed to have **7** is designed (by someone) **8** are paid for by a local company **9** are hidden **10** is owned by a film star

UNIT 16 ZERO AND FIRST CONDITIONAL

ZERO CONDITIONAL

1 **1** feels, 's/is **2** earns, spends **3** get, gives **4** don't like, don't watch **5** do, give **6** 's/is, don't enjoy

FIRST CONDITIONAL

2 **1** I don't go, I won't be able **2** I'll buy, is **3** You'll pass, you don't forget **4** We'll phone, we need **5** finds out, he'll be **6** You won't feel, you put

UNLESS

3 1 I can't get up in the morning unless I have enough sleep. / Unless I have enough sleep, I can't get up in the morning .
2 We'll all have dinner together unless my mum gets home too late. / Unless my mum gets home too late, we'll all have dinner together.
3 My parents will go mad unless we clear up this mess. / Unless we clear up this mess, my parents will go mad.
4 We'll miss the train unless we find a taxi soon. / Unless we find a taxi soon, we'll miss the train.

UNIT 17 REPORTED COMMANDS

1 1 You should try a new hairstyle.
2 Show me your tickets, please. / Please show me your tickets.
3 You shouldn't put your address on the website.
4 You mustn't text me in the morning.
5 Please get out of your car. / Get out of your car, please.
6 Please help me with the washing-up. / Help me with the washing-up, please.
7 You should join the sports club.
8 You should phone the school.
9 You mustn't go into the house.

2 **1** ordered the thief to put the gun on the floor. **2** warned us not to open the box. **3** advised me not to use that shampoo. **4** reminded my friends to come to my party. **5** asked the students to tell him/her their names. **6** asked my brother not to tell anyone. **7** encouraged me to tell my mum about my problem. **8** persuaded my brother to apply for another job. **9** told my dad not to invite the neighbours on Saturday.

UNIT 18 SECOND CONDITIONAL

1 **1** c **2** b **3** d **4** e **5** a

2 Students' own answers

3 1 What would you do if you won lots of money?
2 Who would you ask if you didn't understand some grammar?
3 What would you do if you saw a burger for $50?
4 What would you do if someone asked you about advanced physics?
5 Who would help you if you missed the school bus?

4 **1** 'd/would have, didn't tell **2** were/was, 'd/would take **3** stayed, 'd/would learn **4** wouldn't get, did **5** ate, wouldn't be **6** saved, 'd/would have

UNIT 19 REPORTED SPEECH

1 **1** 'm/am texting **2** can't find **3** laugh at **4** can borrow my **5** buy a newspaper **6** 'm/am looking for **7** 'll/will design

2 **1** said **2** told **3** told **4** said **5** told

3 **1** (that) she was starting **2** could get **3** didn't know **4** (that) he would take **5** (that) they were making **6** were sitting

UNIT 20 PAST SIMPLE PASSIVE

1 I have lived in my apartment for five years, but it is much older than that. The building that my apartment is in <u>was built</u> over 100 years ago. It <u>was designed</u> by a famous architect who also designed many other buildings in the city. It <u>was created</u> for a local businessman who wanted his own building. It <u>was used</u> by his family for about 50 years. Then, it <u>was sold</u> and it <u>was made</u> into lots of smaller apartments.

2 **1** interviewed **2** didn't do **3** the students copy **4** didn't make **5** didn't describe

3 **1** were reminded about the school trip by our **2** were copied, was stolen **3** was given a good luck card by **4** these salads prepared by you **5** wasn't told where

4 **1** was given **2** started **3** were left **4** were pushed **5** decided **6** were covered **7** noticed **8** was almost hidden **9** showed **10** were painted **11** wasn't signed **12** was probably painted **13** paid **14** took **15** discovered **16** was sold

WORKBOOK ANSWER KEY AND AUDIOSCRIPTS

UNIT 1 All about me

VOCABULARY

1 weight**politecareless**town**funny**book**friendly miserableconfident**buy**carefulcheerfulrude** car**serious**run**shyunfriendly**friday

2 **1** careless **2** rude **3** cheerful **4** unfriendly **5** shy **6** miserable **7** polite **8** careful

3 **1** b **2** a **3** b **4** b **5** c

4 **a 1** late thirties **2** straight **3** attractive **b 4** middle-aged **5** handsome **c 6** elderly **d 7** fair **8** good-looking **e 9** pretty **10** blonde **11** early twenties **f 12** teenage **13** dark **14** curly **g 15** bald

READING

1 **1** Eldest child **2** Middle child **3** Youngest child **4** Only child

2 **1** your **2** don't **3** everyone **4** with **5** the **6** at

3 **1** eldest **2** only **3** middle **4** youngest

4 **1** clear **2** surprises **3** consider **4** planning

GRAMMAR

1 **1** gets up **2** are watching **3** is wearing **4** finish/are finishing **5** runs

2 **1** hate **2** don't believe **3** am having **4** want **5** am sending **6** don't understand **7** owns **8** like

3 **1** Every year **2** this term **3** Next month **4** later today **5** always **6** Tonight **7** never **8** tomorrow **9** sometimes **10** right now

4 **1** When we are together, we have fun.

2 I am writing to tell you I have a new computer.

3 I am sending you this email to invite you to my birthday party on Saturday.

4 ✓

VOCABULARY

1

un-	in-	im-
unfair	incorrect	impatient
unfriendly	inexpensive	impolite
unhealthy	invisible	
unkind		
unknown		
unlucky		
unwell		

2 **a** inexpensive **b** unlucky **c** impatient **d** unfriendly **e** unhealthy **f** impolite

3 **1** unwell **2** invisible **3** unkind **4** incorrect **5** unfair **6** unknown

WRITING

1 Students' own answers

2 **1** Sam **2** Rita **3** Sam **4** Rita **5** Sam **6** Rita

3 **1** a bit **2** quite **3** really **4** very **5** fairly

4 Students' own answers

5 Students' own answers

UNIT 2 In fashion

VOCABULARY

1 **1** badly-dressed **2** second-hand **3** unfashionable **4** casual **5** uncomfortable

2 **1** c **2** d **3** e **4** a **5** f **6** g **7** b

3 **1** uncomfortable **2** second-hand **3** unfashionable **4** badly-dressed **5** casual

4 **1 A** skinny **B** uncomfortable **2 A** second-hand **B** brand new **3 A** trendy **B** unfashionable **4 A** smart **B** badly-dressed **5 A** casual **B** well-dressed

READING

1 3 a teen magazine article

2 **1** T **2** T **3** T **4** T **5** F **6** T

3 **1** d **2** a **3** b **4** c

4 **1** protect **2** comments **3** essential **4** collection

GRAMMAR

1 **1** wore **2** wanted **3** forgot **4** went **5** bought **6** enjoyed **7** Did **8** looked **9** got **10** loved

2 **1** What did you do?

2 Did your dad buy a new shirt?

3 Did you go to the cinema with your parents?

4 Did you wear your new jumper?

5 How long did the film last?

6 Did you eat at the restaurant after the fashion show?

7 Did you get home late?

8 Did your parents buy you a new skirt?

9 What did you have for your birthday?

3 **1** took **2** didn't enjoy **3** flew **4** gave **5** didn't want **6** drank **7** didn't visit **8** sent

4 **1** went **2** caught **3** spent **4** visited **5** asked **6** bought **7** saw **8** looked **9** told **10** smiled

5 **1** b **2** a **3** a **4** b **5** b

VOCABULARY

1 **1** badly **2** carefully **3** yearly **4** fast **5** well **6** healthily **7** heavily **8** early

2 **1** early **2** healthily **3** heavily **4** fast **5** well **6** yearly **7** badly **8** carefully

LISTENING

1 2 a party at the end of high school

3 **1** sister **2** last year **3** American **4** isn't **5** café **6** going to

4 **1** beautiful **2** photo **3** remember **4** party **5** good-looking **6** black **7** wait **8** finish **9** America

01

Lara: Hey Rob, is that your sister? She's beautiful!

Rob: Yeah, that's Denise! And that's a photo from last year. Do you remember, Lara, she went to that end-of-year party, the prom?

Lara: Yes. And is that Andy Patterson with her? He's very good-looking, isn't he?

Rob: Yep! In his black tie!

Lara: I can't wait till our prom, can you?

Rob: Do you think I'm going to wear a tie like that?

Lara: Yes, you have to! Everyone does when they finish school.

Rob: Hmm. I think the prom comes from America. I don't like it.

Lara: Oh, Rob! Everyone loves the prom! It's the last time we're together as a group, and it's an important party! You have to go!

Rob: Really? But you know, I think it's silly that girls spend so much money on a dress for one night! I mean, you can get a dress that you can wear again! Denise had a Saturday job in the café – she worked really hard for about a year, and then bought a dress!

Lara: Hmm, I know what you mean. But it's good she didn't ask your parents because it is a lot of money. Mind you, you have to look lovely! And boys have to look nice too!

Rob: I guess, but I'm not wearing a jacket!

Lara: It's OK – we have to wait for a few years yet. And I have to get a job to pay for my dress!

UNIT 3 My way of life

VOCABULARY

1 **1** be born **2** get a degree **3** get a driving licence **4** get a job **5** have children **6** retire **7** leave home **8** start school **9** get married **10** go to university **11** leave school **12** move home **13** vote

2 **1** start school **2** leave home **3** get a degree **4** get married **5** have children

3 **1** go to university **2** voted **3** was born **4** moved home **5** leave school **6** get a driving licence **7** retired **8** got a job

4 **1** c **2** b **3** f **4** a **5** e **6** d **7** g **8** h

READING

1 1, 2, 3 and 6

2 **1** b **2** a **3** b **4** a **5** a **6** b

3 **1** focused on **2** knowledge **3** skills **4** employment **5** practical

4 **1** employment **2** skills **3** practical **4** knowledge **5** focused on

GRAMMAR

1 **1** bigger, biggest **2** greater, greatest **3** safer, safest **4** easier, easiest **5** more exciting, most exciting **6** better, the best **7** worse, the worst

2 **1** latest **2** best **3** cheapest **4** tastiest **5** most scary **6** most amazing

3 **1** the most popular **2** happier **3** the shortest **4** more expensive **5** younger

4 **1** Valentina's university isn't as modern as Charly's.
2 Your city isn't as big as Marco's.
3 I don't have as many apps as my friend.
4 Zoe isn't as tall as Louis.
5 People say that New York isn't as dangerous as New Orleans.
6 Here in the countryside, the internet speed isn't as fast as in the city.

5 **1** Swimming is not as fast as running.
2 Germany is not as hot as Mexico.
3 Antonia's sister is not as friendly as her.
4 Playing video games is not as healthy as playing sports.
5 Dogs are not as intelligent as cats.
6 The science exam was not as hard as the maths exam.

6 **1** My older sister invited her to go out with us.
2 My granddad became happier.
3 We go horse riding together but I am not as good as her.
4 He's a bit taller and thinner than me.
5 We saw the latest film with Tom Hiddleston. I liked it!

VOCABULARY

1 **1** This phone isn't big enough.
2 This jacket is too tight.
3 We have enough space for the baby.
4 This computer isn't fast enough.
5 My mum's car is too small for our bikes.
6 We have enough players in the team.

2 **1** too **2** enough **3** too **4** enough

WRITING

1–2 Students' own answers

3 **1** He hasn't got his phone with him.
2 She doesn't know anyone here.
3 We're going to leave soon.
4 I'm bored.
5 What's your friend's name?

4–5 Students' own answers

UNIT 4 Champions

VOCABULARY

1

x	v	o	l	l	e	y	b	a	l	l
w	m	a	t	h	l	e	t	i	c	s
d	h	s	u	r	f	i	n	g	s	g
w	i	n	d	s	u	r	f	i	n	g
u	s	w	i	m	m	i	n	g	r	a
r	c	l	i	m	b	i	n	g	u	b
j	o	g	g	i	n	g	m	k	g	o
i	t	e	n	n	i	s	i	q	b	x
f	t	e	l	h	n	w	u	a	y	i
g	y	m	n	a	s	t	i	c	s	n
w	p	t	e	c	y	c	l	i	n	g

2

In/on water	Usually indoors	Usually outdoors
surfing	boxing	athletics
swimming	gymnastics	climbing
windsurfing	swimming	cycling
	volleyball	jogging
		rugby
		surfing
		tennis
		windsurfing

3 **1** go **2** does **3** go **4** go **5** play **6** goes **7** play **8** play **9** go **10** goes **11** plays **12** play **13** do **14** play **15** go **16** play

READING

1 2 Snowboarding has great benefits for teens

2 **1** B **2** F **3** A **4** C **5** G

3 **1** succeed **2** advice **3** techniques **4** get hurt **5** benefit

4 **1** succeed **2** get hurt **3** benefit **4** techniques **5** advice

GRAMMAR

1 **1** was **2** were **3** was **4** weren't **5** were **6** was **7** wasn't **8** weren't

2 **1** Chris was playing computer games when the phone rang.

2 Were you visiting your grandparents when I texted you?

3 I was carrying the cat when it jumped from my arms.

4 I was cleaning my bedroom when I found my old diary.

5 We were going to watch the hockey match but it rained.

6 They were listening to music while revising for their exams.

7 Were you talking to Peter about the maths test?

8 I was just thinking about you when you called.

3 **1** b **2** b **3** a **4** b **5** a

4 **1** was swimming **2** was watching **3** Were you going **4** were not/weren't trying **5** was waiting **6** was playing **7** was laughing **8** was living **9** was doing **10** was preparing

VOCABULARY

1 **1** exercise, exercises **2** trainers, trainer **3** match, matching **4** pointed, points **5** fits, fit **6** work out, Working out **7** training, train

2 **1** fit **2** points **3** match **4** coach **5** trainers **6** exercises

LISTENING

1 3 On Saturday you can try different sports for free.

2 **1** ✓ **2** ✓ **3** ✓ **4** ✓ **5** ✓ **6** ✓ **7** ✓

3 **1** T **2** F **3** T **4** T **5** T **6** F **7** T

4 **1** Bank Sports Centre **2** (the) gym **3** hot yoga **4** ice skating, ice hockey **5** beach volleyball **6** everyone / all the family

5 **1** it's different and it's the same **2** we also want to introduce people to other sports activities **3** it's a lot of fun **4** are there any new sports for me? **5** a day for all the family **6** it's free

02

Interviewer: Hello, and welcome to the show. Today we have Hank Rogers from the new sports centre in the studio. Welcome Hank.

Hank: Thank you for having me!

Interviewer: Hank, tell us a bit about the sports centre. How is the Bank Sports Centre different from others?

Hank: Well, it's different and it's the same! Let me explain. So many favourite sports are there, for example, the gym, the swimming pool, classes – but we also want to introduce people to other sports activities.

Interviewer: Tell me more!

Hank: Imagine doing yoga in a room where the temperature is a hot 40 degrees. That's called hot yoga! We also have aerial yoga – that is yoga that you do in the air! It's a lot of fun!

Interviewer: OK, well that's good. Now what about team sports – are there any new sports for me?

Hank: Well, we're also able to have an indoor ice rink in winter. That's just great so we can have ice skating or ice hockey for instance.

Interviewer: Now that sounds great! And in summer?

Hank: In the summer we move the roof back so that you can see the sky, and we put sand down!

Interviewer: Oh, wow! That's amazing!

Hank: I know, and we can do beach volleyball! We're really excited about that.

Interviewer: And you have an open day soon?

Hank: Yes, on Saturday. It's a day for all the family and it's free. So everyone will have the opportunity to try out all these new sports and activities. We open at 9 in the morning and will be there until the evening. And we have some free prizes!

Interviewer: That sounds great! So it sounds like a good place …

UNIT 5 Call the police!

VOCABULARY

1 **1** burglary **2** vandalism **3** theft **4** shoplifting **5** pickpocketing **6** hacking

2 **1** B **2** E **3** F **4** D **5** A **6** C

3 **1** burglary **2** pickpocketing **3** shoplifting **4** hacking **5** vandalism **6** theft

4 **1** hackers **2** vandals **3** Burglars **4** pickpockets **5** thief **6** shoplifters

5 **1** hacker, hacking **2** vandals, vandal **3** burglary, burglar **4** pickpockets, pickpocketing **5** theft, thieves **6** shoplifters, shoplifting

READING

1 c

2 **1** T **2** F **3** F **4** F **5** T **6** F

3 **1** aims **2** cash **3** nasty **4** weaknesses **5** spam

GRAMMAR

1 **1** b **2** a **3** a **4** a **5** a

2 **1** I answered questions about vandals at the police station.

2 Those boys stole money from my bag.

3 Mum was telling us a story about Grandma when her phone rang.

4 Mark did not / didn't wave at Julie because he did not / didn't see her.

5 In the newspaper it said that in our city theft was increasing this year.

3 **1** was **2** was running **3** were singing **4** was thinking **5** looked **6** saw **7** got **8** took **9** imagined **10** loved

4 **1** They were stealing chocolate from the shop when I saw them.
2 ✓
3 We were sitting on the bus when the vandals wrote on the windows.
4 It was snowing when I woke up this morning.
5 I arrived home in the morning, but then I slept all day.

VOCABULARY

1 **1** d **2** a **3** c **4** e **5** b
2 **1** ourselves **2** himself **3** themselves **4** yourselves **5** each other

WRITING

1–2 Students' own answers
3 **1** ✓ **2** ✓ **3** ✓ **4** ✓ **5** ✓ **6** × **7** ✓ **8** ×
4 **Adjectives:** loud, scared
Adverbs: quietly, slowly, immediately, soon
5 **1** immediately **2** loud **3** soon **4** quietly **5** scared **6** slowly
6–7 Students' own answers

UNIT 6 City life

VOCABULARY

1 **1** pollution **2** public transport **3** traffic jam **4** crowds **5** graffiti **6** rush hour **7** green spaces **8** rubbish **9** power cut
2 **1** pollution **2** traffic jam **3** rubbish **4** green spaces **5** crowds **6** public transport **7** graffiti **8** power cut **9** rush hour
3 **1** graffiti **2** rubbish **3** green spaces **4** pollution **5** traffic jam **6** rush hour **7** public transport **8** crowds **9** power cut

READING

1

Barcelona	Bogotá	Singapore	Adelaide
public transport bicycles pollution parks	bicycles pollution public transport	animal life pollution rubbish	pollution parks recycling bicycles public transport

2 **1** C **2** B **3** A **4** A **5** C **6** C
3 **1** Kelly **2** Kelly **3** Winston **4** Poppy **5** Winston **6** Kelly

GRAMMAR

1 **1** some **2** any **3** any **4** some
2 **1** much **2** many **3** much **4** many
3 **1** a few **2** a little **3** a little **4** a few
4 **1** a **2** c **3** c **4** b **5** a **6** c **7** b **8** a **9** b **10** c
5 **1** Many **2** any **3** some **4** a few **5** A lot of **6** much **7** a little
6 **1** many **2** many **3** a few **4** a lot of **5** some **6** much **7** any
7 **1** b **2** a **3** a **4** b **5** a

VOCABULARY

1 **1** apartment building **2** post box **3** speed limit **4** taxi rank **5** pedestrian crossing **6** recycling bin **7** bus stop **8** road sign
2 **1** pedestrian crossing **2** road sign **3** Recycling bins **4** speed limit **5** apartment building **6** bus stop **7** post box **8** taxi rank

LISTENING

1 Students' own answers
2 3 interesting clean-up projects

03
Teacher: OK, we know that cleaning up projects are really popular at the moment. We've all heard of 'clean up the world', 'clean up the beach', erm, 'clean up your computer', and so on. I asked you all to find out about a clean-up project that you didn't know about and that you think is interesting.

3 **1** game **2** turtle **3** problem **4** museum **5** website

04
Teacher: OK, we know that cleaning up projects are really popular at the moment. We've all heard of 'clean up the world', 'clean up the beach', erm, 'clean up your computer', and so on. I asked you all to find out about a clean-up project that you didn't know about and that you think is interesting. Jenny, can you tell us about your project?
Jenny: Sure. I found this project on an Australian website called 'clean up the river'. It's a game for children. You choose your avatar and your transport – how you're going to travel on the river. I chose a turtle – they are such great animals! Then you have to clean up the dirty river. It's cool because it teaches young children about a problem but in a fun way, you know, it's a game. I really liked it – and I learnt a lot too! And of course, what you do next is get a group of friends together and go and clean up a real river.
Teacher: Interesting! I like that and it's a fun idea. OK, next, Greg, what have you got?
Greg: Well, I just typed in 'clean up' and there were a lot of 'clean up' days as you said but I found one website that was really interesting – Museum Clean-up Day! – at a history museum in the United States. They ask for people to help them to clean up the museum. I think that when you do this you help people paint and things. But you can also visit the museum for the day – and it's free! I really like that idea. And if you enjoy the day, you might go back to the museum. I really like history so I would love that!
Teacher: That's new to me too! And I agree, it sounds interesting to do.

4 **1** the **2** crowd **3** met **4** told **5** plastic **6** rubbish **7** groups **8** fun **9** drop **10** bin

05
Teacher: OK. Now you, Meg.
Meg: Well, I actually took part in a 'clean up the beach' day. There was a big crowd of people and we all met at the bus stop in front of the beach. There was a man who told us what to do. We had big plastic bags and we collected any rubbish that we found. We were in different

groups and we worked together. It was a really fun day but it's a pity people drop all this rubbish. It's easy to put it in the bin!

5 **1** F **2** T **3** T **4** F **5** F **6** T **7** F

06 **Teacher:** OK, we know that cleaning up projects are really popular at the moment. We've all heard of 'clean up the world', 'clean up the beach', erm, 'clean up your computer', and so on. I asked you all to find out about a clean-up project that you didn't know about and that you think is interesting. Jenny, can you tell us about your project?

Jenny: Sure. I found this project on an Australian website called 'clean up the river'. It's a game for children. You choose your avatar and your transport – how you're going to travel on the river. I chose a turtle – they are such great animals! Then you have to clean up the dirty river. It's cool because it teaches young children about a problem but in a fun way, you know, it's a game. I really liked it – and I learnt a lot too! And of course, what you do next is get a group of friends together and go and clean up a real river.

Teacher: Interesting! I like that and it's a fun idea. OK, next, Greg, what have you got?

Greg: Well, I just typed in 'clean up' and there were a lot of 'clean up' days as you said but I found one website that was really interesting – Museum Clean-up Day! – at a history museum in the United States. They ask for people to help them to clean up the museum. I think that when you do this you help people paint and things. But you can also visit the museum for the day – and it's free! I really like that idea. And if you enjoy the day, you might go back to the museum. I really like history so I would love that!

Teacher: That's new to me too! And I agree, it sounds interesting to do.

Teacher: OK. Now you, Meg.

Meg: Well, I actually took part in a 'clean up the beach' day. There was a big crowd of people and we all met at the bus stop in front of the beach. There was a man who told us what to do. We had big plastic bags and we collected any rubbish that we found. We were in different groups and we worked together. It was a really fun day but it's a pity people drop all this rubbish. It's easy to put it in the bin!

UNIT 7 Getting on

VOCABULARY

1 **1** a **2** c **3** b **4** a **5** b **6** a **7** a **8** b **9** c **10** b

2 **1** e be **2** c wasn't **3** b have **4** f having **5** a do **6** d makes

3 **1** have fun **2** do me a favour **3** be wrong **4** are annoyed with **5** having problems with **6** being on my own

4 **1** fault **2** angry **3** argument **4** on my own **5** friends **6** in common **7** wrong **8** something

READING

1 Students' own answers

2 2

3 **1** F **2** F **3** T **4** T **5** T **6** T **7** F **8** T

4 **1** silly **2** making faces **3** abroad **4** sharing **5** realises **6** dish

5 **1** dish **2** silly **3** sharing **4** makes faces **5** abroad **6** realise

GRAMMAR

1 **1** Zoe has to practise the piano every day.
2 You must be quiet in the library.
3 You mustn't run in the dining room.
4 Grandma had to cycle 5 km to school.
5 We don't have to go to school tomorrow.
6 I had to make my own lunch yesterday.

2 **1** a **2** c **3** c **4** b **5** a **6** a **7** b **8** c **9** b **10** a

3 **1** should **2** shouldn't **3** should **4** should **5** shouldn't **6** should

4 **1** You should bring a ball if you want to play football.
2 ✓
3 It should be fun if we go together.
4 The rules of this game are that you have to help the monkey to find her home.
5 So you have to believe me – this game is the best.

VOCABULARY

1 **1** hang out **2** get on **3** get together **4** fall out **5** split up **6** look after **7** make up **8** come around

2 **1** getting on **2** split up **3** fell out **4** make up **5** Come around **6** looking after **7** get together **8** hang out

WRITING

1 in the summer; three questions

2 Yes

3 **a** 3 **b** 1 **c** 2 **d** 4 **e** 5

4 **1** great **2** idea **3** should **4** forward

5–6 Students' own answers

UNIT 8 Going away

VOCABULARY

1 **1** check-in desk **2** passport **3** ticket **4** customs **5** sign **6** baggage **7** queue

2 **1** c departure gate **2** d passport control **3** a security check **4** e boarding pass **5** b baggage hall

3 **1** b **2** c **3** c **4** b **5** b **6** c **7** a

4 **1** boarding pass **2** baggage **3** check-in desk **4** sign **5** passport control **6** passport **7** security check **8** queue **9** departure gate **10** customs **11** baggage hall **12** tickets

READING

1 2 Going on holiday? What to take and how to take it

2 **1** b **2** a **3** b **4** a **5** a **6** a **7** b

3 **1** pop … in **2** sponsoring **3** tops **4** playlist **5** reach

GRAMMAR

1 1 We're going to visit Paris next year.
2 Mum's going to clean her car because it's dirty.
3 My parents are having a holiday in Bali without me!
4 I'm going to do my homework now.
5 Tom is going to buy a new phone.
6 James and Noah are playing basketball for the school team next week.
7 Zac is going to the ticket office to buy our tickets for the music festival.
8 I'm going to sit down and have a cup of coffee.

2 **1** are you doing **2** I'm filling in **3** are you going **4** are going to have **5** is returning **6** are taking me

3 **1** going to visit **2** flying **3** going to watch **4** leaving **5** going to buy **6** going to cook **7** studying **8** going to be

4 **1** a **2** a **3** b **4** a **5** a

5 **1** catching **2** going to find **3** are going to have **4** going to rain **5** staying **6** travelling

VOCABULARY

1 **1** go away **2** set off **3** get in **4** check in **5** get back **6** look around **7** pick up **8** take off

2 **1** are you going away **2** 're setting off **3** picking up **4** to check in **5** take off **6** gets in **7** look around **5** getting back

LISTENING

1 **1** ✓ **2** ✓ **3** × **4** ✓ **5** × **6** × **7** ✓ **8** ✓

2 **1** 7 / seven **2** magazines **3** aeroplane **4** song **5** deserts **6** first part

07 I started writing about travelling fourteen years ago when I was a student. Then, for five years, I worked as a teacher, and I wrote about my holiday trips. I decided to give up teaching and just travel and write seven years ago.

At first, I mainly wrote parts of guidebooks, but after a while I started to do articles for some websites, and also newspapers from time to time. The majority of work I do, though, is for magazines. Luckily, there are plenty that have sections about travel.

In the past, my trips were fairly short – just one or two weeks – and I flew a lot to save time. These days, though, I go away for longer – sometimes three months – and if I can, I go by bus or by train rather than aeroplane. I prefer to travel slowly.

What I like best is getting to know people in the places I visit. On each trip, I ask someone to teach me a local song – it gives me a feeling for the culture. I'd love to learn a new language whenever I travel, but that's not realistic. I try other things, though. In Napoli, I learned a recipe for real Italian pizza.

I love cities and I've always written about them, but recently I've focused on other things. I've done several articles on rainforests around the world, and in the next couple of years there are some deserts I'd like to go to and write about.

I have an amazing job, but not all of it's easy. The most challenging thing for me is making the first part of an article interesting. If it doesn't catch readers' attention, they probably won't read the middle part, and certainly not the end.

If any of you would like to try travel writing, my advice would be to …

UNIT 9 Shop till you drop

VOCABULARY

1 **1** change **2** save up **3** take back **4** special offer **5** give away **6** checkout **7** bank account **8** price **9** receipt

2 **1** saving up **2** bank account **3** special offers **4** price **5** take it back **6** checkout **7** give away **8** change **9** receipt

3 **1** special offer **2** price **3** saved up **4** bank account **5** checkout **6** change **7** receipt **8** take … back **9** give … away

READING

1 2 Staying safe when shopping online.

2 **1** D **2** B **3** C **4** B **5** A

3 **1** at your leisure **2** seller **3** lock **4** fairly

GRAMMAR

1 **1** sang **2** made **3** stole **4** saw **5** gone **6** spent **7** won **8** been

2 1 I have written a letter to the newspaper.
2 Sam has lost his wallet.
3 Jayde has never borrowed any money.
4 Jan has never used a credit card online.
5 Louise has caught a bad cold.
6 Have you ever bought shoes from a second-hand shop?

3 1 I have never read that book about South America! Can you buy it for me?
2 Mum has never bought this much food from the supermarket before. I don't think we can eat it all!
3 Have you taken back that shirt that was too big for you?
4 Right! I have saved up enough money to get my new bike. I'm going to buy it!
5 My aunt has never asked for the change when she has given us money to buy sweets. She's so kind!
6 I have never shopped online before. Can you show me how to do it?

4 1 Have you <u>sold</u> it or not?
2 Have you ever <u>met</u> a famous person?
3 Today I am very happy as I <u>have received</u> my new computer game.
4 I have <u>paid</u> for all our tickets to see the football match.
5 The shop assistant <u>has charged</u> me too much money!

5 **1** gone **2** gone **3** been **4** been **5** gone **6** been

6 **1** gone **2** been **3** been **4** gone

VOCABULARY

1 **1** cost **2** pay **3** charge

2 **1** charging **2** costs **3** paid

WRITING

1–3 Students' own answers

4 **1** raced **2** spotted **3** set out **4** amazed

5 just, Then, Later, While, suddenly
1 as soon as **2** later **3** suddenly **4** while

6–7 Students' own answers

UNIT 10 Taste this!

VOCABULARY

1 lion**juicysour**happy**deliciousraw**never **disgustingspicybitter**april**horriblesweetfrozen** car**tastyfresh**

2 **1** juicy **2** delicious **3** fresh **4** sour **5** bitter **6** spicy **7** disgusting **8** frozen **9** sweet **10** tasty **11** raw **12** horrible

3 **1** spicy **2** fresh **3** raw **4** sour **5** juicy **6** sweet **7** frozen **8** bitter

4 **1** delicious **2** horrible **3** disgusting **4** tasty

READING

1 **Hotter:** banana, pineapple, mango
Cooler: apple, pear, strawberry

2 **a** 2 **b** 6 **c** 1 **d** 4 **e** 3 **f** 5

3 **1** with her parents **2** do her homework **3** they didn't know **4** tasty **5** didn't realise **6** positive

4 **1** recently **2** dull **3** pudding **4** variety **5** odd

GRAMMAR

1 **1** has worked **2** have eaten **3** has prepared **4** hasn't invited **5** cooked **6** didn't like **7** has … lived **8** have loved **9** stayed **10** Have … tried

2 **1** for **2** since **3** since **4** for **5** for **6** since **7** for **8** since **9** for **10** since

3 **1** walked **2** said **3** came **4** have seen **5** ate **6** has written **7** appeared **8** lived **9** met **10** have lived

4 **1** b **2** a **3** a **4** b **5** b

VOCABULARY

1 **1** looks **2** tastes **3** tastes **4** smells **5** smells **6** looks

2 **1** looks **2** looked **3** tasted **4** smell **5** tasted

LISTENING

1 Students' own answers

2–3 **1** C **2** C **3** A **4** A **5** B **6** A **7** B

08

1

M: What did you think of the food in Brazil?

F: We were only there for two weeks, and we couldn't go to different parts of the country. But I liked what I had.

M: Did you try that dish with black beans, meat and rice?

F: Yes, it's called feijoada. I had it once and it was very good. What I liked more than anything though was the seafood. It was great.

M: That's interesting.

F: Yes, and we had lots of different types of pasta too. I think they like Italian food there.

M: Everyone likes Italian food.

2

M: Hi Chris. It's Ben. I'm going to the beach with my mum and my brother and sister later. Would you like to come with us? We're leaving at about two after we've had some lunch. If you could come round to my house at about that time, we could give you a lift. Just bring your swimming things and a towel. We'll probably get a drink or an ice-cream at that café we've been to before later in the afternoon. Call me or send me a message. Bye.

3

M: What's your favourite breakfast food?

F: Well, last summer when we stayed in a hotel I had omelette every day. I could see the cook making it and it was delicious. At home, though, we're all in such a hurry at breakfast that no-one has the time to cook.

M: That sounds like my family.

F: Most days, we just have toast and a glass of orange juice. It doesn't bother me, though.

M: Don't you get bored?

F: Not really. I have cereals from time to time as well. But not that much.

4

F: Hi Susie. It's Emma. I wondered if you'd like to come to my house for dinner this Saturday. My auntie and cousins are coming, and Dad said I can invite a friend. He's cooking actually. He doesn't cook very often, but when he does, it's usually good. He does some brilliant chicken dishes with different sauces. This time, though, it'll be fish. If you don't fancy any of that, there'll be vegetable soup – I think Mum's making that. Anyway, I hope you can come. Maybe you can message me? Bye.

5

M: Do you have cooking lessons at your school?

F: Yes. They call it Food Science. Do you?

M: Yeah. I love it. We do a lot of baking – you know, biscuits and pastries – and this week we made a fruit cake, which wasn't bad at all.

F: Sounds good. Can you take stuff home?

M: Usually. I baked some bread which you couldn't really eat because it was too hard. So I left that at school. But I did a pizza once that my mum said was better than anything she could do.

6

F: That smells nice. What is it?

M: It's a ratatouille.

F: That French dish with lots of vegetables?

M: That's right. My grandmother used to make something like this and I always loved it, so I thought I'd try it.

F: Have you followed a recipe for it?

M: Yeah, I looked it up online. It tells you all the different vegetables you need and how small you need to cut them. My sister gave me a really good cookery book for my birthday, but it's mainly Asian food. Anyway, it should be ready soon.

7

F: Did you see Teenage Chef yesterday?

M: Yes, it was great. And the final's next week. Who do you think will win?

F: They've all done well. But Rachel's fried banana dish yesterday looked amazing, and over the whole series, I'd say she's been the best.

M: Rachel? The girl with long hair? She's good, but that guy Mark – with very short hair – made a great risotto.

F: True. But he's good one week and then makes mistakes the next. He's like that girl with curly hair.

M: Jessie?

F: Yeah. She has great ideas, but they don't always work.

UNIT 11 A healthy future

VOCABULARY

1 **A** forehead **B** chin **C** throat **D** thumb **E** shoulder **F** chest **G** elbow **H** back **I** finger **J** knee **K** ankle **L** toe

2 **1** throat **2** ankle **3** chin **4** shoulder **5** knees **6** finger **7** thumb **8** forehead **9** toothache **10** cough **11** chest **12** back

3 **1** e **2** c **3** d **4** b **5** f **6** a

4 **1** toothache **2** earache **3** ache **4** throat **5** headache **6** flu **7** temperature **8** fever

READING

1 **1** ✗ **2** ✗ **3** ✓ **4** ✓ **5** ✗ **6** ✓

2 **1** yoga instructor **2** not as slow as **3** learn how to concentrate **4** get well sooner **5** prepare your body

3 **1** Itzel **2** Diego **3** Celine

4 **1** c **2** a **3** b **4** e **5** d

GRAMMAR

1
- **1** We're going to have dinner together later.
- **2** Josie's going to visit her grandma in hospital after school.
- **3** I hope our teacher will give us a tennis lesson today.
- **4** Mum says she'll pick us up after football practice.
- **5** Stephanie is going to have an operation on her leg.
- **6** It's a bit hot in here, so I'll open the window.
- **7** I think I'll bring some pizza to your party.
- **8** All the boys are going to enter a competition.

2 **1** 're/are going to **2** will **3** will **4** will **5** is going to **6** will **7** will **8** 'm/am going to **9** 're/are going to

3 **1** are you going to do **2** 'll/will do **3** 'm/am not going to answer **4** 'll/will check **5** 's/is going to have **6** Are you going to go **7** 'll/will **8** Will you help **9** will explain

4 **1** 'm/am going to take you **2** 'll/will go **3** 's/is going to look **4** 'll/will get **5** 'm/am going to stay **6** 'm/am going to get **7** 'll/will drive **8** 'll/will be

5 **1** I <u>will send</u> you a message tonight. **2** ✓ **3** We <u>will look</u> at the map tomorrow and decide where to go. **4** I enjoy spending time with her because they're moments that <u>will not happen</u> again. **5** ✓

VOCABULARY

1 **1** caught **2** hurts **3** broke **4** injured **5** cut **6** feeling

2 **1** is **2** injured **3** hurts **4** broken **5** got **6** caught **7** cut **8** gets **9** feel

WRITING

1 Students' own answers

2 Students' own answers

3 Students' own answers

4 **1** B **2** C **3** A

5 2

6 Students' own answers

7 Students' own answers

UNIT 12 Incredible wildlife

VOCABULARY

1 **1** fly **2** bat **3** worm **4** shark **5** ant **6** wolf **7** fox **8** butterfly **9** frog **10** mosquito **11** donkey **12** deer **13** bee **14** eagle

2 **1** shark **2** ant **3** bat **4** donkey **5** deer
Hidden word: snake

3 **1** wolf **2** frog **3** butterfly **4** eagle **5** fox **6** worm

4 **1** C **2** A **3** E **4** B **5** F **6** D

READING

1 1

2 **1** B **2** D **3** A **4** C **5** B

3 **1** take care of **2** join in **3** rescue **4** hold

GRAMMAR

1 **1** might **2** can't **3** could **4** must

2 **1** a **2** b **3** a **4** a **5** b **6** a **7** b **8** a

3 **1** might **2** can't **3** must **4** might **5** might **6** must **7** could **8** can't

4 **1** must **2** might/could **3** might/could **4** might

5 **1** b **2** a **3** a **4** a **5** b **6** a

VOCABULARY

1
- **1** This is definitely not my cat.
- **2** Perhaps your brother can help you with your work.
- **3** That is probably a very famous painting.
- **4** We're probably going to see the dolphins tomorrow.
- **5** Mum and Dad are definitely not going to buy me another phone.
- **6** I'm not certain but perhaps the zoo opens in the summer.

2 **1** probably **2** definitely **3** perhaps **4** definitely not

LISTENING

1 Students' own answers

2 **1** ✗ **2** ✓ **3** ✓ **4** ✗ **5** ✓

3 **1** b **2** a **3** b **4** a **5** b

09

Interviewer: Kate, you've written about a boy and his pet fish. Can you tell us something about your story?

Kate: Well, it's about a boy in London who has nothing but his fish. You know, he thinks that his parents don't understand him but his fish do. And then in the end, his parents … well, I can't say the end or no one will buy my book!

Interviewer: Sure. But why did you write about fish? I mean, we don't exactly think of them as good pets, do we?

Kate: Well, I think that was it – people don't really think of them as pets because they don't show their feelings. But I got interested in fish when my Mum gave me some for my birthday three years ago. Now I love them more than anything else – and they're different from other animals because they don't need a lot of looking after!

Interviewer: Right, so coming back to your story, you entered a competition and won! Why did you enter the competition?

Kate:	I wrote the story and my teacher really liked it. I love writing stories. And then I saw the competition and I thought 'why not?' – just to try something completely different.
Interviewer:	The boy in the story, Marco, really needs an animal to understand him. Do you think that's true for all teens?
Kate:	No, of course not! But, you know, sometimes people, not just teens, might feel that no one understands them. They say things but people don't really understand what they're trying to say. With animals, you don't need to talk. In the story, Marco usually feels sad, but when he goes into his room and he's alone with his fish, he's much happier and more relaxed.
Interviewer:	And what do you do to feel calm?
Kate:	Well, writing stories doesn't usually work! I often get upset and angry if I can't think of a good ending! What I really like doing is going for long walks with my best friend in the countryside. The sounds of nature make me feel very calm. It's great.
Interviewer:	Interesting! Well, thanks Kate …

4 **1** ✓ **2** × **3** × **4** ✓ **5** ✓ **6** ×

UNIT 13 Mixed feelings

VOCABULARY

1

e	d	t	f	h	c	r	s	y	o	r	i
x	n	e	b	e	o	u	t	p	l	h	q
h	a	u	t	b	n	p	r	o	p	q	r
a	m	m	h	q	f	x	e	c	r	y	e
u	y	f	a	n	u	n	s	f	o	m	l
s	l	f	f	z	s	q	s	n	u	s	a
t	b	r	a	v	e	l	e	i	d	l	x
e	d	x	c	r	d	d	d	g	f	d	e
d	i	s	a	p	p	o	i	n	t	e	d
e	m	b	a	r	r	a	s	s	e	d	f
o	x	h	g	r	a	t	e	f	u	l	a
s	c	a	r	e	d	r	d	h	w	n	l

2 **1** amazed **2** proud **3** grateful **4** confused **5** hopeful **6** disappointed **7** exhausted **8** brave **9** relaxed **10** scared **11** stressed **12** embarrassed

3 **1** scared **2** confused **3** disappointed **4** relaxed **5** proud **6** amazed **7** embarrassed **8** hopeful **9** exhausted **10** stressed

4 **1** a, c **2** b, c **3** b, c **4** a, c **5** a, b

READING

1 Students' own answers

2 **1** ✓ **2** × **3** ✓ **4** ✓ **5** × **6** ✓

3 **1** F **2** H **3** B **4** G **5** D

4 **1** record **2** entry fee **3** annual **4** encouraged **5** charities

GRAMMAR

1 **1** The film hasn't started yet.
2 Shelly has just uploaded the photos.
3 He's already finished that game.
4 Mum and Dad have just gone out.
5 I've already done my homework.
6 I'm not ready to go out yet.

2 **1** e **2** b **3** a **4** f **5** c **6** d

3 **1** just **2** already **3** yet **4** yet **5** just **6** yet **7** just

4 **1** just **2** yet **3** yet **4** just **5** already/just **6** just **7** already **8** yet **9** just **10** yet

5 **1** I have just found a very interesting game online.
2 I haven't seen my new house yet.
3 I haven't bought a book to take on holiday yet. What do you think I should take?
4 ✓
5 ✓

VOCABULARY

1 **1** bored **2** annoying **3** relaxed **4** surprising **5** confused **6** embarrassed **7** tired **8** disappointing **9** boring **10** surprised

2 **1** bored **2** confused **3** annoyed **4** embarrassed

WRITING

1–2 Students' own answers

3 Are you one of those people who …?; I absolutely love music.; When I wake up, it makes me feel more alive.; It makes me want to move.; For me, …

4 **1** c **2** b **3** a

5 **a** 1 **b** 2 **c** 3 **d** 2 **e** 3 **f** 1

6 Students' own answers

UNIT 14 On screen

VOCABULARY

1 **1** horror **2** animation **3** chat show **4** action **5** crime drama **6** the news **7** reality show **8** documentary **9** period drama **10** comedy **11** soap opera **12** science fiction

2 **1** comedy **2** animation **3** reality show **4** documentary **5** science fiction **6** period drama

3 **1** action **2** horror **3** crime **4** soap opera **5** chat show **6** the news **7** science fiction **8** documentary **9** period drama

READING

1 Students' own answers

2 **1** b **2** a **3** c **4** c **5** a

3 **1** talent **2** manage **3** crew **4** social life **5** willing

4 **1** social life **2** willing **3** crew **4** talent **5** managed

GRAMMAR

1 **1** a, c **2** b, c **3** b, c **4** a, c **5** a, b **6** a, c

2 **1** that **2** where **3** who **4** where **5** which **6** who

3 **1** that / which **2** that / which **3** where **4** who **5** who **6** where

4 **1** that / which have Daniel Craig in them. **2** where my mum and dad first met. **3** that / which takes place on a beach. **4** who was in a film about dancing. **5** that / which Carole was reading. **6** that / which is showing at the City Theatre.

5 **1** a **2** a **3** b **4** b **5** a

VOCABULARY

1 **1** soundtrack **2** plot **3** character **4** review **5** trailer **6** clip **7** series

2 **1** series **2** clip **3** trailer **4** plot **5** soundtrack **6** character **7** review

LISTENING

1 Students' own answers

2–3 **1** B **2** C **3** A **4** C **5** C **6** A

10

1

F: I saw *Miracle Street* yesterday.

M: The film with all the rap music? I thought that was great.

F: There are actually quite a lot of films with rap soundtracks. For some reason, it goes well with certain kinds of story.

M: What did you think of the ending?

F: It was sad when the guy had to leave all his friends and look for a new life.

M: It had to end like that, didn't it?

F: I suppose so. And the whole film was very realistic – the main characters all seemed like real people.

M: So the actors did a good job?

F: Yes, I think they did.

2

M: I went to the new cinema on Sunday.

F: Is that the one with six screens?

M: Yes. There was only one film that I wanted to see. But I suppose people have different tastes.

F: Are the seats comfortable?

M: Yes, and the screen was big. We had some bad luck, though – the people sitting in front of us talked really loudly during the film.

F: That's annoying. Were the tickets expensive?

M: About the same as in other cinemas. We had to queue for ages to get them, though. The people in the ticket office apologised but they need to do something about that.

3

M: Don't you think being a film actor would be cool?

F: Oh, I wouldn't like it. I'd hate the idea that loads of people were seeing my face on films, on the internet, in magazines and newspapers all the time.

M: That wouldn't bother me. But it's not about being famous. I just think all sorts of interesting people must work in the film business and you'd get to know many of them.

F: Maybe. But don't forget, it's really hard to become a successful actor.

M: I know. The top film stars get very well paid, but that's not what I'm interested in.

4

F: Hi Peter. Joe and Sally told me you're not going with us on Saturday to see the new *Zookeeper* film.

M: No, I don't really fancy it.

F: But don't you remember last year when we all went together see the first *Zookeeper* film? We all had a great time.

M: I'm not so keen on films like that anymore. I'm into more serious stuff now.

F: Well, I know *Zookeeper Two* won't be serious. It's supposed to be a comedy. But I'm sure it'll be fun. And we'll all go and have a burger or something afterwards.

M: Listen. I'll think about it.

5

M: Do you watch *Future Stars*?

F: Everyone our age watches it – teenagers, I mean. I doubt if older people like it much.

M: I watch it with my parents and they enjoy it.

F: Anyway, I really admire those people who go onto the stage and sing, knowing thousands of people around the country are watching.

M: I'd never have the courage to do that. Especially when you think of how cruel some of the comments can be.

F: From the judges, you mean?

M: Yeah. They can be really nasty.

F: I think they're just honest. And anyone going on the programme knows what it's like.

6

F: Did you watch the dinosaur film last night?

M: No. I haven't watched TV for three days.

F: Really? You usually watch lots of TV, don't you?

M: Yeah. But I realised I've wasted so much of my life in front of the TV rather than actually doing more interesting things. So I've set myself a limit of four hours a week.

F: Wow. What do your mum and dad think about it?

M: They're big TV fans themselves. I'm hoping they'll do the same as me. If you think about it, however interesting or uninteresting some TV might be, it can never compare with real life.

UNIT 15 Digital life

VOCABULARY

1 **delete**hot**passwordshare**never**filepodcast**car **doasearchappupload**lemon**installdownload**sun **viruslink**

2 **1** deleted **2** password **3** podcast **4** virus **5** doing a search **6** upload **7** an app **8** sharing

3 **1** app **2** podcast **3** virus **4** file **5** password **6** delete **7** link **8** install

4 **1** share **2** file **3** password **4** uploaded **5** links **6** app **7** download **8** install

READING

1 **1** Home + Away **2** TravelZoom **3** Jump the Queue

2 **1** Go-Go City **2** Jump the Queue **3** TravelZoom **4** 4caster **5** Travelator

3 **1** route **2** forecast **3** host **4** stands out

GRAMMAR

1 **1** is locked **2** are given away **3** are written **4** is spoken **5** are taken **6** is known **7** are asked

2 1 Several types of fruit juice are offered on the menu.
   2 Real fruit is used.
   3 The drinks are made in the kitchen behind the café.
   4 The drinks are brought to your table.
   5 Uniforms are worn by the waiters.
   6 The café is closed on Sundays.

3 **2** are intended **3** is designed **4** aren't deleted **5** is stored **6** are shared **7** is created **8** are used **9** are watched **10** is seen

4 **1** My best friend is <u>called</u> Sean.
   2 You are <u>invited</u> to the picnic next Saturday.
   3 It will be <u>held</u> in Tao Dan Park.
   4 ✓
   5 She <u>is called</u> Michelle.

VOCABULARY

1 **1** d **2** g **3** f **4** e **5** b **6** c **7** h **8** a

2 **1** off **2** up **3** down **4** off **5** on **6** out

WRITING

1 She wants recommendations for new music apps for her phone.

2 Yes

3 **1** For me, … **2** You should definitely try it **3** I would say … is a good choice **4** I prefer **5** If you ask me, … **6** I'd also recommend

4 Students' own answers

5 Hey Sophie! / Happy listening!

6 Students' own answers

7 Students' own answers

UNIT 16 Amazing science

VOCABULARY

1 **1** blow **2** boil **3** cover **4** fill **5** pour **6** rub **7** shake **8** stir **9** tie **10** wrap

2 **1** blow **2** fill **3** pour **4** shake **5** stir

3 **1** boiled **2** tying **3** cover **4** Wrap **5** rubbed

4 **1** c **2** e **3** a **4** b **5** d

READING

1 **1** × **2** × **3** ✓ **4** ✓

2 **1** damage **2** bookmarks **3** sweet **4** sugar **5** bacteria **6** serious illness **7** chocolate **8** mix

3 **1** dough **2** glue **3** mould **4** sweetener **5** laboratory

4 **1** mould **2** sweetener **3** laboratory **4** dough **5** glue

GRAMMAR

1 **1** see, feel **2** heat, boils **3** am, go **4** close, drops **5** walks, thinks **6** enjoys, works

2 **1** pours **2** makes **3** become **4** get **5** go **6** says

3 **1** c **2** d **3** e **4** b **5** a

4 **1** is **2** believes **3** is **4** will watch **5** reads **6** helps **7** will share

5 **1** b **2** b **3** a **4** b **5** a

VOCABULARY

1 **1** cut up **2** carry out **3** work out **4** blow up/out **5** take away **6** add up

2 **1** blow up **2** work out **3** add up **4** take away **5** carry out **6** cut up

LISTENING

1 **1** A **2** C **3** C **4** B **5** C **6** A

11

Interviewer: Today we're talking to Anna Millward, who is an expert on fish. Welcome Anna. How did you first become interested in fish?

Anna: Well, my mum often took me to the zoo, and I probably saw fish there – I'm not sure. One thing I remember, though, is that when I was eight, I persuaded my teacher to get some fish in a tank for our classroom. The idea came from a novel I had – the main characters were fish, and I think that's where my love for them started.

Interviewer: Did you ever want to be a vet?

Anna: Yes. I actually started a course to become one. It was a long course – six years. But I only completed two of them before I switched to biology. It wasn't that I didn't care about animals that were ill – I just wanted to focus on other things, like why are there so many different animals? And how's one fish different from another?

Interviewer: Are you mainly a researcher now?

Anna: Yes, though I also teach. Right now, I'm collecting information about the lakes that are home to a particular type of fish. Most of my research is about that sort of thing. This fish is one that I discovered two years ago – scientists didn't even know it existed. Hopefully, by studying these fish, we'll be in a better position to protect them.

Interviewer: I imagine your work can be difficult sometimes.

Anna: I love my work. I've looked for fish in the freezing waters of northern Russia and in Australian rivers where huge crocodiles live. I deal with all sorts of people – scientists, students, fishermen – with different cultures and languages. And I spend months on end studying fish in a laboratory. I find that part of my work more challenging than anything else – it requires great concentration.

Interviewer: What do you talk to fishermen about?

Anna: They often know more than anyone else about the fish in the waters where they work, and I learn a lot from them. They'll often tell me where I can find a particular type of fish, and they know all about the numbers of fish in a particular area and how they're getting smaller – they're directly affected by it.

Interviewer: Finally Anna – do you eat fish?

Anna: Yes. I like it and it's good for me. But I don't buy fish that's imported from faraway countries – I choose fish that comes from local waters, and I think it's important that everyone does that. The biggest problems for fish populations are caused by huge businesses which catch enormous numbers of fish and sell them all over the world.

UNIT 17 Talented

VOCABULARY

1 **1** author **2** painting **3** gallery **4** studio **5** sculpture **6** artist **7** writer **8** biography **9** novel **10** poetry **11** actor **12** audience **13** poet

2 **1** poet **2** novel **3** artist **4** sculpture **5** author **6** painter

3 **1** exhibition **2** gallery **3** painter **4** sculpture **5** paintings **6** drawings **7** poet **8** poetry

READING

1 Lorde – a rising star with a bright future

2 **1** up **2** At **3** because **4** the **5** One **6** has

3 **1** I **2** C **3** I **4** I **5** I **6** NM **7** I **8** NM

4 **1** voice **2** contract **3** charts **4** fade away **5** stage name

GRAMMAR

1 **1** warn **2** ask **3** order **4** tell **5** advise **6** persuade **7** remind **8** convince

2 **1** He warned us not to go near the water.
2 We asked the teacher to explain the artist's ideas.
3 The headteacher ordered us to be quiet.
4 Billy told me not to open my eyes.
5 Lorraine advised me not to argue with her again.
6 Felix persuaded his parents to buy the latest PlayStation.
7 Dad reminded us to give him the details about the school trip.
8 Mum convinced me to go to the school film night.

3 **1** The man advised us to
2 The security man asked us to show him
3 ordered us to wait
4 warned us not to walk
5 told us to remove
6 persuaded us to go
7 reminded me to take my guitar
8 convinced me not to go to

4 **1** told **2** to help **3** reminded **4** to add **5** asked **6** to go **7** persuaded **8** not to get

5 **1** She told me to look out of the window to check the weather.
2 She told me to give back the money.
3 We were in the same class and the teacher asked us to do a project together.
4 ✓
5 We were talking and a boy in front of us told us to be quiet.

VOCABULARY

1 **1** helpful **2** natural **3** environmental **4** professional **5** peaceful **6** stressful **7** painful **8** cultural **9** political **10** musical **11** successful **12** traditional **13** colourful

2 **1** original **2** cultural **3** financial **4** national **5** cheerful **6** hopeful **7** useful **8** central **9** wonderful

WRITING

1 Students' own answers

2 **Possible answers**
began acting as a four-year-old child / moved to Los Angeles as a teenager / became highest paid actress in the world (2017)

3 1988 – she was born
2000 – first real performance in *The Wind in the Willows*
2004 – first television show
2017 – highest-paid actress in the world

4 **1** at **2** when **3** as **4** Nowadays **5** By ... time

5–6 Students' own answers

UNIT 18 The world of work

VOCABULARY

1 **1** coach **2** politician **3** architect **4** lawyer **5** builder **6** babysitter **7** vet **8** journalist **9** pharmacist **10** presenter **11** firefighter
Hidden word: hairdresser

2 **1** firefighter **2** journalist **3** architect **4** presenter **5** babysitter **6** lawyer **7** builder

3 **1** coach **2** lawyer **3** vet **4** model **5** babysitter **6** politician

READING

1 Students' own answers

2 **1** f **2** e **3** d **4** a **5** c

3 **1** B **2** B **3** B **4** A **5** B **6** B **7** A

4 **1** either way **2** level **3** select **4** decisions **5** challenge

5 **1** Either way **2** decision **3** challenge **4** level **5** selected

GRAMMAR

1 **1** g **2** d **3** f **4** a **5** b **6** e **7** c

2 **1** wouldn't catch, were **2** did, would feel **3** would add, knew **4** had, wouldn't get **5** would take, won **6** would go, didn't feel **7** met, would ask **8** Would you go, gave

3 **1** looked **2** would I see **3** studied **4** would get **5** happened **6** would go to **7** studied **8** would become **9** practised **10** would I become

4 **1** wasn't raining, could go to the beach **2** had a bike, would cycle to your house **3** had the money, would buy that video game **4** wasn't on too/so late, would watch it **5** wasn't so expensive, would buy it

5 **1** a **2** a **3** b **4** a **5** b

VOCABULARY

1 **1** film director **2** guitarist **3** musician **4** blogger **5** receptionist **6** runner **7** supporter **8** actor **9** baker **10** goalkeeper **11** novelist **12** comedian

2 **1** headteacher **2** composer **3** visitor **4** vegetarian **5** cleaner **6** artist **7** electrician

3 **1** banker **2** driver **3** footballer **4** author **5** competitor **6** dentist **7** pianist **8** scientist

LISTENING

1 **1** c **2** b **3** a

2 **1** Sebastian needs advice on meeting a deadline; Nicola needs help with managing her time.
2 Sebastian asks his colleague Sarah; Nicola asks her manager/boss Amy.
3 Students' own answers

3 **1** T **2** T **3** T **4** F **5** T **6** T **7** F **8** F

4 **1** I'm really behind with the work. **2** extend the deadline **3** willing to help you **4** I don't feel I'm making any progress. **5** leave things until the last minute **6** I have a very busy schedule this week

12 **1**

Sebastian: Hi Sarah.

Sarah: Hi Sebastian. Are you ok? You don't look very happy.

Sebastian: My boss gave me a deadline to meet by the end of this week. I'm really behind with the work. I just don't know how I'm going to do it. Can you give some advice?

Sarah: How about sitting down with your boss and finding out if she will extend the deadline? Make a list of everything you need to do and think about how long it will take – then explain the situation to her.

Sebastian: It's a good idea, but I don't really get on with my boss, so I don't think she'll want to help me.

Sarah: Just tell her how you feel, I'm sure she'll be willing to help you – it's her job, don't forget!

Sebastian: Thanks Sarah, that's definitely the best advice. I'll go to see her tomorrow morning.

2

Nicola: Amy, can I just ask your advice about how to improve my organisational skills?

Amy: Yes, no problem, Nicola. What type of things are you trying to improve?

Nicola: I'm not really very good at managing my time, and as hard as I try, I don't feel I'm making any progress.

Amy: Have you tried using sticky notes to remind you about important things?

Nicola: Yes, I do – sometimes it works, sometimes it doesn't. I'm often late for meetings or leave things until the last minute because I often forget.

Amy: Out of ten, how often do you forget?

Nicola: Err … probably five or six.

Amy: Yes, well, that is a bit of a problem, isn't it?

Nicola: Yeah, I really need someone to explain to me where I'm going wrong.

Amy: Right, I have a very busy schedule this week – I'm training the sales team. But I can help you for an hour each day next week if you like. Say 2 pm in my office? But you must promise me that you'll be here on time!

Nicola: Thanks Amy, don't worry, I won't be late!

UNIT 19 The written word

VOCABULARY

1

R	B	J	M	B	Y	M	D	G	S	S	I
K	P	E	-	B	O	O	K	R	Y	S	C
S	T	A	B	J	D	Q	K	A	B	T	F
E	D	U	P	B	R	P	N	P	K	I	C
S	N	Z	E	E	D	B	O	H	K	C	S
P	O	S	T	E	R	R	C	I	T	K	A
G	T	A	A	N	B	O	G	C	Z	E	R
K	E	R	D	O	D	C	A	N	U	R	T
Q	Q	Q	U	V	S	H	C	O	U	F	I
A	X	Z	I	E	E	U	C	V	B	K	C
F	D	W	S	L	A	R	T	E	C	L	L
O	N	O	T	I	C	E	T	L	S	T	E

2 **1** brochure **2** notice **3** e-book **4** paper **5** poster **6** advert **7** graphic novel **8** article **9** sticker **10** note

3 **1** e-book **2** note **3** paper **4** advert **5** brochure **6** article **7** poster **8** notice **9** graphic novel **10** sticker

READING

1 Students' own answers

2 **1** A **2** C **3** B **4** C **5** B

3 **1** display **2** application **3** alarm clock **4** protective **5** enter

4 **1** enter **2** alarm clock **3** display **4** protective **5** application

GRAMMAR

1 **1** c **2** b **3** d **4** a

2 **1** Emma said she was reading an interesting article.
2 Ben said Mrs Jones would help him next week.
3 Fatima said she didn't want to buy a new computer.
4 My brother said he loved downloading free e-books.
5 Mum said Dad couldn't get here on time.
6 My mum said she would get some holiday brochures for Japan.
7 Alison said Jo's dad could pick us up.
8 They said they wouldn't be there.

3 **1 Possible answer**

Cassie said she was 15 and lived in the USA. She said she was studying for her exams now. She said she'd go to Camp Kanosia in the summer. She said she loved it there because she could swim and do lots of water sports.

2 Possible answer

Paolo said he was 14 and was from South Africa. He said he was making this video profile at the moment. He said that he would go to a different school next year. He said it was an art school and he could study drawings, paintings and sculpture there.

4 **1** Jane called me, and she said that she and her brother were going to buy some graphic novels. **2** He said that he was going to put the notice in the students' room. **3** I want to tell you that I got a new e-book. **4** She saw me and she said that she knew me, and we began to talk. **5** ✓

VOCABULARY

1 **1** speaking **2** say **3** said **4** Tell **5** tell **6** talking

2 **1** b **2** c **3** c **4** a

WRITING

1 Students' own answers

2 1, 2, 4, 6 and 8

3 all features are in the review

4 **1** main **2** alien **3** professor **4** comfortable **5** absolutely

5–6 Students' own answers

UNIT 20 Seeing is believing

VOCABULARY

1 **1** make up your mind **2** use your imagination
3 cross your mind **4** have a thought
5 have second thoughts **6** give someone a hint
7 lose your concentration

2 **1** have a thought **2** give them a hint
3 lose your concentration **4** use your imagination
5 make up your mind **6** have second thoughts
7 crosses your mind

3 **1** make up my mind **2** lost my concentration
3 gave her a hint **4** crossed your mind
5 had second thoughts **6** used my imagination
7 had a thought

4 **1** crossed my mind **2** make up my mind
3 lost my concentration **4** give me a hint
5 use my imagination **6** had a thought
7 had second thoughts

READING

1 Students' own answers

2 by drawing images with chalk and then taking photographs of them

3 **1** F **2** F **3** T **4** F **5** T **6** F

4 **1** masters **2** angle **3** portraits **4** tiles **5** pavement

GRAMMAR

1
1 The first Ames room was constructed by Adelbert Ames Jr.
2 It was built in 1946.
3 An Ames room was created for the film star's latest film.
4 The actor was told not to move.
5 This trick was used in/by many films.
6 My photo was taken in the Ames room in a museum in San Francisco.

2 **1** was won **2** is read **3** were paid **4** was asked
5 is designed **6** was created **7** was done **8** were made

3 **1** was built by **2** is delivered by someone
3 were shown the illusion by **4** was done by
5 graphics were used **6** were designed **7** was won by
8 was made to disappear

4 **1** was shown **2** was called **3** was directed **4** was based
5 was written **6** were told **7** was directed

5 **1** b **2** a **3** a **4** b **5** a

VOCABULARY

1 **1** Look at **2** watch **3** see **4** look at **5** watch **6** see
7 see **8** look at

2 **1** watch **2** see **3** watch **4** Look at **5** watched **6** see
7 look at **8** see

3 **1** watched / saw **2** looked **3** saw **4** seen / watched
5 watching **6** seeing **7** looking at

LISTENING

1 **1** ✓ **2** ✓ **3** × **4** × **5** ✓ **6** ✓

2 **1** A **2** C **3** B **4** A **5** B **6** B

13

Interviewer: In the studio with us today we have the young magician, Jerry Tweed. Jerry, who encouraged you to start doing magic?

Jerry: Well, I was only three when my dad took me to a magic show. The man on stage was wearing a suit with stars on it and that's all I remember. We went to my aunt's house afterwards and she said 'Jerry, why not do magic when you're older!' I never forgot those words. That's how it all began.

Interviewer: How did you learn your first tricks?

Jerry: In primary school, I had a teacher who showed us some simple tricks, but I couldn't really do any until I was old enough to go to a Young Magicians' Club – they have great courses there and I really got into it. I know some people have a private teacher but I've never felt I needed one.

Interviewer: And what do you do now to develop your skills?

Jerry: A few years ago, I used to go to as many live shows as possible, and I watched videos on the internet. These days, though, I'm busy performing my own magic, so I don't have much free time. But I still learn a lot from books written by magicians.

Interviewer: You left school early to concentrate on magic. How do your parents feel about that?

Jerry: They were worried when I decided to leave school at 16. They thought I should carry on until I was at least 18 and finish all my exams. But they've seen how successful my shows are and they realise I'm talented enough to make a living from them. They haven't had to support me financially, which I think they're glad about.

Interviewer: You've performed on television recently, haven't you?

Jerry: Yes, it was in the middle of the day so I doubt if it attracted a huge audience. I started with a few traditional tricks. Maybe that was a mistake – doing tricks people have seen before, I mean. But for my last trick, I made a card disappear and the presenter found it in her sandwich. She was amazed and I think that really impressed people.

Interviewer: What are your plans for the future, Jerry?

Jerry: Well, next year I'm performing in various places around Europe and Asia – that tour's already booked. I've thought about making boxes of tricks to sell in shops – they'd be for children who want to learn some basic magic. It's just an idea, though. A friend of mine has set up a school for young magicians – that sounds interesting but it might not suit me. I don't know – we'll see.

STUDENT'S BOOK AUDIOSCRIPTS

01 Unit 1, Student's Book page 10

Lucas: This person is younger than me. He's got dark hair – and it's really curly. He's playing a game on his tablet in this photo.

Alfie: This person is a teenage girl. She's got straight, fair hair – almost blonde – and she's two years younger than me. I guess she's quite attractive – well, she certainly thinks so!

Grace: The person that I want to describe has dark hair, but now he's in his forties he's going bald.

02 Unit 1, Student's Book page 10

1 **Woman:** I think Lucas is really polite. For instance, when he wants to borrow something, he always says please.

2 **Boy:** My brother's called Alfie. He takes my things without asking. He thinks he's funny, but he doesn't make me laugh!

3 **Man:** Grace is very friendly. I see her every morning on her way to school. She always says hello.

4 **Alfie's dad:** Alfie talks a lot – like his mum! He's sometimes a bit careless with homework. I try to encourage him to check it, but he doesn't always do it.

5 **Lucas:** Grace is a great friend. She's always smiling, and she's never miserable. She really makes me laugh.

6 **Lucas's mum:** Lucas knows what he's good at, so he's quite a confident boy. He can also be quite a lazy person though. His room is always really untidy!

04 Unit 2, Student's Book page 14

A **Boy:** This is Jaden Smith. I like him a lot. His dad's Will Smith. Jaden Smith's a singer and he's been in a few films too. He's wearing a denim jacket, a white T-shirt and skinny white trousers. He's got a black cap and a small red bag. He's got some gold necklaces as well.

B **Girl:** This is Taylor Swift. She always looks really trendy. Here, she's walking along a city street. She's wearing a smart black shirt and black trousers. It looks like she has a handbag as well.

C **Girl:** Ed Sheeran isn't normally this well-dressed! He usually wears casual clothes, but here he's wearing a black suit, a white shirt and a black tie. The suit looks brand new. He looks very smart!

D **Boy:** Rihanna is one of my favourite singers. She's wearing trainers, loose-fitting trousers, and a black-and-white blouse with very long sleeves.

05 Unit 2, Student's Book page 14

Presenter: This morning we're at Charlbury High School to find out what's in fashion at the moment.

Ashley

Presenter: What clothes do you like wearing, Ashley?

Ashley: Mmm, I love sports clothes. I never wear anything very smart. I just wear trainers and tracksuits, that kind of thing.

Presenter: Why?

Ashley: Tracksuits are soft on your skin, they're comfortable and easy to wear and you can wear them anywhere. I love this one. It's a great colour!

Molly

Presenter: You look very well dressed today, Molly. Can you tell me about your clothes?

Molly: I really like this top. I saw it in a trendy market stall and I fell in love with it straight away.

Presenter: It's lovely. Very smart.

Molly: Thank you. It's brand new. I bought it yesterday.

Luke

Presenter: Luke, can you tell me what fashions and clothes you like?

Luke: Sure. I like clothes that are quite simple and not too colourful. I'm not interested in what's trendy. My boots are old but I love them. I don't like wearing stuff that's brand new. I love these skinny jeans too – I don't find loose-fitting jeans comfortable. And this is my favourite sweatshirt. It's from a music festival.

Presenter: Did you buy your clothes second-hand?

Luke: No, I bought them new … but quite a long time ago!

07 Unit 2, Student's Book page 17

Sara: Grandma, did you listen to pop music when you were young?

Grandma: Oh, yes! There were all kinds of exciting bands in those days.

Sara: Really? What did you listen to?

Grandma: I remember when I was a teenager. It was a summer's evening in 1969. My parents had a colour TV. Colour TVs were fairly new in 1969. Before then, television was only in black and white.

Sara: Black and white TV?

Grandma: Yes! So this colour TV was rare in those days. There was a music show called *Top of the Pops* and The Beatles were on. They played songs from their new album, *Abbey Road*. Oh, it was an amazing performance! They played really well. *Abbey Road* is still my favourite album of all time.

Sara: I know that album. Dad still plays it. It's cool. But I didn't know it was so old.

Grandma: I loved The Beatles … everyone loved The Beatles. The whole world went crazy when that album came out.

Sara: Oh, Grandma, there's something I want to ask you. Can I borrow your jacket again?

Grandma: The blue one? But it's really old.

Sara: I know it's old, but that style's fashionable again now, and it matches my jeans.

Grandma: I'll just go and get it for you …

Sara: Thanks, Grandma. So what kind of clothes did you wear when you were my age?

Grandma: Girls wore dresses in those days. Short dresses and colourful tights are what I remember from the early 1960s. I had a cool pair of trousers too, with quite short legs.

Sara: And the guys?

Grandma: The men wore smart clothes at the start of the 1960s but by the time *Abbey Road* came out in 1969, the fashion for men was for long hair and beards, and colourful, loose-fitting clothes …

Sara: And – er – the jacket?

Grandma: Oh, yes, the jacket. Here it is. I made this jacket in … I think it was … 1965!

Sara: No way! That's amazing! I never knew you were so clever, Grandma.

Grandma: Well, now you know!

08 Unit 2, Student's Book page 17

Track 08 is taken from Track 07. It is from the beginning of the track to Grandma's line "The whole world went crazy when that album came out."

09 Unit 2, Student's Book page 17

Track 09 is taken from Track 07. It is from Sara's line "Oh, Grandma, there's something I want to ask you. Can I borrow your jacket again?" to the end of the track.

10 Unit 2, Student's Book page 17

Interviewer: What clothes do you like wearing?

Harry: I like wearing jeans. They're very comfortable, and I think jeans always look good.

Interviewer: How often do you buy new clothes?

Harry: Well, I don't go shopping every week, but I suppose I go shopping two or three times a month. I do jobs for my parents to earn money.

Interviewer: Where do you usually buy your clothes?

Harry: I usually go to the market because the clothes are quite cheap. I don't like shopping in department stores because the clothes are too expensive.

Interviewer: How much do you spend on clothes?

Harry: I'm not sure … I probably spend about £30 a month. And I always spend more when I get money for my birthday.

12 Culture: Traditional clothes, Student's Book page 19

Teacher: OK, everyone. Quieten down, please. OK. Now the first presenter today is Julia and she's talking about …

Julia: The Beefeaters at the Tower of London, and their uniforms.

Teacher: Excellent. Go ahead, Julia.

Julia: The Beefeaters are the King or Queen's traditional guards. You can see them at the Tower of London, where they're very popular with the tourists. Everyone wants to take a selfie with them! King Henry VIII created this special group of royal guards more than 500 years ago, in 1509. They've got an unusual name – Beefeaters. Some people say they're called that because they always had beef to eat, because they worked for the royal family. Beef and other meat was very expensive in the past, so only the most important people could eat it very often. Not like today, when beef isn't a very special food.

Teacher: That's very interesting! And what about their uniforms, Julia? Do they always wear the same thing every day of the year?

Julia: No, they don't. In fact, the Beefeaters have got two different uniforms. On most days, they wear a dark blue coat and blue hat, which have some bright red decorations, and they wear dark blue trousers. This is a photo. They call this the undress uniform because it's not so special. But for more important occasions, the Beefeaters wear the state dress uniform. Here's a photo …

Teacher: And that's a much fancier uniform of course …

Julia: Yes, it's their formal uniform. It's got a long, red coat … and you can see the coat's got lots of bright gold decorations, and there's a big white collar at the top of the coat. They also wear long red stockings on their legs, and a special black hat or bonnet on their heads. I think the state dress uniform looks very impressive, especially when you see lots of Beefeaters standing together.

Teacher: Very good, Julia. Any questions? Yes, Michael …

13 Unit 3, Student's Book page 20

Charlie: What are you reading?

Lily: It's a quiz about different countries and various stages of life. I got four out of eight. Do you want to try?

Charlie: Sure. In England, most children start school when they are … Hmm… I can't remember. I'm fairly sure it's four.

Lily: OK. So A.

Charlie: Yeah. So, question 2. In Belgium and Germany, students cannot leave school before they are … Well, it's 16 in most countries. But this is a quiz … so it's probably higher.

Lily: OK. So are you saying C?

Charlie: Yes, 18. C.

Lily: OK. Question 3.

Charlie: In some states in the USA, the youngest age you can get a driving licence is … I can't believe it's 14 – that's too young. It's 17 here. Maybe it's younger in the US. I say B.

Lily: OK. Question 4.

Charlie: In England, around … per cent of young people go to university. Hmm … this quiz is getting harder. I don't think that most people go to university. So it's probably A or B. I'm not sure it's as high as 43%. So that leaves the first one.

Lily: OK. Number 5. So who leaves home earlier?

Charlie: Let me think. I think women probably. They're better at saving money so they can leave home earlier.

Lily: I'm not sure that's true for me, but OK. Question 6. Have you got a job of any kind?

Charlie: No, my mum doesn't want me to have one. Let me read the question … In the UK, children of … are allowed to get a part-time job. I don't think there are any rules. I mean, you can only work part-time, of course – because you can't leave school until you're 16.

Lily: OK. Question 7. This one's about marriage.

Charlie: In … OK. India doesn't seem like the right answer. It's quite a traditional country, I think. So … Spain or Japan. I know Japan's really expensive. Maybe they can't afford to get married until they're in their thirties.

Lily: Maybe.

Charlie: I reckon it's C. I think they get married at a younger age in Spain.

Lily: Eight. This one's quite difficult.

Charlie: In Brazil, you can vote in elections from the age of … Well, it's 18 here, I know that. And in lots of other countries. So I think it's probably the same in Brazil.

Lily: B. Right. Let's see how many points you got …

16 Unit 4, Student's Book page 24

1

Woman: Where do you go windsurfing?

Girl: We live a long way from the sea, but luckily there's a big lake near here, and we go windsurfing on the lake. We go swimming sometimes, too.

2

Woman: How often do you do gymnastics?

Boy: Once a week. I don't like it, but gymnastics is part of our PE lessons at school. We do athletics in the summer instead.

3

Woman: Do you play ice hockey?

Girl: No way! I don't play ice hockey, I don't even go ice-skating – I can't skate! I love watching it on TV though. I go climbing a lot with friends from school. I like that!

4

Woman: What sports do you do?

Boy: I usually do boxing after school on Thursdays. I go jogging quite often, too, because I need to be fit for boxing!

5

Woman: Do you like cycling?

Girl: Yes, I think bikes are brilliant. This is my new road bike – I love it! My mates and I go cycling all the time.

6

Woman: Do you enjoy sport?

Boy: Yes. I love playing football, and I like squash and tennis, too. My sister plays tennis, but she hates losing, so we never play tennis together!

18 Unit 4, Student's Book page 27

Steve: I'm Steve Ross – welcome to *Sports Review*. My guest in the studio in Manchester this evening is Chloe Fuller. Good evening, Chloe, and thank you for coming.

Chloe: Hi, Steve. It's a pleasure.

Steve: OK. Let's look at your photo of the week! What was happening here, Chloe?

Chloe: This photo is brilliant. It's from a match between Sunderland and Liverpool. In the fourth minute of the game, a Liverpool fan threw a red beach ball onto the pitch right next to the Liverpool goal. At the same time, a Sunderland player was running towards the goal with the ball. He kicked the ball – the football, I mean – it hit the beach ball and then went into the net.

Steve: Really?

Chloe: Yes, really! The poor goalkeeper didn't know which way to look – at the beach ball or at the football!

Steve: The referee didn't actually allow the goal, did he?

Chloe: Well, I didn't think it was a goal, but the referee allowed it! Thousands of fans were watching the match on TV, of course. The TV pictures showed quite clearly that the football went into the goal because it hit the beach ball.

Steve: No way! Didn't Liverpool complain?

Chloe: Yes, but the referee didn't change his mind, and Sunderland won the match one–nil!

Steve: That isn't fair, is it?

Chloe: Well, maybe the referee made a mistake, but you can't change the result after a match. Anyway, the Liverpool players were playing really badly. I think Sunderland were a much better team that night.

19 Unit 4, Student's Book page 27

Max: I watched the Champions League final on TV last weekend. It was an amazing game! Real Madrid were playing against Manchester City. Manchester City were winning for most of the game, but Real Madrid scored two goals in the last five minutes. I was very happy because I support Real Madrid. It was really exciting!

Rachel: I do athletics, and two weeks ago I raced in a schools athletics competition. I really enjoyed taking part because it was my first time. Lots of people were watching the competition, and it was so cool when people cheered for me. I ran in two races. I didn't win any, but I came third in one race. I think that's quite good!

20 Life Skills: Keeping fit, Student's Book page 28

Tom: Hey, Anna. I'm going to the park. Are you coming?

Anna: Just a minute, Tom, I'm reading an article.

Tom: What's it about?

Anna: Physical fitness. Did you know that most teenagers in the USA don't do enough exercise?

Tom: Really? And how much is enough?

Anna: Well, the World Health Organisation says teenagers need one hour of physical activity every day.

Tom: That's not a lot! I usually play basketball after school, or I go to the gym with friends.

Anna: Yes, but do you exercise *all* that time at the gym? You and your friends rest and chat a lot too. In an hour at the gym, you probably exercise for about 20 minutes.

Tom: Well, that's true. And what about you? You don't exercise for more than an hour *every* day, do you?

Anna: No, not *every* day, but I do about an hour of exercise most days. I've got volleyball practice after school on Mondays and Wednesdays, and that's not easy. And then I've got swimming on Tuesdays and Fridays.

Tom: That's pretty good. But you don't do very much at the weekend …

Anna: Well, I don't sit at home all the time. I go out with friends and we usually walk around a lot. That's exercise too, you know. And you? You're not very active at weekends, are you?

Tom: Well … I sometimes go skateboarding with Paul.

Anna: Not that much! You and Paul usually play computer games in your room. You should call Danny. He's really into cycling. You and Paul could go cycling with him.

Tom: You're right. And I don't use my bike enough. I could ride it to school more often too.

Anna: Good idea. Hey! You and I could cycle together in the morning. That's more exercise for me too. And we should always walk up the stairs – that's really good exercise.

Tom: OK. How about we start tomorrow morning. I want to get super fit!

Anna: OK, Mr Fitness. We'll see what happens tomorrow. I mean you're not really a morning person!

Tom: What do you mean…?

22 Unit 5, Student's Book page 32

1

Woman: Three weeks ago a [*BLEEP / hacker*] stole over 100 million email addresses and passwords from a bank in the United States. Experts believe that [*BLEEP / hacking*] costs businesses over two trillion dollars every year.

2

Boy: We have a problem with [*BLEEP / vandalism*] in our area. [*BLEEP / Vandals*] have smashed the window of my parents' car three times in the last year. It's unbelievable. They don't even steal anything from the car. I mean, what's the point?

3

Presenter: And what type of person does this regularly?

Guest: We think that only 10% of [*BLEEP / shoplifters*] are professionals. For these people [*BLEEP / shoplifting*] is a job. Professional [*BLEEP / shoplifters*] typically rob large stores and steal expensive items like designer clothes or bags. Then they sell them, often online.

4

Police: This is the police. Can I help you?

Caller: Hello. I'd like to report the [*BLEEP / theft*] of a car. I saw it happen, and I can describe the [*BLEEP / thief*].

Police: OK. Where are you?

Caller: I'm in a car park on Queen Street.

5

Announcer: This is an announcement for all passengers. Please be careful of [*BLEEP / pickpockets*] in crowded areas. [*BLEEP / Pickpocketing*] is common at stations. Make sure valuable items such as phones and wallets are safe and out of sight when you are not using them.

6

Girl: My neighbour doesn't know when the [*BLEEP / burglary*] happened. They were on holiday until this morning and they only discovered it when they got home. The [*BLEEP / burglars*] took TVs, computers, things like that.

23 Unit 5, Student's Book page 32

Track 22 is repeated with the answers [in brackets] for students to listen and check.

26 Unit 6, Student's Book page 36

Speaker 1

Woman: It's probably the worst thing about living in London. It lasts for about two hours in the morning and the same in the evening. There are people everywhere – on the streets, in train stations, shops … The worst place is the Underground. I avoid it after work – especially in the summer. I'd rather walk or catch a bus.

Speaker 2

Boy: There is a serious problem with this where I live. There's nothing to do at weekends, so we go out to the city. There *are* buses from here – but not many. My parents give me a lift and sometimes I have to get a taxi home. But it's expensive. I can't wait until I'm old enough to get my driving licence.

Speaker 3

Man: There's a bus stop near my house and it's got writing all over it. It's horrible. Really ugly. I sometimes clean it myself, but then a few days later it comes back again. I think I know who is doing some of it. But I'm not completely sure and I don't want to start an argument. We're a small community. Everyone knows everyone here.

Speaker 4

Girl: There aren't enough of these where I live. One of my favourite places is the park, but the nearest one to our house is over 20 minutes' walk away. It's too dangerous to cycle there because the roads are really busy. When I was younger, we lived in a village. It was safe enough to walk to school and there were lots of fields all around my home.

27 Unit 6, Student's Book page 36

1 **Man:** There's a bus stop near my house and it's got writing all over it. It's horrible. Really ugly. I sometimes clean it myself, but then a few days later it comes back again. I think I know who is doing some of it. But I'm not completely sure and I don't want to start an argument. We're a small community. Everyone knows everyone here.

2 **Girl:** There aren't enough of these where I live. One of my favourite places is the park, but the nearest one to our house is over 20 minutes' walk away. It's too dangerous to cycle there because the roads are really busy. When I was younger, we lived in a village. It was safe enough to walk to school and there were lots of fields all around my home.

3 **Boy:** There is a serious problem with this where I live. There's nothing to do at weekends, so we go out to the city. There are buses from here – but not many. My parents give me a lift and sometimes I have to get a taxi home. But it's expensive. I can't wait until I'm old enough to get my driving licence.

4 **Woman:** It's probably the worst thing about living in London. It lasts for about two hours in the morning and the same in the evening. There are people everywhere – on the streets, in train stations, shops … The worst place is the Underground. I avoid it after work – especially in the summer. I'd rather walk or catch a bus.

29 Unit 6, Student's Book page 39

Presenter: So for this week's teacher–student debate, we invited Bess from Year 10 and Mr Evans, our chemistry teacher.

Bess: Hello!

Mr Evans: Um, hello.

Presenter: Now, Mr Evans lives in Carrington. It's a village about twenty minutes by car from school. Bess actually lived in the same village when she was younger, but now she lives here in the city, quite near our school. It takes her a few minutes to cycle here in the morning. She's never late for school!

Mr Evans: Well, I'm not sure I agree …

Presenter: OK. So our questions this week are about life in the country and in the city. Mr Evans, you're first. What do you think about living in the country?

Mr Evans: I love it in my village. It's green, there aren't many traffic jams, and there isn't much crime. I know all my neighbours, and there are lots of things to do.

Presenter: Do you agree, Bess?

Bess: I don't think so. I mean, I agree about traffic and crime. And there's a lot more pollution where I am now. But I don't agree that there are lots of things to do. There aren't any cinemas or anything like that in Carrington.

Mr Evans: That's true. It isn't as interesting for people your age in Carrington. Personally, I think the problem is public transport. There aren't many buses, and until you're old enough to drive, it can be difficult to get around.

Presenter: Bess?

Bess: Yes, maybe you're right. I definitely have a lot more fun here than I did in the village … Young people in Carrington just hang out by the river. It's a bit boring.

Presenter: Bess. Is there anything you don't like about living in the city?

Bess: Well, the worst thing about living here is the rubbish. It's everywhere. I really noticed it when I moved here.

Presenter: Have you got any good solutions?

Bess: Yes, it's simple. There aren't enough rubbish bins, especially outside school. And we need more recycling bins. I went to Germany in the summer. It was really clean and every bin was a different colour. There were always four or five different recycling bins, and they recycle almost everything!

Presenter: What do you think about that, Mr Evans?

Mr Evans: Well, I completely agree with Bess. In fact, after this interview I'm going to …

30 Unit 6, Student's Book page 39

Alice: So, which of these two places would you like to live in, Oliver?

Oliver: Personally, I think it's better to live in the city. There are a lot of things to do, like going shopping, going to the cinema or seeing exhibitions. The countryside is boring. What do you think?

Alice: I'm not sure I agree. Of course, there aren't many shops or cinemas in the countryside, but you can do other things. You can go biking, or walking, or have a picnic.

Oliver: But what about people? It seems to me that you meet more people in cities, so you have more friends. Do you agree?

Alice: Yes, that's true. But if you ask me, a lot of people isn't always positive. There are the crowds, too, and rush hour is terrible.

Oliver: Yes, maybe you're right.

Alice: I think that the biggest problem in cities is the pollution. There's too much traffic and too many cars, and there's a lot of rubbish.

Oliver: I completely agree with you about that!

32 Culture: New York City, Student's Book page 41

Dan: Hey, Fiona! How was your trip to New York City last weekend?

Fiona: It … was … *amazing*! I had such a good time!

Dan: I'm not surprised! I love the Big Apple. And you had good weather too!

Fiona: I know! That was lucky because we wanted to visit Coney Island on Saturday morning. I love amusement parks.

Dan: Me too. Coney Island isn't very big or new, but it's fun. And what about baseball? Did you see a game?

Fiona: No, we didn't have enough time, but my dad and I took a tour of Yankee Stadium on Saturday afternoon. That was cool!

Dan: What other things did you see in New York?

Fiona: Well, we visited Times Square, of course! That was Saturday evening. I took lots of selfies! And after that I went up to the top of the Empire State Building. The view was incredible!

Dan: What about MoMA? You know, the Museum of Modern Art. Did you go? That's one of my favourite places.

Fiona: No, we didn't go there this time. I love MoMA, but my parents wanted to go shopping…

Dan: Where? On Fifth Avenue?

Fiona: No! Things are too expensive on Fifth Avenue! We went to Brooklyn on Sunday. I love the second-hand clothing shops there.

Dan: And for lunch? Where did you go?

Fiona: To Chinatown! You know I love Chinese food! It was delicious. And after lunch, we decided to visit the Museum of Chinese in America. We learned a lot about Chinese immigrants in the 19th century.

Dan: And what else? Did you visit Liberty Island?

Fiona: No, we were only there for two days and I've seen the Statue of Liberty before.

Dan: I wonder … When did they build the Statue of Liberty?

Fiona: They finished the statue in 1886, but did you know that it came from France? It was a gift from the French government.

Dan: Yes, I know that! Well, it sounds like you had a busy time in New York.

Fiona: We did! Oh, and I didn't tell you about Sunday evening. We went out for dinner to the Hard Rock Café, and you won't believe who I saw there!

Dan: Who? Lady Gaga? Come on, tell me!

33 Unit 7, Student's Book page 42

Conversation 1

Zac: Hi, Megan. How are you?

Megan: I'm OK, Zac.

Zac: You don't sound OK. What's wrong?

Megan: It's my brother. He makes me angry!

Zac: You're always having problems with him!

Megan: I know. We had an argument this morning.

Zac: What did he do this time?

Megan: He took my phone without asking me and then he dropped it. Now it doesn't work and I can't listen to my music! So I'm bored *and* I'm annoyed with him!

Zac: Are you on your own?

Megan: Yes.

Zac: Well, why don't we do something later?

Megan: You mean go out?

Zac: Yeah. It sounds like you need to have fun! Let's go out after dinner.

Megan: Thanks, Zac. I wish my brother was like you!

Zac: That's OK. … Oh, Megan, can you do me a favour?

Megan: What is it?

Zac: Can I borrow your phone?

Megan: Ha, ha.

Conversation 2

Rachel: Hi, Thomas. Where are you?

Thomas: Oh, hi, Rachel. I'm on my way home. I was running.

Rachel: Oh, what's the running club like?

Thomas: It's OK. I like going running, but the people in the club …

Rachel: What's wrong?

Thomas: Well, it's hard to make friends.

Rachel: But you're really friendly. You've got loads of friends at school!

Thomas: I know. It isn't my fault. Everyone in the club's older than me. We've got different likes and dislikes – we don't have anything in common.

Rachel: You have lots in common – like running!

Thomas: Hmm. You're right.

35 Unit 8, Student's Book page 46

Man: And for those of you that are new to international travel, click here to watch our introduction to getting through the airport …

Woman: You start by checking in at the check-in desk. They check your passport and tickets, and they weigh and label your baggage. Then you get your boarding pass.

Next, you go through the security check. There are often quite long queues these days at the security checks at international airports. Security officers look at what passengers are taking onto the plane, just in case someone tries to take something dangerous.

After that, you have to wait for your flight in the departure lounge. There are restaurants and you can go shopping for local products! Half an hour before the flight, you follow the signs to the departure gate. There, your boarding pass and passport are checked again before you board the plane.

After your plane lands, you have to go through passport control. Then you collect your baggage in the baggage hall and go through customs. There are lots of rules about things you mustn't take to other countries. Customs officers look inside some people's bags and check. Finally, you walk out into Arrivals.

37 Unit 8, Student's Book page 49

Teacher: OK class – listen carefully! I want to tell you about a fantastic travel writing competition I've heard about. The company holding the competition is called 'World Explorer' and they are offering some amazing prizes. They're well known for running expeditions for young people to places like Cambodia, Peru and South Africa, but the winner of this competition is going to join an expedition to Canada!

The expedition is going to take place next year and is going to last for two weeks. You're going to spend two days in the town of Churchill and then trek out to a research centre on skis or snow shoes, where you're going to study local plants and wildlife with a group of scientists.

It really is an amazing opportunity!

To enter, you need to write an article about a place you have travelled to. You must include information about the people you met, the culture and the local environment. Make it as interesting and entertaining as you can!

Based on how popular the competition was last year, the judges are expecting around 3,000 entries, so that gives you an idea of how good your article must be! You should write around 1,000 words, and definitely no more than 1,500. The judges won't even read it if it's longer than that, so be careful.

Today's date is the 19th of January, so you've got a few weeks left to write your article. It must arrive by the 19th of February, and the results are going to be sent out on the 19th of April.

One last thing – as long as you are under 16, the competition is free to enter. You must include your email address, as this is how they're going to contact winners. Photographs will only be needed if your article wins, so no need to send those yet. Good luck everyone!

38 Unit 8, Student's Book page 49

Girl: What shall we do on Saturday?

Boy: What about going ice skating?

Girl: Mmm, the problem with that is the tickets are quite expensive and I don't have much money at the moment. Why don't we go for a bike ride around Hollingworth Lake?

Boy: I'm not sure. I don't think the weather's going to be very good at the weekend. Cycling isn't fun in the rain! How about visiting the National Football Museum?

Girl: That's a good idea. It's free and it's only 15 minutes on the train into Manchester. And we could see if Ahmed and Oliver want to come, too.

Boy: That sounds great! Yes, let's do that.

40 Life Skills: Dealing with conflict, Student's Book page 51

Michael: Aggh! It's half past five. Where *are* you, Amy?

Amy: Michael! Michael!

Michael: Amy! You're late … again! And where's your bike?

Amy: That's the problem! I couldn't use my bike. My sister took it, so I had to walk here.

Michael: Of course! You've *always* got an excuse. Every time we meet, you're late or you forget, or *something happens*. I'm getting tired of this!

Amy: Hey! Relax! I told you what happened. Why are you so angry?

Michael: I'm not angry. I'm annoyed because you're 30 minutes late! And I *always* have to wait for you. Do you care about my feelings? I mean … it's not very nice!

Amy: Hey, hey, wait a second… Look, I know I'm late, and I'm sorry about that. Really! But this time it wasn't my fault!

Michael: I know that. But you have to admit, you're usually late for everything!

Amy: Well … maybe … I'm always late for school … but I need to try harder.

Michael: Yes, you do! But honestly, what's your problem?

Amy: Well, I usually forget about the time. I listen to music or I chat on my phone … and I don't check the time.

Michael: Well, I've got an idea. When we make plans, I can send you a text message before I leave home.

Amy: OK … or maybe I can set an alarm on my phone, so it rings to remind me.

Michael: That's a good idea. And you can *call* me when you're going to be late. Please?

Amy: OK! That's a deal! Now what can we do? I haven't got my bike, so we can't go cycling.

Michael: Let's go for a walk. And we can stop at the comic shop on Queen Street. OK?

Amy: The comic shop? Are you crazy?

Michael: Come on! You were late so you have to be extra nice to me …

Amy: Oh, no … here we go again.

41 Unit 9, Student's Book page 54

Gemma: Hi, Leo. What's that you're reading?

Leo: I'm just finishing this quiz about money. *Money Wizard or Money Waster*? Which are you, Gemma?

Gemma: What do you think?

Leo: I know what *you* think but let's find out. Question 1 is about saving. Do you save up for things?

Gemma: All the time. At the moment I'm saving up for a new computer.

Leo: Really? I've never saved up for anything in my life! Question 2. What about a bank account? Have you got one?

Gemma: My dad opened one for me a few years ago. But I don't use it.

Leo: Hmm … maybe I should get one. I didn't think I was old enough. Anyway, question 3. Do you always look at the price of things before buying them?

Gemma: Always. You know that shop near school? They charge $1.50 for a small bottle of water!

Leo: Yeah, I know. I never buy anything there.

Gemma: How am I doing? I'm a money wizard, yeah?

Leo: Hold on. Four. What about special offers? Do you look for them?

Gemma: Of course! Everyone loves a special offer! But I'm not like my brother. He buys stuff he doesn't need – just because it's on special offer.

Leo: Hmm … I do that sometimes. Here, read question 5.

Gemma: Do you ever decide *not* to buy something while you're waiting at the checkout? No, I never do that.

Leo: No, I don't. OK. Six. What about checking your change?

Gemma: I don't always check it. Sometimes I'm in a hurry. But most of the time, yes, I do.

Leo: Ah! I *always* do!

Gemma: What's the next one?

Leo: Receipts. Do you keep them?

Gemma: Not really. But sometimes for big things. I might need to take them back.

Leo: OK. And the last one. What about your old things? You know, DVDs and stuff like that. What do you do with them?

Gemma: The internet is great for selling things like that. I've sold a lot of my stuff.

Leo: OK. That's the end. Now, let's look in the key and see what it says …

43 Unit 10, Student's Book page 58

Isla: Hi, Ali. We're doing a project in our science class. It's about what we eat and drink.

Ali: Oh, yeah. What do you want me to do?

Isla: Well, it's a taste test. I'm going to give you eight things to taste. But I'm going to cover your eyes with a scarf … so you can't see them. Is that OK?

Ali: Er … OK.

Isla: All you have to do is describe their taste and say what you think they are.

Ali: What kind of foods are they?

Isla: Don't worry. There isn't anything horrible. You really don't need to be worried.

Ali: OK then. I'll do your taste test.

Isla: Really? Great! I'll just tie this around your eyes … there!

44 Unit 10, Student's Book page 58

Isla: Here's number 1.

Ali: Mmm, this is delicious! It's a fruit. Pineapple, I think. It's really juicy!

Isla: OK. Number 2.

Ali: Ugh! That's really sour. What is it? Lemon juice? It's horrible. I need a drink now …

Isla: Here's some water. This is number 3.

Ali: Argh! This is disgusting. It's cold and tastes like rice and raw meat! Hold on, it's not as bad as I thought. It tastes fishy. Is it sushi? You know, raw fish. Salmon or something like that?

Isla: Number 4.

Ali: Well, it's obviously curry and it's really tasty, but it's also quite spicy. I love spicy food. Oh, it's very spicy …

Isla: Now, number 5. It's a drink, so be careful.

Ali: Mmm … It's warm and oh, it's really bitter! What is it? A strong coffee? It tastes like coffee … Like black coffee …

Isla: Number 6.

Ali: Nice. Something sweet after that bitter coffee. It's just cake, I think. Is that right?

Isla: OK, number 7.

Ali: Mmm. It's hard and very cold. It doesn't really taste of anything. Is it some type of frozen vegetable? A pea or something like that? It feels like a pea but I can't taste anything …

Isla: And finally, number 8.

Ali: Mmm … this tastes like bread. Mmm, delicious. It's still warm – it must be really fresh.

45 Unit 10, Student's Book page 58

1 Juicy pineapple
2 Sour lemon juice
3 Raw salmon
4 Spicy curry
5 Bitter coffee
6 Sweet cake
7 Frozen vegetables
8 Fresh bread

46 Unit 10, Student's Book page 58

1 **Ali:** This is delicious. It's a fruit. Pineapple, I think.

2 **Ali:** Argh! This is disgusting. It's cold and tastes like rice and raw meat! Hold on, it's not as bad as I thought. It tastes fishy. Is it sushi?

3 **Ali:** What is it? Lemon juice? It's horrible.

4 **Ali:** Well, it's obviously curry and it's really tasty.

48 Unit 10, Student's Book page 61

1 What did the girl cook when she was young?

Man: So, do you cook a lot at home?

Girl: Not really. My dad taught me how to make a good omelette recently. And I often make one when I need a quick snack. When I was young, I did a lot of cooking with my dad. We made sweet things like cakes.

Man: Have you ever made dinner for your family?

Girl: I've tried. I roasted a chicken once. I followed the recipe carefully, but when we cut into it, it was raw in the middle!

2 Where does the boy get his recipes from?

Boy: Everyone in my family is really into cooking and food in general. My dad actually teaches food technology at a secondary school. I usually cook once or twice a week for everyone at home. I don't have any of my own recipe books. I use ones I find on the internet. I can make a very good chicken and vegetable soup, but my sister is better. She makes a fantastic lamb curry. It tastes incredible but she won't tell me the recipe!

3 Who is a vegetarian?

Boy: So who does most of the cooking in your family?

Girl: My mum, I guess. But I cook quite a lot too. I have to.

Boy: Why? Don't you like your mum's cooking?

Girl: It isn't that. She makes some really tasty meals. But I don't eat meat or fish. So sometimes the three of us – Mum, Dad and me – have a vegetarian meal together, but sometimes she makes something with meat … or fish. And then I try to cook my own meal. I can't really expect her to cook twice.

4 Which dish is only available today?

Woman: And this is the cafeteria where students have their lunch. It's usually open every day from 12.30 until 2, but today we're closing early at 1.30 because of exams. There's always a selection of hot and cold food – burgers, chips, salads, and so on. And we have a special every day too – it's Wednesday today, which means it's pizza. If you just want a snack, they always have soup and lots of different sandwiches to choose from.

5 Which food does Lizzie dislike?

Girl: Hi, James. Mum wants me to check that you and Lizzie can still come for dinner tomorrow evening.

James: Yes, that's fine. We're looking forward to it.

Girl: Oh, good. I was just wondering if there's anything you or Lizzie don't eat? I think we might have roast lamb.

James: Yes, lamb would be fine, or chicken. Lizzie isn't keen on fish, so it might be best to avoid that.

Girl: OK, great.

6 Which ingredient do they need to buy?

Mum: Do you want to give me a hand with dinner?

Boy: Sure. Is this the recipe? Oh. That looks delicious! I really love curries.

Mum: I've never made it before. Well, I've done something similar with chicken, but lamb will be good too. We've got all the ingredients I think. One chilli, two onions, some garlic. Can you check?

Boy: There's plenty of garlic … there's one chilli and … one onion. I guess we need to get one more. I'll go if you like.

7 What do the couple decide to have for dinner?

Man: I'm not in the mood to cook tonight. What about going out for dinner? We could go to that Italian place. I feel like some good pasta.

Woman: I'm not really that hungry and they're closed on Tuesdays, remember? What about something light, like the Japanese, opposite the café? Sushi would be perfect. Then after we could get some ice cream from the café and bring it home. They do amazing quality ice cream.

Man: Mmm… Let's not have any dessert today.

Woman: OK.

49 Unit 10, Student's Book page 61

Server: Hi. What can I get you?

Emma: Could I have a veggie pizza, please?

Server: Of course. Would you like a salad?

Emma: Yes. I'll have a green salad, please.

Server: OK. And to drink?

Emma: I'd like a cola, please.

Server: Large or small?

Emma: Small, please.

Server: OK. Eat in or take out?

Emma: Eat in, please.

Server: That's £12.50, please.

Emma: Here you are.

Server: Thanks. Here's your change.

Emma: Thanks.

Server: Your meal will be ready in about 15 minutes.

Emma: Thanks.

51 Culture: British food, Student's Book page 63

Emily: OK, Andrew. What do you want for lunch today?

Andrew: I don't know. How about beef burgers?

Emily: Oh no! You're only here in London for a week, so you have to try some English food.

Andrew: I know! And what do you suggest? Fish and chips? Or maybe roast beef?

Emily: Well, no … I was thinking some chicken tikka masala would be good.

Andrew: What? Isn't that a curry dish?

Emily: Yes, but curry is one of the most popular dishes in the UK! Didn't you know that?

Andrew: No! When did curry become a British dish?

Emily: Well, the first curry restaurant opened in London more than 200 years ago. But it got *really* popular in the 1960s, when lots of people moved to the UK from India and Pakistan and opened hundreds and hundreds of restaurants with food from their countries.

Andrew: That's cool! But I'm not a big fan of spicy food. What other food is typical here?

Emily: Umm … well, you could try bangers and mash. That's very British.

Andrew: What's that?

Emily: It's sausages – bangers – with mashed potatoes. It's my dad's favourite.

Andrew: OK … and what else?

Emily: Maybe cottage pie? And no, it's not a sweet dish! It's a type of meat pie, with beef and vegetables, and with mashed potato on top.

Andrew: That sounds good. And what about for dessert? You know I've got a sweet tooth!

Emily: Yes, I know! So, you might want to try some English trifle.

Andrew: That sounds interesting. What is it?

Emily: It's a dish made with fruit, cake, jelly and cream. It's delicious!

Andrew: Mmm! And where can we eat all that? At a restaurant?

Emily: No, we can go to a café near here. I think you'll like it. It's really cool!

Andrew: OK, should we go now? Talking about food has made me hungry!

Emily: Sure! Let's go…

53 Unit 11, Student's Book page 64

Conversation 1

George: Hi, Sam. Do you fancy watching a film this evening?

Sam: Oh, no thanks. I played two tennis matches yesterday and I've got aches everywhere – my arms, my legs, my back – everything hurts! I'm going to be asleep by nine o'clock!

Conversation 2

Pedro: Hi Kelly. Are you OK? I heard you fell over at school yesterday. What happened?

Kelly: Oh, it was really silly. I was running along a corridor at school. Suddenly, this girl walked out of a classroom and I ran straight into her.

Pedro: So, how are you?

Kelly: Well, I've got a headache … I hit my chin on the floor, so I've got a cut inside my mouth, and my cheek's a bit sore. And I think I need to go to the dentist. I've got toothache.

Pedro: Oh, dear. And what about the other girl?

Kelly: She hurt her shoulder and her hand – well, her thumb, actually, but it wasn't broken. She's going to be all right.

Conversation 3

Dora: Are you OK, Josh? You look really tired.

Josh: Yeah, I'm not feeling great, actually, Dora. I feel really hot – I think I've got a fever.

Dora: Maybe you're getting a cold. Have you got a sore throat?

Josh: Yeah, I've got a sore throat and a cough, and last night I had earache, too.

Dora: It sounds like you should be at home in bed! I had a headache last night, too.

Josh: Yeah, I think you're right. I hope it's just a cold, and not flu!

55 Unit 11, Student's Book page 66

Conversation 1

Doctor: What seems to be the problem?

Zac: My finger really hurts. I injured it last night when I was playing football.

Doctor: Let me see. Can you move it at all?

Zac: Yes, a bit.

Doctor: OK, so you haven't broken it. But we need to …

Conversation 2

Niall: What are you going to do this weekend?

Anna: Not much! I've got flu. I started to feel ill on Thursday, and now I'm exhausted. I've got a fever at the moment, and aches in my arms and legs.

Niall: Is anyone else in your family ill?

Anna: No, but my sister was ill last week, so maybe I caught it from her.

57 Unit 12, Student's Book page 68

1 **Man:** Ants are very organised animals. They live in groups of many thousands and they've even got farms where they grow mushrooms to eat!

2 **Man:** Sharks and wolves attack humans, but not very often. However, when mosquitoes bite humans, they can give us a disease called malaria. Malaria from mosquitoes kills more than one million people every year.

3 **Man:** Bats have very poor eyes, so they use sound to find their food. They produce a high sound, which bounces off objects that are close to them. Bats use this sound to find where small insects are so they can catch them.

4 **Man:** Brown bears love the sweet smell of toothpaste! Bears sometimes go into tents when people are camping in the mountains because they want to eat the toothpaste! It's a good idea to leave your food and your toothpaste outside your tent if you're camping in the mountains.

5 **Man:** Frogs and butterflies move their feet a lot, but only the bee communicates by dancing. A bee's dance can tell other bees where there is food.

6 **Man:** Dolphins, elephants and monkeys have got big brains, like humans. They can recognise themselves in a mirror. Dogs have got smaller brains and they can't recognise themselves.

7 **Man:** People think that camels don't drink much. But, in fact, when they do drink, they drink a lot. Giraffes drink very little because there's already a lot of water in the leaves of the trees that they eat.

8 **Man:** Whales live in family groups of up to 20. Bats and bees live together in very large groups, but flies don't live with a group of other flies. They live on their own, wherever they find food.

9 **Man:** Most animals are frightened of lions, but donkeys aren't. Donkeys don't run away when there's a lion nearby. Nobody knows why!

10 **Man:** Bats and parrots can fly. Some ants can fly as well. Penguins are birds and they've got wings, but they can't fly.

60 Unit 12, Student's Book page 71

Animals at work.

Woman: We're always hearing stories in the news about how we need to save the planet's wildlife. But sometimes humans need help too. In today's show, we look at how clever creatures can help people to live normal lives – for example, people who are blind, or wheelchair users – as well as how animals help the emergency services and army to keep us safe.

Man: We all know that dogs can make a big difference to blind people, but now they can help others as well. I spoke to a schoolgirl called Donna Hunt. She's disabled and she's been in a wheelchair for three years. How does your dog help you, Donna?

Donna Hunt: My dog, Riley, is amazing. She can open and close doors. She can get things for me, like the remote control. She's even learned to pick up my clothes from the floor!

Man: Does Riley go to your school as well?

Donna Hunt: Yes. Before I had Riley, I was 'the girl in the wheelchair'. Now I'm 'the girl with the amazing dog'! I can't imagine living without her. She can give me my books at school, she can get money out of the bank for me, and she can even give shop assistants my money at the checkout.

Man: That's really clever! Thank you, Donna, for talking to us about Riley.

Donna Hunt: That's OK.

Woman: What a wonderful story!

Man: Yes. Dogs help us more than most other animals. They can smell really well, so the emergency services often use them to find people, for example, under badly damaged buildings. But they aren't the only animals that help in dangerous situations. After a war, there are often bombs buried in the ground. Now the army is using specially trained rats to find these bombs. And the rats are light, so the bombs don't explode.

Woman: That's interesting! I never knew that.

Man: Well, did you know that bees also have a very good sense of smell? They can recognise different chemicals, and they even change their buzzing noise depending on which chemical they find. So now scientists are training them to recognise and find poisonous chemicals, so they can warn us if there are dangerous chemicals in the air. Bees are much cheaper to train than dogs and rats, so scientists hope that they'll be used more in the future.

61 Unit 12, Student's Book page 71

Examiner: Now I'd like you to talk on your own about something. I'm going to give you a photograph and I'd like you to talk about it. It shows two people and a dog on a mountain. Please tell us what you can see in the photograph.

Girl: It looks very cold because they're wearing warm clothes and thick gloves. There's deep snow on the ground. I think the people are probably in the emergency services, and the dog is probably a rescue dog.

On the left, one person is digging down into the snow. Maybe they're looking for someone; they must think someone is under the snow.

The other person's on the right. He's kneeling next to the dog. He might be the dog's trainer. Perhaps the dog has found the person, and now these men are going to dig them out.

I think dogs are amazing animals, and we're very lucky that they can rescue people like this.

63 Life Skills: Respecting the environment, Student's Book page 73

Marcus: Good afternoon everyone, and welcome to *Green Teens*. Our podcast today is about environmental campaigns that people can do at school. We've invited Hannah Carson to talk with us today. Hello Hannah, and thanks for coming.

Hannah: Hi Marcus. It's nice to be here.

Marcus: Now, Hannah, you've organised lots of campaigns at school, haven't you? I mean, you've helped organise them, because you're a teacher, correct?

Hannah: Yes, I'm a science teacher and I help my students do campaigns every year. It's always something different.

Marcus: Sounds interesting! What have your students done this year?

Hannah: Well, we haven't finished yet, but they're making a video about a nature park near the school. It's very popular with young people, especially for hiking and camping, but there have been some problems recently.

Marcus: Problems? Such as …

Hannah: Well, people are leaving a lot of litter, so the park doesn't look very nice. And some people are also breaking the smaller trees, if you can believe that. It's terrible, really.

Marcus: Breaking the trees? Why in the world are they doing that?

Hannah: Oh, I don't know. For fun, maybe? But we're trying to inform people and improve the situation.

Marcus: With a video?

Hannah: Yes! My students have written a film script. It's a comedy about superhero teenagers who want to save a nature park. There are two main characters called Treeboy and Greengirl. It's quite funny!

Marcus: And they want to show the video at school?

Hannah: At school, and they want to upload it to the internet too. Who knows? The video might go viral!

Marcus: Well, that would get lots of attention. And what else are your students doing?

Hannah: Well, they're collecting donations for the park, to plant some new trees and put up signs saying "Don't drop litter" and "Please use the bins".

Marcus: That's a great idea! Good luck to your students!

Hannah: Thanks! They're probably listening to this podcast right now!

Marcus: Let's hope so!

64 Unit 13, Student's Book page 76

Conversation 1

Mum: That was amazing tennis, Ben. You played really well.

Ben: Thanks, Mum. But I didn't win.

Mum: Don't be like that. You got to the final. I'm really proud.

Ben: I know. Thanks. But I'm just disappointed that I didn't win.

Mum: I know what you mean.

Conversation 2

Dad: Vicky, can you go down to the shop for me? We haven't got any milk. It closes in ten minutes. If you hurry, you'll get there in time.

Vicky: But I'm exhausted, Dad. I had football training all afternoon.

Dad: Please, Vicky.

Vicky: OK …

Dad: I'm really grateful, Vicky. I've got a lot to do.

Conversation 3

Freddy: Wow! Did you design that poster?

Sadie: Yes. We're trying to encourage more people to join the rugby team.

Freddy: I didn't know you were so creative. It looks really professional! I'm amazed.

Sadie: Thanks.

Freddie: But I'm confused. Why are you interested in rugby?

Sadie: Read the poster, Freddie …

Freddie: Oh, sorry. It's for the *girls'* rugby team. I didn't know the school had a girls' rugby team!

Sadie: We only started training last week.

Conversation 4

Anna: Hi, Harry.

Harry: Hi, Anna. How is everything?

Anna: Oh, I'm really stressed. I've got a geography exam tomorrow and I haven't started revising yet.

Harry: Have you got lots to do?

Anna: Loads! It's going to take me all night!

Harry: OK. Try not to worry. You'll work better if you're relaxed.

Anna: I know but …

Conversation 5

Chloe: Hi, Lucas. How was your history exam today?

Lucas: Don't ask! I made loads of stupid mistakes! I'm really embarrassed about some of the things I put!

Chloe: Oh, don't worry. It's always easy to remember all the wrong answers you gave. I'm sure you gave some good ones too.

Lucas: Sure. I'm still hopeful that I've passed, but it wasn't my best exam.

Conversation 6

Dan: Oh no!

Mum: What's wrong, Dan?

Dan: I was moving some books. I didn't notice Clara's phone. It fell on the floor. Look. The screen is broken.

Mum: Oh, dear. You should tell her.

Dan: I'm scared, Mum. She's going to be really annoyed with me.

Mum: Yes, she might be. But it's only a phone. Be brave and go and tell her now.

Dan: OK.

68 Unit 14, Student's Book page 83

1 You will hear two friends talking about a film.

Girl: I wonder what's on at the cinema?

Boy: I'll have a look. Mmm … What about *After Dark*?

Girl: Isn't that the horror film that Matt was talking about? He said he'd never seen anything as scary as that.

Boy: I know. He said he was terrified! I've read comments about it online, though, saying it's worth seeing, and that's from people who tell you if they think a film's rubbish.

Girl: Wait a minute. It says here you have to be 18 to watch it.

Boy: Oh well, that's it then. We'll have to find something else to watch.

2 You will hear two friends talking about reality shows.

Boy: Did you see *Soundbites* last night?

Girl: No, I can't stand reality shows! I know they're very popular and they probably make the TV companies loads of money, but they're not for me.

Boy: Which shows have you watched then?

Girl: Well *none*, but there are always stories about reality stars online and I've watched the clips.

Boy: But how can you say that you don't like something when you've never really watched it?

Girl: I don't need to. It's well known that the people who appear in reality shows don't have anything interesting to say and they shouldn't really be on TV at all.

3 You will hear two friends talking about taking part in a short film.

Girl: Did you see the ad for that short film they're making?

Boy: No. What short film?

Girl: They're making a short film and it's about our school – you know, facts and information about what it's like to study here. It sounds quite cool. They're looking for students to interview. Do you want to be in it?

Boy: Oh, I dunno. Maybe. Are they offering any money?

Girl: The ad didn't say! My guess is no. I think you'd do it just for the experience. Are you interested? There's going to be a presentation by the producer.

Boy: Hmm. Might be. When's the presentation?

Girl: Tomorrow at 7.30, before school, in the assembly hall …

Boy: Before school? I'm not getting up that early!

4 You will hear two friends talking about a sci-fi film they've seen.

Boy: Wow! That film went on for ages!

Girl: Did you think so? It was only an hour and fifty minutes.

Boy: It felt much more than that! I nearly fell asleep. But I have to say, the music was pretty cool for a sci-fi movie.

Girl: Yeah, I'm not a big fan of the typical music in sci-fi films. That wasn't true in this case, though. I thought it was pretty original.

Boy: I saw your face when the alien's head exploded!

Girl: What do you mean?

Boy: You looked terrified!

Girl: No, what happened was, I felt my phone starting to ring in my pocket, and it was a bit embarrassing, that's all.

5 You will hear two friends talking about the news.

Boy: Are you following what's happening in Florida?

Girl: You mean with the storm? Yes, I can't stop watching the news. It's absolutely awful.

Boy: I know. I've never really been into what's happening in the news, but I feel so sorry for all the people who've lost their homes.

Girl: I know. It's the first time I've ever paid attention to world events. Usually it's all politics and business, but this makes you realise how we need to pay attention to what's going on around us.

Boy: I totally agree. I'm going to keep up with the news more in future.

6 You will hear two friends talking about going to the cinema.

Boy: What shall we watch then …? Er …

Girl: What about *Silly Money*? It's a comedy.

Boy: That sounds good. I love comedies.

Girl: Me too. It's on at … 4.30, 7.15 and 10.30.

Boy: Mm, ten thirty's too late. Shall we go at 7.15?

Girl: Yes. Good idea.

Boy: I wonder if it will sell out?

Girl: Maybe we should get the tickets before we go.

Boy: Good idea. My mum's booked things online for my sister before. I'll see if she'll do it for us.

Girl: Great. I can't wait.

69 Unit 14, Student's Book page 83

Girl 1: So, what shall we watch for our movie night? What about *Planet Alpha*?

Girl 2: Mmm, I'm not sure. I don't really like science fiction films. I don't think it'll be very good. It looks too violent for me.

Girl 1: How about *Superdog*?

Girl 2: I'm not really a fan of animated films, and I'm not sure about this one. It's for younger kids really, don't you think? But I guess it's a possibility. What else is there?

Girl 1: OK. Well, I don't really want to see *Watching You*. It sounds too scary to me.

Girl 2: I agree. I really don't like thrillers because I just want to relax when I watch a film. Do you think *Jerry's Vacation* sounds good?

Girl 1: Yeah, I think it might be funny.

Girl 2: OK, so let's decide. It's between *Superdog* and *Jerry's Vacation*.

Girl 1: Well, I'd prefer to watch *Jerry's Vacation*.

Girl 2: OK. I think we're both happy with that.

Girl 1: Yes, that's a good choice.

70 Culture: The film industry, Student's Book page 84

Woman: Question 1. The Lumière brothers invented film-making in France in 1895. The first films didn't have any sound, and the pictures were black and white.

Question 2. The Australian silent movie, *The Story of the Kelly Gang*, from 1906, was the first full-length movie ever made. It told the story of Australia's most famous gangster, Ned Kelly.

Question 3. The first film with speaking and music was the 1927 American film *The Jazz Singer* and most films were in black and white until the 1950s.

Question 4. Sherlock Holmes has appeared in the most films. He has appeared in more than 215 movies and he has been played by more than 75 actors.

Question 5. There are more cinema visits per person in Iceland every year than in any other country, with more than five visits per person. The world average is one point five cinema visits per person per year. The USA has four point three cinema visits per person per year.

71 Culture: The film industry, Student's Book page 84

Teacher: All right, Jack. Go ahead, when you're ready, please.

Jack: Thank you. My presentation today is about a classic film called *The Hidden Fortress*. I love classic films – I watch them all the time with my dad. He's a cinema fan and he's got a huge collection of films.

Anyway, *The Hidden Fortress* is a film from Japan. It's a typical action-adventure story with martial arts and samurai battles. They became popular in Japan in the 1950s, and one of the most popular directors was Akira Kurosawa. He was already famous when he made *The Hidden Fortress*, in 1958. It was filmed in many different locations, but all of them were in Japan, because that helped to save money.

Umm …

Teacher: And what about the setting of the film, Jack? Can you tell us where and when it takes place?

Jack: Yes, it's a historical film, and it takes place in Japan during the 16th century, so about 500 years ago, when there was a civil war. The two main characters of the film are a princess and one of her generals, who protects her. Their names are Princess Yuki and General Rokurota. At the beginning of the film, they are travelling to a hidden fortress in the mountains, where they will be safe. They are also carrying a lot of gold, but they must keep it secret.

Teacher: And what other characters are important in the story?

Jack: Well, there are also two poor men who travel with the General and the Princess. I like the farmers because they're quite funny characters – they're always arguing, having problems and making mistakes. And they're also *very* interested in money, so the general promises them a big reward for their help.

Teacher: And did the film do very well?

Jack: Yes, it did. It was the 4th most popular film in Japan in 1958, and Kurosawa's most successful film until that time. It also became famous in other countries, and it won the award for the best foreign film at the Berlin Film Festival, in Germany.

Teacher: And why did you like the film so much?

Jack: Well, I love the action scenes, especially with samurais. I'm really into martial arts. The story is quite exciting, but there are some funny moments that always make me laugh. I really recommend the film. It's a great classic and it had a big effect on many other action films that came after it.

Teacher: Thank you, Jack. Are there any questions?

73 Unit 15, Student's Book page 86

1 **Alex:** Have you ever deleted an important file by mistake?

2 **Alex:** Have you ever had a virus on your computer?

3 **Alex:** Do you have a different password for each website you use?

4 **Alex:** Do you often share links to interesting websites with friends?

5 **Alex:** Have you ever done a search for your own name online?

6 **Alex:** Do you upload photos or videos to the internet to share with friends?

7 **Alex:** How many new apps have you installed on your phone this week?

8 **Alex:** Do you ever download podcasts?

74 Unit 15, Student's Book page 86

1

Alex: Have you ever deleted an important file by mistake, Jack?

Jack: Yes, I have. I was working late one night and I deleted a school project.

Alex: What did you do?

Jack: I got really stressed about it. Fortunately, my dad managed to get it back.

2

Alex: Have you ever had a virus on your computer?

Jack: Only once but yes, I have.

Alex: How did you get it?

Jack: The virus was in a game that I downloaded. I installed the game and suddenly my computer warned me that I had a virus.

3

Alex: Do you have a different password for each website you use?

Jack: Always. Each website has a different one!

Alex: How do you remember them?

Jack: I write them down! There's a really long list on my desk at home!

4

Alex: Do you often share links to interesting websites with friends?

Jack: Yes, all the time. I often share links on social networking websites or in messages.

Alex: What kind of things do you share?

Jack: They're usually funny videos or photos. Anything that makes me smile, really.

5

Alex: Have you ever done a search for your own name online?

Jack: Yes. Lots of times!

Alex: What did you find?

Jack: I found my name on our school website. There are reports of important football matches that I've played in.

6

Alex: Do you upload photos or videos to the internet to share with friends?

Jack: Yes, I upload photos several times a day. I love taking photos of interesting things and sharing them.

Alex: Which apps do you use to share them?

Jack: I mainly use Instagram.

7

Alex: How many new apps have you installed on your phone this week?

Jack: Probably about ten. There are hundreds of apps on my phone. I love finding interesting stuff.

Alex: How many do you have altogether?

Jack: Over 200, I'm sure. But I probably only use five regularly!

8

Alex: Do you ever download podcasts?

Jack: Sometimes. I like listening on the way to school.

Alex: Which ones do you listen to the most?

Jack: I like the ones about science. But I haven't listened to any for a few weeks.

76 Unit 16, Student's Book page 90

A Man: Blow air into the balloon and tie the end.

Rub the balloon on your hair or on a tissue.

Put the can on the floor and hold the balloon near it.

Now … Move the balloon away from the can, just pull the balloon slowly along the floor, and the can will move towards the balloon!

How does this work? Well, the can moves towards the balloon because of static electricity. When you rub the balloon, it gets a negative electrical charge. When you put the balloon near the can, the metal in the can gets a small positive electrical charge. The result is that the static electricity in the balloon *attracts* the can – it pulls the can towards the balloon.

B Woman: Fill the glasses with water.

Put two large spoons of salt into the first glass and stir it.

Add a few drops of food colouring into the other glass.

Cover the glass of coloured water with the cardboard or plastic. Turn it upside down and put it on top of the glass of salt water. Pull the cardboard or plastic out from between the glasses. Now … The coloured water and the salty water won't mix! The two liquids stay apart.

How does this work? Well, salt water is heavier than normal water. Have you ever noticed that your body floats more easily in the sea than in a swimming pool? Try it and you'll see. In the same way, the heavier salt water stays at the bottom of the glass and the lighter coloured water floats at the top.

C Man: Boil the egg for four minutes until the white of the egg is hard but the yolk is soft. The yolk is the yellow part in the middle of an egg. Then peel the egg.

Pour the hot water into the bottle. Put on the lid, wrap it in a towel and shake it well. The bottle will feel very hot, so the towel protects your hands.

Take off the lid and pour out the water.

Put the egg in the opening of the warm bottle.

After a few minutes, the air in the bottle cools and contracts, and the egg is pulled into the bottle.

How does this work? Well, the hot water in the bottle makes the bottle warm, and the air *in* the bottle gets warm too. Hot air expands – in other words, it gets bigger and fills more space than cold air. Cold air contracts – in other words it gets smaller and fills less space than warm air. So, as the air in the bottle goes back to room temperature, it gets smaller, and so it pulls the egg into the bottle.

78 Unit 16, Student's Book page 93

Interviewer: Lauren, you've made a documentary about a young man called Taylor Wilson. Tell us about him. Er, how did you *find out* about him?

Lauren Phillips: Actually, it was luck. I saw a clip of Taylor Wilson talking and – he inspired me. And his story made me realise that your dreams won't come true unless you make them come true. We have to work out what we really want to do, and we have to do it.

Interviewer: Wow! Tell me more!

Lauren Phillips: Well, as a kid he was really into science. By his early teens, Taylor had enough equipment to carry out simple experiments in his parents' garage. One time when he was showing a radioactivity experiment to his family, he nearly blew up the whole house! He was lucky, and no one was hurt, though all the neighbours ran out of their homes because they were worried it was a gas explosion!

Interviewer: Did he get into trouble?

Lauren Phillips: No, luckily for him, his parents forgave him. In fact after that, they sent him to a special school for super-intelligent kids. Neither his parents nor his school could teach Taylor much by the time he was in his teens. He was just much too clever.

Interviewer: Uh huh. A lot of very successful adults are the same – they scored in the top one per cent of tests at the age of 12. Steve Jobs, Mark Zuckerberg, Lady Gaga … they all scored in the top one per cent.

Lauren Phillips: Yes, Taylor scored the same … Anyway, this special school was located next to a university so that school students could use the university's facilities. Soon Taylor spent all his time hanging out at the university's nuclear physics department. And that's when he decided to make a star in a jar.

Interviewer: 'A star in a jar'?

Lauren Phillips: Yes. He worked out how he could build his own nuclear fusion reactor. So the 'star' is the burning nuclear reaction and the 'jar' is the reactor – the container for the nuclear reaction.

Interviewer: Uh-huh.

Lauren Phillips: And *then* he announced that he was going to build this nuclear reactor at home!

Interviewer: What?

Lauren Phillips: Exactly! The nuclear physics teachers were like, 'Oh, no, that is *not* a good idea!', but nothing would stop Taylor, so they helped him to *move* his nuclear reactor to their laboratory at the university. And at the age of 14, Taylor Wilson became the 42nd person on earth to create their own nuclear fusion reaction.

Interviewer: That's incredible.

Lauren Phillips: I know! Next, he had an idea for using radiation to find hidden guns or bombs. He helped the US Government to make a bomb-detection machine to use at airports. He was even asked to show it to President Obama!

Interviewer: What *is* this guy gonna do next?

Lauren Phillips: I don't know, but I hope he continues to give lectures like the one I saw. He makes you realise that if you have an idea, you need to act on it now. He's an amazing speaker and he really gets people excited about science. His lectures have had four million views and there are plans for a Hollywood movie about him!

79 Unit 16, Student's Book page 93

Girl: It looks like the people are school students or they might be visitors at a science fair. There's some scientific equipment in the photo. I'm not really sure, but it looks like some sort of experiment with electricity.

There are some purple lines coming from the equipment. I don't know what they're called, but the lines are electrical, like lightning in a thunderstorm.

The girl in the middle of the photo is wearing a white lab coat and it looks like she has special gloves as well. She looks surprised by what she is touching.

The people behind her seem very interested in the experiment.

81 Life Skills: Staying safe online, Student's Book page 95

Melissa: I've had some problems with bullies because I'm different. I like wearing unusual clothes, so some people make fun of me. Two months ago, a group of popular girls found out my phone number and started sending me nasty messages. Some days, I got more than 20! Finally, I talked to my parents and that helped! They bought me a new phone and now only my friends have the number. I also block any calls from strangers.

Justin: Have I ever been cyberbullied? Yes, I have! Last year, I got into a fight with this boy at school, and he got really angry about it. He started writing about me on a social network that all my friends use. He posted comments on my profile, calling me names, and he sent me private messages, saying, 'I'm going to get you' and things like that. I never answered him, and I changed the privacy settings on my profile, so only my friends could post comments or send me messages. I'm lucky, because that was the end of the problem.

Laura: I had a bad time last year because a boy started saying nasty things about me at school. He also sent emails about me to other people. It was bad, and some people stopped talking to me. After a month or so, he finally stopped, and now things are back to normal, but it was difficult for a while. I didn't tell my parents, but I think that was a mistake. If it happens again, I'll tell them right away.

David: I don't think I've been cyberbullied, but I've had problems with the internet. I started getting lots and lots of junk mail and other emails from strangers, and lots of adverts from websites all over the world. In the end, I closed that email account and opened a new one, but then the same thing happened again, and again, and again! I've changed my email account five times now, and I tell my friends to keep it secret, but the same keeps happening. I don't know what to do! Maybe someone is putting my email on a public website. I don't know.

82 Unit 17, Student's Book page 98

Conversation 1

Girl: Well, this room obviously belongs to some sort of artist.

Boy: Yeah. A painter, maybe. Look at those pots of paint and the brushes.

Girl: Yeah … There are a few drawings and a painting, but there are sculptures at the back there too.

Boy: Oh, yeah, so there are. And it must be the artist's studio. It's too messy to be a gallery.

Girl: That's a good point.

Conversation 2

Boy: This office obviously belongs to an author. Look at all those novels. Maybe he –

Girl: Or 'she'!

Boy: Yeah – maybe he or *she* – is a poet. I can see a few books of poetry on one of the shelves.

Girl: Or it could be someone who's into historical fiction.

Boy: Or someone who loves reading about other writers' lives. Look at that title over there … *Gabriel García Márquez – A Life*. That's a biography.

Girl: I can't believe the size of the bookcase!

Conversation 3

Boy: This looks like a film set in the desert. The person sitting on the high chair might be the director.

Girl: Yeah, you can see actors and the film crew.

Boy: And all sorts of equipment.

85 Unit 18, Student's Book page 102

Speaker 1

Woman: I've always loved animals. Even at school, I knew this was the job I wanted to do. I work with small animals – pets. That means anything from rabbits to … um, rats. I really enjoy meeting their owners too. And they're always so grateful for my help.

Speaker 2

Man: I'm very proud of what I do. It's a dangerous job, and it's very hard physically, especially when there's a big fire and we have to go in with special clothes and safety equipment. It feels good when we've finished a job, though, and made a place safe again.

Speaker 3

Woman: I usually only work in the evenings, often at weekends. I like playing with the children, especially doing creative things. They usually behave well, but sometimes they think that because their parents are out, they can do what they want! It isn't fun then!

Speaker 4

Man: I started working at my dad's shop when I was a teenager. I only did cleaning then. I wasn't allowed to even touch any scissors! But when I left school, my dad taught me how to cut hair. A few years later, I opened my own place. I generally really enjoy my job. I'm quite sociable, so love chatting to people while I work.

Speaker 5

Woman: I love sport, and I love teaching, so this job is really ideal for me. I usually work with groups of about 20 children. We practise some skills, like running with the ball, and then they have a match.

Speaker 6

Man: I never wanted to sit in an office all day. I prefer being outside, doing things with my hands. We work on everything from flats to offices and shops, places where people will live and work. That's pretty cool, I think.

87 Unit 18, Student's Book page 105

Conversation 1

Allie: Hi, Ben.

Ben: Hi, Allie. You sound a bit miserable. What's up?

Allie: It's money. I've never got any. I'm always asking my parents for more.

Ben: What about getting a job at the weekend? My sister's a babysitter for our neighbours on Saturday nights. I was thinking about doing something similar. Maybe in a year or so.

Allie: The problem with that is my parents might say 'no'.

Ben: Explain to them that you don't want to ask them for money all the time … And if that doesn't work, maybe they've got some jobs you could do. You know, cleaning, cooking or stuff like that. For money, of course!

Allie: Thanks, Ben. That's great advice. I'll speak to them tonight about it. Anyway, you didn't phone me to hear my problems. What's up?

Ben: Oh, yeah. Do you want to go …

Conversation 2

Evan: Mrs Shaw. Please can I ask your advice about something?

Mrs Shaw: Of course, Evan.

Evan: I've got to choose ten subjects to study next year. And I'd like to choose the best subjects for my future. But …

Mrs Shaw: … you're not sure what you want to do?

Evan: Um, no, that's not the problem. I know that I'd really like to do a film degree at university. I just want to choose the best subjects for that.

Mrs Shaw: What about doing some research online? There's lots of information there.

Evan: Yes, you're right. I'll do that.

Mrs Shaw: I know you love films, Evan … , but if I were you, I'd choose a good mix of subjects. It's good to have lots of options. You might change your mind in the future.

Evan: Yeah. I see what you mean.

Mrs Shaw: And also, Evan … Ten is quite a lot of subjects. Eight or nine might be better – especially if that means better marks.

Evan: Maybe you're right. Thanks very much, Mrs Shaw. I should go to my next lesson …

88 Unit 18, Student's Book page 105

Girl: OK, let's talk about the jobs that this girl could do. What about walking dogs for people? That's pretty easy and probably quite fun.

Boy: I'm not so sure. It wouldn't be much fun in bad weather.

Girl: That's true. And cutting the grass or gardening would be the same. What do you think about doing jobs around the house for your parents? For example, ironing and cleaning.

Boy: Well, those jobs would be indoors, at least. But the problem with ironing and cleaning is they're boring.

Girl: Yes, you're right. And I think that working in an office might be boring, too.

Boy: That's true. Working with young children might be better.

Girl: Yes. Babysitting can be easy, especially if the children are well behaved. But the pay isn't very good.

Boy: Hmm. Maybe you're right. If I were her, I'd work in a café. It might be fun, and she would earn a lot of money in tips.

Girl: Yes, that's a good choice.

90 Culture: Special training, Student's Book page 107

Presenter: Today we're talking to talented seventeen-year-old Carolina Woods. Hi, Carolina.

Carolina: Hi.

Presenter: Tell us a little bit about yourself. What's your special talent?

Carolina: Well, since the age of three, I've always loved ballet. That's not quite true actually. When I was seven, my first real teacher was scary and I didn't want to go back to class after the first lesson. My parents promised to buy me a pink ballet dress if I went back, so I did!

Presenter: What happened next?

Carolina: When I was 11, I went to the Royal Ballet School in London. I had to stay there during the week. I was away from my family for the first time in my life, so it was hard at first.

Presenter: But you were doing something that you enjoyed?

Carolina: That's right, and I was with other young people with the same interests.

Presenter: But you didn't stay there, did you?

Carolina: At 15, I got the chance of a place at both the Royal Ballet Upper School in London and also the Vaganova Ballet Academy in Russia. I had to decide whether to go with some of my classmates to the best school in London or leave my family and friends and move to Russia to study at one of the best ballet schools in the world.

Presenter: And you decided to go to Russia. Why?

Carolina: I couldn't speak Russian and I didn't know anyone there, but it seemed like a fantastic opportunity.

Presenter: So what is your life like now in Russia?

Carolina: I train every day with some of the best dancers in the world. My whole body hurts by the end of the day but I never complain because I'm doing something that I love.

Presenter: Do you miss your friends and family?

Carolina: Yes, of course I do, but we speak online all the time and my parents often come to Russia to see my shows.

Presenter: Well, thank you, Carolina. Next week …

92 Unit 19, Student's Book page 108

Conversation 1

Girl: Is that a novel you're reading? I mean, I didn't realise you liked books!

Boy: I guess it's a *kind* of novel.

Girl: Let's see. Oh, so it has pictures the same as a comic.

Boy: Yes, but it's much longer than a comic. And it's more fun to read than a novel!

Conversation 2

Boy: What are you doing?

Girl: Uh? You told me to give my sister the details …

Boy: I didn't mean *write* a message! There's no time.

Conversation 3

Girl: Have you decided what after-school classes to apply for next year?

Boy: No, but I've been meaning to look at the list and see what they all offer.

Girl: Yes, take a look at this. I've already chosen mine so you can keep it.

Conversation 4

Boy: Have you returned all of your library books?

Girl: I'm not sure. Why?

Boy: You have to take them back a week before the end of term or they'll fine you.

Girl: No way! How do you know that?

Boy: There was something about it on the board.

94 Unit 20, Student's Book page 112

Conversation 1

Girl: OK. Green … red … blue …

Boy: Can you go a bit quicker?

Girl: OK … yellow, blue, black,

Boy: Good!

Girl: Purple … Argh. That was your fault. I lost concentration!

Boy: Never mind. Start again.

Conversation 2

Girl: This is impossible. I can only see one animal – a rabbit. Can you give me a hint?

Boy: OK … Look at the rabbit's ears …

Girl: Oh, I see it now. A duck!

Boy: That's right.

Conversation 3

Boy: This one's good.

Girl: OK. Give me a second … OK. There are … No. Wait. I've changed my mind. There are others … 16, 17, 18. Yes! OK. There are 18.

Boy: Sorry! You missed one.

Girl: Oh, no way! Where?

Boy: One of the letters below the big four is actually a three.

Girl: Oh, yeah! It didn't cross my mind to look there!

Boy: I got it *completely* wrong the first time.

Conversation 4

Boy: I don't know the answer to this one. Surely it's the one on the right.

Girl: Yes, but this *is* an optical illusion, remember? That can't be the correct answer.

Boy: But the one on the left *looks* smaller.

Girl: Hold on. I've just had a thought. Are they the same size?

Boy: That's a good guess. Have you got a ruler?

Conversation 5

Boy: OK, she's old – very old, and she's got a huge nose.

Girl: Can you see anyone else?

Boy: Um … no. Wait. Yes, I think I can see … No … Oh, wait.

Girl: Make up your mind!

Boy: No. No, I can't see anyone else.

Girl: OK. You have to use your imagination to see the second person. Look at the old woman's nose and imagine it's someone's chin.

Boy: Oh, wow. That's incredible! It's another woman, she's younger and we can't see her face.

96 Unit 20, Student's Book page 115

You will hear an interview with a young magician.

Presenter: Hi, Amelia. Welcome to the university podcast. So, how did you get started as a magician?

Amelia: Well, ten years ago my older brother gave me his old magic set. It was brand new, really – he never played with it. I was nine then, and more interested in computer games, but I practised some of the tricks and showed them to my family. They were amazed and said I had a talent for it. From then on, magic became a big part of my life.

Presenter: So, where have you performed?

Amelia: I used to do talent shows at school. I was called 'Amazing Amelia'! They've been the ones I've enjoyed the most – especially the two years I came first. I've also done tricks at young children's birthday parties. They were useful practice but they aren't the easiest audience. Now, I've left school and I'm doing my degree, I'm in the Magic Club and we do shows every few months. We've done two so far and they've been really popular.

Presenter: And have you created any of your own tricks?

Amelia: If you read biographies of famous magicians, it's clear they spend a lot of time inventing new tricks. But for less experienced magicians, their advice is always the same: being a good magician is more about the way you speak to your audience. So I spend a lot of time thinking about how I present my tricks. But, no, none of my tricks were created by me. I found them in books or online.

Presenter: And do you practise tricks a lot?

Amelia: A lot! I mainly do it at home by myself, but also at our club, and *wherever* I am, I always have a trick or two in my pocket. I love trying new tricks on friends – even if they're not always successful. And fortunately they never seem to get bored of seeing them!

Presenter: Do you ever tell anyone how you do your tricks?

Amelia: It depends. In our university club we obviously tell each other everything. But, of course, we're very good at keeping secrets! In the past, I was persuaded by a few of my non-magician friends to explain one or two tricks. And amazingly, they haven't told anyone … yet! But nowadays, I don't tell them anything. I might give them a *tiny* hint. But that's it.

Presenter: And would you like to be a professional magician one day?

Amelia: Umm … A few years ago that was definitely my plan. And I feel certain that a career in magic would be a lot of fun. I even study languages, which would be useful for performing in other countries. But recently I've started having second thoughts. I'm only 19. At the moment, I think I need to keep magic as a hobby and make sure I get a good degree. I don't need to make my mind up now.

Presenter: Thank you, Amelia. We wish you lots of luck!

97 Unit 20, Student's Book page 115

Mark: Hey, Lucy, you know Thomas – he's in my maths class. He's really into magic. One of his tricks is incredible. You won't believe this, but he floats above the ground!

Lucy: Are you serious? You're saying that he can levitate – he can rise into the air, above the ground? That just isn't possible, Mark.

Mark: I know. I couldn't believe my eyes!

Lucy: How far was he above the ground?

Mark: I don't know. Ten centimetres? He stayed there for about five seconds.

Lucy: No way! Did you ask him how he does it?

Mark: Of course I asked him. Everyone did. He said we couldn't keep a secret and would tell everyone …

Lucy: Well, he's completely right, of course. Where is he? I want to see this incredible trick …

98 Life Skills: Identifying reliable news, Student's Book page 116

Speaker 1, Jade

Jade: One day I saw a story about the Hubble space telescope, and I'm a fan of astronomy, so I had to read it. The headline asked, 'Has Hubble discovered life in space?', which sounded cool, but when I read the story, I knew it was fake. It said the telescope had photographed a secret city on Mars, but NASA wasn't saying anything because it would scare people. And the article didn't give any names, of course! I read lots of scientific articles, and that's not the way real scientists write about their work!

Speaker 2, Marc

Marc: Fake news? Well, there've been many cases involving celebrities. One time I was at the supermarket and I saw two magazine cover stories about a famous Hollywood actor. One headline said he had secretly married a supermodel, and another magazine said they had just broken up. But the funniest part is – they were never together. The model gave an interview and said she had never met him before. You can't believe anything you see in magazines!

Speaker 3, Ben

Ben: Hmm. Well, it can be a serious problem. There was a case in the USA about a company that made burgers. A TV programme said the company was using a 'strange pink liquid', which sounds horrible! During the show, the reporter used the phrase 'strange pink liquid' many, many times, and the company said that was bad for their business. In the end, the TV programme had to pay the company for damaging its image.

Speaker 4, Katy

Katy: Well, it's quite an important issue. I think fake news can be dangerous when it's about health and medicine. I mean you often see stories about some amazing plant or food that can make you healthier and more beautiful. Or maybe a fantastic exercise machine that helps you lose 10 kilograms in a week. Of course, they're only adverts, and they want to sell you a product and take your money. I think that's horrible. Some people believe these crazy stories, and they might do things that are bad for their health.

Acknowledgements

The authors and publishers acknowledge the following sources of copyright material and are grateful for the permissions granted. While every effort has been made, it has not always been possible to identify the sources of all the material used, or to trace all copyright holders. If any omissions are brought to our notice, we will be happy to include the appropriate acknowledgements on reprinting and in the next update to the digital edition, as applicable.

Teacher's Book

All the texts, photographs and illustrations used are from the Student's Book.

Front cover photography by Priscilla Gragg/Getty Images.

Videos

Key: C = Culture.

Photography

All the photographs are sourced from Getty Images.

C4: StockLapse/Creatas Video+.

Video Clips

The following video clips are sourced from Getty Images.

C1: Mont Blanc Films/Photodisc; HeroImagesFootage/Creatas Video; eclipse_images/Vetta; RubberBall Productions LLC/Verve+; Image Source Ltd/Jupiterfootage; DonHammond/Vetta; saskami/Creatas Video; thisnight/Creatas Video; HeroImagesFootage/Creatas Video; fstop12/Vetta; valentinrussanov/Creatas Video; Sladic/Creatas Video; xavierarnau/Creatas Video; Caiafilm/Vetta; ReeldealHD Ltd./Verve+; xavierarnau/Creatas Video; simonkr/Vetta; konstantynov/Creatas Video; selected-takes/Creatas Video; JohnnyGreig/Creatas Video; **C2:** simonkr/Creatas Video; Schroptschop/Vetta; RoosterHD/Vetta; thisnight/Creatas Video; Erik Van Ingen/DigitalVision; zxvisual/Creatas Video; Alex Potemkin/Creatas Video; AERIALDAILY/Creatas Video; Toshi Sasaki/Photodisc; Erik Van Ingen/Photodisc; piola666/Creatas Video; Toshi Sasaki/Photodisc; Mageed/Creatas Video; cjp/Creatas Video; franticstudio/Creatas Video; onuroner/Creatas Video; Photo and Co/DigitalVision; halbergman/Creatas Video; Erik Van Ingen/DigitalVision; Nz_b/Creatas Video; Toshi Sasaki/Photodisc; simonkr/Creatas Video; **C3:** gilaxia/Creatas Video; topnatthapon/Creatas Video; commandoXphoto/Creatas Video; 4kodiak/Vetta; piola666/Creatas Video; querbeet/Creatas Video; invizbk/Creatas Video; Peresmeh/Creatas Video; LPETTET/Creatas Video; querbeet/Creatas Video; Tolga_TEZCAN/Creatas Video; HOsiHO/DigitalVision; Caiafilm/Vetta; TODCHAMP/Creatas Video; topnatthapon/Creatas Video; FreedomMAN/Creatas Video; visualspace/Creatas Video; VikramRaghuvanshi/Creatas Video; funky-data/Creatas Video; jxfzsy/Creatas Video; topnatthapon/Creatas Video; GCShutter/Creatas Video; GKinion/Creatas Video; khanoglu/Creatas Video; Mindklongdan/Creatas Video+/Getty Images Plus; Copyright Unscripted Films/DigitalVision; **C4:** saskami/Creatas Video; LPETTET/Creatas Video; selected-takes/Vetta; T-Bone Films/Photodisc; Silverwell Films/Archive Films: Creative; DutcherAerials/Creatas Video; Petrified Films/ Archive Films: Creative; LPETTET/Vetta; Petrified Films/Archive Films: Creative; Alphotographic/iStock Unreleased; StockLapse/Creatas Video+; Craig McCourry/Verve+; TODCHAMP/Creatas Video; RubberBall Productions LLC/Verve+; Frank Perl/Verve; Laurence Dutton/Vetta; selected-takes/Creatas Video; Allstar Picture Library/Photolibrary Video; Luka Lajst/Vetta; fehimeren/Creatas Video; **C5:** Andersen Ross/Verve+; RoosterHD/Creatas Video; FatCamera/Creatas Video; Pressmaster/DigitalVision; kali9/Creatas Video; Andersen Ross/Verve+; kali9/Creatas Video; perinjo/Creatas Video; Blend Motion/ Verve+; Andersen Ross/Verve+; simonkr/Creatas Video; SolStock/Creatas Video; Steve Debenport/Creatas Video; ContentWorks/Creatas Video; kali9/Vetta; HeroImagesFootage/Creatas Video; kali9/Vetta; SolStock/Creatas Video; simonkr/Creatas Video; fstop123/Vetta; perinjo/Vetta; ReeldealHD Ltd/ Verve+; TuiPhotoengineer/Creatas Video; komisar/Creatas Video; HeroImagesFootage/Creatas Video.

Audio

All the music clips are sourced from Getty Images.

Intro: LP_MUSIC/SoundExpress; **C1:** juqboxmusic/SoundExpress; **C2:** omin_13/SoundExpress; **C3:** MagnusMoone/SoundExpress; **C4:** Dmitriy Shironosov/SoundExpress; **C5:** juqboxmusic/SoundExpress.

The publishers are grateful to the following contributors:
author of *Cambridge English Prepare! First Edition* Level 4 Teacher's Book: Helen Chilton; cover design and design concept: restless; typesetting: Mouse Life, S.L; videos in units 2, 3, 6, 10, 11, 13, 17 and 18 produced by Purple Door Media Ltd.